D1241570

THE SAGE HANDBOOK
of
FIELDWORK

THE SAGE HANDBOOK
of
FIELDWORK

Edited by
DICK HOBBS and RICHARD WRIGHT

SAGE Publications
London ● Thousand Oaks ● New Delhi

First published 2006

SAGE Publications Ltd
1 Oliver's Yard
55 City Road
London EC1Y 1SP

SAGE Publications Inc.
2455 Teller Road
Thousand Oaks, California 91320

SAGE Publications India Pvt Ltd
B-42, Panchsheel Enclave
Post Box 4109
New Delhi 110 017

British Library Cataloguing in Publication data

A catalogue record for this book is available from
the British Library

ISBN 0 7619 7445 8

Library of Congress Control Number available

Typeset by C&M Digitals (P) Ltd., Chennai, India
Printed on paper from sustainable resources
Printed in Great Britain by The Cromwell Press Ltd, Trowbridge, Wiltshire

To Bridgette Mack and Janet Lauritsen, for their wise counsel and enduring friendship

Richard Wright

To Sue, Pat and Nik

Dick Hobbs

Contents

Preface   x

PART ONE: LOCATING FIELDWORK   1

1   The Fieldwork Tradition   3
George J. McCall

2   Praxical Reasoning and the Logic of Field Research   23
Gary Shank

PART TWO: SITUATING FIELDWORK   37

3   Jelly's Place: An Ethnographic Memoir   39
Elijah Anderson

4   Your Place or Mine: The Geography of Social Research   59
Michael Stein

PART THREE: SITUATING THE RESPONDENTS   77

5   Fieldwork with the Elite: Interviewing White-Collar Criminals   79
Mary Dodge and Gilbert Geis

6   Entering the Field: Recruiting Latinos for
Ethnographic Research   93
C. H. Browner and H. Mabel Preloran

PART FOUR: FIELDWORK AS A REFLEXIVE ENTERPRISE   107

7   Self-Narratives and Ethnographic Fieldwork   109
Ben Crewe and Shadd Maruna

8   'You Don't Do Fieldwork, Fieldwork Does You':
Between Subjectivation and Objectivation in
Anthropological Fieldwork   125
Bob Simpson

PART FIVE: THE FIELD OF EMOTION   139

 9   Aural Sex: The Politics and Moral Dilemmas of Studying the
     Social Construction of Fantasy   141
     Christine Mattley

10   The Case for Dangerous Fieldwork   157
     Bruce Jacobs

PART SIX: FIELDWORK AND SEXUALITIES   169

11   Fieldwork on Urban Male Homosexuality
     in Mexico   171
     Joseph Carrier

12   Knowing Sexuality: Epistemologies of Research   185
     Chris Haywood and Mairtin Mac an Ghaill

13   Researching Sex Work: Dynamics, Difficulties,
     and Decisions   201
     Teela Sanders

PART SEVEN: EMBODIMENT AND IDENTITY   223

14   Fieldwork and the Body: Reflections on an
     Embodied Ethnography   225
     Lee F. Monaghan

15   Sport Ethnography: A Personal Account   243
     Susan Brownell

16   Hidden Identities and Personal Stories: International Research
     about Women in Sport   255
     Jennifer Hargreaves

PART EIGHT: FIELDWORK IN ORGANISATIONS   275

17   Fieldwork and Policework   277
     Nigel Fielding

18   An Ethnographer's Tale: A Personal View of Educational Ethnography   293
     Robert G. Burgess

PART NINE: FIELDWORK, SCIENCE AND TECHNOLOGY   307

19   Software and Fieldwork   309
      Susanne Friese.

20   Seeking Science in the Field: Life Beyond the Laboratory   333
      Steve Fuller.

PART TEN: LOCATING FRESH FIELDS   345

21   Postmodern Fieldwork in Health Research   347
      Nick J. Fox

22   Fieldwork in Transition   361
      Peter Kirby Manning

Author Biographies   377

Name Index   383

Subject Index   392

Preface

Fieldwork refers to the research practice of engaging with others on their own turf, exotic or otherwise, in order to describe their cultural practices, understandings and beliefs. It takes many forms and is conducted in a myriad of settings by social scientists working within a wide variety of academic disciplines. Common to all fieldwork is a desire to understand the social worlds inhabited by others as *they* understand those worlds, that is, in terms of the meanings they ascribe to their everyday actions and experiences. As such, fieldwork is a profoundly personal research strategy; even in its most passive forms, it typically requires some participation in the lives of others, often on unfamiliar ground, with all of the unforeseeable contingencies that characterise any human interaction.

As a result, fieldworkers operate on uncertain terrain, in essence acting as 'professional strangers', though the extent of their marginality will depend on such things as their personal history and the specific culture being studied. Strangeness and distance were distinguishing characteristics of nineteenth century anthropology. The colonial context of anthropological studies carried out during this era meant that fieldworkers typically did their 'research' abroad and seldom shared cultural perspectives with members of the studied population. Fieldworkers were detached from their informants and tended to regard native cultures as exotic and essentially inferior. As a consequence, the gathering of data often comprised little more than the acquisition of cultural artefacts.

A more self conscious, less colonially-oriented approach to fieldwork emerged during the first half of the twentieth century. This development can be linked to the rise of the so-called Chicago School of sociology, which combined the rigour of European theory and classical anthropology, with a concern to locate and engage with the social problems of rapidly evolving urban settings. Fieldworkers became members, associates and fringe members of urban subcultures, groups, and gangs. They lived in urban neighbourhoods and filtered cultural activity through the lens of their own experiences of complex and rapidly changing social settings. Echoing Henry Mayhew's forays into nineteenth century London, and influenced by the campaigning work of Jacob Riis and Lincoln Steffens, a fertile academic tradition was born.

That tradition is alive and well, as the contributions to this volume amply demonstrate. Today, even the quantitatively oriented social scientists are beginning to recognise the critical importance of fieldwork for understanding how people perceive and interpret their own actions and experiences in the context of distinct cultural and subcultural settings. They have come to understand that fieldwork can expose and explain social worlds that are veiled by their cultural or geographical remoteness or camouflaged by over-familiarity. This is not to suggest, however, that fieldwork is without its problems and critics. The inevitable involvement of fieldworkers in the lives of those they study poses vexing methodological and ethical questions. In regard to method, for example, there is a longstanding concern that the presence of a fieldworker unavoidably alters the social situation being studied, and that the more successful fieldworkers are in reducing the perceived distance between themselves and those they are studying, the less 'objective' they become in gathering and reporting their data. In writing up accounts of their research, fieldworkers inevitably must pick and choose what to report and serious questions have been raised about the extent to which such choices reveal more about the observer than the observed.

But the methodological questions associated with fieldwork pale in relation to the ethical dilemmas arising from its practice. Immersion in the field implicates the fieldworker and places a range of responsibilities on the fieldwork enterprise that are not apparent in the everyday practices of alternative, less personally involving methodologies. In addition, the ethnographic realities of everyday physical and emotional existence in the field can involve negotiating hazards that are often exacerbated by the fieldworker's non-familiarity with the physical and cultural environment.

Many of the contributors to this volume have struggled with these issues in real world fieldwork settings and their reports make for compelling and instructive reading. Perhaps more than any other social science research methodology, fieldwork can only be fully appreciated through the interpretive lens of the investigator, which is hardly surprising given that it is the only method in which researcher and instrument are one and the same. That realisation is what prompted us to propose a handbook devoted exclusively to the practice of fieldwork. Part science, part art, there likely will never be an accepted standard for what constitutes first-rate fieldwork. Instead, that ground will remain hotly contested, with various ethnographic camps offering differing perspectives on and approaches to the fieldwork enterprise. All of those camps are represented in the chapters that follow, as are the new and emerging fields in which they have staked their claims.

Part 1

Locating FieldWork

1

The Fieldwork Tradition

GEORGE J. MCCALL

WHAT IS FIELDWORK?

In the research community generally, fieldwork refers to primary research that transpires 'in the field' – that is, outside the controlled settings of the library or laboratory. The importance of field studies in a wide range of disciplines, like geology or botany or the social sciences, is quite evident.

Of course, the methods of field research (McCall, 1978) frequently do, and should, include 'field experiments'. Does applying fertilizer to a prairie increase the number of insects? Does street lighting reduce crime? Yet, in virtually every discipline, field methods lean very heavily toward the non-experimental – toward observational studies, in the statistical sense of that phrase. Much of that work employs 'systematic field observation' (McCall, 1984); for example, the number of plant species occurring in a square meter may be empirically ascertained, as might the frequency of expressions of disagreement within a troubled marital pair. Many other field studies employ a more naturalistic, more open-ended style of observation that emphasizes discovery or pattern recognition; for instance,

a field botanist might come to see that her observations can be usefully summarized by the concept of *brousse tigrée*. A second meaning of 'fieldwork', then, has reference to the period of preliminary work and/or of data collection that does take place in a field setting, as distinguished from other phases of those same studies (such as design, analysis, write-up) that take place in more conventional and researcher-controlled settings. For instance, an old-fashioned face-to-face survey study would exhibit a period of fieldwork, and even the decennial census by mailed questionnaire involves a period of fieldwork in which block maps are constructed and updated.

A third and key meaning of 'fieldwork' is peculiar to the social sciences, such as sociology and anthropology. Some of the distinguishing characteristics of fieldwork in this sense stem from the phenomenon of reflexiveness, that is to say, inclusion of the observer in the subject matter itself. Reflexiveness does not occur in, for example, geology or botany, since the observer is neither a rock nor a plant, but it typically does occur in ecology, where the observer's species of animal often is a member of an ecological community being studied. In disciplines that take for their subject matter some aspect of human society, this phenomenon of reflexiveness is quite inevitable. Another source of the distinguishing characteristics of social science fieldwork is the fact of symbols – all thought and action of human beings is, or can be, framed in systems of meanings and symbols. Possession of true language enables humans to inhabit symbolic universes. A final source is the fact of cultures – the sharing of lifeways within the limits of social aggregation. When some but not all humans share any particular language, they come to inhabit differing symbolic universes, which in turn tend to lay claim to specific geographical territories as well.

THE PARTICIPANT-OBSERVATION TRADITION OF FIELDWORK

Responding quite directly to these three sources of peculiarity is the social science version of fieldwork:

- fieldworkers will need to depict those symbolic universes in order to understand the thought and action of those humans who live therein;
- to depict such a symbolic universe requires learning the focal language and the attendant lifeways of the corresponding speech community;
- any study of (some aspect of) that speech community will reflexively require study of self as well as others, so that the observer also becomes an observed participant;
- the phrase 'in the field' takes on further meaning, since for a human to study humans *in situ* is to venture onto the latter's turf, a territory they control numerically so that their ways dominate there.

Fieldwork that exhibits these characteristics is considered 'ethnographic'. Whereas pure ethnography attempts to focus on representing all or most of such a 'culture', much ethnographic research focuses instead on documenting and illuminating some culturally embedded social system.

At the methodological heart of ethnographic fieldwork lies 'participant observation'. Some commentators construe participant observation in a narrow sense, as being one distinctive method of collecting qualitative data, 'in which a researcher takes part in the daily activities, rituals, interactions, and events of a group of people as one of the means of learning the explicit and tacit aspects of their life routines and their culture' (DeWalt and DeWalt, 2002: 1). In that view, this core method is traditionally supplemented by some variety of other data collection methods, such as interviewing, document analysis, census-taking, etc.

Other commentators – myself included (McCall and Simmons, 1969) – view participant observation in a broader sense, as naming not a single method but a necessarily multimethod, mixed-method (quantitative and qualitative) mode of social research in which both participation and observation figure prominently.

In either case, most commentators can agree that the key elements of participant observation include:

- living in the context for an extended period of time;
- learning and using local language and dialect;
- actively participating in a wide range of daily, routine, and extraordinary activities with people who are full participants in that context;
- using everyday conversation as an interview technique;
- informally observing during leisure activitities (hanging out);
- recording observations in field notes (usually organized chronologically); and
- using both tacit and explicit information in analysis and writing. (DeWalt and Dewalt, 2002: 4)

Of these several elements, perhaps none is so defining of fieldwork as the punctilious writing of fieldnotes, carefully recording all that one did, saw, heard, and experienced out in the field on that day. Of the elements not enumerated above, perhaps none is so defining as (1) the perpetual monitoring of the research process for possible problems or biases, and (2) the fact that aspects of that research process – design (formulation of questions and plans), data collection, data analysis, write-up – do not comprise a linear sequence of stages, as in most other social research, but a rapidly rotating wheel, in which all four aspects are performed virtually every day while in the field.

THE SCIENCE TRADITION OF FIELDWORK

None of us can recall the shock that the brutality of the First World War created among all intellectuals, as the absurdity of a belief in human progress was painfully revealed. With the idea of progress rejected, social scientists in particular abruptly abandoned the stage theories of human evolutionary progress that had guided them since earliest days. A new resolve to start all over again from a more scientific foundation of careful, empirical, descriptive studies rapidly took their place (Hinkle and Hinkle, 1954). Indeed, attempts were made to develop observational languages distinct from theoretical languages. But although both behaviorism and logical positivism enjoyed some vogue in the social sciences, no reputable sociologist or anthropologist ever fully subscribed to either program. Objects such as cultures, roles, and selves were considered real and potentially knowable. Objectivity in their study was considered to be a virtue, something worth striving for even in the face of great difficulty. The tradition of fieldwork

as science is an important heritage of that post-First World War resolve.

EARLY ROOTS

Among sociologists, both in Europe and in the United States, much field research of good quality had already been undertaken long before the First World War. In the front ranks stood the intensive, first-hand field studies of the English poor by Charles Booth (1892–97) and Sidney and Beatrice Webb (1898). But as transplanted to the United States, their 'social survey' movement (Harrison, 1918–20; Kellogg, 1909–14) became principally a social movement openly advocating particular reforms. The Chicago department (Park and Burgess, 1921; Small, 1921) instead proclaimed science to be the true aim of sociology, over social change.

Among anthropologists, similarly, research of good methodological quality amply predated the First World War. Yet, too much of what passed for ethnography remained essentially second-hand, relying on one or two informants reporting on the 'verandahs' of missions or colonial stations. The science tradition in anthropology post-First World War dates from a new insistence on complementing informant reports with first-hand observation – not just in rapid surveys of an extensive area, but in intensive studies of particular communities. Although such studies had occasionally been executed earlier (for example, Frank Cushing's studies of the Zuñi in the 1880s and the Spencer and Gillen study of the Arunta in the 1890s that so influenced sociologist Durkheim), the scientific tradition of ethnography is usually dated (Wax, 1972; Stocking, 1983) to the Pacific Island studies of Bronislaw Malinowski (1922) and Margaret Mead (1928).

Following the First World War, reputable social scientists not only repudiated stage theories of human progress, they also largely abandoned all other single-factor explanations of human affairs and thus tended to embrace 'multiple causation'. At the extreme, this emphasis on multiplicity of influences took the form of a doctrine of 'holism' – that is, studying the entirety of an object in all of its aspects. Indeed, such was the rationale for the 'case study method', seeking an understanding of the total individual, group, institution, community, or society. First of all, as pointed out by Waller (1934), such a holistic approach fit well with the then prevailing 'Gestalt psychology', which emphasized that systems are self-organizing and greater than the sum of their parts. Many have similarly noted that a holistic approach also fits well with the dictates of Malinowski's functionalist theory. Second, the case-study method fit the call for careful, empirical studies because it was seen as an inductive method that begins with the accumulation of concrete data. Focusing on qualitative interrelations, it can discover causal sequences, processes of change in time, and complex mechanisms of interrelationships of social phenomena (Hinkle and Hinkle, 1954: 25). Even though sociologists of this early period came up with the label of 'participant observation' (Lindeman, 1924), it was the alternative label of 'case-study method' that dominated sociological discussions of this approach throughout the early days.

And those discussions were quite heated indeed, since some other prominent social scientists interpreted the call for scientific, objective research as clearly supporting the very different 'statistical method'. Its proponents considered the statistical method more scientifically respectable, since the hallmark of esteemed sciences at that time seemed to them to be quantification.

Statistical conclusions are precise, verifiable, valid, useful in prediction, less elaborate, less costly than those arrived at by qualitative methods, and, finally, are objective in that they cannot be biased by prejudiced interpretations of the data. Opponents reminded statisticians of the limitations of their research tool. They contended that statistics cannot express causal sequences or mechanisms but only cross-sectional views; they cannot reveal dynamics of action but only the presence or absence of selected factors; they cannot describe an entity as a whole; and they can never reach the inner, subjective elements in the mental life of man (Hinkle and Hinkle, 1954: 25).

From today's perspective of the highly differentiated university, it can fairly be asked why the sociological and anthropological roots of fieldwork were not actually more different from one another than they were. To start with, both disciplines initially derived their notion of 'fieldwork' from the natural-history disciplines. In fact, many of the early anthropologists actually began their fieldwork careers as zoologists and only gradually drifted into the study of human societies. During this period the early textbooks in both disciplines relied heavily on conceptions borrowed from natural history – a framework that remained popular in sociological analyses well into the 1950s. A second reason for so little differentiation in the early days is that joint departments of sociology and anthropology were then very common indeed in the United States, and British anthropologists were known for their 'sociological school', relying on the inspiration of Emile Durkheim. Although from the beginning anthropologists probably took holism a bit more seriously than sociologists, members of joint departments did closely evaluate one another's work. Traditionally, 'the field' was, for a department's anthropologists, some little-known spot remote from Western societies while, for its sociologists, it was most often some quite accessible place where it was convenient to study some little-understood segment of US society.

The University of Chicago is exemplary in this respect, as it exerted considerable influence on the development of both disciplines. At Chicago, the department remained a joint affair up until 1929. Before that splitting away, its key anthropologists included not only Edward Sapir but also, and more influentially, Robert Redfield (a follower and son-in-law of sociologist Park) and Lloyd Warner. For several years, the new anthropology department was headed by A.R. Radcliffe-Brown, whose structure-functionalism approach struck Park as perhaps even more sociological than that of the sociology department. Even after the separation, sociology graduate students were required to take coursework in anthropology – so that anthropologists commonly served on sociological dissertation committees – and the continuing sociologists in charge of research training were highly conversant with contemporary developments in anthropology (Chapoulie, 1987).

Beginnings

Because they reflect these several characteristics of post-First World War social science, the many fieldwork studies of the 1920s and 1930s can truly be said to constitute the beginnings of the scientific participant-observation tradition of sociological/anthropological fieldwork.

Park, as an old newspaperman who reckoned that he had walked more streets of the world than any man alive, required that his graduate students closely observe urban settings. But as a student of William James, he also placed the strongest emphasis on documenting and illuminating the subjective, or mental, aspect of life. Under Park's direction, and with little textual material to guide them

(Martineau, 1838; Webb, 1926; Webb and Webb, 1932), a set of highly influential participant-observation fieldwork studies soon appeared, including such classics as Nels Anderson's (1923) study of the hobo, Frederick Thrasher's (1927) study of Chicago gangs, Harvey Zorbaugh's (1929) study of that city's Near North Side, Clifford Shaw's (1930) study of a delinquent boy, Everett Hughes's (1931) study of the Chicago Real Estate Board, and Paul Cressey's (1932) study of the taxi-dance hall. Partly through the initiative of his better-trained colleague Ernest W. Burgess, Vivian Palmer was engaged to record and codify the fieldwork methods of these early studies (Palmer, 1928). At the same time and in the same department, anthropologists Redfield and Warner were already undertaking their path-breaking fieldwork studies – Redfield in a series of small Mexican communities and Warner in his 'Yankee City' studies of Newburyport, Massachusetts.

But as vital as the Chicago department was, the fieldwork tradition initially developed and flowered at a variety of locations. Within sociology, perhaps the most important of these other locations was the Lynds' study of Middletown (1929) that did so much to institutionalize the participant-observation approach to the holistic case study of communities. Within anthropology, similarly, Mead's Samoan fieldwork was pursuant to her degree at Columbia University, and Malinowski's was European inspired.

Traditional participant-observation fieldwork is organized by a whole series of antinomies, tensions, and stresses (Hughes, 1960), many of which were posed and essentially worked out during this earliest period.

From the beginning, issues concerning the social role of the participant observer centered on the researcher's cultural standing, on the antinomy of 'insider' versus 'outsider'.

Some student sociologists were urged to make sociological capital of their membership in, and cultural understanding of, some understudied segment of society (anthropologists who were also natives did not emerge until considerably later). More typically, however, fieldworkers had to enter from outside, to take up life among the natives in order to develop a cultural understanding. In either case, the participant observer exemplified the social type Park had identified, the 'marginal man'. Of course, just how marginal that individual was depended on the degree of 'culture conflict' between the culture of the natives and that of the academy.

The researcher's perspective on native society could easily range from that of an ordinary member (later termed an 'emic' perspective), to that of a complete stranger (later termed an 'etic' perspective). The great risk of holding tightly to the member perspective is that of 'going native', and retaining a strict stranger perspective is that of 'ethnocentrism'. The necessity of transcending those opposing perspectives was established very early; the fieldworker must remain open to native views while simultaneously seeking an academic understanding; a balance must be attained between description and explanation, between the idiographic and the nomothetic. Such a transcendent perspective is especially vital in view of fieldwork's commitment to examine not only the objective behaviors of natives but also the subjective, meaningful aspect of those behaviors. The fieldworker's participation in many native activities is a direct source of knowledge about the subjective aspects, while simultaneous observation of those activities is a source of knowledge about their objective aspects; hence, the 'double consciousness' that is distinctive of participant observers.

Almost always, some native activities are found to be accessible even to outsiders, while certain other activities are not so initially, but can become accessible to the participant observer as trust and rapport are achieved. Because some activities occur only rarely, they are directly accessible only to that participant observer who stays around for a long period of time. Early trials soon showed that a fieldworker should stay at least a year, and that the expense of doing so was much less for the solo fieldworker than for a team of observers (despite the potential for reliability checks provided by the latter).

The Jekyll/Hyde character of social theory in all this was discovered very early. Grand theory was rejected from the beginning, as too abstract and as leading to overemphasis on deductive reasoning and the logic of proof. Fieldwork was instead meant to be heavily inductive and to emphasize a logic of discovery. The dilemma was that to transcend the descriptive and the idiographic, to achieve some balance with the explanatory and the nomothetic, does require social theory of some sort; what we now call 'theories of the middle range' were just modest enough for that balancing act.

It is perhaps not so widely recognized today just how self-critical these early fieldworkers were, methodologically speaking. Not only did it become correct and necessary, in those post-First World War days, for fieldworkers to describe within their monographic reports the methods they had employed, but fieldworkers also began writing separate articles that raised and explored more systemic problems encountered (Webb, 1926; Cressey, 1927/1983; Thrasher, 1928; Mead, 1933; Lohman, 1937; Reimer, 1937).

Succeeding generations

The 'cohort effect' is quite evident among scholarly researchers in every field, so that the problems and approaches of each succeeding period-cohort are fairly distinct from those who came before or after. And because the demands of participant observation are so rigorous, nearly all commentators agree that traditional fieldwork is an undertaking for the young and the not-yet highly encumbered. As a result of both these factors, the tradition of fieldwork bears the clear marks of succeeding generations, about every decade or so.

Imagine the following sort of branching diagram, with a time scale running from left to right along the bottom, beginning at the year 1920. An individual's actual conduct of fieldwork can be represented by an upward oblique line for roughly a decade, plus or minus. That individual's shift into the subsequent roles of commentator, codifier, and mentor typically helps to shape the fieldwork of the next couple of decades – diagrammatically represented by a horizontal line spanning twenty to thirty years. Overall, then, the diagram presents a continuous line of fieldwork running obliquely upward to the right, with a series of fairly short horizontal branches also to the right. This mode of diagramming emphasizes the discontinuity between faculty cohorts while perhaps exaggerating the continuity of the fieldwork enterprise. In reality, that enterprise also experienced significant intergenerational differences and trends, many of which are missed in most histories of the tradition (Richards, 1939; Wax, 1972; Platt 1983, 1994, 1995, 1996; Bulmer, 1984) because those histories do not extend much beyond 1960 (but see Emerson, 2001).

In the first place, fieldwork is a way of doing sociology/anthropology, and thus it reflects the ongoing struggles of those fields to more usefully define the nature of society and, especially, of culture; during each generation, those struggles have been distinctive. To some extent, those struggles in turn reflect the social context of the times. Second, fieldwork generations tend to specially concern themselves with one or two aspects of the research process (design, data collection, data analysis, write-up). Third, the fieldwork issues central to a generation (role issues, epistemic issues, phenomenal issues, methodological issues, ethical issues) reflect which of those several antinomies of fieldwork (or their consequences) most engage its concern.

Since I am more familiar with these developments in sociology, the account here will naturally emphasize those (especially at the University of Chicago), though with some attention to developments in anthropology as well.

The 1940s

At Chicago, Park had long since retired and Radcliffe-Brown had returned to England, but by then Hughes, Redfield, and Warner had become established as key faculty mentors in fieldwork. In addition to their own ethnographic publications (Hughes, 1943; Redfield, 1941; Warner's entire 'Yankee City' series), they were able to draw upon a sprinkling of new fieldwork commentaries and codifications – by Florence Kluckhohn (1940), Jesse Bernard (1945), Ernest Burgess (1945), Burleigh Gardner and William Foote Whyte (1946), and John Bennett (1948) – that focused mainly on the data collection aspect of the research process.

For much of the decade of the 1940s, of course, the pool of graduate students in all fields was heavily depleted by the manpower demands of the Second World War. The great outpouring of military applied social research, exemplified by *The American Soldier*, tends to obscure the fact that some of this military research took the form of fieldwork, as aspiring social scientists found themselves in novel situations – for example, Bruno Bettelheim (1943) published his study of the Nazi concentration camp, Ralph Turner (1947) analyzed the navy disbursing officer as a bureaucrat, and George Homans (1947) examined the social system of the small warship. Anthropologists, such as Clyde Kluckhohn, Margaret Mead, and Ruth Benedict, also served the national interest through necessarily 'quick and dirty' construction of ethnographies of enemy and ally societies alike. Not surprisingly, as many of these sociologists and anthropologists found themselves 'insiders' within personally unfamiliar circumstances, issues of the researcher's social role proved of central interest to this generation of fieldworkers.

But of course, not all the major works in this genre were military. At Chicago, Whyte (1943) published his seminal account of street corner life in an Italian slum, and Allison Davis, Burleigh Gardner, and Mary Gardner (1941) brought out their fieldwork analysis of caste and class in the Deep South.

The 1950s

Nationally, this decade saw functional theory, already well developed in anthropology, make vast inroads in sociology, especially through the writings of Talcott Parsons and Robert K. Merton. It is not accidental that this decade was also the heyday of interdisciplinary work and programs – in social relations, behavioral sciences, policy sciences, and social psychology – perhaps underlain by the experience of military teamwork during the Second World War. Furthermore, all the social sciences shared a strong focus on psychiatry and mental disorders; culture and personality, still with a strong interest in national character, had become a major subfield of anthropology.

In the Chicago sociology department during the 1950s, the key faculty trio was supplemented by Anselm Strauss, as students everywhere flocked to graduate school under the GI Bill of Rights. At Chicago, this cohort of students – including Howard S. Becker, Morris Schwartz, Donald Roy, Erving Goffman, Ray Gold, Joseph Gusfield, Robert Habenstein, Fred Davis, Julius Roth, and Murray Wax – flowered into what is often regarded as 'a second Chicago School' (Fine, 1995). Fine and Ducharme (1995) emphasize this generation's obsession with the origins and manifestations of totalitarianism, and the fact that much of its best sociological fieldwork explores themes of institutional control.

The textual materials even in fieldwork reflected the major methodological advances made in the course of military studies during the prior decade. Chief among these new resources was an enduring special section on fieldwork techniques in the interdisciplinary journal *Human Organization*, eliciting dozens of first-rate articles, including Wax (1952), Vidich and Bensman (1954), Becker and Geer (1957), and Dean and Whyte (1958). Their popularity lent support to the appearance of similar articles in leading sociological journals, including Arensberg (1954), Becker (1956, 1958), Gold (1958), Miller (1952), Schwartz and Schwartz (1955), Vidich (1955), Vidich and Shapiro (1955), and Wax (1957).

As a group, these articles covered rather evenly all four aspects of the research process, but focused on a smaller number of fieldwork issues. Methodological issues reflect a morphing of the earlier case-study versus statistical methods controversy into one between participant observation and modern survey research. To clarify relations among the latter two required revisiting the tensions between validity and reliability; instructive here is renewed attention to the 'community restudy problem' (Lynd and Lynd, 1929, 1937; Wierzbicki, 1982), as Redfield (1930, 1955) and Oscar Lewis (1951) confronted the significance of their differing views of a particular Mexican village. The central epistemic issue of the decade – the handling of biases – revealed a desire of this generation to go beyond Gunnar Myrdal's rather passive approach of listing one's known biases to more active attempts to countervail at least some common biases. Role issues reflected a concern for management of 'field relations' in striving for trust and rapport.

Anthropological and sociological fieldworkers alike drew inspiration from the methodological chapters by Paul (1953) and Lewis (1953) in the Kroeber-edited handbook on *Anthropology Today* and from Spencer's edited volume on anthropological methods, particularly the chapter by Herskovitz (1954).

Not to be overlooked was a new generation of quite general, interdisciplinary textbooks on the range of research methods – Jahoda et al. (1951), Goode and Hatt (1952), Festinger and Katz (1953), Doby et al. (1954) – each with attention to fieldwork, under various labels. (Whyte's contributions to those chapters – including his own (1951) – inspired publication of a new and more influential 1955 edition of his earlier monograph, and Dean's (1954) contribution was especially acute.) The importance of these general textbooks lies in the fact that, though participant observation enjoyed a standing as *the* method in cultural anthropology (even today), it was, in the 1950s, only one among many ways of doing research in the other social sciences. Everyone did participant observation back then, at least occasionally (Merton, 1947; Blau, 1954; Wolff, 1960), including some sociologists who later radicalized field research, such as Alvin Gouldner (1954; Stein, 1954) and even psychologists such as Festinger, Riecken, and Schacter (1956).

Indeed, the most important community study during this decade – Vidich and Bensman's (1958) *Small Town in Mass Society* – was conducted by the Harvard-trained Vidich and the Columbia-trained Bensman.

The 1960s

Fieldwork mentoring in the Chicago department was effectively eliminated for most of the 1960s, as Hughes and the others were forced out by the administration (Abbott and Gaziano, 1995). Nationally speaking, however, in many ways this decade represents the highwater mark of the fieldwork tradition, with many new resources. First of all, those who had emerged as leaders in sociological fieldwork dispersed more widely as faculty mentors – Hughes to Brandeis and later Boston University, Becker to Stanford and later Northwestern University, Strauss to the University of California's Medical School in San Francisco, and Vidich still with Whyte at Cornell. Very important ethnographies were published during the 1960s by these leaders: Becker, Geer, Hughes, and Strauss (1961) on medical school; Becker, Geer, and Hughes (1968) on college students; Strauss, Schatzman, Bucher, Erlich, and Sabshin (1964) on ideologies in psychiatric institutions; and Glaser and Strauss (1965) on awareness of dying. The major new systematic text was that of Glaser and Strauss (1967) on discovering grounded theory, an idea that was to subsequently revolutionize sociological fieldwork.

Second, many of those students comprising 'the second Chicago school' finally published their major ethnographic works, including those highlighted by Fine and Ducharme (1995) – Fred Davis's (1963) book on polio victims and their families, Julius Roth's (1963) book on tuberculosis treatment, and Erving Goffman's (1961) book on total institutions.

Third, mentors everywhere now had access to the Junker (1960) report on the Hughes/Warner study of learning to do fieldwork, as well as the Adams and Preiss (1960) anthology of articles from the *Human Organization* series – including new or expanded papers by Whyte (1960) on interviewing, Wolff (1960) on collecting and organizing data, and Becker and Geer (1960) on analyzing fieldwork data. Major new journal articles along these lines included Bensman and Vidich (1960) on the roles of theory in fieldwork, Zelditch (1962) on some methodological problems of fieldwork, Janes (1961) on phases of the participant-observer role, Smalley (1960) on making fieldnotes, and Glaser (1965) on analyzing fieldwork data. The main new specialized textbooks, however, were anthropological, including that of Thomas Williams (1967) and that of Raoul Naroll (1962), which formalized within ethnography the idea of data quality control, a notion subsequently extended by McCall (1969).

Fourth, a relatively new resource for sociological mentors that emerged during this decade – supplementing career reflections of fieldworkers such as Powdermaker (1967) – was the special compilation of explicit reflections on the experience of major fieldwork studies. The Vidich, Bensman, and Stein (1964) volume focused largely on studies of communities, and included an important new contribution by Becker (1964) on problems in publishing fieldwork reports. The Hammond (1964) volume, on the other hand, contained reflections on a wider range of fieldwork studies, including reflections by Blau (1964) and Dalton (1964).

A fifth major resource was the journal *Social Problems*, especially under Becker's early editorship. That journal was the official publication of the Society for the Study of Social Problems, which became an unofficial scholarly home for many fieldwork sociologists in their opposition to both functional theory and abstract empiricism.

Having come of age during the conformist decade of the 1950s, the large generation of fieldwork students of the 1960s, mainly explored themes of deviance including John Lofland, George McCall, Jerry Simmons, Sherri Cavan, John Irwin, Julian Roebuck, Jack Douglas, Erich Goode, Jim Henslin, Laud Humphreys, Peter Manning, Marvin Scott, David Sudnow, Sam Wallace, Jackie Wiseman, James Spradley, and Robert Keiser. In doing so, they often followed the lead of 'labeling theories' such as that of Becker (1963) and pursued the notion of 'subcultures' (supported by the likes of Oscar Lewis (1959)). (Although, of course, deviance did not completely dominate the interests of that generation of fieldworkers, for the decade also saw brilliant community studies in the work of Herbert Gans (1962), Elliot Liebow (1967), and Gerald Suttles (1968).)

The central issues of the decade, fittingly enough, concerned ethics – especially the ethics of covert participant observation, with its issues of informed consent (Roth, 1962; Dalton 1964; Erikson, 1967; Bulmer, 1982), and the ethics of publication, with its issues of confidentiality and the objectification of relationships (Becker, 1964). Role issues similarly centered on the covert participant observer and on the many stresses experienced by the overt fieldworker (Henry and Saberwal, 1969).

The 1970s

At the urging of Morris Janowitz, the Chicago sociology department during the 1970s brought in Suttles and David Street to restore the fieldwork tradition for which that department had long been famed. Although these two certainly succeeded in restoring the tradition – as witnessed by the fieldwork studies of Elijah Anderson (1978), Michael Burawoy (1979), and William Kornblum (1974) – it was already too late to restore departmental dominance within that fieldwork tradition; even across town, at Northwestern University, Becker was quite their equal as a mentor. All across the land, the previous generation of graduate students had become enthusiastic faculty mentors, and many had written specialized textbooks or compiled useful anthologies. Among these were (in sociology) books by Lofland (1971, 1976), McCall and Simmons (1969), Schatzman and Strauss (1973), and Filstead (1970), as well as (in anthropology) the textbook by Pelto and Pelto (1970) and the methods handbook edited by Naroll and Cohen (1970).

Compilations of reflections on the experience of major fieldwork studies remained quite useful, including those by Habenstein (1970) and the anthropologists Golde (1970), Freilich (1970) and Spindler (1970). A useful supplement, again, was the career reflection of sociologist Rosalie Wax (1971).

A key new resource for fieldwork mentors everywhere was convenient outlets for small fieldwork studies. The most enduring of these was the new journal *Urban Life and Culture*, but equally enlightening for students was the student fieldwork anthology edited by Spradley and McCurdey (1972).

The new generation of graduate students had come of age during the traumas of the Vietnam War and related tragedies, and had experienced a tumultuous episode of university turmoil. These students sharply questioned the work of their mentors, especially with regard to the ethics and the 'relevance' of such work. Neo-Marxian 'critical theory' had already radicalized some segments of social research, and fieldwork too was made

(by some) into a political problem. For a couple of decades already, some anthropologists had found overseas fieldwork to be entirely problematic for political reasons. And now some sociological textbooks in fieldwork, such as Johnson (1975), were already edging toward political radicalization; even Becker's (1967) SSSP presidential address had asked whose side are we on.

The political critique of fieldwork focused on the aspect of design – the kinds of question that fieldworkers had asked and not asked – and on related issues of social role and ethics. At the same time, and perhaps not coincidentally, epistemic issues were commonly raised that tilted fieldwork toward the purely emic perspective, as the new 'cognitive anthropology' (Tyler, 1969) advocated study of folk categories, and toward emphasis on tacit culture, as the new 'ethnomethodology' (Garfinkel, 1967) called for study of folk practices. These political and epistemic critiques came together in the critical volume by Dell Hymes (1974) seeking to 'reinvent' the discipline of anthropology.

The 1980s

Perhaps in reaction to the development of critical anthropology, the journal *Urban Life and Culture* twice changed its title during the 1980s, first dropping the term 'culture' and subsequently renaming itself *Journal of Contemporary Ethnography*. In any case, the new Spradley (1980) text sought explicitly to harness many of the new techniques of cognitive anthropology to the service of traditional participant observation, which was explicated for that generation in the Burgess (1984) text.

Methodological issues of the 1980s reflected yet another morphing of the primordial case-study versus statistical-methods controversy, this time into a controversy between qualitative and quantitative (experimental and quasi-experimental, rather than survey) methods of social research. This new controversy raged most heatedly in the field of program evaluation (Cook and Reichardt, 1979), with some commentators going so far as to reject the relevance of validity and reliability to qualitative research and to invent new parallel concepts founded on 'member validation', a highly emic perspective (Guba and Lincoln, 1989). That struggle eventually reached a resolution in which most researchers conceded the value of both qualitative and quantitative methods, often advocating 'mixed-method' studies. Perhaps as a result, a whole variety of different qualitative approaches split off at this time, often taking refuge under the flag of grounded theory.

Another central issue of this period was epistemic, as some commentators (Denzin, 1989) took to an extreme the interpretive approaches of Herbert Blumer (1969) and Clifford Geertz (1973), arguing that all the fieldworker ever obtains are interpretations (rather than descriptions), so that 'texts' take the place of reality. On that ground, methods of textual analysis developed in literary criticism were considered more appropriate than traditional participant observation.

Furthermore, ethnography was made (by some) into a moral problem. Seizing upon the reflexiveness of participant observation, some commentators (particularly in anthropology, where cultural relativism had expanded to moral relativism) contended that because the observer is among the observed, the fieldworker has no right to claim any authoritative voice in the final product and no right to endorse any other particular voice.

Both the epistemic and the moral critiques focused attention squarely on the write-up aspect of the research process, concluding that a 'crisis of representation' existed, in that

traditional 'realistic' ethnographic reports were viewed as imposing inappropriately 'scientific' standards. In the eyes of such commentators (Clifford and Marcus, 1986), virtually any sort of alternative reporting format offered new opportunities worth exploring.

This 'new ethnography', with its excessive focus on the lived experience of the fieldworker and its 'anything-goes' approach to analysis and reporting, seems to have appealed greatly to many who had come of age during the days of the openly self-indulgent 'Me Generation', as did a variety of 'agency theories' in anthropology.

The 1990s

The graduate students of the 1990s, on the other hand, had generally come of age in a cultural climate driven by the media-centered 'Generation X', and many of their subsequent writings analyzed movies and other forms of popular culture. The social movement of postmodernism, in its skepticism and its culture critique (mainly of Western societies), seemed to strike an important chord among such analysts, some of whom split off to form new departments of 'cultural studies'.

Perhaps as a result of Generation-X interests, role issues emerged as fieldworkers confronted again how demographic characteristics like gender, race, and age influence field relations, with some commentators (such as Murray, 1991) openly advocating the use of sexual relationships (straight or gay) as a key source of data. The epistemic and methodological issues raised during the previous decade continued the splintering and the separatism within fieldwork, as both feminists and gays proclaimed distinctive methodologies (Reinharz, 1992). The persistence of those issues also gave rise to two important new mentoring resources, the reinvigorated journal *Field Methods* and the *Handbook of Qualitative Research* (Denzin and Lincoln, 1994).

Reconsiderations of the write-up aspect of the research process continued in the 1990s, extended at that time to the proper forms and uses of fieldnotes (Sanjek, 1990; Emerson et al., 1995). But it was the analysis aspect of the research process that received dominant attention, as the by-then-universal availability of powerful personal computers led nearly all fieldworkers to consider the use of software programs to assist them in the management and analysis of large ethnographic datasets (Miles and Huberman, 1994; Weitzman and Miles, 1995). Responding to this renewed interest in analysis, Becker (1998) and Werner and Schoepfle (1987) codified some of the techniques of traditional analysis, while Burawoy (1991) proposed an analytic alternative to grounded theory and Hodson (1999) explored application of meta-analysis to sets of ethnographies.

During that decade, adherents of traditional fieldwork began mounting more explicit and more vigorous epistemic defenses against the inroads of postmodernism (Harris, 1995; Katz, 1997; Kuznar, 1997), while still other commentators (such as Hammersley, 1992) tempered their understandings of realism in response to the relativist concerns of constructivists.

Trends

Over the course of these generations, the shape of the fieldwork conducted has certainly been influenced by: (1) pressures from competing modes of social research, (2) societal happenings – wars (hot or cold), depressions, boomtimes, etc. – that condition both cohorts and universities, (3) the experiences and interests of mentors, and (4) the nature and content of teaching resources. All these influences have been at least briefly addressed in the previous subsections.

What I have not yet addressed is how the generational shape of fieldwork is influenced by (5) fads and fashions of intellectual life, which are often longer-term and hence give rise to 'trends' over the span of a few decades.

For example, a romance with psychoanalysis characterized intellectual life over the first few decades of this particular span but later faded dramatically, and with it the concomitant obsession of the social sciences with psychiatry and, especially, personality. In fieldwork particularly, the 'cases' to be studied were less often individual personalities and more often groups, institutions, or communities. The life histories and personal documents that played such a prominent part in early ethnographies became ever harder to find in later ethnographies.

Similarly, the diachronic interests of early anthropologists like Boas, rather soon gave way to an emphasis on synchronic accounts – the 'ethnographic present'. Cultural history moved from center-stage in the fieldwork drama to the less prominent role of context (although historical context never became any less important in fieldwork than physical or social context).

Of course, as mentioned, much of the impetus for synchronic accounts stemmed from early theoretical approaches such as functionalism (in anthropology and later in sociology). The long romance of those fields with functionalism very much guided fieldwork studies, but that intellectual fashion went out of style after the 1960s.

In a similar manner, holism receded as Gestalt psychology became less fashionable in intellectual life. Indeed, toward the latter part of our span, even the appropriateness of four-field anthropology came to be questioned by some. Even earlier, anthropological fieldwork less often addressed whole small-societies in favor of a more frequent focus on segmental problems, and sociological fieldwork came to focus less on institutions and more on social settings (Lofland, 1976). However, even though fieldwork gradually came to place less emphasis on holistic accounts, the importance of the whole context of phenomena remained a key principle in fieldwork analysis.

Finally, the sociology of knowledge gained increasing foothold in intellectual life over this span, especially from the 1960s onward. Its emphasis on the social construction of reality initially lent supportive detail to the idea of cultures, but later such constructivism was construed by some as more importantly supporting a notion of relativism. The neo-Marxian aspect of sociology of knowledge, meanwhile, lent support instead to a political critique of social science.

As a result of these five factors, each fieldwork generation has had to struggle to achieve some sort of reasonable balance with respect to each of the antinomies and tensions of participant observation, especially those between emic and etic perspectives, between tacit and explicit sorts of cultural knowledge, between subjective and objective aspects of native actions, between participation and observation as sources of knowledge, between descriptive and explanatory aims, between idiographic and nomothetic interests, between inductive and deductive reasoning, between the logic of discovery and the logic of proof.

THE FUTURE OF TRADITIONAL FIELDWORK

In view of all these developments and challenges, is traditional fieldwork dead? Only in the triumphalist claims of various anti-science factions! Indeed, the tradition ends only when, and where, anti-science becomes fashionable. Today, as the remainder of this *Handbook* makes clear, there are postmodern varieties of 'fieldworkers' who reject the scientific participant-observation tradition in favor of non-ethnographic (yet still qualitative) alternatives. The point is that each of these anti-science factions remains surrounded by traditionalists, who rather quickly absorb any useful points these factions may contribute.

Scientific participant-observation fieldwork still lives today in numerous traditional ethnographic reports (such as Leach, 2003; Wolcott, 2003), in compilations (Emerson 2001), and in many chapters of the Atkinson et al. (2001) *Handbook of Ethnography*. More importantly, scientific participant-observation fieldwork is still being taught in many of today's how-to-do-it textbooks (e.g., Agar, 1996; Bailey, 1996; Becker, 1998; DeWalt and DeWalt, 2002), thus assuring that this tradition has not only a past and a present, but also a twenty-first-century future.

REFERENCES

Abbott, Andrew, and Gaziano, Emanuel (1995) 'Transition and tradition: Departmental faculty in the era of the Second Chicago School', in G.A. Fine (ed.), *A Second Chicago School? The Development of a Postwar American Sociology*. Chicago: University of Chicago Press. pp. 221–72.

Adams, Richard N., and Preiss, Jack J. (eds) (1960) *Human Organization Research: Field Relations and Techniques*. Homewood, IL: Dorsey.

Agar, Michael (1996) *The Professional Stranger: An Informal Introduction to Ethnography* (2nd edn). Thousand Oaks, CA: Sage.

Anderson, Elijah (1978) *A Place on the Corner*. Chicago: University of Chicago Press.

Anderson, Nels (1923) *The Hobo: The Sociology of the Homeless Man*. Chicago: University of Chicago Press.

Arensberg, Conrad (1954) 'The community study method', *American Journal of Sociology*, 60: 109–24.

Atkinson, Paul A., Coffey, Amanda Jane, Lofland, Lyn H., Lofland, John, and Delamont, Sara (eds) (2001) *Handbook of Ethnography*. Thousand Oaks, CA: Sage.

Bailey, Carol A. (1996) *A Guide to Field Research*. Thousand Oaks, CA: Pine Forge.

Becker, Howard S. (1956) 'Interviewing medical students', *American Journal of Sociology*, 62: 199–201.

Becker, Howard S. (1958) 'Problems of inference and proof in participant observation', *American Sociological Review*, 23: 652–60.

Becker, Howard S. (1963) *Outsiders: Studies in the Sociology of Deviance*. New York: Free Press.

Becker, Howard S. (1964) 'Problems in the publication of field studies', in A.J. Vidich, J. Bensman, and M.R. Stein (eds), *Reflections on Community Studies*. New York: Wiley. pp. 267–85.

Becker, Howard S. (1967) 'Whose side are we on?', *Social Problems*, 14: 239–47.

Becker, Howard S. (1998) *Tricks of the Trade: How To Think About Your Research While You're Doing It*. Chicago: University of Chicago Press.

Becker, Howard S., and Geer, Blanche (1957) 'Participant observation and interviewing: A comparison', *Human Organization*, 16(3): 28–32.

Becker, Howard S., and Geer, Blanche (1960) 'Participant observation: The analysis of qualitative field data', in R.N. Adams and J.J. Preiss (eds), *Human Organization Research: Field Relations and Techniques*. Homewood, IL: Dorsey Press. pp. 267–89.

Becker, Howard S., Geer, Blanche and Hughes, Everett C. (1968) *Making the Grade: The Academic Side of College Life*. New York: Wiley.

Becker, Howard S., Geer, Blanche, Hughes, Everett C., and Strauss, Anselm L. (1961) *Boys in White: Student Culture in Medical School*. Chicago: University of Chicago Press.

Bennett, John W. (1948) 'The study of cultures: A survey of technique and methodology in field work', *American Sociological Review*, 13: 672–89.

Bensman, Joseph, and Vidich, Arthur (1960) 'Social theory in field research', *American Journal of Sociology*, 65: 577–84.

Bernard, Jesse (1945) 'Observation and generalization in cultural anthropology', *American Journal of Sociology*, 50: 284–91.

Bettelheim, Bruno (1943) 'Individual and mass behavior in extreme situations', *Journal of Abnormal and Social Psychology*, 38: 417–52.

Blau, Peter M. (1954) 'Co-operation and competition in a bureaucracy', *American Journal of Sociology*, 59: 530–35.

Blau, Peter M. (1964) 'The research process in the study of The Dynamics of Bureaucracy', in P. Hammond (ed.), *Sociologists at Work*. New York: Basic Books. pp. 16–49.

Blumer, Herbert (1969) *Symbolic Interactionism*. Englewood Cliffs, NJ: Prentice-Hall.

Booth, Charles (1892–97) *Life and Labour of the People of London* (17 vols). London: Macmillan.

Bulmer, Martin (ed). (1982) *Social Research Ethics: An Examination of the Merits of Covert Participant Observation*. London: Macmillan.

Bulmer, Martin (1984) *The Chicago School of Sociology*. Chicago: University of Chicago Press.

Burawoy, Michael (1979) *Manufacturing Consent*. Chicago: University of Chicago Press.

Burawoy, Michael (1991) 'The extended case method', in M. Burawoy (ed.), *Ethnography Unbound: Power and Resistance in the Modern Metropolis*. Berkeley: University of California Press. pp. 271–87.

Burgess, Ernest W. (1945) 'Sociological research methods', *American Journal of Sociology*, 50: 474–82.

Burgess, Robert G. (1984) *In the Field: An Introduction to Field Research*. London: Routledge.

Chapoulie, Jean-Michel (1987) 'Everett C. Hughes and the development of fieldwork in sociology', *Urban Life*, 11: 407–20.

Clifford, James, and Marcus, George E. (eds) (1986) *Writing Culture: The Poetics and Politics of Ethnography*. Berkeley: University of California Press.

Cook, Thomas D., Reichardt, Charles S. (eds) (1979) *Qualitative and Quantitative Methods in Evaluation Research*. Beverly Hills, CA: Sage.

Cressey, Paul G. (1927/1983) 'A comparison of the roles of the "sociological stranger" and the "anonymous stranger" in field research', *Urban Life*, 12: 102–20.

Cressey, Paul G. (1932) *The Taxi-Dance Hall: A Sociological Study of Commercialized Recreation and City Life*. Chicago: University of Chicago Press.

Dalton, Melville (1964) 'Preconceptions and methods in Men Who Manage', in P. Hammond (ed.),

Sociologists at Work. New York: Basic Books. pp. 50–95.

Davis, Allison, Gardner, Burleigh B., and Gardner, Mary R. (1941) *Deep South: A Social Anthropological Study of Caste and Class.* Chicago: University of Chicago Press.

Davis, Fred (1963) *Passage Through Crisis.* Indianapolis, IN: Bobbs-Merrill.

Dean, John P. (1954) 'Participant observation and interviewing', in J.T. Doby, E.A. Suchman, J.C. McKinney, and J.P. Dean (eds), *An Introduction to Social Research.* Harrisburg, PA: Stackpole. pp. 225–52.

Dean, John P., and Whyte, William F. (1958) 'How do you know if the informant is telling the truth?', *Human Organization,* 17(2): 34–8.

Denzin, Norman K. (1989) *Interpretive Interactionism.* Newbury Park, CA: Sage.

Denzin, Norman K., and Lincoln, Yvonna S. (eds) (1994) *Handbook of Qualitative Research.* Thousand Oaks, CA: Sage.

DeWalt, Kathleen M., and DeWalt, Billie R. (2002) *Participant Observation: A Guide for Fieldworkers.* Walnut Creek, CA: AltaMira Press.

Doby, John T., Suchman, Edward A., McKinney, John C., and Dean, John P. (eds) (1954) *An Introduction to Social Research.* Harrisburg, PA: Stackpole.

Emerson, Robert M. (2001) 'Introduction: The development of ethnographic field research', in R.M. Emerson (ed.), *Contemporary Field Research: Perspectives and Formulations* (2nd edn). Boston: Little Brown. pp. 1–26.

Emerson, Robert M., Fretz, Rachel I., and Shaw, Linda L. (1995) *Writing Ethnographic Fieldnotes.* Chicago: University of Chicago Press.

Erikson, Kai T. (1967) 'A comment on disguised observation', *Social Problems,* 14: 366–73.

Festinger, Leon, and Katz, Daniel (eds) (1953) *Research Methods in the Behavioral Sciences.* New York: Dryden Press.

Festinger, Leon, Riecken, Henry W., and Schacter, Stanley (1956) *When Prophecy Fails.* Minneapolis, MN: University of Minnesota Press.

Filstead, William J. (ed.) (1970) *Qualitative Methodology: Firsthand Involvement with the Social World.* Chicago: Markham.

Fine, Gary Alan (ed.) (1995) *A Second Chicago School? The Development of a Postwar American Sociology.* Chicago: University of Chicago Press.

Fine, Gary Alan, and Ducharme, Lori J. (1995) 'The ethnographic present: Images of institutional control in second-school research', in G.A. Fine (ed.), *A Second Chicago School? The Development of a Postwar American Sociology.* Chicago: University of Chicago Press. pp. 108–35.

Freilich, Morris (ed.) (1970) *Marginal Natives: Anthropologists at Work.* New York: Harper & Row.

Gans, Herbert J. (1962) *The Urban Villagers.* New York: Free Press.

Gardner, Burleigh, and Whyte, William F. (1946) 'Methods for the study of human relations in industry', *American Sociological Review,* 11: 506–11.

Garfinkel, Harold (1967) *Studies in Ethnomethodology.* Englewood Cliffs, NJ: Prentice-Hall.

Geertz, Clifford (1973) *The Interpretation of Cultures: Selected Essays.* New York: Basic Books.

Glaser, Barney (1965) 'The constant comparative method of qualitative analysis', *Social Problems,* 12: 436–55.

Glaser, Barney, and Strauss, Anselm L. (1965) *Awareness of Dying: A Study of Social Interaction.* Chicago: Aldine.

Glaser, Barney, and Strauss, Anselm L. (1967) *The Discovery of Grounded Theory.* Chicago: Aldine.

Goffman, Erving (1961) *Asylums.* Garden City, NY: Doubleday Anchor.

Gold, Raymond L. (1958) 'Roles in sociological field observations', *Social Forces,* 36: 217–23.

Golde, Peggy (ed.) (1970) *Women in the Field: Anthropological Experiences.* Chicago: Aldine.

Goode, William J., and Hatt, Paul K. (1952) *Methods in Social Research.* New York: McGraw-Hill.

Gouldner, Alvin (1954) *Wildcat Strike.* Yellow Springs, OH: Antioch Press.

Guba, Egon, and Lincoln, Yvonne (1989) *Fourth Generation Evaluation.* Newbury Park, CA: Sage.

Habenstein, Robert W. (ed.) (1970) *Pathways to Data: Field Methods for Studying Ongoing Social Organizations.* Chicago: Aldine.

Hammersley, Martyn (1992) *What's Wrong with Ethnography?* London: Routledge.

Hammond, Philip (ed.) (1964) *Sociologists at Work.* New York: Basic Books.

Harris, Marvin (1995) 'Anthropology and postmodernism', in M.F. Murphy and M.L. Margolis (eds), *Science, Materialism, and the Study of Culture.* Gainesville, FL: University Press of Florida. pp. 62–77.

Harrison, Shelby (1918–20) *The Springfield Survey* (3 vols). New York: Russell Sage Foundation.

Henry, Frances, and Saberwal, Satish (eds) (1969) *Stress and Response in Fieldwork*. New York: Holt.

Herskovitz, Melville J. (1954) 'Some problems of method in ethnography', in R.F. Spencer (ed.), *Method and Perspective in Anthropology*. Minneapolis: University of Minnesota Press. pp. 3–24.

Hinkle, Roscoe C. Jr., and Hinkle, Gisela J. (1954) *The Development of Modern Sociology*. New York: Random House.

Hodson, Randy (1999) *Analyzing Documentary Accounts*. Thousand Oaks, CA: Sage.

Homans, George C. (1947) 'The small warship', *American Sociological Review*, 11: 294–300.

Hughes, Everett C. (1931) *The Growth of an Institution: The Chicago Real Estate Board*. Chicago: Society for Social Research.

Hughes, Everett C. (1943) *French Canada in Transition*. Chicago: University of Chicago Press.

Hughes, Everett C. (1960) 'Introduction: The place of field work in social science', in B.H. Junker (ed.), *Field Work: An Introduction to the Social Sciences*. Chicago: University of Chicago Press. pp. v–xv.

Hymes, Dell (ed.) (1974) *Reinventing Anthropology*. New York: Vintage.

Jahoda, Marie, Deutsch, Morton, and Cook, Stuart W. (eds) (1951) *Research Methods in Social Relations* (2 vols). New York: Holt.

Janes, Robert W. (1961) 'A note on phases of the community role of the participant-observer', *American Sociological Review*, 26: 446–50.

Johnson, John M. (1975) *Doing Field Research*. New York: Free Press.

Junker, Buford H. (1960) *Field Work: An Introduction to the Social Sciences*. Chicago: University of Chicago Press.

Katz, Jack (1997) 'Ethnography's warrants', *Sociological Methods and Research*, 25: 391–423.

Kellogg, Paul U. (ed.) (1909–14) *The Pittsburgh Survey* (6 vols). New York: Russell Sage Foundation.

Kluckhohn, Florence (1940) 'The participant observer technique in small communities', *American Journal of Sociology*, 46: 331–43.

Kornblum, William (1974) *Blue Collar Community*. Chicago: University of Chicago Press.

Kuznar, Lawrence A. (1997) *Reclaiming a Scientific Anthropology*. Walnut Creek, CA: AltaMira.

Leach, James (2003) *Creative Land: Place and Procreation on the Rai Coast of Papua New Guinea*. New York: Berghahn.

Lewis, Oscar (1951) *Life in a Mexican Village: Tepoztlán Revisited*. Springfield: University of Illinois Press.

Lewis, Oscar (1953) 'Controls and experiments in field work', in A.L. Kroeber (ed.), *Anthropology Today*. Chicago: University of Chicago Press. pp. 452–75.

Lewis, Oscar (1959) *Five Families: Mexican Case Studies in the Culture of Poverty*. New York: Basic Books.

Liebow, Elliott (1967) *Talley's Corner: A Study of Negro Streetcorner Men*. Boston: LittleBrown.

Lindeman, Eduard C. (1924) *Social Discovery: An Introduction to the Study of Functional Groups*. New York: Republic.

Lofland, John (1971) *Analyzing Social Settings: A Guide to Qualitative Observation and Analysis*. Belmont, CA: Wadsworth.

Lofland, John (1976) *Doing Social Life: The Qualitative Study of Human Interaction in Natural Settings*. New York: Wiley.

Lohman, Joseph D. (1937) 'The participant observer in community studies', *American Sociological Review*, 2: 890–98.

Lynd, Robert S., and Lynd, Helen Merrell (1929) *Middletown*. New York: Harcourt, Brace, & World.

Lynd, Robert S., and Lynd, Helen Merrell (1937) *Middletown in Transition*. New York: Harcourt, Brace & World.

Malinowski, Bronislaw (1922) *Argonauts of the Western Pacific*. London: Routledge.

Martineau, Harriet (1838) *How to Observe Morals and Manners*. London: Chad Knight.

McCall, George J. (1969) 'Data quality control in participant observation', in G.J. McCall and J.L. Simmons (eds), *Issues in Participant Observation: A Text and Reader*. Reading, MA: Addison-Wesley. pp. 128–41.

McCall, George J. (1978) *Observing the Law: Field Methods in the Study of Crime and the Criminal Justice System*. New York: Free Press.

McCall, George J. (1984) 'Systematic field observation', *Annual Review of Sociology*, 10: 263–82.

McCall, George J., and Simmons, J.L. (eds) (1969) *Issues in Participant Observation: A Text and Reader*. Reading, MA: Addison-Wesley.

Mead, Margaret (1928) *Coming of Age in Samoa*. New York: William Morrow.

Mead, Margaret (1933) 'More comprehensive field methods', *American Anthropologist*, 35: 1–15.

Merton, Robert K. (1947) 'Selected problems of field work in the planned community', *American Sociological Review*, 12: 304–12.

Miles, Matthew B., and Huberman, A. Michael (1994) *Qualitative Data Analysis: An Expanded Sourcebook*. Thousand Oaks, CA: Sage.

Miller, S.M. (1952) 'The participant observer and "over-rapport"', *American Sociological Review*, 17: 97–99.

Murray, Stephen O. (1991) 'Sleeping with natives as a source of data', *Society of Gay and Lesbian Anthropologists Newsletter*, 13: 49–51.

Naroll, Raoul (1962) *Data Quality Control*. New York: Free Press.

Naroll, Raoul, and Cohen, Ronald (eds) (1970) *A Handbook of Method in Cultural Anthropology*. New York: Natural History Press.

Palmer, Vivien M. (1928) *Field Studies in Sociology: A Student's Manual*. Chicago: University of Chicago Press.

Park, Robert E., and Burgess, Ernest W. (1921) *Introduction to the Science of Sociology*. Chicago: University of Chicago Press.

Paul, Benjamin (1953) 'Interview techniques and field relationships', in A.L. Kroeber (ed.), *Anthropology Today*. Chicago: University of Chicago Press. pp. 430–51.

Pelto, Pertti J., and Pelto, Gretel H. (1970) *Anthropological Research: The Structure of Inquiry*. Cambridge: Cambridge University Press.

Platt, Jennifer (1983) 'The development of the "participant observation" method in sociology: Origin myth and history', *Journal of the History of the Behavioral Sciences*, 19: 379–93.

Platt, Jennifer (1994) 'The Chicago School and first-hand data', *History of the Human Sciences*, 7: 57–80.

Platt, Jennifer (1995) 'Research methods and the second Chicago School', in G.A. Fine (ed.), *A Second Chicago School? The Development of a Postwar American Sociology*. Chicago: University of Chicago Press. pp. 82–107.

Platt, Jennifer (1996) *A History of Sociological Research Methods in America, 1920–1960*. Cambridge: Cambridge University Press.

Powdermaker, Hortense (1967) *Stranger and Friend: The Way of an Anthropologist*. New York: Norton.

Redfield, Robert (1930) *Tepoztlán, A Mexican Village: A Study of Folk Life*. Chicago: University of Chicago Press.

Redfield, Robert (1941) *The Folk Culture of Yucatan*. Chicago: University of Chicago Press.

Redfield, Robert (1955) *The Little Community*. Chicago: University of Chicago Press.

Reimer, Hans (1937) 'Socialization in the prison community', *American Prison Association Proceedings*, 151–55.

Reinharz, Shulamit (1992) *Feminist Methods in Social Research*. New York: Oxford University Press.

Richards, Audrey I. (1939) 'The development of field work methods in social anthropology', in F.C. Bartlett, M. Ginsburg, E.J. Lindgren, and R.H. Thouless (eds), *The Study of Society*. London: Kegan Paul. pp. 272–316.

Roth, Julius A. (1962) 'Comments on "secret observation"', *Social Problems*, 9: 283–84.

Roth, Julius A. (1963) *Timetables*. Indianapolis: Bobbs-Merrill.

Sanjek, Roger (ed.) (1990) *Fieldnotes: The Making of Anthropology*. Cornell, NY: Cornell University Press.

Schatzman, Leonard, and Strauss, Anselm L. (1973) *Field Research: Strategies for a Natural Sociology*. Englewood Cliffs, NJ: Prentice-Hall.

Schwartz, Morris S., and Schwartz, Charlotte Green (1955) 'Problems in participant observation', *American Journal of Sociology*, 60: 343–53.

Shaw, Clifford R. (1930) *The Jack Roller: A Delinquent Boy's Own Story*. Chicago: University of Chicago Press.

Small, Albion W. (1921) 'The future of sociology', *Publications of the American Sociological Society*, 15: 174–93.

Smalley, W.A. (1960) 'Making and keeping anthropological field notes', *Practical Anthropology*, 7: 145–52.

Spindler, George D. (ed.) (1970) *Being an Anthropologist: Fieldwork in Eleven Cultures*. New York: Holt, Rinehart & Winston.

Spradley, James P. (1980) *Participant Observation*. Fort Worth, TX: Harcourt Brace.

Spradley, James P., and McCurdy, David W. (eds) (1972) *The Cultural Experience: Ethnography in a Complex Society*. Chicago: Science Research Associates.

Stein, Maurice R. (1954) 'Field work procedures: The social organization of a student research team', in A.W. Gouldner (ed.), *Patterns of Industrial Bureaucracy*. Glencoe, IL: Free Press. pp. 247–69.

Stocking, George W. Jr. (1983) 'The ethnographer's magic: Fieldwork in British anthropology from

Tylor to Malinowski', in G.W. Stocking Jr. (ed.), *Observers Observed: Essays on Ethnographic Fieldwork*. Madison: University of Wisconsin Press. pp. 70–120.

Strauss, Anselm, Schatzman, Leonard, Bucher, Rue, Erlich, Danuta, and Sabshin, Melvin (1964) *Psychiatric Ideologies and Institutions*. New York: Free Press.

Sudnow, David (1965) 'Normal crimes: Sociological features of the criminal code', *Social Problems*, 12: 255–76.

Suttles, Gerald D. (1968) *The Social Order of the Slum*. Chicago: University of Chicago Press.

Thrasher, Frederic M. (1927) *The Gang: A Study of 1,313 Gangs in Chicago*. Chicago: University of Chicago Press.

Thrasher, Frederic M. (1928) 'How to study the boys' gang in the open', *Journal of Educational Psychology*, 1: 244–54.

Turner, Ralph H. (1947) 'The naval disbursing officer as a bureaucrat', *American Sociological Review*, 12: 342–48.

Tyler, Stephen A. (ed.) (1969) *Cognitive Anthropology*. New York: Holt, Rinehart & Winston.

Vidich, Arthur J. (1955) 'Participant observation and the collection and interpretation of data', *American Journal of Sociology*, 60: 354–60.

Vidich, Arthur J., and Bensman, Joseph (1954) 'The validity of field data', *Human Organization*, 13(1): 20–7.

Vidich, Arthur J., and Bensman, Joseph (1958) *Small Town in Mass Society*. Princeton, NJ: Princeton University Press.

Vidich, Arthur J., Bensman, Joseph, and Stein, Maurice R. (eds) (1964) *Reflections on Community Studies*. New York: Harper & Row.

Vidich, Arthur J., and Shapiro, Gilbert (1955) 'A comparison of participant observation and the collection and survey data', *American Sociological Review*, 20: 28–33.

Waller, Willard (1934) 'Insight and scientific method', *American Journal of Sociology*, 40: 285–97.

Wax, Rosalie H. (1952) 'Reciprocity as a field technique', *Human Organization*, 11(3): 34–7.

Wax, Rosalie H. (1957) 'Twelve years later: An analysis of field experience', *American Journal of Sociology*, 63: 133–42.

Wax, Rosalie H. (1971) *Doing Fieldwork: Warnings and Advice*. Chicago: University of Chicago Press.

Wax, Rosalie H. (1972) 'Tenting with Malinowski', *American Sociological Review*, 37: 1–13.

Webb, Beatrice (1926) *My Apprenticeship*. London: Longmans, Green.

Webb, Sidney, and Webb, Beatrice (1898) *Problems of Modern Industry*. London: Longman.

Webb, Sidney, and Webb, Beatrice (1932) *Methods of Social Study*. London: Longmans, Green.

Weitzman, Eben A., and Miles, Mathew B. (1995) *Computer Programs for Qualitative Data Analysis*. Thousand Oaks, CA: Sage.

Werner, Oswald, and Schoepfle, G.M. (1987) *Systematic Data Analysis*. Newbury Park, CA: Sage.

Whyte, William F. (1943) *Street Corner Society: The Social Structure of an Italian Slum*. Chicago: University of Chicago Press.

Whyte, William F. (1951) 'Observational field methods', in M. Jahoda, M. Deutsch, and S.W. Cook (eds), *Research Methods in Social Relations* (Volume II). New York: Holt. pp. 493–513.

Whyte, William F. (1955) *Street Corner Society: The Social Structure of an Italian Slum* (enlarged edn). Chicago: University of Chicago Press.

Whyte, William F. (1960) 'Interviewing in field research', in R.N. Adams and J.J. Preiss (eds), *Human Organization Research: Field Relations and Techniques*. Homewood, IL: Dorsey Press. pp. 352–74.

Wierzbicki, Zbigniew T. (1982) 'Methodological issues concerning restudies in local rural communities', in H. Mendres and I. Mihailescu (eds), *Theories and Methods in Rural Community Studies*. Oxford: Pergamon. pp. 193–221.

Williams, Thomas R. (1967) *Field Methods in the Study of Culture*. New York: Holt.

Wolcott, Harry F. (2003) *The Man in the Principal's Office*. Walnut Creek, CA: Sage.

Wolff, Kurt (1960) 'The collection and organization of field materials: A research report', in R.N. Adams and J.J. Preiss (eds), *Human Organization Research: Field Relations and Techniques*. Homewood, IL: Dorsey Press. pp. 240–54.

Zelditch, Morris, Jr. (1962) 'Some methodological problems of field studies', *American Journal of Sociology*, 67: 566–76.

Zorbaugh, Harvey (1929) *The Gold Coast and the Slum: A Sociological Study of Chicago's Near North Side*. Chicago: University of Chicago Press.

2

Praxical Reasoning and the Logic of Field Research

GARY SHANK

In many ways, the history of research is also a history of the application of logic to our efforts to understand the world (see Kneale & Kneale, 1962, for a comprehensive review of the history and development of logic and inquiry). The efforts of such famous Greek natural historians as Pliny the Elder and Aristotle to understand and explain their findings were in part made possible by the discovery and refinement of the techniques of deductive reasoning (Parry & Hacker, 1991). The emergence of the scientific revolution in the sixteenth and seventeenth centuries CE would not have been possible without prior efforts (extending back as far as the twelfth century CE) in grasping the nature and uses of inductive reasoning (see Coppleston, 1962, 1963 for a description of the development of these ideas; and Holland et al., 1986, for a contemporary understanding of induction). In our current era, precise simulation programs and the very functioning of the digital computer are based on pioneering work in symbolic logic (cf. Langer, 1953, for a basic review of symbolic logic).

One area that seems relatively independent of logical theory and application, however, has been the practice of fieldwork. Fieldwork has always prided itself as an experiential and tactical enterprise (Shank, 2002: 102–106). Novice fieldworkers are warned about taking too many theoretical notions and preconceptions into the field (Glaser & Strauss, 1967; Schatzman & Strauss, 1973; Glaser, 1978; Hammersley & Atkinson, 1983; LeCompte & Preissle, 1993, among many others). Fluidity and flexibility of thought and action, keeping an open mind, applying eclectic methods, and taking careful and precise records that are as free as possible from pre-existing theory, have been held up as ideals for those who seek to understand societies and cultures on their own terms (see, among numerous others, Geertz, 1973, 1983; Spradley, 1979, 1980). These principles are evident in works that are considered classics of field research, including the major works of such historically important researchers as Boas (1911/1965), Malinowski (1914–18/1967; 1922/1961), Goffman (1959, 1961) and Whyte (1955). Even in today's atmosphere of nuanced understandings of the textual and political natures of field research, there is still the sense that the field researcher is guided and illuminated, rather than structured and consequential (see Clifford, 1986; Van Maanen, 1988; Stake, 1995; Ellis & Bochner, 2000; among others).

Does this mean that there is no logic, *per se*, to fieldwork? In this chapter, I would like to argue to the contrary. Not only is there a logical framework to fieldwork, but there has always been a logical framework to fieldwork. We are only just now in a position to be aware of the nature of that framework, because of advances in fundamental logical theory over the past 100 years or so. The logical place for us to start, then, is with the nature of these relatively recent breakthroughs in logical theory.

RECONSTRUCTED LOGIC AND LOGIC-IN-USE

One important point of departure is to make clear the distinction between the notions of reconstructed logic and logic-in-use. These terms were the brainchild of Abraham Kaplan (1964) in his explication of how inquiry is actually performed in the behavioral sciences.

Reconstructed logic is the tool we use to summarize our actions in as scientific a fashion as possible. It is found, in most research reports, in those sections where we build a careful argument that leads up to, and supports, a research question. From that careful argument and consequential question, actual hypotheses are derived and put to the test. The analysis and discussion of those tests leads to further careful argumentation, reasoning, and deduced conclusions.

Reconstructed logic is nice and neat, but is it a faithful map of the actual actions and paths of empirical inquirers? More often than not, the actions of such inquirers are much less linear, less structured, and far less

neat and orderly. They play hunches, or get inspired in the shower or in their dreams, or make guesses or take gambles. This seeming hodgepodge of actions and strategies are the sorts of things that Kaplan called logic-in-use. Logic-in-use is just as important to empirical inquirers as the reconstructed logic used to bring the fruits of that inquiry into final form.

One way to look at the relation of logic-in-use to reconstructed logic is to say that logic-in-use is a sort of creative pre-logical precursor to the act of nailing down the inquiry first with more precise procedures and then with using reconstructed logic to characterize and report the findings. This approach consigns logic-in-use to the category of those sorts of preliminary tools we use to rough sketch and rough frame the final elegant act of inquiry. By privileging reconstructed logic in this fashion, however, we are forfeiting any chance of finding systematic principles at play in the operation of logic-in-use.

Here is a key thesis of this chapter: logic-in-use, as described by Kaplan (1964), is just a provisional way to look at a process which is actually as precise and systematic, in its own way, as any other mode of logic. That is, logic-in-use is just another name for what others have called 'abductive reasoning'. Abductive reasoning, as applied to and used by field researchers, will be characterized in this chapter under the title of praxical logic (for reasons that will hopefully be clear later on).

Before we sketch out the nature of praxical logic, let us first spend a bit of time laying out its more generic form – abductive reasoning.

THE NATURE OF ABDUCTIVE REASONING

There is a small but growing body of literature on abduction and abductive reasoning.

It first began to take its current systematic form in the work of Charles S. Peirce (1955, 1992, 1998). Peirce (1839–1914) is most famous as the founder of the philosophical school of Pragmatism and as one of the early founders of semiotic inquiry.

In Peirce's prodigious body of work (much of which remains unpublished), there are two themes that arise and interact over and over again. These are the themes of logic and meaning. We see these themes joined in the conceptions of abduction and abductive inferences.

In his work as a logician, Peirce comes to realize that current models of inference are incomplete, particularly as applied to efforts in empirical inquiry. He therefore introduces the concept of abductive reasoning to address this 'gap' in our systematization of logic. An abductive inference, for Peirce, takes the following form (Peirce, 1955: 151):

> The surprising fact, C, is observed;
> But if A were true, C would be a matter of course,
> Hence, there is reason to suspect that A is true.

There has been very little work based on examining Peirce's work on abduction. Fann (1970) is one of the exceptions. Sebeok & Eco (1983) have also collected a number of essays that explore abduction from a Peircean foundation.

Much of the current work on abduction is based on two important secondary sources. Hanson (1958) built upon Peirce's work to talk about the logic of discovery, and Harman (1965) extended Peirce's model to talk about reasoning to the best explanation. The notions of discovery and reasoning to the best explanation serve as the basis of most contemporary research into abduction, particularly in the areas of expert systems and artificial intelligence. An excellent summary of that work can be found in Josephson and Josephson (1994).

In this chapter, we want to turn away from Hanson's and Harman's more specific applications of abduction, and return to the basic notion of making abductive inferences in general. One way to look at an abductive inference is to say that it is reasoning toward meaning. In this fashion, it is quite different from the other two modes of reasoning. This is best shown via the use of practical examples.

We will look at a series of three syllogisms. The format of these syllogisms will follow Peirce's notion. Instead of talking about major and minor premises, and conclusions, Peirce prefers the alternate notions of, respectively, rule, case, and result. These notations are particularly useful in pointing out the differences between deduction, induction, and abduction.

Let us start with a simple deductive syllogism:

> Rule: All dogs bark.
> Case: Spuffy is a dog.
> Result: (It is therefore certain that) Spuffy barks.

If we rearrange our basic terms, then we get a different sort of inference. In this next case, we will come up with an inductive inference. Notice that, in this syllogism, our final qualification is very different in nature from the claim for certainty derived in our first example:

> Case: Spuffy is a dog.
> Observation: Spuffy barks.
> Rule: (It is likely, to some degree of probability, that) All dogs bark.

In essence, we have abandoned certainty in order to create, instead, a probabilistic law. The strength and value of that law, as a tool to guide inquiry, will be very dependent upon the quality and likelihood of the evidence we come to accumulate. That is, if we base our general law on just Spuffy alone, we have a pretty weak case. The more cases we observe barking, the more likely our general law becomes. This logic is at the very heart of scientific reasoning.

Peirce realized that there was yet one more (and only one more) general combination of these terms in a syllogistic manner. Here it is:

> Observation: (We are surprised or puzzled to find out that) Spuffy barks.
> Rule: (But we know that) All dogs bark.
> Case: (It is plausible to suppose that) Spuffy is a dog.

In this situation, we are going from the circumstances of making a unique observation to being able to explain that observation in a meaningful way. This reasoning to the case, or reasoning to meaning, is at the heart of abduction. As I have pointed out elsewhere (Shank, 1998), it is at the very heart of, and is indeed the ground state or default mode of, ordinary cognition. This fact alone makes abduction worthy of extensive research.

However, there is another very valuable use for abduction for field researchers. To understand this application, we need to talk about the link between abduction and the theory of signs, or semiotic theory.

ABDUCTION AND SEMIOTICS

There are two major founders of contemporary semiotics. The linguistic branch, pioneered by the work of Saussure (1959), has led to social research that focuses on code systems and structures of meaning. These approaches also use language as the premier code-modeling system. Propp (1928/1968), Barthes (1957), Lévi-Strauss (1966), and Eco (1976) are prominent examples of the

linguistic form of semiotic research in the social sciences.

The other type of semiotics, based on the work of Peirce, tends to look at signs as reflections of logical processes. That is, a sign is a 'map' of a type of inference that depends upon signification and which cannot be reduced to a simpler 'if–then' kind of statement. To illustrate this process, Peirce talked about each sign consisting of three components – the object, the sign, and the interpretant. These were linked using the following simple diagram:

> Object – Sign – Interpretant

We can put this into an operational form as follows (Shank, 1987, 1993, 1998, 2001; Shank and Cunningham, 1996):

> If Object – By Sign – Then Interpretant

Putting the above diagram into a narrative form, we get: If we have an object, which is not actually present, being made manifest by an actually occurring thing acting as a sign of that object, then we have, as a consequence, some interpretant whose nature is mediated by the fact that the object was presented only by virtue of its representing sign.

Hopefully, a simple example can clarify this. Suppose we are driving along on a steep, narrow and windy road. We come to a sharp bend, and as we slow down a bit to make the turn, we see dead ahead that a bridge on the road has collapsed. We slow down as fast as we can, locking our brakes if we have to. We can represent our actions as follows:

> If 'BRIDGE OUT' – Then 'SLOW DOWN QUICKLY'

Now, suppose we are on the same road, but this time, halfway up the hill and well before the turn, we see a sign that says 'Bridge out around the next turn'. In this case, we act in a different way. We start slowing down gradually, since we suspect that there is a bridge out ahead, but we are not totally sure. Maybe the sign is a joke, or an old sign that needs to be removed. But as we make the turn very gradually, we see that the bridge is indeed out, and now we begin the act of turning around. We can represent these actions as follows:

If 'BRIDGE OUT' – By 'SIGN' – Then 'SLOW DOWN GRADUALLY'

This time, our consequent is qualitatively different from the case where we had no sign to warn us. Therefore, the interpretant is nothing more than a consequent as mediated by a sign. Sometimes that consequent is the same. Sometimes it is slightly different, as in this case. Other times, it is completely different.

Peirce began looking at ways that these three components (object, sign, and interpretant) could be combined to create different classes, or types, of signs. He concluded that there were ten such classes (Peirce, 1955). For years, Peirce scholars tended to look at these classes as interesting formal curiosities, with little practical value or applicability.

In my own work (Shank, 1987, 1993, 1994, 1998, 2001; Shank & Cunningham, 1996; Moss & Shank, 2002), I decided to explore the possible application of these ten classes toward acts of inference. Suppose we conclude that the ten classes of signs can be used to map out the types of act of inference we use as inquirers? If Peirce is right, there will be ten and only ten types of inference that inquirers use as they seek to perform their acts of inquiry.

THE TEN CLASSES OF SIGNS

First, what do these ten classes look like, as a group? Moving away from Peirce's rather arcane categories, I chose the following clusters to help categorize these classes of signs.

Open – Single – General. In this case, we are looking at what our sign stands for, or how it represents some object.

If a sign is open, this means that it represents the potential of an object, rather than an actual object. A good example of an open sign is a dark cloud. If we see a dark cloud, then we take that cloud as representing the potential for rain.

If a sign is single, this means that it represents one specific actual. A good example of a single sign is a footprint in the mud. If we find such a footprint, then we take it as representing the fact that a single actual foot had been placed there.

If a sign is general, this means that it represents a class or category of objects. A good example of a general sign is a stop sign. If we see a stop sign, then we take that sign as representing a general command to stop.

Icon – Index – Symbol. Here, we are looking at just how the sign signifies its object.

If a sign is iconic, this means that it stands for its object by imitating or resembling that object. A good example of an iconic sign is a photograph. If we see a photograph, then we pay attention to the image portrayed more than to the photograph as something on its own terms.

If a sign is indexical, this means that it points to, or serves as evidence for, some object. A good example of an indexical sign is a fingerprint. If we see a fingerprint, then we pay attention to the print as evidence regarding someone's finger.

If a sign is symbolic, this means that it stands for its object in some law-like, or strictly conventional fashion. A good example of a symbolic sign is a word. If we see a word, we think of the object represented more than we think of the word as something on its own terms.

Tone – Token – Type. Finally, we need to consider the nature of the sign itself, and the role that it is playing as a sign.

If a sign is a tone, then it is acting as a potential portal for the consideration of some possibility. That is, we cannot be sure if this potential sign is actually a sign at all. A good example of a tone is a nearly subliminal shift of light in our visual periphery. Does it signify some change in light patterns, or did some retinal neuron misfire? While we cannot be sure, it alerts us for something that may or may not happen.

If a sign is a token, then it is acting, by its unique nature, as a sign of one single thing. A good example of a token is a signature. When we have a signature, it is a unique rendering (no two signatures are exactly alike) of a specific individual's autograph.

If a sign is a type, then it is meant to be taken as an example of an entire group or class of objects. A good example of a type is the sign 'MEN'. If we see such a sign on a door, then we know that this is a public restroom designated for use by males. We also acknowledge such variants as 'GENTLEMEN', 'GUYS', and little stick figures without stylized dresses.

In review, we have three sets of categories to help specify any given sign. These categories, according to Peirce, are monotonic. By monotonic, he meant that they 'unfold' in one direction. Each set unfolds in a monotonic fashion, and the entire set also unfolds as well.

The first process of unfolding occurs around the open category. Since an open sign has only the potential of representing an object, many modes of objects and interpretant relations are allowed. In fact, there are six types of open sign: open iconic tones, open iconic tokens, open iconic types, open indexical tokens, open indexical types, and open symbolic types.

Why are there no open indexical tones, or open symbolic tones? This is because tones deal only with the potential of interpretants, and when we have indexical or symbolic conditions, we have already established or assumed that there is a link between the object and the interpretant. This is part of the monotonic process described earlier. In a similar fashion, there is no such thing as an open symbolic token, since we only have tokens under iconic or indexical circumstances. That is, when we have a symbolic process, we have already moved beyond the possibility of considering any single one token.

When we move to the single category, we find that we have to abandon all considerations of tone and the notion of a symbolic token, for the same reasons as discussed above. We also abandon all iconic considerations, since single signs go beyond mimesis or resemblance, and require some sort of actual presence or rule. Therefore, we find that there are three categories of single signs: single indexical tokens, single indexical types, and single symbolic types.

Finally, when we arrive at the general category, we see that only the symbolic and the type conditions are available. Icons and indexes are not general categories, nor are tones and tokens. Therefore, the only type of general sign is the general symbolic type.

In review, here are the ten classes of signs, in monotonic order:

Open Iconic Tone
Open Iconic Token
Open Iconic Type
Open Indexical Token

	OPEN		SINGLE		GENERAL
Iconic tone	conjectural		*No single icons –* *single requires presence*		*No general icons or indices;* *icons and indices represent* *a specific*
Iconic token	divinatory/omen				
Iconic type	metaphoric				
Indexical token	investigative/clue		evidential		
Indexical type	pattern	ABDUCTION	factual	INDUCTION	
Symbolic type	explanatory		formal		DEDUCTION

Figure 2.1   *Forming the ten classes of signs and their reasoning categories*

Open Indexical Type
Open Symbolic Type
Single Indexical Token
Single Indexical Type
Single Symbolic Type
General Symbolic Type

This formation process is also illustrated in Figure 2.1. Note how the monotonic nature of selection is reflected in the figure.

MAPPING THE TEN CLASSES INTO EMPIRICAL INQUIRY

Here is where the nature of praxical logic really begins. As we said earlier, these classes have long been regarded as interesting logical curiosities. It has been part of my work and my intentions to map common activities within empirical inquiry into this class structure. When we do, we find that it provides a completely adequate map of all the sorts of inferences that any empirical inquirer might need to draw upon to do research.

Let us take a slightly different approach to make this clear. What sorts of inferences can we empirical inquirers make? We already know that we make inferences based on logic-in-use and reconstructed logic. But can we get more specific than that?

First, we know that we can make deductive inferences, but what sorts of things can we make deductive inferences about? First, we need rules that are true. The only rules that can be certainly and completely true are those that are true by convention. If they are true by convention, then they are symbolic in nature, and are applicable to entire classes of objects. Because it is applicable to an entire class of objects, then we can represent any object in a formal, or conventional fashion.

This leads us to our first category: anytime we make a deductive inference, that inference will point us, inevitably, to some general symbolic type. That is, the product of a deductive inference in empirical inquiry is a general symbolic type. Since 'general symbolic type' is a long name, let us shorten it to a deduction. Therefore, we are saying that all deductions have the characteristics of being general symbolic types, or that when we deduce we are reasoning to a deduction. This also leads us to realize that, when we have general signs, we must address them deductively in the empirical world.

If we must address general signs deductively in the empirical world, how then do we treat single and open signs? Simply, single signs are treated inductively and open signs are treated abductively.

We know that there is one form of deduction, just as there is only one form of general sign, the general symbolic type. But there are three forms of single signs. Does this mean that there are really three types of induction? Surprisingly, this does seem to be the case. Let us look at each form of induction in turn.

First, there is the type of induction associated with the single indexical token. Here we have one single thing, in its uniqueness, acting as a sign for an object. We know that there is a sign, and we know that this sign stands for an object. But we cannot be as sure of the link between the sign and the object as we are when we are using deduction, since we do not have some certain law or rule to fall back upon. But this given sign is evidence, to some degree or other, of the object. We can call this form of induction, where we study one given thing to determine its likelihood of being a sign of an object, as evidential induction, or reasoning toward evidence.

When we can put together enough individual pieces to get a better picture of the object involved, then we are going beyond the mere consideration of one thing as being a piece of evidence or not. We are now in the position of dealing with single indexical types, or a family of things that all seem to point in one direction. When we can take enough things together in this fashion to make a case for an object, we are beyond evidence gathering. We are now engaged in factual induction, or reasoning toward facts.

Finally, we have the case where we have so much evidence that seems so factual in its totality that we can begin to approximate formal-looking, empirically-based laws to account for their operations and forms. Unlike the deductive case, though, we can never be sure if our laws are truly correct.

They always remain available for revision, like any other form of inductive inference. We can label this most complex and sophisticated type of induction as formal induction, or reasoning toward theory (or in some lesser cases, hypothesis).

The final six classes of signs represent the broad and largely unexplored domain of abduction. We will move from the most diffuse to the most formal types of abduction.

First, there is the form of abduction that centers around the open iconic tone. What sort of a sign is an open iconic tone? It is an indicator of the possibility that something might possibly be a sign.

Here is an example. Suppose I own a shop with a picture window. Across the street is a vacant house, with a rock garden in the front yard. I see a moving van pull up, and movers start unloading items. One of the items is a tricycle. Immediately, I start getting nervous, but why? In fact, I am abducing that people might be moving in across the street, and they might possibly have a small child, and that the child, when combined with the rock garden, might possibly represent a threat to my picture window.

We might be tempted to dismiss all of this as idle conjecture, but upon careful analysis we see that it conforms to legitimate abductive reasoning given the degree of likelihood that is involved. While no one should take these pieces as evidence of any serious threat, it is reasonable to take them together as one potential consequence of this sequence of conditions and events. In fact, field researchers use these sorts of processes all the time. We can say that the shopkeeper has inferred an abductive hunch. Hunches are important in fieldwork, and now we can say that they have some inferential validity as well, so long as we stay within the rules of abductive reasoning. Therefore, open iconic tones often lead to hunches, or conjectural abduction. Another way to capture this is to say that this is an example of reasoning to a hunch.

The next form of abduction centers around the open iconic token. What sort of a sign is an open iconic token? It represents those situations when an actual thing, because of its resemblance to a second thing, might possibly signify something else.

Here is an example. Imagine a farmer standing in a field. All of a sudden, the wind picks up and the sky gets a little darker. The farmer knows that, sometimes, when this happens, dark clouds move in. Furthermore, sometimes those dark clouds blow over, but sometimes it rains. Therefore, he starts paying more attention to the sky in the direction of the wind. The farmer's actions are a form of abductive inference. He is treating the open iconic token, or the wind and slight darkening, as a possible omen of some future situation; namely, clouds and rain. He is not so sure that he is driving his tractor into the barn; he would rather get some plowing done if he can. But he is also paying attention, since he does not want to get his expensive tractor trapped in the rain either.

We tend to associate omens with arcane or occult thinking, but they are perfectly common and ordinary types of inference. Fieldworkers are always reading omens as part of their efforts. We can call these examples of divinatory abduction, or reasoning to an omen.

The third form of abduction centers around the open iconic type. What sort of a sign is an open iconic type? It represents those situations where one thing can be said to possibly resemble another thing by virtue of some possible real or imagined conceptual link.

When we are dealing with open types, we are often actively looking for rules of combination or relation that can help us gain new insights. Open iconic types represent the most diffuse and open circumstance, and so any rule becomes more conjectural and 'playful' than specific or empirically-based. But playing around with possible rules has always been a part of empirical research, and certainly a key part of fieldwork in particular.

Let us consider an example. Suppose I am watching people working in a factory, and I am trying to understand when and why they take breaks. I am looking as hard as I can, but nothing is simply revealing itself to me. So I take a different tack. How are people working in factories, I muse, like, say, ants in an anthill? When would an ant take a break? I don't know all that much about ants, but I do know that they serve a queen. Is there a correlation to the queen on the factory floor? I start seeing workers nod to one individual, who then nods back, before they take their break. I perk up; I may finally be on to something here.

In this case, the open iconic type is something I created as an aid to help me understand what is happening. It is, in fact, a metaphor. Metaphors are actually rule-like abductive inferences we make in order to get a fresh look at something else. Metaphors have a long tradition in empirical inquiry and in fieldwork, as does metaphoric abduction, or reasoning to a metaphor.

By the time we get to the fourth form of abduction, things are getting more specific. We have left behind the iconic categories, and have moved on to the open indexical token. What sort of a sign is an open indexical token? It is an individual thing that may or may not be evidence for something else.

Actually, the open indexical token is one of the most familiar signs to fieldworkers. It is that tiny bit of reddish liquid in the bottom of a cup that may or may not be wine. It is the dirt on the hands of the person who may be a crop harvester. It is any sort of thing in the environment that may or may not open up our understanding of a situation or process. In other words, an open indexical token is a clue. Clues are so important in all field-oriented forms of empirical inquiry that we need not dwell on them further here. We can simply say that the inference that something might indeed be a clue is an act of investigative abduction, or reasoning to a clue.

The last two forms of abduction both deal with types, and so there is the dimension of researcher control in these inferences. The first form centers around the open indexical type. An open indexical type is an actual thing that might serve as evidence for a larger system of organization or order.

Here we have the case where we have gathered actual things together because we suspect they may be related to each other in some possibly systematic way. We are no longer interested in what individual signs have to tell us. We are interested in how they work together. Fortunately, human beings are very good at this sort of abductive reasoning. We are skilled at bringing things together so that we can find patterns. When we do this, we are doing pattern abduction, or reasoning to a pattern.

The final form of abduction centers around the open symbolic type. An open symbolic type is a sign that is part of a possible larger system of order. When we put this into practical terms, we are talking about gathering together all our hunches, omens, metaphors, clues or patterns, and creating an overall system that is coherent and can possibly inform us about what is going on. These larger systems are called explanations. We are then said to be conducting explanatory abduction, or reasoning to an explanation.

It does not take much effort to see how this system of praxical logic has an almost unlimited set of possible applications for field researchers. Because of the systematic ways that all these classes of signs were defined and created, there are new and potentially fruitful systematic paths for comparison. For instance, metaphors, patterns, and explanations are all abductive processes centered around type signs. How can we use this information to create modes of inquiry that allow us to take advantage of these connections in systemic ways? Questions like these are manifold. We will conclude this chapter by briefly exploring one dimension. How can praxical logic be viewed as a way to sort out and understand the sorts of logical commitments researchers make in the field?

PRAXICAL LOGIC AS A SERIES OF COMMITMENTS

For our purposes as field researchers, one of the best ways to look at the potential use of praxical logic is in terms of its role in helping us make various sorts of commitments to our unfolding data as part of the ongoing research process. Commitment to unfolding data is an intricate balancing act for field researchers. On one hand, we want to make sure that we are sensitive to even the most subtle nuances in the data field, lest we overlook something that might inform us. On the other hand, we have to be careful at all times not to foreclose our emerging theoretical understanding in terms of what we are finding. That is, we do not want to have a theoretical understanding too soon, lest we subsequently tune out important data that do not fit our models.

Praxical reasoning can help us in this commitment process by allowing us to parse our commitment efforts into three separate, albeit interrelated, categories. These are commitments to meaning, coherence, and theory. We will consider each in turn.

The first area that we need to examine is our commitment, as field researchers, toward meaning. One lesson we learn early on is that any setting is rich in meaning. How do we tap into that meaning, without running the risk of simply seeing what we want to see?

This is where the abductive element of praxical reasoning is most important. Given that meaning is most likely to be diverse and complex, we are fortunate that abductive reasoning, or our ability to reason to meaning, comes equipped with most aspects and facets of potential use.

One temptation might be to use our abductive tools in a linear and developmental fashion. That is, we might start first by drawing hunches, then working up to omens and clues, and finally ending with metaphors, patterns, and explanations. This, however, is a constrained use of what is meant to be a very flexible set of tools. We must let our level of understanding be our guide. If we cannot put our finger on any clear trend or situation, then we need to work with what we have before us, and see where our hunches take us, inference-wise. If we are inundated with data, then we need to start finding out if these data fit into patterns. If we feel like we have headed up a dead end, then perhaps a handy metaphor or two can spring us on a new path. The pursuit of meaning is rarely linear, so why should our reasoning toward meaning be any different?

Once we feel that we have made a commitment to examining field-oriented settings in terms of understanding how these settings are meaningful on their own terms to the people who are most directly involved, we must then press our efforts even further. It is not enough for us to be able to reconcile meaning for individual settings and situations. Do these individual acts of meaning cohere? In other words, what is our commitment to discerning an overall, coherent picture of our given field setting?

Here is where we realize that, on a very practical level, inductive reasoning is, among other things, an act of reasoning to coherence. The simplest level of coherence is toward any given piece of potential data we might find. Is this piece of data just a random thing that happened to be there, or is it actually evidence of a possible sort of orderly phenomenon? This is a critical sort of evidential inference that we make, as field researchers, hundreds if not thousands of times in the life of a project. But do these inferences allow us to build a more coherent whole, via the process of factual induction? That is, have we turned bits and sets of evidence into bodies of facts that can be used not only to understand our field settings but also to make predictions and extrapolations from them? As these predictions and extrapolations become richer and take on a life of their own, we can then be there to build further, more formal, patterns of inferences. At last, if we are lucky, a coherent picture of the complex whole starts to take form.

Finally, we have developed a rich, complex, meaningful, and coherent picture of the people, places, and things in our field settings. If we feel compelled to stay bound to the empirical roots of our research, then we can reason in a formal manner toward an inductively based set of hypotheses that, with any luck, we can pull together under the broader heading of theory. If these theories, rooted as they are close to the data, persist, then we can even take the final step of treating them like quasi-deductive sets of rules.

CONCLUSION

There are many interesting conceptual and formal things that can be done with the combination of praxical logic and field research. But I want to leave us with one last practical consideration.

Praxical research, by its very nature, helps us to think of the aspects, pieces, and facets of field settings and field life in new ways. Because we are free to move logically in a number of flexible but finite ways, we can look upon everyday data in new ways. Here is the way I look at them; I hope you find this useful. It is my firmest belief as a researcher that there are whole modes and levels of order in the empirical world that we have not only not found, but that we do not even suspect exist. But if we are oblivious to these levels of order, how can we ever hope to find them? The answer is simple; each and every thing in the empirical world is a potential portal to these levels of order. All we need are the keys. These keys are not only crafted by our skills as observers and investigators, but also by our ability to infer from our observations and investigations. Praxical logic gives us ten new keys to use to open some of these new locks. Who knows what we might find?

REFERENCES

Barthes, R. (1957) *Mythologies*. New York: The Noonday Press.

Boas, F. (1911/1965) *The Mind of Primitive Man*. New York: Free Press.

Clifford, J. (1986) 'On ethnographic allegory'. In J. Clifford & G.F. Marcus (eds), *Writing culture: The poetics and politics of ethnography*. Berkeley, CA: University of California Press. pp. 98–121

Coppleston, F., SJ (1962) *A History of Philosophy: Volume 2. Medieval Philosophy. Part II: Albert the Great to Duns Scotus*. Garden City, NY: Image Books.

Coppleston, F., SJ (1963) *A History of Philosophy: Volume 3. Late Medieval and Renaissance Philosophy. Part I: Ockham to the Speculative Mystics*. Garden City, NY: Image Books.

Eco, U. (1976) *A Theory of Semiotics*. Bloomington, IN: Indiana University Press.

Ellis, C. & Bochner, A.P. (2000) 'Autoethnography, personal narrative, reflexivity: Researcher as subject'. In N.K. Denzin & Y.S. Lincoln (eds), *Handbook of Qualitative Research* (2nd edn) Thousand Oaks, CA: Sage. pp. 733–68.

Fann, K.T. (1970) *Peirce's Theory of Abduction*. The Hague, Netherlands: Martinus Nijhoff.

Geertz, C. (1973) *The Interpretation of Cultures*. New York: Basic Books.

Geertz, C. (1983) *Local Knowledge: Further Essays in Interpretive Anthropology*. New York: Basic Books.

Glaser, B.G. (1978) *Theoretical Sensitivity*. Mill Valley, CA: The Sociology Press.

Glaser, B.G. & Strauss, A.L. (1967). *The Discovery of Grounded Theory: Strategies for Qualitative Research*. Chicago: Aldine.

Goffman, E. (1959) *The Presentation of Self in Everyday Life*. Garden City, NY: Doubleday.

Goffman, E. (1961) *Asylums*. Garden City, NY: Doubleday.

Hammersley, M. & Atkinson, P. (1983) *Ethnography: Principles in Practice*. London: Routledge.

Hanson, R.N. (1958) 'The logic of discovery'. *Journal of Philosophy*, LV(25): 1073–89.

Harman, G.H. (1965) 'Inference to the best explanation'. *Philosophical Review*, LXXIV: 88–95.

Holland, J.H., Holyoak, K.J., Nisbett, R.E. & Thagard, P.R. (1986) *Induction: Processes of Inference, Learning, and Discovery*. Cambridge, MA: MIT Press.

Josephson, J.R. & Josephson, S.G. (1994) *Abductive Inference: Computation, Philosophy, Technology*. Cambridge: Cambridge University Press.

Kaplan, A. (1964) *The Conduct of Inquiry: Methodology for Behavioral Science*. San Francisco, CA: Chandler.

Kneale, W. & Kneale, M. (1962) *The Development of Logic*. Oxford, UK: Clarendon Press.

Langer, S.K. (1953) *An Introduction to Symbolic Logic* (2nd edn). New York: Dover.

LeCompte, M.D. & Preissle, J. (1993) *Ethnography and Qualitative Design in Educational Research* (2nd edn). San Diego, CA: Academic Press.

Lévi-Strauss, C. (1966) *The Savage Mind*. Chicago: University of Chicago Press.

Malinowski, B. (1914–18/1967) *A Diary in the Strict Sense of the Term*. Stanford, CA: Stanford University Press.

Malinowski, B. (1922/1961) *Argonauts of the Western Pacific.* New York: E.P. Dutton & Co.

Moss, C.M. & Shank, G. (2002) 'Using qualitative processes in computer technology research on online learning: Lessons in change from "Teaching as Intentional Learning" [79 paragraphs]'. *Forum Qualitative Sozialforschung/Forum: Qualitative Social Research* [Online Journal], 3(2). Available at: http://www.qualitative-research.net/fqs/fqs-eng.htm

Parry, W.T. & Hacker, E.A. (1991) *Aristotelian Logic.* Albany, NY: SUNY Press.

Peirce, C.S. (1955) *Philosophical Writings of Peirce.* New York: Dover.

Peirce, C.S. (1992) *The Essential Peirce: Volume 1 (1867–93).* N. Houser & C. Kloesel (eds). Bloomington, IN: Indiana University Press.

Peirce, C.S. (1998) *The Essential Peirce: Volume 2 (1893–1913).* The Peirce Edition Project (eds). Bloomington, IN: Indiana University Press.

Propp, V. (1928/1968) *Morphology of the Folktale.* Austin, TX: University of Texas Press.

Saussure, F. (1959) *Course in General Linguistics.* New York: Philosophical Library.

Schatzman, L. & Strauss, A.L. (1973) *Field Research: Strategies for a Natural Sociology.* Englewood Cliffs, NJ: Prentice-Hall.

Sebeok, T.A. & Eco, U. (1983) *The Sign of Three.* Bloomington, IN: Indiana University Press.

Shank, G. (1987) 'Abductive strategies in educational research'. *American Journal of Semiotics,* 5(2): 275–90.

Shank, G. (1993) 'Abductive multiloguing: The semiotic dynamics of navigating the Net'. *The Electronic Journal of Virtual Culture* [Online Journal], 1(1).

Available at: http://www. infomotions.com/serials/aejvc/aejvc-vln01-shank-abductive.txt

Shank, G. (1994) 'Shaping qualitative research in educational psychology'. *Contemporary Educational Psychology,* 19: 340–59.

Shank, G. (1998) 'The extraordinary ordinary powers of abductive reasoning'. *Theory and Psychology,* 8: 841–60.

Shank, G. (2001) 'It's logic in practice, my dear Watson: An imaginary memoir from beyond the grave [96 paragraphs]'. *Forum Qualitative Sozialforschung/Forum: Qualitative Social Research* [Online Journal], 2(1). Available at: http://qualitative-research.net/fqs/fqs-eng.htm

Shank, G. (2002) *Qualitative Research: A Personal Skills Approach.* Saddle River, NJ: Prentice-Hall.

Shank, G. & Cunningham, D.J. (April, 1996) 'Modeling the six modes of Peircean abduction for educational purposes'. Paper presented at the Seventh Midwest AI and Cognitive Science Conference, 28, April 1996, Bloomington, IN. Available online at: http://www.cs.indiana.edu/event/maics96/Proceedings/shank.html

Spradley, J.P. (1979) *The Ethnographic Interview.* New York: Holt, Rinehart and Winston.

Spradley, J.P. (1980) *Participant Observation.* New York: Holt, Rinehart and Winston.

Stake, R.E. (1995) *The Art of Case Study Research.* Thousand Oaks, CA: Sage.

Van Maanen, J. (1988) *Tales of the Field: On Writing Ethnography.* Chicago, IL: University of Chicago Press.

Whyte, W.F. (1955) *Street Corner Society: The Social Structure of an Italian Slum.* Chicago, IL: University of Chicago Press.

Part 2

Situating Fieldwork

3

Jelly's Place: An Ethnographic Memoir

ELIJAH ANDERSON

This project began as an assignment in a graduate course in field methods at the University of Chicago, taught by Gerald Suttles. Students studied a variety of settings, among which were neighborhoods, hotels, and a church, and mine was a corner tavern and liquor store: I studied Jelly's. I didn't think about this conceptually at the time, but one of the reasons I may have gravitated to this setting was that it gave me an opportunity to think about my own background, my own story, so to speak, even with important aspects of my identity.

I was born in the Mississippi Delta during the Second World War. My father went through the fourth grade, my mother through the eleventh. After I was born, they migrated to the North, he to work in the foundry of the Studebaker Corporation, she to work as a domestic. While growing up in the segregated black community of South Bend, from an early age, I was curious about the goings on in the neighborhood, but particularly streets, and more particularly, the corner taverns that my uncles and my dad would go to hang out and drink in.

As I matured, I did in fact love to be out 'in the streets'. I was independent and free-spirited, and did many of the things that street kids do. By the time I was ten, I had the run of the town. At ten and eleven, I sold papers on the downtown streets. At twelve and a half, I set pins at a bowling alley. It's all automatic now, but in my day, bowling alleys had pin boys who were paid ten cents a game; I set two alleys at a time for spending money. At the bowling alley, I met other young boys, and saw the winos who hung around in the background. They generally ignored us, but we were quite impressed by them. We had many experiences on the streets, but luckily I never got into serious trouble. Later, at the age of thirteen, I got a job at a typewriter store in downtown South Bend, doing odd jobs and learning to repair typewriters; yet I had enough spare time to be a boy scout and a school athlete until I graduated from high school and went off to college. There, I took an undergraduate sociology class in which I remember being very impressed by Liebow's *Tally's Corner*, so much so that I dreamed of doing a similar study in Chicago.

Hence, my selection of Jelly's as a field setting was a matter of my background, intuition, reason, and the result of a little bit of luck. In seeking a site for initiating my study, I visited a number of establishments on the Southside of Chicago, including carry-outs, bars, and simply streetcorner gathering places. While wanting very much to study black streetcorner men, I did not really want to risk my physical safety. As I drove around the Southside, each place I visited had its unique qualities. Some looked very rough and foreboding; others seemed overly quiet and safe. After spending a few hours there, Jelly's seemed to bridge the two extremes. It seemed inviting.

In fact, however, 'getting in' at Jelly's required work, work which ultimately turned out to be provocative, revealing, and rewarding. Initially, I was a 'strange cat,' an outsider, for whom 'getting in' became a long and drawn-out process that provided rich ethnographic research experience. The following fieldnote represents the beginning of my journey.

> As I entered, sat down at the bar, and ordered my first drink, I drew the attention, direct and indirect, of most of the other patrons. Their eyes followed me, they lowered their voices and stopped interacting so freely with one another, as they listened attentively to what I was saying to the barmaid, even observing the way I said it. They desired information about me, and I gave it, however unwittingly, through my interactions with them. As I ordered my first tall Bud at Jelly's, I broke the social ice, and the others, seemingly temporarily satisfied, returned to their preoccupations, but now with an inattentive awareness of my presence. As the barmaid brought my beer, I promptly paid her, just as the sign ('Please pay when served') on the large mirror in front of me directed. She eagerly accepted my payment. As a stranger, I had to pay when served, while the people around me, presumably regular customers, received round after round on credit. It was clear that the rule was for outsiders like me.

As I began my fieldwork, I had no absolute idea where the research would lead, nor where each possible direction might take me.

In part, this open-ended approach was a conscious act; in part it was a sensible and natural way to proceed. To be sure, I had read the classic sociological literature and was familiar with the issues of the day, but for Jelly's social setting, I had no explicit sociological problem or question and, of course, no set answers. At this early stage of fieldwork, I felt, to generate set notions about the field study in the form of questions or assumptions could preclude certain lines of inquiry that might prove valuable later.

Most of all, I was curious about Jelly's and the people there, and I really wanted to learn as much as I could about their social world. With this motivation, I was simply satisfied to hang out, observe, and keep notes. But mainly, I grappled with the immediate issues of 'getting in' and establishing myself as a viable participant in the setting. My research questions and problems emerged over time. I understood that I needed to be as open to new experience as possible, but also to maintain a sense of 'structure,' or organization, to bring sociological meaning to the finished work.

GETTING IN

After spending a couple of weeks at Jelly's, I met Herman and I felt that our meeting marked a big achievement. We would come to know each other well. And, in time, he would become an important sponsor of my entree, serving both as a kind of coach – smoothing my way by introducing me to others there and speaking up for me in my absence – and as an informant, consistently briefing me on the ins and outs of group life on the corner.

Over time, I had observed Herman and had come to see him as something of an informal leader at Jelly's. A kind of 'top cat,' he would light up the tavern with his presence, and through our close association, I could borrow from his status there. Forty-five years old, about 5'9", and brown-skinned, he was a happy-go-lucky sort, always ready with a joke, a laugh, or a disarming smart remark. From my early conversations with him, I found out that Herman worked as a janitor in a Chicago office building, and he would often 'come by Jelly's to drink and carry on'.

Herman was also curious about me. In an early meeting, I told him I was a student at the University, and he thought that was 'very nice'. At that point, I did not disclose that I wanted to do a study of the corner. I hesitated before declaring myself as a researcher because I frankly did not know how much it would matter, but also because I had somewhat tentative relations with the Jelly's crowd. In addition, at that point my project amounted to little more than a paper for a class; I did not yet know that it would become a major study. So I did not disclose my intentions to him until later.

Through our conversations, Herman and I exchanged much information and became fairly well acquainted. We were becoming friends. We would discuss local politics, Mayor Daley, Herman's workplace, our backgrounds, families, and friends. On many of my return visits to Jelly's, he'd be there, and we'd always catch up with each other. He seemed to genuinely like me, and he was one person I could feel comfortable with.

Another person whom I met early on was Rose, the barmaid. Rose was a heavy-set, chocolate-colored woman of 32, with sparkling brown eyes and a ready smile that revealed perfect white teeth. She had a history of 'man trouble' and presently lived with a man named Derrick, who was not the father of her three children. Their relationship was a running story around Jelly's, particularly Derrick's apparent selfless support of Rose's children.

People would joke about what Rose was 'putting down' to keep Derrick so committed to her. After many return visits to Jelly's, Rose and I became familiar enough for me to receive my beer on 'credit', instead of having to 'pay when served' as the sign on the mirror directed. She, too, liked me, and was always ready to help in any way she could. From the beginning, she would address me as 'baby' and 'honey', and I simply called her 'Rose', just as others did. She made me feel welcome at Jelly's.

In time, I increased the circle of people I 'knew' and made slow if incremental progress in getting to 'know' ever more of the local denizens. When I returned, some would engage me again, building on the initial relationship we had established. I began to meet people they knew, slowly building a web of informal relationships.

More and more, I would simply use the place as a kind of watering hole. Sometimes after my classes, I'd go there and drink beer and then return to the University of Chicago library and write up my field notes. Sometimes, one of my fellow students and friends would be there to debrief me, asking, 'What happened today? What happened last night?' I would respond by relating the goings-on at Jelly's. Their questions showed helpful interest, but also gave me a form of support for this work. By relating my experiences to my fellow students, I began to develop a coherent perspective or a 'story' of the place which complemented the accounts that I had detailed in my accumulating field notes.

Perhaps no situation was more critical to my entree than the following occurrence. One evening after several weeks of visiting Jelly's, I walked into the bar room and took a seat at the bar. The juke box blared, as it often did, and people were laughing and talking and drinking. An open doorway connected the bar room and the liquor store, and I spied

Herman on the other side. The bar room side was a more open scene that allowed strangers to come and go without really 'belonging' to Jelly's. Such people could come and hang out for the simple price of a drink, as I had been doing. The liquor store side differed in this important respect.

When outsiders walked in to buy liquor, clerks encouraged them to leave as soon as they had made their purchase, and few lingered. This practice reflected an unwritten rule and virtually everyone understood it. Hence, the men who actually hung out, as distinguished from 'customers,' on the liquor store side derived a license to do so by virtue of being insiders or having standing in the group; Jelly, the owner, would not allow those he considered to be the lowliest people on the corner to hang in the liquor store, not simply for reasons of status but because such men tended to be unruly and capable of 'making trouble,' and thus posing a threat to his livelihood. These men were required to take their liquor outside, on to the corner itself or into the neighboring park. It could be said that the insiders had 'hanging rights', and were thus allowed to come and use the place as a kind of club house, even retiring to the back room on occasion to drink and talk 'serious business'.

So when I walked into the bar that day and saw Herman on the other side, which I felt was off limits, I encouraged him to come to me. But he beckoned to me while I beckoned to him. My gesture indicated, 'I'm not going over there. Come over here.' But his gesture said, 'No, come over here.' But I finally deferred and walked over to join him and the other fellows standing around the liquor store, marking my first visit to that side.

Importantly, Herman's gesture served as a sort of symbolic invitation for me to join the club. And as I approached the gathering that stood just through the open door, Herman said, 'Hey, Eli, meet Uncle Rip, and this here is Sleepy, this is so-and-so.' And to them he said, 'This is Eli, this is the cat I've been telling y'all about. He's getting his PhD.' On the corner around Jelly's, typically a good amount of boasting occurs, and one comes to realize that people often exaggerate and outright lie about themselves and their accomplishments, or are expected to do so. So the men received Herman's information about me with a certain incredulity, saying somewhat mockingly, 'Yeah, yeah, yeah, he's getting his PhD.' After this had died down, the men resumed telling war stories and other tales. A few minutes passed, and then seemingly out of the blue, and in front of the others, Herman asked me directly, 'Eli, you want to come to a Christmas party tomorrow?' Surprised at this invitation, I was taken aback, but then accepted, saying, 'Sure. Where and when?' And he said, 'There's gonna be one where I work at. Come around about 4:30.' Soon after that, Herman gave me the address, I promised to come and meet him there, and I went home to write up my field notes on the day's remarkable events.

The next day, I found the building, walked in, and asked for Herman. Well, Herman was located in a cubicle in the basement among the Ajax, the light bulbs, and other maintenance supplies. I wandered down, and when he saw me, he was elated. 'Hey, man, glad you came. This is where I work. This is my office.' He was obviously proud of the setting and the work he did, and the fact that he was responsible for keeping 'this place sparkling clean.' We made small talk for a while, but then before leaving his 'office', suddenly, he asked, 'Eli's what's your mama's name?' I hesitated. For me, there was something inappropriate about his question. Where I grew up, young people played 'the dozens,' competitive games of 'signifying' or personal attribution. And if a player knows the name of another's mother, that person is disadvantaged, and losing at such games can be emotionally hurtful – which is ultimately the object. The players make witty rhymes and effectively personalize them with a mother's name. Hence, my background conditioned me to be careful about letting my mother's name out; only trusted and close friends are privy to this rivileged information. So when I heard, 'What's your mama's name?' I naturally hesitated. Picking up on my hesitation, Herman knowingly offered, 'Well, my mama's name is like Jesus's mama's name.' 'What's that? Mary?' I responded. He said, 'Yeah, yeah.' So with that, I reciprocated with my mother's name. Strikingly, this exchange of mother's names became an important bond in our relationship. 'OK, your mama and my mama are sisters, so that makes us first cousins. So if anybody asks, we're cousins,' he explained.

The upshot of all of this was that Herman wanted to avoid trouble on his job. He understood that bringing a strange black man into his place of work might arouse suspicion, but it was all right to have a cousin come, because cousins are presumed to be responsible to one another. Herman needed to be able to vouch for me or to pass me off as someone who could be taken as trustworthy. Although it was highly unlikely that someone would ask detailed questions about me, he wanted to be prepared.

We then left his 'office' and walked through the halls toward the Christmas party. As we moved along, he told me repeatedly, 'See how clean this place is? This is what I do, man. See how clean it is.' Clearly, he took great pride in his work. As we approached one office, he stopped and knocked on the door, and the occupant opened up and invited us in for a drink of Jack Daniels. Herman introduced me: 'This is my cousin Eli. This is so-and-so.' We drank

and talked for a while and then went to another office, where we were offered more drinks. Finally we arrived at the Christmas party. There were a lot of people there, but two secretaries, Herman, and I were the only blacks. The workers shared much camaraderie and seasonal good cheer, along with mistletoe. He introduced me to everybody there as his cousin: 'This is my cousin, Eli. He goes to the University of Chicago. He's getting his PhD.' He told the black secretaries that I was the cousin he had been telling them about, revealing to me that he had possibly already been using our relationship to enhance his standing with his co-workers. Eventually, as the party wound down, we left and headed back to his cubicle where Herman changed into street clothes. A sharp dresser, he put on his keen-toed, two-tone shoes, his black cashmere coat, and highboy hat, while I wore a wide-brimmed hat, an old army jacket, and cowboy boots. I complimented him on his nice clothes and, offering me his coat, he replied, 'Feel that, Eli. Feel that. Soft as a baby's ass.' 'Yes,' I said.

As we walked out of the building and toward my car, Herman said to me, 'You know, Eli, I'm really so glad you came. I feel like a man among men. You're my best friend, hear? I'm glad you came.' As we walked along, I said, 'I'm glad I was able to come. The party was nice. But, say Herman, tell me something. Why did you ask only me to come to the party, and none of the other guys?' Collecting himself, he said, 'Well, uh, Eli, I can't be lettin' just anybody come up on my job. I warn't too sure about them, 'course I ain't too sure of myself sometimes around these intelligent folks. But I knew you, with all that education, that you'd know how to talk to them.' To Herman, unlike the other men at Jelly's, I could be trusted to behave appropriately among these downtown, middle-class people.

His speech clearly demonstrated that he recognized the increased sense of status that my presence had given him among his co-workers. At the same time, Herman wanted to take advantage of my presence at the party to bolster his status on the corner. As we continued our trek to my car, he continued, 'You know, Eli, when you get back to Jelly's, don't forget to tell ol' fat-assed Jelly what we did. That we really did kiss all them women under the mistletoe. And we had good booze to drink. And we were around intelligent folks.' Apparently, Herman had been boasting about the upcoming Christmas party, and wanted me to be a witness to the good times. We soon reached my car and drove to Jelly's, and as I pulled up to let him out, he asked, 'Ain't you comin' in?' I declined as I was anxious to get home and write this rich experience up as a field note. 'Aw' right, but when you come back, don't forget to tell ol' fat-assed Jelly and the fellas what we did at the party!' Agreeing to do so, I let him out, and we parted company.

A few days later, I returned to Jelly's and entered the tavern but with a new feeling of confidence. I asked Rose, the bar maid, where Herman was, and when she told me he was on the liquor store side, I boldly went over there. When Herman caught sight of me, he greeted me warmly, saying, 'Hey, Eli, how you doin'?' In the course of the conversations, Herman would ever so slightly or even directly inform people of our activities at his Christmas party, and then, when prompted, I would bolster his account of the party. But equally important, whenever the opportunity arose, Herman would introduce me to people around the corner as his cousin: 'Hey, this is my cousin Eli. Eli, this is so-and-so,' calling me his cousin to people I had only recently met in a different guise. But calling me cousin was not a matter of deception; he was not trying to fool the men as to the nature of our blood relationship. They knew that I wasn't his real cousin.

And equally important, he knew they knew. In effect, Herman and I were 'going for cousins,' and in doing so, we passed as 'fictive kin' or as 'play' cousins, which symbolized our close bond of friendship. It said to the others that we were 'tight,' or close, that we had bonded, and importantly, that 'to mess with Eli is to mess with me.' In these circumstances, I effectively borrowed from his status around the corner. And in turn, he accepted some social responsibility for me. At least, this is how both he and the men around Jelly's seemed to understand our developing relationship.

Increasingly, I was considered 'one of the fellas,' and slowly learned what it meant to have the run of both sides of Jelly's establishment. Now I could venture into the back of the liquor store, where the 'serious business' that the men engaged in turned out to be an ongoing crap game and other forms of gambling. The fact that I could be present meant that I was gaining the trust of the others there. I now felt comfortable enough to move around freely in Herman's absence, and the men generally accepted my presence. Largely I had this growing feeling of being increasingly accepted in my own right.

Around this time I found an opportunity to 'come clean' about my intention to do a study of Jelly's. Herman visited me in my dorm room in an old hotel that the university had remodeled into a dormitory. We were drinking sherry and talking about Jelly's when I first broached the subject. Herman loved to come over and drink sherry, because that was something he could not do on the corner. Drinking wine in public was something the most 'no-count' people did; anyone worthwhile drank hard liquor. I told Herman that I had to write this paper for a class and that I wanted to do it on Jelly's. 'What do you think of that?' I asked him. In between sips of sherry and without hesitation, he replied, 'Fine. Do it, man. Do it.' We then moved on to other topics. By the end of the evening, I wasn't sure how much of this had registered with him. But when I returned to Jelly's the next afternoon, he announced to the group, 'Alright, ya'll. Eli's studying ya'll, so do somethin', do somethin'!' A number of the men momentarily paid attention, but most were left unfazed. The announcement was akin to a pebble dropping into a pond: ripples followed, but soon everything became calm again. The people there did not pay my presence the attention that a more middle-class group might have. Moreover, the men did not seem to relate to the concept of 'researcher'. As the following narrative shows, my identity on the corner was very often associated with that of Herman, but as a 'student' or an 'educated' friend of Herman's, or at most a 'school teacher.' On the corner at Jelly's, people were most concerned about outsiders who might somehow physically threaten the group, so mild-mannered students had very little significance for the denizens of the corner.

Meanwhile, Herman and I spent more and more time together, going to movies and local restaurants in Hyde Park. He met some of my friends, and I met his family. His 20-year-old stepson, Carl, was having problems at his school, and I would go have dinner with them and talk to him. Herman's wife, however, remained slow to accept his explanation of who I was, as the following field note shows:

One evening, after I had been hanging around with Herman and the others at Jelly's for about six months, while Herman and I were sitting around his house drinking beer his sister telephoned. Herman's common-law wife, Butteroll, answered the phone. After talking for a long time, she gave the phone to Herman. As Herman talked with his sister, he referred to me as his friend, Dr. Eli Anderson (exaggerating my status, since I was still a graduate student at the time). 'Come on, Eli. Talk to my sister. Here,' said Herman, as he handed me the telephone. After talking for a while, I gave the phone back to Herman, who then proceeded to brag about me to his sister. Then he returned the phone to Butteroll. She said, 'Aw, Sis. Don't believe that mess. That man ain't no doctor! He ain't nothin' but one o' them wineheads that hang up at that ol' tavern with Herman.'

Embarrassed, Herman grew silent. Soon we left.

At the same time, like almost anyone undertaking such a project, I myself had moments of doubt about what I was doing. On one occasion, I stood on the main thoroughfare outside of Jelly's front window on a weekday at about 5pm when a full Chicago Transit Authority bus was slowly passing by. Just at the instant when I turned up a can of tall Bud wrapped in a brown paper sack, a middle-aged, proper-looking black woman who reminded me of my middle-class and very proper Aunt Freddie looked down at me as the bus passed by. She turned her head my way, our eyes meeting as she looked dead at me, slowly shaking her head with a look of mixed pity and disgust. With that I had an instant of self-doubt about what I was really doing on the corner, who I was hanging out with, and whether 'research' was enough to justify it. The issue would come up on occasion, but not very often, and would be quickly resolved when I would connect with the other students for support and friendship.

Gradually, I came to know the men at Jelly's and the way they interacted with each other. I didn't feel a great need to understand everything at once but felt content to render the setting and its people through my field notes. Throughout this period, I engaged the denizens of the corner and wrote detailed field notes about my experiences, and from time to time looked for patterns and relationships in my notes. In this way, an understanding of the setting came to me in time, especially as I participated more fully in the life of the corner and wrote my field notes about my experiences; as my notes accumulated, and as I reviewed them occasionally and supplemented them with conceptual memos to myself, their meanings became more clear, while even more questions emerged.

THE CLOSING

About six months into the study, in the middle of March, the whole place closed down. I never learned the truth of the matter, but the story was that Jelly had failed to pay off the right inspectors, and they closed him down. At that point, I really thought the study was over and would not amount to more than a course paper. But then during this time, Herman called me up and said, 'Eli, where you been, man? Let's go up to Jelly's.' I said, 'Jelly's is closed.' 'That's OK, let's go see what's happenin'.' And I agreed to pick him up and go to Jelly's. When we got there, we saw the fellows standing around in the front even though Jelly's was closed. So we joined them. On this day, we simply stood around – in a cold drizzle – just socializing and talking with the fellows, hands in pockets, smoking cigarettes, face to face. And they said to Red Eddy, 'Go get us a taste, man.' Red Eddy had no standing and really no money, as well, so he went and got the taste, and when he returned, everyone passed it around, while he drank the leftovers.

For more than a month, the whole place was closed. But this situation, which was something of a social crisis for the men, turned out to be important for my understanding of the group. Almost daily, rain or shine, the men would gather, sometimes in shifts, on the corner outside Jelly's. The men did not come to Jelly's just to drink; they could go anywhere to drink. But it seemed they could not find the peculiar quality of sociability just anywhere. Moreover, their statuses and identities were not easily transferable to other street corners. These were really the people they most cared about, and who cared about them. They came seemingly in an effort to guard their turf, to be present, and to barter in sociability, exchanging favors, news, and other basic elements of

social life. I paid close attention to all this, capturing much of the social activity in my field notes, while beginning to raise what later became the most penetrating questions of the study. Why did men really come to and return to Jelly's corner? What did they seek to gain? What was the nature of the social order there? What was their basis for social ranking? And how and in what circumstances did the men make and remake their system of social stratification?

During this time it became so clear to me that the group was stratified in socially important ways and that such stratification was a critical aspect of the sociability occurring there. For during this time, the men had to be outside on the corner and without their normal props for expressing their local sense of place in the group. If during normal times, the bar room door separated the 'outsiders' from the 'insiders' at Jelly's, this was no longer the case. If during normal times, women visited Jelly's tavern, sitting at the bar, this was no longer the case; women stopped coming around. If during normal times, the lowliest members of what I was coming to see as an 'extended primary group' were refused admission to the place, this was no longer the case, as everyone now had to be outdoors and was free to associate with whomever he could, with whomever would have him. Consequently, the closing of Jelly's exposed the social organization of the group, and I could view it in a somewhat different light, in a different perspective. The social dynamics of who did what with whom in what circumstances was available for me to rather freely observe.

I could see the social pyramid, how certain guys would group themselves and say in effect, 'I'm here and you're there.' During this time the concept of 'crowds' and their uses became clearer for me. As a young sociologist, maybe as a result of some form of 'anticipatory socialization,' I wanted very much to think sociologically, and so I made sense of these crowds as the 'respectables,' the 'non-respectables,' and the 'near-respectables.' These made sense, and I became somewhat comfortable making these distinctions and imposing them on the social reality that I observed. Even though I heard the men refer to one another in other terms, my labels provided a tidy structure, giving the impression of stable categories, which was what I thought I was striving for. To the question of why the men came to Jelly's, I began to see that the answer that they came here to drink, while partly true, would require greater elaboration, but gave me a good start. With the passage of time, as well as deeper involvement with the men at Jelly's, my early distinctions came to be surpassed and relegated to mere working conceptions.

THE REOPENING

Within a month of the closing of the whole place, the liquor store side reopened, while the bar room side remained closed for the duration of the study. From a research perspective, this development too proved to be advantageous, placing things in an even more revealing light. For, in these new circumstances, the liquor store more fully replaced the corner as a setting for sociability. If, during the closing, sociability became more available outside on the corner, it had split between outside and inside, but it occurred in a way and in circumstances that I could more ably witness than had been the case previously. For one thing, the status hierarchy remained more visible since Jelly remained worried about being closed down again and was more adamant than ever about keeping out the 'no-counts' who were prone to cause trouble. What it came down to was

that if you drank cheap wine, which the others pejoratively called 'the oil,' you had to take it outside, but if you drank hard liquor or beer, which took on positive connotations, you were allowed to do so inside. Inside, such non-respectables might sit on the crates, but if a respectable came along and wanted to sit there, the lower status person would have to move.

In a word, as the local status system became more clear to me, Jelly's itself became more of a male club house. Strikingly, the women did not return, in part because there was still no decent place for them to sit. Inside, most of the men would stand around, with the lucky few able to sit on upended soda bottle crates or one or two chairs that were very quickly occupied, all of which discouraged the presence of women. The noise levels and the harsh language were another disincentive for women. Whenever a woman would enter the store, the word would go out, 'Lady in the house!' and this signaled the men to stop cursing and show respect for the woman. Things would then quiet down, but when she left, the noise levels would quickly rise and the decorum would all but disappear.

During evenings and weekends, the liquor store became especially active, with people arriving after work to spend their leisure hours there. The place would usually buzz with conversation and loud talk, helped along by heavy consumption of alcohol. Typically, Jelly himself served as a kind of bartender/clerk who would serve up pints as well as tall Buds to people who would then promptly drink them on the premises or outside.

All the while, Herman and I were becoming better friends. We would hang out together more, sometimes venturing far beyond Jelly's, to different neighborhoods, barbershops, or even to movies or to restaurants downtown. We would go to the movies, to ball games, to restaurants such as Unique and Velois's, even to the lounge on the 96th floor of the John Hancock building where we could look out over the city while having a few drinks.

During this time, Herman became for me more and more of a kind of teacher of the streets. With great pride, he would sometimes announce and document his checkered past, which included pimping, heroin use, and jail time, as if to say he was uniquely suited for this role. And I, as a young doctoral student, but also someone who wanted to learn what he had to teach, was a willing student. On one Saturday morning, for instance, we ventured over to the Westside, a place thought by many of the men at Jelly's to be especially lawless and violent. We were on a mission to meet up with one of Herman's cousins who lived in the Robert Taylor projects there. For some reason, we rode the bus rather than take my car, which usually afforded a certain amount of safety. As we got off the bus and headed up a main thoroughfare on the Westside, we spied a group of young men about a block away.

As we approached them, Herman said to me, 'Looks like trouble. Just dig me.' As we walked along, Herman began to behave completely out of character, assuming the pose of a junky. As we approached the rough-looking group, Herman moved up to the big front window of the tavern they stood in front of. In an instant, Herman pressed his face against the glass and placed his right hand to his forehead and peered through the window as though he were looking for someone. I simply stood by and watched. The other men looked on. After a few minutes of this 'looking,' Herman opened with, 'Ya'll seen LeRoy?' A young man who seemed to be the leader of the group then responded, 'I don't know no LeRoy, man.' Herman then engaged the young man, who was smoking a cigarette, further. 'Lemme smoke with you, man. You got another square (cigarette)?'

With this Herman pulled the collar of his coat up on him as though he was shivering from the cold and displayed this strange wall-eyed look. The man took in this show, but then promptly went into his shirt pocket and came up with the cigarette. 'You got a light, partner?' persisted Herman. The man reached for a book of matches, lit the match and placed it to Herman's cigarette. The others, seemingly taken aback, simply looked on. Herman then took a deep drag of the cigarette, and motioned to me, 'C'mon, Eli, let's go.' With that, we went on our way searching for 'LeRoy.'

Later Herman and I spoke about what had just transpired. Clearly, he created this ruse to get out of what could have turned into a tense situation. By signaling that he was familiar with the neighborhood, but also that he was looking for something, perhaps drugs, or someone he knew, he threw the small group off balance. If they were planning to move against us, they had then to regroup or rethink their plan, which gave us just enough time to get away, or so he believed. We then proceeded on our way toward the projects.

As the ethnography progressed, I felt increasingly included in the activities of the group members, especially the regulars. I felt this inclusion especially during times when the group members would call my name in a familiar manner, implying that I was one of the boys. People seemed to become more at ease with me, as I did with them. They told jokes and stories more frequently in my presence, and followed them with easy laughter and talk. I noted that such laughter was often, though not always, directed at a 'no-count.' Once I told a no-count head story which was a hit and supported one of my early notions concerning group inclusion for putting down a lesser member of the group. But I did not test this notion for a long while.

In thinking about my own inclusion into the group and how this might be facilitated, I observed that even well-established members of the general group would often make ritual greetings to one another by asking for a third person who was usually not present at the time. By such an act, I thought, the membership and affinity of both men could be affirmed. Usually, the person 'cutting in' (as I later heard the men describe it) seemed not really to be concerned with the person asked for. Such an act could serve as a person's claims on what could be called 'passage rights.' It seemed that such people negotiated their way anew each time they came to the corner by engaging in such actions. In employing this ritual, I would sometimes ask for Herman and sometimes for others.

Through such actions I was making claims on rights of membership. After performing this ritual, I would exercise other rights by boldly walking up to the large window and looking through it as though I were looking for Herman or someone else. After this, I would walk through the front door, look around, and perhaps go into the back room. Afterwards, I would emerge from the back room or move on through the front room to the street and join the others standing outside on the corner. Such acts of familiarity with the place, and the group, contributed to my entree. As I would accomplish such acts without incident, I began feeling more and more secure about my own acceptance and inclusion.

Probably the most important sign of the progress of my own inclusion was the presence and subsequent initiation of new group members. With each successful entree by a new member, I could feel my own position within the group becoming that much more secure. Over a period of three years, I had the good fortune of being among group members as others were coming around as new people. This fact helped my own sense of group standing in important ways, for now there were new people whom I could show around, which I proceeded to do. People could now ask me questions, and I could act as a kind of informant. In doing so with certain 'new' people, I became less circumspect about my own position within the group and at times would even forget myself and just simply hang out around Jelly's, absorbing the ambiance of the area.

As this process of inclusion progressed, I could feel that I was being treated and defined as a certain kind of person. I was gaining a more secure place. At first I was associated with Herman. But later, as mentioned, I began establishing my own independence, which made for a more generalized identity within the group. It seemed that the more generalized this identity became, the more secure and durable it became; and the less vulnerable it was to accusations or misunderstandings between and among the members. In a word, group members began to trust me, and freely allowed me rights of membership. Almost suddenly, I became able to 'associate' with hoodlums and wine heads without being taken for one by the regulars and others, doing so to gain a better perspective on the group. Relative independence was thus slowly being achieved.

But as the inclusion progressed, I felt myself to have many sides. Group members communicated to me, in part, by the ways in which they treated me and attempted to treat me. One side of me, especially to the regulars, was that of college student. To some, particularly the regulars, I represented the height of propriety, for I was 'in college' and getting a PhD. For those who took this side of my identity seriously, I should do no wrong, and they often had a problem with having their own presuppositions about me coincide with what they could observe about me. For instance, once, after I had been around Jelly's for about seven months, I attempted to carry a wine bottle in my back pocket. At this, Herman became upset, pulled me aside, and began quietly reprimanding me, saying that people could get the wrong idea about me if I were not careful, that 'carrying wine bottles in yo' pocket is what wine heads do.' And on another occasion, I tried to use foul language, and again, Herman reprimanded me with, 'Eli, you ain't supposed to talk like that. Man, you got all that education, you ain't supposed to cuss like that.' I stood corrected, but with a certain better understanding of my place in the group and a sense of what Herman thought I owed him. And, on another occasion, I joined in the banter of the moment by attempting to do what some of the regulars were doing by using the word 'motherfucker.' Again, Herman reprimanded me: 'Now, Eli. You didn't go to school for no eight years to talk like that!' In *Street Corner Society*, Whyte similarly reports that Doc, his main informant, chastised him for swearing on the same grounds. This kind of corroboration between settings allows us to posit more general theories on social behavior.

I had to face reprimands such as these during much of the first year I hung out at Jelly's. But as time passed, and the more I hung around, I became more able to be like the others, which undoubtedly had to do with my growing general acceptance among the men, so that I had somewhat more freedom to engage in certain kinds of behavior without being totally defined by it. But my freedom also had to do with my sponsors' growing confidence in my acceptance by the group, and their corresponding feeling that they did not have to be as responsible for me as they had once been. With a growing sense of freedom, I ventured to make more and deeper contacts with the wine heads and the hoodlums without seriously risking being identified with them. During the social interactions we all experienced, other members reminded me of my own entitlement to such freedom. As I attempted to make room for myself, Herman and the others simply let me be. I had this freedom because I successfully negotiated for it, and they allowed me to have it.

ON MY OWN

My inclusion into the group at Jelly's was brought home to me one Friday night when a number of us were sitting and standing around in Jelly's, drinking, laughing and talking, as we normally did. I was standing near Jelly and a couple of others when a customer approached the counter and asked for a six pack. Without missing a beat, Jelly ordered, 'Eli, get this man a six pack.' I was close to the cooler which was behind the counter. I promptly went behind the counter to get the six pack and gave it to Jelly, who then rang it up for the customer. As simple as that may sound, to go into the cooler as many others had done was to feel more included. I felt as though I had the license to go into a friend's refrigerator. I felt such liberty was reserved for those who had standing, and thus I felt as though I was really becoming one of the boys.

As Herman and I became increasingly better friends, the other men certainly took note, as did Herman himself. 'You alright now, Eli,' commenting on my supposed acceptance by the group. 'You some of Herman, you some of Tonk, you some of

Taylor,' he would declare, attesting to my progress at being included as one of the regular group members.

Some of what I learned came through trying to initiate projects myself. I once planned a trip to the movies for the men, and they agreed to meet me on the corner at 9:30 in the evening. No one showed up. When I asked several of the men later on what had happened, the answer I got was, 'I got hung up.' This taught me that people talk big on the corner but can't be counted on to follow through.

Herman, however, surprised me once. One summer I took my fellowship money and rented an apartment in Madison, Wisconsin, about two hours away. The city has a lovely lakeside setting where I could relax and do my reading in peace. I shuttled back and forth between Madison and Chicago, and one day I invited Herman to come visit me on his week off from work. I was at Jelly's when he showed up with his packed bags and told the men he and I were headed for California, all the while giving me furtive winks. I let him tell his story. I left before him, and the plan was for him to come later on the bus. Based on my past experience, I didn't expect him to follow through, but to my surprise he showed up. My apartment was an efficiency, so he got a room at the YMCA and we saw the sights of Madison, Herman with his ear to his transistor radio to catch the game. When we went out to the lake, he wouldn't go on the water, but we sat on the terrace of a fancy hotel and waitresses in bikinis served us drinks. Herman was delighted. A whole different world had opened to him, and he was eager to document it. He had his picture taken with the waitresses and later had one of them take our picture in front of a Cadillac in the parking lot. However, instead of a week he only stayed the night, because he was so anxious to get back and tell the men at Jelly's about it. This showed me how important the group and his place in it was to him. He showed the pictures to everyone and in general played off the trip for a long time.

By this time, I felt I was developing a good sense of what was going on sociologically at Jelly's. About a year and a half into the study, when I began working with Howard Becker, I gave him an account of my work up to that point, including my discovery of the three groups – the 'respectables,' the 'non-respectables,' and the 'near-respectables.' Howie required more clarification of those terms. And he asked me a critical question, 'But, Eli, what do they call themselves?' Up to now, I had been comfortable imposing my 'sociological' labels on the men, but now, with greater scrutiny, my understanding increased dramatically. I reviewed my field notes, closely noting and responding to the question of what the men called themselves and what they meant by such words. From my notes, the folk concepts 'winehead,' 'hoodlum,' and 'regular' stood out.

Armed with this perspective, I returned to the corner to investigate, and to try anew to better understand who was who. I first verified this with Herman, and he agreed, 'Sure, those are the crowds. You got that right.' And I then ventured to test these labels in the field. One day I pulled TJ over for a talk. I asked him about the labels, and said, 'What are you?' 'I'm regular, man, you know that,' as if something was wrong with me. He thought it was weird that I would be asking him something like this. I might add here that over the course of my time at Jelly's, people would allow me to blend into the woodwork so to speak, but when I would begin to inquire about the nature of the group, they would seem to be jarred into thinking, What's wrong with Eli? There he goes again, asking all those weird questions.

Clearly, as someone who was presumably closely involved, or 'in,' with the men, I should 'know what's happening,' or be fully aware of the local knowledge of the corner. Hence, it was 'strange' for me to ask 'so many questions' that I should already know the answer to. In these circumstances, I played the role of the 'cultural dope,' or from time to time, 'played dumb.' Playing such a role made some people suspicious of me. One of shadiest characters there thought I might be an undercover cop, but Herman vouched for me, saying I was 'just a student over at the University,' and that I was 'studying ya'll.'

Despite such questions, I persisted, asking person after person. 'So what are you?' 'I'm a regular.' And 'What are you?' 'I'm a regular.' 'What are you?' 'I'm a regular.' Finally, I got to Red Eddy, one of the most well-known wineheads around, and even he declared, 'I'm regular!' Virtually, everyone was a regular! But then I began to ask how they viewed one another, or what they thought of others in relation to themselves. So I asked, 'What is he?' 'Oh, he's a hoodlum' or who is he, and the answer would be, 'He's a winehead.' It came out that while group members would declare themselves as 'regulars,' absolutely no one would identify themselves as a 'hoodlum' or as a 'winehead.'

In these circumstances I began to appreciate and make note of the fluidity of the group, but particularly the way in which people labeled themselves in comparison with one another. Especially interesting was the role of competition in the determination of status, and how that lent a precarious aspect local ranking. From this perspective and such questions, the whole corner opened up to me anew. The word 'regular' had at least two connotations. One had to do with the fact that every one was regular in the sense that they came regularly to Jelly's and were actually a part of the extended primary group. But in another sense, the word 'regular' was a mere folk label for my sociological imposition of the 'respectable.'

In this usage, the 'regulars' basically valued 'decency.' They associated decency with conventionality but also with 'working for a living,' or having a 'visible means of support.' The regulars had relatively stable families, and they valued those families as well as traits such as churchgoing and law-abiding-ness. They used the corner mainly as a recreational place, as they had other options, of which they would remind the others from time to time.

The hoodlums in general were concerned about an invisible means of support. They too were often employed, but they tended not to make such a big deal of it, and compared to the regulars, were more alienated. They weren't especially proud of the fact they had to 'slave for the man,' or to labor in jobs they labored in. If working at all, they did so with certain ambivalence. Generally, it was important to their identities to be able to get by in some kind of slick way. They would pride themselves on encounters with the police or time in the county jail, at times enthralling others with their death-defying tales.

The wineheads constituted a residuum of the wider group, even a group that others, possibly suffering a loss in resources, could fall into. If the regulars were mainly concerned with 'decency,' and the hoodlums were primarily concerned with 'being tough' and 'getting by invisibly,' the wineheads were concerned essentially with 'having some fun' and 'getting a taste.' And the taste they would get was very often wine. And as indicated throughout this work, Jelly, the owner of the liquor store, would discourage their presence and let them know up front, 'Get out of my place!' or 'I done told you about coming in here. Out!' he would say. So they ranked really low in the social hierarchy. But the hoodlums, who were somehow marginally better in his mind, could be around. And the regulars were certainly the most welcome.

As I considered where I fit, or who I was to the people of Jelly's, and came to see myself as a certain kind of person, I gained a sense of timing for displaying certain emblems important to the culture of Jelly's for the desired effect. My dress for Jelly's was similar to that of the others of the setting. I often wore jeans, an army jacket, a work shirt, and boots. Sometimes I wore dressy shirts and dress pants. For me, there was no single way to dress; my dress was varied, just like that of the others, though a few seemed rather set in their ways of dress. I wanted to be taken as ordinary, and reflected this intent in my dress, my speech, and my general demeanor. At times, I purposely did things to see what reaction I would elicit from people. For instance, on occasion I would wear a broad-rimmed bordello hat cocked 'acey-deucy' (to the side) just to get reactions from others. Of course, this was after I had been hanging around for a long while. After dressing this way, it occurred to me that I had possibly earned the right to wear such a hat.

In my developing relationship with the men, as an ethnographer, I strove to learn how the rules of the group applied to me, what I could and could not do with each person with whom I interacted and came to know and who came to know me. In this connection, I see those rules as developing in situations, as actions expressed and then legitimated through responses to my conduct, behavior which in effect told all concerned that they could either continue or should discontinue a certain line of action. The rules were not stable and knowable in the sense that they were a part of some stated code that could be simply given to someone, but rather they were unwritten, intangible, amorphous, and heavily dependent upon the situations in which the actors found themselves. The rules for different individuals emerged from competing senses of powerfulness maintained by various people within the group. It was from this sense of power, and self-confidence, that personal actions by particular individuals were attempted and then either accepted or rejected by others. The people of Jelly's spent much time discussing their observations of such events. Through this kind of social commentary, continuously occurring within the group, the social order of the group was made known to its respective members, as well as to me. Indeed, through often intense involvement of myself, I gained an understanding of the social organization of the group. This became all the more a matter of socialization as I became increasingly involved in the daily round of group life, the various transactions, and social bargains being made or broken within the group.

About a year and a half after my entree, I began using my tape recorder and thus gained direct conversational data. The most important reason for my waiting so long was my need to establish my own identity within the setting, a goal which would not have been furthered by my use of the tape recorder early on in the process of getting to know Jelly's. I could not take for granted some right to use a tape recorder in the setting but had to earn this right with the people of the corner. The right to use a tape recorder, just as the right to hang around, was negotiated and earned. This, of course, took a certain amount of time. To have used a tape recorder prematurely would have opened me up for suspicion and the possible enmity of others on the corner, thus making my entree difficult at best and impossible at worst. I had to gain a certain degree of trust and friendship with the men before I felt able to broach my wish to tape-record. When I did begin to do so, I used a combined tape recorder and radio. I did not tape surreptitiously but did so in the open. I asked for the men's permission and they granted it. I felt it would have been counterproductive to disrupt the research situation before each taping; the resulting tapes might have appeared contrived rather than natural and authentic.

I gained such rights through my participation and involvement in the social setting. By hanging out at Jelly's, on the street corner, 'doing what they do,' others in the setting could take me for granted, as just 'one of the boys.' Through this process, I became a fixture of sorts as I gained a place in the minds of the men. I drank with the men. I laughed with the men. I talked with them about all kinds of things. I adopted their speech habits and ways of speaking, their gestures, and even their ways of walking. But probably the most important thing about my getting the trust of the men was my continued presence at Jelly's. I was around, and endured, which probably more than anything else, accounted for my general acceptance. Perhaps it did not matter so much what I did, but my presence was so important for gaining the groups' growing trust and for holding a particular place in their minds.

The dialogue, physical and verbal, that I was conducting with the men was crucial for the advancement of the work, for it allowed me to sort out the most important themes for an understanding of Jelly's, thus defining the study. One plays with ideas, as they emerge, in relationship to reality as one sees it. This meant sitting down with people, talking with them, hearing them out, but viewing the situation as data from which to interpret and evaluate the hypothesis one already has. Ultimately, I felt the analysis

must be my own, an analysis which could differ from that of the subjects themselves. Such a difference does not negate the study, but hopefully uncovers a reality of which the subjects may have been unaware.

In a process commonly known as 'analytic induction,' I would come up with an idea, hold it for a while, look for negative cases which would require its revision. And if I found such cases, I would then revise my thinking to take into account the new information, incorporating that into my hypothesis and developing perspective. For example, in observing the relationship between regulars and wineheads, it was clear that the wineheads' constant begging annoyed the regulars. To deal with this, they developed a habit of 'buying off' certain wineheads. They would simply 'loan' the problematic winehead a sum they knew he couldn't or wouldn't pay back. The winehead in debt would then avoid the regular who had made the loan, since the regular could then simply remind him of his debt as a pretext for not lending him more. After 'discovering' this practice, I looked for negative cases in my notes, but instead found positive ones, which then encouraged me to make the proposition. The following field note is relevant.

> One evening six regulars, including Herman and myself, were gathered in front of Jelly's liquor store. Tiger and Mack were the only wineheads there. Tiger was trying to 'get up the money' for some wine. He asked me, 'Eli, lemme hold somethin'. I'll see you straight when my check comes' (meaning lend me some money and I'll repay you when I get it). I then went into my pocket and came up with fifty cents. I gave it to him, and he went inside the liquor store. I asked Herman what he thought of the loan I had just made. Herman laughed matter-of-factly. 'He sold himself cheap.'

I asked other regulars as well as a few wineheads about this practice, and time after time found mostly positive evidence in support of the assertion that those with money engage in the practice of 'buying off' those who annoy them with their constant begging. I thus felt safe about holding on to the idea and incorporating it into the work. From in-depth consideration of such ideas, larger questions emerged. Patterns formed and could be observed, giving the work a somewhat inductive character, ever holding out the possibility of growth of new ideas and emphasizing the tentative nature of the ideas thus formed. In this way, my analysis seemed to resonate with the understandings of the people themselves.

As I was preparing to leave Jelly's, the hoodlums were taking over; they began to dominate the scene as the regulars slowly faded away and did not come around as much. Part of this had to do with Jelly's sporadic openings toward the end of my stay on the corner of Jelly's. He might open on a Monday, not open on Tuesday, and then not open again until Thursday. This sporadic opening and closing simply would not do for the regulars, many of whom came to Jelly's after work; thus, some of them found other places to hang out, though they would sooner or later return to Jelly's corner to rejoin their consorts. The ties they had made there were too important just to let go, though over time they did so, however slowly. Meanwhile, the activity around the corner became increasingly street-oriented. The level of fighting increased. The hoodlums asserted themselves more, and the regulars who continued to come around confronted the prospect of having to display their 'tough' sides more than they desired. This helped some to find excuses not to visit Jelly's corner, encouraging them to think of the corner as a place 'to stay away from.' In so doing, the regulars increasingly defined Jelly's as a place for hoodlums and wineheads, a definition which was certainly not wasted on those 'decent' people of Jelly's immediate

environment, people who knew all along what 'kind of place it was.'

Much later, when I made a return visit to Jelly's, the place had closed down and Jelly himself had retired. Indeed, many of the people were 'new' and 'hoodlums' in the minds of those people I knew on the corner. Shortly before the publication of the book, Herman told me that the place had indeed changed, that 'the hoodlums had taken over' and seemed to be everyplace.

In reflecting on my experiences at Jelly's, it became clear that I always experienced a certain amount of tension within me in carrying out the study, a tension based on my awareness that I lived in two social worlds, that of the University and that of Jelly's. I never completely resolved this tension, or ambivalence. I simply became more aware of the existence of both worlds. Perhaps experiencing this duality was very positive, for it highlighted each social world and clarified my own sense of self and personal identity.

WRITING IT UP

Writing is not just the last stage of a study, but an integral part of an ethnographic work from the outset. From my very first visit to Jelly's, the documenting of my experiences through writing field notes was a primary concern. In writing these notes I tried to record experiences and observations of social life in prose, writing up as much detail as possible, particularly actions and conversations. We used typewriters in those days, and I would fill up legal-sized paper with single-spaces. I tried to recapture what had just happened, writing down as much detail as I could recall. A great aspect of the process of writing these field notes was that you wrote them and that was it; it was somewhat like keeping a diary that could be reviewed later with benefit. And after the day's entry, you could put it aside in favor of going off to do some more fieldwork.

My teachers encouraged me to 'write down what was happening in fine detail' and to make these notes as free of judgments and pre-suppositions, including the unexamined use of adjectives and evaluative nouns, as possible. For example, to write down simply that 'the men were shabbily dressed' obscures much detail about specifically how the men dressed, or exactly which details led to the generaliza-tion of 'shabbily dressed.' In theory, such details in my field notes would be quite infor-mative and useful when it was time to review them for analysis.

Moreover, I had to be cognizant of the effect of bias creeping into the work and, when discovered, to work to make the most effective use of it: to question my developing knowledge and to field test it whenever possi-ble. The rule for writing notes required me to convey as realistic as possible a sense of local events that included the actions and words of people as best I could remember them. In this effort to be true to the social world, I trained myself to remember whole conversations that occurred in the field and then to replicate them in my field notes.

Usually, I wrote these notes immediately after spending time in the setting or the next day. Through the exercise of writing up my field notes, with attention to 'who' the speak-ers and actors were, I became aware of the nature of certain social relationships and their positional arrangements within the peer group. And during my first weeks in the field, I was particularly aware of such people and their immediate situations.

Throughout the study, I also wrote con-ceptual memos to myself to help me sort out my findings. Usually no more than a page long, they represented theoretical insights that emerged from my engagement with the data in my field notes. As I gained tenable hypotheses and propositions, I began to listen and observe selectively, focusing in on those events that I thought might bring me alive to my research interests and concerns. This method of dealing with the information I was receiving amounted to a kind of dia-logue with the data, sifting out ideas, weigh-ing new notions against the reality with which I faced there on the streets and back at my desk.

My ultimate goal of the study was to make sense of the experience of being part of the group on Jelly's corner, but also to understand how the people there made sense of their world. In fact, I had been trying to make sense of what was going on from the beginning, but in writing the study up, I tried to get even more of a handle on it. Any study requires these two kinds of understanding. One is gained 'on the hoof' and involves appreciating the local knowledge and learning how to behave in the local setting: the everyday rules of local life. One comes to appreciate what is expected and what reactions are likely to result from one's actions. In effect, the ethnographer is being resocialized. The other sort of under-standing is sociological sense-making. One tries to pull all the material together so as to represent the situation in a way that makes sense sociologically and adds to the general fund of knowledge. This requires blending the local knowledge one has learned with what we already know sociologically about such set-tings. This dynamic movement is one of the most challenging problems in doing ethno-graphic work.

To make sense is to communicate with people, the readers, who have not been in the particular research setting, and allow them to comprehend what is going on there. Realizing this goal is fraught with difficulties because representation of the setting is essentially the ethnographer's personal statement that becomes valuable to the extent that it resonates with the presuppositions of the people who haven't been there. That is when it becomes able to be taken seriously as knowledge. As a young sociologist, contributing to the field very much concerned me. In trying to blend the knowledge I was gaining at Jelly's with accepted sociological thinking, I wrote hundreds of pages of field notes. I also wrote conceptual memos to myself, in which I began to see patterns develop that pointed to a sociological question, and this question had to do with how these men, in coming together, were making and remaking their stratification system. What were its components? How did it operate in face-to-face interactions? How do the various principles of status contradict or support one another?

I began the process of writing up the study by simply putting down whatever came to mind in terms of the stories and issues that I had gathered from my time at Jelly's, basically emptying my head of all the things I had learned. This included the insights that came out of the conceptual memos as well as material from my field notes. In time, this free writing, which took the form of a narrative that eventually amounted to 100–plus pages, resulted in a kind of crystallization of issues. I then went over this document and took notes on it by placing each major idea in the form of a declarative statement on a 5x7 index card, one idea to a card. Finally I sorted the cards by category and arranged them on the floor of my apartment. I had separate categories on the regulars, the hoodlums, the wineheads, etc. I left the cards there for several weeks, playing with the arrangement until I felt I had it right. When I ultimately picked

them up, row by row, I had the guts of respective chapters. My task then was to sit with each row and develop a chapter out of each set of cards.

The final step necessitated relating my findings to the literature. That meant reading what other sociologists had to say about issues similar to those I had uncovered among the men at Jelly's and seeing how my assessment agreed with or differed from theirs. Of course, I had already done a lot of this reading in preparation for going into the field. Through my initial reading I discovered that I wanted to do this kind of study. Now I read as a matter of relating what went before me with my own findings, in essence fitting my own work into the literature.

This ethnographic study was twofold. In one sense, it addressed the question of how these black men live on this corner, and in another, it considered how the local people organized themselves according to values, norms, and rank. The first question concerned a specific group of black men, but the second has significance for human group interaction in general. I did not start with the general question. I simply wanted to get to know these men, but as I did so, status and rank became salient issues. These considerations piqued my interest and I was drawn to ask what status and rank meant to them. But I was also interested in how they met the exigencies of life. These questions emerged as the study progressed. Ultimately, I as the researcher became a communication link – between the men at Jelly's and the wider world, between their practical skill in constructing social organization and our general understanding of how social organization works. That, I believe, is our job as students of social life – to learn from those we study and then teach others the lessons we have learned.

At the same time, the study provided me with the personal satisfaction of developing adult relationships with the sorts of men whom I had seen and been intrigued by as I was growing up. Gaining an understanding of the social dynamics of the men at Jelly's required me to find my own place in the setting, and in representing this process of inclusion ethnographically, I started to come to terms with my own story. I believe another researcher would have come to many of the same conclusions as I did, but ethnography always contains a subjective element that can only be corroborated by other fieldworkers in similar settings. I was both observer and participant, dual but integrated roles that were so critical for the ethnographic work on Jelly's Corner.

4

Your Place or Mine: The Geography of Social Research

MICHAEL STEIN

It is often the case that when methods texts consider fieldwork, more emphasis is given to the work than the field. This includes texts exclusively devoted to ethnographies, which focus on the work because it represents a set of teachable skills governed by widely accepted standards of appropriateness. The work has a history, then, and lies before the researcher waiting to be done. The physical, social, and psychological space where research is conducted is less subject to consideration. Places are usually already there, seemingly completed, but they cannot be taken for granted. The field itself, the places wherein observed behavior occurs, needs to be considered in its own right. Issues of place affect social research throughout the process. This is true for the researcher as well as those being studied.

This chapter will treat these assertions in turn. After establishing the case that greater focus on the work than the field dominates social research, attention will turn to issues of place and the relevance of these issues to social behavior. The implications for theory,

method and, specifically, ethnographic research will then be explored. Appreciation of the field will thus be better joined with the work to be done, and an equality of importance of the terms will be attained.

ESTABLISHING THE CASE

Although there is a clear emphasis on quantitative techniques in texts that present a general survey of methods, a single chapter will often be devoted to ethnography or other field-based research (Adler and Clark, 1999; Agnew and Pyke, 1994; Babbie, 1998; Wysocki, 2001). On rare occasions, several chapters may be given over to the epistemological debates concerning the appropriateness of field-based, ethnographic research (Goldenberg, 1992). In these cases, ethnography is something of a sidelight, a brief contrast to (or respite from) the quantitative methods that dominate the social sciences.

There are, of course, texts devoted entirely to ethnographic fieldwork. One common form is that of the 'cookbook' which provides step-by-step procedures for conducting such research (Agar, 1980; Berg, 1989; Hammersley and Atkinson, 1983; Jackson, 1987; Spradley, 1980). In addition there are readers, which likewise offer guidance by means of experience and cautionary tales (Filstead, 1970; Hesses-Biber and Leavy, 2004; McCall and Simmons, 1969; Shaffir and Stebbins, 1991; Shaffir, et al. 1980). As would be expected, greater appreciation for fieldwork will be found in these texts. Concerns with the processes, strategies and techniques of fieldwork are featured, and a logical sequence is followed. Topics such as entering the field, cultivating rapport, gathering, recording and organizing data, and leaving the field are typical. Often the issue of ethics – frequently held to be of particular concern to ethnographers – will be covered in these texts.

For all this detailed focus on strategy and technique, it is presented to the near exclusion of the dimensions, conditions, and contingencies of the places in which such research is conducted. There is a geography of social research which requires its own exploration.

The place(s) where research is conducted inform the entire enterprise. Because humans take note of their surroundings, place may represent a critical dimension regardless of the method employed. The laboratory experiment, for example, is often cited as a contrived, artificial environment that may arouse the curiosity or other forms of self-consciousness among subjects, and thereby affect behavior (Goldenberg, 1992: 284). For the ethnographer, consideration of place is paramount since research is conducted in settings natural to the behavior being observed, and may in fact play a part in its determination. Thus the 'scene' becomes something more than mere background.

Rather, place assumes a centrality and texture, whether stated or not, that shape the research, the researcher, and the researched. The call by Stimson (1988) to bring the notion of place back into methods involving fieldwork would seem self-evident, but has largely gone unheeded. The near exclusive focus on work has left the field untended and fallow.

CONSIDERATION OF PLACE

As discussed here, place refers to 'meaningful space' (L. Lofland, 1998; Relph, 1976; Seamon, 1979; Tuan, 1977; Walter, 1988). That is, ascribed individual or collective definitions, associations, attitudes, sentiments, intentions, reputations, and other bits of consciousness are an important part of the creation and sustenance of place. These subjective elements are mediated by human experience, whether real or imagined, concurrent or in memory.

Although most of the attention in this chapter is on the built environment, it is also true that places largely devoid of human constructed things, actions or habitants conjure meaning, sometimes dramatically different in nature. Some places, such as Shangri La or Middle Earth, may be sited in the imagination only, but be evocative of certain values, attitudes and style of life. Excitable children and some people in therapy are sometimes told to find their 'quiet place' – which may or may not include a specific physical location – and to go there. Through processes of time, over succession, by design, decree or circumstance, meaning accrues to place. Territories may come to have an identity or character through human imputation and, like people, become known as good, bad, desirable or unsavory (J. Lofland, 1969: 168). This human imputation of meaning is necessary to give any physical setting a sense of place. Such definitions may differ, and are subject to change for both the natural and built environment. Differences in definition may be a product of experience, culture, social class or other social groupings. The Australian desert experienced by many outsiders as barren and hostile, is for Aborigines a place of wonder and excitement (Walter, 1988: 137). Changes may involve nothing more than redefinition, or more likely result from a process of intended, physical transformation. Science or other forms of expertise may create a sense of place. Once the true source of the Mississippi River was isolated from among a number of small inconspicuous pools of water, the surrounding area was made a park and a tourist destination was thereby created (Tuan, 1977: 162). Times Square in New York City has been transformed over the last twenty years from a den of iniquity to a place of considerably more wholesome pursuits (Traub, 2004).

Cognitive dimensions are more essential to place as it is discussed here than physical properties, although physical features may play a critical part as well. Places are defined and differentiated by means of boundaries, which may, like the space they demarcate, be literal, figurative or metaphorical. Physical boundaries are the most evident and may be natural, such as rivers, mountain ranges, and the like, or be part of the built environment, such as walls, buildings or streets. The significance of the these boundaries may be legal and political, such as borders between municipalities, states, or countries, or social and cultural like the 'other' side of the railroad tracks that separates the good and bad parts of town.

Places can also be metaphorical, their boundaries more amorphous, even as they suggest a general, and often generic, physical locale. The 'Middle West' of the United States – much of which is characterized as the 'fly over' by travel agents from other parts of the country – is variously perceived as greater or lesser portions of the middle of the North American continent, and suggestive of rural, 'heartland' values (Shortridge, 1989). Far less bucolic are 'the streets,' and the culture assumed to accompany them (Anderson, 1990; Wright and Decker, 1994, 1997).

If persons are admonished to 'keep' or 'mind' their place, social status is implied, an abstraction frequently associated with place. A whole host of status meanings is strongly suggested by the physical locations where given groups may typically be found. References to such places as the Ivy League or a trailer park indicate very different sorts of persons, values, attitudes, interests, and lifestyles.

Time and space are intimately related (Jakle, 1987: 4–5; Tuan, 1977: 179–98). Urban dwellers frequently measure the distance between places in units of time: 'I live 20 minutes from the airport.' Time, on the other hand, is thought of as 'length' or 'volume' (Tuan, 1977: 118). Legends, fairy tales and myths are often both 'a long time ago' and 'far away.' A temporal dimension can alter the meaning of a place, sometimes radically so. As noted above, the meaning of place may change over time intentionally or otherwise. It is also true that the meaning of a given place may be altered temporarily. Tourist destinations may be dynamic or 'dead', depending on the season. Night often adds a layer of atavistic menace to settings, and has been likened to a 'frontier' (Melbin, 1987). The passing of time through aging can change our perception of place as well as the propriety of our presence there. The metaphorical 'open road', for instance, seems especially suited to youth.

Whether primarily by means of physical features, imputed reputation, time, or in combination, the objective (if any) and subjective elements of place conjure meaning, sentiments, and attitudes, and become imbued with them. Place, persons and behavior are linked through meaning and experience. Places do not 'act', but they do contain and shape action, and may be strongly associated with it. It is humans who create the sense of a place through the imputation of meaning. Places are thus part of the social construction of reality (Berger and Luckmann, 1966), which act back upon their creators by exerting influence over behavior.

It is axiomatic when purchasing a house that the three most important considerations are 'location, location, and location.' Place in this case refers usually to neighborhood, and it is widely held that for reasons of investment and more, a modest house in a good neighborhood will make more economic sense than a fine house in a bad neighborhood. As noted above, the meaning of places is subject to change, and through processes of discovery, renewal, and redevelopment, the reputation of neighborhoods can be transformed, and greatly increase the value of properties within, just as earlier social and economic processes may have lead to a decline in value. In either case, it remains true that the meaning of a place – in this case the perceived character of a neighborhood – will inform purchase decisions and add or detract from a sense of easefulness.

The purchase of a house is usually the most significant single economic decision to be made in a lifetime, and also infrequent. A more routine, day-to-day commercial activity – shopping – takes place in a more public sphere of commerce, and here too the importance of location is evident. This is true for both owner/operator and consumer. As with housing, social class has a clear effect upon where businesses locate and where consumers go. If an area is perceived as in some way 'bad,' neither owner nor consumer is likely to venture there. One chain of grocery stores in metropolitan St Louis, Missouri is exclusively suburban, and does not build and no longer operates anywhere within the city limits, their move being a commercial version of 'white flight.' A British journalist has suggested that English supermarket chains appeal to different social classes and thus by interests, lifestyle, and consumption patterns (Jeffries, 2004). Other types of commerce are oriented toward those of lesser means. Just as most shopping malls want to be close to affluent neighborhoods, so too will pawn shops, currency exchanges and 'rent-to-own' furniture stores locate in poorer areas. In addition to issues of social class, other factors of place, such as zoning laws, visibility or access have an impact on location. Interior arrangements are also considered by many places of commerce. Malls will suggest appropriate locations for specific types of business as well as the placement of food courts and such natural elements as water and plants.

The world of work comprises a major portion of economic activity, and plays a large part in where people will live. Location and interior design are again important dimensions. Various categories of work are associated with particular places. High-tech 'corridors' are firmly established on the east and west coasts of the United States, and close to major research universities, and may bring other categories of work with them.

Typically, the world of work makes all manner of demands upon appearance and behavior in varying degrees. The interior of the workplace has been subject to various manipulations as a way of maximizing efficiency. Social science in the early twentieth century was at times put to use by industry to increase output. The Hawthorne effect suggested that almost any physical change in factory décor would improve productivity. The more recent replacement of offices with cubicles in corporations is also seen as a way of affecting work behavior.

Although the economy is a major force in the modern world, there are other motives for behavior. Spiritual matters, and the places associated with them, can exert a powerful influence on social action. The transcendent nature of spiritual beliefs imbue sacred places with special and refined meaning, ritual and personages (Walter, 1988: 69–95). Rituals reflect and reinforce the various attitudes of reverence, awe, respect, gratitude (and sometimes fear) that attend the sacred. Familiarity with these rituals can also help to distinguish insiders from outsiders. Transcendence may also suggest mythic places not of the earth. Perceptions of heaven and hell over time and across cultures have variously suggested locales – sometimes of a literal, physical nature – 'up above' and 'down below' (Turner, 1993). This verticality is frequently reflected in earthly notions of social status – religious and otherwise – and is often reinforced by place (Tuan, 1977: 37–8). Sacred places also have a literal and physical presence in both the natural and built environment. For animists, mountains, deserts, forests and other natural features will be invested with sacred meaning. 'The Holy Land' consists of both natural and built places. Cities such as Mecca, Jerusalem and the Vatican (and particular places within them) are destinations for a multitude of pilgrims. 'Houses' of worship, be they churches, temples, mosques, or other edifices, are perhaps the most conspicuous sacred places in the built environment. They can range from soaring cathedrals to storefront churches. Through processes of de-sanctification, the meaning of some sacred places can be changed. Thus, as some

churches in poor urban neighborhoods have been created from abandoned stores or theaters, former churches have been remade into restaurants, other commercial venues, or residences; the edifice remains, but has been re-placed. It is also true that outsiders may display ignorance, disrespect or indifference toward places held to be sacred by insiders. The mountain setting treated as sacred by a group of Native Americans may be seen simply as a commercial opportunity to a property developer.

A quality of sacred meaning, sentiment and emotion is sometimes given to places in the secular world. Although no serious claim is made concerning supreme beings, creation, theodicy and the like, such places will evoke awe, reverence, and other signs of respect from adherents who often make pilgrimages to them. Entertainment and other forms of popular culture are replete with examples of secular saints and places associated with them. Ryman Auditorium in Nashville – a former church – is considered a 'holy' place of a different sort, and a shrine of country music. Yankee Stadium is accorded a similar sacred-like status by many baseball fans. In these cases, too, the outsider may have a disdainful attitude about such place. Places may be sanctified as memorials to lives lost, especially in war. The Alamo, Gettysburg, and the battleship *Arizona* are examples in the United States. Places for the dead are generally accorded sacred status. Overturning tombstones or otherwise defacing cemeteries is typically seen as moving beyond vandalism by involving sacrilege. Nationhood itself is sometimes elevated to sacred status (Tuan, 1977: 177). Places such as Plymouth Rock, Independence Hall, The Alamo, and others are celebrated as emblematic of the 'American way' and are part of a mythos that elicits the kind of awe, reverence, respect, and loyalty once reserved for God(s) alone. Physical or behavioral displays of a lack of patriotism is in these cases becomes a kind of secular heresy. By such means outsiders may again be identified.

The interaction between place and person is mutually reinforcing. This reciprocity means that knowledge of place gives one some idea of the sorts of people, and kinds of behavior, to be encountered there. Likewise, some knowledge of a person can indicate the sorts of places where one is likely to be found. Through the process of being defined and identified, places are inevitably social, whether part of the natural or built environment, physically real or vividly imagined. Economic and sacred places are but two broad categories among many. To these could be added places of politics, art, and recreation to name but a few. The meaning given to places can vary widely due in part to differences in social structure and personality. Social class, race, gender, age, education, and religion, as well as attitudes, interests, and personal experience, will all play a part in defining place and the attitude and expected behavior toward and within them. Thus places can have simultaneous meanings (Hiss, 1990: 3–26; Meinig, 1979: 33–48; Relph, 1976: 29). The Mississippi River, for example, can flood the imagination with geographic, economic, historical, religious, mythical, cultural, poetic, literary, and recreational meaning. The notion of 'home' as opposed to 'house' is enriched with meaning, emotion and sentiment that has few analogies in languages other than English (Sopher, 1979: 129–45). In the idealized form, these meanings usually revolve around familiarity and security captured by the phrase 'there's no place like home'. Yet the home that there is 'no place like' can clearly transcend that single enclosed, bounded, private dwelling of the nuclear family. The meaning of home can radiate to increasingly larger scale. In street culture, the term

'homeboy' indicates a person (personally known or not) who is familiar with the 'hood' of which one is a part. 'Hometown,' whether the small, physically fictional but emotionally real, Grover's Corner of 'Our Town,' or the in-your-face hyper-reality of New York City, equally convey a sense of a familiar, comfortable knowledge and security. The notion of home refers to the level of nation and invokes the sense of a patriotic, sacred status with the term 'homeland.'

Because of differences in social structure, culture and personality, the meaning and response toward and within place can differ. A fundamental consideration of place could first focus on a general attitude about it. The relative attachment to or avoidance of a given place provide an elemental and essential understanding of it, the persons within, and the sort of behavior that might be expected from them. Indifference to a place will not be visited here. Given what has been said so far, merely 'passing through' some places with no experience, affect or effect, means it's no place at all. Unless it is preceded by reputation, or changed through experience, there will be places for some (though not others, of course) whose existence is shorn of meaningfulness and thus an essential quality.

Love is a strong, multifaceted emotion that usually leads to some sort of attachment. Love of place, such as the aforementioned manifestations of 'home,' can be given to settings in the real, physical world, or those of imagination. The attachment may be to the physical place where one was raised, or extended to a homeland (Tuan, 1977: 149–60). Emotional or physical meanings less intense than love may also create an attachment to place. From a profound sense of comfort and familiarity to mere convenience, we may be attracted to a place. These attitudes may likewise provide behavioral cues. The loyalty to a place, by means of support or abandonment, the means and fierceness by which a place may be defended, the degrees to which one may miss or feel nostalgia for a place, all indicate the degree of attachment.

Fear of place also warrants consideration. Although not the precise opposite of love, fear is likewise enriched with meaning, sentiment, emotion and attitude. These meanings and attendant behavior could include hatred, repulsion, avoidance, denial, or suspicion, to name a few. Such places, be they scary, deviant, or otherwise ominous (Walter, 1988: 159–75), can motivate individual or collective action, from picking up one's pace in an unfamiliar neighborhood (or avoiding it altogether) to policies of urban renewal. Fear of place may be sited in direct, personal experience, or reside only in the imagination; it may manifest itself in physical structures or be created out of reputation only. In any case, the fear of place can have as profound consequences as love of place. Both, it may be added, can be understood and accepted or irrational and uninformed.

One other extreme mode should be considered. Alienation from place is more likely a product of disillusionment than fear but also results in avoidance. It is in complete and direct contrast to attachment. Alienation from a place generally means that one was once in some way part of it. As with forms of attachment, the places one fears or otherwise avoids can be as intimate as home or as abstract as society.

PLACE AND SOCIAL SCIENCE

The consideration of place is not foreign to social science. There are a number of disciplines, or at least factions within them, where place assumes some importance. As a consequence, a clear overlap between these works, theoretical and otherwise, can be found. The prominence of place found within these disciplines is the result or focus of research. Seldom, however, is the importance of place in conducting research examined. Rather, the focus is upon theoretical meditation, ethnographic narratives that include descriptions of places and their importance to participants, or works which include practical applications in the form of planning or design. From these works lessons may be drawn which inform the process of research as well as the findings.

Anthropology typically details place both in terms of culture and structure. This is especially evident when an exotic group is under investigation, but is hardly restricted to them. In these cases, certainly some description, and often analysis, is given to specific places, such as shelter, places of public meeting, recreation, ritual and the like. Area studies, which consider places such as Southeast Asia or the Modern World, for instance, suggest that cultural place may transcend national boundaries and identities (Appadurai, 1996). Whether the setting of interest is exotic or familiar, or is of a scale that transcends nations or is circumscribed by a given tribe or neighborhood, descriptions of place, at the very least, are inherent to anthropology.

The importance of human experience and meaning to the creation of place is a central component of cultural geography. In these works, then, something more than mere physical description is offered. This can include unified theoretical statements (Seamon, 1979; Tuan, 1977), collected essays about various landscapes (Meinig, 1979), strictly visual aspects of place (Jakle, 1987), consideration of a specific area (Shortridge, 1989), or the spaces that surround or are between places and thus help define them (Ford, 2000).

The 'city' is a place at times considered by anthropologists, and cultural geographers, and specifically so by urban sociology. Inherently rich in physical and social texture, complexity, experience, and meaning, urban settings are the predominant social form of the modern world. As a container and generator of economic, political, social, and cultural life, the city is unparalleled. Whether one is attached to, repulsed by, or alienated from urban life, the sheer physical and social presence and impact of the city is undeniable. The city has a place in imagination as well as a physical reality. It is frequently an important focus of myth, fable, and cautionary tale, as well as song, film, and other media of popular culture. Within the city, imagined or real, are places of excitement, and danger, opportunity and despair. The wealth of meaning and emotion associated with the city can be contradictory and simultaneous. By convenience or necessity, the city is also a setting for a wide variety of research.

Like any place, the city can be distinguished from other places by boundaries which may in turn be legal/political, cultural and social, as well as physical. Within these boundaries, the complexity of cities is such that distinct areas can also be discerned. It is also true that the distinction between the specific places may over time or through other processes natural or intentional, become blurred or changed entirely. Whether enduring, changed or in flux, the nature of these places will have an impact on the behavior that occurs within them.

The contrast between the generic city and other places is sometimes starkly clear. A strong anti-urban bias in the United States has been noted (L. Lofland, 1998; Palen, 1995; Whyte, 1988). Where the rural countryside or small town are portrayed as places of pure innocence and virtue, the city is contrasted as evil and corrupting. Just as the city has been characterized as 'unheavenly' (Banfield, 1970), the term 'God's country' is invariably applied to rustic rather than urban settings. Regions such as the Middle West and the New England village are often conceived by insiders and outsiders alike as rural in nature and thus characterized by pastoral values revolving around an uncomplicated honesty, and wholesomeness (Meinig, 1979: 164–92; Shortridge, 1989), virtues never applied to cities. Cities are frequently thought of as dangerous places, generating fear and complete avoidance, or retreat into places that are variously 'defended' (Francis, 1989; L. Lofland, 1998: 101–75). 'Street culture' (Anderson, 1990; Wright and Decker, 1994, 1997), which encompasses such physical locales as corner hangouts, alleys, project gangways, and entire neighborhoods, as well as a host of menacing values and behaviors, is distinctly urban. Other unsavory, if not dangerous, places, such as 'skid row' (Spradley, 1970) and a variety of undesirable populations (Whyte, 1988: 156–64), are also associated in most people's minds with the city.

To others, of course, the city is a dynamic place of excitement, culture, and other pleasures often exclusive to these settings (L. Lofland, 1998: 77–96). The diversity of the city creates a cosmopolitan environment. Urban enclaves (Abrahamson, 1996) provide a sense of familiarity, comfort, belonging and identity to a wide array of economic, ethnic, or lifestyle groups. For denizens of urban life, the rural is synonymous with naiveté, lack of sophistication, and other forms of provincialism.

Although the suburb is physically an extension of the city, it too has evolved into a place of distinct meaning of myth, ideology and imagery for both booster and critic (Palen, 1995: 68–100). Strongly associated with family and attendant values, the 'home' is especially stressed. Seen as a 'great place to raise kids,' and featuring a pace and lifestyle promoted as a contrast to the hurly-burly of city life, the growth of suburbs was hastened by a number of social forces. In the 1960s and 1970s, the succession of urban neighborhoods by poorer ethnic groups created a condition of 'white flight.' Recent retreats to the suburbs by corporate headquarters, workplaces, and other generators of economy have exacerbated this trend (Palen, 1995: 184–7; Whyte, 1988: 285–97). The kind of people who could live in the suburbs, and thus the sort of activity likely to be encountered there, was at one time restricted by law and various local covenants. Although these laws have been struck down, an economic, social and cultural contrast between suburb and city – especially 'inner city' – is clear and conveys dramatically different experience, meaning and emotion.

The city was the birthplace and impetus of American sociology. The University of Chicago was not only the site of the discipline's first department, but was also the setting of many early classic studies whose ecological approach suggested a link between urban places and behavior (Park et al., 1925; Zorbough, 1929). The focus of these classic works was often with the effects of urban social disorganization and such resulting social problems as deviance, delinquency and crime (Shaw and McKay, 1942), a theme with a more contemporary resonance (Stark, 1987). The level of analysis in these studies is usually the disorganized neighborhood, places in the city where the aforementioned 'street culture' thrives. Whether viewed as a source of problem or pleasure, the city, and places within them have long been linked with certain sorts of people and behavior.

The theorized effect of place on behavior has also been a source of urban planning. These efforts have been of a scale large and small, involved both commercial and residential plans, and been directed toward the poor and affluent alike. Champions of city living,

such as Jacobs (1961) and Whyte (1988), have examined the length of blocks, size and scale of buildings, types of commercial establishment, natural elements of wind, water and trees, and their effect upon the liveliness and perceived safety of streets and neighborhoods. The changing character of given commercial or residential places within cities can be a direct function of this planning or through gradual succession. In some cases such efforts will be buttressed by policies of tax or other financial incentives. The results sometimes involve the close proximity and occasional tense interaction between populations not accustomed to one another, as when urban 'pioneers' move from the suburbs or more affluent parts of the city to gentrified neighborhoods (Anderson, 1990). Whether urban areas change from the direct consequence of planning, or other, more gradual social forces are at work, outcomes will create places perceived as more or less attractive, to be sought out, hurried through, or avoided altogether.

The city, of course, is not the only place that is of common interest to anthropologist, geographer, and sociologist. The physical and social complexity of cities, and thus the variety of experience, emotion and meaning they are imbued with, make them an especially rich environment for the consideration of place, person and behavior.

PLACE, THEORY AND METHOD

The central importance of human experience, emotion and meaning for place finds unity in theories and methods employed by the social sciences noted above. Those theories that stress subjective features of human behavior are not dominant, but have a rich tradition in the social sciences. A broad assumption here would be that human action is premised by the meaning a setting and situation has for a given participant. To fully understand a given behavior, then, a fundamental appreciation of the meaning it has for participants is critical. This would include, of course, the meaning of the places in which behavior is enacted.

To the extent that the generation of meaning is in part a cultural process, any attention paid to place would likewise consider elements of culture. Culture, writ large or small, is shared with others, and thus these meanings may often show broad agreement. The complexity of culture, and experience within it, can create simultaneous meanings of place. Differences in culture and experience may result in radically different meanings applied to the same place. The meaning of place is also subject to change, whether intended or not. Thus an emergent quality of place may also be noted. From these meanings imputed to place and 'given off' by them, human behavior is contained and shaped.

Several theories or theory groups (Mullins, 1973) can be mentioned in these regards. A number of the anthropologists, geographers, and sociologists noted in this chapter have been classified under the rubric of phenomenology, which stresses subjective experience. More common to sociology is symbolic interaction, which generally makes note of place. It might first be pointed out that this theory itself has a strong association of academic place. Nurtured at the University of Chicago, it also has strong 'bases' at Berkeley and Iowa (Mullins, 1973: 75–104). The 'definition of the situation' is of fundamental concern to interactionists; these definitions will, in part, be dependent upon the places in which they occur (Cardwell, 1971: 46). Likewise, identity is socially bestowed and sustained, and the identity one is given will derive partly from the kinds of place where one may be found

(J. Lofland, 1969: 234). These definitions and meanings are subject to validation, negotiation and change, and are thus 'emergent' in nature.

The dramaturgy of Erving Goffman is most often considered part of the interactionist tradition, and frequently makes note of place. In a general sense, a successful presentation of self (1959) involves the right person doing the right things in the right setting. 'Frontstage' and 'backstage' regions (1959: 106–40), which are roughly analogous to public and private places, guide requisite behavior for both the individual and collective. Violations of these guidelines, or mixing one with the other, whether intended or not, can result in breakdowns of social order. Access to a backstage and the privacy it suggests is an indicator of social status and is reflected in physical arrangement of homes or social establishments (Goffman, 1959: 123; Schwartz, 1968: 745–8). In large part, Goffman's interest is in behavior in public places (1959, 1963, 1971). The special conditions of 'total institutions,' and the specific setting of various asylums (1961) also received his discerning attention.

The distinctiveness of place is maintained through boundaries. The defense of territorial boundaries from various forms of encroachment (Lymon and Scott, 1967) is evident from the territory of self, through neighborhood enclaves to the nation-state. Boundaries, however, may not always be clear, including those between public and private places. Rather, some intermediate form may be found. Home territories (Cavan, 1963; L. Lofland, 1985; Lymon and Scott, 1967: 238–40), ostensibly public places in which some seem to have special, more private privileges, provide one example. In these settings any member of the public may have access, but a clear distinction between insiders and outsiders is apparent. 'Third places'

(Oldenburg, 1982) involve relationships which are less intimate and demanding than those of a primary nature, but in which participants are not strangers to one another and share a conviviality. In a similar fashion, Lyn Lofland (1998) suggests a parochial realm of casual acquaintances as well as the private realm of intimates, and the public realm of complete strangers or those known to us only categorically. There is a fluidity of meaning and boundary at work in these cases. Commercial establishments such as bars or coffee shops may by law be open to anyone, but may be more parochial than public, and considered more exclusively part of a neighborhood. Regulars may be allowed to go behind the counter or have a proprietary claim on seating. The key here is the quality of relationship to be found. Thus any number of specific settings may be third places or part of the parochial realm. In any of these cases, insiders and outsiders may be distinguished by their knowledge of the public or parochial nature of these places and the boundaries that define them. A continuum of private, and especially parochial, and public realms, suggests areas of ambiguity. In addition, transformations from one kind of place to another can occur through concerted action, public policy, or other means. As these transformations may result in different participants and consequent behavior, they may be subject to pride or divisiveness.

The sources cited in this chapter are united by a focus on place. They also share an appreciation of the importance of human experience, emotion and imputed meaning as a defining element of place. There is also congruence between these theories and the method of ethnographic fieldwork. The theories share a focus on subjective aspects of behavior, the meaning that behavior has for its participants, and that this is essential to understanding human action. It is further assumed that this information is best gathered – as a primary source, at least – by means of direct observation of behavior in the natural setting in which it occurs. Since particular places will likely contain certain kinds of people and behavior, the description and analysis of these places is critical to the ethnography. Goldenberg (1992) suggests that social research can be divided into relative camps of 'detached outsider,' and 'sympathetic insider.' The former does not view meaning as problematic, maintains distance from the data which is assumed to be structural in nature, and assumes the researcher to be the 'expert' as participants may be misinformed or even unaware of these external forces. The laboratory, with the attendant environmental and social manipulations of the experiment, is seen as a quintessential place for research. In contrast, the sympathetic insider sees meaning as a central concern and thus finds it necessary to get 'close' to the data by observing social life as it is lived and where it is lived. Participants are 'expert' as it is an appreciation of their experiences, emotions, and meanings that is necessary to a complete understanding of any social situation. Ethnographic fieldwork assumes that data must be taken as it is found and where it naturally occurs, and this is as true for the prosaic as the exotic. The place for ethnographic research is the setting where the behavior of interest is to be found.

RELATED ISSUES FOR FIELDWORK

The standard approach for conducting fieldwork broadly involves a sequence of selecting and entering the field, gathering and recording data, and leaving the field. As with any social research, ethical concerns are also important. It is the contention of this chapter that place can have an important effect on the entire sequence. It is clear that fieldwork needs to be sympathetic to the places where behavior occurs and the meaning the places have for participants. That these issues apply to the researcher as well as the researched has not been typically stressed and will be considered here. The selection of the place where research will be conducted most obviously depends on the research question, which in turn may be guided by theory or previous research. It might be first briefly noted that it is the 'detached outsider,' as described above, who is most likely to receive funding for research in the United States. This is due in part to the fact that such an approach usually results in faster results which can be reported with the sorts of statistics, pie charts, tables, and other indicators of 'real' science that satisfy national values of efficiency, economy, and objectivity. The association between place, person and behavior means that theoretical interest in a particular population or behavior can strongly suggest place. Casinos and racetracks contain gamblers and exclude children, young singles are not likely to be encountered in bingo parlors, and those interested in street culture will be better served heading to the inner city than the outer suburb.

For the ethnographer, some level of culture is being examined (Spradley, 1980: 1–10). Whatever the level and scale of the culture under investigation, there will be physical places where the culture is enacted. The study of everyday life in public settings provides certain advantages. Routine settings offer not only data which is familiar and close at hand, but public places have the real advantage of easy accessibility (Goffman, 1959: xi; 1974: 14–17). This is much more so than those places of the private and parochial realm. Observation of such places will require permission which, if granted, will take some time in obtaining, or conducting the research under false, misleading or other surreptitious conditions. This, while defensible, raises a number of ethical issues that do not arise in many public settings. As previously noted, places of the parochial realm may ostensibly be public, but acceptance into a 'home territory' sufficient for gaining an insider's cultural knowledge of the place requires a level of trust not required of observations in strictly public realms. Misidentification at the boundaries of these realms may happen to researcher and researched alike. Lyn Lofland (1998: 45–6) suggests that Elijah Anderson's (1990) observations of conflicts between gentrifying newcomers and adjacent ghetto-dwellers may be a case of both observed and observer confusing quasi-private behavior in a parochial realm as meaning aggressive behavior in the public realm. Of course, access to these places can be negotiated, trust can be gained, and realms correctly discerned, but the nature and condition of a place must be considered for this to occur. What's 'out there' and how easily the researcher may enter is dependent on a number of things.

More exotic locales, such as adult bookstores (Weatherford, 1986), tattoo parlors (Sanders, 1989), soup kitchens (Stein, 1989) or 'street culture' (Wright and Decker, 1994, 1997), may require special or prolonged negotiation and more time to build trust in order to elicit or understand an insider's view of the culture. Another option is for the researcher to enter in 'disguise,' or otherwise not revealing the research intent. The observer as 'known' or unknown (Hammersly and Atkinson, 1983: 68–72; J. Lofland, 1971: 93–6; Spradley, 1980: 49–50) can affect what may be seen, or allowed to be seen. In some instances, observing children playing in a public park for example, there is no real ethical or other imposition. There are more problematic situations when the option of disguise may be nonetheless justifiable.

Humphreys (1970) simply could not at the time and place of his research have been able to enter the field or observe the behavior of interest without this tactic. A variety of deviant places, legal or otherwise, may commonly require some form of negotiation or disguise, and thus especially careful consideration in their selection. There has been more research conducted in dangerous places than consideration of them as research settings, but such consideration can clearly have an effect on selection and entry.

Whatever the nature of the places where research takes place, they will likely contain front and backstage regions, which are relevant to subject and ethnographer. Access to the dramaturgical backstage is always revealing and potentially disruptive. Thus the researcher needs to be aware of their existence, whereabouts, rules of entry, management and control, and the like. Clearly, the more exotic a setting is relative to the researcher, the more consideration, time, trust and learning will be required in these regards.

Having selected the field and become firmly ensconced in it, there are issues of gathering and recording data. Some of this follows from the degree of accessibility. Access to backstage regions means one becomes privy to some of the 'secrets' of those under observation. This includes the physical location as well as the behavior that occurs within. Here, the development of rapport and the cultivation of informants can be critical. This in turn will depend on the degree to which the ethnographer as sympathetic insider is viewed as such by participants. The 'fit' between the background and personality of the researcher and the physical and social properties of the place where the research is conducted is thus an important consideration. It would seem safe to assume that the further the distance between researcher and place of research, the more time will be required for this sort of access, and the gathering of such information.

Although much of the organizing and writing of data will be carried out away from the places where they are observed, and some may be stored in memory until that time, some recording may be done on premises. A number of the issues noted above are relevant here. The degree to which the research is known, and whether it is known to all or only a select few informants, is one example. If the researcher is known as such to all, formal interviews can be conducted at appropriate time and places, and note-taking or electronic recording may be engaged. Even if the research is known to all those being observed, some time and places – a religious service, for example – will be less conducive to formal interviewing, and note-taking or the use of recording devices would be highly intrusive. If the ethnographer is to any extent disguised, more caution would be required. In either case, but especially with those when the research is disguised, note-taking is a backstage activity relative to the ethnographer. As a disruption to the normal frontstage flow of activity, such recording would in some way need to be 'behind the scenes.' Thus, even if an observation was of backstage activity of the persons being observed, the ethnographer would need access to a remote, private region to make note of it. Some places and roles that may be assumed by the ethnographer make interviewing and note-taking less conspicuous in that they may appear to be routine activity. In many places in the public realm where many strangers will congregate, notes may be taken fairly discreetly, with little chance of raising suspicion or other sorts of disruptive concern. Places in the private or parochial realms will generally require more care. In some cases negotiations prior to entering the field may include the creation of space where the ethnographer may go for the expressed purpose of recording observations or conducting interviews. Public, private and parochial places, front and back regions are common issues of place that the ethnographer will find relevant while observing social life. It is equally true that these same issues may have an impact on the very process of conducting such research. A related point may be noted here. Whatever the degree of being known or disguised as a researcher, the observer of scenes, however exotic or mundane, will not be in a position to see everything. The unseen will be part of any scene. Even with recording devices, other things are going on out of frame and range. Thus the physical proximity of the ethnographer to the action can at times be restricted by place. A 'bird's eye view' offers broader perspective, but may lose important detail. Here too, if possible, some negotiation regarding access may be in order.

Earlier discussion suggested research strategies of the detached outsider and sympathetic insider. The problem of the detached outsider, at least from the view of ethnography, is one of literal and figurative distance from the data. Initially at least, and especially in exotic settings, the ethnographer is something of a 'tourist' or 'sightseer.' With time, however, this should become less the case. Although the ethnographer is, or becomes, by definition a sympathetic insider, there are issues of ethics and practicality that may arise. Over identification with the culture and group under observation, getting too close, or a sense of being too much 'at home' in the places of research, can lead to going native, compromising ethics and validity. This may be true of places frequently defined as deviant or even dangerous. There is often an attraction and romance to the ethnography that is

seldom, if ever, found in the laboratory or in the computation of chi squares. More practically, a time comes for the ethnographer to leave the field. There are some safeguards against going native or staying too long at the places where the ethnography is being conducted. Awareness of these possibilities is aided by having other places to go. One example would be those places reserved or negotiated for note-taking, or otherwise organizing the data. This often literally removes one from the scene, and supplies a necessary perspective. In addition, the focus of organizing data reinforces the role of observer over that of participant. In some instances, formal arrangements may be made to ensure against going native. A former colleague engaged in ethnographic research of a religious cult made arrangements with a friend to be forcibly removed from the setting in the unlikely event of his being won over by the acolytes.

In some cases ethnographers may study their own place, and become one of their own informants (Anderson, 1990; Reimer, 1977). However much of an insider the ethnographer is or becomes, though, it is likely that differences in background, experience, and outlook will offer some separation between researcher and researched. The regular or even occasional retreat to places common to the ethnographer as person is beneficial for perspective. The irony of the sympathetic insider retaining some degree of being an outsider is usually realistic and practical. A professor is not a hobo, and the occasional foray back home or to campus, will reinforce this fact. In addition, being a bit of an outsider guards against a sense of curiosity about a place of research being replaced by complacency. Ultimately, when the scene becomes predictably routine to the researcher, when observations seem redundant or satisfy descriptive and theoretical demand, the time to leave the scene and return to one's real home has arrived.

Being 'in' or 'out' of place is relevant to both participants and the ethnographer observing them. As the usual object of ethnography is to study subjects in their natural settings, a good deal of attention will be paid to behavior that is 'in place.' In these cases much behavior will be routinized or become so over time. Much ethnographic description will have an 'in-house' character. It is also true that outsiders may pass through (including the ethnographer if for just a time), or insiders of one place will find themselves as outsiders in another. This 'fish out of water' motif is more than just a common generic storyline. The complexity and fluidity of modern society means it is likely to occur. Either case is a mismatch between person and place, and has implications for behavior. Wright and Decker (1994) interviewed a burglar who, as an inner-city black, recognized how out of place he would be trying to hide or be inconspicuous in a wealthy suburb. A counterpart can be found in their study of armed robbers (1997). In this case another denizen of street culture noted that when he saw a white guy in his neighborhood, then it was 'payday.' In this case researcher and robber can assume a white guy was not in this place to pick up a friend or look for housing. Rather, a search for drugs located him out of place and carrying a good deal of cash. Other examples of participants being out of place need not be as dramatic. Lyn Lofland (1998: 12) suggests that if a realm is of a clearly dominant form, any attempt to impose another means social territories can also be out of place. All such instances underscore the assonance or dissonance of person, place, and dynamics of behavior.

The ethnographer needs to establish and be aware of being in or out of place as well. In order to appreciate the meaning places and behavior have for participants, some degree of being in place is essential. Safeguards against going native, on the other hand, may require an intentional effort at going out of place. The 'fit' between researcher and researched may again be at issue. Being completely out of place, a middle-aged man studying 'rave' concerts, for example, does not preclude such research. It does, however, mean that certain strategies may have to be abandoned, and that the social and experiential distance between researcher and place become a noted and attended element of the research. A danger of disguised research is that the researcher's hidden intent may become exposed to participants. A likely result is that an assumed insider suddenly and permanently becomes out of place.

Place is an essential aspect of ethnographic fieldwork. Meaning, experience and emotion are essential characteristics of place. This is as true for the ethnographer as for those being observed. The assumptions of fieldwork as a method generally assure that descriptive and analytical attention will be paid to places and the meaning they contain and emit for participants. What is needed in texts that advise the ethnographer is a greater focus on the part place plays on the research process itself. The necessary attention given to the work involved needs to be joined by an appreciation for the effects the field can have on the work.

REFERENCES

Abrahamson, Mark (1996) *Urban Enclaves: Identity and Place in America.* New York: St Martins Press.

Adler, Emily Stier and Clark, Roger (1999) *How It's Done: An Invitation to Social Research.* Belmont, CA: Wadsworth.

Agar, Michael (1980) *The Professional Stranger: An Informal Introduction to Ethnograhpy.* New York: Academic Press.

Agnew, Neil and Pyke, Sandra W. (1994) *The Science Game.* Englewood Cliffs, NJ: Prentice-Hall (1st edn, 1969).

Anderson, Elijah (1990) *Street Wise: Race, Class, and Change in an Urban Community*. Chicago: University of Chicago Press.

Appadurai, Arjun (1996) 'Sovereignty without territoriality: notes for a postnational geography', in P. Yeager (ed.), *The Geography of Identity*. Ann Arbor, MI: The University of Michigan Press. pp. 40–58.

Babbie, Earl (1998) *The Practice of Social Research* (8th edn). Belmont, CA: Wadsworth.

Banfield, Edward C. (1970) *The Unheavenly City: The Nature and Future of Our Urban Crisis*. Boston: Little Brown.

Berg, Bruce L. (1980) *Qualitative Research Methods for the Social Sciences*. Boston: Allyn and Bacon.

Berger, Peter and Luckmann, Thomas (1966) *The Social Construction of Reality: A Treatise on the Sociology of Knowledge*. New York: Anchor.

Cardwell, J.D. (1971) *Social Psychology: A Symbolic Interaction Perspective*. Philadelphia: F.A. Davis.

Filstead, William J. (ed.) (1970) *Qualitative Methodology*. Chicago: Markham.

Ford, Larry R. (2000) *The Spaces Between Buildings*. Baltimore, MD: The Johns Hopkins University Press.

Francis, Mark (1989) 'Control as a dimension of public-space quality', in Irwin Altman and Ervin Zube (eds), *Public Spaces and Places*. New York: Plenum.

Goffman, Erving (1959) *The Presentation of Self in Everyday Life*. Garden City, NY: Doubleday.

Goffman, Erving (1961) *Asylums*. Garden City, NY: Doubleday.

Goffman, Erving (1963) *Behavior in Public Places*. New York: Free Press.

Goffman, Erving (1971) *Relations in Public*. New York: Harper & Row.

Goldenberg, Sheldon (1992) *Thinking Methodologically*. New York: Harper Collins.

Hammersly, Martyn and Atkinson, Paul (1983) *Ethnography: Principles in Practice*. London: Tavistock.

Hesse-Biber, Sharlene and Leavy, Patricia (eds) (2004) *Approaches to Qualitative Methods*. Oxford: Oxford University Press.

Hiss, Tony (1990) *The Experience of Place: A New Way of Looking at and Dealing with Our Radically Changing City and Countryside*. New York: Vintage.

Humphreys, Laud (1970) *Tearoom Trade: Impersonal Sex in Public Places*. Chicago: Aldine.

Jackson, Bruce (1987) *Fieldwork*. Urbana: University of Illinois Press.

Jacobs, Jane (1961) *The Death and Life of Great American Cities*. New York: Plenum.

Jakle, John (1987) *The Visual Elements of Landscape*. Amherst: The University of Massachusetts Press.

Jeffries, Stuart (2004) 'I'm rich and I'm living well: shopping here is part of that', *Guardian Unlimited*, 11 March.

Lofland, John (1969) *Deviance and Identity*. Englewood Cliffs, NJ: Prentice-Hall.

Lofland, John (1971) *Analyzing Social Settings*. Belmont, CA: Wadsworth.

Lofland, Lyn (1985) *A World of Strangers: Order and Action in Urban Public Space*. Prospect Heights IL: Waveland.

Lofland, Lyn (1998) *The Public Realm: Exploring the City's Quintessential Social Territory*. New York: Aldine.

Lymon, Stanford M. and Scott, Marvin B. (1967) 'Territoriality: a neglected sociological dimension', *Social Problems*, 15: 236–49.

McCall, George J. and Simmons, J.L. (eds) (1969) *Issues in Participant Observation*. Reading, MA. Addison-Wesley.

Meinig, D.W. (1979) 'Models of American community' in D.W. Meineg (ed.), *The Interpretation of Ordinary Landscapes: Geographical Essays*. New York: Oxford University Press.

Melbin, Murray (1987) *Night as Frontier: Colonizing the World After Dark*. New York: Free Press.

Mullins, Nicholas (1973) *Theories and Theory Groups in Contemporary American Sociology*. New York: Harper & Row.

Oldenburg, Ray (1982) 'The third place', *Qualitative Sociology*, 5(Winter): 265–84.

Palen, John J. (1995) *The Suburbs*. New York: McGraw-Hill.

Park, Robert, Burgess, Earnest, and McKenzie, R.D. (1925) *The City*. Chicago: University of Chicago Press.

Reimer, Jeffery (1977) 'Varieties of opportunistic research', *Urban Life and Culture*, 5: 467–78.

Relph, Edward (1976) *Place and Placelessness*. London: Pion.

Sanders, Clinton (1989) *Customizing the Body: The Art and Culture of Tatooing*. Philadelphia: Temple University Press.

Schwartz, Barry (1968) 'The social psychology of privacy', *American Journal of Sociology*, 73(6): 741–52.

Seamon, David (1979) *A Geography of the Lifeworld.* New York: St Martin's Press.

Shaffir, William B. and Stebbins, Roberta (eds) (1991) *Experiencing Fieldwork: An Inside View.* New York: Sage.

Shaffir, William B., Stebbins, Roberta, and Turowitz, Allan (eds) (1980) *Qualitative Research.* New York: St Martin's Press.

Shaw, Clifford and McKay, Henry (1942) *Juvenile Delinquency and Urban Areas.* Chicago: University of Chicago Press.

Shortridge, James R. (1989) *The Middle West: Its Meaning in American Culture.* Lawrence: University Press of Kansas.

Sopher, David E. (1979) 'The landscape of home', in D.W. Meinig (ed.), *The Interpretation of Ordinary Landscapes.* New York: Oxford University Press.

Spradley, James P. (1970) *You Owe Yourself a Drunk: An Ethnography of Urban Nomads.* Boston: Little Brown.

Spradley, James P. (1980) *Participant Observation.* New York: Holt, Rinehart & Winston.

Stark, Rodney (1987) 'Deviant places: a theory of the ecology of crime', *Criminolgy*, 25(4): 893–909.

Stein, Michael (1989) 'Gratitude and attitude: a note on emotional welfare', *Social Psychology Quarterly*, 52(3): 242–8.

Stimson, Gerry V. (1988) 'Place and space in sociological fieldwork', *The Sociological Review*, 34(3): 641–56.

Traub, James (2004) *The Devil's Playground: A Century of Pleasure and Profit in Times Square.* New York: Random House.

Tuan, Yi-Fu (1977) *Space and Place: The Perspective of Experience.* Minneapolis: University of Minnesota Press.

Turner, Alice K. (1993) *The History of Hell.* New York: Harcourt Brace.

Walter, E.V. (1988) *Placeways: A Theory of the Human Environment.* Chapel Hill: University of North Carolina Press.

Weatherford, Jack (1986) *Porn Row.* New York: Arbor House.

Wright, Richard and Decker, Scott (1994) *Burglars on the Job: Street Life and Residential Break-In.* Boston: Northeastern University Press.

Wright, Richard and Decker, Scott (1997) *Armed Robbers in Action: Stickups and Street Culture.* Boston: Northeastern University Press.

Wysocki, Diane Kholos (ed.) (2001) *Readings in Social Research Methods.* Belmont, CA: Wadsworth.

Zorbaugh, Harvey (1929) *The Gold Coast and the Slums.* Chicago: University of Chicago Press.

Part 3

Situating the Respondents

5

Fieldwork with the Elite: Interviewing White-Collar Criminals

MARY DODGE AND GILBERT GEIS

There are some notable differences involved in interviewing white-collar criminals compared with getting information from criminals on the lower rungs of the offence ladder. For one thing, white-collar criminals pose no physical danger to the researcher. Violence is not their thing, though there is no doubt that their criminal negligence in regard to matters such as the illicit pollution of the atmosphere and neglect of mine safety regulations causes more deaths than the total number of homicides tabulated in the Uniform Crime Reports. A left-leaning attorney summarized this point well: 'I don't defend right-wing murderers,' he said. 'If I wanted to defend right-wing murderers, I'd become a corporate lawyer' (Applebome, 1995: B10).

On rare occasions, however, white-collar criminals may use their power and resources to strike back at an unpopular outsider who is gathering information that they would prefer to keep private. Probably the most notorious example involved General Motors' extensive investigation of the personal life of Ralph Nader. Nader had published a heavily-documented book, *Unsafe at Any Speed* (1965), that was an indictment of the automobile industry for massive failures to protect the public from hazardously designed automobiles. General Motors picked on the wrong man. Nader, legally-trained (Harvard Law School), filed a lawsuit that was settled for $450,000. More than half that sum was used to start the Public Research Interest Group, which served as the base for Nader's extraordinary career as an ardent foe of exploitation of the common folk by big business, lobbyists, and politicians (McCarry, 1972; Whiteside, 1972).

As we use it here, the term 'white-collar criminal' refers to law-breakers who occupy a position that carries with it a reasonably high status in the world of work. Today, of course, the association of a white collar with prominence and respectability is somewhat outmoded. Presidential candidates campaign in sweat shirts and jeans, and collarless women increasingly have come to occupy seats of power. The possible disconnect between dress style and social position was brought home to us when we interviewed a parolee from the federal prison system about the crime that had led to his incarceration. He told us that he had been drinking a good deal on that particular day. When he returned from the bar to his car he was surprised, he said, to find a wig and a gun on the front seat. He took this to be a signal from a higher power that he was supposed to rob a bank. He was dressed in a suit, white shirt, and tie. The hold-up was short-circuited by a long-haired hippie making a bank deposit who slapped the gun out of the robber's hand and then chased after him as he fled the scene. Passers-by kept waylaying the hero instead of the villain, figuring he was the culprit, until matters were sorted out and the robber captured (Geis and Huston, 1981).

In traditional criminological understanding, a white-collar criminal is a person who violates the law by committing an offence tied to his or her work (Sutherland, 1949; Geis, 1992). An accountant may have embezzled company funds, a state legislator may have taken bribes in connection with a building project, a physician may have submitted false claims to a medical benefit program or performed unnecessary surgery in order to obtain the fee. There also are more arguable white-collar offences in which people of wealth and position violate the criminal law in somewhat more oblique ways. Martha Stewart exemplifies this cadre. Suspected of insider trading, often a difficult charge to prove before a jury (Szockyj and Geis, 2002), she was convicted of lying to federal investigators and thereby obstructing justice rather than of trading on non-public information to her personal financial advantage. Presumably, unless they immediately admit guilt, virtually all federal offenders lie to investigators and by doing so obstruct justice. We would, perhaps somewhat arbitrarily, regard Martha Stewart as a white-collar criminal, just as for research purposes we would regard Al Capone as a murderer and kingpin of organized crime rather than as an income-tax violator.

Unlike drug dealers, burglars, and other street offenders, white-collar offenders will not come to an interview zonked out on drugs. On the other hand, their social background may very likely be superior to yours, the interviewer, and they often are both smarter and shrewder than you are. This can make dealing with them for research purposes an especially challenging enterprise. Typically, the better part of wisdom is to accept the status and the possible IQ discrepancies and to use them to your advantage by assuming the role of an informed innocent, a babe in the woods. You can unearth material beforehand about the person and the situation that interests you from readily available sources and perhaps from earlier interviews and use it to demonstrate with a few offhand remarks that you have done your homework. Now you want to sit at the feet of a particularly knowledgeable insider and allow that person to 'teach' you, as only he or she would be able to do. You will be aided by the fact that, as Holstein and Gubrium (1995: 18) put it, the United States has become 'an interview society' marked by 'the increasing deprivitazation of personal experience.' Besides, as those prone to look on the sunny side of things, interviews of white-collar criminals, however difficult to arrange, are a good deal easier to set up than interviews with murder victims.

Of course, the 'babe in the woods' approach will hardly work if you are an older, professorial type who may be condescended to by the white-collar offender or, on the other hand, could be regarded as something of a threat, so that tension pervades at least the earlier stages of the interview. We might recommend trying the tactic of A.J. Liebling, the legendary writer for the New Yorker, who would 'sit facing the person from whom he intended to elicit information; and then sit there and sit there, silently':

> Soon the person being interviewed would begin to break down. Most reporters plunge into an interview asking too many questions, among which the interviewee is free to pick and choose, concentrating upon the questions that are easiest to deal with and skirting without seeming to do so those that might prove embarrassing to him. Liebling's method left the interviewee unnerved and at a loss about what he was supposed to defend himself against; by the time Liebling put the first question to him, he was ready to babble almost any indiscretion. (Gill, 1975: 320–321)

But then Liebling was an overpowering presence; heavy-set with a big belly, a bald head, lively eyes behind thick-lensed, metal-rimmed glasses, and a razor-sharp mind, besides representing a very powerful media outlet (Remmick, 2004).

Getting to talk with white-collar offenders often presents issues that are unlikely or less likely to arise in connection with interviews with street offenders. In the best of all possible worlds, it can be interesting to conduct a longitudinal study to seek to learn what things either predetermine or catapult a person into white-collar law violations. Sample populations can be surveyed and subsamples interviewed in business schools or perhaps when they enter a Fortune 500 firm. The problem is that a huge number of interviews would be necessary to achieve an adequate sample of later offenders, since there are relatively few discoveries of white-collar crime. Besides, of course, unlike, say, murder, we have no assurance regarding whether the subsample is representative of the much greater number of upperworld law-breakers that assuredly exist. Besides, our best information indicates that a large part of the incentive to engage in white-collar crime is formed after a person joins a company or takes up a profession, not before. It has been found, for instance, that

the theft of corporate secrets almost invariably takes place only when an executive becomes discontented, perhaps because he/she finds themselves an outsider in a family business, his/her advancement blocked by diverse (and less qualified) children and other relatives of the owner (Sarbin, 1994).

Attempts to gain access to white-collar offenders before the legal system has (or does not have) its way with them is a daunting task. If they are high enough on the business, political, or professional totem pole, they have receptionists, aides, secretaries, and other factotums who screen those to whom they will grant an audience. Crossing these barriers will require persuasive powers far beyond the reach of most of us. If you persist, they typically will refer you to their lawyers who, if they are so gracious as to answer your telephone call (or your fourth or fourteenth such call), will interdict any access to their client and offer, at best, platitudinous observations regarding the absurdity of the authorities' case and the blameless position of the accused, not to mention his or her extraordinary contributions to the well-being of all of us.

Even when there are promising interview possibilities, problems can arise. We once obtained a list of telemarketing shills who had been involved in a clearly fraudulent scheme. The case had never gone forward because the serious illness of the accountant who had worked on it for several years delayed matters until the statute of limitations foreclosed any possibility of prosecution. We drafted a letter requesting interviews, saying that we had chosen names at random from the state registry of accredited telemarketing agents. But one of the members of our research team demurred, arguing that there was something disquieting about using a fraudulent approach in a study of fraudulent behavior. We amended the letter to comport with the true facts, and then, unthinkingly, sent it out on university stationery that indicated we were housed in a department of criminology. We received but one response from our 100 solicitations. That person agreed to be interviewed, but when we appeared at the company's luxurious, somewhat intimidating headquarters he was ill at home with an ulcer that was acting up, a not uncommon affliction in the telemarketing business. Another man cheerfully filled in, feeding us lies with consummate skill. Our only suspicion that he might be conning us came when he adroitly turned aside our request to see the boiler room in the basement from where calls were made, casually indicating that he couldn't imagine that it would really interest us. Less than a month later the company was raided, went into bankruptcy, and reopened a while later in a nearby city with most of the same personnel (Doocey et al., 2001).

If there is a trial of a white-collar crime case that you contemplate researching, the court setting is an exceptional venue for gathering information. For some reason, criminologists have not exploited these naturalistic settings for what they are worth: in the area of white-collar crime we are aware only of Croall's (1988) courtroom observations in the United Kingdom. Courts are public forums, and they offer an opportunity to observe the emotions and hear the words of the leading players, both in formal proceedings and in informal moments during court recesses and lunch breaks. Here will be gathered veteran courtroom observers (the retirees who haunt these judicial halls), who can often provide particularly telling observations about what is taking place. Besides, if the trial is long, there will be ample opportunities to interview witnesses, kin of the accused, and court functionaries, and sometimes even the accused and the accusers. In addition, of course, transcripts of the proceedings offer what can often be extremely useful information and direct quotations.

Then there are the incarcerated white-collar criminals. Imprisoned street offenders, especially juvenile delinquents, often seem to be bored and willing to break the monotony by responding to queries from a diverting outsider, although often with their mind and tongue attuned to how a parole board member might respond to what they say. White-collar offenders, even if they are willing to cooperate, appear reluctant to be seen inside a prison, a setting that they find particularly degrading. In our study of the General Electric antitrust case, for instance, we learned that the most prominent of the offenders refused to have any of his family visit while he was locked up in the Montgomery County, Pennsylvania, jail (Geis, 1967).

White-collar offenders do not linger long in prisons, in the unlikely event that their highly skilled and exorbitantly paid attorneys have failed to keep them from that fate (Mann, 1985). The best bet is to attempt to talk to them when the case is completed and/or they are out of prison and back at home, often rather unnerved by the sudden public disinterest in them and, perhaps, by their former colleagues' disdain. The best approach almost invariably is to say that you want to learn their side of the story, that the other side has already been given a thorough airing. We once saw this approach work wonders when a *New York Times* reporter called a friend of ours, seeking information on a piece of investigative journalism that he was putting together. Our friend's response was unhesitating: 'I have no comment,' he said. The reporter answered, almost indifferently. 'That's okay with me,' he said, 'but we have gotten some files through the Freedom of Information Act and your role in this business is at best unclear and may be damaging to your reputation. I thought you might be able to clarify the matter for me.' Our friend quickly decided that, indeed, he might well be able to do so – and did.

Because white-collar criminals, in their working roles, are not accustomed to being challenged or contradicted, their greatest vulnerability from an interviewer's viewpoint is that they usually have come to believe that they are clever enough to persuade others, whom they assume are less clever, of the accuracy and value of what they have to say. Like most of us, they will respond to flattery if it is not too blatant, and especially when it comes from a person – especially a charming person – who seems to be reasonably open-minded and truly interested in what they have to say. The matter of objectivity requires amplification. White-collar criminals understand that the person interviewing them is very likely to be unsympathetic to their plight. In terms of social science neutrality and hyper-objectivity, we are reminded of the academic woman who saw her husband and a grizzly bear locked in combat and wondered whether she was obligated, as a 'neutral' professional, to call out: 'C'mon, husband; c'mon bear.' A skillful interviewer can use his or her ideology and predilections as a springboard for challenging but tactful questions, always conveying the idea that his or her original beliefs are open to amendment.

The wording of questions can be crucial. The best example of this that has come our way is found in a discussion of tryouts for performances by the Marx brothers. In successive appearances they would alter the wording of a joke and note the audience reaction. They found, for instance, though they never understood why, that the use of the word 'nauseating' in one quip invariably drew howls from those in the theater, while employment in the same joke of other terms – such as 'disgusting,' and 'disagreeable' – was

met with only a few chuckles (Kanfer, 2000). Schumann (1982: 22–23) puts the matter more formally: 'Too much can be inferred from answers taken at face value to questions of dubious merit. ... All answers depend upon the way the question is formulated. Language is not a clean logical tool like mathematics that we can use with precision.'

Whether one or a pair of interviewers provides the best results in elite interviews remains an unsettled issue, though there is compelling anecdotal evidence favoring what Kinkaid and Bright (1957b) call the 'tandem interview', which they found particularly effective with business elites 'whose time is generally at a premium, a fact our respondents seldom allowed us to forget.' They summarize their conclusion in these words:

> Probably the underlying factor making tandem efforts so successful in this study was the level of ability of the majority of our respondents. They were as a rule highly articulate persons capable of thinking through complex issues and expressing their views quickly and economically. With two interviewers this source of data was much more efficiently explored than would have been possible with the lone interviewer, no matter how well trained. We also have the impression that our respondents felt their time was more justifiably spent with two interviewers than one. (Kinkaid and Bright, 1957b: 308)

They note that the corporate executives seemed to get some satisfaction from the fact that at least one of the interviewers was paying full attention to him rather than having to be diverted by note-taking. They also felt that a post-mortem of the interview by a pair who had participated in it would yield better insights than either one alone would likely have achieved, especially in terms of nonverbal cues that cannot be gleaned from a tape recording (see also Kinkaid and Bright (1957a) and note Riesman's (1954) earlier use of two interrogators to talk to the interviewers who worked on Lazarsfeld's study of academic freedom (Lazarsfeld and Thielens, 1958).

Bechhofer and his colleagues believe that two interviewers are more likely to create a relaxed atmosphere and a greater sense of natural conversation that will elicit more worthwhile information than a one-on-one interview format. They describe the procedure this way:

> After the customary introduction, pleasantries and opening remarks, one person would take up the interview, making only brief notes as it went on. The other would take extensive notes, carefully observe the reactions of the respondent and the other interviewer, nod sagely from time to time, or grunt as is the way of interviewers. (Bechhofer et al., 1984: 97)

The interviewers can switch roles in midstream and the more 'passive' partner is able to add a further dimension to the conversation when he or she feels that a subject has been overlooked or needs further attention. It is taken for granted that the extra person hikes the cost of the research, but the reduced need to tape record and transcribe the tape may compensate at least somewhat for the added expense.

These observations have been strongly seconded by Braithwaite on the basis of his interviews with 131 senior pharmacy executives in five countries (Braithwaite, 1985). Braithwaite focuses on the value of having a second person's testimony when, as happened in an unsettling number of instances with his study, the companies threatened to file or actually did file libel and defamation suits. Braithwaite also had to omit a great deal of very important data from his book because the publisher's lawyers were wary of legal actions which he felt were totally unwarranted. He also had to defend himself against allegations sent to his boss at the Australian Institute of Criminology and to the country's Attorney General. Had he had someone who could corroborate that what he had written accurately reflected what was said, he believes that matters would have gone much more smoothly.

Braithwaite endorses the idea that two interviewers make for more worthwhile informal converation and allow each to more readily keep abreast of the flow of information. Those interviewed, he believes, more often found the two-person interview to involve 'normal dialog rather than a conspiracy to extract information from them' (Braithwaite, 1985: 137).

White-collar criminals generally hold condescending and sometimes scornful attitudes toward social science and its practitioners, who are deemed not to be citizens of the 'real world.' Dexter, a seasoned interviewer of elites, offers Theodore Reik's *Listening with the Third Ear* (1948) as a particularly valuable guide for interview interactions, and observes that 'a large part of listening with a third ear is noting and adapting to a frame of reference different from one's own' (Dexter, 1970: 20). Listening with the third ear means hearing not only what is spoken but one's own 'inner voice' to ascertain 'what speech conceals and what silence reveals' (Reik, 1948: 126). As a further example, Reik notes that when he accompanied a patient to the door, she, unlike the other women he treated, never looked into the large mirror on the nearby wall, a matter he found telling about her personality and condition.

It is recommended by Dexter that a start be made with the 'easier' interviews in order to get oriented before proceeding to the more difficult sessions. Valuable advice is also offered by John Dollard in his classic study of southern race relations: 'The researcher learns,' Dollard points out 'by fleeting empathy which is followed by reflection and distance' (Dollard, 1949: 15–17).

Most often these days reliance in white-collar crime research is placed on sophisticated statistical analyses of legislative hearings and newspaper reports. Diane Vaughan, whose exemplary study of the *Challenger* spacecraft disaster (Vaughan, 1996) drew upon interviews with scientists who arguably were negligent in their oversight, notes the difficulties involved in efforts such as hers:

> Documentation of misconduct within an organization prior to an enforcement action or public investigation is and always has been difficult for researchers to obtain. After a violation becomes public knowledge, an offending organization is understandably reluctant to have a sociologist unleashed in its midst, and evidence documenting internal activities that is obtained by social control agents is not always admissible in judicial proceedings let alone open to perusal by social scientists. (Vaughan, 1992: 132)

Vaughan also points out that barriers to obtaining personal interviews with white-collar criminals often induce reliance on press reports and she warns that researchers studying a well-publicized white-collar crime should approach mass media sources warily:

> We tend to see the media as our colleagues, for in keeping with our critical stance toward the power elite, journalists tantalize us with exposes that attack the powerful. In our enthusiasm for the bounty of information that the sensational case produces, we must remind ourselves of what we know about the manufacture of news and the social construction of knowledge for public consumption. (Vaughan, 1995)

A major reason why we are short on true understanding of the personal dynamics of white-collar criminal behavior relates to the failure to learn from the source, the thoughts, motives, rationalizations and other concomitants associated with persons who engage in such illegal acts. Note, for instance, Szwajkowski's (1985: 566) encouragement of efforts to resolve conflicting evidence on corporate law-breaking by means of empirical studies which, he declares, are 'especially attractive because the indicators cited can be readily computed or accessed without gaining entry to the firms themselves.' Heeding such advice, scholars of white-collar crime have preferred to park themselves in front of computers in temperature-modulated environs and crunch out elegant correlations between this and that characteristic of a corporation and whether or not it and/or its officers have been prosecuted for a white-collar offence. But the profit-and-loss statement of a corporation, neatly correlated with industry-wide conditions, need not be of any consequence to a crooked executive unless the person interjects and reacts to it. Information on how white-collar offenders understand and interpret their actions can only be acquired by moving into the field and learning at firsthand those considerations that trigger individual actions within the corporate sphere. Posner (1970: 413–414), a federal appellate court judge with impeccable intellectual credentials, has suggested that interviews with businessmen and their lawyers might well reveal a good deal more about the deterrent effect of antitrust law than what is found in log-linear regressed statistical reports.

The rocking-chair research approach advocated in the previous paragraphs allows the accumulation of data, which can be subjected to statistical manipulations that today find favor with editors of most of the behavioral science journals, the lifeblood appendages to a successful academic career. This, plus the often seemingly insurmountable barriers and the time demands that obstruct the path to extensive interview opportunities, has resulted in the fact that the white-collar crime scholarly literature offers but few examples of insights obtained directly from the offenders themselves. There is a burgeoning library of books by upper-class offenders, often ghost-written, telling their story, but only infrequently do they attend in a forthcoming manner to concerns that criminologists regard as substantively and theoretically informative.

In the criminological world, Marshall Clinard, a pioneer in white-collar crime research, sought out a sample of retired middle managers now living in Arizona trailer parks to obtain their views about the relationship between corporate wrongdoing and the ethos of their former workplace, learning that they regarded the example set by the company's chief executive officer as the key factor in inhibiting or encouraging corporate crime (Clinard, 1983). Michael Benson contributed an interview-based article on the techniques employed by white-collar offenders to deny their criminality. He talked with a non-random, self-selected sample of 30 incarcerated offenders and found that proffered 'explanations' varied with the type of violation and that the offenders sought to resist degradation, most commonly by denying criminal intent (Benson, 1985). More than two decades later, Benson looked back upon his interviewing experiences:

> I got out the interview transcripts and looked them over. I was surprised at how clearly I could remember many of the men I had spoken with. I could readily recall how I felt about them – sorry for some, skeptical of others. The interviews were an intense experience for me. Fieldwork affects you as a person in ways that secondary data analysis or survey research never do. It requires an involvement of your person.
>
> My interviews typically lasted an hour or slightly more. I soon learned never to schedule more than two in a day; otherwise, it was too draining. The interviews required an enormous amount of concentration. They required me to really, really listen to what people are saying, while retaining enough detachment to keep track of what you wanted to cover.
>
> I started my work with a list of written questions, but I abandoned this approach after only a few interviews. Looking down at a piece of paper and checking off questions destroyed the flow. I identified a few broad questions that I raised in each interview: how did you get involved in this situation, how did you feel about the investigation, how did your family and friends react, and how are you doing now? Sometimes I would change the order in which I asked the questions because of the spontaneous flow of the discussion.
>
> You will find it easier to do field interviewing if you really care about the question you are looking for an answer to.
>
> There was great variation in how the subjects responded to me. Some sat with their hands folded and

waited for me to ask them something. They answered with a few sentences and then stopped talking unless I prodded them to expand on what they had said. Others began talking the minute I entered their office and hardly allowed me to get a word in. No matter what I asked they continued on their own terms while I sat, frustrated, trying to wait out the monologue. (Benson, 2004: personal communication)

Benson adds that it often is essential to find a sponsor if you are going to endeavor to do work with white-collar offenders. In his case, Rita Simon, his dissertation advisor, introduced him to a judge who was a friend of hers; this judge passed him along to the chief judge, who liked the idea of the project, and told the federal probation office to cooperate with the research (Benson, 2004).

INTERVIEWING EMBEZZLERS

Two complementary research probes stand out among the few endeavors to interview white-collar offenders: Donald Cressey's (1953) study of 133 male embezzlers in three penal institutions and Dorothy Zietz's (1981) research on 100 female embezzlers at the California Institution for Women in Fontana. Cressey's sample, though generically identified as embezzlers, embraced all inmates who had taken a position of trust in good faith and then violated that trust, so that, in addition to persons charged with embezzlement, it included confidence men, forgers, and other law-breakers. Cressey's guiding framework was 'analytical induction,' an approach that called for a theoretical formulation that fit every case. The location of a single exception demanded a restatement of the causal explanation. For this reason, initial interviews were free-floating, seeking regularities. Subsequently, they focused on determining if the responses of the interviewees meshed with the explanatory mode – that they had a non-shareable problem, realized it could be resolved secretly by fraud, and possessed a becalming rationalization to justify to themselves what they were going to do (for a critique of this postulation see Nettler, 1974).

Initially, the men to be interviewed had to be reassured that Cressey in no way was connected with the prison authorities or with a law enforcement agency. He had frequent interviews with each subject, each running from half an hour to three times that length, 'depending on the subject's willingness to talk without being questioned and with a minimum of encouragement or prompting' (Cressey, 1953: 23). Only a few interviews were taped; otherwise, the procedure followed these lines:

> In some cases verbatim notes could be written during the interviews without disturbing the subject, but in other cases it seemed appropriate to make only outline notes, and in some cases no notes could be taken at all. In the last two instances, the content of the interview was written down in the subject's own words as soon as he left the room. (Cressey, 1953: 26–27)

Zietz provides no details of her interview procedures, though she points out that the inmates she talked to may be a skewed sample of all who engage in similar behavior because authorities may be reluctant to incarcerate women with young children. Her work with 100 female inmates who shared the offence patterns of the men in Cressey's sample showed that the women were driven to violate the law by a felt need to resolve problematic family concerns rather than by the self-aggrandizement that characterized Cressey's male sample.

FACING PHYSICIANS

Most of our own research interviewing has been done with medical doctors who have become ensnared in a legal net because of two particular forms of law-breaking: a violation of the laws and regulations applicable to the treatment of Medicaid patients (Jesilow et al., 1993); and failure to obtain consent for the transfer of eggs and embryos from one woman to another. These alleged actions were at best arguably proscribed under federal or state law. The authorities went after the three fertility clinic physicians with charges of violating Medicare laws by naming colleagues as assistants in operations when the assignment was done by medical residents who were ineligible for Medicare compensation, and for false income tax returns (Dodge and Geis, 2003).

Physicians are regarded as particularly difficult interview subjects. Sir William Osler, the preeminent medical figure of the nineteenth century, believed that physicians were prone to arrogance because their work often lacked leavening influences. 'No class of men needs friction so much as physicians – no class gets less,' Osler wrote. He declared that 'the daily round of a busy practitioner tends to develop an egotism of a most intense kind to which there is no antidote. The few setbacks are forgotten, the mistakes often are buried and ten years of successful work tends to make a man touchy, dogmatic, intolerant of correction, and abundantly self-centered' (Cushing, 1940: 447).

That such conditions often translate into discomforting interview situations is testified to by Manning (1967: 307), who found that the physicians he interviewed during his doctoral dissertation research believed that '[s]ince the interviewer is presumed to lack intimate knowledge, the higher-status respondent may feel that the etiquette of the encounter leaves him free to be rude through evasiveness or implausibility, free to ignore the demands of the questioner who is stepping out of the confines of his deference role.' There is some evidence that the movement of a considerable number of women into the practice of medicine has, at least in terms of their interactions, moderated the arrogance often manifest by physicians (R. Geis et al., 1991).

Medicaid fraudsters

We used two interviewers, wise beyond their years, during our study of physicians who had been prosecuted for crimes against the Medicaid benefit program (Jesilow et al., 1993). Their recollections of what they went through are notably instructive about interviews with white-collar criminals.

Stephen Rosoff drew these conclusions from his work on the project:

> Interviewing offenders of any hued collar is a tricky proposition. It's a textbook case of social exchange. The interviewer wants something of value; but so too does the interviewee – validation, a sympathetic ear, a soapbox, whatever. The difference between higher-status offenders and underclass street criminals, I believe, is that the latter are trying to achieve a respect they've never enjoyed. White-collar criminals presumably have enjoyed respect (often great respect) in the past, a respect they have unwillingly forfeited. My take is that this loss makes the higher-status offenders' need for respect greater. My experience teaching in prison left me with a sense that while most convicts proclaim their 'innocence,' it's usually a pro forma ritual. On the other hand, my experience years ago with 'peculating physicians' left me with a different sense. These guys not only proclaim their innocence, they believe it – or, at least, they desperately want you to believe it. They hunger for the respect they once had.
>
> The first challenge in interviewing an elite offender is to extract information without being overtly adversarial. If I were interviewing a convicted burglar, I would probably call him Charlie (or whatever his first name is), while he might call me 'Doc.' There is a role reversal when the offender is an elite deviant. I respectfully called the Medicaid fraud subject Dr So-and-so, as I would similarly do with Mr Milken and Ms Stewart. And I might well be called Steve in return – or called nothing at all. No problem. When the interview ends, I'm still the one without a parole officer.
>
> I've talked with my colleague Steve Egger, who conducted numerous interviews with serial killer Henry Lee Lucas (Egger, 2003). He's an ex-cop, but he recognized that he couldn't interrogate Lucas. He realized that every question could be the last question he would get to ask. Lucas would respond only as long as the interview served whatever purpose he desired. Such was also the case with the Medicaid doctors. I once took a long drive to Bakersfield to interview a doctor from a foreign country who had been convicted of fraud. The first question – date of birth? – went uneventfully. But I never got past the second question – medical school and date of degree? He apparently found this question insulting and refused to proceed. So I had made an arduous trip to learn the physician's birthday. I should have saved the objectionable question for last.
>
> Interviewing a fallen elite is a game of thrust and parry. Most white-collar criminals have gargantuan egos. As any skilled martial artist can tell you, the way to defeat a stronger opponent is to turn his strength against him. I would suggest manipulating the subject's egomania and using it as a means of stimulating self-revelation. (Rosoff, 2004)

Connie Payne, the other interviewer on the project, notes, among other things, that being a young female interviewing physicians introduced additional complications:

> I approach my subjects sympathetically, not wanting to shame them even more while questioning them. Remaining respectful and echoing their sentiments of having been wronged by 'the system' supported an open discussion of the fraudulent claims they filed. Meeting the doctors on their own turf – in their homes, clinics, at a restaurant – also helped. Despite their fall from grace, many still come across as pleased with themselves, even if bitter about their setbacks. I also feel that who I was – a young woman, serious but rather mild-mannered – made the doctors open up, to present their cases to an understanding audience.
>
> Their stories attributed their problems to bookkeeping oversights, unclear and especially unfair regulations that practically forced them into breaking the rules in order to stay in business. None would admit that their standards were deficient. Some said that their minority status, the location of their practice, or the volume of their work were why they were targeted. I cannot recall any who admitted to knowingly violating the law. They wanted to get their story out, something they felt they were unable to do during court proceedings. Some came across as wounded by their experience, others as determined to get into the next money-making venture. Most seemed to be struggling to regain the status and the income they had been accustomed to. Many had been trained in 'offshore' medical schools and were a bit defensive about it. A memorable exception was a graduate of Johns Hopkins, who was now living in

a Hollywood flophouse, unemployed, and appeared (and smelled) one step from homelessness. He agreed to the interview only if I would buy him a meal. Illegal drugs and alcohol seemed to be linked to his professional demise.

Then there was the smug abortionist who tried to shock me by emerging for our interview with a jar of body fluid; and another doctor who tried to recruit me to what he said was a Playboy movie production.

Most of the doctors declared that they were not hurting anybody; rather they were doing old and poor people a service by flaunting oppressive government regulations. The victim mentality of these guys was pervasive. I think part of the reason they were so open with me was that they thought people also viewed Medicaid with disdain. Perhaps they assumed the purpose of my research was to expose the outrageous nature of the medical assistance plans. We did not tell them this; nor did we tell them otherwise. (Payne, 2004)

A fertility clinic scandal

The study that the two present authors conducted, regarding a fertility clinic scandal involving world-renowned doctors working at the medical school, relied very heavily on interviews with the physicians (Dodge and Geis, 2003). They had been accused of taking commandeered eggs and embryos from non-consenting patients and implanting them in other patients, who remained unaware of their source. One of the doctors had also been accused of using non-FDA (Federal Drug Administration) approved drugs. Two of the physicians had left the country before indictments were handed down, and therefore steadfastly maintained that they were not 'fugitives.' Both doctors – one in Mexico City and the other in Santiago – had obtained positions in highly prestigious clinics. The third doctor, who remained in the United States, had been convicted in a jury trial in a federal court of mail fraud in regard to billing insurers for assistants who were not, by law, qualified to receive fees. Everybody we talked to regarded him as a scapegoat, the sacrificial lamb offered up by university authorities to deflect attention from their own oversight failures. He was

extremely cooperative because he wanted his story to be told.

Mary Dodge did the interviews with the relocated doctors – Ricardo Asch in Mexico and Jose Balmaceda in Chile. Both of us talked several times with Sergio Stone. This is Mary's memories of her experiences:

The difficulties that arose were numerous, some probably predictable, others unforseen. They involved ethical considerations concerned with talking to pre-adjudicated doctors. Any information they might give me could be subject to subpoena by investigating agencies. I also had to be alert to doing a case study rather than a 'tell-all' journalistic story. And I had to be on guard against succumbing to the abundant persuasive powers and good looks of both doctors.

There was strong but not definitive evidence of their wrongdoing. For me, the nagging question was the doctors' version of what had gone on.

Access was the initial problem. Letters sent to their many attorneys typically were ignored, though once in a while a lawyer would meet with me and set out what he saw as his client's defense. We then moved to e-mailing the doctors, playing upon the idea that as academics themselves they ought to be supportive of a scholarly attempt to set the record straight. The initial interview was with the third doctor – Sergio Stone – and his cooperation seemed to make an impression on his two former colleagues.

When Asch finally agreed to meet with me in Mexico City, friends expressed concern about my safety, stereotyping Asch as a dangerous criminal type. I had problems resisting Asch's charm. The hotel he directed me to was one of the finest in the city, where I received a steep discount through a deal he had prearranged. Asch was accommodating and attentive during the four days we talked together. He largely stuck to his own conversational agenda, and I was always mindful of not alienating him with questions that he might consider offensive. His denials of wrongdoing were logical. The tapes I made were invaluable in locating nuances and possible flaws in what he had claimed, though I found that the tapes I had made in restaurants were indecipherable because of background noises.

The interview with Jose Balmaceda was the most difficult to arrange. He had quickly distanced himself from the scandal when it erupted and he had avoided intramural inquiries because, since he was untenured, there was no need to hold hearings to determine whether he should be dismissed. Finally, he agreed to see me, under certain conditions. 'I can collaborate with your project but I still hold as a condition that I have relatively little knowledge of other people's versions (especially the university's). I should be able to comment on any part of the story that concerns me'.

After I had purchased non-refundable plane tickets, Balmaceda notified me that his plans had changed and that he would be out of town on the day we had scheduled. On his return there would be a one-day window of opportunity for an interview. I had an awful case of food poisoning the day before the interview, and I was about as focused on not vomiting on Balmaceda's elegant shoes as on our conversation. Even his surprising admission that egg misuse actually had taken place seemed at that time anticlimactic. When I got home I thought of many more questions that I wished I had asked.

Mary indicates that when she reflects today on her eight years of interviews regarding the fertility clinic scandal she often asks herself, and answers, the following questions:

- Did I manipulate the circumstances to gain access? Perhaps.
- Did I fabricate or exaggerate the potential benefits to the interviewee? Never.
- Did I include in the book their version of the truth? Absolutely.
- Is qualitative interviewing different from journalism? Yes.
- Can a researcher maintain objectivity? Not easily. (Dodge, 2004)

Mary Dodge's and the other personal reports of the ups and downs of interviews with white-collar criminals heed the advice of Stephen Jay Gould about the manner in which scholars ought to report their work:

The messy and personal side of science should not be disparaged, or covered up, by scientists for two major reasons. First, scientists should proudly show the human face to display their kinship with all other modes of creative human thought. The myth of a separate mode based on rigorous objectivity and arcane, largely mathematical knowledge vouchsafed only to the initiated may provide some immediate benefits in bamboozling a public to regard us as a new priesthood, but must ultimately prove harmful in erecting barriers to truly friendly understanding, and in falsely persuading so many students that science is beyond their capabilities. (Gould, 1995: 94)

GETTING FEEDBACK

Our usual policy is to submit to the person we interviewed a copy of what we intend to put into print as a result of that particular encounter. Rare exceptions have occurred when the write-up was so critical that all it could lead to was unremitting verbal warfare. But even in such instances, we ordinarily checked the direct quotes while self-protectively omitting interpretations and observations. Our rule was that if the reader disagreed with what we had written, we would very seriously consider any changes that were suggested. If we did not feel that the changes were in order, we nonetheless would place whatever comment the person desired verbatim in a footnote on the page involved. We have never had to add such a footnote in our work and have had fewer than a handful of eventful disputes over substance. The most intractable dispute was in a report to the California Department of Corrections in regard to an evaluation of a halfway house for drug addicts. In the report, we had said 'many' and they thought the proper word should be 'some.' We gave in on that one, though Howard Becker had to make a trip to Sacramento at the expense of our grant to mediate the standoff. Persons who review our material often add very worthwhile further observations. And on some, perhaps many, occasions, the reviewer has spared us later embarrassment by catching errors of fact for which we alone were responsible, either out of carelessness or our misunderstanding of what had been said to us.

CONCLUSION

There are a number of things that need saying – briefly – about white-collar crime research in general. First, that it is unusually demanding when contrasted to many other aspects of the criminological enterprise. We have noted some of the barriers to obtaining first-hand data. There are also problems associated with getting control of the subject, since it incorporates law and regulatory processes and economics, among other disciplines, in addition to the behavioral sciences. Second, true understanding of the dynamics of white-collar crime does not lend itself easily to the fashionable statistical manipulations that so much more readily find a home in today's academic journals. Nonetheless, we would echo the theme of the famed physical anthropologist Mary Leakey, who preferred the nitty-gritty of fieldwork, spending long hours under the boiling African sun unearthing fossils, then carefully measuring, sketching, and cataloging them. 'Theories come and go,' Leakey insisted, 'but fundamental data always remain the same' (Golden, 1996: 33).

Finally, the challenge posed by obstacles hindering fieldwork on white-collar crime can be compensated for some by the fact that they are dealing with persons who can be seen as notably repugnant. Juvenile delinquents and street criminals characteristically themselves suffer the slings and arrows of outrageous fortune. White-collar offenders typically have a great deal and grasp for much more. We need not condemn them – they are humans fashioned by the same values that to a more or less degree motivate us all. But many of us get more satisfaction from trying to expose the usual greed and self-righteousness of the upper-class lawbreaker and, by our research, hope to level the playing field.

REFERENCES

Applebome, Peter (1995) 'The pariah as client: Bombing case rekindles debate for lawyers', *New York Times* (April 28): B10.

Bechhofer, Frank, Elliott, Brian and McCrone, David (1984) 'Safety in numbers: The use of multiple interviewers', *Sociology*, 18(1): 97–100.

Benson, Michael L. (1985) 'Denying the guilty mind: Accounting for involvement in a white-collar crime'. *Criminology*, 23(4): 583–607.

Benson, Michael L. (2004) Personal communication (31 March).

Braithwaite, John (1984) *Corporate Crime in the Pharmaceutical Industry*. London: Routledge & Kegan Paul.

Braithwaite, John (1985) 'Corporate crime research: Why two interviewers are needed', *Sociology*, 19(1): 136–138.

Clinard, Marshall B. (1983) *Corporate Ethics and Crime: The Role of the Middle Manager*. Beverly Hills, CA: Sage.

Cressey, Donald R. (1953) *Other People's Money: A Study in the Social Psychology of Embezzlement*. Glencoe, IL: Free Press.

Croall, Hazel (1988) 'Mistakes, accidents and someone else's fault: The trading offender in court', *Journal of Law and Society*, 15(3): 293–315.

Cushing, Harvey (1940) *The Life of Sir William Osler*. London: Oxford University Press.

Dexter, Lewis Anthony (1970) *Elite and Specialized Interviewing*. Evanston, IL: Northwestern University Press.

Dodge, Mary (2004) Personal communication (10 April).

Dodge, Mary and Geis, Gilbert (2003) *Stealing Dreams: A Fertility Clinic Scandal*. Boston: Northeastern University Press.

Dollard, John (1949) *Class and Caste in a Southern Town*. Garden City, NY: Doubleday.

Doocey, Jeffrey H., Shichor, David, Sechrest, Dale K. and Geis, Gilbert (2001) 'Telemarketing fraud: Who are the tricksters and what makes them trick?', *Security Journal*, 14(3): 7–26.

Egger, Steven A. (2003) *Need to Kill: Inside the World of the Serial Killer*. Upper Saddle River, NJ: Prentice-Hall.

Geis, Gilbert (1967) 'White-collar crime: The heavy electrical equipment antitrust cases of 1961', in Marshall B. Clinard and Richard Quinney (eds), *Criminal Behavior Systems: A Typology*. New York: Holt, Rinehart & Winston. pp. 139–150.

Geis, Gilbert (1992) 'White-collar crime: What is it?', in Kip Schlegel and David Weisburd (eds), *White-collar Crime Reconsidered*. Boston: Northeastern University Press. pp. 31–51.

Geis, Gilbert and Huston, Ted L. (1981) 'Bystander intervention into crime: Public policy considerations', *Policy Studies Journal*, 11: 398–408.

Geis, Robley, Geis, Gilbert and Jesilow, Paul (1991) 'The Amelia Stern syndrome: A diagnosis of a syndrome among female physicians', *Social Science & Medicine*, 13(8): 967–971.

Gill, Brendan (1975) *Heard at the New Yorker*. New York: Random House.

Golden, Frederic (1996) 'The first lady of fossils', *Time* (International edition) (23 December): 33.

Gould, Stephen Jay (1995) *Dinosaur in a Haystack: Reflections in Natural History*. New York: Harmony Books.

Holstein, James A. and Gubrium, Jaber F. (1995) *The Active Interview*. Thousand Oaks, CA: Sage.

Jesilow, Paul, Pontell, Henry and Geis, Gilbert (1993) *Prescription for Profit: How Doctors Defraud Medicaid*. Berkeley: University of California Press.

Kanfer, Stefan (2000) *Groucho: The Life and Times of Julius Henry Marx*. New York: Knopf.

Kinkaid, Harry V. and Bright, Margaret (1957a) 'Interviewing the business elite', *American Journal of Sociology*, 63(3): 304–311.

Kinkaid, Harry V. and Bright, Margaret (1957b) 'The tandem interview: A trial of the two-interviewer team', *Public Opinion Quarterly*, 21(2): 304–312.

Lazarsfeld, Paul F. and Thielens, Jr., Wagner (1958) *The Academic Mind: Social Scientists in a Time of Crisis*. Glencoe, IL: Free Press.

Mann, Kenneth (1985) *Defending White Collar Crime*. New Haven, CT: Yale University Press.

Manning, Peter K. (1967) 'Problems in interpreting interview data', *Sociology and Social Research*, 51(3): 302–316.

McCarry, Charles (1972) *Citizen Nader*. New York: Saturday Review Press.

Nader, Ralph (1965) *Unsafe at Any Speed: The Designed-in Danger of the American Automobile*. New York: Grossman.

Nettler, Gwynne (1974) 'Embezzlement without problems', *British Journal of Criminology*, 14(1): 70–77.

Payne, Connie (2004) Personal communication (3 April).

Posner, Richard (1970) 'A statistical study of anti-trust enforcement', *Journal of Law and Economics*, 13(2): 365–419.

Reik, Theodor (1948) *Listening with the Third Ear: The Inner Experience of a Psychoanalyst*. New York: Farrar, Straus.

Riesman, David (1954) *Individualism Reconsidered and Other Essays*. Glencoe, IL: Free Press.

Remmick, David (2004) 'Reporting it all: A.J. Liebling at one hundred', *New Yorker* (20 March): 52–61.

Rosoff, Stephen M. (2004) Personal communication (4 April).

Sarbin, Theodore R. (1994) 'A criminological approach to security violations', in Theodore R. Sarbin, Ralph M. Carney and Carson Eoyang (eds), *Citizen Espionage: Studies in Trust and Betrayal*. Westport, CT: Praeger. pp. 107–126.

Schumann, Howard (1982) 'Artifacts are in the mind of the beholder', *American Sociologist*, 17(1): 21–28.

Sutherland, Edwin H. (1949) *White Collar Crime*. New York: Dryden.

Szockyj, Elizabeth and Geis, Gilbert (2002) 'Insider trading: Patterns and analysis', *Journal of Criminal Justice*, 30(4): 273–286.

Szwajkowski, Eugene (1985) 'Organizational illegality: Theoretical integration and illustrative application', *Academy of Management Review*, 10(3): 558–567.

Vaughan, Diane (1992) 'The macro-micro connection in white-collar crime theory', in Kip Schlegel and David Weisburd (eds), *White-Collar Crime Reconsidered*. Boston: Northeastern University Press. pp. 124–145.

Vaughan, Diane (1995) 'Sensational cases and flawed theories: Lessons from the Challenger case', paper presented at the American Society of Criminology, Annual Meeting, Boston (16 November).

Vaughan, Diane (1996) *The Challenger Launch Decision: Risky Technology, Culture, and Deviance at NASA*. Chicago: University of Chicago Press.

Whiteside, Thomas (1972) *The Investigation of Ralph Nader: General Motors vs. One Determined Man*. New York: Arbor House.

Zietz, Dorothy (1981) *Women Who Embezzle or Defraud: A Study of Convicted Felons*. New York: Praeger.

6

Entering the Field: Recruiting Latinos for Ethnographic Research

C.H. BROWNER AND H. MABEL PRELORAN

Urban field research rests as much on in-depth interviewing as participant observation, yet finding qualified participants for either endeavor provides a unique set of challenges. Surprisingly, however, standard sources on field methods skip the subject of recruitment entirely (e.g., Taylor and Bogdan 1998; Bernard 1998, 2002; Patton 2002). Instead they discuss issues that arise after recruitment has been successful, such as how to establish and maintain rapport, negotiate the parameters of the researcher's own role in a field setting, and the importance of being unintrusive. Similarly, accounts on how to choose key informants merely stipulate that the cardinal rule is that they be knowledgeable about their culture and able to describe it to an interested listener – not how to generate interest in your own project to begin with. Similarly, analyses of sampling leave off after they describe the logic behind common sampling strategies and procedures for ensuring that they are representative.

Yet recruiting study participants for field-based and other types of social scientific research has become more difficult as researchers increasingly compete with public opinion pollsters and other telemarketers for potential subjects' time and attention. Recruitment difficulties are usually compounded when the design calls for recent immigrants or individuals from ethnic minority backgrounds (Blumenthal et al., 1995; Arrom et al., 1997; Naranjo and Dirksen, 1998), or more than one member of a family group (Bonvicini, 1998). Recruiting participants for field research can also present more of a challenge than for surveys because the former tends to involve a longer-term commitment and may be seen as too time-consuming with insufficient rewards (Arcury and Quandt, 1999). Difficulties may be compounded when recruiting study participants for health-related research that does not offer therapeutic benefits (Wilcox, Wesnes et al., 1994; Wilcox, Heiser et al., 1995; Wilcox, Kats et al., 1996).

Of course, recruitment in and of itself is not the only problem qualitative researchers face. Sample bias is another criticism field-based studies invariably encounter. And while any recruitment strategy will work better for some participants than for others, the measures taken to raise the recruitment rate might also skew it, attracting some types of people at the expense of others. This may be inevitable to a certain extent in all studies and researchers should be cognizant of how their recruitment strategies are influencing sample composition. Our goals therefore are to discuss the strategies we developed to overcome the problems of recruiting immigrant Latino couples for a qualitative study on decisions about fetal diagnosis and prenatal care.

BACKGROUND

Our study of the amniocentesis decisions of Latino couples (Browner et al., 1999) makes for a revealing test case because it posed a combination of obstacles to recruitment. We were trying to enroll an immigrant group that customarily has low participation rates in social research; we were trying to recruit couples, not just individuals; and we were approaching them at a sensitive time in a medical setting without offering any medical benefits.

The investigation focused on a group of Mexican-origin women in Southern California who were offered amniocentesis because they had screened positive on a routinely offered prenatal blood test (Crandall et al., 1983). A positive result indicates an increased risk of fetal anomaly (including neural tube defects, Down syndrome and other chromosomal anomalies) (ACOG, 1996). In and of itself, however, it is merely a screening test and a positive result indicates only that there may be a problem. Further testing is offered to women who screen positive, typically a high-resolution ultrasound and sometimes amniocentesis, an invasive procedure that carries a small risk of miscarriage. In California, these tests are performed at a state-license prenatal genetics center. The risk inherent in amniocentesis and the fact that most anomalies detected by fetal diagnosis have neither treatment nor cure, often leads pregnant women to experience intense anxiety should they screen positive. It was during the period when couples were deciding about amniocentesis or waiting for their results that we had our first recruitment contacts.

Participation in our study required a minimum of one face-to-face interview, lasting a little over an hour, with each member of the couple, as well as a willingness to respond to one or more requests for additional information in person or by telephone. Although the original design called for separate interviews, some candidates would agree to participate only if they and their partner could be interviewed together.

Although we were aware that recruiting couples would be more difficult than just women, we wanted to include males in our study of amniocentesis decisions in order to redress a significant lacuna in most existing work on the subject. As a result of this research gap, we know little about men's values, attitudes, and needs in relation to prenatal care, particularly fetal diagnosis or how they might affect women's decisions. We wanted to test our hypothesis that male partners' roles in Latinas' reproductive decisions are often underestimated (Browner, 2001). Anecdotal accounts revealed that couples often differ in their views about prenatal testing (Rothman, 1987; Rapp, 1991), but we knew little about how differences within couples are resolved (Resta, 1999). These issues promised to be particularly salient in Latino populations where evidence suggested that men's wishes can be decisive in women's fertility decisions (Browner, 1979, 1986; Tucker, 1986).

The woman and her male partner remained the analytical unit throughout our investigation, but our conception of 'couple' changed as the study advanced. In our initial conception, a 'couple' was defined as two people who shared the biological parenthood of the fetus, constituted a social and economic unit (with a shared residence and family budget) (Netting et al., 1984; Guyer and Peters, 1987; Wilk and Miller, 1997) and intended to provide emotional and material support to the child after its birth. But early on we found that in the greater Los Angeles area, couples with these characteristics were not easy to find or enroll. Some couples shared social and economic responsibilities and made joint reproductive decisions even though they lived apart. In other cases, men might appear prominently in women's accounts of their amniocentesis decisions while the men themselves were seemingly uninvolved (Preloran and Browner, 1997; Browner and Preloran, 2000). Accordingly, an extra effort was made to include such male partners in our investigation.

STRATEGIES FOR RECRUITING LATINO COUPLES

Over the course of our recruitment efforts, we employed four distinct strategies. In the 'standard' approach, one of the partners, usually the woman, would first be contacted in person, and then the researcher would follow-up by telephone with both partners. In a small number of cases, both partners were successfully recruited 'on the spot' at the genetics clinic without the need for follow-up calls. However, on occasion we were forced by circumstance to resort to two other approaches. In the case of 'co-recruitment,' we would first recruit the woman, she would then broach the issue of participating with her male partner and the researcher would complete the process. Under the

'brokering' strategy, the female partner would independently recruit the male partner without further help from us.

During an approximately twenty-four month period, the recruitment coordinator (H.M.P.) and three assistants, all four of whom are Latina, attempted to contact the 1,305 Spanish-surnamed women who were offered amniocentesis at six genetics clinics, all located in southern California. From the initial pool, 783 (60.0%) did not meet our enrollment criteria for a variety of reasons (e.g., the screening test result was false positive, they were being offered amniocentesis for other reasons, such as advanced maternal age). In addition, 132 (10.1%) could not be recruited for other reasons (e.g., separation or divorce; phone disconnected; failed to answer phone calls; women told recruiter that partner would not be interested; partner deported, imprisoned, or working outside the area).

Three hundred and ninety (29.9%) eligible women remained. Of these, 243 (62.3%) declined participation, either actively – by openly stating they were not interested – or passively – by avoiding more than ten phone contacts or canceling more than five appointments. While we were obligated to respect the candidates' right to refuse, we were concerned that our sample might be biased if the refusals followed a systematic pattern. We could obtain only limited information from candidates about their reasons for declining to participate in our research. The most common explanation was the wish to be left alone. Anecdotal evidence also suggests that various types of fear were significant factors in refusal. For example, some women were unwilling to give us their home address; others said their landlords did not allow them to receive visitors or that their husbands discouraged them from leaving home. Some men said they feared that participating

Table 6.1 *Characteristics of the study population*

	Women (n = 147)		Men (n = 120)	
	#	%	#	%
Ethnicity				
Mexican American	45	30.6	34	28.3
Mexican immigrant	102	69.4	76	63.3
Other Latino	—	—	10	8.3
Education				
Primary or less	37	25.3	31	26.7
Secondary or less	72	49.3	60	51.7
More	37	25.3	25	21.6
Household Income				
Less than $10,000/yr	49	34.5	34	28.8
$10,001–$20,000/yr	42	29.6	43	36.4
$20,001/yr or more	39	27.4	34	28.8
Don't know	12	8.5	7	5.9
Religion				
Catholic	125	85.0	96	80.0
Other	15	10.2	10	8.3
None	7	4.8	14	11.7

Notes: Numbers add up to fewer than 147 (women) and 120 (men) because of missing data.
'Mexican American' was defined as having been born in the United States or having immigrated before completing primary school, 'Mexican immigrant' as having immigrated after completing primary school, and 'other' as from a Hispanic background other than Mexican.

in the study would only add to the distress their partners felt after the positive screening test result. While informative, the number of candidates who provided such explanations is too few to permit generalization.

In recruiters' daily field notes, information about each contact with a potential participant along with the participant's reasons for accepting or declining were recorded. For successfully recruited candidates, reasons for participation were coded inductively. Answers such as 'I don't know;' 'Because I want to' (without specifying why); 'No particular reason,' etc. were categorized as 'No Particular Reason.' Responses (e.g., 'una mano lava la otra' ['one hand washes the other']) were coded as 'Helping Researcher' when respondents expressed appreciation for the interest the researcher had shown in them and wanted to reciprocate by helping. Candidates who said they were interested in learning more about the implications of

their own test results or genetic testing more broadly were classified 'Gain Knowledge.'

Finally, 122 couples were successfully recruited (although 120 couples actually completed the study). They provide the basis for the following analysis of successful recruitment approaches. In addition, 27 women who were part of a couple when they agreed to enroll in the research but became single before we could interview their partners are also included. (See Table 6.1 for general characteristics of the study population.) We retained these 27 newly 'single' women in part to examine the effect of marital status on recruitment efforts and study variables, which would have been impossible had the sample consisted only of couples. Among these 27 were six who, by circumstance, happened not to be living with their partners at the time of the interview due, for instance, to a partner's unexpected trip to Mexico. The relationships of the other 21 were genuinely 'unstable' in that the men had practically disappeared or were otherwise indifferent to the pregnancy. As we discuss later, this fact had a significant effect on our ability to recruit those men.

Enrollment rates varied at different stages of our research. During the pilot phase, they were extremely low, at 3.3%. At that time we were bound to and restricted by an approach that made direct contact with candidates difficult. Our clinic sponsors insisted that candidates be formally introduced to us by medical personnel, who would also explain the aims and benefits of our study and ask for the client's collaboration. The slow pace of recruitment prompted us to request more direct contact with candidates. Our request was eventually granted on the condition that candidates be approached in the presence of medical personnel. Enrollment rates rose to 8.0% once this change was implemented. Over time we gained greater trust from our medical sponsors and were eventually allowed to recruit more independently. Yet although we now had the visible support of clinic staff, for the most part we were left to recruit on our own. We found that the key to achieving this level of staff cooperation was to follow the rules of each field site but to as be 'invisible' as possible. When we were given the freedom to use all four of our recruitment strategies we were able to achieve an enrollment rate of 37.7%.

It is important to note that our greater success at recruiting did not necessarily mean that our new strategies were cost-effective (Patrick et al., 1998). Our procedures were often very time-consuming for both researchers and participants, since motivation to participate was usually low, and the need to enroll both partners made the effort more difficult (Bonvicini, 1998). On-the-spot recruiting was the least labor-intensive strategy, while brokering proved to be the most demanding. Co-recruitment was somewhat less labor-intensive than our 'standard' approach.

Given that most of our candidates were not particularly interested in participating in our investigation, we needed to find ways to motivate them. Assigning bilingual-bicultural recruiters was very helpful in building trust, as other researchers working with ethnic minority groups have found (LeVine and Padilla, 1980; Arean and Gallagher Thompson, 1996; Casey et al., 1996; Arrom et al., 1997). But our research went a step further. Taking a cue from the candidates themselves, we found we could motivate them by appealing through aspects of the 'traditional' gender roles found in Latino culture.

CULTURAL SCRIPTS FOR MOTIVATING WOMEN

Couples were our target population, but most of our initial contacts were made with women – not least because nearly half of the female candidates came for genetic counseling alone or with partners who were occupied elsewhere watching their children. In the clinic waiting rooms, it quickly became clear to us that many of the women we sought to recruit for our sample, especially those who were relatively new immigrants, were anxious, ill at ease, or reluctant to ask questions of clinic staff, especially if they did not appear to speak Spanish. In addition, many had brought young children with them. We found it possible to be helpful in both situations by offering to perform small favors (*favorcitos*) for them, such as listening to a woman's complaints about the long hours of waiting, helping her to communicate with clinic staff, complete hospital or insurance forms, find a pay phone, or watch her children while she was otherwise occupied attending to medical or administrative matters. Occasionally, we would also offer emotional support to women who were upset about the prenatal genetic testing decisions they were facing. Sometimes we sought to establish friendly ties by providing information or offering help even before introducing ourselves as researchers.

It is important to note at this point that some may question whether the approach to recruitment used here may have been unethical because we began to develop friendly relationships with potential participants before completely disclosing the details of our research (Singer et al., 2000). However, it is safe to assume that potential study participants would not mistake us for clients nor staff. Although we were present in the waiting room for several hours at a time, it was clear we were not waiting to be seen by a clinician. We did not dress like clinicians, nor perform formal clinical responsibilities. Moreover, in compliance with IRB (International Review Board) ethical requirements, any interested candidates were given a comprehensive explanation of all aspects of the project before any participation began. That is, we explained their prenatal care was in no way connected with participation in our study, that they could decline to answer questions that made them uncomfortable, and that they could withdraw from participation at any time. We did make minor modifications in the sequence of our recruitment protocol from time to time. For example, with women we brought up the $40 monetary incentive, and the fact that the interview could give them a chance to talk about their feelings about amniocentesis, earlier than we did with the men. But in all cases, we invariably provided full disclosure of the research goals and procedures. Participants always read and signed the consent form detailing the study's objectives and what participation would involve prior to any formal interview. In our experience, these measures minimized the possibilities for misunderstanding between researcher and candidates, and provided an environment in which concerns by study participants could be freely raised.

Turning back to our recruitment approaches, two conversation topics that also often helped 'break the ice' were their children (who were sometimes playing near their mothers while we were chatting) and women's hopes and beliefs about the sex of the fetus. Although conversations could be helpful in establishing rapport, offering small services was more effective. These interactions followed a 'cultural script' that we came to call *comadrismo*, a term derived from '*madre*' or 'mother' and commonly used by Latinas to describe relationships of trust and mutual support among women. In doing so, we employed the classical anthropological approach of participant observation.

The participant observation approach involves engaging in the same activities as those of study participants or as close as it is possible for an outsider to do so (Spradley, 1980; Russell, 1994). Sometimes, nurses, rushing to fulfill multiple demands, asked us to show patients how to fill out forms, or walk them to the room where they would have their next appointment. On other occasions, patients who had already seen us doing those small tasks similarly requested our help, or we offered it to them. From time to time, in the course of chatting with candidates who unfortunately found themselves with an unusually long wait at the hospital or clinic, we indicated that we were involved in a research study that might interest them. In other cases, we introduced ourselves in the waiting room and asked if we might talk more with them after they finished their medical appointment. We believe these diverse approaches did not obscure our intentions, but rather were used to sensitively discover the 'right time' in which the request to participate in our research would be most sympathetically heard.

Usually, after we had established an initial rapport with a woman, we proceeded to introduce ourselves as social researchers interested in talking with them at greater length about their pregnancies. While we alluded to our interest in issues surrounding prenatal diagnosis, we placed more emphasis on wanting to talk with them about their feelings rather than their decisions *per se*. When women seemed receptive but non-committal (i.e., responding with 'I'd prefer to think about it'), we waited until they had completed their genetic consultation and ultrasound testing before continuing our recruitment efforts. At that point, we explained that we could conduct the inter-view in a more relaxing environment, such as their home, and emphasized that we did not intend to be a burden. This was suffi-ciently reassuring for several women, who then agreed to enroll in the investigation. We also introduced the incentive of financial compensation for their time, characterizing it as a 'small amount' offered as a token of our appreciation ($20 per person, $40 per couple; all participants were compensated at the conclusion of their interviews). Some who had initially hesitated expressed more interest once they learned of this incentive. At this point, we explained that participation in the study would also require an interview with their male partner. A number of women continued to show interest but said they were still undecided. We therefore asked permission to call them at home, reminding them that they were under no obligation and that their refusal would in no way jeopardize their prenatal care.

Becoming *comadres* (i.e., offering resources and services, including $40 com-pensation) appears to have been significant in motivating some women who had been otherwise reluctant to enroll in the research. The financial incentive was not, in and of itself, the decisive factor in most cases, but it did make a difference for women who seemed less inclined to participate and may have been politely trying to refuse by saying they would 'think about it' or 'call back.' After learning that they would be compensated for their time, several women responded more positively, giving more precise instructions like, 'Call me tomorrow after 9 am, or better, after dinner if you also want to speak to my husband.'

INVISIBLE MEN

Once women agreed to participate, we turned to the task of recruiting their part-ners. In about 12% (17 of 147) of cases, this was an easy task; both partners attended the genetic consultation and both agreed on the spot to be part of our investigation. In an additional 58 cases, the woman said she was interested and agreed to let us call her partner at home. All men contacted under these circumstances, which we called our 'standard' procedure, agreed to enroll in the research. In the remaining cases, how-ever, we found we needed the woman to col-laborate in recruiting her partner. To facilitate these efforts, we developed the strategies of 'co-recruitment' and 'brokering,' which we describe below.

Our hopes of recruiting most men 'on the spot' at the genetics clinics went unfulfilled. About half the men did not attend their part-ners' prenatal genetics consultation, and a large proportion of those present tended to be physically separated from their partners, either taking care of their children, pacing in the corridors, or outside in the parking lot check-ing on their automobiles. As a result, most male recruitment was done by telephone. Unfortunately, however, the men were usually not available when we called and many did not return our phone calls. (We had planned on making a maximum of six follow-up calls, but ultimately chose to increase this to ten.)

The difficulty we had recruiting men for our study was in itself instructive, casting a revealing light upon some of the attitudes we hoped to investigate in the study proper. The men's failure to attend their partner's prenatal genetic consultation and their reluctance to communicate with us may have indicated a more general disengagement from their partners' amniocentesis decisions. Since men's roles in such decisions were central to our research, we became even more concerned to recruit men in order to explore the meaning of their apparent lack of interest and distance from the process. We also faced an obvious danger of sample bias, if the only men who agreed to participate in the study were those who were involved in the amniocentesis decision to an unusual degree.

In comparison with the face-to-face relationship of *comadrismo*, which proved effective in recruiting women, indirect contacts worked better with most men. This led us to develop the 'co-recruitment' and 'brokering' approaches. In co-recruitment, the researcher and the female candidate, sometimes with the help of other family members, shared responsibility for motivating the man to participate. We recruited 29 couples in this manner. This recruitment strategy was, in fact, first suggested to us by several women who offered to 'soften up' their partners prior to our contacting them. Co-recruitment was also used as a secondary strategy when women realized that their own efforts to recruit their male partner were not enough. On one such occasion, a woman helped us to recruit her reluctant husband by instructing her mother-in-law to leave the house at the time of our call so that her husband would be forced to answer the phone to us. Similarly, another woman offered to 'kidnap' her husband by having her eldest son ask him to stay home to work on the family car until we could meet him at home to request his participation. In a third instance, the sister-in-law of a female candidate agreed to organize a meeting between us and her brother. These examples illustrate how the female candidates enlisted other members of their family in the co-recruitment process.

'Brokering' was the other strategy that was successful in recruiting male partners. In these cases, the women offered to recruit their partners themselves, and our own role was a passive one. Forty-five female candidates offered to act as brokers and 43 of these women completed the study. Initially, this approach seemed cost-effective as it involved no additional time investment on our part. Unfortunately, however, brokering also had the highest male withdrawal rate (22/45 or 48.9%), far exceeding the other three approaches (7/104 or 6.7%) and attempts to re-enlist those men were time-consuming. Nevertheless, our experiences observing women acting as recruitment brokers with their male partners were instructive in that they helped us develop a 'cultural script' which proved fruitful in our own attempts to recruit men.

CULTURAL SCRIPTS FOR MOTIVATING MEN

At first we thought we could 'train' women for the task of recruiting their male partners. We suggested they emphasize the benefits of participation, that is, we were offering to pay them to discuss issues of interest to them, without them having to leave their homes. For the most part, our suggestions were dismissed with polite smiles, but one woman told us directly, 'No se preocupe, yo sé cómo darle la vuelta a mi marido' ('Don't worry, I know how to turn my husband around'). When asked how she would do it, she replied, 'I'm going to tell him (the study) is for the good of the children. … I know that if we want to convince him, we should forget the talk about money – don't even mention it to him – he is too proud to accept money for something like this.' Similarly, another potential broker observed, 'My husband won't understand getting paid for answering some questions. What I have to do is convince him that the person who will come is working for the good of the barrio. Besides, he needs to be sure you won't make any trouble. He is afraid I will open the door to strangers.'

These responses prompted us to ask other women how they had approached their partners. Two themes recurred in the women's testimony: altruism – toward the child they were expecting or the community – and home security. Learning from the women, we incorporated both of these themes into our general approach to male recruitment. When contacting men we emphasized the altruistic aspect of 'collaborating with the research for the good of the children and the Latino people.' We also took care to allay men's security concerns by explaining that we would send an interviewer, generally a woman, who could be trusted.

Just as we had drawn upon the culture of Latino women to develop the comadrismo script, we sought to couch our approaches to Latino men in a cultural script that was familiar to them. We developed an approach that we termed poderismo (powerism) in which men were assured that they would retain control of the research process at all times, deciding when and where to meet and, should they wish, when to withdraw from the study. Under poderismo, men were encouraged to express their concerns about

participating and to suggest ways to resolve these concerns. Instead of anticipating problems and offering solutions, as we often did with women, we would pose the question, 'What should we do about this?'

The following excerpt of a recruitment interaction between C (a male candidate) and R (researcher) helps to illustrate central characteristics of the poderismo approach – reassuring men that they are in control of the situation, acknowledging the importance of home security, and showing a concern for their partner's well-being.

C: I don't think I could participate [in the study]; here at home it is always too crowded and many times I have to work at night and I need to rest during the day.

R: I see you have these problems. … What should we do?

C: Could you meet any place?

R: Yes…

C: I don't know … it would be too difficult. … And, besides, I don't want a stranger to come … you know these days…

R: Right …

C: And … besides … I don't want her to be sad talking about these things again.

R: I don't know … maybe she will feel better if she could talk.

C: I don't know…

R: If you decide to give it a try and you don't like it, or you see she is sad, and you decide to stop the interview … for any reason, we will stop, no questions asked.

C: Well, I have to talk with my wife.

R: I hope you'll join us, and remember that in this study we will follow your commands. If you decide to help us, we'll appreciate it, but if you don't … [it's fine] we understand your reasons.

Using this combination of co-recruitment and brokering, together with the poderismo script, we were able to recruit many otherwise reluctant men, who were not necessarily present at the genetic consultation. Ultimately, our study population consisted of nearly equal numbers of men who were present at the genetics consultation and men who were absent, allowing us to account for the role men play in their partners' amniocentesis decisions.

Table 6.2   *Percentage of women endorsing reasons for participation in the study (by recruitment approach)*

	On the spot (n = 17)	Co-recruitment (n = 29)	Standard (n = 58)	Brokering (n = 43)
Gain knowledge	52.9	24.1	13.8	18.6
Help researcher	23.5	20.7	39.7	81.4
No reason	23.5	55.2	46.6	—

Note: Minimum pairwise comparison, t =1.98, p < .05 – in the 'On the spot' versus 'Co-recruitment' groups

Table 6.3   *Percentage of men endorsing reasons for participation in the study (by recruitment approach)*

	On the spot (n = 16)	Co-recruitment (n = 26)	Standard (n = 55)	Brokering (n = 23)
Gain knowledge	87.5	34.6	38.2	34.8
Wife asked	—	42.3	5.5	26.1
Help community	6.3	19.2	27.3	4.3
No particular reason	6.3	3.8	29.1	34.8

Note: Minimum pairwise comparison, t = 3.26, p < .01 – in the 'On the spot' versus 'Brokering' groups.

ASSOCIATIONS BETWEEN RECRUITMENT APPROACH AND REASONS FOR PARTICIPATING IN THE RESEARCH

When a variety of recruitment strategies are employed, it is possible to examine statistically whether the attitudes, characteristics and circumstances of study participants vary systematically with the recruitment techniques that brought them into the sample.

There were no statistical associations between the way a participant was recruited and such basic sociodemographic characteristics as their age, birthplace, religion, household income, education, or degree of acculturation. But other study variables were statistically associated with the recruitment approach.

We found strong statistical associations between recruitment approach and women's and men's reported reasons for participating in the investigation ($\chi^2_{(6)} = 50.44$, p < .001 and $\chi^2_{(9)} = 41.61$, p < .001 respectively). Categories for reported reasons for participating in the study were created inductively and

open-ended responses were coded into them. We found that male and female respondents who were recruited 'on the spot' were much more likely than others to indicate 'gaining knowledge' as their principal reason for participation. On the other hand, women recruited through the standard approach or through brokering were more apt to say that they agreed to participate in order to help the researcher. In contrast, men enrolled through co-recruitment said that their main reason was because their wife had asked them to, while men recruited by the standard approach typically said they agreed either to gain knowledge or to help their community (see Tables 6.2 and 6.3).

DISCUSSION

Overall, our strategies raised our recruitment rate to just under 38%, a respectable figure given all of the difficulties associated with recruiting immigrants and couples during a sensitive time. We were even more successful at retaining participants: only one man and two couples dropped out of the study once we had begun interviewing them. Nevertheless, because our study population was made up of individuals who were predisposed to seek biomedical prenatal care, we cannot generalize our results to those who did not do so.

Our experiences prove that rapport is as vital to recruitment as it is to qualitative research itself. This fact was starkly illustrated by the extremely high rates of refusal that dogged us at the beginning of the research, when we were required to contact candidates through medical intermediaries. Our recruitment strategies required relatively extensive and unimpeded access to the potential candidates prior to securing their consent. Candidates who agreed to enroll in the study said they felt we were genuinely concerned about them as individuals and sensitive to the realities of their lives and they wanted to reciprocate. Asking some who were initially reluctant how they overcame their concerns, one woman replied, 'When you asked me to participate I said to myself, "Here it goes again," (but) when you kept calling me day after day ... chatting (with you) made me see you were really interested in what happened to me there (at the genetics center).' Another woman had a similar reaction: 'I like it when things are more personal ... (and) when Jeff (the interviewer) told my husband he would love to go with him to the restaurant (the participant had invited Jeff out for dinner) we liked that ... we said, "Fine," and we would do it (participate).' When asked what had made one particularly skeptical man change his mind, he explained, 'She (partner) convinced me (to participate) because she said that talking to the girl (the recruiter) made her feel good.' In addition, some participants indicated that learning that emotional support and psychological referrals

Table 6.4   *Percentage of endorsed reasons for participation in the study (by sex)*

	Men (n = 120)	Women (n = 147)
Gain knowledge	43.3	21.8
Wife asked	16.7	—
Help researcher	3.3	46.3
Help community	15.0	0
No particular reason	21.7	32

Note: As the code categories for this variable differed for the men and women, these data are presented for descriptive purposes only.

would be available for the duration of their pregnancies were important factors in their decision to enroll in the study.

To raise the recruitment rate to 38%, it was necessary to use a variety of strategies. There was no 'one-size-fits-all' recruitment strategy that could, on its own, ensure the participation of a high proportion of male and female Latino candidates. The strategies we have outlined here are complements not substitutes: they were not simply better or worse than each other, they were better or worse for specific subgroups of the population, according to their circumstances and inclinations. To achieve an overall recruitment rate of 38%, the entire gamut of on the spot, standard, co-recruitment, and brokering was needed.

While aspects of our approach, such as financial incentives and expressions of genuine caring, have been successful in other investigations, the 'cultural scripts' of *comadrismo* and *poderismo*, developed here, made a real contribution. Why were these cultural scripts effective? We can shed some light on this issue by looking at the different reasons men and women gave for participating in the study (see Table 6.4). Of the women recruited through *comadrismo*, 46% indicated that they had enrolled in the study as a way of reciprocating the support and assistance we had provided. On the other hand, 43% of the men enrolled in order to gain more knowledge. Many men, even those who attended the genetic consultation, felt unsure about the genetic information they had been given and seemed to regard the interview as an opportunity for clarification. For example, one man said, 'I didn't understand the chart with the black spots that come in pairs [chromosomes], so if you come with it and explain it to me, I'll do the interview.'

In both cases, the cultural scripts served to recast an unfamiliar relationship into one that was culturally familiar. Most of our candidates were uncertain, concerned, and confused about prenatal diagnosis. They tended not to feel sure of themselves or in command of their situation. If we had not recognized this fact, our recruitment efforts might have added to the confusion: we were approaching candidates at a clinic, but we were not doctors; we were asking questions related to medicine, but we were not offering any medical services. However, by framing our requests in terms of *comadrismo* and *poderismo* we encouraged our male and female candidates into roles that were familiar and perhaps sometimes even comforting to them. Many female participants felt close enough to us to talk very openly about what it meant to them to be labeled a high-risk pregnancy and what was involved in their decision to accept or decline amniocentesis. Likewise, by putting men 'in charge' of the research proceedings, *poderismo* gave men a reassuringly familiar role in an otherwise unfamiliar domain.

Our decision to employ multiple recruitment strategies was necessary not only to boost the recruitment rate, but also to *balance* the recruitment rate, ensuring that our study did not over- or under-sample people on one side of an important research question. As it was, there was no significant difference between the rate of amniocentesis acceptance in our interview sample and the rate among all the Mexican-origin women offered amniocentesis at the six participating genetics clinics because they had screened positive (Browner and Preloran, 1999).

CONCLUSIONS

While exploratory in nature, our investigation has drawn needed attention to some of the challenges field researchers face and some techniques that have proven successful in one study with Latino couples. Our findings certainly highlight the challenge of eliciting information from non-participants, while respecting their desire to be left alone. Although in our case recruiters' ethnic backgrounds matched those of participants, our recruitment strategies were successful not for this reason alone. By taking time to consider the potential impact of cultural differences on participant–researcher interaction, investigators from backgrounds different from those of study participants can also develop recruitment strategies that are sensitive to participants' ethnic backgrounds.

By offering more effective ways to begin field research with Latinos we hope this chapter will promote a better understanding of how to meet the needs of this and other understudied populations. And by analyzing the strengths and weaknesses of the different approaches we used to recruit participants in a 'real world' medical setting, we also hope it provides researchers with an overview of the first steps of the fieldwork enterprise.

ACKNOWLEDGMENTS

Funding for this research was provided in part by the National Center for Human Genome Research (1RO1 HG001384–01), the Russell Sage Foundation, UC-MEXUS, the UCLA

Center for the Study of Women, and the UCLA Center for Culture and Health. Maria Christina Casado, Nancy Monterrosa and Ricardo Rivera provided invaluable assistance at all stages of the research. Eli Lieber performed the statistical analyses and Simon J. Cox helped sharpen the argument. We also wish to thank Silvia Balzano, Susan Markens, Melissa Pashigian, Betty Wolder Levin, and Arthur J. Rubel, and members of the UCLA Latino Mental Health Research Group: Kimlin Ashling-Giwa, Victor Diaz, Victoria Hendrick, and Marvin Karno for their helpful comments on an earlier draft of the chapter and the directors and staff of the participating genetics clinics both for facilitating the research and providing us with access to their patients. Permission was obtained from the institutional review board of each participating genetics clinic and interviewees signed consent forms. Some of the data appear in Preloran, H.M., Browner, C.H. and Lieber, Eli (2001). 'Strategies for motivating Latino couples' participation in qualitative health research'. *American Journal of Public Health*, 91(11): 1832–41.

REFERENCES

ACOG (American College of Obstetricians and Gynecologists) (1996) 'Maternal serum screening'. *International Journal of Gynaecological Obstetrics*, 55: 299–308.

Arcury, T.A. and Quandt, S.A. (1999) 'Participant recruitment for qualitative research: a site-based approach to community research in complex societies'. *Human Organization*, 58: 128–133.

Arean, P.A. and Gallagher-Thompson, D. (1996) 'Issues and recommendation for the recruitment and retention of older ethnic minority adults into clinical research'. *Journal of Consulting and Clinical Psychology*, 64: 875–880.

Arrom, J., Giachello, A.L. and Carroll, R. (1997) 'Issues of recruitment and retention of minorities into

clinical trials'. Paper presented at the Annual Meeting of the American Public Health Association, Indianapolis, IN.

Bernard, H.R. (ed.) (1998) *Handbook of Research Methods in Anthropology*. Walnut Creek, CA: AltaMira Press.

Bernard, H.R. (2002) *Research Methods in Anthropology: Qualitative and Quantitative Approaches* (3rd edn). Walnut Creek, CA: AltaMira Press.

Blumenthal, D.S., Sung, J., Coates, R., Williams, J. and Liff, J. (1995) 'Recruitment and retention of subjects for a longitudinal cancer prevention study in an inner-city black community'. *Health Service Research*, 30: 197–205.

Bonvicini, K.A. (1998) 'The art of recruitment: the foundation of family and linkage studies of psychiatric illness'. *Fam Process*, 37: 153–165.

Browner, C.H. (1979) 'Abortion decision making: Some findings from Columbia'. *Studies in Family Planning*, 10: 96–106.

Browner, C.H. (1986) 'The politics of reproduction in a Mexican village'. *Signs: Journal of Women in Culture and Society*, 11: 710–724.

Browner, C.H. (2001) 'Situating women's reproductive activities'. *American Anthropologist*, 102(4): 773–788.

Browner, C.H. and Preloran, H.M. (1999) 'Male partners' role in Latinas' amniocentesis decisions'. *Journal of Genetic Counseling*, 8: 85–108.

Browner, C.H. and Preloran, H.M. (2000) 'Latinas, amniocentesis, and the discourse of choice'. *Culture, Medicine, and Psychiatry*, 24: 353–375.

Browner, C.H., Preloran, H.M. and Cox, S.J. (1999) 'Ethnicity, bioethics, and prenatal diagnosis: The amniocentesis decisions of Mexican-origin women'. *American Journal of Public Health*, 89(11): 1658–1666.

Casey, K.M., Cohen, F. and Hughes, A. (1996) *ANAC's Core Curriculum for HIV/AIDS Nursing*. Philadelphia: Nursecom Inc.

Crandall, B.F., Robertson, R.D., Lebherz, T.B., King, W. and Schroth, P.C. (1983) 'Maternal serum alpha-fetoprotein screening for the detection of neural tube defects'. *Western Journal of Medicine*, 138: 524–530.

Guyer, J.I. and Peters, P.E. (1987) 'Introduction: conceptualizing the household: issues of theory and policy in Africa'. *Development and Change*, 18: 197–214.

LeVine, E. and Padilla, A. (1980) *Crossing Cultures in Therapy: Pluralistic Counseling for the Hispanics*. Belmont, CA: Wadsworth.

Naranjo, L.E. and Dirksen, S.R. (1998) 'The recruitment and participation of Hispanic women in nursing research: a learning process'. *Public Health Nursing*, 15: 25–29.

Netting, R.M., Wilk, R.R. and Arnould, E.J. (1984) 'Introduction'. In R.R. Wilk, R.M. Netting and E.J. Arnould (eds), *Households: Comparative and Historical Studies of the Domestic Group*. Berkeley, CA: University of California Press. pp. xiii–xxxviii.

Patrick, J.H., Pruchno, R.A. and Rose, M.S. (1998) 'Recruiting research participants: a comparison of the costs and effectiveness of five recruitment strategies'. *Gerontologist*, 38: 295–302.

Patton, M.Q. (2002) *Qualitative Evaluation and Research Methods* (3rd edn). Newbury Park, CA: Sage.

Preloran, H.M. and Browner, C.H. (1997) 'Rol de la tradición en las prácticas del embarazo: efectos e la información genética entre mexicanos residentes en Estados Unidos'. *Revista de Investigaciones Folklóricas*, 12: 67–75.

Rapp, R. (1991) 'Constructing amniocentesis: maternal and medical discourses'. In F. Tsing and A.L. Ginsburg (eds), *Constructing Gender in America*. New York: Beacon. pp. 28–42.

Resta, R.G. (1999) 'Just watching'. *American Journal of Medical Genetics*, 83: 1–2.

Rothman, B.K. (1987) *The Tentative Pregnancy: Prenatal Diagnosis and the Future of Motherhood*. New York: Viking Penguin.

Russell, B.H. (1994) *Research Methods in Anthropology: Qualitative and Quantitative Approaches*. (2nd edn). Thousand Oaks, CA: Sage.

Singer, M., Huertas, E. and Scott, G. (2000) 'Am I my brother's keeper?: A case study of the responsibility of research'. *Human Organization*, 59(4): 389–400.

Spradley, J.P. (1980) *Participant Observation*. New York: Holt, Rinehart & Winston.

Taylor, S.J. and Bogdan, R. (1998) *Introduction to Qualitative Research Methods: A Guidebook and Resource* (3rd end). New York: Wiley.

Tucker, G. (1986) 'Barriers to modern contraceptive use in rural Peru'. *Study of Family Planning*, 17: 308–316.

Wilcox, C.S., Heiser, J.F., Crowder, A.M., Wassom, N.J., Katz, B.B. and Dale, J.L. (1995) 'Comparison of the effects on pupil size and accommodation of three regiments of topical dapiprazole'. *British Journal of Opthalmology*, 79: 544–548.

Wilcox, C.S., Kats, B.B., Morgan, D.L., Morrissey, J.L., Schneider, A.L. and DeFrancisco, D.F. (1996) 'Increasing ethnic diversity and managed care: how will they influence research patient recruitment in the nineties?' *Psychopharmacology Bulletin*, 32: 193–200.

Wilcox, C.S., Wesnes, K.A., Wisselink, P.G., Simpson, P.M., Morrissey, J.L. and Happy, J.M. (1994) 'A double-blind, single-dose, four-way crossover comparison of the effects of abecarnil, alprazolam, and placebo in the evaluation of cognitive functions in male volunteers'. 33rd Annual Meeting of the American College of Neuropsychopharmacology: Abstracts of Panels and Posters, San Juan, Puerto Rico. (11 December).

Wilk, R. and Miller, S. (1997) 'Some methodological issues in counting communities and households'. *Human Organization*, 56: 64–70.

Part 4

Fieldwork as a Reflexive Enterprise

7

Self-Narratives and Ethnographic Fieldwork

BEN CREWE AND SHADD MARUNA

Identity psychologists like Dan McAdams (1985, 1993) argue that if you want to know the answer to the question 'who am I?' (in other words, if you want to know my identity), you first have to know my story. The construction and reconstruction of one's life story narrative (or 'personal myth'), integrating one's perceived past, present, and anticipated future, is the process through which modern adults imbue their lives with unity, purpose, and meaning. Overwhelmed with the choices and possibilities of modern society (Fromm, 1941), modern individuals internalize this autobiographical narrative in order to provide a sense of coherence and predictability to the chaos of their lives.

Over the last two decades, this idea that identity is an internal narrative has achieved a privileged place in the social sciences and humanities, with adherents like Norman Denzin, Paul Ricœur, Roger Schank, and Charles Taylor. The distinguished psychologist Jerome Bruner (1987: 15) argues:

> Eventually the culturally shaped cognitive and linguistic processes that guide the self-telling of life narratives

achieve the power to structure perceptual experience, to organize memory, to segment and purpose-build the very 'events' of a life. In the end, we become the autobiographical narratives by which we 'tell about' our lives.

The equally distinguished UK sociologist Anthony Giddens (1991: 54) agrees, arguing that in modernity, '[a] person's identity is not to be found in behavior, nor – important though this is – in the reactions of others, but in the capacity to keep a particular narrative going'.

Theodore Sarbin (1986: vii) has argued that the narrative should be seen as the 'root metaphor' for the entire field of psychology and that 'narrative psychology' represents 'a viable alternative to the positivist paradigm'. The idea, building on traditions such as symbolic interactionism, hermeneutics and phenomenology, is that human life is essentially and fundamentally narrated and that understanding human interaction, therefore, requires some understanding of these stories. Indeed, Bruner (1987: 21) largely accepts Jean-Paul Sartre's famous claim that the human being 'is always a teller of stories, (s)he lives surrounded by his (or her) own stories and those of other people, (s)he sees everything that happens to him(her) in terms of stories and (s)he tries to live his(her) life as if (s)he were recounting it'.

As a result of this widespread, intellectual consensus, 'life history methodology' has flourished in fields as diverse as anthropology, cognitive science, criminology, education, history, literary criticism, moral philosophy, and theology. An endless list of research articles have analyzed the life stories of teachers, French bakers, deer poachers, trial lawyers, tribal elders, prostitutes, and individuals from every conceivable walk of life (see especially, Bertaux, 1981). There is nothing new to oral history methods, of course. In fact, approaching research 'subjects' and asking them to 'tell me the story of your life' might be among the oldest tools in the short history of social science (see, for example, White, 1943/1989: 289). However, this old practice has been given a new life by the theoretical insights of the narrative identity school.

It would be wrong, however, to assume that traditional life history methodology – usually involving the tape recording, transcribing and analysis of life story interviews conducted one-on-one in a private, non-clinical setting – is the only appropriate strategy for exploring and understanding life narratives. In this chapter, we will argue that life history research can both enhance and be enhanced by ethnographic fieldwork methods. First, we will outline our understanding of narrative psychology, and demonstrate how such self-narratives might be as easily accessed in field interactions as they are in a more formal interview situation. Next, drawing on our own fieldwork experiences, we will demonstrate the value of fieldwork for analyzing and interpreting life history data. Just as importantly, we will demonstrate the value of life history

interviewing for the interpretation of field observations and interactions. Our conclusion is that life history research and fieldwork are highly complementary approaches to social research and that either method used in isolation from the other may miss important insights available with methodological triangulation.

For the sake of clarity, all of the examples throughout this chapter will be drawn from a field-based study of prison social life (see Crewe, forthcoming), conducted over a ten-month period between October 2002 and August 2003. Based in (Her Majesty's Prison) Wellingborough, the project has used the method of sustained immersion in a single establishment that was the standard approach of much early prison sociology (most obviously, Clemmer, 1940; Sykes, 1958; Mathiesen, 1965; Carroll, 1974). The main aim of the study has been to revisit the classic themes of such work within the contemporary context. The prison, a 'Category C' training establishment (medium security) with an operational capacity of 526 prisoners at the time of the research, lies in the East Midlands of England. Most prisoners are serving sentences of between two and six years, for offences such as burglary, robbery and possession (of drugs) with intent to supply. One wing, in the prison's main buildings, holds around 60 life-sentence and long-term prisoners who have been deemed suitable for medium-security conditions.

The first author was provided with keys to enable access throughout the establishment, and was allowed to move freely and without accompaniment. Visits were made around four times per week, including weekends and evenings. The first three months of fieldwork were spent observing everyday practices and interactions, and talking informally with staff and prisoners about daily life in the prison. In the months that followed, and informed by the initial phase, a large number of long, semi-structured interviews were conducted, generating around 300 hours of recorded material. Life history interviews were carried out with around half of the overall sample of 70 prisoners. Most were individuals with whom some kind of relationship had already been established through informal engagement in the early phases of the research.

THE NEED FOR SELF-NARRATIVES

Arguably, self-narratives hold a special place in the type of prison-based research the authors typically conduct. Goffman (1961: 66) notes that the 'milieu of personal failure' in total institutions is such that inmates display a 'peculiar kind and level of self-concern' and tend to develop 'sad tales' or storylines about themselves that explain their current status. Certainly, a great deal of this kind of storytelling occurs in prisons. Many prisoners assert narratives that account for their predicament, differentiate them from other inmates, or provide a plot for a happier future. As Goffman suggests, these tales may have a functional purpose, in protecting those who tell them from anxieties about their moral status, their prospects and their ability to control their environment. Indeed, where they are most forcefully declared, they can help prisoners to negotiate and navigate their way through the prison social world. A prisoner whose plan to pursue a business idea or whose identity as a recovering alcoholic or 'changed person' is most fully formed, exudes a single-mindedness that detaches them somewhat from the bustle of the prisoner community (see Maruna, 2001).

At the same time, it should be noted that the role of self-narratives in the prison environment is little different from their place outside such institutions. All of us tell stories about who we are and what makes us unique, and these stories influence the way we interact in our own environments. The biographical content of prisoner self-stories (most obviously including an explanation of how they came to be there) simply accentuates the role of narratives, and the prison setting has a tendency of exposing and laying bare the human need for sense-making and meaning in life.

Psychologists argue that the self-narrative is what keeps the very human experience of meaninglessness and existential void at bay (McAdams, 1985). Personal myths may also be the primary mechanism through which individuals are able to maintain a sense of self-worth in the face of moral, social and personal failings. We use stories to make sense of, rationalize and account for our experiences, be they successes or tragedies. Not every aspect of a person's life requires such internal explanation. Brushing one's teeth at night or saving part of one's salary in a bank are rarely central features in an identity story, because these behaviours are so common that they require little justification. Generally, narratives focus on deviations from normative behaviours or the experiences in a person's life that, when taken in totality, make them unique as an individual: achievements, predicaments, failings and aberrations. Most critically, narrative reconstruction becomes necessary when a person experiences some threat to his or her identity (see Maruna and Ramsden, 2004). As such, research on narratives has a natural and essential place in the study of deviant or criminal behaviour. For instance, Scott and Lyman (1968: 62), argue: 'Since it is with respect to deviant behavior that we call for accounts, the study of deviance and the study of accounts are intrinsically related, and a clarification of accounts will constitute a clarification of deviant phenomena.'

These stories represent personal outlooks and *theories* of reality, not reality itself. While based on historical fact, the self-narrative is thought to be an imaginative rendering, a sort of myth-making through which the past is reconstructed, edited and embellished in order to create a coherent plot and themes. Like the symbolic interactionist mantra 'if (persons) define situations as real, they are real in their consequences' (Thomas and Thomas, 1928: 572), narrative psychology is premised on the idea that 'stories hold psychological truth' (McAdams, 1999: 496).

The storied identity can be seen as an active 'information-processing structure', a 'cognitive schema' or a 'construct system' that is both shaped by and later mediates social interaction. Giddens (1991: 14) writes: 'Each of us not only "has," but lives a biography'. People tell stories about what they do and why they did it. These narratives explain their actions in a sequence of events that connect up to explanatory goals, motivations, and feelings. Moreover, these self-narratives then act to shape and guide future behaviour, as persons act in ways that accord to the stories we have created about ourselves (McAdams, 1985). Gergen (1971: 2) theorized that the 'way in which a man conceives of himself will influence both what he chooses to do and what he expects from life'.

While our life goals and strategies give us a direction in which to act and our traits give us our behavioural styles, our individual *identities* provide the shape and coherence of our lives. Epstein and Erskine (1983: 135) use this 'need to maintain a coherent, integrated conceptual system' or 'theory of reality' to explain 'behavior that either is manifestly self-destructive or is maintained in the absence of reinforcement'. Caspi and Moffitt (1995) argue that a person's self-narrative may act as a filter for the encoding and processing of social information as different people exposed to the same situation will react differently as they interpret events in a manner consistent with their understanding of self (self-narrative), their understanding of others, and their previous experience. Self-narratives may also act as a filter in the clarification of goals by filtering out goals that are inconsistent with an individual's self-narrative.

Unlike personality traits, which tend to be largely stable over time, the narrative identity can and does change throughout life. In fact, our stories have to be 'routinely created and sustained in the reflexive activities of the individual' (Giddens, 1991: 52). As such, numerous therapeutic efforts have been directed to the possibility of re-creating one's self-narrative in more socially adaptive directions (e.g., White and Epston, 1990). Moreover, these dynamic narratives are not created in a vacuum. Identity theorists argue that identity is very much shaped within the constraints and opportunity structure of the social world in which people live. Rather than stripping individuals of community and macro-historical context, therefore, narrative analysis can inform our understandings by illustrating how the person sees and experiences the world around her. Self-narratives are therefore also excellent data for the analysis of the underlying socio-structural relations of a population (Bertaux, 1981).

HOW ETHNOGRAPHY ENHANCES LIFE HISTORY RESEARCH

The study of self-narratives is, for obvious reasons, linked closely to life history methodology. Research in narrative psychology sometimes draws on existing, written narratives, such as published autobiographies (e.g., Maruna, 1997), or on diaries and other forms of confessional writing (e.g., Stewart et al., 1988). Other researchers have asked research participants (often undergraduate students) to write autobiographical essays specifically for research purposes (Schütz and Baumeister, 1999). Most commonly, however, those interested in self-narratives tend to conduct one-on-one, tape-recorded, biographical interviews with research participants (see Josselson and Lieblich, 1993). These narratives can be analyzed to discern the 'themes' and roles that guide an individual's behaviour. Sometimes this content analysis involves the development or utilization of elaborate coding schemes for systematically recording patterns in the structure and thematic content of narratives (see especially, Smith, 1992). The narratologist's interest in these narratives is not so much the facts they contain (what happened in their lives), but rather in the meanings the person attaches to such facts – how they choose to frame the events of their lives.

This methodological privileging of life history interviewing, however, does not necessarily flow from the theory behind narrative psychology. That is, there is a substantial difference between the internal, personal myths that an individual 'lives by' and the verbal or written accounts they might give about their life in a research situation. The transcribed life histories collected in social scientific research are thought to 'hold the outlines' of these internal narratives (McAdams, 1985), but they are not the identity narratives themselves.

Presumably, then, there are other strategies that are useful for tapping into these internalized narratives. One obvious approach would be the deep immersion into a field setting associated with ethnographic research. The fieldworker who becomes closely involved with individuals in real-world settings potentially has the same access to the 'outlines' of these identity narratives as the researcher who conducts a two-hour interview and then never sees the person

again. Fieldwork allows opportunities for deeper, longer-lasting relationships to emerge, as well as allowing for interactions and observations in a greater variety of situations.

The role of self-narratives in the analysis of field data might be made more clear by looking at concrete examples from the first author's prison ethnography. In prison research, identity issues are often manifest. Prisoners often identify themselves as a 'former drug addict' or as 'different from the other scum in here' almost immediately upon being introduced to a fieldworker, and although time and privacy in interactions might be required in order to work out precisely what such descriptions 'mean', formal interviews may be unnecessary for understanding the self-perspectives of prisoners.

Consider the following two interactions, both occurring on a single night of fieldwork on a prison wing at Wellingborough. The first involves a prisoner whom the first author had met once before in the prison's philosophy class. He politely invites the first author for a cup of coffee in his clean, undecorated cell. The man is older than most inmates, and says that he socializes mainly with a set of 'more mature' prisoners on his wing (the Voluntary Testing Unit), where there is, he says, a 'better quality person' than elsewhere in the establishment. Despite this, he explains, he avoids getting close to anyone, lying about his offence so that no one knows that he is relatively affluent. He does not trust other prisoners, and makes sure that he neither gives anything to nor borrows anything from others. Although he plays cards and snooker with a small number of associates, he would not consider giving his address to anyone. The first author is, he says, the only person with whom he has been honest about his crime. He describes in detail his personal wealth, the houses and businesses that he owns, and the unfairness of his conviction. He is charming and flattering, asking about personal and professional issues, and he expresses regret when the researcher leaves to visit elsewhere on the wing. His self-identity is evident from this brief, but intimate interaction: he is a businessman and a family man, not a 'criminal', and he has more in common with the researcher than with other prisoners.

The second interaction reveals similar themes during an informal conversation on the ground floor of the wing. A prisoner explains that this is his first sentence, related to a pub fight in which someone was seriously hurt: 'It could have been anyone … it happens all the time.' But, unlike most other prisoners, he accepts responsibility for what happened and deeply regrets it. He has a 'different mindset' from most others on his wing, and 'nothing in common with a twenty-one year old car thief'. He is 'a bit of a snob, really', and doesn't think of himself as a criminal. He has always worked and paid taxes, whereas most prisoners have never done so and don't want to. He has only a couple of friends on the wing, 'hardworking lads – not addicts – who have got into trouble through no fault of their own'. Although he has not found prison difficult, it was a shock to get used to: he finds it difficult 'being treated like a second-class citizen', and finds it odd that staff were suspicious of how polite he was. They were used to people being rude, and told him that it would help him move through the system if he started off misbehaving and then changed, because they could then say that he was improving: 'I won't do that – become part of the system.'

Such discourses of distinction from 'this lot' were common. Prisoners who were 'working people' or 'family men', who had found religion or education, or who were recovering drug addicts often recounted their stories publicly, or in private conversations in public spaces, such as the workshops, the segregation unit, or the wings. In doing so in these locations, they could specifically identify those prisoners from whom they wanted to differentiate themselves: 'junkies', 'proper criminals', 'idiots', 'nonces', or 'kids'. Since identity is always relational, that is, defined in everyday context, and interaction, the opportunity that ethnography gives for these relational distinctions to be observed and understood is highly valuable.

Likewise, identity may be mutually confirmed and reinforced through the support of narrative partners. In one work unit, two prisoners recount a shared story of recovery from drug addiction. Placed together in a double cell in their local prison, they had bonded over the discovery of common life circumstances, opening up to each other as they began to get clean and think about their lives. Both had children, and say they had always made sure, even when addicts outside prison, that their families came first: 'A lot (of prisoners) don't give a shit. They'd rather get a bag (of heroin) than a phonecard to call their kids.' They describe how being away from their children is the hardest thing about prison. One has not seen his kids since starting his sentence over a year ago, and is now being divorced by his wife, who is 'fed up with it'. He goes on: 'I'm fed up too. I'm 30, and if I don't stop now, I never will.' Both men are keen to change themselves, working with dedication and supporting each other's proclamations of personal transformation. Here, then, experiences of drug abuse and its impact on family life provide the dominant nodes in life stories that are jointly mobilized to shape institutional behaviour and ambitions about release.

Family narratives were not always used in such ways. In another workshop, a prisoner complains about how little money he will be given when he's released back into society: 'I'm a man with three kids and lots of women. By the time you see your kids, you've got no money left.' He goes on to describe that his daughter now demands designer clothing, and that it is hard to ensure that her demands are met. 'Whatever my kids want, they'll get', he insists. 'It might take a week, but they'll get it. There's people in prison earning more money in here than they ever will outside.' He identifies himself explicitly as 'a provider', and describes how belittling it feels not to be able to support your family as you would like to: 'You can't be there – and every child needs a father.' The researcher asks how he manages: 'I used to sell drugs', he whispers. 'You need at least ten phonecards a week to speak to your children. I won't go without' (fieldwork notes, December 2002).

In interview, two months later, he repeatedly revisits the themes of protecting and providing for his family, using them to justify his involvement in the prison's illicit economy. In highlighting how drug dealing has enabled him to be a 'head' (i.e., a powerful prisoner) inside as well as outside prison, and in boasting of his ability to make money under the noses of his captors, when they 'wouldn't survive two seconds in my world', he also reveals the significance of discourses of status and masculinity in his activities. In such respects, the ethnographic fieldwork and life history interview are complementary in a number of practical and intellectual ways.

Fieldwork is valuable partly because, in generating trust, credibility and familiarity, it makes interviewees more likely to disclose themselves in interviews. Researchers who engage in life history interviewing are consistently surprised and honoured that research participants are so willing to talk about their lives to a complete stranger (and indeed seem to immensely enjoy the experience). Yet, research participants are presumably even more open when they believe their interviewer has some appreciation of their world and their needs. Researchers are evaluated in action, and potential participants make decisions about them accordingly.

This lesson was made manifest in the first author's prison ethnography. One of the first prisoners to take part in the life history interviewing explained his willingness to participate as follows:

> You know, it just happens that we've spoke a few times on the wing and I find you a pretty sensible fella. You know, so I don't really mind – we've spoke on the landing, I see how you've spoke with other people, I've seen how you've dealt with them: you've heard them, you've listened to them, you've got your own points of view.

Knowing before an interview begins where a prisoner is from, the work that they have chosen within the prison, or their attitude towards prison staff, provides a practical 'hook' – a way of naturally starting conversation, rather than rigidly following an interview protocol. Likewise, recalling a past conversation with an interviewee or referring to an interaction that has involved them helps to confirm the sincerity of one's interest.

HOW LIFE HISTORY RESEARCH ENHANCES ETHNOGRAPHY

The benefits of linking life history interviewing to ethnographic research go both ways, however. That is, collecting and analyzing life history narratives from individuals in a research setting can greatly enhance one's understanding of field interactions.

Most obviously, life history interviews can clarify the deeper meanings of incidents that have been witnessed during the fieldwork process (see also Hollway and Jefferson, 2000). This may be especially useful when someone's behaviour appears to deviate from dominant cultural norms. For instance, in the first author's prison study, he observed a striking and unusual episode in which a prisoner named 'Andrew'[1] confronted a large and aggressive fellow prisoner who had been abusing an older inmate for his lack of hygiene. This risky intervention, in support of a distinctly low-status and socially isolated prisoner, against a dominant wing resident, was both brave and uncharacteristically public. The incident only made sense when situated in the context of Andrew's life story and analyzed alongside his biographical interview transcript:

> *Was there a stage in your life when you felt like you were a man, rather than a boy?*
> The only thing close to that I can think is, I got put into care when I was fifteen, still at school. [...] It was then that I met people that hadn't got parents, which were already totally, totally out of control. [...] I got bullied in that kid's home [...] and I did start to hate it for a while, y'know, 'James', he's a big skinhead and he made my life a misery. [...] But then I got locked up and I got four months Detention Centre, and when I was there, you get made to do gym, [and] when you come out, you are fit; and when I finished that I went back to the kid's home, and I remember James, on the stairs with a girl, trying to show off, and he smacked me in the mouth, [and I thought:] 'I ain't takin' this anymore,' and I knocked him clean up with two bangers, [...] and within the space of comin' out of that [Detention Centre], within six weeks they were all terrified of me. I realized I could fight. [...] That's when I grew up, when I went first into Detention Centre, because I was forced, I had no option.

Indeed, Andrew himself was able to draw the connection between his past experiences and his current attitudes during the interview (conducted several weeks after the initial incident):

> Even to this day now I can't abide a bully, I won't see it, y'know, because I know from my own personal experience what it's like. And even if I didn't know you and even in 'ere, even though I'm goin' home in five weeks, if I see somebody bullyin' someone, I'd do something about it, I would. [...] Bad as I am, I've got a heart, and when I see that, I feel so sorry for that geezer [and] there's a big rising anger in me for the bully.

Once the first author raised the issue of the above incident during the interview, Andrew reflected further on its meaning:

> I've nearly been in a few fights over that guy. [...] I understand that he smells and all the rest of it, but you don't have to start shoutin' your mouth off and makin' him feel bad, y'know, makin' yourself try to look big, havin' a go at him in front of everybody else. 'Cos it gets to me that much, y'know. I just, I can't understand how people can be so insensitive, y'know. I'm the same outside, I'm exactly the same outside. If one of my mates has a go at somebody, and [if the] guy's scared, [...] I'll stop my friend. [...] I dunno whether that's because of what happened when I was at the kid's home, but I've always been the same. If I can see somebody's scared, I won't let it happen, I'll do whatever I can, not to let it happen.

An interview with another prisoner, 'Jeff', likewise clarified a conversation that had taken place some weeks earlier. Standing on the prison landings one evening, Jeff had explained the frustration of going to bed at night worrying about his children. He was particularly agitated about a motorbike that he had bought for his son before starting his sentence, whose brakes were not working. His wife had sent it to someone to be fixed, but 'nothing's happened for weeks. The guy's missus keeps saying he's not in', and Jeff expressed considerable annoyance that he could not intervene to sort things out.

The researcher noted the conversation but interpreted it only as an unusual manifestation of free-floating anxiety regarding what is going on 'on the outside' that is typical of prisoners (although somewhat out of character for this particular individual). However, when the individual was formally interviewed, without reference to this prior exchange, a series of autobiographical comments revealed the symbolic significance of motorbikes in Jeff's life story:

> *What did you end up in jail for then?*
> What, for me first offences? Me very first offences was just pinchin' motorbikes. [...] I've started hanging around with lads on my estate, and I started nickin' motorbikes – 12, 13 year old – as a kid, I started nickin'

motorbikes. And me dad started beating me up and things, because of that. [...] With me dad, the way he was brought up was, his dad used to beat him up. And he was the same as me when I was little, pinchin' motorbikes and things like that. If he'd a bought me a motorbike, I wouldn't'a pinched one. My lad won't pinch one, I've bought him one, you know what I mean, he doesn't 'ave to pinch one, he's been *bought* one.

Here, then, the nature of Jeff's frustration became apparent only through the elucidation of his life story.

Interviews can be deliberately used to address apparent inconsistencies from the fieldwork phase and to probe beneath public identities. It may be tempting to regard ethnographic encounters as more 'real' than the representations offered within the more organized environment of the interview. However, interviews provide an opportunity for participants to offer alternative versions of the self. In prison, where putting on a 'front' or 'mask' can be important, it is unsurprising that many interviewees distance themselves from their public personae. 'Dan' had a reputation for aggression and instability, and described a number of incidents from his prison career in which he had acted with 'no inner feelings'. Such acts cannot be discounted from assessments of his character, but Dan explained that there was a difference between his public portrayal and his sense of self:

Once I walk out this door I'll be a totally different person, because I don't want people to think I'm a muppet, they can take the piss. So, I look out for myself, it's how you've got to be when you're in this environment.

So you're different in this environment to the way you think of yourself?
I'm totally different. When I'm banged up behind my door I'm totally different, I'm laid back, chilled out, like a normal person. I'm on my own, I've got no one to argue with, no one can wind me up, I'm happy. That's my time to sit and think about other things instead of your daily routine in here.

What's the identity that you have on the wing that you show to other people?

Everyone just leaves me alone. On that wing there is no one on there that can really cause me any trouble or grief. [...] If you put on a front as though you don't care and no one bothers you, then you're going to sail through your sentence, no one will give you any grief. [...] If I've got a problem I'm not going to walk around looking mopey, sad, because someone is going to look at it as a weakness and try and exploit it.

Dan appeared to be hyper-sensitive to minor slights, such as being talked about behind his back. He railed against another prisoner who, by standing on his foot and not apologizing, he felt had 'taken the piss'. Such sensitivities to weakness and disrespect were striking partly because Dan was largely seen as dangerous rather than vulnerable. As he went on to explain, however, one reason why Dan was so keen not to be disrespected was that he was aware of the extreme nature of his reactions. He admitted to harbouring homicidal fantasies when slighted. Elsewhere in the interview, Dan reported having been subjected to serious physical abuse by his father, for which he claimed to be 'really, really grateful': 'it made me into a person that can take a real good kicking [...] I've not got no pain barrier. There's nothing there now to cause me pain.' Dan's lack of compassion for others, his intense response to minor, personal affronts and his attempt to avoid trouble through inhabiting a psychotic persona would appear to be connected to such life experiences.

Other interviews shed light on apparent discrepancies between self-identities and actions, and between seemingly incompatible public roles, in ways that also illuminated the character of prison life. Thus, when prisoners publicly censured heroin users ('smackheads'), but then admitted in interview to themselves being users, it became apparent that the addict identity was stigmatized: 'Even though I know you've seen me smoking gear (heroin) I ain't a smackhead', claimed one interviewee, in what was a common refrain. As subsequent interviews revealed, for those prisoners with reputations as serious or 'professional' criminals, it was especially important to avoid the 'smackhead' label.

In another interview, with a gregarious and dominant prisoner named 'Paul', probing the values and self-image of his autobiographical interview made it possible to reconcile what had appeared to be his somewhat incongruous public identities. Fieldwork observations and conversations suggested that, on the one hand, having been socialized into prison culture from an early age, Paul held rigid anti-establishment views, and identified himself with traditional inmate values. At the same time, however, he was somewhat detached from mainstream inmate culture, and appeared to have little involvement in the internal economy or in the everyday wing politics between prisoners. Moreover, he was deeply involved in prison education: an activity that could be regarded as 'institutional'.

In interview, Paul recounted coming from a close-knit family, run by 'a group of sort of matriarchs [...] proper old battleaxes', who had taught him to treat women with respect. He was among a minority of prisoners who reported having female friends outside prison. Expanding on how this affected him within prison, Paul noted that '95% of the attitudes towards women you meet in prison are not good', and that a 'prevailing attitude' in prison was to 'class the whole of womanhood as bitches and evil scum'. He had himself been 'betrayed' by a woman during his sentence, but was proud not to have submitted to what was a dominant and 'worrying' misogyny: 'I suppose it's my arrogance speaking but I think that my values, my attitudes and my morals that I hold are far superior to most peoples.' Overall, then, Paul was left feeling somewhat different from other prisoners: 'sort of removed. [...] It puts me in a position where I don't quite understand where a lot of them come from. [...] I have to bite my tongue a lot.'

That Paul managed to maintain a credible prison identity was also interesting given his commitment to prison education. He had discovered education early in his sentence, devouring books and their bibliographies until he satisfied his intellectual curiosity. Asked whether this had influenced his self-image, Paul responded that it had done so 'hugely, in quite a few ways', diverting his attention from other things within the system, in both positive and negative ways: it had 'broaden[ed] the horizons' and prevented him from succumbing to the 'destructive forces' of boredom. At the same time, he believed it had stopped him participating in some of the activities that the prison explicitly recognized as positive contributions, such as work with children and the Listeners scheme. However, Paul expressed considerable ambivalence about such schemes, suggesting that he would not want to 'get involved in something just to get out, just to get tick marks on "he's a good boy" sheet', and distinguishing education from other prison activities: 'education is like a separate entity within the prison because they're not part of the establishment, if you know what I mean'. Through such logic, then, Paul had forged a prison role that allowed him to escape anti-institutional temptations and maintain his self-image as different from the inmate mass, without forcing him to engage directly with the establishment's aims or making him appear 'pro-staff'.

Incidents observed *after* an interview has been conducted may make more sense with the knowledge of powerful life events. Early on in his interview, 'Shaun' recalled his stepfather waiting for him to come home from school, 'watching what I was doing [...] and the way I saw it he was trying to catch me out doing things wrong so he had an excuse then to [...] ground me, slap me, whatever.' He went on to describe being beaten not only for very minor incidents, but also for things which continued to influence his thinking in relation to 'trouble':

> It wasn't that he'd beat the truth out of me, which he did a couple of times; he beat me to tell him I'd done something when I hadn't. [...] Even if it wasn't me, he was going to make me say it was me anyway. And I'd have to go through all that pain, for no reason. Even to this day – it's something I say to a few people on the wings – [...] I'm a person where if I'm going to lose out and something's going to happen to me for no apparent reason whatsoever then I get the infamous 'fuck it' attitude. If something's going to happen to me for *no* reason, then I'll be damn sure to make something happen for *some* reason. I'd rather you smack me in the mouth for something I'd done than for something I hadn't done. [...] I may as well create something or do something wrong, you know, than get the amount of trouble I'm going to get for no reason. At least at the back of me mind then I know I've done something wrong. At least compensate for the beating I'm going to get for something that I never did wrong in the first place. [...] Why get your head kicked in for fuck all, when you can get your head kicked in for something? Why get four years for one burglary, when you can go out and get four years for 15 or 20 odd, you know. So I suppose that's, it's that kind of attitude that's stuck with me for a while you know.[2]

In the eyes of the establishment, Shaun was a 'difficult prisoner', whose behaviour was volatile and unpredictable. Yet, for him, when confronted with the possibility of being disciplined, it was rational to respond belligerently, as he did, twice, in subsequent weeks, in ways that would have been opaque without an understanding of his life story.

NARRATIVE IDENTITY AND SUBCULTURAL RESEARCH

Most of the examples above demonstrate how biographical interviewing can help researchers interpret the actions of individual actors in a research setting. However, a principal goal of much ethnographic research, of course, is to better understand the ways and norms of groups or subcultures. Indeed, one risk in utilizing a narrative psychology framework in field settings is the potential for making overly reductionist interpretations of such social milieus. In other words, repeatedly ascribing the origins of various interactions to the autobiographical understandings of individual participants may ignore the ways in which subcultural involvement itself shapes individual identities and self-understandings.

Nonetheless, the value of narratives for making sense of sociological patterns in institutions or subcultures should not be underestimated. Again, prison research illustrates this point well. The classic literature on prison subculture has been almost entirely sociological in focus, demonstrating how institutional constraints lead to various social behaviours and norms. However, many of these characteristics of prison life may also be illuminated by an appreciation for the autobiographical self-understandings of prisoners.

One recurrent discourse, expressed frequently and vehemently (as in Andrew's case, above), is a hostility to bullying and the exploitation of the vulnerable. Prisoners insist that bullying is not tolerated, and that those who attempt it are quickly and forcefully 'dealt with'. As the following interview quotes suggest, this norm may have roots in prisoners' personal experiences:

> I don't like bullying. I really don't like bullies at all. [...] Because I have been bullied before, and I don't like people violently hurting me. [...] If you've got a big fellow bullying a little kid, then it is something to do with me, because it's wrong. It's wrong in outside society and it's wrong in here.

> 'Steve' was being bullied [...]. Now, if anyone goes near him to give him any grief whatsoever the person that gives him grief will be like out of the jail in hospital, because he's been bullied the whole of his life. I was bullied by my dad up to the age of 18 so I know what

being bullied is like. [...] I walked into the pad of the [bully], the geezer is there with his mates laughing so I grabbed him by the throat up against the window. I said 'why don't you try slapping me?' – he said 'I've got no problem with you' – I said 'but you've got a problem with him because he can't defend himself'. [...] I hate people that pick on the weak in jail, I really do detest bullies in jail.

I couldn't stand fucking bullying. I was bullied in school. And from as early an age as I can remember, even in pubs, if I saw somebody take the piss out of somebody [...] I'd stand by him, and embarrass him. 'How would you feel?'. [...] That was one of my morals. That was one of my codes. Always look out for the vulnerable guys. And I still stick to that rule today. [...] Once upon a time I was little, and I was vulnerable, and I was picked on. And the day I snapped is the day I swore that I won't tolerate it. I will not let that happen in front of me. And I've stuck by my guns ever since. [...] I've been bullied, and being picked on – people don't understand the effect it can have on someone.

This is not to suggest that codes relating to bullying are reducible to the biographical experiences of prisoners. Ideals of mutual aid between prisoners can also be seen as a functional response to the pains of imprisonment (Sykes, 1958). However, for some prisoners in particular, this is an issue which has normative as well as practical significance, rooted in personal histories. For researchers interested in the origins and functions of the 'inmate code', this is an important observation.

Another striking aspect of inmate subculture is a somewhat contradictory attitude towards women, including female officers. As discussed above, women were commonly denigrated as manipulative, unfaithful and malevolent, and were highly objectified as sex objects. Yet they were also held up as beacons of virtue and salvation, particularly mothers and grandmothers, and were treated and talked about in ways that displayed courtesy, chivalry and sentimentalism.[3] Interviews suggested that these patterns were embedded in life experiences and values, as well as being responses to the sexual and emotional frustrations of prison life.

For example, Owen's life story included multiple, contemptuous references to women. Girlfriends, who were often prostitutes, were referred to as 'whores', including Owen's own sister, about whom he expressed passionate, at times confusing, views, that signalled feelings of betrayal as well as disgust:

She started to smoke crack and that and she's a whore now and I hate her guts. [...] Because when I used to go to prison and secure units all over the country, she would come and visit me. [...] She used to be wicked [i.e., great]. Wicked. She was so lovely. [...] Now, it's totally, totally changed. Everything about her. She's just a bitch. She's horrible. She's got three kids. She don't even see them. She don't give a shit about herself. She's just fucked. She's a lost cause, she really is. I mean I love her to bits, it's my sister, I always will, we shared the same bathwater as kids. But I hate her as well. I fucking hate – I hate her. I hate what she's become anyway. I truly hate what she's become. I've been here for three years, she's come to see me once.

His antipathy towards other women, often expressed through violence, also related to notions of being 'disrespected' and anxieties about control:

And a lot of women will suck crack dealers' dicks, basically, for crack. And that's why she'd get a beating, basically. [...] I'm not forcing her to go out there and sell her body. But if she whores about with crack dealers and people I know, then to me, she's disrespecting me. If she wants to go and do a punter, I don't mind that. But if it's people I know, then I'm not having that. I've done some bad things. [...] Saying that, if I didn't do that, they'd run fucking rings round me.

In contrast, Owen described his mother in highly idealized terms: 'the most beautifullest woman I know. The most loving, caring woman I know [...]. Just a beautiful woman. Lovely, in every sense. Just my best mate.' Although she had beaten him as a child, she had also provided unconditional love:

I can always remember my mum saying to me 'Look, you are what you are. You are my first born and I love you to bits. The only thing I ask of you is tell me the truth. Never lie to me. Just tell me the truth and I'll be there for you.' And I respect her for that. And all the shit I've put her through as well. [...] And she's always there for me. Always sends my money. I love her to bits.

Given her unqualified support for him, it was significant that Owen's mother was 'the only person I've got 100 per cent faith in'. Likewise, both of the other people who Owen adulated offered the same unreserved love: a substitute father figure, and – somewhat ironically – a prostitute whom he saw as a 'big sister' rather than a 'whore', and who 'even though she was a crack addict [...] She'd always come and make sure I was alright. [...] She'd just look after me'.

Owen's attitude towards female officers seemed to echo his negative life experiences with women and his anxieties about respect. He described having had confrontations with his female personal officer, reflecting that 'maybe they think I'm a pushover and they can take the piss, and when I snap, they think "well, maybe not"'. One incident involved a female officer having taken down from his window a curtain that we had placed there against the rules. Incensed, Owen challenged the officer, and recalled responding to her explanation as follows: 'I says "look, let me break something down for you. Have a bit of fucking respect." [...] And I said "Look, you're a bitch. Do that again and I'll knock you out. I don't care if you're a woman. I'll punch you in your face."'

Asked if he had a different relationship with female officers than with male officers, he answered: 'I hate them, female officers. I fucking hate them. I hate them. Not because they're women. [...] – I suppose it's got something to do with them being women.' Providing an explanation, he recounted an incident in which a female officer had told him and a friend 'loads of things real personal', but subsequently disciplined the friend without discussing it with them first. Owen clearly resented that, having established some level of intimacy with them, she had then exerted power over them, regarding this as a typically female betrayal: 'How can

you sit there and tell people [things], laugh and joke with him, then when you leave, go up to security and get him [done] for something he said? Fucking bitch. All women screws are like that. [...] They'll go on safe at you, laugh and joke. Then they'll just switch on you.'

Though not typical, such views were not unusual. Prisoners described female officers in terms that were considerably more emotionally charged than those used for male officers. The recurrent labelling of female (but much less often male) officers as 'two-faced' was symptomatic of the way in which many prisoners encouraged them into nurturing or sexual roles, and resented them when they acted in accordance with their official responsibilities. Often, then, prisoners projected on to female officers the terms of actual or desired relationships with women who were not present in the prison, especially mothers and girlfriends. This could entail positive as well as negative sentiments: 'The older female staff, I talk to them like me nan', reported one prisoner; another said:

> You do treat women different. People might find this a bit sexist and that but I treat most women I come across like I'd treat me own mum. [...] It's very rare that I'll swear in front of a woman officer, I wouldn't. I daren't swear in front of me mum, [...] that's how I was brought up [...]. If you sit down and talk to a woman officer, it's like you are talking to them as, you know, as a woman.

At the same time, most prisoners claimed that they would intervene without hesitation in a situation where a female officer was in danger of being attacked, whereas a male officer might not elicit the same response. Prisoners outlined their logic not just in terms of their values ('it's just the way I was brought up ...'), but also life events. Thus, one prisoner explained that he would step in to protect a female officer because his home life meant that he had seen 'enough women getting hit' in his life. Again, then, attitudes towards women were an aspect of prison culture that was inflected by personal experiences as well as general cultural mores outside prison and the inherent characteristics of prison life.

IN SUMMARY

The idea that identity takes the form of a self-narrative has become nearly paradigmatic in the humanities and social science. What this typically means for researchers is that in order to understand why people behave the way they do, it is important to understand the personal myths by which they live. This does not necessarily mean that the best form of research involves the collection of oral history data, however. Indeed, there are numerous reasons to think that ethnographic interactions with individuals in their 'natural environment' provides an equally good, if rather more time-intensive, method for accessing self-narratives. At the very least, fieldwork can greatly enhance a researcher's access to life history information and can be of considerable value in interpreting life stories.

While benefiting from ethnographic work, life interviews also enhance the ethnographic process. Most obviously, they aid further interaction with interviewees and provide interpretive guidance on potentially salient issues. In addition, however, the systematic collection of autobiographical data can even help shed light on unusual aspects of subcultural and institutional behaviour. Although researchers need to avoid the hazards of reductionism in their interpretation of field interactions, the combination of life history methodology with ethnographic observations appears to be a highly complementary form of research triangulation and worthy of greater utilization.

NOTES

1 All names used here are pseudonyms.

2 Another prisoner told a similar story of abuse and its effects on his mentality:

> I was beaten by my dad from a very early age. I think that made me want to rebel even more. I'd sit there and think, at least I'm getting a kicking for something I had done, even if they didn't know I'd done it. [...] I was being beaten by my dad every day, so if I was doing something, even if they didn't know about it, then in my head it would just be that I'd been found out by dad and he was giving me a beating for it, even though he knew nothing, they didn't know for quite a while when I was doing things.

3 Female researchers are almost always referred to as 'miss'; prisoners often apologise for swearing in front of women; and there is little embarrassment about romantic gestures directed towards women, whereas most other forms of emotion are proscribed.

REFERENCES

Bertaux, Daniel (1981) *Biography and Society: The Life History Approach in the Social Sciences.* London: Sage.

Bruner, Jerome S. (1987) 'Life as narrative', *Social Research*, 54: 11–32.

Carroll, Leo (1974) *Hacks, Blacks and Cons: Race Relations in a Maximum Security Prison.* Lexington, MA: Lexington Books.

Caspi, Avshalom and Moffitt, Terrie E. (1995) 'The continuity of maladaptive behavior: from description to understanding in the study of antisocial behavior', in Dante Cicchetti and Donald J. Cohen (eds), *Developmental Psychopathology: Vol. 2. Risk, Disorder and Adaptation.* New York: Wiley.

Clemmer, Donald (1940) *The Prison Community.* New York: Rinehart.

Crewe, Ben (forthcoming) 'Codes and conventions: the terms and conditions of contemporary inmate values', in Alison Liebling and Shadd Maruna (eds), *The Effects of Imprisonment.* Cullompton, UK: Willan.

Epstein, Seymour and Erskine, Nancy (1983) 'The development of personal theories of reality from an interactional perspective', in D. Magnusson and V.L. Allen (eds), *Human Development: An Interactional Perspective.* New York: Academic Press.

Fromm, Erich (1941) *Escape from Freedom.* New York: Farrar & Rinehart.

Gergen, Kenneth (1971) *The Concept of Self.* London: Holt, Rinehart & Winston.

Giddens, Anthony (1991) *Modernity and Self-Identity: Self and Society in the Late Modern Age.* Stanford, CA: Stanford University Press.

Hollway, Wendy and Jefferson, Tony (2000) *Doing Qualitative Research Differently: Free Association, Narrative, and the Interview Method.* Thousand Oaks, CA: Sage.

Josselson, Ruthellen and Lieblich, Amia (eds) (1993) *The Narrative Study of Lives: Vol. 1.* Thousand Oaks, CA: Sage.

Maruna, Shadd (1997) 'Going straight: desistance from crime and self-narratives of reform', *Narrative Study of Lives,* 5: 59–97.

Maruna, Shadd (2001) *Making Good: How Ex-Convicts Reform and Rebuild Their Lives.* Washington, DC: American Psychological Association Books.

Maruna, Shadd and Ramsden, Derek (2004) 'Living to tell the tale: redemption narratives, shame management and offender rehabilitation', in A. Lieblich, D.P. McAdams, and J. Josselson (eds), *Healing Plots: The Narrative Basis of Psychotherapy.* Washington, DC: American Psychological Association. pp. 129–51.

Mathiesen, Thomas (1965) *The Defences of the Weak: A Sociological Study of a Norwegian Correctional Institution.* London: Tavistock.

McAdams, Dan P. (1985) *Power, Intimacy and the Life Story: Personological Inquiries into Identity.* New York: Guilford.

McAdams, Dan P. (1993) *The Stories We Live By: Personal Myths and the Making of the Self.* New York: W. Morrow.

McAdams, Dan P. (1999) 'Personal narratives and the life story', in Lawrence A. Pervin and Oliver P. John (eds), *Handbook of Personality: Theory and Research* (2nd edn). New York: Guilford. pp. 478–500.

Sarbin, Theodore R. (1986) 'The narrative as a root metaphor for psychology', in Theodore R. Sarbin (ed.), *Narrative Psychology: The Storied Nature of Human Conduct.* New York: Praeger.

Schütz, Astrid and Baumeister, Roy F. (1999) *Journal of Language and Social Psychology,* 18: 269–86.

Scott, Marvin B. and Stanford, M. Lyman (1968) 'Accounts', *American Sociological Review,* 33: 46–61.

Smith, Charles P. (ed.) (1992) *Handbook of Thematic Content Analysis.* New York: Cambridge University Press.

Stewart, Abigail J., Franz, C. and Layton, L. (1988) 'The changing self: using personal documents to study lives', *Journal of Personality,* 56: 41–74.

Sykes, Gresham (1958) *Society of Captives.* Princeton, NJ: Princeton University Press.

White, Michael and Epston, David (1990) *Narrative Means to Therapeutic Ends.* New York: Norton.

White, William Foote (1943/1989) *Street Corner Society: The Social Structure of an Italian Slum* (4th edn). Chicago: University of Chicago.

8

'You Don't Do Fieldwork, Fieldwork Does You': Between Subjectivation and Objectivation in Anthropological Fieldwork

BOB SIMPSON

While in the thick of fieldwork in rural Sri Lanka in the late 1970s, I wrote a letter to my supervisor complaining bitterly about the way I was being manipulated by my principal informant.[1] My gatekeeper had turned into something of a gateblocker, who had begun to proscribe the key people I wanted to contact in his community. My supervisor seemed rather amused at my frustrations. He no doubt recognised a point at which he and, no doubt, numerous others had reached as they tried to gain a precarious foothold in other peoples' lifeworlds. In response, he made one of his typically pithy observations, pointing out that 'you don't do fieldwork, fieldwork does you'. At that time, this simple aphorism provided a crucial learning point about the nature of participant observation. However much we might wish to assume the identity of an academic researcher replete with methods, theories and learned degrees, the truth is that once we step into the complex flow of other people's social experience we are novices and bumbling incompetents, largely oblivious to the complex and multiple layering of our informants' lives, identities and histories. Furthermore, it takes months and even years to attain the kind of basic social and cultural competences that are necessary if our descriptions are to derive any 'thickness' in the Geertzian sense. But, competence takes many forms and ones that go well beyond the cultural *faux pas* which feature in the confessional accounts of some anthropologists and what has become a familiar strain of what Geertz once referred to as 'the diary disease' (Geertz, 1988: 89).

In this chapter I am interested to explore a particular kind of incompetence, namely in the management of power and the micropolitics of the field. The realisation of deficit in this regard can be enormously discomfiting for social scientists when in the field because, not unreasonably, we claim to have some expertise when it comes to understanding social life and like to preserve the fiction that our research is carefully planned and executed. However, ethnographic fieldwork is a messy business which can and should puncture these pretensions. It requires us to relinquish expert status and embark on the uncomfortable process of learning about persons and power from scratch and often through mistakes and manifest ignorance. Indeed, the messiness of participant observation once moved Lofland to describe it as 'sprawling, diffuse, undefined and diverse. As a research genre it appears (relative to other domains of social science) organizationally and technologically the most personalized and primitive' (Lofland, 1974 cited in van Maanen 1988: 24. See also Strathern, 1991). For anthropologists, this version of ethnographic practice is both essential and appropriate when it comes to capturing the rich and complex textures of social life as lived in different but increasingly interconnected social and cultural settings, leading Strathern to comment that 'if at the end of the twentieth century one were inventing a method of enquiry by which to grasp the complexity of social life, one might wish to invent something like the social anthropologist's ethnographic practice' (Strathern, 1999: 1). But, at a time when there is a considerable undertow pulling social research practice towards ever more prescribed forms, such strengths are apt to be construed as weaknesses. The idea that one might be 'done', even if heuristically so, by one's fieldwork rather than 'doing' it in accord with some quasi-experimental, managerial model would not go down well on a grant application form. Yet, all ethnographers are, to some degree or other, 'done' by their fieldwork; rather like sex in Victorian society, everybody knows that this goes on, it is just that we prefer not to talk about it in polite company (but see Lareau and Schultz, 1996).

I am interested here in considering process variables, such as these, which are often ignored in the alchemy of turning base experience into communicable knowledge in the form of ethnographic writing. I want to highlight some of the patterns that are discernible when one steps back and looks at a self caught up in processes that can only be understood once out of the field and the ferment of intense engagement with ethnographic enquiry has begun to subside. Such patterns are apt to be startling for the order, symmetries, repetition and consistency they display but, more importantly, they are fundamental when it comes to understanding the way that theory and ethnography merge into and out of one another in academic practice. The device that I use to explore this alchemy of ethnography is a movement back and forth between the notions of subjectivation and objectivation. By subjectivation, I mean the way in which those in the fields in which we work construct the researcher as a person or self who is aspiring to achieve some level of participation, rapport or, in more recent theorisations of fieldwork, 'complicity' (see Marcus, 1997 for a critique). The fieldworker, as a living, social presence, has to be fitted in and made sense of as coming from somewhere, for some purpose and with a good deal of baggage that is of interest to the host community. By objectivation, I follow closely the notion put forward by Bourdieu in his attempt to carve out a scientific reflexivity in social science praxis, as distinct from the 'narcissistic reflexivity' of postmodernism and the 'egological reflexivity' of phenomenology (Bourdieu, 2003). As he explains, his aim in invoking this notion is not to explore.

[the] 'lived experience' of the knowing subject but the social conditions of possibility – and therefore the effects and limits – of that experience and, more precisely, of the act of objectivation itself. It aims at

objectivising the subjective relation to the object which, far from leading to a relativistic and more-or-less anti-scientific subjectivism is one of the conditions of genuine scientific objectivity. (Bourdieu, 2003: 282)

In other words, cold reflection on the personal circumstances of fieldwork is pressed explicitly into the business of making sense of different social and political realities and then rendering this sense into more or less coherent ethnography. However, consideration of objectivation is also heavily implicated in the process of subjectivation; the social conditions of possibility that Bourdieu outlines are not just bracketed by what one takes into the field, but also by the particular forms and circumstances of social interaction once there. In a crude attempt to out-Bourdieu Bourdieu, one might propose that logically we should subjectivise the objective relation to the subject.

To date, participant observation has been the opposition used to frame the subject–object conundrum. However, although a useful umbrella term to capture the general act of 'being there', it remains a vague and uncomfortable oxymoron. The notion of participation is oddly neutral and covers a multitude of possible positions *vis-à-vis* the object of research, while observation carries with it an idea of distance and separation which harks back to natural science models of investigation. Drawing attention to the experiences that connect objectivation with subjectivation takes us a small step further in that it reminds us, first, that the researcher is not simply observing, but observing from precise coordinates within space, time and individual biography and, second, that these play a part in the way that our various interlocutors make sense of us in their worlds. But, outing the animateur of ethnographic research is, of course, nothing new. It has long been the case that basic markers such as gender (e.g., Bell et al., 1993) and ethnicity

(e.g., Kondo, 1990) are recognised as playing their part in determining how one interacts with a field of social relations and in turn how this shapes the resulting ethnography. The theme that I wish to take up here is the rather less considered one of temporality and how the trajectory of the 'ethnographic self' (Coffey, 1999) impacts upon research in different locations across the lifecourse of the academic researcher. In a recent essay, Simon Coleman (nd) has referred to this as the problem of the multi-sited ethnographer, in contrast to the currently influential notion of multi-sited ethnography (Marcus, 1995; Hastrup and Fog-Olwick, 1996). In so doing, Coleman highlights the crucial temporal contrast with the more spatially oriented conceptualizations of how one field relates to another. Ethnographers do not just work in different spatial locations, they also work in those locations across time and are themselves subject to particular lifecourse events and processes which we subsume under the label 'ageing' (Reed-Danahay, 1997). Thus, how one does and is in turn 'done' by fieldwork as a young man or woman is very different from the same process 20 years later (Parkin, 2000: 259).

In what follows, I recount two episodes of ethnographic fieldwork each in a very different context in Sri Lanka. The first was in 1978–80 when I undertook doctoral research into the transmission of ritual traditions among the drummer caste (*beravayo*).[2] The second, carried out over several visits (2000, 2002, 2003) and totalling five months was among doctors, clinicians and other professionals involved in debating and devising strategies for the regulation of new reproductive and genetic technologies.[3] On the face of it, one could not imagine two more different settings in which to conduct ethnographic research. In one I worked with a group of low-caste, marginal and impoverished artisans; in the other I worked among elites of the highest order who command considerable social and economic capital by virtue of their class and profession. Here I describe each of these field settings, comparing and contrasting their distinctive dynamics and how in the oscillation between subjectivation and objectivation fundamental patterns and dynamics have emerged.

DRUMMERS

In October 1978, at the age of 23, I went to Sri Lanka with the intention of carrying out doctoral fieldwork into artistic traditions and indigenous notions of creativity. I was young and inexperienced. Although I had studied South Asian culture and society as part of my undergraduate degree, read pretty widely the social science literature on Sri Lanka, visited several leading anthropologists who had worked in the region and taken two months of lessons in Sinhala from a Sri Lankan PhD student, I had never visited the island before. Needless to say, when I arrived nothing looked or felt quite like it did when, in the months leading up to the fieldwork, I followed Malinowski's advice and 'imagined myself set down'. The richness and complexity of what I encountered left me at once enchanted and terrified. 'Operationalising' plans and intentions for fieldwork was almost impossible and most of my energies seemed to go into the business of simply getting by on a day-to-day basis in a third world country. There was a good deal of trial and error with a propensity for the latter. What was proving to be a rather unfocused ramble through sites of artistic production and creativity was given considerably more definition following a chance meeting with Professor Bruce Kapferer, then of Adelaide University. Kapferer had already

carried out extensive fieldwork among the drummer caste (*beravayo*) in the south of the island (Kapferer, 1983) and instantly made the connection between the kinds of question I wanted to explore and the group with which he was already familiar. On his advice I visited the area north of Akuressa in the southern province and began to establish contact with Berava communities in the area.

The Berava are historically linked with the provision of drumming and dancing to royal courts and temples (Ryan, 1953: 124–5). Largely through their role as temple functionaries and the providers of exorcism and healing rituals, the Berava have been responsible for the maintenance and transmission of a significant portion of the ritual knowledge and skills that underpin Sinhalese popular traditions, and particularly in the southern provinces (Kapferer, 1983; Simpson, 1984). In addition to dancing and drumming, the community are also renowned for mask-making, astrology, temple sculpture, magical use of incantations (*mantra*) and verses (*set kavi* and *vas kavi*) as well as the more mundane crafts of carpentry and house-building.

My point of introduction to the Berava community was a man named Cyril, a drummer and a senior member of the community who Kapferer had recommended I meet. Cyril made me welcome and offered me whatever assistance I wanted. He said he would introduce me to his extensive network of kin, take me to rituals and furnish whatever information I needed. I truly felt I had made an enormous breakthrough. I was at last doing an anthropology which bore some resemblance to what every other anthropologist I had ever read about or spoken to had done. I had arrived! Through the guidance and support of Cyril I began to map out the contours of the Berava community in that area and to see the extraordinary breadth of knowledge and skills that underpinned their ritual performances and artistic productions. However, long-term fieldwork inevitably takes one beyond the frontstage, beyond politeness and apparent openness and into the more complex dynamics of power relations. Things were far from straightforward between Cyril and I, and between Cyril and his own community. The dawning realisation that fieldwork is indeed a messy business is captured in the introduction to my PhD thesis which I reproduce *in extenso*:

> I became an important source of kudos for Cyril in his political machinations within his own community. Consequently, in my interactions with his kinsmen, I became the subject of an explicit and often exaggerated control by him. This issue remained a source of conflict right up until the very final day of my fieldwork: a salutary lesson that the field anthropologist is never a free agent but, as an inevitable result of the sequence and types of relationship made in the initial stages of fieldwork, is the subject of a determinism that carries him or her, whether they realise it or not, along the internal cleavages of a small community. Thus, certain kinsmen and even whole villages were proscribed by Cyril whilst other interactions were encouraged. The picture of the community I eventually arrived at was seen through an aperture of which I thought I was in control but which, in fact, Cyril himself controlled and directed. (Simpson, 1984: 6)

In truth, I still feel a frisson of anger as I recall the occasions when I was blocked and outwitted in my attempts to shape my fieldwork according to the plans that I had rather than those that suited his purposes. However, my overwhelming feeling was, and remains, one of immense gratitude, not only because he introduced me to a version of Berava social networks as they centred on him, but, more importantly, my daily frustrations taught me something far more profound about the inescapable relationship between power and knowledge.

As a novice fieldworker I assumed I had gone to the field to 'collect' data and not become the pawn in power games I could hardly begin to imagine at that stage. Yet, at the outset I had, with Cyril's generous help, successfully opened up a social space within the Berava community. This space was fashioned out of the gradual building of trust, gift transactions and exchange, affection, practical kinship knowledge and being a regular presence in daily life. The problems began when I started to develop pretensions to what might be described as anthropological omnipresence: the idea that having successfully opened up one space in the community I might exercise autonomy and open up similar spaces in other parts of the community. Social mobility and elevation above the particular networks into which I had inadvertently become locked was linked in my mind to the idea that reflexivity was all very well but there also had to be some objectivity in there too. Needless to say, Cyril was not particularly bothered about the finer points of epistemology; what he was concerned about was the day-to-day management of power relations in his community. Being something of a 'big man', he was caught in a round of seemingly relentless demands from kin seeking help (*udava*) and patronage. As a westerner closely allied to him, I was also caught up in this process, a definite source of status and occasional material benefit. To have me stumbling around the community without his guidance and therefore out of his control was a social disaster for him, a wasteful and non-strategic use of the social and economic capital that I evidently represented.

However, the problem Cyril had with the free-floating ethnographer was not just about material resources that might go astray. Of far greater significance in terms of the politics of the community, and what I eventually came to write about, was the question of knowledge – who had it, where it came from and who it would be passed on to. An important lesson that I soon came to learn was that for this community the corpus of knowledge and practice, which we think of collectively as tradition, was not something that attached lightly and evenly to them, but was deeply implicated in questions of social and cultural reproduction and differentiation within the group. It later struck me that what I had assumed was a kind of cultural property, that is, one that is passed on openly and which is widely available, was in fact more like intellectual property for which issues of ownership and retention come into play (Simpson, 1997; and see Strathern, 1996). Indeed, the analogy with property and ownership proved particularly productive in making sense of the dynamics of this community. Those who were rich in knowledge and skills used them not just as the means to a livelihood, but as the basis of marital alliance and hence as a means to achieve cooperation in performance with kin and, crucially, to make demands upon them for the tutelage of their children. Knowledge could be easily lost when over-retentive teachers died, or it could even be stolen by those prepared to crib distinctive items, such as dance steps, verses or stylistic features from another's repertoire. Indeed, performers were keenly aware of who knew what and how they came to know it. In this secretive and turbulent setting, relations of cooperation and conflict held people together and the idea of someone oblivious to all this blithely asking questions could be disruptive and even dangerous. I recall how on one occasion I asked an old teacher (*gurunanse*) if he could recite for me some particular verses (*kavi*) used in a particular ritual. He laughed out loud at the prospect, pointing out that he had not yet even taught the verses to his own son. In other words, knowledge and skill are the basis of hierarchy, distinction and identity, which in turn give cooperation in work its

particular social dynamic, even where a father and son are concerned.

Thus, I did not just collect fieldwork data from the Berava, I entered a world of social relations at a precise point. Furthermore, the coordinates of that point are more usefully located and described by thinking in terms of subjectivation and objectivation rather than by, for example, the notions of participation and observation. To think in terms of the former allows a more explicit articulation with the ethnographic texts that will follow So, what seemed like small-minded power games, when viewed from close proximity, came to form part of a far more interesting interweaving of cultural and political processes when viewed from a distance. What I had hit upon was something fundamental and illuminating regarding the social organisation of knowledge in this community. I had also learnt an important lesson about the way that this knowledge is neither neutral nor anodyne but is highly charged and therefore capable of causing disruption of one kind or another if not handled according to the norms and values of the community. I could have known none of this before going to the field and neither would I have begun to make sense of it in the way that I did had I not experienced a degree of social dissonance with Cyril and his kin.

DOCTORS

In 2000, I returned to Sri Lanka to undertake a very different kind of fieldwork. In the years since my initial fieldwork I had maintained my interest in kinship and had been a researcher into various aspects of divorce and family change in the UK. This work eventually led me into an interest in the new reproductive technologies and their impacts on relationships. In 1999, a chance finding of the website of the Human Genetics Unit at the University of Colombo Medical Faculty prompted me to consider the question of how technologies such as in-vitro fertilisation, paternity testing, gamete donation and new forms of pre-natal testing and selection were being received in a country such as Sri Lanka. The exciting prospect presented itself of tying research ends together, that is, bringing my knowledge of and interest in Sri Lankan culture and society together with my interests in the new reproductive and genetic technologies. Much had been written at that time about the ethical, social and legal implications of the new technologies in Euro-American societies, but virtually nothing had been written about their reception in the developing world.[4] The knot that emerged once I set about tying these ends together turned out to be the question of regulation and what role bioethics played in the construction of a response to these powerful and globally diffused technologies. And so it was that in 2000 I began an ethnographic study of the medical and professional community in the capital, Colombo. I was interested in how these professionals were going about the practical work of ushering in the new technologies as well as the intellectual work of regulating, assimilating and otherwise rendering these technologies socially and culturally meaningful.[5] Unlike the Berava, there was no community as such here, but a network of professionals linked by the challenge of responding to the new and boundary-crossing technologies ushered in by advances in embryology and molecular genetics. These individuals were, in every sense of the word 'elites', the '"makers and shakers": groups whose "cultural capital" positioned them above their fellow citizens and whose decisions crucially shape what happens in the wider society' (Shore and Nugent, 2002: 3). What I was trying to capture in this

fieldwork is neatly summarised by Marcus, who in reflecting on changes in the nature of fieldwork over the last 20 or so years, suggests that 'what ethnographers in this changed *mis-en-scene* want from subjects is not so much local knowledge as an articulation of the forms of anxiety that are generated by the awareness of being affected by what is elsewhere without knowing what the particular connections to that elsewhere might be' (Marcus, 1997: 97).

On the face of it, this piece of work and my earlier work among the Berava could not have been more different, and I approached the new research with this assumption very much in mind. In this context, I was of similar age to many of my informants and fitted into the gerontocratic hierarchy of the medical community in a way that I could never have done as a young man. Also, as a tenured academic with considerable research experience and publications in socio-legal studies of the family in the UK (e.g., Simpson, 1998), I fortunately did not need to invoke my research with the Berava as part of my credentials. From my earlier experience working with the Berava I knew that members of the English-speaking middle classes often viewed such communities with great disdain. Therefore, the following wind that I used to waft me into this new context was my reputation in UK research and not the fact that I had carried out doctoral research with low-caste, magico-ritual specialists in Sri Lanka. In further keeping with Marcus's changing *mis-en-scene*, my second fieldwork was experimental, risky and moved well beyond the located community which features so prominently in classical ethnographic research (Marcus, 1998: 234).

To reiterate briefly, then, at points over 20 years apart, I worked with two communities widely separated in socio-spatial terms. I only thought in terms of difference – apart from the fact that both groups lived in the same nation-state, similarities seemed implausible. The Berava I worked with were low-caste and marginal, while the doctors were elites, wielding considerable power and influence in Sri Lankan society. While the Berava were Sinhala speakers who operated in a rural setting, the doctors I interviewed and mixed with were English speakers and operated in urban settings. The Berava are generally associated with the despised art of drumming and the irrationalities of ritual healing and exorcism. Doctors, on the other hand, are considered the epitome of rationality, dedicated to the project of progress and modernity through the advance of medical science. What these differences amounted to, in effect, was that when working with the Berava I was operating on the anthropologist's more familiar incline and 'studying down', whereas in the latter I was definitely 'studying up' (Nader, 1972).

At root, the distinction between 'studying down' and 'studying up' centres on the question of power. While for the Berava, a white academic in their midst represented *kudos* and therefore a resource that had to be managed, among the doctors there was no question of my serving such a purpose. Indeed, the situation was quite the opposite. I was a 'doctor', but not a medical doctor, and therefore for them counted as one from that world of prolixity and imprecision that is the social sciences. Furthermore, my general impression was that doctors were so preoccupied with their own professional structures of status and hierarchy that a social scientist, even if foreign, had little to offer them by way of *kudos* or anything else. Nonetheless, the medical professionals I encountered were friendly and polite in their responses, as they responded to my evident interest in their views and activities.

While *kudos* may have contributed little to the dynamics of my relationships with

doctors, the fact I was, in academic terms, a fellow traveller did. As a researcher, it was assumed that my gaze would parallel theirs and be focused on the public they served. The prospect that it might stray on to them was somewhat problematic and often triggered strategies of deflection and obfuscation. The reasons for such responses are not difficult to figure. In recent years, the medical profession has come in for much criticism. The gradual move to an open and deregulated economy over the last 20 years has produced a massive rise in private-sector medical provision and a growing place for the profit motive in the relationship of many doctors with their patients. Thus, a profession which once received reverence bordering on the divine has been widely tainted by allegations of greed and negligence. Social scientists are not renowned for their reticence on such issues and doctors are on the look out for those who might cause damage to individual doctors or their professional community. Similarly, allowing a researcher to stray beyond the frontstage of a 'gentlemanly' medical profession and into the turbulent rough and tumble of backstage medical politics is not to be encouraged either. In Sri Lanka, as anywhere else, people don't like to wash their dirty linen in the street.

What all of this adds up to is a difference in the status and impact of the representations that the ethnographer produces. With the Berava, the reality is that, because I published very little from that research, did not have my PhD translated into Sinhala and was unable to return to Sri Lanka for many years, they never got access to the literary representations that I constructed of them. In truth, the fact that I wrote a PhD in which a section of their community figured centrally had little consequence for them then or now. Doctors, on the other hand, present an entirely different proposition. They expect to see the work that I carry out and I, in turn, expect them to see it. Also, in some of the more policy-related aspects of my work, I have co-written with local doctors and academics (e.g., Dissanayake et al., 2002; Simpson et al., nd). If I get my facts wrong or my representations are deemed inappropriate or misleading, I will find out through one channel or another. In this context, because I am both 'studying up' and studying across cultures, the authority of representation cannot be taken for granted in the way that it was when I researched the Berava 25 years ago – representations are, in a real sense, negotiated. Being 'done' therefore does not stop when one leaves the field but goes on into the process of writing.

So much for the differences. As my attempt to develop ethnographic research set amidst the intellectual activity of doctors and other professionals involved with the new technologies got under way, similarities began to emerge between the two settings which were unexpected, illuminating and, on occasion, startling.

Perhaps the most obvious similarity was that in both settings I was dealing with individuals who were elites within their own communities: among the Berava I spent time with virtuoso performers and revered elders; among the doctors it was respected practitioners and those who had reached positions of seniority and influence in the profession. For practitioners in both contexts, the creation of reputation and respect was built upon a rigorous training in which knowledge and skill, and how and from whom these were acquired, played a crucial part. Although constructing genealogies of medical elites was outside the scope of my study, the number of times kin relationships cropped up did lead me to think that this would make a fascinating study. Indeed, in

ways that had powerful resonances with the Berava, kinship, reputation and practice seemed closely intertwined in the professional lives of doctors, creating all-important networks, alliances and status hierarchies which I occasionally glimpsed beneath the relatively featureless exterior of the medical community. As with the Berava, claiming kinship relationship to and professional genealogy from particular teachers proved to be as important for the doctors as it did for the Berava in their ideas about their individual *paramparava* or learning pedigree. Furthermore, although there is no such thing as a caste of doctors, it did strike me how often doctors married doctors, had parents who were doctors and aspired for their children to be doctors in ways which consolidate and perpetuate medical elites.

One rather curious overlap occurred in conversation with a doctor who was highly critical of elites within the medical establishment. He referred to these elites as the *bamunu kuliya*, meaning the Brahmin caste. The use of this term struck me as very interesting as some of my Berava informants would refer to themselves as the *bamunu kuliya*. For them, the use was a device to attribute high-status origins to their low-status existence. Describing themselves as *bamunu kuliya* linked the knowledge and activities of Berava with high-caste Brahmins, who were believed to have brought the arts of exorcism and healing to Sri Lanka at some point before the colonial period. Somehow the caste fell from grace and things that were once 'high' became low and devalued. This narrative was used to explain a number of features of caste and identity among the Berava, such as the refusal of higher castes to share a table with members of the caste: high-caste people see it as an indication of their superior status; the Berava, on the other hand, explain this behaviour not in terms of their lowly status but, on the contrary, as a survival of a Brahmanic tradition in which they would choose, for reasons of purity, not to eat with others. For doctors, to label sections of their profession as *bamunu kuliya* does not carry any notions of impurity, but it does indicate the social identification of a caste-like separateness to medical elites. Thus, for one, the term was attributed by others and was not a little ironic, suggesting a group with an over-blown sense of their own elite status; for the other, the term was self-referential and an attempt to convert their own lowly status into something worthy of greater esteem.

Finally, I was not long into my study when I began to realise that I was being caught up in a dynamic that I had experienced once before. As in my PhD research, the fieldwork I was doing was, in fact, showing every sign of doing me. As previously, I had assumed that as a researcher I was free to range over a community upon which a body of knowledge sat in a more or less public and unproblematic way. However, this community was also fiercely hierarchical and riven with professional schisms and factionalism. As before, it soon became apparent that the aperture which regulated my gaze upon the community was being directed, not to where I wanted it, but to where others wanted it. Becoming aware of this and addressing the difficulties that this created for my research began to throw important light on some of the key dynamics of this community. In addition to kinship, it became apparent that affiliations based on caste, religion, political allegiance and even the school and university attended, all played their part in creating a densely textured structure of social relations within the medical community. However, an ethnography of the medical community was not what I set out to do, and so my research material on the social organisation of the medical community was unintended and necessarily partial. For this

reason, fascinating though it is, I do not intend to write this material up. There is, of course, also the question of the ethics of constructing backstage representations which, predictably, are always thought about more when ethnographers find themselves 'studying up'. What I *did* set out to undertake, however, was an ethnography of a field of ideas and connections centring on the emerging discourse of developing world bioethics. In this regard, my earlier experience of working with the Berava proved instructive in ways I could not have imagined. Principally, that research gave me insight into the ways in which intellectual activity is socialised in Sri Lankan society and the way that knowledge is not splashed indiscriminately across the community but percolates in a highly structured fashion down conduits of a rather more primordial kind. In the context of bioethics and the current spread of global virtues (Rabinow, 2002), such insights are crucial for they provide clues as to how these powerful formations are given distinctive, local inflections.

At the time of writing, my fieldwork among the doctors is not complete and so the narrative is not nearly so fixed as the one that describes my encounter with the Berava over 20 years ago. The story might yet unfold in different and unpredictable ways. Nonetheless, consideration of the point of entry and the processes of subjectivation and objectivation within which this is framed provide vital commentary when it comes to understanding how this new ethnography is assembled and the distinctive forms that it is beginning to take.

CONCLUSION

Using recollection and reflection on two major pieces of fieldwork conducted in Sri Lanka some 20 years apart, I have in this chapter attempted to weave together two processes – subjectivation and objectivation. In highlighting the patterns, some symmetrical and others contrasting, that have emerged across these two pieces of work, I hope to have made explicit how the methodological and epistemological objectives of participant-observation fieldwork are also inescapably framed between processes of subjectivation and objectivation. Yet, to place one's fieldwork within these major parentheses is in no way an abnegation of power and responsibility on the part of the ethnographer, but a necessary and heuristic exploration of the circumstances whereby ethnography is created over time. Here, this has entailed a further opening out of the politics of the field and how the power relations and strategies in which the fieldworker becomes implicated find their way into ethnographic writing. On the one hand, the notion of subjectivation has been used to highlight my induction into two different communities in which knowledge is closely linked to social identity and cultural practice. Part of this induction involved recognising that, among both drummers and doctors, my arrival prompted questions as to why an attempt was being made to capture and convert their knowledge into forms which lie problematically outside familiar contexts of its production, performance and distribution. Furthermore, reflection on this process begins to make it clear precisely why it is necessary, in political and cultural terms, for them, as subjects of anthropological research, to manage the encounter in this way. In both instances, contemplating these familiar dramas of fieldwork helps to move beyond knowledge as detachable information and into the more complex dynamics of a socially grounded knowledge.

The notion of objectivation, on the other hand, makes it possible to countenance descriptions that are not just 'thick', but which are also wide in that they introduce temporal variables that serve to situate and contextualise the production of ethnography. The long, intense and physically arduous immersion in a rural community I undertook in my early 20s as an unencumbered single man is very different from the accelerated, short bursts of fieldwork I undertook in my 40s in the relative comfort of downtown Colombo and in regular telephone and e-mail contact with wife and children. In the former, I had a strong sense of being 'far away' and 'inside' a clearly identified field. In the latter, the 'field' metaphor was hardly appropriate as I was researching networks which were, in communication terms, 'close' and of which I was, as an academic, in some senses already a part. Viewed against this backdrop, the invocation of multi-sitedness in my second round of fieldwork might be seen as being as much to do with personal circumstance as it is a response to a world made up of increasingly interconnected and mobile populations.

Each of the above point to the ways in which we are 'done' once we place ourselves in other people's lifeworlds and provides us with an important reminder of the place of humility in ethnographic research. It serves as a warning that the assumptions of control, prediction, surveillance and omnipresence that increasingly permeate our research designs are often confounded in the face of complex, lived social reality, and, if ethnography is to be a vital tool in the social sciences, this is very much the way it should be.

NOTES

1 My supervisor was David Brooks, who carried out fieldwork among Bakhtiari nomads in Southern Iran. His fieldwork was exceptional in that he was one of the few outsiders to have completed the arduous and highly dangerous summer migration of the tribe. The nature of

this fieldwork brought him into a particularly close engagement with Bakhtiari culture and politics. Although he never completed his PhD, a remarkable visual record of his contribution to the ethnography of the Bakhtiari is to be found in the film 'People of the Wind', for which he was the consultant anthropologist.

2 This research was funded by the Social Science Research Council and resulted in a PhD entitled 'Ritual Tradition and Performance: The Berava Caste of Southern Sri Lanka' (1984).

3 This research was funded by the Nuffield Foundation Social Science Small Grants Scheme (2000) and the Wellcome Trust under the Medicine in Society Programme (Biomedical Ethics GR067110AIA) for the year 2002–03.

4 Notable anthropological contributions in this regard have examined the discourses surrounding IVF and infertility (Franklin, 1995, 1997; Franklin and Ragoné, 1998), ideas of nature and kinship in relation to the new technologies (Strathern, 1992, 1997), the analysis of prenatal diagnostic counselling (Rapp, 2000), popular understandings of the new technologies (Edwards, 1993, 2000), the medicalisation of genetics (Finkler, 2000), and attitudes towards egg sharing and donation (Konrad, 1998, 2005).

5 See Simpson 2000, Dissanayake et al., 2001 and Simpson et al., 2005.

REFERENCES

Bell, D., Caplan, P. and Karim, W.J. (1993) *Gendered Fields: Men, Women and Ethnography.* London and New York: Routledge.

Bourdieu, P. (2003) 'Participant Objectivation', *Journal of the Royal Anthropological Institute,* 9(2): 281–294.

Coffey, A. (1999) *The Ethnographic Self: Fieldwork and the Representation of Identity.* London: Sage.

Coleman, S. (nd) 'The multi-sited ethnographer'. Unpublished manuscript.

Dissanayake, V.H.W., Simpson, R. and Jayasekara, R.W. (2002) 'Attitudes towards the new genetic and assisted reproductive technologies in Sri Lanka: a preliminary report', *New Genetics and Society,* 21(1): 65–74.

Edwards, J. (1993) 'Explicit connections: ethnographic enquiry in north-west England', in J. Edwards et al. (eds), *Technologies of Procreation: Kinship in the Age of Assisted Conception.* Manchester: Manchester University Press.

Edwards, J. (2000) *Born and Bred: Idioms of Kinship and New Reproductive Technologies in England.* Cambridge: Cambridge University Press.

Finkler, K. (2000) *Experiencing the New Genetics: Family and Kinship at the Medical Frontier.* Philadelphia: University of Pennsylvania Press.

Franklin, S. (1995) 'Postmodern procreation: a cultural account of assisted reproduction'. in F. Ginsberg and R. Rapp (eds), *Conceiving the New World Order: The Global Politics of Reproduction.* Berkeley: University of California Press. pp. 323–45.

Franklin, S. (1997) *Embodied Progress: A Cultural Account of Assisted Conception.* London: Routledge.

_____ and Ragoné, H. (eds) (1998) *Reproducing Reproduction: Kinship, Power and Technological Innovation.* Philadelphia: University of Pennsylvania Press.

Geertz, C. (1988) *Works and Lives: The Anthropologist as Author.* Stanford, CA: Stanford University Press.

Hastrup, K. and Fog-Olwick, K. (eds) (1996) *Siting Culture.* London: Routledge.

Kapferer, B. (1983) *A Celebration of Demons.* Bloomington: Indiana University Press.

Kondo, D.K. (1990) *Crafting Selves: Power, Gender and Discourses of Identity in a Japanese Workplace.* Chicago: University of Chicago Press.

Konrad, M. (1998) 'Ova donation and symbols of substance: Some variations of the theory of sex, gender and the partible person'. *Journal of the Royal Anthropological Institute,* 4(4): 643–68.

Konrad, M. (2005) *Nameless Relations.* Oxford: Berghahn.

Lareau, A. and Scultz, J. (1996) *Journeys Through Ethnography: Realistic Accounts of Fieldwork.* Boulder, Co: Westview Press.

Lofland (1974) 'Styles of reporting qualitative field research', *American Sociologist,* 9: 101–11.

Marcus, G.E. (1995) 'Ethnography in/of the world system: the emergence of multi-sited ethnography', *Annual Review of Anthropology,* 24: 95–117.

_____ (1997) 'The uses of complicity in the changing *mis-en-scene* of anthropological fieldwork', *Representations,* 59(Summer): 85–108.

_____ (1998) *Ethnography Through Thick and Thin.* Princeton, NJ: Princeton University Press.

Nader, L. (1972) 'Up the anthropologist', in D. Hymes (ed.), *Reinventing Anthropology.* New York: Vintage Books. pp. 284–311.

Parkin, D. (2000) 'Fieldwork unfolding', in P. Dresch, W. James and D. Parkin (eds), *Anthropologists in a Wider World.* Oxford: Berghahn. pp. 259–73.

Rabinow, P. (2002) 'Midst anthropology's problems', *Cultural Anthropology*, 17(2): 135–49.

Rapp, R. (2000) 'Extra chromosomes and blue tulips: medico-familial conversations', in M. Lock et al. (eds), *Living and Working with the New Medical Technologies: Intersections of Inquiry*. Cambridge: Cambridge University Press.

Reed-Danahay, D. (1997) 'Introduction', in D. Reed-Danahay (ed.), *Auto/Ethnography: Rewriting the Self and the Social*. Oxford: Berg. pp. 1–17.

Ryan, B. (1953) *Caste in Modern Ceylon*. New Brunswick. NJ: Rutgers University Press.

Shore, C. and Nugent, S. (2002) *Elite Cultures: Anthropological Perspectives*. London: Routledge.

Simpson, B. (1984) 'Ritual Tradition and Performance: The Berava Caste of Southern Sri Lanka'. Unpublished PhD'. Durham: University of Durham.

———— (1997) 'Possession, dispossession and the social distribution of knowledge among Sri Lankan ritual specialists', *Journal of the Royal Anthropological Institute*, 3(1): 43–59.

Simpson, B. (1998) *Changing Families: An Ethnographic Approach to Divorce and Separation*. Oxford: Berg.

———— (2001) 'Ethical regulation and the new reproductive technologies in Sri Lanka: the perspectives of ethics committee members', *Ceylon Medical Journal*, 46(2): 54–57.

———— Dissanayake, V.H.W. and Jayasekera, R.W. (2005) 'Contemplating choice: attitudes towards interviewing in human reproduction in Sri Lanka', *New Genetics and Society*, 24(1): 99–118.

Strathern, M. (1991) *Partial Connections*. ASAO Special Publication 8, Savage, Maryland: Rowan and Littlefield.

Strathern, Marilyn (1992) *After Nature: English Kinship in the Late Twentieth Century*. Cambridge: Cambridge University Press.

———— (1996) 'Potential property: intellectual rights and property in persons', *Social Anthropology*, 4: 131–73.

———— (1997) 'The work of culture: an anthropological perspective', in A. Clarke and E. Parsons (eds), *Culture, Kinship and Genes*. Basingstoke: Macmillan.

———— (1999) *Property, Substance, Effect: Anthropological Essays on Persons and Things*. London: Athlone.

van Maanan, J. (1988) Tales of the field: *On Writing Ethnography*. Chicago: Chicago University Press.

Part 5

The Field of Emotion

9

Aural Sex: The Politics and Moral Dilemmas of Studying the Social Construction of Fantasy

CHRISTINE MATTLEY

Much has been written about the moral and political dilemmas of field research, and, as Punch (1998) has observed, there exist certain features that have an impact on fieldwork that are not always articulated in written accounts of research. Among those features he discussed is researcher personality, which influences the choice of topics and the intellectual path taken. 'But we are often left in the dark as to the personal and intellectual path that led researchers to drop one line of inquiry and pursue another. We require more intellectual autobiographies to clarify why academics end up studying what they do' (Punch, 1998: 162). This chapter is an attempt at beginning to fill that need. Specifically, in this chapter I will focus on how I navigated the political and moral terrain of ethnographic research and the intellectual path I took during my own research on phone sex workers and callers. I will also relate my findings on how fantasy was constructed in the context of one particular

phone sex company. Finally, I will discuss what I learned in the process and what I would do differently.

The first personality feature that influenced my fieldwork is perhaps an obvious one: my ongoing interest in the sociology of emotion. I have long been interested in the sociology of emotion and as I continued to teach and research in the area, I became more intrigued with the topic of emotion work in the workplace (Hochschild, 1983). As I thought about how emotion is done in the context of work, I began to think that it would be interesting to research work that is characterized by emotional labor rather than work in which emotion work is just a part; to study work in which the commodity sold is emotion. So it seemed that an obvious choice was the selling of fantasy, specifically the selling of sexual fantasy over the telephone. Of course, the question was where would I find such a research site? I assumed that women staff most of the phone fantasy companies and that, as a woman, I could gain access to such a research site, whereas a man could not (or at the very least would have a very difficult time doing so). Thus, the second personal characteristic I possessed was my gender. However, I also thought that more than simply gaining entry was going to be necessary in order to do this research. I believed that I would need to understand the experiences and emotion work of the women who worked the lines from their point of view. Therefore, I knew I would need to actually do the work as well. The third characteristic I possessed was my ability to carry out a feminist ethnography. Consequently, in 1993 I got a job working for a phone fantasy line, and conducted covert participant observation. The process of how I carried out this ethnography is my focus here.

POLITICS AND MORAL DILEMMAS

The beginning stages of research in general often seem to proceed on multiple fronts. My research was no different. In the beginning I embarked on several paths at once. Of course, I looked everywhere I could for information on phone sex work. I quickly discovered that the only information available was in popular magazines, talk shows, or advertisements telling me to call and spend money talking to someone. There was very little information on the industry or the work itself. I also began to think about how I could approach the topic and decided to look for ads for workers. I formulated basic sociological questions about the work itself and about the emotion work performed by those who worked the lines. At the same time, I began to apply for funding to help support my research. I soon discovered that the topic of phone sex was not necessarily seen as a subject worthy of investigation and other academics (including some feminists) didn't see the merit of such research.

Therefore, funding was going to be difficult to obtain. From my field journal:

> 1–23–93 I have applied for internal funding twice and have been turned down both times. I talked with [the administrator in charge of IRB (Institutional Review Board) and internal funding] and she said the first time that there was some concern as to how I will 'get in'. I can't believe that this would be a concern. I was clear about my procedure. In the second time around I clearly got trashed by one reviewer – it was obviously ([a friend of mine). I am so disappointed in her, I feel betrayed by her – especially since we have talked about this research and she was so supportive face-to-face. Her comments included asking whether I had chosen this research because it is titillating. I guess I expected more from her as a woman and as a feminist.

The concern that was raised was not about the covert nature of the work, but rather entry and doubt about the topic of sex work. I knew then that I would have to support the research myself – I never again tried to obtain funding for my research. I also began to realize the political nature of the work I was about to undertake.

Punch suggests that:

> To a greater or lesser extent all research is suffused by politics – from the micro politics of personal relations to the cultures and resources of research units and universities, the powers and policies of government research departments and ultimately, even the hand (heavy or otherwise) of the central state itself. (Punch, 1998: 159)

The nature of my research and the site/topic is political in several ways. My attempts to fund my research clearly demonstrated to me the politics of those who controlled my university's research resources. It also suggested the debate among feminists regarding sex work. Many feminists believe that sex work is inherently oppressive and that all sex workers are exploited, while others believe that choice extends to a woman's right to use her body as she wishes (Delacoste and Alexander, 1987/ 1998; McClintock, 1993; Nagel, 1997; Segal and McIntosh, 1993 all provide summaries of this debate). Thus, the topic I chose was (and is) controversial. In fact, I was not sure exactly where I stood on the issue. However, I felt confident that as a feminist I could ask the right questions. More importantly, I would let the voices of the women I hoped to study shape my conclusions.

I also became aware that within the discipline of sociology there is ambiguity as to where research on sex work 'fits'. Much of the work on sex workers, particularly prostitutes and strippers, appears in the literature on deviance. However, I was not sure that such a categorization was adequate because it caries with it a value judgment and I believed that such a placement precluded a discussion of the work itself and of the emotional labor involved. This categorization is not unique to the discipline, but is evident in the larger culture as well (McClintock, 1993). Although phone sex is legal, it still falls under the genre of illegal sex work and therefore carries with it the same stigma (Flowers, 1998; Mattley, 1998). I knew that research on phone sex workers would be controversial and thus political on multiple levels.

Not only was the choice of topic political, so was my choice of method. My decision to do covert participant observation was one that emerged in the course of exploring research sites. Early in the process of this research I found a 'help wanted' ad for a phone fantasy line, so I called and talked to the man who owned it. In the course of our conversation he explained that I would be working from home and would need to have an unlisted, unpublished line in my home that was fitted with a device so that I could distinguish 'business calls' from 'regular calls'. He also wanted copies of utilities bills 'so I know you are who you say you are'. I decided not to try to work with this company because I wanted to interact with other women and working from my home would have isolated me from other workers. However, I also learned something important – that an owner

might be wary of outsiders and I needed to be cautious about what I revealed to them. I decided to not reveal my complete identity when I applied for a job as a phone worker. However, could I do this and remain true to my feminist ideals?

Reinharz suggests: 'Feminist ethnography is consistent with three goals mentioned frequently by feminist researchers: (1) to document the lives and activities of women, (2) to understand the experience of women from their own point of view, and (3) to conceptualize women's behavior as an expression of social contexts' (Reinharz, 1992: 51). I knew that as a feminist my goals were to understand the phone workers' experiences, to document their experiences using their own words and perspectives, and to understand how their emotional labor was a part of their work context. I also knew that understanding their experiences from their own point of view was important to challenge the dominant sociological view of sex workers as deviants, which has most often been written by male sociologists. Additionally, Reinharz tells us that:

> Many feminist researchers have written about the ethical and epistemological importance of integrating their selves into their work and of eliminating the distinction between the subject and the object. The complete participant approach fits this particular feminist goal, although it is not shared by all researchers who consider themselves to be feminists. (Reinharz, 1992: 69)

I knew that I needed to do this work.

However, I still grappled with the prospect of doing covert research. I knew that to do covert participant observation was a highly controversial choice because of the long standing debate in sociology over the ethics of this method (see Fine, 1993; Miller, 2001; and Mitchell, 1993, for excellent reviews). The issue of secrecy is at the heart of this debate. As Mitchell (1993) suggests, secrecy is not absolute, but relative. He begins with the assumption that secrecy is socially constructed, negotiated, and maintained by intentional actors. It is also, Mitchell maintains, a pervasive feature of social life. He tells us that:

> when secrecy is understood as a generic and constantly transforming feature of all social action, ethnographers' identities are not so much given roles to be played as they are emergent products of fieldwork itself, forthcoming as researchers and subjects explore each other's cognitive and affective revelations and concealments. (Mitchell, 1993: 4)

I decided that I would be open about who I am, but not why I wanted to be hired. I also decided that exactly how much information I revealed about myself, as well as when I revealed it, would be determined by the situation. Following Mitchell's logic, I felt sure that I would not expose others to any more risk than everyday interaction would. The American Sociological Association's Ethical Standards, Section 12.05, Use of Deception in Research states:

> (d) On rare occasions, sociologists may need to conceal their identity in order to undertake research that could not practicably be carried out were they to be known as researchers. Under such circumstances, sociologists undertake the research if it involves no more than minimal risk for the research participants and if they have obtained approval to proceed in this manner from an institutional review board or, in the absence of such boards, from another authoritative body with expertise on the ethics of research. Under such circumstances, confidentiality must be maintained unless otherwise set forth in 11.02(b). (asanet.org)

Although I knew that my choice was still controversial, I was within the ethical guidelines of the American Sociological Association.

THE PROCESS: GETTING MYS JOB

Now that I had come to conclusions about how I would do the research, I needed a job. I thought about several options, including going to either of the coasts where I knew there was more of a concentration of phone sex operations and more opportunities for

'phone actresses'. Then, one day, I was looking in the newspaper from a nearby city (thinking about buying a new CD player) and I decided to look in the 'want ads'. To my surprise, under the section 'escorts wanted' was the following ad:

> TELEPHONE HELP NEEDED - THE STATE'S LARGEST PHONE FANTASY SERVICE IS ABOUT TO DOUBLE IN SIZE. WE ARE HIRING FOR ALL SHIFTS PLUS WEEKENDS. WE ARE LOOKING FOR ONLY SERIOUS PEOPLE WITH A GOOD PHONE VOICE, RELIABLE TRANSPORT AND GOOD WORK HISTORY. PAY $300-500 PER WEEK. CALL FOR INTERVIEW MON–FRI 10 AM TO 4 PM. (PHONE NUMBER)

I was amazed. At last I had found an opportunity relatively close by. As Punch (1998) suggests, one of the factors that figures into a person's ability to do field research is geographic proximity. This brought me one step closer to getting this research underway. From my field journal:

> 3–22 I called about 2pm. When a man answered, I said that I was calling about the ad in Sunday's [paper]. He said they were interviewing, and asked if I wanted to come up. I said that I had a couple of questions, and he said OK. I said that I live in Athens, but am interested in some extra money. I also said that I am wondering if I can do this work, having never done it, is there training? He said yes. I asked about the pay and he said that you make 30 cents a minute, but if you don't make $8 per hour you get fired because you are obviously not working enough. (That works out to about 26 minutes per hour.) I asked him if there was a minimum number of hours that I had to work and he said 'No, you work as many or as few hours as you want.' I said 'I assume that some shifts are more desirable than others.' He said 'No, we're open 24 hours per day 364 $\frac{1}{2}$ days per year.' I asked about any special abilities and he said, 'If you don't show up on time, if you can't follow instructions and you don't work enough minutes you won't make it, you'll get fired.' He also said that 'You have a great phone voice, otherwise I wouldn't have taken the time to even talk to ya.' I set up an appointment for Wednesday the 24th. He gave me directions to the address, and we said goodbye.

After the conversation I felt yet another step closer and was cautiously excited. I was apprehensive about the interview itself because I felt as though this was a unique opportunity and I really wanted to be hired. From my field journal:

Interview day: On my drive I kept thinking what if I fail? This is my first try and I really hope that I am successful. I am nervous. What will they be like? What will the building be like? What will the interviewer be like? What will I say? What sorts of things will they ask? Obviously about work history, why I want to do this. What will I say? Probably that I am wanting to earn some money, and that I am not sure that I have any other talents, except that I love to talk. On one hand I think this is great experience just for the interview, but on the other hand I feel like this is a perfect setup and I really hope that it works out. My appointment is for 1pm and I arrive about 10 minutes early, park and go inside. The building is a two-story brick building and still says Professional Building on the outside. I walked inside and found myself in a foyer with a flight of stairs to my right that went up and one flight went down. I saw a youngish dark-haired woman who asked, 'Are you here for an interview?' I said, 'yes', and she replied, 'Through that door, someone will be with you in a minute.' I said 'thank you' and walked through the glass door in front of me. I waited a couple of minutes and then a woman appeared, asked me if I was here for an interview, I said yes. She gave me an application and then disappeared through a door at the opposite end of the room. The outer office was somewhat small maybe 10×12, contained a couple of bookcases, a filing cabinet, a desk and chair, and a chair on the other side of the desk, where I sat down to fill out the application. The application was very simple. On the top of the page was written Private Contract Application and it had spaces to list my social security number, my driver's license, my name, address, phone number. It also asked if I was ever arrested, if so why, if I was ever convicted of a felony and if so for what, if I knew anyone working for the company and if so who, if I had ever worked for an adult-oriented business, if currently employed, if they might contact my current employer (although it did not ask who my current employer was), the name of someone to contact in case of emergency and phone number, where I had heard of the company, last year enrolled in school, where last enrolled in school. It was only one page long (front only). I thought to myself that this application was so different than what I am used to. None of my academic credentials were of interest here – it felt really foreign. I sat waiting for about 10 minutes and while I waited I noticed that on the wall there seemed to be instructions about Visa and Mastercard although I couldn't tell why. I also noticed that as a couple of women came and went each time the door opened I could hear voices coming from the other side. The voices were laughing and talking, clearly on the phone. The office was neat but threadbare. After about 10 minutes a young woman emerged and asked if I was there for an interview, I said yes and she said for me to follow her. We went through the door and turned left into an office that had a large desk, brass lamps, leather chairs, a collection of knives on the wall behind the desk, and a couple of them on the desk. She sat behind the desk, told me to sit, that the man I spoke with on the phone (John I think) was not there, she didn't know when he would return, so she would conduct the interview.

She – 'Give me a minute to look over this (motioning to the application).'

Me – 'Sure.'

She looked up and said, 'Oh, I know where Athens is, I went to school in (a town nearby).' She said, 'We are a phone fantasy line, with very, very explicit sex conversations.'

Me – 'I know.'

She – 'Why are you interested in this type of work?'

Me – 'Money.'

She – 'Well let me tell you a little about this work – you have to have an imagination, and be a good bullshitter. We are one of the lowest-costing lines, we charge 1.25 per minute with a 10-minute minimum. The callers call our phone number, so the charge shows up on their phone bill, and we pay 30 cents per minute. You get paid every Friday but you won't get paid for the first couple of weeks, so you will be on the same schedule as the rest of the girls. You'll get regular checks, and they won't say phone sex on them or anything. We're a legit company, you'll fill out a W–2, so we will withhold taxes. You can make pretty good money. I've been doing this for eight years and it's been very lucrative.'

Me – 'Eight years in this work?'

She – 'Yeah, eight years in phone sex. This is a growing business, we have about 70 girls working here and we've done 1 million minutes since the beginning of the year.'

Me – 'Since Jan. 1?'

She – 'Yeah!' She went on to say, 'We are a coed line, so we are all 18–23. We're a laid back place, but have some rules. You cannot meet any of these guys outside of here, you will put yourself in danger, get you, the other girls and us in trouble.'

Me – 'I assume that it would be scary do that' and she agrees.

She asked again, 'Why do you want to do this kind of work?'

Me – 'Well, since I'm an academic, I'm not sure I have a lot of skills. I like to talk on the phone, and I'm not easily embarrassed so I figure this looks like pretty good money, why not? I need money.' I ask about shifts she says, 'There are four 6 hour shifts per day 8am–2pm, 2pm–8pm, 8pm–2am, and 2am–8am. What shifts would you be interested in?'

Me – 'I could work any shifts but would probably like afternoons or evenings.'

She – 'Which one?'

Me – 'I don't care.'

She – 'When could you start?'

Me – 'Anytime.'

She – 'God, you're so easy to get along with!'

Me – 'I want a job.'

She – 'It's a pretty long drive from Athens for just 1 shift.'

Me – 'I have friends in Columbus I can crash with if I need to if I am pooped' (I didn't tell her my friends are Motel 6!).'

She – 'Well, I'm willing to give you a try.'

Me – 'Oh, good!'

She – 'Well what shifts do you want to do?'

Me – 'Well the ad said all shifts but since I'm driving up from Athens I'd like afternoons.'

She – 'What days?'

Me – 'Well, I'm on a two-day class schedule, Monday and Wednesday, so Thursday through Sunday I'd be available.'

She – 'Great, weekends are hard to fill.'

Me – 'Really? That surprises me.'

She – 'Well college students want to party, and some women have kids so need to be home.' She asks if I have questions and I say, 'The gentleman I spoke with said you provide training.'

She said, 'You get trained by a supervisor, and then they work with you for a couple of weeks after you're ready to go to the phones.'

I couldn't believe that was all there was to the interview process – just a one-page application, a quick conversation and I was hired. As we concluded our conversation the afternoon supervisor walked in. We were introduced, chatted for a few minutes and then a very heavy set man walked in, who was introduced to me as 'Big Boy'. He was the man I spoke with on the phone. The supervisor offered to show me around the building and we made arrangements for me to begin work the following Saturday.

DOING THE WORK

I began working the following Saturday (and continued working for almost a year). The supervisor trained me for about a day and a half and then I was on my own. As a new

'girl', I got lots of help from the other workers. Everyone seemed open and helpful, although I didn't immediately forge any friendships. The supervisor knew that I was an academic, and if the other workers asked what I did for a living, which of course they did, I told them. Although they were intrigued, they didn't seem to care; they readily accepted me and treated me as they treated the other women. As other new 'girls' were hired, I observed the same process of workers asking questions of the new person followed by acceptance. During the time I was in the field, I worked between three and five days per week, for a minimum of six hours per day. I did almost, 2000 calls, 1,983 to be exact, got to know other workers, the management, and spent many hours talking with all the people working there. Some of the women became friends, with whom I occasionally socialized after working hours; others were merely acquaintances.

I kept a field journal during the entire process of my work, from trying to find such a business, to trying to acquire funding for my project, to trying to gain access, and, of course, during the entire time I was in the field. I not only recorded field notes, but I also included my own reactions, emotions, and thoughts. During the first half of my time in the field, I recorded data secretly. However, about midway through my time in the field I was talking to the supervisor and she said, 'God, you should do a study of these callers!' We talked about it and I decided to approach the manager and the owner. When I approached the manager, she said 'It's OK with me if it's OK with John' (the owner). Just then John walked in and I thought 'now or never'. I told him I wanted to do research on the callers, but that I would let him read anything before I published it. He said, 'I hate to read that fucking stuff, I trust you, you won't fuck me over. It's about time someone tell this story, the media's got it all wrong.' I again offered to let him read anything and he said, 'I told you, I hate to read that kind of stuff, just go ahead.' From that point on, I recorded data in a more blatant way while I was working the lines. I had just acquired another advantage for doing my research – the owner liked and trusted me. I didn't particularly like him, but I knew that I wouldn't betray his trust in me. I would tell the story without 'fucking him over'.

When I first started this research, I was anxious about being 'one of the girls'. I knew my research pivoted on being able to become friends with the other workers. I wasn't nervous about the actual work; my nervousness was more about not standing out – just passing. At first the work was novel but soon it became just work. It was often mind numbing: I came to think of it as an emotional assembly line. That other women faced the same challenge of routinization was evident. For instance, the supervisor did all her paperwork – checking our call sheets, credit card charges, and entering call data in callers' files on the computer, and the like – while she was taking calls. Another woman routinely read novels and newspapers while she took calls. Most of us regularly carried on whispered conversations while we were doing calls. It was not unusual for the women to use humor to break the monotony – usually in the form of jokes, pranks, or making fun of the callers. From my field journal:

> Since it was April Fools today the women seemed to be teasing each other all day. At one point Mia (who was sitting in the cubicle next to me) flipped the intercom of her phone on so we could all hear her caller. It was really funny and everyone around was laughing. I thought it funny that even though we all hear this many times a day we all laughed when she did it.

However, most days were mundane. I wanted to be sure that the routinization of the work was not an artifact of the shift and the days I usually worked so I decided that I needed to experience each of the shifts and all of the weekdays. Consequently, during the time I was in the field, I worked all of the various shifts and I worked each day of the week at one time or another. Often workers needed to find someone to work their shift for them and I did. This was not seen as unusual. Women often did these favors for each other or women worked extra shifts to make more money.

MORAL DILEMMAS IN THE FIELD

I experienced two different types of moral dilemma while I was in the field. The first type had to do with doing research in a workplace. Specifically, I knew that if I didn't make lots of money during a given shift, my life wouldn't be negatively impacted: I was not totally dependent on the work for my livelihood. At the same time I needed to be engaged enough in the work so that I was a 'real worker' and that I understood the work in the same way as did the other workers. I resolved this in a couple of ways: by being sure to be able to give calls to other workers when appropriate and by not being too aggressive about taking calls. In other words, I was a good worker, but not pushy in terms of taking calls. I was also keenly aware of leading two lives. I felt as though I was traversing them, never fitting in either place (and since I was basically living in a motel I felt suspended, as though I had no home). On the one hand, I was immersed in the work, but because of my covert research I never felt as though I really revealed my entire self – I always held back somewhat. On the other hand, I was still an academic and member of my department but I felt removed from the daily activities of the department. I was a woman with a foot in two very different worlds.

I never fully resolved this dilemma; I used my commute back and forth as a reentry into each of my worlds.

The second type of dilemma I experienced was really more of a dilemma for those around me. As I have noted elsewhere (Mattley, 1998), I was accorded a (dis)courtesy stigma as a result of studying phone sex workers. While doing this research I was often asked about it. I got comments and questions such as, 'I could never do that sort of work'. Or 'How can you do that? How can you sell something so intimate? Something so private?' Or 'Don't you feel like you're selling part of yourself?' I've even been asked if I became aroused while doing calls. These questions and comments were usually delivered in such a way as to make it clear to me that while they could never do 'that sort of work' there must be something about me that made it easy for me to do the work. The application of this (dis)courtesy stigma cast me into the role of the 'other'. The realization that I was being cast as the 'other' led me to work the hyphen. Michelle Fine has described this in the following way: 'By working the hyphen, I mean to suggest that researchers probe how we are in relation with the contexts we study and with our informants, understanding that we are all multiple in those relations' (Fine, 1998: 135). Workers were aware of the stigma of sex work and it was occasionally a topic of discussion. Talking to other workers helped me understand how they navigated this stigma and helped me deal with the one applied to me. I also came to recognize how similar my friends and I were to the phone sex workers; as women we all shared many issues.

There was another consequence of being accorded a (dis)courtesy stigma that was more of a methodological lesson. I was repeatedly surprised when people across campus would ask about my research or colleagues would bring it up in front of strangers (like job candidates). I realized how important it is to try to control 'talk' about research while it is being conducted. I typically tried to steer the conversation away from my research. If that didn't work, I would simply say that I didn't want to discuss it while I was still in the field. This methodological lesson is that I still continue to try to impress on others the importance of not discussing the fieldwork of others while they are in the field.

RESEARCHING FANTASY

As I started this project, I was interested in the emotion work of the workers. During the course of my research I also began to think about the suspension of disbelief. What was really going on with callers? Surely, if they really thought about it, they couldn't actually believe what was being said. Then it began to dawn on me that belief didn't matter – we were jointly constructing fantasy. This led me to think about the fantasy sociologically. However, as I investigated the literature I found that most writing on fantasy relied on a Freudian/psychological conception of fantasy that portrayed it as an individual phenomenon that is emanating from some deep psychic flaw. I only found two exceptions to this pattern: Fine's (1983) sociological work on a fantasy gaming subculture, and Caughey's (1984) anthropological work on imaginary social relationships. Caughey is especially important for my work because his is a rare in-depth work on fantasy that recognized the social nature of fantasy. Since there exists no sociological precedence for the examination of fantasy, his work is especially significant here. He approached the issue of individuals' fantasies from a non-psychological angle. In fact, he suggests: 'Often fantasies are seen as pathological and unnatural. This is erroneous. Like psychotics, normal people characteristically live simultaneously in two different worlds, one of fantasy and one of reality' (Caughey, 1984: 156). 'The evidence shows that most Americans experience vivid fantasies daily, but that they rarely talk about them to others. This taboo on disclosure is based in part on the cultural assumption that fantasy reveals "pathology"' (Caughey, 1984: 188). I believe that the paucity of sociological attention to fantasy reflects a cultural metanarrative which suggests that fantasy is a waste of time and quasi-pathological, the implication being that it must therefore be the purview of psychology.

However, I believe that fantasy is a topic worthy of sociological examination because fantasy is a form of subjective experience during which a person is transported to another world where they find themselves as an actor-participant in another reality. Sociologists do have a long tradition of theorizing and writing about the subjective life of the individual. Subjective experience has figured prominently in sociological writings and, from the time of Mead, the internal life of the individual has been seen as richly constituted and active.

Consistent with this tradition, I believe that fantasies, and particularly sexual fantasies, are social. They consist of encounters between the fantasy self and imagined others and are governed by the sociocultural construction of individual experience. 'To an important extent, fantasy is a cultural phenomenon. It reflects individual desires, but only as these have been shaped, twisted, and structured by cultural forces' (Caughey, 1984: 163). The fantasy world is a conspicuously social world and is clearly a worthy sociological topic. I wondered, though, how

are phone fantasies constructed and governed by cultural norms?

THE CONSTRUCTION OF PHONE FANTASY

The social construction of fantasy operated on two levels. The first level included the 'girls' themselves, and the context of the call. The phone identities of the workers were fictitious, as was the place we supposedly worked. The second level was the phone fantasy itself. The phone fantasy was often constructed by or requested by the caller, but often the worker controlled the construction of the fantasy or shared in the control so it was jointly constructed during the call.

WORKERS' CONSTRUCTIONS

Turning to the first level of fantasy construction, not only were the workers' identities constructed, but also the history and the setting of the work was a fantasy constructed for the benefit of the callers. It was, in a sense, the 'public face' of the workers. The day of my interview, when I met 'Blair', the shift supervisor, she told me that before I started working I would need to come up with a name and a description. From my field journal:

'While we were talking she said, 'God you're tall!!'

I say, ' Yeah.'

She asks, 'How tall?'

I say, 'Almost 6 feet.'

She replies, 'You should use that in your description. You need to think of a description. Tall is good, men seem to like that.'

Me – 'Should I be blond, black hair or what?'

She – 'It doesn't matter, mine is that I am tall, green eyes, auburn curly hair, 150 lbs. When I say 150 some guys hang up, but some really like it. Make your boobs

C cause D makes men think dumb. Think of a name, but you may not be able to use it because we have so many girls here, some may be taken.'

Me – 'What else?'

She – 'Well, we should probably make you a grad student, be a sociology grad student so if you get someone who knows something you'll be OK. We get some pretty intelligent men. There is one guy who calls that is a medical professor who spends more than a thousand a month, and he is really smart, I have really learned a lot from him. Some of these guys really like intelligent women, so you shouldn't hide it.'

Thus, the descriptions that women assumed on the phones were constructed and in the case of this company, women were coached according to assumptions about what men are thought to find attractive. In addition, the descriptions of all of the other workers were posted by shift in each cubicle. This was necessary so that if we were asked about other workers at any time we all would be able to give consistent descriptions of one another. Actually, it often happened that we were in fact asked about other women and we were expected to act as though we were friends with some of them. If we described an activity with another 'girl', we were supposed to tell the other worker or leave her a note so that she wouldn't get caught in our fabrication. Thus, not only did the management of the company heavily influence our descriptions, but also we were all careful to orchestrate our fantasy activities with other workers.

Not surprisingly, women's fantasy descriptions were quite consistent. As I have described elsewhere (Mattley, 2002), we were portrayed as being of varying heights, ranging from 104 to 135 pounds, as having long hair regardless of color, possessing what could be best described as ideal bodies (none were small busted), and all of the workers were supposedly students. Finally, although there were a few African Americans and Asian Americans working there, all but three were supposedly white (the three exceptions were supposedly Asian Americans). This consistency was due to the preferences of the owner.

My first day I was given a manual that outlined procedures, prices, items offered for sale, rules, and most interestingly 'the College Coeds story', which was quite detailed. Part of the 'history' was that we were located in a huge old house, similar to a sorority, and that many of us lived in the house. We ostensibly had our own bedrooms and we took phone calls in the privacy of our own rooms. In fact, we worked out of building that had been a professional building not unlike those that doctors and dentists commonly use. It had three large offices and eighteen cubicles spread out over three levels. I was told that everyone must know the story because sometimes new callers are curious as to how 'College Coeds' was established, and obviously all the workers needed to say the same thing. In essence, we had to share the company fantasy with the callers. Long-time callers often quizzed new workers about how they came to work there, if they lived there, and why they did the work. However, such probes were not limited to new workers. Sometimes my repeat callers would ask me time after time about why and how I worked there, who my best friends there were, and many questions about my personal life.

In summary, each of our descriptions was a fantasy constructed in consultation with the management and given to other workers. We were required to learn the company fantasy and to fit ourselves into it. Finally, these fantasies were structured by what the management perceived to be men's fantasies and were governed by what I have described as gender performances (Mattley, 2002).

THE PHONE FANTASY

In terms of the work itself, the actual calls were socially constructed in three ways. First, my shift supervisor trained me. During my first couple of shifts I sat by the supervisor's desk and she trained me how to answer the phones (what to say), literally how to work the phones, how to do the paperwork for each call, how to verify phone numbers, how to verify credit cards, and so on. More importantly, I listened to her calls, and she told me what she thought men liked to hear, shared with me fantasies she had constructed, and how to know which direction to take calls. It is useful to note that often when men called they would request particular women, various types of woman or types of call, and whoever answered the phone would direct the call. Other times callers would not request anything or anyone specifically so it was very useful to be able to 'read' the caller, which was done by listening carefully to the language the caller used.

The second way that calls were socially constructed was that the workers often shared with one another the fantasies they had used with callers. We listened to one another's calls, and we talked about the callers. Sometimes this was in a very informal way, just chatting with one another, but other times callers' favorite fantasies were entered as part of their computerized files. At one point, one of the other workers offered to teach me how to do domination calls. I literally sat by her desk and listened to several calls before doing domination calls myself. The process of learning domination involved learning the attitude of domination, the activities the dominatrix demands of the slave, and the pace and control of the call. I found other workers eager to share their fantasies and expertise not only with me, but I observed the same teaching among other workers as well. There were sexually oriented magazines scattered throughout the workplace and women often picked them up, read them and used ideas from them in subsequent calls. We also pointed out to one another stories we thought useful, funny, or outrageous. The point is that we all used them and therefore they shaped our work.

The third way that phone fantasies were constructed was by the workers and the callers jointly or by the callers alone – that is, they would call in and tell the worker exactly what fantasy they wanted and/or they would control the construction of the fantasy in the call. My data suggest that callers controlled the calls 21 percent of the time, we jointly constructed the call 38 percent of the time, and I controlled the call 41 percent of the time (Mattley, 2002).

Regardless of who controlled the construction of the fantasy, or what kind of mood the workers were actually in, the workers were supposed to be perpetually 'ready', easily aroused, and never in a bad mood – the fantasy of the always eager partner. This observation is consistent with Caughey's suggestion that '[f]antasy others are fully appreciative of the excellent qualities of the fantasy self … fantasy beings are also highly cooperative. Enthusiastically, reliably, and untiring, they also do just what the fantasy self wants' (Caughey, 1984: 162).

It became apparent to me that no matter how women described themselves or what activities they described, callers never questioned the truth of what was being said. In fact, callers would comment on my voice, my 'looks', tell me I was beautiful, and how that excited them. I think that the willing suspension of disbelief is a necessary part of jointly constructed fantasy. 'The appeal of the fantasy world is clear. One enters a perfect setting, assumes a perfect self, and interacts with perfect others' (Caughey, 1984: 163).

THE CALLS

Before turning to the content of the fantasies, let me speak briefly of the calls I controlled

(41 percent of all the calls I did). Such calls fell into two broad categories. The first and larger category was composed primarily of new or first-time callers. These callers didn't really know what to do or expect so I constructed the fantasy. The second, smaller category (12 percent of my total calls) was comprised of callers wanting domination. Even if these callers briefly told me their fantasy, it was up to me to embellish it and control the fantasy completely.

It was not unusual, I found, for the callers to talk to me about why they used phone sex lines. Many of the men expressed feeling safe about sharing their fantasies (which they took to be unusual, perverted or sick) and feeling that their wives or girlfriends would be horrified by their fantasies. In actuality, their fantasies were variations on a theme and very few were startling or outlandish. Typical of what some callers told me follows (from my field journal):

4–16   Although I didn't prompt him, 'Sam' began to talk about 'these phone lines', and said that he 'really likes them' because its 'really safe sex and it is better than real sex.'

Me – 'Why?'

He – 'Because I can share my fantasies, I can say them out loud to you and I probably wouldn't tell my girlfriend them.'

Callers' fantasies were amazingly consistent, rarely individualized, and for the most part were what could be described as conventional. I kept detailed data on the fantasies callers requested or constructed. Calls typically included several different activities, but clear themes emerged. As I have reported elsewhere, the predominant fantasies were receiving oral sex (39 percent), intercourse with the man behind the woman (19 percent), intercourse with the man 'on top' (14 percent), hearing the worker orgasm (12 percent), me dominating (12 percent), cunnilingus (9 percent), sex in unusual places (8 percent),

fetishes (4 percent), and homosexual fantasies (3 percent)' (Mattley, 2002).

Sometimes callers would call while they were watching a movie and use it as a basis for the call. Occasionally, they would call and describe something they had read in a magazine or a book and that story would become the starting point for the fantasy. Flowers has noted: 'The consumers of phone sex enjoy an illusion of great freedom and adventure, but their actions are considerably constrained. ... With few exceptions, phone sex fantasies follow standard scripts' (Flowers, 1998: 84). '[P]hone sex appears to be utterly dependent on the same old symbols and visualization rituals that characterize the stereotypical images provided by traditional pornography and society in general' (Flowers, 1998: 114). In their 1993 study of 84 'dial-a-porn' recorded fantasies, Glascock and LaRose found two dominant themes: reciprocal sexual activities in which each participant has an equal role, and subservience, defined as one party portrayed as actively encouraging or soliciting sexual behaviors primarily for the satisfaction of others.

Whether it was the worker using stories from magazines or callers using movies or magazines, both sometimes relied on sex materials as the inspiration for the fantasies they constructed. This clearly underscores the power of social influence – used as a starting point, sex materials frame the fantasy. This is in line with Caughey's assertion:

First, the fantasy is partly determined by the particular cultural norms it attempts to transcend. Second, even anticultural fantasies are typically structured by cultural rules for breaking rules. Finally, such fantasy indirectly contributes to social order. (Caughey, 1984: 186)

In other words, even fantasies callers consider to be outlandish are patterned or constructed by culture.

Despite the fact that calls were consistent, workers still endeavored to make each caller feel as though his fantasy was unusual, exotic, and exciting. We all acted as though each question was unique, each call was arousing, and each caller interesting. No matter how many times a day we described ourselves, our preferences, our abilities, we still had to be passionate. The ability to maintain this excitement was crucial to the construction of the fantasy – our fantasy selves needed to be eager and willing. So, no matter how many times we heard the same thing from callers, we all knew that we needed to act as though it was novel. From my field journal:

> 9–12   While I was talking to (one of my regulars) today he asked me what I thought of phone sex lines. I told him I thought it wasn't any different than movies, magazines, or books; all part of the same genre. He said 'Yeah, but it's better.' I asked why and he said, 'Because it's a different movie every time I call.'

CALLERS' DESCRIPTIONS – FANTASY SELVES

While I was in the field I sometimes wondered whether the callers were telling the truth about their appearances. Then I realized that it didn't matter: their descriptions of themselves might be part of their fantasies. Physical descriptions are like props in a fantasy. The vast majority of callers (71 percent) described themselves as being between 5'10' and 6'2'. Almost half (47.7 percent) said they weighed between 165 to 190 pounds. Forty-five percent said they were between 29 and 35 years old. Finally, 57 percent claimed to have what is best described as white-collar or managerial jobs. Often callers would also describe their physique to me by telling me how much they worked out, how strong they were, or how muscular they were. In general, then, callers described themselves as tall, relatively young, well-muscled and white-collar or professional – a very masculine image to be sure.

Whether or not these descriptions were accurate, they conformed to cultural ideals of masculinity (Mattley, 2002).

> Good as the fantasy world is as an accommodating place, it has another even stronger appeal. Entry into a fantasy world involves not only a transformation of setting, but also a transformation of self. ... The fantasy identity is significantly different because the self is modified in various ways. (Caughey, 1984: 161)

RULES FOR FANTASY MAINTENANCE

Once the fantasy selves were constructed/ presented and the fantasy was constructed by one or both of us, the fantasy needed to be maintained (at least for the duration of the call). In other words, just as other forms of interaction have rules and boundaries, phone fantasies also have rules. Some rules were unspoken, like a form of tacit knowledge, and foremost among them was that the fantasy selves were not to be questioned for accuracy. Callers accepted workers' descriptions of themselves and didn't question them except to hear them each time they called. Likewise, workers never questioned callers' descriptions of themselves. That is not to say that workers didn't question and talk about callers' descriptions with other workers; they did, and often it was in a joking or derogatory manner. However, workers and callers alike all knew that the calls were fantasy and that the descriptions were part of the fantasy, so they were not open to verification. Equally important was the unspoken rule that we were not available for 'real' relationships. Callers often teasingly said things like, 'Geez, I'd love to meet you!' but we knew that the callers weren't serious. Occasionally, however, a caller would express a sincere desire to meet us. From my field journal:

> 7–15 While I was talking to 'Vern' today, he asked, 'If I send you the money will you come and visit me?

I mean I'll really do it – I'm dying to meet you and spend time with you.' I was so disappointed – I thought he 'got it'.

I felt as though the fantasy had been breached.

In theater there is a technique known as 'breaking the third wall'. The third wall refers to the invisible line at the end of the stage that separates the audience from the actors. Breaking that wall refers to the practice of getting the audience directly involved in the play, by doing things like talking to them, or even starting a scene with the actors in the audience. Vern's request was like breaking the third wall. This occurrence was not unique to me; it happened to other women as well. When we talked about callers doing this, other workers expressed feelings similar to mine; we were disappointed in their breaking the third wall because it ruined the call (the fantasy). It also revealed their disregard for the unspoken rule and labeled them as pitiful.

WHAT I LEARNED

There is much that I learned that I believe is valuable to other researchers. I gained two types of knowledge, one about fantasy and one about doing this type of fieldwork. In terms of fantasy, my fieldwork revealed these fantasies to be social (and socially constructed) in several ways. From the descriptions of the workers to the calls themselves, the fantasies were clearly jointly produced. Whether or not one believes these fantasies to be vulgar, they are nonetheless social. It is time that we free fantasy from the dominion of pathology and move it squarely into the social realm. As such, I believe that fantasy is clearly a topic that warrants more sociological investigation. As a starting point, we need information regarding the construction of other types of fantasy as well as the rules governing fantasy maintenance.

The second type of knowledge I gained was methodological. Clearly, I possessed several advantages that allowed me to do my fieldwork. Chief among them were my gender and my personality. Had I been a man or had I been a shy woman I could never have done this work. That I am a feminist helped keep me focused on understanding women's experiences and how they were tied to this particular context. I was also attuned to my emotions in the course of this research and it helped me recognize one of the dilemmas I faced – the application of (dis)courtesy stigma that led me to work the hyphen. A realistic assessment of personal strengths and weaknesses need to be part of the decision-making process in choosing a method.

Although I agree with Punch's assertion that all research is suffused with politics, I was able to navigate this terrain. When I realized that I was not going to be able to find funding for my research I supported it myself with the money I made working the phone lines. I believe that funding for controversial topics is increasingly difficult to find and therefore we need to be able to find creative ways to support our work. My solution was an obvious one, and in that respect I was lucky. It is a topic that undoubtedly warrants more attention.

There were, however, other dilemmas I faced while researching a controversial topic. For me, the topic and the method are inextricably bound. Since phone sex is a part of sex work, access was problematic. I felt that the only way for me to gain access to the site was through covert participant observation. After being in the field, I firmly believe that had I simply approached the owner and asked for access, I would have been turned down. Additionally, actually doing the work and being just one of the 'girls' allowed me to establish a relationship with other women that would have been otherwise impossible.

So, would I do it differently? Absolutely not. Did it bring its own problems? Definitely. The primary problem of covert work is obviously secrecy. The secrecy didn't cause me to feel the difficulty of traversing two lives; we workers all did that to a certain extent and we talked about the stigma of the work and ways to cope with keeping work a secret from others. The secrecy prevented me from talking to them about the (dis)courtesy stigma of the research. Fortunately for me, I had a colleague that I used as a sounding board and that is who I talked to regarding the dilemma I faced. I believe that it is crucial to have someone who can act as a sounding board and that you can talk to throughout the research.

As discussed earlier, secrecy is a part of social interaction, but while I was in the field the secrecy of my work was always in high relief for me. Secrecy demands attention in as much as we always have to worry about the possibility of it breaking down. There were times when I was aware that my research was being gossiped about. Since I was in the field covertly, I was worried that my research was in danger. One of the women who started working after I did was a student at my university in a department where I have several friends. I worried that she would hear gossip about my work, and my cover would be blown. Controlling talk about field research is critical. My advice is to keep to a minimum the people who know about the work. However, talk can not be completely controlled and questions cannot be ignored or brushed off but need to be faced head-on with well-prepared responses so the research cannot be trivialized. I hope that qualitative research training more systematically addresses this issue. Graduate advisors and senior mentors should make sure that preparation for the field includes 'practice' in answering difficult questions about the research site. In the same way that we prepare for an interview or lecture, close colleagues or mentors can prepare a researcher by asking probing questions in private, to prepare her for navigating these difficult questions in public (Mattley, 1998).

I believe that doing covert participant observation carries with it numerous dilemmas, but they are not insurmountable. The choice as to whether or not to do covert work is not a capricious one. All methods are selected according to their appropriateness for the research question. The decision to use covert participant observation is more difficult because, as Miller points out, it is 'the truly least used of all the qualitative methods' (Miller, 2001: 13). Therefore, it comprises a smaller share of the body of qualitative research and, as a result, researchers have fewer guideposts to help them in their decision-making process. One thing is certain: only more discussions by those of us who have done covert participant observation will make the decision clearer.

REFERENCES

Caughey, John L. (1984) *Imaginary Social Worlds.* Lincoln, NE: University of Nebraska Press.

Chancer, Lynn Sharon (1993) 'Prostitution, Feminist Theory, and Ambivalence: Notes from the Sociological Underground'. *Social Text*, 37 (Winter): 143–71.

Delacoste, Frederique and Alexander, Priscilla (eds) (1987/1998) *Sex Work: Writings by Women in the Sex Industry.* San Francisco, CA: Cleis Press.

Fine, Gary A. (1983) *Shared Fantasy: Role-playing Games as Social Worlds.* Chicago: University of Chicago Press.

Fine, Gary A. (1993) 'Ten Lies of Ethnography: Moral Dilemmas of Field Research', *Journal of Contemporary Ethnography*, 22: 267–94.

Fine, Michelle (1998) 'Fine Working the Hyphens: Reinventing Self and Other in Qualitative Research,' in Norman K. Denzin and Yvonna S. Lincoln (eds),

The Landscape of Qualitative Research. Thousand Oaks, CA: Sage. pp. 130–55.

Flowers, Amy (1998) *The Fantasy Factory.* Philadelphia, PA: University of Pennsylvania Press.

Glascock, Jack and Robert, LaRose (1993) 'Dial-A-Porn Recordings: The Role of the Female Participant in Male Sexual Fantasies', *Journal of Broadcasting and Electronic Media,* 37(3): 313–24.

Hochschild, Arlie R. (1983) *The Managed Heart.* Berkeley, CA: University of California Press.

Mattley, Christine (1997) 'Field Research with Phone Fantasy Workers: Managing the Researcher's Emotions', in Martin D. Schwartz (ed.), *Researching Sexual Violence Against Women: Methodological and Personal Considerations.* Thousand Oaks, CA: Sage. pp. 101–14.

Mattley, Christine (1998) '(Dis) Courtesy Stigma: Fieldwork among Phone Fantasy Workers', in Jeff Ferrell and Mark Hamm (eds), *Ethnography at the Edge.* Boston, MA: Northeastern University Press. pp. 146–58.

Mattley, Christine (2002) 'Voicing Gender: The Performance of Gender in the Context of Phone Sex Lines', in Patricia Gagne and Richard Tewskbury (eds), *Gendered Sexualities: Advances in Gender Research* (Vol. 6). London: JAI/Elsevier Science. pp. 79–102.

McClintock, Anne (1993) 'Sex Workers and Sex Work: Introduction', *Social Text,* 37(Winter): 1–10.

Miller, J. Mitchell (2001) 'Covert Participant Observation: Reconsidering the Least Used Method', in J. Mitchell Miller and Richard Tewksbury (eds), *Extreme Methods.* Needham Heights, MA: Allyn and Bacon. pp. 13–20.

Mitchell, Richard G. (1993) *Secrecy and Fieldwork.* Newbury Park, CA: Sage.

Nagle, Jill (ed) (1997) *Whores and Other Feminists.* New York: Routledge.

Punch, Maurice (1998) 'Politics and Ethics in Qualitative Research', in Norman K. Denzin and Yvonna S. Lincoln (eds), *The Landscape of Qualitative Research.* Thousand Oaks, CA: Sage. pp. 156–84.

Reinharz, Shulamit (1992) *Feminist Methods in Social Research.* New York: Oxford University Press.

Segal, Lynne and McIntosh, Mary (1993) *Sex Exposed: Sexuality and the Pornography Debate.* New Brunswick, NJ: Rutgers University Press.

10

The Case for Dangerous Fieldwork

BRUCE A. JACOBS

People to whom I describe my research with street-level crack dealers, especially students, are intrigued by what I discovered but more often surprised by the way I obtained the data. 'How did you do it?,' they ask. 'I went up to them,' I respond. Well, they continue, 'How did you get them to talk to you? Wasn't it dangerous?' The last question is always poignant, partly because I was robbed at gunpoint myself during the study, partly because I realize that most 'everyday people,' particularly sheltered undergraduates, are afraid of getting close to serious criminals in the wild. They share this fear with many of my fellow criminologists, though possibly for different reasons, so I understand it.

What I tell them is that fieldwork with active criminals is surprisingly easy and reasonably safe. Easy in the sense that no community, regardless of size, has a shortage of offenders; safe because most of the time even serious criminals are doing non-criminal things and want to help out people who are genuinely trying to understand them. It may not seem this simple, but really it is.

In the same breath, I tell them that my story as a qualitative researcher is one of

evolution because of the dangers I have faced. This evolution represents my attempt to manage danger. If danger can't be avoided in fieldwork, it can be lessened without making substantial sacrifices in what one studies or the results s/he ultimately obtains. That is the point of departure for the current chapter.

DANGER IN FIELDWORK

Danger is thought to be an unavoidable part of criminological fieldwork. This is because the researcher associates with high-risk people who are doing marginal things and lacks legal recourse in the event that something untoward happens to him or her, unless s/he wants to breach confidentiality and be labeled a snitch, both of which will bring a quick end to the research.

Danger takes on two principal forms in work of this kind. Personal danger is the most obvious and menacing form. By personal danger I mean violations that threaten the researcher's safety and well-being, like the robbery I experienced. No ethnographer is totally immune, and the literature is filled with tales of investigators who confronted it and 'lived to tell us' (Kleinman and Copp, 1993: 17, quoted in Blee, 1998: 383; see also Van Maanen, 1988). Bourgois (1995: 30), for example, was privy to countless acts of serious rule-breaking – aggravated assaults, bombings, and police shootouts – during a five-year study of the New York drug trade. Wright and Decker (1994) almost got caught in a burgeoning dispute between two warring street offenders as they performed a 'walk-about' with one of the men. James Inciardi (1993) landed in volatile drug houses inhabited by desperate people whose behavior could deteriorate into psychopathy at any moment. Stephen Lyng (1998) took a spill on a Kawasaki Ninja motorcycle as he skirted a corner pushing 100 mph during research on voluntarily reckless activities, resulting in a permanently disabling injury. Gary Armstrong (1998) was involved in a number of violent incidents while carrying out his ten-year ethnography of British football hooligans, and James Patrick (1973) was forced to fight with a gang member while covertly studying Glasgow gangs. Ken Pryce, whose ethnography of street hustling is an outstanding example of the genre (1979), was murdered when he turned his attention to organized crime in the Caribbean. In addition to being robbed at gunpoint, I was involuntarily detained on at least two occasions, stalked, defrauded numerous times, and had someone try to punch out my car window as I sat inside with the motor on. I also unwittingly drove into a running gun battle in which the 'pop' of the gun was so loud and so close I nearly lost control of my vehicle in ducking for cover and speeding away.

Less threatening to the researcher in an immediate physical sense but no less menacing are the legal dangers s/he can face. Witnessing criminal behavior or simply having knowledge that specific crimes have taken place makes you an accessory to their commission whether you like it or not

(Hobbs, 1988: Chapter 1). Social scientists enjoy no privileged relationship with their respondents (Adler, 1990), like physicians do with their patients or attorneys with their clients. Many of criminology's most respected ethnographers 'could well be considered a rogues' gallery of common criminals' for this reason alone (Ferrell, 1998: 24).

Graduate student Rik Scarce learned this painful lesson in 1993 during research on the radical environmental movement. The authorities demanded his data, he refused, and he served 159 days in jail before a sympathetic judge let him go. Scarce told his subjects that he was going to protect them, and that is what he did (see Scarce, 2002). Though rare in the actual practice of field research, Scarce's ordeal makes it clear that ethnographers studying hidden or illegal populations uncover things that authorities want to know about and if they want to badly enough, they will force it out of you, or try to. The biggest risk to fieldworkers, Polsky justifiably contends, comes not from the 'cannibals and headhunters' but from the authorities, for the 'criminologist studying uncaught criminals in the open finds sooner or later that law enforcers try to put him on the spot – because, unless he is a complete fool, he uncovers information that law enforcers would like to know…' (Polsky, 1967: 147).

I too have had run-ins with the authorities, although none, thankfully, resulted in anything close to what Scarce had to endure. What was ironic about these confrontations was their role in helping to generate access to the rule-breakers I wanted to study. The worse the police treated me, the faster my credibility rose.

I began my research on street crack dealers knowing no one in the setting, having no connections, and with no one to vouch for me. I identified an active, open-air drug market in which I thought I could blend and to which I thought I could gain access. Owing to my race (white) and age (late 20s) at the time I did this research, I picked an area near a major local university. Dressing the part of college student, I assimilated quite readily. After observing the scene for a while, I approached individuals whom I suspected were involved in dealing. I told them I was a university professor who wanted to do a study of dealing and street life. They were more surprised than suspicious, but surprise seemed to express itself as suspicion. They told me to get the hell away from them, or something like that. They sneered. They cursed. They called me a cop. But I persisted – long enough, crucially, for the police to start hassling me.

Presuming I was just another addict looking to buy drugs and unaware of my research objectives, the police stopped, interrogated, and searched me on at least four occasions. Sometimes these searches occurred in the presence of the offenders I wanted to talk to, sometimes not. But this treatment was the key to my acceptance. Early on in a project of this nature, arguably the greatest threat that the ethnographer of active criminals has to face is the belief that s/he is working undercover. The police are known to use the research role to gather incriminating information about targeted subcultures, and researchers, as outsiders, are unknown quantities who can not be trusted. The authorities' detention of me, therefore, was absolutely essential for solidifying my credibility for the remainder of the project and setting up the snowball sampling procedure I would use to recruit additional respondents (Wright et al., 1992; for a complete discussion of these and other relevant issues, see Jacobs, 1998).

RE-EVALUATING ACCESS

'Cold access,' such as the kind I negotiated, is for the desperate or, some say, the stupid.

Perhaps I was both, but I wanted to do the work. That admission notwithstanding, I am now delighted to convey how easy it is to identify serious offenders in one's midst and even more delighted to relate how open they can be in talking to you about their lives. Ned Polsky (1967: 124) revealed this over three decades ago, but I remained painfully ignorant at the time I initiated the crack study:

> Getting an introduction or two [to active offenders] is not nearly so difficult as it may seem. Among students whom I have had perform the experiment of asking their relatives and friends to see if any could provide an introduction to a career criminal, fully a third reported that they could get such introductions. ... Moreover, once your research interests are publicly known you get volunteer offers of this sort. From students, faculty, and others, I have have more offers of introductions to career criminals ... than I could begin to follow up. (Polsky, 1967: 124)

As Polsky implies, the academic criminologist's most powerful resource is his or her students. If you're in a big program with lots of undergraduate majors, you teach dozens of students every year, semester after semester. Your store of potential contacts grows exponentially and may well be unlimited over time. These contacts can vouch for who you are and what you're doing because they see it for themselves in class every lecture day. You don't need to counter the perception that you're a cop, nor need you give an extensive justification of why you want to do the research. You are a criminologist so that is self-evident. Nor do you want to offer an elaborate explanation. Too much specificity can expose the people you want to talk to. 'I'm writing a book about crime and street life,' I might say, or something more vague than that.

I used a variation of this technique for a small, post-crack study of heroin I conducted (Jacobs, 1999). One of my student's cousins was an active user and occasional dealer. Within days of establishing contact with this man, offenders started showing up to my office in bunches. The technique was so successful that I had to put the brakes on recruitment. At one point, would-be respondents were appearing at the university's administration building asking for directions to my office. My experience does not appear to be isolated:

> on several occasions, it almost became problematic when marginal members of [the crime] network [I was studying], and even outsiders, accosted me angrily for never tape-recording them [for an interview], claiming that they 'deserved to be at least a chapter' in my book. (Bourgois, 1995: 46, commenting on his research with New York drug dealers)

Recruitment has a powerful tendency to take on a momentum of its own, particularly if you emphasize the academic nature of the research. People in general are flattered when you want to talk to them about their lives, but especially when it is in the interest of 'science.' This may strain credibility but it's true, and especially when you're researching active offenders. Where others fear or ignore them or want to lock them up, you're trying to tell their story (Solway and Waters, 1977). These are people marginalized in virtually every other aspect of their lives. Your interest is refreshing and empowering. It affirms that what they have to say is important and that they have something genuine to contribute. As Harrington (2003: 609–10) notes: 'Researchers must be categorized in ways that are not only relevant to participants ... but also identity-enhancing. ... [T]he interest of the researcher can be interpreted as conferring a flattering aura of "specialness" ...'

This doesn't give you license to drop your guard. You have to remember who you're dealing with, lest you lose the edge that helps you identify trouble before it bites you. I say this from my street-based experience. One of my initial contacts for the crack study was a young man I'll call Luther. He was one of the first to trust that I was a university professor doing research on street life, not a cop, and helped initiate a chain of referrals that ultimately netted 40 respondents. After Luther could no longer provide referrals, I moved on, cutting him loose too quickly I suppose, and without adequate debriefing. He felt wronged, he was mad, and he took it out by robbing me. I described the incident in detail in an earlier report (see Jacobs, 1998).

I believe the robbery would never have happened had I been more attentive to the special referral role he had come to play in my research and had I communicated my gratitude and reasons for moving on more clearly. Nobody deserves less, particularly an active criminal with a fragile ego, but in my quest for more data, I lost sight of this. It won't happen again.

MEDIATED ETHNOGRAPHY

Recognizing that recruitment of offenders is less daunting than I imagined but safety more precarious than most reasonable researchers feel comfortable with, I have now moved away from street-based research and toward more strictly interview-focused work of criminals, where I (or a co-investigator) conduct the interviews but where indigenous fieldworkers arrange them in a controlled setting removed from the streets. I like to call this approach mediated ethnography. As I indicated early in this chapter, my shift in research strategy is in no small part a danger-reduction strategy. Reduction is the operative word because I remain very much engaged with street offenders and their formidable law-breaking.

Indeed, the offenders I have interviewed since being robbed are, as a group, more unstable and potentially violent than those I interviewed prior to the incident. In a study performed by colleagues drawing offenders from roughly the same St Louis neighborhoods from which I draw my samples, respondents showed up bleeding from a recent knife or gunshot wound or toting weapons (see Wright and Decker, 1997). I have not confronted freshly wounded respondents in my personal experience, and interviewees may be toting firearms, but I generally don't ask and they generally don't tell. Not uncommon, however, is for interviewees to show up under the influence of powerful psychoactive drugs. Questions that might seem innocuous to me may be perceived as quite threatening during an opiate 'nod,' and I ask a lot of questions. Your data are only as good as your questions, but the things you have to ask when you're studying drug robbery or car-jacking or violent retaliation – topics of my recent research – typically are not innocuous.

Who you talk to is at least as important as the setting in which those conversations take place, and in mediated criminological ethnography, respondents obviously remain serious offenders who may well decide to test you. During the retaliation study, a muscular African-American offender in his middle 20s came up to my office for an interview. Wearing a red 'do-rag' (bandana), fashioned gang-member style around his head, and a white sleeveless T-shirt that showcased a sinewy frame (and several tattoos, if I remember correctly), his appearance was ominous. Just before the interview started – in the quad of my university – he began speaking loudly in what others would perceive to be a menacing tone but which I interpreted to be bravado. His exact words escape me at present, but it was something like he was going to rob someone right then and there, that he was a bad man, and that everybody should look out. He made these statements in a rather bold way, but I

responded matter-of-factly. 'You're going to spook someone talking that way around here,' adding that 'if you really were going to rob someone, you sure as heck wouldn't be talking about it.' He looked at me wryly, knowing, perhaps, that he had only the vaguest intentions of committing such a crime, surprised, it seemed, that I had called his bluff. Some small talk followed, we went into my office, and nothing more of the sort occurred.

In an incident with a car-jacker some months earlier, I had the respondent tell me at the interview's close that of the four people questioning him that day (in this particular interview, a PhD student, postdoctoral fellow, and a colleague all were present), I was the only one he wouldn't target for a robbery. 'You looked at me eye-to-eye this entire time. You ain't scared. I wouldn't jack you,' or something like that. The implication, perhaps, was that people who averted his gaze were 'intimidatable.' My associates in the room that day may have been looking down for very good reasons – to collect their thoughts, write down notes and questions, or something else essential to the research – but his perception is all that matters. I do remember this interviewee being particularly aggressive in his description of things, and I do recall looking straight at him during this description precisely because I wanted him to know that there was nothing wrong with what he was saying or how he was saying it, and that, to me, he may as well have been describing a trip to the local supermarket. Reacting normally to what is graphic or extreme or intimidating is expected in their world and it behooves the researcher to react in precisely that way. It also helps to show that you're not making value judgments about what they're reporting, which encourages them to see you as someone only who wants answers.

SAFER OR LESS DANGEROUS?

The prospect of someone sneaking up on me or being caught in a running gun battle or getting car-jacked is decidedly remote in the cozy confines of a sealed interview room. This is comforting when I think about the places where I might otherwise be conducting a given interview. Paradoxically, the mediated approach lacks the protective power of informal social control, and informal social control is one of the reasons I felt oddly safe during my street-based research. On a typical interview day, there would be activity all around. Residents might occupy a front stoop next door. Cars rode up and down the streets. An occasional school bus, city bus, or utility truck would pass by. Children might approach and talk to me. I didn't feel isolated. If something happened, somebody would see it, which made me feel safer. The perception of safety – even if it's not a reality – is what allowed me to go back to the field time and again. And the more times I went out there without anything bad happening, the more confident I became that nothing would. Even when I did get victimized or experienced some kind of confrontation, I always labeled it a freak thing, an exception, not something to worry about.

Research as I now undertake it is quite solitary. No one's in the interview room beside me or perhaps a colleague who's doing the interview with me (or perhaps my field recruiter). The door is shut. The shades are drawn. If a respondent wanted to try something, s/he easily could. I have cash, not a lot, but enough. Like everyone else, I carry a wallet. In that wallet is an ATM card and ATM cards can be used in a number of machines close by. The principal danger, I suppose, is being abducted by a respondent high on crack or heroin or PCP, who's had a very bad day or week, who is desperate, and who wants to make somebody pay. Mind

you, this never has happened, and I have interviewed scores of active offenders using this method, but it's possible I suppose.

If personal dangers remain, legal dangers do diminish substantially. Despite having 'guilty knowledge,' I can't be jailed for loitering, trespassing, or any number of other offences I could be charged with *in situ*. More importantly, the police cannot interrupt a street-based interview to seize my notes and tapes. My principal fear is that the authorities could confiscate completed transcripts and computer files, which is why I am careful not to record the real names of respondents, specific locations in which they have committed crimes, or other identifying information. These data are not important anyway. The criminal act is my unit of analysis, not the crime and its identifying players, and I am concerned about specific events only insofar as they permit elaboration of broader patterns that bring new conceptual meaning to my research topic. Seizing my transcripts would be unlikely to tell the police something they don't already know anyway. I have found the police to be arrogant in their perception of academic fieldworkers and what they do. Typical in their thinking is that a college professor cannot tell them anything they don't know or haven't experienced in their thousands of hours of patrol and interrogation. Besides, they have their own snitches to provide names and locations of specific crimes. Felony arrests are all that matter, and their informants provide them in bunches. Forcing this information out of me is too much trouble and hassle for a payoff that is questionable at best.

DANGER AND VALIDITY

Perhaps the most vexing concern I now face revolves around the issue of validity. That is, how do I know that respondents are giving me the 'straight story?' The question becomes more consequential as the deviantness of the study population increases because the stakes are higher and respondents have more to lose by disclosing what 'really goes on.' It is amplified further when you decide not to immerse yourself physically in the setting because you can not prove first-hand that everything respondents are telling you is true. At face value this may stand in stark contrast to the practices of those fieldworkers who immerse themselves totally in a criminal culture (Archard, 1979; Armstrong, 1998; Hobbs, 1988, 1995; Irwin, 1970; Wolf, 1991). Yet even the most ardent, deeply immersed ethnographer cannot be where the action is all the time, and to say that something is not valid or true or accurate just because you didn't witness it yourself is just wrong. Is it possible to apprehend the explosive power of an atomic bomb without detonating one yourself and sitting sufficiently close by to see, feel, and hear its destructive consequences? Before chiding me for my churlishness, remember that this is coming from a person who has spent a considerable time in the field. It is possible to approximate thick description, and have a good handle on its validity, without actually 'being there.'

'Being there' can bring validity problems of its own. The researcher's very presence can 'create' the data s/he reports – a phenomenon referred to as methodogenesis (Stoddart, 1986; see also Harrington, 2003) – and if participation in the field is too thoroughgoing, it can dull the analytic sensitivity necessary to provide a value-free account. On this dilemma, Harrington (2002) observes:

> depth of participation in a group is a signal of researchers' credibility ... the more time a researcher spends with a group, the farther he or she gets into the 'backstage' area (Goffman, 1959), and the more convincing the resulting account (Glesne and Peshkin, 1999). [Yet] credible ethnography also requires evidence of analytic distance on the part of the researcher. Credible ethnographies must be 'more than a personal document' (Stoddart, 1986: 104). Researchers must demonstrate an ability to be both immersed in a group and separate enough to view it with a critical eye. This poses an inevitable dilemma for which there is no entirely satisfactory solution. (Jorgenson, 1989; quoted in Harrington, 2002: 50)

A balance can be achieved with the right strategy, and it is upon this balance that the validity of one's data may well hinge. In the mediated approach, balance hinges on help from an indigenous 'paraprofessional,' a person entrenched in the criminal subculture who enjoys a solid reputation for street integrity and trustworthiness, and who can vouch for the researcher's legitimacy. As a researcher, I infiltrate by proxy, riding the fieldworker's credibility and coattails with a tight grip. The benefits of immersion coupled with the neutrality of distance make for a powerful combination.

The importance of the so-called gatekeeper to criminological fieldwork cannot be overstated, but its role in mediated criminological ethnography is especially notable. Research of this kind cannot be undertaken without an 'individual who will establish the (researcher's) credentials (and who is) well thought of by the other participants in the system' (Walker and Lidz, 1977: 115). This person is justifiably designated 'the "hero" of the research – the person without whom the research could never have been conducted' (Shaffir et al., 1980: 128). I have interviewed scores of hardened criminals with the help of my fieldworker, yielding richly descriptive data. I would not be surprised if respondents were to disclose things in an arranged interview they might keep concealed if I were to accompany them in their natural setting. I don't have a reliable 'baseline' with which to offer this conclusion, but it's a hunch based on a combination of experience and understanding human behavior.

A respondent in a forthcoming study on violent retaliation told me about a highly sensitive and very serious crime he committed, notable given the sensitive nature of the topics I study. 'Red,' as I will call him, reportedly knocked into another man accidentally at a bar one night, spilling his drink on the man's clothing. Angered, the man, who was on a date with a female companion, 'knocked the shit' out of Red, giving him no chance to explain the incident or apologize for it. Other patrons inside the tavern witnessed the assault, as did the female companion, whom Red vaguely knew. Embarrassed and incensed, Red left the bar and went to his vehicle, where he retrieved his handgun and sat waiting for several hours. When the violator exited – inebriated and ignorant of Red's presence – Red attacked, shooting the man several times in the back. I stopped the interview and asked Red why he was telling me this. I hear about a lot of serious wrongdoing in interviews, but respondents tend to 'draw the line' when it gets too serious. I can't remember exactly what Red told me, but it was something like, 'I had to get it off my chest. It makes me feel better.'

I have examples of other such revelations, none perhaps as sensitive, but the fact remains that serious criminals often have no one to disclose transgressions to in confidence. Many have long since burned up ties with people they could realistically confide in – family members in particular – through their own irresponsible and malicious behavior. And associates typically are not an option. Not only do they fear a contemporary snitching about something they disclose, revealing something to 'get it off one's chest' can make you look weak, and weakness is not something you ever want to show, especially when your associates are other criminals who may view it as an invitation for victimization. More often than not, street criminals' associates are indeed offenders.

The social distance between researcher and respondent empowers the latter to speak freely. With anonymity comes comfort and with comfort comes candor. Of this 'stranger phenomenon,' Georg Simmel (1908/1950: 404) wrote almost a century ago on the 'most surprising openness' among otherwise distant parties who reveal 'confidences which sometimes have the character of a confessional and which would be carefully withheld from a more closely related person' (quoted in Harrington, 2003: 600). Qualitative research is filled with anecdotal accounts of respondents who claim to seldom or never share information they offer in an interview (see, for example, Arendell 1997), yet the interview's liberating potential has garnered relatively scant methodological attention, especially in criminological work where it may be most valuable of all. This probably derives from the dominant social scientific understanding of how interviews proceed and should be conducted:

> Most methods textbooks treat interviewing as a conversation between two people – the interviewer and the interviewee. The interviewer asks questions, and the interviewee responds to them. But if you think about it, this is a peculiar kind of conversation. In an interview, one person – the interviewee – reveals information about him- or herself; the other does not. One person – the interviewer – directs the conversation, often with expectations for what should happen during that conversation and for what constitutes a 'correct' answer; the other does not. One person – the interviewer – decides when the questions have been satisfactorily answered and closes the conversation; the other does not. In this sense, an interview is an odd type of conversation indeed. In what other kind of conversation is there such a lopsided exchange? (Esterberg, 2002: 84)

Qualitative interviews with offenders are all about empowerment. The researcher develops general questions, offers these questions, and then sits back with a receptive ear to give interviewees the opportunity to teach him or her – someone supposedly 'smarter' than them (in terms of educational attainment) – about their day-to-day lives. The dialogue that emerges is 'loose,' 'mutual,' and, most importantly, respondent-dominated (Warren et al., 2003). Most people don't take the time to hear what offenders have to say. Many more are too afraid or just don't care, especially members of respectable society, which people like me represent. Teachers, principals, bosses, business owners, police officers, and other authority figures not only fail to afford offenders the respect they think they deserve, they actively disrespect them. Researchers' interest validates offenders as experts on a topic of genuine scholarly interest. Researchers provide a forum for demonstrating competencies that can be demonstrated nowhere else (Wright and Decker, 1994). Though researchers may remunerate offenders for their time, as I do, the sum is small in relation to what they could be making at the same time 'hustling.' The fieldwork exchange remains very much 'symbolic and nonmaterial' (Jorgenson, 1989; Harrington, 2003).

THE DANGER OF TOO LITTLE

Perhaps the most overlooked danger of carrying out fieldwork with active criminals is that too little of it is indeed carried out. Any impartial observer to the study of crime can readily see that the field, particularly in the United States, is dominated by a quantitative discourse that speaks almost exclusively in numbers and formulas. Such observers, especially students new to the field and eager to understand the 'mind of the criminal,' are at first stunned, then stupefied, by a domain of inquiry that professes to study rule-breaking without studying the subjectivity that drives it – the motives, thoughts, emotions, rationalizations, and vicissitudes of the rule-breakers. One cynic comes close to suggesting that criminologists are more likely to study each other – each other's 'theories' of crime that is – than they are criminals (see Fleisher, 1998: 55–6). Though this may be a reach, criminology, especially in the United States, remains very much a discipline fixated on technical, statistical, and theoretical proficiency to the exclusion of the immediate phenomenological foreground in which decisions to offend are activated.

Numbers and formulas provide the aura of scientific legitimacy that qualitative research simply cannot offer. If, as some criminologists will tell you, the discipline has an inferiority complex – bestowed by natural scientists who don't consider social scientists real scientists – such an aura becomes important. But aura comes at a price. Numbers and formulas detach social life from its situated meaning and transform 'flesh-and-blood' people into lifeless variables and categories for quantification and measurement (Fleisher, 1998: 49). The cost of legitimacy is real understanding.

Perhaps technical proficiency derives from fear, fear of some of the dangers outlined in this chapter or maybe something less exotic: the fear of being 'unproductive.' Criminological fieldwork can be frustratingly time-consuming. If you're starting a project 'cold,' you have to enter the setting and establish a presence (or identify and train fieldworkers to do it for you), develop rapport, cultivate key informants, and gain respondents' trust, among other things, all before any data are even collected and coded. This requires patience and persistence but, most of all, the abiding faith that what you are doing will ultimately pay off. This faith is significant because it is in the early periods of research that it appears nothing is being accomplished, or will be:

> The first few days or even weeks of a study may bring in only superficial information, along with bits of data that either do not seem to make sense or do not fit together. One who has become accustomed to measuring progress in terms of pages read or written, naturally finds this beginning stage frustrating. Unless obviously dramatic [things] are unfolding before our eyes, it may seem that nothing is happening. (Whyte, 1984: 69)

Emergent answers don't fit into neatly prescribed categories. Some answers don't come at all. Others simply raise tougher questions.

There's lots of unpredictability. No matter how tightly controlled your recruitment strategy or research design, the work can be messy. It's not that these problems cannot be overcome, but rather that many social scientists 'are temperamentally unsuited … to leave the role of Ph.D., Professor, Expert, (and) Teacher … (to muck) around in the real world outside the academy' (Lofland, 1976: 13–14, quoted in Broadhead and Fox, 1990: 329).

This is especially true when the alternative is so much more convenient. Quantitative data frequently exist for you, perhaps collected and archived in downloadable format for maximum efficiency. Research, in some cases, can be a matter of formulating hypotheses, arranging concepts, and crunching the numbers. This greatly reduces the time it takes to complete a viable manuscript. Because data sets can be used over and over again, there's no shortage of material for future studies. Scholars can make entire careers out of secondary data analysis, and some unabashedly proclaim that they might do just that (see Geis, 2001, on this point). Because so many other criminologists are doing the same thing with the same or similar data sets, one's work can get cited and re-cited. This increases your 'impact factor' – an important measure of your influence in the field. Scholars with the biggest impact factors are the most marketable, and this translates into cushier offices, bigger salaries, and fancier titles.

Ethnographies of criminals also rarely get funded or funded significantly. Funding is critical because manuscripts in the discipline's flagship journals are less likely to be completed without it. In the United States, without publications in these journals, you will be hard-pressed to get tenure, and without tenure, your academic career will come to a halt. Tenure, and more generally academic advancement, increasingly depends on grantsmanship itself. The ability to secure external funding is rapidly becoming one of the most important requisites of promotion from, for instance in the United States, assistant professor, ranked coequally at some institutions with peer-reviewed publications. But the relationship is reciprocal, and reciprocally reinforcing. Successful grantsmanship depends in no small part on your publication record – funding agencies generally do not throw big money at unproven scholars, nor should they – and publications usually don't come without funding. Publications lead to external dollars, external dollars help generate more articles, which makes you even more viable for additional external dollars so you can publish yet more articles.

Then there is the fear that many researchers of active criminals rarely talk about or perhaps are even aware of. The fear that what they study, how they study what they study, or some combination of the two, will in some way taint them. Tainting is a very real possibility in sociological, anthropological and criminological field research (see Archard, 1979). Scholars who inhabit the same social space as rule-breakers,

> who intentionally place themselves in situations of shady legality and unconventional morality, push at the very boundaries of professionally acceptable scholarly inquiry. They risk having their research denigrated on grounds of bias, subjectivity, over-involvement, and overrapport. They in turn risk informal censure from colleagues who feel that this sort of research, by directing close attention to criminal or deviant groups, in effect stamps these groups with an imprimatur of scholarly legitimacy. (Ferrell and Hamm, 1998: 4)

Related is the widely-held, though often unstated belief, that what a field researcher studies, to some degree, reflects his or her personal values, interests, or preoccupations. Translation: If you're studying deviants, you must want to be one of them or, at the very least, you sympathize with their activities and perhaps even approve of them. During a study of phone sex operators, Professor Christine Mattley (1998) thus became the object of 'workplace giggles, double entendres, and references to dirty movies' from colleagues who presumed she wanted a legitimate way to indulge her own 'perverted' and 'voyeuristic' tendencies (see Hamm and Ferrell, 1998: 258). The more immersed the researcher gets in a deviant setting, or the more deviant the topic itself, the more convincing this perception can become. The researcher may even be suspected of being the very thing s/he is studying. When the topic is drug use, homosexuality, or some other stigmatizing behavior, the consequences can be far-reaching (Henslin, 1972; Sluka, 1990). The researcher's legitimacy itself may fall into question (see Tewksbury and Gagne, 1997: 147).

CONCLUSION

Danger of one sort or another will always be present in fieldwork-based studies of active criminals. But danger must be accommodated if we are to make the strides we need to make to really understand offender behavior. There are more or less direct ways to go about the business of field research and, over the years, my approach has become 'less direct' because of the dangers I've faced. The compromise that danger has forced me to strike is one that I believe balances competing concerns – about access, safety, and validity – in a manner consistent with the core mission of social science. Deeper explanation and understanding may come at a price, but the structure, process, and contingent forms of serious rule-breaking cannot be specified without it.

REFERENCES

Adler, Patricia (1990) 'Ethnographic Research on Hidden Populations: Penetrating the Drug World.' In Elizabeth Y. Lambert (ed.) *The Collection and Interpretation of Data from Hidden Populations.* NIDA Research Monograph. Washington, DC: US Government Printing Office. pp. 96–112.

Archard, P. (1979) *Vagrancy, Alcoholism and Social Control.* London: Macmillan.

Arendell, Terry (1997) 'Reflections on the Researcher–Researched Relationship: A Woman Interviewing Men,' *Qualitative Sociology* 20: 341–68.

Armstrong, G. (1998) *Football Hooligans: Knowing the Score.* Oxford: Berg.

Blee, Kathleen M. (1998) 'White-knuckle Research: Emotional Dynamics in Fieldwork with Racist Activists,' *Qualitative Sociology* 21: 381–99.

Bourgois, Philippe (1995) *In Search of Respect: Selling Crack in El Barrio.* Cambridge: Cambridge University Press.

Broadhead, Robert S. and Fox, Kathryn J. (1990) 'Takin' It to the Streets: AIDS Outreach as Ethnography,' *Journal of Contemporary Ethnography* 19: 322–48.

Esterberg, Kristin G. (2002) *Qualitative Methods in Social Research.* Boston: McGraw-Hill.

Ferrell, Jeff (1998) 'Criminological *Verstehen:* Inside the Immediacy of Crime.' In Jeff Ferrell and Mark Hamm (eds) *Ethnography at the Edge: Crime, Deviance, and Fieldwork.* Boston: Northeastern University Press. pp. 20–42.

Ferrell, Jeff and Hamm, Mark S. (1998) 'True Confessions: Crime, Deviance, and Field Research.' In Jeff Ferrell and Mark Hamm (eds) *Ethnography at the Edge: Crime, Deviance, and Fieldwork.* Boston: Northeastern University Press. pp. 2–19.

Fleisher, Mark S. (1998) 'Ethnographers, Pimps, and the Company store.' In Jeff Ferrell and Mark Hamm (eds) *Ethnography at the Edge: Crime, Deviance, and Fieldwork.* Boston: Northeastern University Press. pp. 44–64.

Geis, Gilbert (2001) 'On Cross-disciplinary Qualitative Research: Some Homilies.' Paper presented at a symposium on interdisciplinary research, University of California, Irvine.

Glesne, C. and Peshkin, A. (1999) *Becoming Qualitative Researchers.* Reading, MA: Addison-Wesley.

Hamm, Mark S. and Ferrell, Jeff (1998) 'Confessions of Danger and Humanity.' In Jeff Ferrell and Mark Hamm (eds) *Ethnography at the Edge: Crime, Deviance, and Fieldwork.* Boston: Northeastern University Press. pp. 254–72.

Harrington, Brooke (2002) 'Obtrusiveness as Strategy in Ethnographic Research,' *Qualitative Sociology* 25: 49–61.

Harrington, Brooke (2003) 'The Social Psychology of Access in Ethnographic Research,' *Journal of Contemporary Ethnography* 32: 592–625.

Henslin, James M. (1972) 'Studying Deviance in Four Settings: Research Experiences with Cabbiess, Suicides, Drug Users, and Abortionees.' In Jack Douglas (ed.) *Research on Deviance*. New York: Random House. pp. 35–70.

Hobbs, D. (1988) *Doing the Business: Entrepreneurship, the Working Class and Detectives in the East End of London*. Oxford: Oxford University Press.

Hobbs, D. (1995) *Bad Business: Professional Criminals in Modern Britain*. Oxford: Oxford University Press.

Inciardi, James A. (1993) 'Kingrats, Chicken Heads, Slow Necks, Freaks, and Blood Suckers: A Glimpse at the Miami Sex-for-Crack Market.' In Mitchell S. Ratner (ed.) *Crack Pipe as Pimp*. New York: Lexington Books. pp. 37–67.

Irwin, J. (1970) *The Felon*. Englewood Cliffs, NJ: Prentice-Hall.

Jacobs, Bruce A. (1998) 'Researching Crack Dealers: Confessions, Dilemmas, Strategies.' In Jeff Ferrell and Mark Hamm (eds) *Ethnography at the Edge: Crime, Deviance, and Fieldwork*. Boston: Northeastern University Press. pp. 160–77.

Jacobs, Bruce A. (1999) 'Crack to Heroin?: Drug Markets and Transition.' *British Journal of Criminology* 39: 555–74.

Jorgenson, D. (1989) *Participant Observation: A Methodology for Human Studies*. Newbury Park, CA: Sage.

Kleinman, S. and Copp, M. (1993) *Emotions and Fieldwork*. Newbury Park, CA: Sage.

Lofland, J. (1976) *Doing Social Life: The Qualitative Study of Human Interaction in Natural Settings*. New York: Wiley.

Lyng, Stephen (1998) 'Dangerous Methods: Risk Taking and the Research Process.' In Jeff Ferrell and Mark Hamm (eds) *Ethnography at the Edge: Crime, Deviance, and Fieldwork*. Boston: Northeastern University Press. pp. 221–51.

Mattley, Christine (1998) '(Dis)courtesy stigma: Fieldwork among Phone Fantasy Workers.' In Jeff Ferrell and Mark Hamm (eds) *Ethnography at the Edge: Crime, Deviance, and Fieldwork*. Boston: Northeastern University Press. pp. 146–58.

Patrick, J. (1973) *A Glasgow Gang Observed*. London: Eyre Methuen.

Polsky, Ned (1967) *Hustlers, Beats, and Others*. Chicago: Aldine.

Pryce, K. (1979) *Endless Pressure: A Study of West Indian Lifestyles in Britain*. Harmondsworth: Penguin.

Scarce, R. (2002) 'Doing Time as an Act of Survival.' *Symbolic Interaction* 25: 303–21.

Shaffir, Wiliam B., Stebbins, Robert A. and Turowetz, Allan (1980) *Fieldwork Experience: Qualitative Approaches to Social Research*. New York: St Martin's Press.

Simmel, Georg (1908/1950) *The Sociology of Georg Simmel*. Edited and translated by Kurt H. Wolff. New York: Free Press.

Sluka, Jeffrey A. (1990) 'Participant Observation in Violent Social Contexts.' *Human Organization* 49: 114–26.

Solway, I. and Waters, J. (1977) 'Working the Corner: The Ethics and Legality of Ethnographic Fieldwork among Active Heroin Addicts.' In R. Weppner (ed.) *Street Ethnography*. Beverley Hills: Sage.

Stoddart, K. (1986) 'The Presentation of Everyday Life: Some Textual Strategies for "Adeqate Ethnography."' *Urban Life* 15: 103–21.

Tewksbury, Richard and Gagne, Patricia (1997) 'Assumed and Presumed Identities: Problems of Self-Presentation in Field Research.' *Sociological Spectrum* 17: 127–55.

Van Maanen, John (1988) *Tales of the Field: On Writing Ethnography*. Chicago: University of Chicago Press.

Walker, A. and Lidz, Charles (1977) 'Methodological Notes on the Employment of Indigenous Observers.' In R. Weppner (ed.) *Street Ethnography*. Beverly Hills, CA: Sage. pp. 103–23.

Warren, Carol A.B., Barnes-Brus, Tori, Burgess, Heather, Wiebold-Lippisch, Lori, Dingwall, Robert, Rosenblatt, Paul C., Ryen, Ann and Shuy, Roger (2003) 'After the Interview.' *Qualitative Sociology* 26: 93–110.

Whyte, William Foote with King Whyte, Kathleen (1984) *Learning from the Field: A Guide from Experience*. Beverly Hills, CA: Sage.

Wolf, D. (1991) *The Rebels: A Brotherhood of Outlaw Bikers*. Toronto: University of Toronto Press.

Wright, Richard and Decker, Scott (1994) *Burglars on the Job*. Boston: Northeastern University Press.

Wright, Richard and Decker, Scott (1997) *Armed Robbers in Action*. Boston: Northeastern University Press.

Wright, Richard, Decker, Scott, Redfern, A. and Smith, S. (1992) 'A Snowball's Chance in Hell: Doing Fieldwork with Active Residential Burglars.' *Journal of Research in Crime and Delinquency* 29(2): 148–61.

Part 6

Fieldwork and Sexualities

11

Fieldwork on Urban Male Homosexuality in Mexico

JOSEPH CARRIER

In a thoughtful 'Afterword' to *Understanding Social Research: An Introduction*, Orenstein and Phillips (1978) point out to their readers that they hope their book has made them more methodologically sensitive and better able 'to think about a sociological problem in a way that is researchable' and 'more cautious and concerned about the quality of the evidence upon which conclusions are based.' They note, however, that in their guide to research activities they 'have tried not to present a set of recipes ... (and) have tried to avoid the implication that there are set, standard, and uniform ways of conducting a research project.' They further assert that in any particular research project, 'the issues being investigated, and the people being studied, may force the researcher to violate important methodological cannons in the interest of answering – to the extent possible – important and relevant questions.' They conclude that 'a good researcher knows how to make the compromises in methodological elegance which may be necessary to study important issues' (Orenstein and Phillips, 1978: 418).

This chapter deals with some of the realities that I have had to face while conducting ongoing ethnographic fieldwork on male homosexuality in Mexico since the summer of 1968. I will review the preliminary fieldwork I did to get my study underway, my original research design, the compromises I had to make in methodology over time, and the ethical issues that surfaced as a result of some of the methodological changes. My intention is to provide fledgling researchers with some knowledge about the real world of field research and to reassure them that all is not lost when they find they have to make important compromises in their study over time. I realize, of course, that times have changed and that field researchers nowadays have to follow much stricter guidelines with respect to the protection of human subjects than I did at the beginning of my research project over 30 years ago in the late 1960s. Nevertheless, I am sure anyone doing fieldwork on human sexual behaviors at present will still have to deal with the real world and make significant compromises over time in the design of their research.

PRELIMINARY FIELD RESEARCH

The major part of my field research was carried out from late fall 1969 to early spring 1972 while I lived in Guadalajara, the second largest city in Mexico. Prior to that time – mostly during the summer of 1968 – I conducted preliminary field research using participant observations and interviews of selected respondents in western and southern Mexico to help me determine the feasibility of studying Mexican male homosexual behaviors, narrow the scope of my planned research, and select the best location for fieldwork.

Based on findings from my preliminary fieldwork I concluded that research on male homosexuality was doable as a topic for a doctoral dissertation but that, because almost no research data were available on Mexican male homosexual behaviors and I had only a limited amount of time available for the dissertation fieldwork, I needed to limit the scope of my study as much as possible. My preliminary findings also made clear that although sex between adult men in Mexico is not illegal, it is censured behavior in Mexican society and I therefore had to maintain a certain anonymity with respect to my study and respondents.

In response to these conclusions I decided to base my study in Guadalajara – a metropolis where I could move about more or less anonymously – and to limit my research population to urban mestizo Mexican men living there who were involved in homosexual encounters. Over time, as a result of serendipity, I enlarged my research population to include Mexican men living in some cities and towns in the northwestern states of Baja California, Sonora, Sinaloa and Nayarit. But I wisely kept my original plan to exclude rural and Indian Mexican populations from my study and continued to mainly focus my fieldwork on mestizo urban Mexican men living in Guadalajara.

In retrospect, it is quite clear that the findings from the preliminary fieldwork I did in Mexico during 1968 helped me come up with a far better research design for my study than I would have had otherwise. And since I was starting from scratch – no meaningful studies of male homosexuality in Mexico had been done when I started my study – my preliminary participant observation and interview data about Mexican male homosexual encounters notably facilitated the launching of my fieldwork in Guadalajara. On recently rereading the unpublished paper I wrote about my preliminary findings in the fall of 1968 – 'On urban Mexican male homosexual encounters' – I was surprised as to how much I had already learned about Mexican male homosexuality by the beginning of my study in the fall of 1969.

A PERSONAL ETHICAL PROBLEM

There was yet another benefit to be had from my preliminary fieldwork when I arrived in Guadalajara in the fall of 1969, but before taking advantage of it I had to rethink and come to terms with what I knew was going to be a major ongoing ethical problem: the separation of my private sex life from my study. While doing my preliminary fieldwork I had already been confronted by the problem and had resolved it by setting up a rule that I would not have sex with study respondents recruited for interviews, but would, if the occasion warranted, have sex with insistent cantina men 18 years of age and older who targeted me as a sexual partner (see Carrier, 1999, for a more complete discussion of this early ethical issue). I adhered to this 'cantina rule' up to the time I moved to Guadalajara in December 1969.

But at that point in time it became clear that this ethical problem was going to be far more complex than I had imagined.

Shortly after my arrival in Guadalajara, for example, I had to deal with the following ethical problem. While trying to find a suitable apartment where I could live and yet still have enough anonymity to use it as a base of operations for my fieldwork in Guadalajara, I was living in a small hotel located adjacent to Parque de la Revolucíon – one of the largest parks in the city and a noted cruising place. To assist me in the search for an apartment I contacted a former sex partner, a 25 year-old Mexican man named Pablo, whom I had met in the park in July 1968 and who had visited me the following fall at my house in California. He lived with his family just a short walking distance from the hotel in an older, traditional neighborhood. I told him that I had returned to gather information about Mexican male homosexuality that would be used as a basis for my PhD dissertation in anthropology at the University of California/Irvine and that it would take me at least a year and a half to complete my study. He quickly understood my need for a very special apartment.

After a few days of looking for an apartment, however, it became obvious to Pablo and me that we were not going to be able to find a place quickly that I could afford and where my future study respondents could, out of sight of nosy neighbors, discreetly come and go. Worried about my financial situation, he suggested I move from my hotel to his house where I could stay until I found an apartment. I thanked him for inviting me and privately thought nothing would come of it since I had met his middle-class family in 1968 and knew that he lived in rather crowded circumstances with his parents, nine siblings, and grandmother. I was wrong. The next day Pablo returned to the hotel and took me to his house to have lunch with his parents. During lunch they invited me to stay at their house while apartment hunting. I thanked them but did not immediately accept the offer. There were some important ethical concerns that I had to resolve before I accepted their invitation and lived in their house for even a short period of time: I had had sexual relations with their son and I was about to embark on a study of Mexican male homosexuality.

Pablo walked back with me to the hotel after lunch and urged me to move to his house. I told him about my ethical concerns but he dismissed them straightaway because he said we were now just friends and no longer sex partners, and there would never be a need for me to tell his parents or his family about my study, which was to be carried out discreetly. And he said he had already told his parents before lunch that I was just a graduate student studying Spanish in Guadalajara. After two days of indecision I decided that, given Pablo's level of comfort and his complete knowledge about my study, it was ethically okay to live with his family temporarily until I found an apartment.

Living with Pablo's family turned out to be an exceptionally rewarding experience and provided me with many useful insights about the family relations of a closeted, homosexually oriented young Mexican man at first-hand. But the most important benefit of my having met him in the summer of 1968 was his willingness to serve as a key informant at the outset of my study in Guadalajara in the fall of 1969. With his help I was able to map out the local homosexual scene in a relatively short period of time. And through his friendship network I was able to establish contact with behaviorally homosexual men from varying social classes who eventually gave me access to seven different circles of friends who agreed to participate in my study. He thus provided me with invaluable assistance in the crucial beginning phase of my study. And, even though he had a full-time job, he developed a special interest in my research and continued to be extremely helpful in recruiting new respondents for my study until I left Guadalajara to return to Los Angeles in the spring of 1971.

ORIGINAL RESEARCH DESIGN

My principal research question at the outset of my study was: How do urban Mexican males cope with their homosexuality? A major premise of the study was that a majority of male human beings who have other males as primary or secondary sexual objects and who engage in overt sexual experiences with other males are able, over time, to come to terms, that is cope, with a pattern of sexual behavior that is considered deviant in their urban society. Underlying this premise is the belief that homosexually behaving males utilize an indeterminate number of ways to cope with their homosexuality and that male homosexuality is not necessarily a symptom of pathology (see Hooker, 1957).

As a means of understanding how Mexican males cope with their homosexual behaviors, I also assumed that there was a need to know something about the impinging social forces that make coping necessary and a need to know something about their order of importance. A related research question of interest to the study, therefore, was: What social forces are most important to the individual male's coping with homosexuality and in what order are they important?

A review of the literature available in 1968 suggested that few data were available with which to answer either of the above research questions in any urban society, let alone Mexico. With the exception of a handful of important studies (Kinsey et al., 1948; Schofield, 1960; and Hooker, 1965), most of the research data that were available on male homosexuality at that time were limited to psychological studies of patient populations in the Anglo worlds of the United States and England.

I chose Mexico as the location of my study because it offered an untapped research resource for the study of male homosexual behaviors in a natural setting and would make possible an eventual cross-cultural comparison with the available data on male homosexual behaviors in the United States and England. The implied research question here was: Are there important cultural differences between Anglo and Latino urban male homosexual behaviors? Still another advantage of studying Mexican male sexual behaviors was that I also knew that the influence of a variable considered a significant deterrent to the satisfactory adjustment of urban homosexual males in the United States, legal harassment, would be removed from my project study data collected in Mexico.

In my original research design I divided my proposed 16 months of fieldwork in Guadalajara into qualitative and quantitative phases. During the first nine months I planned to do participant observation fieldwork. Using the data collected in that phase, I then planned to construct a questionnaire using a mix of forced-choice and open-ended questions and during the last seven months of fieldwork interview a stratified quota sample of, hopefully, 100 respondents. Assuming that it would not be possible to develop a random sample, my objective was to interview a selected group of respondents from the largest socioeconomic segment of the urban Mexican male population that would at least be representative of the major 'sex role' categories of homosexually behaving men identified during the qualitative participant observation phase of the fieldwork.

An important objective of my original research design was to include as prospective respondents *all men* who were involved in *homosexual encounters.* I decided early on that I did not want my study to be limited to only *gay, ambiente,* or *homosexually* identified Mexican men. My preliminary fieldwork had revealed quite clearly that in the world of men who have sex with other men only a small minority of that population identified themselves as being *homosexual.* In addition, by using this research strategy I also finessed the questions of: Who is *homosexual* and what is *homosexuality?*

In designing my research I assumed that *homosexual encounters* were the basic unit of homosexuality. I defined them as an interaction between two (or more) males that has as a terminal objective the fulfillment of the sexual desire of at least one of the males involved in the encounter. They were narrowly interpreted to mean encounters in which there is an intent on the part of the males involved to terminate the encounter with a physical sex act. I thus considered homosexual encounters to be one of the primary energizing forces that motivated individuals to act. And it was the desire for and/or carrying out of these sexual encounters in conjunction with society's disapproval of them that brought about a general need for individuals of interest to my study to cope with their homosexuality.

Finally, with respect to my original research design for recruiting respondents, during the start-up phase in Guadalajara I planned to initially enlist several key homosexually identified informants and then over time use their friendship networks to provide me with some additional informants. By the time I finished my study, I visualized having close social contact with several different circles of friends, some of which would be overlapping, from the lower and middle social classes. Using the participant observation data collected in Guadalajara, I also planned over time to recruit additional key informants with behavior patterns that differed from those men already participating in the study. The data I had collected about Mexican male homosexuality during my preliminary survey suggested that a large majority of heterosexually identified participants in homosexual encounters, most of whom I had met in *straight* bars and cantinas, would not be active participants in friendship circles of homosexually identified men. I thus assumed I would have to recruit and socialize with this category of respondent on a one-to-one basis.

LOCATION OF OFFICE/APARTMENT

After searching for two weeks, Pablo and I found a two-bedroom, third-floor walkup apartment with a very private side entrance that was perfect for my study. The apartment house was located on the corner of a busy main thoroughfare in an upper-middle-class neighborhood that was in transition to becoming commercialized, with several of the old mansions already converted to restaurants. There were three commercial establishments on the ground floor of the apartment house, and there was only one other apartment which was rented to four university students, on the third floor. Pablo told me that since it was not a large, crowded, family-oriented apartment house or neighborhood, my respondents could visit me without having to worry about what people might say – they would not have to run a gauntlet of nosy neighbors. Since most of my respondents would be traveling by bus, another important feature of the apartment was that it could be reached from the center of Guadalajara by three different bus lines in 5–10 minutes. And, since most buses stopped operating at midnight, its location also had the advantage that it was within a reasonable walking distance from the center of town.

RECRUITING INFORMANTS

Finding informants during the early months of my fieldwork turned out to be much easier than I had anticipated. As soon as I got established in my apartment Pablo started introducing me to his homosexual friends. I was thus able to meet and establish friendly relationships with three new respondents in a relatively short period of time and, lucky for me, they did not know each other. This meant that with their help I was then able over time to establish contacts with three different circles of friends. And through individuals met in those friendship circles I was eventually able to establish contact with four more new friendship circles of homosexual men. While getting acquainted with the men making up these seven friendship circles, I also met and developed friendships with ten independent homosexual men who were essentially loners, usually searched for sex partners alone, and at most socialized with only one or two homosexual friends. They were not part of any circle of friends or homosexual network.

Although I was quite pleased with the progress I was making and believed that I had developed social contacts with a sufficient number of informants for the participant observation phase of my study, I decided that I needed still more informants as a backup but from a homosexual network that had no contact with the one that Pablo had gotten me into and preferably one that was operating in a lower-class neighborhood

on the other side of the city. I eventually succeeded in adding three new overlapping circles of friends who met these criteria to my study but before doing so I had to resolve ethical doubts about the way in which I gained access to them and would be socializing with and observing them.

ANOTHER PERSONAL ETHICAL PROBLEM

When I put my research design together in the fall of 1969, I was still uncertain as to how I was going to be able to separate my private sex life from my study during the 16 months of my fieldwork in Guadalajara. Because homosexuality at that time was not yet considered to be a legitimate research topic for graduate students in anthropology, I decided it was unwise to discuss any of my personal ethical concerns in my dissertation proposal. Needless to say I never mentioned my 'cantina rule' or the circumstances that brought it about. In fact I was so uneasy about what my committee and fellow graduate students would think about my using 'participant observation' as my primary field research method that I noted I envisioned it to be similar to that defined by Zelditch (1962: 568–579): 'The field worker directly observes and also participates in the sense that he has durable social relations in the social system under investigation.' It is an innocuous definition and for me to quote it was a real 'cop-out' since I already knew that being a 'participant observer' of Mexican male homosexual behaviors in Guadalajara would most likely lead to still unforeseen ethical dilemmas. For example, I knew my cantina rule would be helpful in establishing an ethical guideline but I also knew that it would be of limited utility since it set ethical limits only to participant observations that I would make while in drinking establishments. What did I have to do to separate my private sex life from my project?

For ethical reasons, I did not want to target prospective study informants as sex partners, so a few weeks after settling down in my office/apartment I started looking for an individual whom I could have as a friend and steady sex partner during the 16 months I would be doing fieldwork in Guadalajara. I believed that having a steady relationship with someone would allow me to totally separate my private sex life from my research project.

After a couple of false starts, I ended up initiating what I hoped would be a long-term friendship and sexual relationship with a young man named Arturo (see Carrier, 1995: 99–100, for a detailed description of this relationship). Early on in our affair, however, it became obvious to me that it was going to be difficult to separate my personal life with him from my study. Arturo turned out to be an incredibly good informant not only about his personal sex life but also about the homosexual behaviors of all the Mexican men he had had sex with up to the time we met, and the information he was giving me was too valuable to ignore. Moreover, as his fictive husband, I became part of his circle of homosexual friends and socializing with them provided me with additional valuable information about Mexican male homosexuality.

I finally came to the conclusion that unless I was celibate during my 16 months of fieldwork there was no way in which I could separate my private sex life from my study. Since celibacy was not a reasonable option for me, I decided that I would continue my affair with Arturo and use him and his friends as a special group of informants for my study. As it turned out, his circle of friends provided me with access to two additional circles of friends. And since these three circles of friends were completely separate from the seven that I had already recruited and were from working-class families, they ended up being my backup group of respondents. With Arturo's permission, I resolved my personal ethical concerns about their being linked to my private sex life by letting them know that they would be part of my study of Mexican male homosexuality. None of them dropped out of their friendship circle or avoided me as a result of becoming informants for my study. In fact over time many of them sought me out in private and gave me detailed personal information about their sex lives, past and present.

SERENDIPITOUS FIELDWORK

An unexpected and oftentimes excellent payoff for long months of fieldwork is the expansion of one's project and knowledge due to serendipity. During my 33 years of working in the field in Mexico, for example, I added to my investigation two extremely valuable and totally unanticipated research components that were not part of my original research design. They provided some important findings about Mexican male homosexuality that would not have been made had I kept rigidly to my original research plan.

MINI STUDIES IN COASTAL WESTERN MEXICO

One valuable research component came about as a result of my driving 1,650 miles back and forth between Los Angeles and my research site in Guadalajara. Since I only drive in Mexico during daylight hours, the trip required three and a half days of driving in either direction. This meant that *en route* via National Highway 15, which goes in a southeasterly direction from Nogales at the

US–Mexican border to Guadalajara, I had to make three overnight stays in coastal western Mexican cities or small towns, such as Hermosillo, Ciudad Obregon or Navojoa in the State of Sonora, and Los Mochis, Culiacán or Mazatlán in the State of Sinaloa. After having supper and before returning to my motel to sleep, I usually passed time by checking out the local gay scene. I almost always found some homosexual cruising in parks and in certain bars and cantinas, and usually ended up drinking and socializing with one or two young Mexican men. Occasionally I would take someone I met back to my room.

After making a number of these trips in the 1970s I began to realize that with just a little more time and effort I could systematically gather some interesting data on male homosexual behaviors in these urban areas of coastal western Mexico that would provide additional insights for my ongoing study of male homosexuality in Guadalajara. So *en route* back and forth to Guadalajara in the 1980s I focused on four urban areas – Hermosillo in Sonora and Los Mochis, Culiacán, and Mazatlán in Sinaloa – and spent some extra time in each place to do in-depth interviews and participant observations. And in the spring of 1987, as a result of my car breaking down *en route* back to Los Angeles from Guadalajara, I was also able to gather some fascinating data in Tuxpan, a small farm town located near the Pacific coast some 400 miles southeast of Los Mochis in the state of Nayarit. I spent two weeks there while waiting for parts and the overhaul of my car's engine.

The mini study in Hermosillo, a city with a population of about half a million and the state capitol of Sonora, took place in the *zona roja* (the red light district) during the summer and fall of 1980. I learned about the unusual goings-on in the bars, nightclubs, and cantinas in the *zona* one summer night through a chance meeting with a Mexican professor and his lover while visiting the only gay bar in downtown Hermosillo. I told them about my study of male homosexuality in Guadalajara and asked them about their gay scene. They told me that the *zona*, located on the outskirts of the city, was the best place for cruising at night and offered to accompany me there. While *en route* to the *zona* in a taxi, the professor told me that we would go first to a straight dance bar, unlike any other in Mexico, where homosexual male transvestites had taken over and played the roles of waitress, dance hostess, and prostitute. He had accurately described the bar. When we arrived it was packed with macho ranchero men dancing with the 'hostesses' and being waited on by the 'waitresses'. One could only guess as to whether the men knew they were dancing with and being waited on by men in drag. Afterwards, we strolled around the *zona* and I was astonished by the large number of male transvestites to be seen working in other drinking establishments. I returned for several days the following fall to gather additional information about the transvestite men and their experiences working in the Hermosillo *zona roja*.

Another mini study, of a late afternoon and early evening drinking establishment called La Luna, took place during the summer of 1982 in Los Mochis, a large agricultural town about 300 miles south of Hermosillo. I learned about La Luna late one afternoon while looking for a motel to spend the night. My traveling companion had shouted at me to stop the car, jumped out, and walked fast to catch up with what appeared to be an ordinary-looking heterosexual couple ambling down the side of the road holding hands. He saw something I had not noticed – the 'lady' was a man in drag. On arrival in a Mexican town for an evening layover, my eagle-eyed Latino friend from Colombia was always on the lookout for 'drag queens' since they were usually willing to give him a good rundown on the local homosexual scene. This time he struck gold. The 'lady' was a waiter at La Luna. Located on the outskirts of Los Mochis, the bar encouraged local homosexual and bisexual men to congregate and cruise. We ended up spending the rest of the afternoon and evening there. Three weeks later, *en route* back to Los Angeles from Guadalajara, we made another weekend stopover in Los Mochis to spend more time at La Luna and interview some of the transvestite waiters.

Some additional research findings were made during stopovers in Mazatlán and Culiacán on ten round-trips by car from Los Angeles to Guadalajara. During these visits I gathered some useful information about the similarities between Mexican male homosexual behaviors and the gay scene in urban areas distant from each other but connected by Highway 15. One of my original Guadalajara respondents moved to Mazatlán, so I was also able to use his assistance in mapping out the gay scene over time in a popular beach city that attracts many foreign as well as Mexican tourists.

The Tuxpan mini study began shortly after having my car towed into the town and finding the best engine mechanic. My traveling companion and respondent José and I went to a popular open-air restaurant facing the river that runs through Tuxpan for a late Saturday afternoon lunch. As soon as we walked into 'La Vitamina' and saw it filled with men drinking beer and eating grilled fish tidbits, we knew we had made a good choice. We had no idea, however, of the good luck we were about to have in being befriended by our waiter, Vicente, who within the space of an hour gave us a complete rundown of the homosexual behaviors of the young men in Tuxpan. Vicente also told us to have supper in a nearby restaurant

that was run by a bisexual man named Beto, who would give us many first-hand details about his many sexual adventures with the young *mayates* in town. Since we were to be there at least two weeks, José and I were pleased to hear that so much was going on. I knew then that the time spent waiting for engine parts and repairs could be put to good use. José proved to be a valuable research assistant and along with Vicente and Beto helped me map out the surprisingly extensive homosexual scene in Tuxpan. Several days before leaving I also had the good luck to run into Gilberto, one of my original respondents in Guadalajara, who had returned to his hometown to live with his mother. He provided some invaluable historical information about the gay scene in Tuxpan and took it upon himself to make sure I clearly understood what was going on sexually and politically in his hometown and that town officials were relatively tolerant about 'gay activities'. As examples, he pointed out that a gay bar was allowed to operate in the small farm town's *zona roja* and, since it was viewed as a spoof, a group of gay men were allowed to conduct an annual 'Queen of Tuxpan' contest and that the Chief of Police usually attended the fiesta with the crowning of the queen.

A BARRIO STUDY IN GUADALAJARA

Another valuable research component – a small field study of homosexual behaviors in a poor *barrio* (neighborhood) located near downtown Guadalajara – was added to my investigation in the summer of 1982 as a result of my re-establishing contact with Alberto, one of my original informants in Guadalajara. We met again by chance one night in the spring of 1982 while I was having a beer in Bar Poncho, the most popular gay bar in Guadalajara at the time. We had not seen each other for a long time (about eight years, we thought), and we were both happy to be back in touch again.

I had lunch with Alberto the next day and afterward went home with him to give my regards to his parents and his many brothers and sisters. I had visited them only a few times in 1970 during the early months of my friendship with Alberto, who was only 17 years old at the time. I was surprised and pleased to receive such warm and friendly greetings. Later in the afternoon he gave me a tour of his *barrio*, pointing out that, like many old neighborhoods close to downtown Guadalajara, it dated back to the early eighteenth century when the small Catholic Church located at its center was built. He told me that even though his neighbors were poor, they still thought of themselves as being middle class and maintained most of the old Mexican traditions. He said that a lot of social activities in the *barrio*, for the young as well as the old, are intertwined with church activities. As is the case in many old *barrios*, for example, the church's student choir (referred to as the *estudiantina*) not only performs music for Sunday masses and special occasions but also provides *barrio* youth a means of getting together for all kinds of social activities.

Sensing my interest in knowing more about male homosexuality in his *barrio*, Alberto suggested I spend some time studying it and volunteered to help as much as possible. I told him I wanted to do the study, but it would just be a small one since I would be able to do it only sporadically during my annual visits to Guadalajara. I also wanted to focus it narrowly on how it felt to be known as a *joto* (a common derogatory term used to designate an effeminate male as homosexual) by men in the *barrio* and to be the butt of their homosexual jokes. Alberto replied

that we could do it together and I could get information first-hand, since he could spread the word that I was also a *joto*.

I started the small field study when I returned to Guadalajara for a month in the summer of 1982. At Alberto's suggestion, I drove down so I could have a car available to take his friends around the city on their many social outings. It turned out to be a clever strategy for both participant observation and acceptance by Alberto's friends. One of the most sought-after uses of my car was to take young men and their friends to serenade their girlfriends late at night. Since the serenades often ended after the buses stopped running, and because the girlfriends sometimes lived several miles away, the young men were quite happy to be taxied back to the *barrio*. As a result of being able to use my car for *serenatas* and many other different kinds of social outings, I was quickly accepted as an adjunct member of their group. By the end of my month-long visit they felt comfortable enough having me around to start making me the butt of their homosexual joking. I had established my reputation in the *barrio* as a *joto*.

As a 54-four year-old *norteamericano*, I was initially uneasy hanging around with Alberto and his younger group of *barrio* friends. He was 25, and they ranged in age from 15 to 27. I wondered what their parents and older siblings thought about my constant presence in the *barrio*. What did they think I was doing? By the time I left, however, it became clear that no one seemed hostile to my presence and I was usually invited along with Alberto to attend family-sponsored fiestas and ceremonies. It was Alberto's *barrio*, so I decided at the end of the first month of study to let him decide whether I should continue. I made it clear to him that I wanted to go on with the study and felt comfortable being around his family, friends, and neighbors, but that if it was causing him any problems at all, I wanted to stop the study straightaway. When I posed the question to Alberto, he responded immediately: 'Please, don't stop now. My friends and I will be very disappointed if you don't come back next year.'

I continued the study for six more years, driving down to Guadalajara and spending about a month on each visit. I was unable to return in 1983, so I resumed the study in the summer of 1984 and returned to the *barrio* every year until 1989. I sampled all the seasons: a winter, spring, and fall – and three summers. During 1983 three *barrio* youths moved to southern California to work, and we kept in touch through visits and by telephone. All but one became homesick and returned to Guadalajara before the year ended. The third youth stayed on but finally moved back home in 1995. I have kept in touch with Alberto and his *barrio* friends up to the present through letters and e-mail, and through occasional visits to Guadalajara.

All in all, for this study I totaled close to six months hanging around the *barrio* with Alberto and his friends. Each year I returned for a visit I was greeted warmly, as though I was one of their older relatives working in Los Angeles for the money although preferring to live in Guadalajara. Because the families lived in such crowded circumstances, I was never able to find a place to stay in the *barrio*. The truth is that some of my young friends in the *barrio* really liked my staying in a hotel so they could hang out with Alberto and me there and take warm showers, watch television, and drink beer. Luckily, I was always able to get the same back room in a small hotel, and the desk clerks never complained about my constant stream of male visitors.

Although Alberto and his group of friends remained relatively close and the same over the six years my study took place, each year I was able to see differences in attitudes and behaviors related to age (Alberto was 25 when I met him again in 1982 and 32 by the end of the study in 1989). There were also some changes in group cohesiveness related to work, marriage, and different interests. Yet the core *barrio* group remained essentially the same at the end of the study as it was at the beginning in 1982. Alberto at present (2005) keeps in touch with many of his old friends but is no longer as close as he once was with them because he and his family had to move, for financial reasons, to another *barrio* located on the outskirts of the city, and because several of his close friends also had to move to different parts of the city and so they now live long bus rides from each other.

DISCUSSION

Pioneering ethnographic research on human sexual behaviors requires investigators to spend months in the field gathering data about their subjects. Shortcut research methods, like the use of focus groups or questionnaires, may provide some interesting insights about sexual behaviors but they still cannot replace time-consuming interviewing and participant observations of subjects in the field (Carrier, 2001). A good example of using only focus groups and interviews is the research done by Michele Shedlin and her Nicaraguan colleagues in their study of high-risk sexual behaviors and HIV/AIDS in Nicaragua, but in a recent paper (Shedlin et al., 1996) they carefully point out the need for more extensive fieldwork 'on the cultural context of homosexuality and prostitution.'

Given the long time period needed to conduct reliable fieldwork and gather data on human sexual behaviors through participant observations, interviews, and other research methods – both qualitative and quantitative – the prospective researcher must take into account the fact that one can never predict with certainty the practicality of any given research design until it is implemented in the field. Because of the need for privacy, when carrying out a study of human sexual behaviors in a foreign country, it is even more difficult to know how well a given research design will fare over the life of the project. One thing is certain: modifications of the research design will be needed as the investigation progresses over time. And issues related to the conduct of the research and its effect on the respondents and population being studied will have to be carefully monitored by the researcher and decisions made with respect to its ethicality. Special attention will also have to be given to the effects that the researcher's private sex life may have on respondents and on the investigation over time.

I have used my personal experiences in Mexico to illustrate the many ways in which the real world may affect an original research plan for conducting fieldwork on human sexual behaviors in a foreign country and the need for resiliency in adjusting the original plan as the fieldwork is initiated and progresses over time. It would be worthwhile for readers to look at the different ways in which other researchers have had to deal with the realities of conducting fieldwork in their studies of human sexual behaviors in Mexico and of Mexican immigrants in California. Although only a relatively few field studies have been carried out to date, the spread of HIV and AIDS has motivated an increasing number of medical anthropologists to conduct this kind of research in the past ten years.

I suggest that the reader looks at some of the following PhD dissertations or books and carefully examine the methods used by the researchers in conducting their fieldwork: Ayala (1999), Cantú (1999), Carrillo (2002), Noriega (1994), Prieur (1998), Taylor (1978) and Wilson (1995). Unfortunately, the amount of information they provide about their original research design, how it changed over the life of their fieldwork, and how they dealt with the ethical issues they faced in conducting their fieldwork is uneven. Enough information is given, however, for readers to ask themselves the important questions I have raised in this chapter.

REFERENCES

Ayala, A. (1999). 'Mexican immigrant women, sex work, and health'. PhD dissertation. Los Angeles: University of Southern California.

Cantú, L. (1999). 'Border crossings: Mexican men and the sexuality of migration'. PhD dissertation. Irvine: University of California.

Carrier, J. (1995). *De los Otros: Intimacy and Homosexuality among Mexican Men.* New York: Columbia University Press.

Carrier, J. (1999). 'Reflections on ethical problems encountered in field research on Mexican male homosexuality: 1968 to present'. *Culture, Health & Sexuality,* 1(3): 207–21.

Carrier, J. (2001). 'Some reflections on ethnographic research on Latino and southeast Asian male homosexuality and HIV/AIDS'. *AIDS and Behavior,* 5(2): 183–91.

Carrillo, H. (2002). *The Night is Young: Sexuality in Mexico in the Time of AIDS.* Chicago: The University of Chicago Press.

Hooker, E. (1957). 'The adjustment of the male overt homosexual'. *Journal of Projective Techniques,* 21: 18–31.

Hooker, E. (1965). 'An empirical study of some relations between sexual patterns and gender identity in male homosexuals'. In John Money (ed.) *Sex Research: New Developments.* New York: Holt, Rinehart & Winston. pp. 24–52.

Kinsey, A, Pomeroy, W. and Martin, C. (1948). *Sexual Behavior in the Human Male.* Philadelphia: Saunders.

Noriega, G. (1994). *Sexo Entre Varones: Poder y Resistencia en el Campo Sexual.* Mexico: El Colegio de Sonora.

Orenstein, A. and Phillips, W. (1978). *Understanding Social Research: An Introduction.* Boston: Allyn and Bacon. pp. 416–19.

Prieur, A. (1998). *Mema's House: On Transvestites, Queens, and Machos.* Chicago: The University of Chicago Press.

Schofield, M. (1960). *Sociological Aspects of Homosexuality.* Boston: Little Brown & Co.

Shedlin, M., Molina, R.A. and Ortells, P. (1996). 'Research on high-risk behavior in Nicaragua'. Paper presented at American Public Health Association Annual Meeting, New York City, November.

Taylor, C. (1978). 'El Ambiente: Male homosexual social life in Mexico City'. PhD dissertation. Berkeley: University of California.

Wilson, C. (1995). *Hidden in the Blood: A Personal Exploration of AIDS in the Yucatan.* New York: Columbia University Press.

Zelditch, M. (1962). 'Some methodological problems of field studies'. *American Journal of Sociology,* 67: 568–79.

12

Knowing Sexuality: Epistemologies of Research

CHRIS HAYWOOD AND MAIRTIN
MAC AN GHAILL

As in the nineteenth and twentieth centuries, sexuality in the twenty-first century continues to fascinate, abhor, excite and astonish. For many societies in the northern hemisphere, sexuality has developed as a private and public erotic template that enables us to make sense of our emotions, intimacies and passions. It is a form of eroticism that has, as Foucault (1980) suggests, come to designate the 'truth of ourselves', a conduit through which flows the essence of our human nature. Over the last three centuries researchers and their field studies have played, and continue to play, an indispensable role in facilitating a growing popular cultural anxiety to find, identify and establish the nature of sexuality.

In this chapter we draw upon a growing number of studies (including our own) that have been researching sexuality in several educational arenas. More specifically, we explore a number of the most common research approaches towards sexuality in education, namely, empiricist, culturalist and standpoint epistemologies. It is suggested that although these have provided useful and productive insights and knowledge about sexuality, such research frameworks may serve to limit the possibilities of sexual research in schools. In other words, our knowledge of sexuality is limited by the very methodologies we use to increase or improve our knowledge.

In response, this chapter considers transgressive research approaches to sexuality that are mainly developed by post-structuralists. These transgressive approaches argue that appeals to truth, validity and reliability are 'chimeras', where the scientizing of social knowledge 'is thus inextricably linked to the suppression of other ways of knowing' (Richardson, 1997: 208). They further argue that methodologies need to deconstruct or to queer ('open up') previously closed analytical categories. Finally, the chapter, based upon our own experience, contextualizes these approaches by examining the difficulty of investigating sexuality in the current social and cultural climate. We begin by looking historically at the emergence of sexuality as an object inquiry.

MAKING SEXUALITY POSSIBLE

Modernist assumptions about schools as a secure site and safe haven for children have been challenged by the proliferation of 'sexual' issues that include Clause 28,[1] HIV/AIDS, increasing sexually transmitted infections, growing awareness of sexual violence, a rising numbers of teenage pregnancies, the age of consent and paedophilia. In response, the state, the media and the academy have focused on tackling these issues through a traditional social scientific empiricism. A characteristic of this approach is that the source of sexual behaviours is identifiable. Once located, the source can be altered to produce a set of different sexual behaviours. This approach to human nature has a long tradition. It has been argued that since the Enlightenment, humanity was repositioned as the object of inquiry, a new conduit through which things became knowable but also as subjects that could become known. Part of this broader transformation in ways of knowing, understandings of reality and consequent research frameworks begin to be incorporated into organic structures. This means that scientific inquiry was:

> … no longer content to designate one category of beings among other categories; it no longer merely indicates a dividing-line running through the taxonomic space; it defines for certain beings the internal law that enables a particular one of their structures to take on the value of a character. Organic structure intervenes between the articulating structures and the designating characters – creating between them a profound, interior, and essential space. (Foucault, 1970: 251)

The focus on the interior spaces of individuals not only marks a shift in the object of inquiry but also a generation of new methodological challenges. Rabinow (1988) argues that the questions of modern philosophy are different from previous forms because older philosophical tendencies did not differentiate between internal representations and external reality. With objects of inquiry being located within interiors or essential space, according to Rabinow (1986: 235) 'knowledge became internal, representational and judgmental' and the emphasis shifted towards establishing truths. As a result, epistemology emerged as a means to represent accurately what is outside the mind; so to understand the possibility and nature of knowledge is to understand the way in which the mind is able to construct such representations' (Rorty, 1979: 3). The reconfiguration of epistemology as central to the scientific process intensified the importance and centrality of social research methods as the means to establish truth.

A range of historical studies have traced how, from the mid-1800s, an interior and essential space of human nature was designated as 'sexuality' (Foucault, 1981; Laqueur; 1986, Weeks, 1995, 1994; Bland and Doan, 1998). It was this 'essential space' of sexual behaviours that medicine, biology, physiology neurology and psychology began attempting to identify, categorize and explain. Although discussions about anatomy and behaviour had been taking place since the Renaissance, investigations by figures such as Karl Ulrichs (1825–95), Richard von Kraft-Ebing (1840–1902), Havelock Ellis (1859–1939), Magnus Hirchsfield (1868–1935) and, later, Sigmund Freud (1856–1939) began to develop a separate epidemiology of sexual being. Such explanations established objective sexual states, pre-dispositions and tendencies, and, as a result, could separate the normal from the abnormal. At the same time, sexologists adopted a range of methods, that were used to access the locus of the sexual. Alongside traditional scientific methods, such as physical examinations, observations and experiments, sexologists began to use techniques including life history accounts, interviews and case studies. These methods were seen to produce data that would reveal the truth of sexuality. For example, Looby (1999) provides an example of a self-observational diary that was used to document an individual's sexual behaviour.

During the twentieth century these later methods became the mainstay of sexual research. For example, central to Kinsey's approach was an emphasis that the truth about sexual behaviour can be achieved through accumulating large numbers of interviews. For the *Sexual Behaviour in the Human Male* (1948) Kinsey, Pomeroy and Martin collected over 5,300 accounts. The purpose of the interviews was their ability to identify a range of practices that would enable extrapolations that would be valid and reliable. Frequency patterns became the methodological premise of the research. As such, these frequencies could be compared across other social categories, such as sex, occupation and age. In this account, truth contained within the appeal of the natural was embedded in the frequencies of such practices. For example, from his frequencies Kinsey was able to extrapolate that one in three men had a homosexual experience. The object of inquiry, sexual behaviour, could be objectively identified through stringent research methods. The need for a objective scientific approach to sexuality meant that earlier sexological research attempted to produce data that could be extrapolated and replicated across populations.

Bristow (1999) suggests that not only did this period generate ways of seeing the erotic, it developed a language that continues, within conditions of late modernity, to be applied to sexual behaviours, such as sexuality, bisexuality, homosexuality, heterosexuality and a diverse range of paraphilias that includes sadism, masochism and voyeurism. As a result, research on sexuality in education has adopted many of the epistemological

frames of early sexological research. In short, conventional studies of sexuality in schools adopt a modernist approach that depends upon a concept of *verisimilitude*. This means that sexual meanings, behaviours and practices are representative of an underlying sexual state or condition. Methodologically, researchers have tended to rely upon verisimilitude as a means to explain what is going on in schools. This means that the sexual requires little explanation of *why* it is sexual because meanings, behaviours and practices are fundamentally reflective of a sexual interior. This chapter engages with this theme by examining the following three approaches: empiricist, culturalist and standpoint epistemologies.

EMPIRICIST EPISTEMOLOGY: DOCUMENTING THE SEXUAL

An example of this approach can be found in Francis and Skelton (2001). They clearly identify the heterosexual nature of schooling by detailing how male teachers interacted with girls in the classroom and/or by the comments that were made about women. These are as follows:

> The children are told to meet up in the hall for PE after they have got changed. Phillip Norris (the teacher) adds, 'You'll want to be quick girls because I've got my sexy shorts with me today' and he wiggles his hips. (Skelton: Fieldnotes)

> As I go in to Nathan's woodwork class to get him, a youngish male teacher is working with a big group of boys including Nathan. I say, 'Can Nathan come with me for an interview, if he's willing?' Teacher eyes me roguishly and then the boys and says loudly, 'Now there's an offer you can't refuse, Nathan'. The boys in the group laugh and tut and one says, 'Oh sir' reprovingly. (Francis: Fieldnotes) (Francis and Skelton, 2001: 16)

It is not disputed that in their different ways, the two extracts are working across erotic fields of being and doing. These episodes do appear to be capturing social relations that contain an erotic dimension. What is contentious is that the frames of reference that are used to establish the 'sexualness' of a situation arise as a result of common-sense understandings of what constitutes the sexual. As verisimilitude, the sexual flows from teacher's verbal and bodily language.

However, this empiricist-informed, embodied 'sexualness' can only operate through a specific cultural matrix. This means that the adoption of an interior essential space of sexuality operates to conceal the cultural nature of their conceptualizations. When educationalists filter what is and what is not sexual they are implicitly inscribing historically and culturally received notions of what constitutes the sexual. In other words, educational researchers are often caught up in their own culturally determined sexual scenarios. Simon and Gagnon (1999) consider thinking about sexual realities in terms of sexual scripts. These scripts enable people to negotiate sexual worlds. It is argued that educationalists transpose their own sexual scripts into the conceptual frameworks of their practice. They thus operate a number of cultural filters that 'specify appropriate objects, aims and desirable qualities of self/other relations, but also construct in times, places, sequences of gesture and utterance and, among the most important, what the actor and the co-participants (real or imaginary) are assumed to be feeling' (Simon and Gagnon, 1999: 31). Francis and Skelton know that the above fieldwork episodes are 'sexual' because the filter used to detect and identify the category is generated by their own cultural rules and norms of what constitutes the 'sexual'. At the same time, the semiologies that operate through these sexual articulations are inscribed by a feminist reading. In summary, the sexualness of a

situation is constituted by the cultural templates being used. This means that the sexual materiality of a situation is pre-defined and can be read off when particular cultural associations are activated. Thus the researcher, in capturing 'the sexual', refers to the expression of the culturally negotiated meanings of the sexual as the evidence of their interiority.

In much educational research, the 'sexual' is deemed to flow veridically from the individual. In doing so, a number of sexual truth effects have been activated that are central to how the sexual is seen to appear in schools. Although it could be argued that this is simply a conceptual quibbling, the impact of the philosophical position on how we make sense of sexuality is crucial. Eisner (1993) provides us with a way of exploring the kinds of educational research claims of which Francis and Skelton are exemplary. Furthermore, as Eisner argues, 'ontological objectivity' purports to accept things as they are, with phenomena existing in its 'ontological state'. In educational studies, the sexual exists unproblematically, with a direct correspondence between the ontology of sexuality and the researcher's sensibility. Usher (1997: 27) outlines this empiricist methodology, where '[t]he categorisation of the sexual, reproductive or mental health disorders is based entirely on what can be measured or observed, thus reinforcing the focus on material phenomena in these different spheres'.

It appears that in educational research practices, there is a recourse to more traditional sexual sciences, that is the materiality of the sexual through the measurement and observation of physiological, psychological or behavioural processes. According to Weeks (1986: 80), sexologists 'naturalize sexual patterns and identities and thus obscure their historical genealogy'. In contemporary educational studies, individuality takes on a similar process: sexual patterns become individualized, which in turn obscures the historicity of the sexual. In short, individuality has become the new essence of the sexual (Callero and Howard, 1989). By positing the source of sexuality as emerging from individuals, philosophical debates between essentialism and social constructionism appear to be avoided (Stein, 1994; Dean, 2000). For example, in the above extracts, it is not necessary to establish whether teachers' talk is physiologically located or culturally generated. What matters is what pupil or teacher talk is doing *educationally*. As Francis and Skelton suggest, it is important to establish whether the sexual in the above extracts is seducing or harassing. However, by focusing on individuals, the sexual becomes something 'bodily' or, more specifically, something that is embodied. Such a disarming conceptual move produces a series of particular truth effects where the presence of the sexual can only exist through the materiality of the body (see Jeffcutt, 1993). Indeed, from an empiricist perspective, schooling operates to limit, control and hold in check the sexual. A position that connects with common sense. For instance, in a recent study by one of us, it was documented how one teacher talked about a recent episode of 'wagging', where a pupil missed school in order to spend time with her boyfriend:

TEACHER: She's besotted ... she can't get enough of him, missing classes, not doing homework, wearing make up ... you see that is when you have to hold it in check.

C: Hold what?

TEACHER: Her hormones! You get them coming in all their make up, lippi, nails done, short skirts and they prance around ... the boys the same ... they come in like peacocks, strutting around ... if you want to do some proper research in sexuality develop an antidote for hormones. (Haywood, 2006: 247)

Thus, in documenting the sexual in schools, talk, interactions and behaviours not only become displays of sexual materiality

but operate to *become* the sexual materiality. As a result, the logic follows that the more an individual talks about sex, the more the individual displays sexual behaviours and practices, the more we are able to make sense of sexuality and schooling. Thus, the educationalist fixes and establishes the possibilities of the sexual. In challenging this empiricist approach to sexuality, it is argued that conceptually, educationalists tend to draw upon received maps of meaning when they research sexualities in schooling. These maps of meaning provide the cues and the directions about how we make sense of what is deemed as sexual (Money, 1988). Thus empiricists draw upon their own experience as a technique of collecting data and making it meaningful. In the process, reality becomes reassembled in a way that limits the thinking through of sexuality and schooling (Jeffcutt, 1993).

CULTURALIST EPISTEMOLOGY: LOCATING THE SEXUAL IN CULTURAL MEANING

Another methodological approach in conceptualizing sexuality and schooling has been to prioritize the epistemological significance of school cultures. The focus on configurations of meaning and ways of life have provided rich understandings of sexuality within schools. Many educationalists use teacher, peer, youth or childhood cultures as a way of making sense of sexual formations in schooling contexts. However, many of these studies draw upon a traditional cultural anthropology as their methodological navigation of the sexual. It is argued that this form of navigation provides a limited account of the nature of the sexual in schooling. Cultural studies of schooling are not new. For example, the work of the Centre for Contemporary Cultural

Studies, in Birmingham, provided a number of ways of linking school cultures to broader social relations of class, ideology and gender. More recent studies of cultural formations of sexuality in schools have adopted North American anthropological perspectives. According to Atkinson et al. (1993), North American ethnographic studies have two main features. One feature is that these approaches focus on the cultural uniqueness of the research setting. This means that various locations with differentiated groups generate a unique set of cultural practices. The second feature is that pupil subcultures clustered around ethnicities, genders and sexualities, rather than socio-economic location, are a source of counter cultural-conflict with the school. In this way, pupil meanings stand in opposition to the institution of the school. It is the contention of this section that by locating sexuality as generated by cultural configurations, the locus of the 'sexual' becomes contained and fixed.

By focusing on sexual cultures in traditional anthropological ways, educationalists have taken on both the productiveness and limitations of the discipline. In much of the cultural studies of sexuality in schools there is a tendency to identify cultural specificities through otherness and difference. Bowman (1997), in a critique of traditional anthropology, argues that by identifying cultural difference, people are placed within pre-existing cultural norms and, as a result, become culturally immobilized. This can be clearly seen in Mary Kehily's work on masculinity and heterosexuality. Despite acknowledging Foucault's notion of the institutional organization of bodies, Kehily posits 'culture' as the epitome of the sexual in schooling: 'The ethnographic evidence discussed in this chapter suggests that heterosexuality is constituted in the everyday practices of young

men in school' (Kehily, 2000: 32). In Kehily's work the cultural norms of a group of boys are collected. These, in turn, allow access to the sexual. She argues that in 'sex-talk, masturbation and pornography' young men constitute a version of heterosexuality that is collectively achieved. Again, it should be pointed out that pupil cultures are important for the negotiation and expression of the erotic and that they are significant in establishing, ordering and normalizing an economy of sexual forms. What is contested is that by focusing on cultural groupings, pupils' meanings become the exclusive epistemological assembler of reality. In doing so, it establishes that sexual forms only really exist in collective subjectivities.

Buchanan (2000) suggests that contemporary cultural studies can only engage with 'what is said' rather than identifying what 'can be said'. Subjectivities become the place where the sexual writes itself and is written – philosophically presenting itself as constituted by its presence. Interestingly, in terms of the exploration of culture, the researcher operates as a bricoleur, deciphering and decoding what constitutes the sexual nature of group interactions. It is assumed that when the researchers collect explicit talk about sexual matters, they are closer to the truth. In one way, the focus on culture has been translated into an over-concern with the sexual details of research participants' attitudes and behaviours. An unintended effect of this focus is a disconnection from the context. It becomes unimportant to know about the school context. Where the context does become important is in the ways that shape the essential sexual articulation of pupil cultures. Alongside other social locations, such as the family, the recreational ground and the neighbourhood, schooling becomes a sexual location because it is inhabited by sexual being and doing. The importance of this way of looking at sexuality is that any place in the school or wider society can operate as sexual as long as the sexual is present in collective subjectivities. For example, nursery schools can be understood as sexual places because younger children speak about sexual matters (Walkerdine, 1981).

A further limitation to empiricist and cultural studies, research approaches is the assumption that the sexual exists outside the researcher. Hence, the researcher has to get as 'close' to the data as possible. Therefore, correspondence between the researcher's account and the object of the research is underpinned by concepts of space and distance. Thus the quality of the research is based upon whether the representation accurately reflects the truth of the object that it is deemed to represent. Research evaluations tend to be made up of metaphors of near and far, closeness and distance, surface and depth. Traversing the distance between the object and the resulting representation has been well mapped, with error or bias checks being developed that enable a valid and reliable reconciliation between interpretation and object (Maxwell, 1992). Therefore, epistemologically, conventional researchers argue that a number of dangers at various points of the research have the potential to impede or disrupt the researcher making valid and reliable observations and interpretations. Importantly, distance concepts in methodology are not simply characteristic of positivistic criteria, they are as equally central to qualitative research. For example, 'validation hermeneutics' is a methodological approach that tends to be underpinned by Weber's (1930) notion of *Vehstehn*. It is a perspective that attempts to uncover and establish the meanings of those being studied. In this way, norms and values

exist independently of the researcher. In order to gain access to 'what is going on', the research has to document social actors' meanings. As a result, validity and reliability are measured by the correspondence between the researcher's accounts and those of the social actors.

Almost similar to the televisual wildlife documentary, the researcher of sexual cultures attempts to get close to the action, picking up what is really happening. Often research quality is measured by the quality of revelations – 'were their most intimate secrets discussed' or 'did they tell the researcher something that they would not have told anyone else'. Alongside maintaining sexuality as a discrete object, there is a further tension embedded in this approach, as exemplified in Bolton's (1995) research. In his work on gay male sex practices in Belgium, the need to get close to participants was a central concern. Often, he would use his participation in the sexual culture as a research tool:

> By experiencing them, I came to learn of blow jobs from bar tenders when the door was locked at closing time, of jacking off in cruising spots in a park near the Grand Place in partially public view, of sexual encounters in alleyways between someone heading home from the bars, someone on their way to work at dawn, of sexual action in the dunes along the coast and on the piers in Ostende and in the backrooms of discos and in the bathrooms of ordinary bars. (Bolton, 1995: 148)

Bolton assumes that the truth about sexuality can be accessed via intimate contact with his participants. Again, these accounts operate veridically. For Bolton, after-sex relaxed conversations provided the perfect platform for the participants to open up, and for him to get close to the data. Importantly, he suggests that he did not use the participants as research objects, rather in the process of conducting relationships with gay men, he was presented with information that was important for his study.

STANDPOINT EPISTEMOLOGIES: SEXUAL STRUCTURES OF OPPRESSION

A more critical research approach to sexuality in education has been to adopt standpoint epistemologies. Gay and lesbian researchers have suggested that in order to generate knowledge, the adoption of a gay or lesbian standpoint is necessary. It is not, as McIntosh (1997) suggests, about the way that you perceive the world, but rather how the world is seen if you take a particular perspective. Harding (1991: 252) acknowledges the complexity of this position, as a lesbian standpoint may be taken up by anyone who is 'able to think from the perspective of lesbian lives'. Integral to the standpoint position in general is that meanings, beliefs and values do not operate independently of social reality; rather they are constituted through the structured relationships that groups have with reality. A lesbian or gay standpoint epistemologically does a number of things, including: making visible the perspectives of groups that are socially marginal; providing legitimacy of interpretation produced by those who are marginalized; enabling the exploration of these marginalized experiences and enabling access to the views of social majorities. Thus, by claiming knowledge as constitutional, it demonstrates the existence of a lesbian or gay oriented reality. In this way, shared knowledge is a result of shared social situations as historical conditions generate patterns of thought.

Quinlivan and Town (1999) highlight, in their research, that schooling was not a neutral sexual environment. By taking young gay men's standpoint, the researchers identified how sex education curricula affected young gay men in ways that the institution did not acknowledge. The researchers became aware of the implicit pathologization of sexuality (that some sexualities are naturally normal and acceptable) and how homosexuality was only mentioned in the context of disease. One effect of this for the young gay men was that, within this context, they felt uncomfortable with their sexual identities, perceiving the curriculum as preventing them from expressing their sexual feelings at a physical level. At the same time, depictions of female sexuality, as an over-used focus for sex education lessons, generated particular feelings for lesbian students. Female sexuality was often portrayed as a passive sexuality. As their lesbian identities were defined through an active sexuality, these lessons disturbed them as they implicitly portrayed them as doubly deviant. Alongside this, the formal curriculum naturalized heterosexuality, with its emphasis on reproductive technologies. Furthermore, adopting a specific lesbian standpoint, as Rogers (1994) points out, there is a greater intensity of silencing for lesbians in schools than for gay men. For while schools situate male sexuality as active, thus creating the possibility of gay sexualities, female sexuality is situated as passive, making lesbianism even more invisible. Her research in a North American secondary school highlights that the support structures for young gay men mirrored the structures for support of heterosexual young people. However, these support structures were absent for young lesbians.

Similar to the empiricist approach, the standpoint epistemology operates as a neutral, transparent conduit that enables 'true' accounts to be heard. As Fawcett and Hearn (2004: 207) suggest: 'It is understood that by listening to the voices of women and others oppressed made "other", and taking full account of their experiences in their struggle against oppression, the "truth", or at least a form of truth, can be revealed and action "taken".' The researcher locates the identities of the researched and then uses those identities as a means through which to gather specific and located knowledge about the contradictions that these marginal groups face and experience. Research on sexuality has highlighted how schooling practices generate experiences of fear, marginalization, trauma and silencing for lesbian, gay and bisexual young people (Rofes, 2000; Trotter, 2001).

In order to get close to participants' meanings, researchers have endeavoured to capture sexual lives in the making. It appears that the pressure on lesbian and gay students is similarly felt (albeit in different ways) by gay and lesbian teachers. Sparkes' (1994) thoughtful life history of a lesbian teacher (Jessica) provides an insight into how heterosexuality and patriarchy work through relations of inequality. It captures the emotional distress that gays and lesbians feel as a result of the strongly marked heterosexual and homosexual boundaries of school life. In conversations and interviews, Jessica brings to our attention the tensions and anxieties formed by the institutional surveillance and self-policing that encumbers a teacher who self-identifies as lesbian in a heterosexual arena. Sparkes argues that the sexual category of lesbian, a category of sexual belonging, is immediately structured by the social arena. Such an experience circulates through the homophobia that is present in schools. This anxiety is heightened by Jessica's position as a PE teacher, a teaching position that tends not to occupy traditional authority within administrative structures. This coincided with teaching colleagues who were homophobic or unsupportive of sexuality equality. As a result, a number of avoidance practices were taken up and adopted by Jessica.

One of the unintended effects of research that focuses on marginal groups is that it can portray their experiences as negative. Stanley and Wise (1993), in their work on feminist

epistemology, argue for an 'ontology of the oppressed'. By suggesting that reality is constituted through frameworks, lesbian standpoints can operate as ways of seeing the world that are within the frame of forbidden pleasures and thoughts. Central to the identity of these oppressed groups is the notion that there is a reality, which defines and constructs their membership, although there may be plurality across standpoints: 'It involves knowledge of how to tell apart what is lesbian and what is heterosexual, and what are the behaviours, emotions and persons that link these supposed binaries, for all is continuum and almost nothing composes the extremities of these categories' (Stanley and Wise, 1993: 225). Furthermore, standpoint epistemology often relinquishes academic privilege and authority over the research as a means to avoid reproducing the conventional power relations found in wider society. At the level of sexuality, if sociological researchers were not engaging research participants in reciprocal relationships and allowing their voices to be heard, research methods could be understood as oppressive. As such, power relations within the fieldwork situation have to be broken down, so that research participants can be equally involved in the formation of research questions, the research schedule, data analysis, coding and dissemination of results. A critical aspect of standpoint epistemology, then, is to validate the authenticity of research subjects' oppressive experience by refusing the authority of the expert. In many ways, this process also involves a process of praxis, where marginal groups can be supported and freed from oppressive social structures. As Bensimon suggests:

A lesbian standpoint is critical. Not only does it expose the compromises, the unmediated actions, and the performances of closetedness that the institution of compulsory heterosexuality forces on lesbian professors, but it also awakens consciousness about our own and others' unexamined privileges. (Bensimon, 1992: 111–12)

FORGING TRANSGRESSIVE RESEARCH: BEYOND SEXUALITIES

A number of developments have taken place within social and cultural theory that have major implications for how we research sexuality. One of the most important developments could be described as the 'cultural turn' which has prompted researchers to re-examine the methodological bases of their research (Schwandt, 1994; Kvale, 1996; Lincoln and Guba, 2000). Importantly, such writers do not simply locate social and cultural theoretical developments as something that implicates methodological practices. Rather, methodology becomes central to a broader engagement with social and cultural arenas. Too often, studies make claims about the transgressive nature of their research while rarely allowing such transgressiveness to filter into an engagement with methodology. As a result, studies that posit the fluid, floating and fragmented nature of reality are cohered by relatively stable and fixed ontological and epistemological foundations. Unproblematically, the appeal to the socially constituted nature of knowledge and understanding is often backed up by traditional methods of data collection, such as interviews, ethnography and questionnaires. The issue is not that these techniques are inappropriate, but rather that if we are experiencing transformations of the modern subject, how are social scientists responding to such changes, in terms of rethinking their methodological approach? This section tentatively suggests ways in which this might be addressed by considering research frames that do not hold on to sexuality. Furthermore, the argument is not necessarily one of methodological purism. Rather, it is about rethinking the configuration of the relationship between knowledge generation and the object of inquiry.

As the earlier sections suggested, approaches to sexuality in schooling have outlined the different ways that sexuality manifests itself within schooling institutions. Such understandings are highly relevant and important. However, it might be appropriate to reconsider how sexuality is used. This means that a particular epistemology is employed that designates how the sexual in schools can appear. For example, as we have seen, a main way of understanding sexuality has been through identifying sexual identities. What coheres these studies is the necessity of sexuality itself. In other words, is it possible to make sense of sexual experiences that stand outside sexuality? And how can we develop an epistemology of the sexual that is not dependant on sexuality? It could be argued that contemporary writers on schooling and sexuality have become subject to criticisms that were levelled at earlier sexological researchers. As Weeks suggests:

> The sexological descriptions and aetiologies yanked together into broad categories many disparate sexual practices, to create sexual dichotomies which, while seeming to help us understand human sexuality, actually trapped individuals in mystifying compartments, where morality and theory, fear and hopes were inextricably and dangerously enmeshed. The gap became a void filled by contending moral and political values. (Weeks, 1986: 74)

As we have seen, studies depend upon an *object of desire* to explain the nature of the sexual. Alongside this, the object of desire is predominantly gendered. This means that the experience of the sexual can only take place and make sense through the regulatory category of sexuality. As a consequence, the demonstration of sexuality always tends to be marked by particular ways of being male or female. At present there is little research evidence of sexual experiences in schooling that considers the object of desire as not marked by a notion of sexuality. In short, there is no eroticism or sexual desire without sexuality.

One of us has empirically examined this issue while carrying out research at a middle school in the northeast of England that focused on exploring the relationship between sexuality and schooling (Haywood, 2005). As part of that research, interviews, observations and audio diaries were collected from a group of young people (aged 10–12). During the course of the research a number of themes began to emerge and one of these focused on the relationship between children and their sexual identifications. It appeared that the children did not have the language to make sense of their sexual understandings and experiences without drawing upon adult-centred/oriented categories. One of the research participants was implicated in a 'school rumour' that was circulating at the time that the research was conducted. The rumour focused on the claim that Carole Ann was sexually different. The researcher heard other students calling her a bisexual, a 'hetero', and a lemon (lesbian). The basis of the rumour was that she had 'fingered' (digitally penetrated) a girl from another school. Although Carole Ann had not been isolated by her close friends – they appeared to be protective of her and keen to defend her – many of the other girls continued to talk and gossip about the incident, causing Carole Ann much distress. In one lesson, a piece of paper with a sticker picture of a lemon with the name Carole Ann underneath was passed around between the girls and the boys. The teacher had intercepted this and, unaware of the situation, asked Carole Ann to explain herself. Carole Ann refused to answer the teacher or even make eye contact with him. The silence between them was broken when one of the boys shouted out that it was one of the other girls who had drawn it.

At lunchtime the researcher saw Carole Ann, who was standing on her own smoking behind the tennis courts. Initially she seemed awkward as the researcher approached her and the researcher was conscious that the conversation might perpetuate the harassment she was experiencing. The defensiveness of Carole Ann could not be avoided in the space of five minutes and the conversation was marked by its rigidity and aggression. In the conversation, which was intended to be supportive, it was revealed that the rumour was connected to another issue of oral sex:

C: So … why did you go down on him …
CA: He said he'd give me some money for some ciggies.
C: What did you say?
CA: Nothing. I just did it.
C: How did it make you feel?
CA: … erm … I weren't going out with him and he had the fiver in his hand. He wanted me to … so er … I … I did.
C: Because of the money?
CA: Yeah. I did it with my mate as well. Gary said he'd pay us a tenner if me and my mate tongued each other.
C: Tongued?
CA: French kissed.
C: You didn't care …?
CA: No.
C: …and …
CA: Nothing … just did it. I don't fancy her …. Does that make me a slag? … Is that what you think?
C: Why would I think that?
CA: 'Cos they say I do anything.
C: And you don't fancy them?
CA: I don't fancy him or her. I don't fancy them …
C: … and not fancying them … doing it … did you feel …?
CA: …nice … good … liked it.
C: I'm sorry, I am not getting at you, but when you say 'good'…
CA: I don't fancy them, I'm not a fucking lemon.

With that, Carole Ann threw her cigarette butt into the bush and walked off, running into a younger boys' football game, pinching the ball and threatening to punch anyone who tried to get it back. Traditional perspectives might argue that Carole Ann was in denial or that, given a more safe and supportive space, she would have been able to come out as a lesbian.

However, Carole Ann's experiences resonated with other experiences in the school that suggested the inappropriateness, confusions and guilt induced by adult-defined sexual categories. Leck (2000), exploring the sexual in American schools, offers a critique of the pervasive gender/sexuality diacritic explanations of sexuality and schooling. She argues that when formal studies of sexuality and schooling reduce their analysis to dualistic categories such as hetero–homo, the everyday complexity of the lived out erotic is compromised by such simplistic categories. She also argues that although placing hetero and homo into a sexuality taxonomy provides the conceptual space for other sexualities, this binary generates more confusion and is 'destructive for those individuals who are caught up in the politicization, the oversimplification, and the embedded misunderstandings about adolescent sexualities' (Leck, 2000: 323).

It is argued that the extract demonstrates that there is the possibility of a phenomenologically erotic space outside sexuality operating within the cultural resources of age, gender and sexuality. Further research is urgently needed to explore sexual experiences and understandings that might generate other ways of knowing. Perhaps, as Dean (2000) suggests, once we escape an understanding of sexuality as genitally focused, we are more likely to gain a more succinct insight into what the sexual means and how it is lived. Furthermore, the rejection of a bodily sexuality also allows the possibility of an understanding of the sexual that goes beyond an identity politics.

DOING SEXUALITY RESEARCH IN CONTEMPORARY CULTURE

In previous work we have highlighted the difficulties of conducting research on masculinity in prevailing social and cultural contexts (Haywood and Mac an Ghaill, 2003). Alongside others working in the area, we have been privately advised that researching sexuality is a bad career move, experienced marginalization because of our assumed sexualities and been accused at conferences that discussing sexuality was akin to rape and homophobia. In his *Confessions of a Sex Researcher*, Fisher points out:

> ... the public assumes that one's speciality area is related to one's behaviour. Hence it is usually assumed that anyone doing research on homosexuality is gay, or that anyone doing research related to teenage pregnancy must have been a pregnant teenager. This is not a problem that is typically encountered by researchers in other areas. Memory researchers are not usually asked if they are trying to improve their own memories, and medical researchers are not typically assumed to be suffering from the diseases which they are studying. (Fisher, 1989: 144)

Work on sexuality is taking place at a time when schools are socially projected as the guardians of morality. Goode and Ben-Yehuda (1994: 29) stress that: 'moral panics are likely to "clarify [the] normative contours" and "moral boundaries" of the society in which they occur, and demonstrate that there are limits to how much diversity can be tolerated in a society'. Sexual episodes in education, reported by politicians and the media, do this by simultaneously activating understandings of childhood and the social responsibilities of schooling. Research on sexuality in schools is not taking place in a neutral context. Rather, schooling has become an arena where cultural anxieties are being continually projected and temporarily resolved. Researchers are operating as part of this dynamic. For example, the cultural intensification of childhood innocence is systematically producing sexual significances within schooling practices as institutional roles and responsibilities become sharply defined. The researcher does not stand outside this. Rather, it could be argued that research practices are actually being constituted by it.

In light of the current sexual concern over schooling and children, getting access to participants (children) is producing increasing challenges to researchers in the field of sexuality. This can occur at a number of levels. Sex and schooling is an extremely problematic and anxiety-producing couplet, and the researcher is often engaged in an intensive process of neutralizing the emotional charges that this field of inquiry generates. An example of this was found by Haywood (2006) conducting research in a mixed-sex secondary school. After successfully negotiating access to the school through the head teacher (notifying parents of the pupils involved), interviews with pupils on their social and personal development were undertaken. During the interviews, pupils provided accounts of their sexual development. Furthermore, the diversity and prevalence of their sexual experiences was intriguing. By approaching a former teacher of the school, a colleague in the university department, comparisons were sought about the uniqueness of the research context. It appeared that indeed, from the colleague's experience, it was surprising that these pupils were reporting to me and/or participating in sexual behaviours.

By this time, information and advice on risk prevention became part of the research process. As the interviews became frequent, such advice and information enabled these issues to be openly discussed with an adult. However, abruptly, the research was stopped. The Head of Department at the university summoned the researcher to his office whereupon he was asked: 'Have you been talking to underage girls about sex?' In response, the researcher responded that yes during the interviews issues about sex and relationships, among a wide range of other issues (friendships, alcoholism, family life, bullying) had

been discussed. The Head of Department suggested that urgent action had to be taken as they had had a complaint from the school Principal. The researcher and the Head of Department went to the school to talk to the Principal about the research. After the meeting, the Principal approached the researcher and said that he did not see what the problem was. Issues of sex and sexuality arose quite frequently and he couldn't understand why the university had got in contact *with the school.* It appeared that the Head of Department, alongside the colleague who had been approached for clarification, had concerns about the research being with underage girls. By talking about sex, the researcher was potentially actively engaged in a sexual activity.

This resonates with a cultural process suggested by Judith Butler (1997), where language is becoming increasingly metonymic. This means that spoken or written words constitute the very actions that they intend to describe. So, in the case above, talking about sex with children becomes the practice itself. The case is reconceived as the researcher wanting to carry out this practice. In this way, words do not merely describe; they are figured as performing what they describe, not only in that they constitute the speaker as sexual, but also in that they constitute the speech as a sexual practice. Researchers are reconfigured to carry sexual desire not only through the space they occupy or their physical contact, but also through the words that they speak. Butler has suggested that words themselves have become contagious, through their metonymic rush: 'In effect, a desirous intention is attributed to the statement *or* the statement is itself invested with the *contagious* power of the magical word, whereby to hear the utterance is to 'contract' the sexuality to which it refers' (Butler, 1997: 113). Butler goes on to suggest that the spoken word becomes the 'vehicle of desire, transferring that desire, arousing that desire' (Butler, 1997: 113). Therefore, the intensification of a discourse of abuse has sexualized research practice and reshaped acceptable and appropriate forms of behaviour. Poole et al. (2004) have highlighted that much ethical debate has focused on the effects of the research on their participants. Importantly, they argue that what remains under-considered are the unseen effects on those carrying out the research. In the context of the current sexual moral panic, it will be interesting to examine the dynamics of future research practices that take place with children in schools.

CONCLUSION

We are in a contemporary cultural context where finding out about sexuality is not simply a research priority but has emerged as part of a late modern reflexivity surrounding our sexual selves. Commercially, the economic return in promoting a conspicuous consumption of the sexual has been phenomenal (Stranack, 2002). Sexual research has become mainstream, with a burgeoning selection of self-help guides that offer to reveal our secret natures, alongside the emergence in popular scientific magazines of an evolutionary psychological argument that genetics is the basis of social behaviour. This is seen most clearly in the celebration of the discovery of the 'gay gene'. At the same time, popular television programmes provide 'sex tips' to a national audience, while e-mail spam interrupts daily routines with revelations of how to optimize our sexual performances. Popular culture commends that we should all become experts in sexual knowledge and fluent in sex talk. As sexual researchers,

we are constantly faced with dealing with such common-sense assumptions. The concern in this chapter has been that existing methodological approaches to sexuality mirror common-sense understandings that the sexual is somewhere out there to be found.

We have argued that conventional conceptualizations of sexuality connect with a broader, historical, Western understanding of sexuality. Central to this approach has been what Callero and Howard (1989) call liberal philosophies. They identify five effects of this philosophy: that most research goals around sexuality are intent on explaining sex behaviours; that the individual is the ultimate level of analysis; that explanation is achieved by identifying a series of key causal variables; that such variables tend to be physiological, cognitive or part of a personal socio-historical biography; and finally that intervention is the result of the application of findings. The implication is that sexuality is not seen as a social process but as an emergent force that has a natural state and is, in itself, value free. We conclude by suggesting that a general re-orientation towards sexuality might be needed that engages not simply with getting the correct answers or representative samples, but rather with establishing a re-interrogation of the underlying epistemological frames that are used when exploring sexuality in social and cultural arenas.

NOTE

1 In UK law, section 28 of the Local Government Act 1988 prohibits local authorities from promoting homosexuality by publishing material, or by promoting the teaching in state schools of the acceptability of homosexuality as a 'pretended family relationship'. In 2000 the Labour government paradoxically outlawed the teaching of sexuality but legislated for the promotion of 'family relationships'.

REFERENCES

Atkinson, P., Delamont, S. and Hammersley, M. (1993) 'Qualitative research traditions', in M. Hammersley (ed.), *Educational Research: Current Issues*. London: Paul Chapman.

Bensimon, E.M. (1992) 'Lesbian existence and the challenge to normative constructions of the academy', *Journal of Education*, 174(3): 98–113.

Bland, L. and Doan, L. (eds) (1998) *Sexology in Culture: Labelling Bodies and Desires*. Cambridge: Polity Press.

Bolton, R. (1995) 'Tricks, friends and lovers, erotic encounters in the field', in D. Kulick and M. Wilson (eds), *Taboo, Sex, Identity and Erotic Subjectivity in Anthropological Fieldwork*. London: Routledge.

Bowman, G. (1997) 'Identifying versus identifying with "the Other": Reflections on the siting of the subject in anthropological discourse', in A. James, J. Hockey and A. Dawson (eds), *After Writing Culture*. London: Routledge.

Bristow, J. (1999) *Sexuality*. London: Routledge.

Buchanan, I. (2000) *Michel de Certeau: Cultural Theorist*. London: Sage.

Butler, J. (1997) *Excitable Speech: A Politics of the Performative*. New York: Routledge.

Callero, P.L. and Howard, J.A. (1989) 'Biases of scientific discourse on human sexuality: Toward a sociology of sexuality', in K. McKinney and S. Sprecher (eds), *Human Sexuality: Social and Interpersonal Context*. Norwood, NJ: Ablex.

Dean, T. (2000) *Beyond Sexuality*. Chicago: University of Chicago Press.

Eisner, E. (1993) 'Objectivity in educational research', in M. Hammersley (ed.), *Educational Research: Current Issues*. London: The Open University.

Fawcett, B. and Hearn. J. (2004) 'Researching others: Experience, participation and material reflexivity', *The International Journal of Social Science Methodology*, 7(3): 201–218.

Fisher, T. (1989) 'Confessions of a sex researcher', *Journal of Sex Research*, 26(1): 144–47.

Foucault, M. (1970) *The Order of Things: An Archaeology of the Human Sciences*. New York: Routledge.

Foucault, M. (1981) *The History of Sexuality*. Harmondsworth: Penguin.

Francis, B. and Skelton, C. (2001) 'Men teachers and the construction of heterosexual masculinity in the classroom', *Sex Education: Sexuality, Society and Learning*, 1(1): 9–21.

Goode, E. and Ben-Yehuda, N. (1994) *Moral Panics: The Social Construction of Deviance*. Oxford: Blackwell.

Harding, S. (1991) *Whose Science? Whose Knowledge? Thinking from Women's Lives*. Buckingham: Open University Press.

Haywood, C. (2006) *Sexuality and Schooling: A Politics of Desire*. Unpublished PhD thesis, University of Newcastle-upon-Tyne.

Haywood, C. and Mac an Ghaill, M. (2003) *Men and Masculinities: Theory, Research and Social Practice*. Buckingham: Open University Press.

Jeffcutt, P. (1993) 'From interpretation to representation', in J. Hassard and M. Parker (eds), *Postmodernism and Organizations*. London: Sage.

Kehily, M. (2000) 'Understanding heterosexualities: Masculinities, embodiment and schooling', in G. Walford and C. Hudson (eds), *Genders and Sexualities in Educational Ethnography: Studies in Educational Ethnography* (Vol. 3). Oxford: JAI Press.

Kinsey, A.C., Pomeroy, W.B and Martin, C.E. (1948) *Sexual Behavior in the Human Male*. Philadelphia: W. B. Saunders.

Kvale, S. (1996) *Interviews: An Introduction to Qualitative Research Interviewing*. Thousand Oaks, CA: Sage.

Laqueur, T.W. (1986) *Making Sex: Body and Gender from the Greeks to Freud*. Cambridge, MA: Harvard University Press.

Leck, G. (2000) 'Heterosexual or homosexual?: Reconsidering binary narratives on sexual identities in urban schools', *Education and Urban Society*, 32(3): 324–48.

Lincoln, Y.S. and Guba, E.G. (2000) 'Paradigmatic controversies, contradictions, and emerging confluences', in N.K. Denzin and Y.S. Lincoln (eds), *Handbook of Qualitative Research* (2nd edn). Thousands Oaks, CA: Sage.

Looby, C. (1999) 'Sexual self-observation', in R.A. Nye (ed.), *Sexuality*. Oxford: Oxford University Press.

Maxwell, J.A. (1992) 'Understanding and validity in qualitative research', *Harvard Educational Review*, 62(3): 279–300.

McIntosh, M. (1997) 'Seeing the world from a lesbian and gay standpoint', in L. Segal (ed.), *New Sexual Agendas*. London: Macmillan.

Money, J. (1988) *Lovemaps: Clinical Concepts of Sexual/Erotic Health and Pathology, Paraphilia, and Gender Transposition in Childhood, Adolescence, and Maturity*. New York: Prometheus Press.

Poole, H., Giles, D.C. and Moore, K. (2004) 'Researching sexuality and sexual issues: Implications for the researcher?', *Sexual and Relationship Therapy*, 19(1): 79–88.

Quinlivan, K. and Town, S. (1999) 'Queer as fuck? Exploring the potential of queer pedagogy in researching school experiences of lesbian and gay youth', in D. Epstein and J.T. Sears (eds), *A Dangerous Knowing: Sexuality, Pedagogy and Popular Culture*. London: Cassell.

Rabinow. P. (1986) 'Representations are social facts: modernity and post-modernity in anthropology', in J. Clifford and G.E. Marcus (eds) *Writing Culture: The Poetics of Ethnography*. Berkeley: University of California Press. pp. 234–61.

Rabinow, P. (1988) *French Modern: Norms and Forms of the Social Environment*. Cambridge, MA: Harvard University Press.

Richardson, L. (1997) *Fields of Play: Constructing on Academic Life*. USA: Rutgers University Press.

Rofes, E. (2000) 'Young adult reflections on having an openly gay teacher during early adolescence', *Education and Urban Society*, 32(3): 399–412.

Rogers, M. (1994) 'Growing up lesbian: The role of the school', in D. Epstein (ed.), *Challenging Lesbian and Gay Inequalities in Education*. Buckingham: Open University Press.

Rorty, R. (1979) *Philosophy and the Mirror of Nature*. Princeton, NJ: Princeton University Press.

Schwandt, T. (1994) 'Constructivist, interpretivist approaches to human inquiry', in N. Denzin and Y. Lincoln (eds), *Handbook of Qualitative Research*. Thousand Oaks, CA: Sage.

Simon, W. and Gagnon, J.H. (1999) 'Sexual scripts', in R. Parker and P. Aggleton (eds), *Culture, Society and Sexuality*. London: UCL Press.

Sparkes, A.C. (1994) 'Self, silence and invisibility as a beginning teacher: a life history of lesbian experience', *British Journal of Sociology of Education*, 15: 93–118.

Stanley, L. and Wise, S. (1993) *Breaking Out Again: Feminist Ontology and Epistemology*. London: Routledge.

Stein, E. (1994) 'The relevance of scientific research concerning sexual orientation to lesbian and gay rights', *Journal of Homosexuality*, 27: 269–308.

Stranack, J. (2002) 'Are we all trash?', *Blueboy*, 10: 26–27.

Trotter, J. (2001) 'Challenging assumptions around sexuality: services for young people', *Youth and Policy*, 71: 25–43.

Usher, R. (1997) 'Telling a story about research and research as story-telling: Postmodern approaches to social research', in G. McKenzie, J. Powell and R. Usher (eds), *Understanding Social Research Perspectives in Methodology and Practice*. London: The Falmer Press.

Walkerdine, V. (1981) 'Sex, power and pedagogy', *Screen Education*, 38: 14–23.

Weber, M. (1930) *The Protestant Ethic and the Spirit of Capitalism*. London: Allen and Unwin.

Weeks, J. (1986) *Sexuality*. London: Routledge.

Weeks, J. (1995) *Invented Moralities: Sexual Values in an Age of Uncertainty*. Cambridge: Polity Press.

13

Researching Sex Work: Dynamics, Difficulties and Decisions

TEELA SANDERS

The sexual behaviour and lifestyles of others are entrenched in anthropological and sociological studies. Classic works from Malinowski (1929/1987) and Mead (1928/1949) both explore the sexual activities of so-called 'primitive' societies. More recent, somewhat controversial work places sexual behaviour at the centre of sociological inquiry. Bolton (1995) had sex with gay informants; Goode (2003) became a member of the Fat Civil Rights Organization by admitting and pursuing his sexual attraction to large women, while Blackwood (1995), Altork (1995) and Killick (1995) all reveal their involvement in erotic field relations. 'Going native' is not uncommon in the sexual setting. Douglas (1977) left his clothes behind to partake in the nude beach scene, Parry (1982) became a naturist in order to understand the codes and practices of the subculture, and Humphreys (1970) became a 'watch queen' outside public toilets in a park while men engaged in homosexual rendezvous.

One sexual fieldwork site that has not received due attention and reflection from a methodological, ethical or epistemological stance is that of the sex industry. The economy that facilitates the matching of female sexual services and male custom has been in the background of deviancy studies from the outset (see Cressey, 1932; Reckless, 1933). Due to the expansions of the contemporary sex entertainment economy, the term 'sex industry' refers to direct sexual services, such as prostitution, and non-direct sexual services, such as fantasy telephone lines, erotic dancing, strip shows and pornography. In this chapter, the term 'sex work' is applied broadly to include activities where access to women's body parts is sold for cash. Unless otherwise stated, the chapter will discuss research into female adult prostitution, excluding male and transgendered sex markets and child prostitution.

This chapter contributes several insights into researching the sex industry and adds generally to the wider complexities of how the researcher is positioned in field relations. First, the gatekeepers who offer an 'assisted passage' to the deviant sex markets are explored alongside the wealth of qualitative methods that are employed as data collection techniques. Second, the role of the participant observer is deconstructed to find out different types of 'participation' in the context of the sex industry. Third, the research bargain and experiences of initiation rituals that form part of the access deal are explored. Fourth, researchers in the sex industry engage in a series of real-life dilemmas that are specific to the sexualized, suspicious and volatile nature of sex markets. Managing the 'researcher' identity, the emotional consequences of investigating a sensitive and sexual topic and the potentially dangerous nature of the environment deserve attention. Fifth, and finally, this chapter explores how fieldwork in sex industry research is often characterized by nakedness. This creates opportunities for the researcher to move away from the periphery to the inside yet at the same time creates complexities in terms of the embodiment of the fieldwork experience.

The chapter has provided the opportunity to comb through my own ethnographic experiences of researching the street and indoor prostitution markets in England. Examples will be drawn from this work (see Sanders, 2001, 2004a, 2004b, 2005) as well as a range of other studies in the sex industry, mainly in Britain and the United States. However, one point for discussion is the reluctance of researchers of the sex industry to analyze or, perhaps more accurately, write about their position as a collector, observer and recorder of commercial sexual behaviour. Such 'confessional tales' (van Mannen, 1988), although acknowledged as epistemologically and methodologically necessary, are too briefly scattered among the work on the sex industry.

THE RELUCTANT REFLECTIVE RESEARCHER

There is now a detailed body of research that begins to uncover the extent, nature and organization of prostitution and other sex markets. The majority of findings are qualitative in nature, where the researcher has gone into the native environment, often for long periods of time, and immersed themselves in the cultural setting. Yet, despite the intensity of the popular ethnographic methods, there is limited reflection on fieldwork practice, the researcher's experiences or how the observer's role affects the process (for exceptions, see Maher, 2000; Miller, 1997; O'Connell Davidson and Layder, 1994; O'Neill, 1996; Sharpe, 2000). For example, Edwards (1993: 100) mentions visiting and observing sex clubs in European cities but no explicit acknowledgement of the methodology is offered. Similarly, in Murphy's (2003) astute and thorough observations of women who perform striptease acts exposing the dancers' use of impression management, there is no deconstruction of the researcher's own place as an observer among naked women, dim lights, thudding tunes and drooling men.

So, why not reflect on the sexual or intimate nature of researching the sex economy? Coffey (1999: 83) reminds the sociologist that 'sexual reputation is a gendered sexual concept' and that revealing antics in the field could be somewhat damaging for those who are not white, male and heterosexual. We can therefore ask whether reputation, career aspirations and 'face' hold back the researcher from 'spilling all'? Are researchers shy of what Goffman (1963) and later Mattley (1998) calls 'courtesy stigma', fearing that we will be cursed by the stereotypes and myths of those we study? The lack of published material on fieldwork practices is probably not only due to an individual unwillingness to engage in reflective evaluations, but also because of 'academic prudery' that has traditionally kept prostitution out of academic circles (Ashworth et al., 1988). Mattley (1997) confirms such prejudices are still alive among the decision-makers of institutions as her funders objected to the sex industry as a research site because the endeavour was considered voyeuristic. In my own work to date, like others, reporting the findings had been prioritized, leaving little time for reflection on the intricacies of the sexual field. However, such prioritizing is an excuse for admitting that the real barriers to critical methodological evaluation stem from the constraints of institutional expectations that favour a less subjective approach to presenting data, as well as a subtle masculine research culture where reflexivity sits uncomfortably at the margins.

It appears, then, that the researcher of erotic settings has sometimes overlooked the recent trend in what Denzin (1997) has called the fifth phase of interpretative inquiry, where deconstructing the researcher's place in the process is a critical means of sociological understanding (Albesson and Skoldberg, 2000; Coffey, 1999; Plummer, 1995). This chapter argues that just as the researcher's body is integral to the ethnographic process because 'fieldwork is necessarily an embodied activity' (Coffey, 1999: 59), the subjectivity of the researcher shapes and is inevitably shaped by the presence of sexual activity, desires, emotions and identities in the field. The privilege and advantage of fieldwork is that it is a live interaction, free from the constraints of scientific procedures. Yet field relations are still subject to the same laws of human interaction as other types of relationship. This chapter unpacks the taken-for-granted and assumed interactions between researcher and respondent to reveal what really happens when researchers, for professional purposes, go into the sex industry.

CHAPERONS, CONTACTS AND COURTESANS

Traditionally there have been some difficulties collecting data on prostitution because of the simple problem of locating and contacting sellers, buyers and organizers, who are cleverly hidden from the urban landscape. Yet there are some tried and tested gatekeepers that support the journey from the academic institution to the backstreets of brothels and peep shows. As Maher (2000: 209) documents in her journey to 'Crack Row' in a Brooklyn neighbourhood, sociologists who seek to locate hidden cultures must first find an 'assisted passage'. The criminal justice system, particularly courts and prisons, provide a captive audience of both buyers and sellers from the sex trade (see Faugier, 1996; Kinnell, 1991; Miller, 1997; Norton-Hawk, 2004). Monto (2000: 71) surveyed men who had been arrested for kerb crawling and had opted to enrol at a 'John's school' to reform their behaviour rather than receive a sentence. In Britain, the police have enabled fieldworkers to link into the street prostitution scene (Benson and Matthews, 1995; Faugier, 1996), enabling Sharpe (2000) to become an 'honorary member of the vice squad'.

Described as a common access route into all deviant communities (Hobbs, 2001: 214), the most popular gatekeeper into prostitution is specialist health and welfare services. Genitourinary clinics provide a self-defined population of respondents (Boynton, 2002; Day and Ward, 1990; Green et al., 2000; Ward et al., 1999) and throughout the world researchers have worked alongside outreach provision (for descriptions, see Cooper et al., 2001; and Kirkpatrick, 2000) to observe the indoor and street sex markets (Church et al., 2001; Evans and Lambert, 1997; Lever and Dolnick, 2000; O'Neill and Barbaret, 2000; Porter and Bonilla, 2000; Whitaker and Hart, 1996; Wojiciki and Malala, 2001). However, not all gatekeepers are formal. O'Connell Davidson was introduced to an entrepreneurial sex worker by one of her students who worked as a receptionist (O' Connell Davidson and Layder, 1994: 176) and Jewell Rich and Guidroz (2000: 36) came to know the phone sex industry through a personal acquaintance. Ultimately, whether the gatekeeper is formal or informal, the literature highlights that the researcher must have an insider to initially introduce a world where individuals are understandably suspicious, untrusting and weary of disclosing information. For these reasons, cold calling without prior introduction appears to result in failure (O'Connell Davidson and Layder, 1994: 213), while e-mailing unexpectedly is equally fruitless (Sanders, 2004b).

The popularity of the health or welfare agency as the primary gatekeeper could falsely give the impression that access was relatively straightforward. Trying to access female sex workers through a health project, Hubbard (1999: 233) learned that sex workers only comply if the following four principles are evident. First, that the research will produce knowledge to help reduce stigma surrounding prostitution; second, that the researcher has an insight into reality; third, a recognition that prostitution is a legitimate form of work; and fourth, a belief that health and safety risks should be minimized. As Smart (1984: 153) describes, once access has been gained at an official level, the researcher is then faced with the task of convincing others further down the ranks that their quest is legitimate. In my own project, there were three levels of access. First, the managers of the National Health Service in the city; second, health professionals who worked on a day-to-day basis with women on the street and indoor prostitution establishments; and third, owners, managers and workers in each licensed sauna, illegal brothel or escort agency. This experience of 'layered access' is not specific to researching the sex industry, but may well be symptomatic of the complexities of entering into an illegal and illicit activity. However, what is specific to the sex industry is that after each level of access has been secured the researcher is brought closer to the sexual world of the commercial exchange. Therefore the researcher must learn to quickly move between the clinical world of protocols, policies and public health remits to the equally clinical but commercially erotic world where women exchange access to parts of their bodies for cash from strangers.

A MYRIAD OF METHODS

The spectrum of methods available in the social sciences and humanities has been applied to all corners of the sex industry. Historical and contemporary documents, newspapers and archive data are lucrative sources of detail (Finnegan, 1979; Hausbeck and Brent, 2000; Lowman, 2000; Matthews, 1997; Walkowitz, 1980). Autobiographical accounts provide rich insights into the daily routines and experiences of those working in the trade (Cockington and Marlin, 1995; Delacoste and Alexander, 1988; Efthimiou-Mordant, 2002; Jaget, 1988; Kempadoo and Doezema, 1999; Levine and Madden, 1988; Nagel, 1997). In contrast, scientific-based clinical methods rely on quantitative methods to develop instruments for the collection of large-scale data (Brewer, 2000; Farley et al., 1998; James, 1974; McKeganey et al., 1992; Monto and Hotaling, 2001; Morgan Thomas et al., 1989; Romans et al., 2001; Silbert and Pines, 1982; Ward et al., 1999). Sociological and epidemiological approaches have been combined to explore specific questions relating to health, social interaction and 'risky' behaviour (Asamoah-Amu et al., 2001; Barnard, 1993; Barnard, McKeganey and Leyland, 1993; Campbell, 1991; Gossop et al., 1994; Green et al., 2000). In general, though, the absence of large numbers of respondents deters the use of quantitative methods, and because this topic is in the infancy of establishing a research agenda 'exploratory qualitative investigation' is needed (Jewell Rich and Guidroz, 2000: 37).

Some studies of the sex industry take on both qualitative and quantitative methods of data collection. In her book, *Prostitution, Power and Freedom* (1998), O'Connell Davidson presents a case study of one entrepreneurial British prostitute, 'Desiree', plus participatory observation as a receptionist and in-depth interviews with clients, receptionists, and other sex workers. These combined ethnographic techniques were applied to 'explore some of the contradictions of control within the prostitute–client relationship' (O'Connell Davidson and Layder, 1994: 210). Questionnaires were considered a 'blunt and unresponsive instrument' that was not appropriate to tease out the complexities of prostitution. Yet systematic recordings of the range, pattern and nature of the sexual demand from clients was gained through a questionnaire, combined with an analysis of letters and other documents provided by clients. Original and innovative textual material, including sex workers advertisements, phone kiosk cards, pornographic videos and magazines and specialist contact magazines, informed the

research along with observations in a magistrates court, peer support groups, internet sites and some e-mail interviews. Triangulation can generate an abundance of data. Having spoken to 211 women and conducted in-depth interviews with 45, Maher's (2000: 214) final data set consisted of 5,000 pages of transcribed interviews, a field diary, photographs, and items such as letters, poems and drawings from individual women.

It is the interview that is most widely employed to elicit information about the sex industry (Campbell, 1991; Day, 1994; Epele, 2001; Lewis and Maticka-Tyndale, 2000; May, Horcopos and Hough, 2000; McKeganey and Barnard, 1996; McLeod, 1982; Miller, 1995; Montemurro, 2001; Murphy, 2003; Rickard, 2001; Sterk, 2000). This usually takes the form of unstructured conversations – what O'Neill (1996: 131) calls 'guided conversations'. Abbott (2000: 19) describes how informal discussions were the main method among pornography producers and actors. The life history method is applied so individual stories can illustrate broader social processes (Heyl, 1979; Hoigard and Finstad, 1999; Mansson and Hedin, 1999; O'Neill, 2001; Phoenix, 1999) and occasionally focus group discussions have been a successful method of understanding concepts such as risk, disease and contagion (Downe, 1999). Gysels et al. (2002) researched sex workers in a Ugandan trading town and combined life history interviews with income and expenditure diaries and a diary of commercial sexual transactions. Porter and Bonilla (2000: 107) found that interviewing women in their work environment was an advantage because they could observe the realities of the working day. Equally, Pasko (2002: 51) reports how varying interview locations between work, home and leisure settings with the same female dancers enabled 'different levels of reflection and retrospection of their stripping experiences'. Porter and Bonilla (2000: 107) also note that gathering data is not a series of structured interviews but broken contact, resulting in snippets of material gathered during women's working hours.

It is widespread within prostitution studies to include indigenous people, or what Gossop et al. (1994) call 'privileged access interviewers' in the design or execution of the research (Kinnell, 1991; Norton-Hawk, 2004; Plumridge et al., 1997; Pyett and Warr, 1997: 540; Rao et al., 2003; Raphael and Shapiro, 2004: 129; Silbert and Pines, 1982). This methodological approach stems from a political standpoint that places peer education and empowerment at the centre of the research process. O'Neill (1996: 130) reflects on how the principles of her research have been 'women-centred', locating 'women prostitutes as key players' and 'active participants in the social construction of knowledge'. Epistemological justifications for using insiders as chief data collectors conveniently negotiates the problems of accessing a closed society, which is sometimes difficult to engage with because of chaotic lifestyles and the consequences of substance misuse (Hart, 1998; Miller, 1997; Sanders, 2001).

Issues associated with sampling a hard-to-reach population have been well documented (Atkinson and Flint, 2001; Bloor et al., 1991; Faugier and Sargeant, 1997; Kaplan et al., 1987; van Meter, 1990). In the sex industry, non-random or opportunistic samples are sought to achieve an 'intensive analysis of a limited number of cases which represent … the central objectives of the research' (O'Connell Davidson and Layder, 1994: 174). Innovative sampling techniques, such as media campaigns (Lever and Dolnick, 2000) and 'time sampling' over a range of days and hours (Barnard, 1992: 143), enable snowball sampling to generate a chain of referrals. Despite some attention to the difficulties of sampling this population, researchers have questioned the need to be concerned with the scientifically imposed notions of rigour on groups who are dislocated from the mainstream. Maher, (2000: 29) states that 'the search for representativeness also obscures what the anomalous or the marginal can reveal about the centre' and goes on to describe how the selection process in ethnographic work is not unlike the way we include and exclude those in our friendship circle. Establishing field relations is essentially a personal affair that requires lengthy periods of time and significant investment on the part of the fieldworker.

Being in the field no longer means leaving the safety of the office, campus or institution as the internet means that computer-mediated communication can be applied to understand electronic erotica and sexual behaviour (Durkin and Bryant, 1995). Monto (2004) refers to bulletin boards as an avenue to explore the purchaser's side of the sexual exchange, while Sharp and Earle (2003) describe what they crudely term 'cyberpunting' and 'cyberwhoring'. Yet these suggestions are made with little acknowledgement of the ethical and methodological complications of researching the sex industry online (Hine, 2000, 2004). The anonymous, privatized and asynchronous nature of the internet means that the researcher is potentially even more central to the development of research relations and the quality of the research relationship. As I have demonstrated elsewhere (Sanders, 2004b), establishing research relationships online or 'lurking' in chat rooms reveals how the decision to disclose the researcher's status and motives can be problematic. The ambiguous notion of privacy in the public virtual domain poses a set of ethical dilemmas requiring a more rigorous approach to establishing bona fide status than is usually necessary in face-to-face situations.

PARTICIPANT OBSERVATION: PEERING INTO THE OBSCENE?

As Maher (2000: 208) notes, there are inherent unequal power relations involved in ethnographic observations of the sex industry, yet despite these contradictions, to achieve the politics of representation more ethnographic work is needed among those who live at the margins. In this sense the essence of ethnography, participant observation, may be the only way to accurately detail the lives of those excluded from the centre. Information gained in this way is 'important both in plugging gaps in our existing knowledge of human sexuality and also as preparatory material' (O'Connell Davidson and Layer, 1994: 167).

It can be derived from the literature that participant observation of the sex industry can be categorized into four different types. First, and less typical, is the 'insider as researcher', whereby a woman is already located as a legitimate member of the sex industry and subsequently adopts the research position while still earning a living from sex work. For instance, Funari (1997) was a peep-show actress when she decided to use her privileged position to research the commodification of her own body, while Ronai and Ellis (1989) exposed the strategies that dancers use to manipulate the audience and control their emotions. Using one's biographical or employment status as a foot into the fieldwork camp has been an acceptable feature of ethnography (Adler and Adler, 1991; Ditton, 1977; Goffman, 1968; Suttles, 1968). Yet as Ronai (1992: 102) admits, the

complication of this insider role lies with 'the difficulty in extricating a researcher self from other selves while involved in participant observation'.

The second type of participant observation involves the researcher actually taking on an authentic role within the sex market, something that pushes the boundaries of the 'professional distance' advocated by some scholars of ethnography (Fetterman, 1991: 94). Mattley (1998) writes an introspective narrative of her emotional experiences during her fieldwork where she became a telephone sex worker. Mattley took on this job for nine months, worked three to five days a week, took 1,983 calls from purchasers of sexual fantasies and became an accepted member of the workforce. Similarly, O'Connell Davidson (1998) became a receptionist for an entrepreneurial sex worker and took on the day-to-day running of the establishment, welcoming clients and answering the phone. Moving into this emic perspective enabled O'Connell Davidson to witness all stages of the negotiations and observe the sex worker in her natural setting.

Adopting what Miller and Tewksbury (2001) call 'extreme methods', a small number of researchers opt for a 'hands-on' approach to sex research by placing themselves at the centre of the commodified environment. Allison (1994), for example, became a waitress in a Tokyo hostess club. Although the customers never touched her, because the club forbade such contact, conversations with men were highly sexualized and concentrated on her physical appearance, especially her breasts. In this way, Allison participated in sexualized banter and her verbal engagement was sexualized although not sexually explicit. Wendy Chapkis (1997) explains how she achieved ethnographic integrity by training and practising as a massage therapist to women clients and bought sex on one occasion. By positioning herself within the deviant occupation, Chapkis was able to convey all sides of the prostitution prism and speak with authority about the emancipatory potential of sex work.

The third type of participant observation is that of actually witnessing sexual activity. In arenas such as strip clubs, erotic dancing bars and pornography studios, explicit sexual interaction or acts are an integral part of the landscape, available for the eyes of any paying customer. Barton (2002), Dodds (1997), Lewis and Maticka-Tyndale (2000), Liepe-Levinson (2002), Thompson and Harred (1992) and Wood (2000) reveal their experiences of entering night time entertainment markets to observe women performing erotic dances, strip shows, and nude waitressing. Smith (2002) and Montemurro (2001) provide a rare snapshot into the world of the male stripper and the female 'screamer'. Murphy (2003: 311) reflects on 124 hours observing the practices of stripping performances at 'Paper Dolls', watching the front stage shows and hanging out in the dancers' room and manager's office. Abbott's (2000: 19) primary data collection site was pornography production sets, industry parties and a trade show, all of which encompassed nudity and explicit sex, such as anal sex and 'double' penetration. It would have been difficult to gain qualitative material on such work-related cultures and identities without going into the field and therefore it can be assumed that the topic dictates the activities the observer is exposed to.

The fourth type of observation is the most popular method of observing an illicit economy and that is essentially at the periphery. Researchers usually locate themselves inside the sex industry, yet their place is normally on the margins of the activity. In San Francisco, Epele (2001) researched drug-using women involved in street work through informal observation on the street, in cafés, hotels and 'hang out' places. Sitting in bars in the red light district has been a successful observation tactic for Nencel (2001) in Peru, Downe (1999) in Costa Rica and Hart (1998) in Spain. In these ethnographies, the richness of the data is a result of the lengthy hours spent watching interactions between workers, clients and the wider sex work community that facilitated an engagement with individuals in their everyday social context. Williamson and Cluse-Tolar (2002: 1077) spent six months on the streets 'learning the culture, language and geographic layout' in preparation for interviews with pimp-controlled prostitutes. Sharpe (2000) describes her 'street corner research' with prostitutes, punters and police in a northeastern English city and offers one of the few insights into the 'problems and pleasures of the ethnographer in this field'. This realistic account admits that the research strategy and interview schedule never actually went to plan as the reality of the setting took on its own momentum. Indeed, Nencel (2001: 73) reveals how the fieldwork's rhythm is dictated by the repetition of daily practices and the '(un)events' of the respondents' lives.

In these different types of observation role, it is generally the case that the gatekeepers and the sex workers are aware of the researcher's status but the clients are not. In Gold's typology of observation (1958, cited in O'Connell Davidson and Layder, 1994: 168–9), observers who attempt to pass as a member of the group – what Gold calls the 'complete participant' – involves some level of covert activity. O'Connell Davidson and Layder (1994: 214) justify their covert observation of clients because they were 'untroubled by (their) uninvited intrusion' since the clients were anonymous, could not be traced and therefore were protected from harm. On the other hand, O'Connell Davidson held a strong ethical commitment and sense of responsibility towards the sex workers who gave informed consent about their participation. Moving between covert and overt observation with different audiences, who may well be present at the same time, highlights how 'field roles are continually negotiated and renegotiated' (O'Connell Davidson and Layder, 1994: 167).

The fluidity of the observing role when studying sexual behaviour poses the question. What actually is 'participant' observation? Is it acceptable to describe observation from the sidelines as participant or is it what Bolton (1995) calls observation without full participation? Adler and Adler (1994: 380) are clear that the researcher is only required to 'interact closely enough with members to establish an insider's identity without participating in those activities constituting the core of group membership'. Goode (2003: 503) criticizes his own sexual involvement with female informants some 20 years previously and asks 'When is ethnography over the edge'? For those who opt to 'go native' by taking on a participant role or by directly witnessing sexual behaviour, moral and ethical decisions are raised that tunnel to the core of the researcher's place in the sexual setting. From my own experiences, the very 'real-life' nature of ethnography meant that observing nakedness and sexual activity was not a calculated decision made in the 'before' stages of the research but a combination of the intensity of the environment and opportunistic events. It was not unusual in the close confines of a busy brothel to hear sexual activities taking place (the cracking of a whip can be heard in the background of the interview tapes), to see men walking naked from one room to the other or to be invited by workers

or clients to earn cash at 'smacking parties'. Indeed, when Astrid, an experienced worker with whom I had sat for many hours, invited me into the room to 'see how clinical it was', I should not have been shocked but perhaps delighted at the chance to move from the periphery where I lurked to the centre as an insider. After all, I grappled, isn't this the ultimate objective of the participant observer? I had to weigh up why watching the sexual interaction was so different from watching other aspects of the commercial transaction and how observing sex would alter the parameters of the research?

It became apparent that being asked to watch a sex worker 'at work' in the full sense was as much about the respondent's experience of the research process as any concern for the validity of the data collection. As Shaffir (1991: 72) comments, 'cooperation reflects less their estimation of the scientific merits of the research than their response to personal attributes'. Astrid asked me into the room as a way of clarifying the in-depth questions I asked about the differences between sex as work and sex as pleasure. Verbally describing the complex strategies and control techniques was not as satisfactory for Astrid as showing me how things were done. Astrid was eager to express her expertise, was proud of having few aggressive incidents and was considered locally to be an excellent mentor and businesswoman. Watching the sex act, which was a routine acted out strategically to minimize time and maximize profits, was not an invitation to voyeurism but an opportunity to confirm the working practices, rules and routines I had painstakingly asked Astrid and others to describe. The chance to observe the interaction was an opportunity to give credence to the skills of the women, recognize their performance at work, and breakdown further stereotypes of the 'prostitute'.

THE RESEARCH BARGAIN
AND EXCHANGE

Methodological accounts of research in the sex industry describe the importance of a 'research bargain' or exchange as a means of legitimating the researcher's presence in an alien territory (Adler and Adler, 1991: 175). As an incentive for potential participants, this has recently taken the form of monetary payment for interviews (Cusick, 1998; Lever and Dolnick, 2000: 89; Pyett and Warr, 1997: 540). Maher (2000: 215) states that not paying the women for their time given during the interview would have been highly exploitative. As I have described (Sanders, 2001), paying interviewees raises difficult parallels between a client paying a sex worker for access to her body and a researcher paying a respondent for access to information about their experiences. This financial agreement can be considered exploitative because 'researchers are sometimes seen as akin to pimps, coming into the field to take, then returning to the campus, institution or suburb where they write up the data, publish and build careers – on the backs of those they took data from' (O'Neill, 1996: 132).

A one-off payment is often supplemented by other exchanges of material goods. Relationships were sweetened between Maher (2000: 212) and street crack smokers through an exchange of small amounts of cash, and commodities such as cigarettes, food, clothing, subway tokens and make-up. McKeganey and Barnard (1996), like Whitaker and Hart (1996), included service provision in the research design that placed the researcher in an advantageous position as well as engaging in what were considered to be ethical obligations by providing sterile needle equipment and condoms to street sex workers in Glasgow (also see Barnard, 1992).

In my research it was part of the deal that I would supply condoms and on several occasions women only agreed to be interviewed if these items were exchanged. Being known as the 'Condom Lady' was symbolic, a simple way of expressing a non-judgemental attitude to their work. By providing an advocate role with health, social and police agencies and practical assistance my observations moved out of the work setting and into the domestic aspects of respondents' lives.

However, aside from these practical bargains that assist the passage into the unfamiliar, the researcher–respondent relationship is built on other forms of exchange. I began the relationship with interviewees by going through the procedures of informed consent, stating the university affiliation and the aims of the study. This unnecessarily formalized the situation because the women were not interested in the academic reasons why I was present in their world. They wanted to know other details from which they could make a judgement about my personality, sexual orientation and history before they decided to disclose information. In order to get to the point of in-depth, accurate detail, women checked that I understood their comparisons and analogies by asking if I had had similar sexual, physical or emotional experiences. Because they knew I could not use sex work as a framework of reference, respondents encouraged me to conceptualize their experiences through my own self-reflection. For instance, amidst giggles and red faces we would discuss the art of faking an orgasm, the 'performance' of the sexual act (the perfect timing of the ohs and arghs) and the difference between 'one-night stands' and long-term relationships. The 'norms of reciprocity' (Adler and Adler, 1991: 175) urged me to contribute something to the relationship. If I was to ask women to reveal their sexual experiences and hope for honest answers, I had to be prepared to share and reflect on mine. Again, this should have been no surprise as feminist scholars have advocated that researchers locate themselves within the same 'critical plane as the women they study' (Harding, 1986: 89), insisting that the researcher invest herself in the research (Edwards, 1993: 183). Through personal investment and an exchange based on disclosure, trust was established. This exchange of information reduced, although would never remove, the power imbalance to achieve what Smith and Wincup (2000: 342) call a 'mutually advantageous' relationship.

TRIALS, TESTS AND TIGHTROPES

It is not uncommon for researchers who attempt to live alongside groups that are outside their own experience to undergo various forms of initiation rituals or tests of their character, credibility or principles (Mitchell, 1991: 102; van Mannen, 1988: 85). What is distinct regarding the trials placed before the researcher in the sex industry is that these 'acceptance rituals' are bound up with sexual innuendo and behaviour that usually falls somewhere between acute embarrassment or a tricky situation for the fieldworker. Reflecting on her own place in a strip club, Murphy (2003: 332) notes that in fieldwork sites, where observing a performance is the main activity, the tables can soon be turned as the ethnographer's role shifts from 'watching the spectacle' to becoming 'part of the show'. Unfortunately relegated to only a footnote, Murphy describes how she took part in an initiation exercise orchestrated by the male

manager, involving an encounter with a female stripper (who was probably topless) where she had to down a cocktail shot from a test-tube that was in the stripper's mouth. This was recognized as a test and when successfully completed was a sign of full acceptance. In my own research, two sauna workers made sure I was left alone with a client who promptly propositioned me, while the women were upstairs watching on closed-circuit cameras as I squirmed my way out of the situation. This was done with good humour on both sides (see Sanders, 2004a) but, crucially, the women had purposely created an awkward situation to test whether I would maintain my covert status and so they could gauge my reactions to an uncomfortable situation.

Other examples of how sex workers test the researcher as a process of establishing their credibility identifies the general suspicious nature of this population. For example, Sterk (2000) encountered problems attempting to enter into the street prostitution networks. Respondents challenged the researcher's ability to keep secrets by revealing a piece of confidential information only to monitor whether she would tell others. Sharpe (2000) recounts how her persistence on the street under conditions of verbal abuse and aggression from passers- by, who assumed she was a prostitute, brought out a show of solidarity from the women who were initially disparaging of her presence. Sharpe evaluates that staying in the alien environment against the odds gained her respect from the sex workers because she demonstrated she was not afraid to be seen as one of them. This gave Sharpe credibility among the community and a 'workable level of acceptance'. From these examples, it can be assumed that from the outset the researcher is subject to a specific set of observations, judgements and monitoring by the respondents which inevitably shapes relationships and the type of data collected.

NAKEDNESS, INTIMACY AND RAW DATA

There is an assumption that in settings where sexuality, sexual activities and bodies are on display, the researcher's experience will inevitably be sexualized. Although, as Coffey (1999: 83) states, 'it is not necessary for sexual activity to be explicit in the setting for it to be conceived as sexual', it is also the case that sex markets are not necessarily erotic environments. For instance, prominent features of street prostitution, such as violence, pimping and drug addiction, dampens any chance of a sexy atmosphere. Equally, contrary to popular opinion, brothels, saunas, and escort agencies do not ooze the sex appeal, erotica or fetishism promised by the neon lights, glossy magazines or phone card advertisements. In the saunas and working premises that I visited, the dialogue was not particularly sexy and initial interactions observed between workers and clients was framed by the overriding emphasis on the business negotiation, exchanging money and establishing a contract. There was never any fondling, kissing, or hugging observed between clients and workers and it could be argued that the sex worker purposely desexualizes her body for the purpose of work (Brewis and Linstead, 2000a, 2000b). Despite a strange absence of sexualization, most of the data collection was conducted with women in various stages of nakedness.

Some sex arenas unnecessarily bring the researcher into close contact with nakedness. Montemurro (2001: 276) describes the four basic ingredients of the male strip club as 'women, men taking off their clothes, alcohol and screaming', which in turn determines the

researcher's experience. Within the sex entertainment economy, hypersexuality is built around partial nudity, alcohol consumption, and digressing expectations of appropriate behaviour. In my fieldwork there was an acceptance of nakedness between the workers, managers and owners that can be paralleled to other workplaces, such as the cat walk or backstage in the theatre where actors and models are in various stages of undress, grooming and re-dressing. Throughout my visits to saunas I became accustomed to spending much of the time among semi-naked women executing various bodily preparations on themselves and each other. For example, I interviewed Beryl over a series of sessions in the 30-minute slot she allocated as 'preparation time'. While bathing, shaving, washing and styling her hair, applying makeup, and dressing in lingerie I conducted a somewhat fragmented but high-quality, in-depth interview (see Sanders, 2005: Chapter 1). In such close proximity the researcher 'is no longer distanced from the action, the discourse, but is implicated unavoidably in its production' (Mitchell, 1991: 108).

Reflecting for the purpose of this chapter, I began to question why I was given access to this intimate state without knowing individuals for any length of time. It became clear that this was not about the skill of the researcher but an implicit understanding between women who were given access to the privileged 'women only' spaces within the establishments. As a temporary member of the informal network that allowed me to pass from one business to another, I had signed up to a tacit set of beliefs about the female body and the meaning of female nakedness in this context. This understanding was based on the following three principles that contextualized nakedness and the female body in a wider framework of femininity. First, those who were allowed access to this space accepted the legitimacy of all women's bodies no matter their shape, size, colour or how their bodies performed labour. Second, there was an understanding of the importance of taking care of the body in relation to health, especially sexual health, where there was a shared awareness around the intricacies of internal examinations, symptoms and treatments of infections, the practice of safe sex and its psychological implications (see Sanders, 2001). This belief was expressed through the familiar routines of self-beautifying that most women in Western society are accustom to. Third, reserved only for sex workers, there was a mutual respect of what they put their bodies through in order to earn money. Non-sex workers can never truly understand the implications of sex work but can respect the decision to work in the industry. Signing up to these implicit beliefs was the reason why nakedness was so openly displayed to an outsider. Conducting the fieldwork among semi-naked women was not sexual but was part of the complex intimate relationships created in the field. Monitoring my reactions to their nakedness was probably another yardstick informants used to judge my character and principles. The truth was I was so concerned with 'gathering data' that the nakedness of the situation often passed me by, only to understand later that this was a clear indication of my immersion in the lived experiences of the sex workers.

MANAGING IDENTITIES, EMOTIONS AND DANGER

Although each research setting and experience is unique, there are three significant issues to take into account in the sex industry. First, the physical presence of the researcher, including the gender of the researcher, needs to be managed at different stages of the project; second, the intense and emotive research experience often leaves the fieldworker with overwhelming, uncomfortable and angry responses; third, the sex industry, in particular the street prostitution market, often sits on the wrong side of the law among other criminal fraternities such as drug markets, human trafficking networks and gun sales (see May, Edmunds and Hough, 1999), making for a precarious and unpredictable environment.

The criminalized nature of the sex industry, coupled with the high levels of suspicion among patrons, has resulted in the researcher being mistakenly identified as plain clothes police (see Barnard, 1992: 145; Sharpe, 2000: 366), journalists (Sanders, 2004b), or accused of spying for rival competitors (Lever and Dolnick, 2000). Trying to reduce the level of conspicuousness can only create further barriers. Maher (2000: 211) wore a baseball hat to hide her blonde hair, a visible sign of her outsider status in a black community, only to be advised later to ditch the cap because her chosen headgear made her look like an undercover cop. As Barnard (1992: 145) notes, it is often a case of establishing who the researcher is not rather than who he/she is before any level of trust is formed.

Once a fieldwork presence has been secured, this does not guarantee successful relationships. Sharpe (2000: 366) remarks that the ethnographer must possess 'flexibility bordering on the schizophrenic' in order to manage the tensions between different audiences. Sharpe had to show loyalties to the police as the initial gatekeepers but at the same time had to develop relationships with street prostitutes which could only be achieved by distancing her associations with the police. The identity of the researcher must be managed at different levels in the 'intracommunity' and inter-agency politics can cause additional pressures (O'Neill, 1996: 132). Miller (1995: 433) found that taking the role of the 'acceptable incompetent' enabled interviewees to adopt a teacher role and she was able to avoid potential tensions.

Sociologists have explained why sharing the same gender with respondents is not enough to establish an effective or more equal research relationship (Horn, 1995; Kohler Riessman, 1991; Logan and Huntley, 2001; Luff, 1999; Oakley, 1981). Although, as Maher (2000: 211) notes, 'gender does not guarantee sisterhood', being a woman is an essential characteristic when researching the female sex industry. Hubbard (1999: 230) found that despite having a well-placed gatekeeper his maleness was a major barrier to accessing female sex workers, who found a male interviewer an 'unwelcome intrusion' into their feminized space. O'Connell Davidson and Layder (1994: 170) maintain that the social identity of the inquirer affects the observation possibilities and it was 'only because I am woman that I am able to participate as a receptionist'. A male researcher could not have assumed such a position because, for instance, he could not legitimately answer the phone or welcome clients in the expected way. Hence, the sex industry is a unique setting that reveals the gendered stratification of 'parts of the social world which are invisible to men simply because they are men' (O'Connell Davidson and Layder, 1994: 219). Yet, in the sex industry, this is further complicated by the misplacement of women in male-dominated environments such as strip clubs, making access a tricky business (see Barton, 2002).

The commodification of bodies and the prevalence of exploitation, violence and stigma make the sex industry an emotionally draining and ethically problematic research topic. O'Connell Davidson and Layder (1994: 216–17) make a rare reference to the negative emotions generated by a two-hour interview with 'Dick', a British sex tourist who visited Thailand to have sex with young girls. O'Connell Davidson reflects: 'talking to him was the most difficult and unpleasant experience I have ever had as a researcher. What he told me sickened and disturbed me. … Listening to such offensive views without attacking them leaves me with a sense of discomfort.' She goes on to reveal that towards the end of the interview Dick 'actually sat back, spread his legs and started masturbating through his trousers'. (O'connell Davidson and Layder 1994) The spectrum of emotions the researcher experiences is captured by Sharpe (2000: 365), who describes her presence in the harsh street world as 'hardwork, dangerous, sole destroying … extremely funny … and too often very sad'. Miller (1997) also notes the stress caused by the voyeuristic nature of listening to prostitutes retelling violent stories of rape and how this fitted uncomfortably when she scuttled back to her safe house to ponder on her doings in the deviant world.

O'Neill (1996: 132) states that there are 'dilemmas and dangers thrown up by doing this sort of close "ethnographic" research with any group, but particularly with "marginalised", "criminalised", and "stigmatised" groups'. Researchers must not only consider the prospect of danger for themselves but the possible exposure of respondents to risks (Stacey, 1988). The time the sex workers share with the researcher ultimately reduces the opportunities available to earn money which can jeopardize their contact with clients and increase pressure from coercive boyfriend-pimps or managers. The presence of a researcher in a tightly knit community can also have unexpected negative impacts. Researching street sex workers in a southwest English city, I found that the presence of a paid research opportunity revealed the hierarchical nature of prostitution and the divisive competition between older and younger workers, experienced and less experienced, drug users and non-drug users (see Sanders, 2001). Yet, as O'Neill and Campbell (2001) have shown, through participatory action research that places all the participants (in this case street sex workers and community residents) at the centre of the knowledge construction, research can be a positive and binding experience producing effective policy solutions.

Maher (2000: 217) categorizes her experience of fieldwork in the drug and sex markets as posing legal risks (witnessing law-breaking activities and intense police scrutiny), health risks (physical contact with a population saturated by intravenous drug use, HIV and Hepatitis B and C), and personal risks (relating to the volatile environment). O'Neill (1996: 132) witnessed a violent assault on a woman who was involved in prostitution during the fieldwork and as a result attended court as a witness on four occasions. At the time of the attack it was too dangerous to intervene so, along with others, she had to stand by while a respondent was robbed and injured. On three occasions, the night before each court appearance, O'Neill's car was vandalized outside her home. The judge reprimanded the perpetrator and placed a curfew on him, banning him from entering the neighbourhood. The night before the final court hearing there was no vandalism. This example flags up the 'tensions between risk and trust' (O'Neill, 1996: 134) and how research directly affects the personal, bringing the risks of ethnography often too close to home.

Sharpe (2000) relays the dangers of the British street prostitution market as a research site and, like Maher's (2000) experience, several participants died brutal deaths during the fieldwork. My own experiences of danger are closer to Maher's, who found that she was not

necessarily at risk in the field but neither was the environment secure. As white, educated, middle-class women we were both afforded some protection that is not shared with other women in the neighbourhood. Nevertheless, Maher notes, like Liebling and Stanko (2001), that it is often the least experienced researchers that receive minimum protection from the academic institution and emphasizes a need for training, preparation and supervision by the institution to ensure that projects are responsible and ethical.

TAKING THE SELF SERIOUSLY

Ethnographic fieldwork in the sex markets demands both 'body work' and 'emotion work' from the researchers as they place their own body alongside that of their respondents as both parties engage in an exchange of watching, analyzing and managing their physical presence and emotional consequences. To make sense of their place in a somewhat risqué yet intricate world, the fieldworker relies on the same strategies as the sex workers who engage in performance, manage risks and employ tactics to get through the work routines. Young and Lee (1997) describe how the fieldworker's engagement in emotion work through sociological studies is legitimate data that should form part of the intellectual analysis. Managing our emotions by putting them aside neglects how 'feelings become resources for understanding phenomena' and if emotions are not analyzed they 'will still shape the research process, but you will not know how' (Kleinman, 1991: 184–5). In studies of the sex industry where immersion in a life world is intense and perplexing, the reactions of the researcher, the details of the field diary and the stories often reserved for friends, should be a celebrated opportunity to understand the complexities of sexual behaviour. Through methodological reflections, fieldworkers can use their own experiences and insights to break down stereotypes and stigma that unnecessarily plague a community which is highly organized, skilled and ethical. Yet, at the same time, the relationships built in the field do not exist in a vacuum and are not exempt from the blurred reality of intimate interaction. Zussman clarifies this sentiment:

> Fieldwork, to be sure, lives in ambiguity. It is often extra ordinarily difficult to disentangle all the threads of relationships, sexual and non-sexual, developed in the field, just as it is difficult to disentangle the threads of all but the most superficial relationships developed in any area of social life. Professional relationships blur into friendships. Friendships blur into professional relationships. This is all part of the messiness of social life. (Zussman, 2002: 470)

The reluctance of the researcher to reflect may lie with the ambiguity of the intimate relationships, and just as the fieldworker never truly leaves the field (Stebbins, 1991), the uncovering of the research experience may be preserved for the personal and exist only outside the academic enterprise.

REFERENCES

Abbott, S. (2000) 'Motivations for Pursuing an Acting Career in Pornography.' In R. Weitzer (ed.) *Sex for Sale*. London: Routledge. pp. 17–34.

Adler, P.A. and P. Adler. (1991) 'Stability and Flexibility: Maintaining Relations Within Organized and Disorganized Groups.' In W. Shaffir and R. Stebbins (eds) *Experiencing Fieldwork. An Inside View of Qualitative Research*. London: Sage. pp. 173–83.

———. (1994) 'Observational Techniques.' In N. Denzen and Y. Lincoln (eds) *Handbook of Qualitative Research*. Thousand Oaks, CA: Sage. pp. 377–402.

Allison, A. (1994) *Nightwork: Sexuality, Pleasure and Corporate Masculinity in a Tokyo Hostess Club*. Chicago: University of Chicago Press.

Altork, K. (1995) 'Walking the fire line: the erotic dimension of the fieldwork experience.' In D. Kulick and M. Wilson (eds) *Taboo: Sex, Identity and Erotic Subjectivity in Anthropological Fieldwork*. London & New York: Routledge. pp. 107–39.

Asamoah-Amu, C., Khonde, N., Avorkliah, M., Bekoe, V., Alary, M., Monder, M., Frost, E., Deceunink, G., Asamoah-Amu, A., and Pepin, J. (2001) 'HIV Infection among Sex Workers in Africa: Need to Target New Recruits Entering the Trade.' *Journal of Acquired Immune Deficiency Syndromes* 28: 358–66.

Ashworth, G., White, P. and Winchester, H. (1988) 'The Red Light District in the West European City: a Neglected Aspect of the Urban Landscape.' *Geoforum* 19: 201–12.

Atkinson, R. and Flint, J. (2001) 'Accessing Hidden and Hard-to-Reach Populations: Snowball Research Strategies.' *Social Research Update* 33.

Barnard, M. (1992) 'Working in the Dark: Researching Female Prostitution.' In H. Roberts (ed.) *Women's Health Matters*. London: Routledge. pp. 141–56.

Barnard, M., McKeganey, N. and Leyland, A. (1993) 'Risk Behaviours among Male Clients of Female Street Prostitutes.' *British Medical Journal* 307: 361–62.

Barton, B. (2002) 'Dancing on the Mobius Strip: Challenging the Sex War Paradigm.' *Gender and Society* 16: 585–602.

Benson, C. and Matthews, R. (1995) 'Street Prostitution: Ten Facts in Search of a Policy.' *International Journal of the Sociology of Law* 23: 395–415.

Blackwood, E. (1995) 'Falling in Love with an-Other Lesbian: Reflections on Identity in Fieldwork.' In D. Kulick and M. Wilson (eds) *Taboo: Sex, Identity and Erotic Subjectivity in Anthropological Fieldwork*. London & New York: Routledge. pp. 51–75.

Bloor, M., Leyland, A., Barnard, M. and McKeganey, (1991) 'Estimating Hidden Populations: a New Method of Calculating the Prevalence of Drug-injecting and Non-injecting Female Street Prostitutes.' *British Journal of Addiction* 86: 1477–83.

Bolton, R. (1995) 'Tricks, Friends and Lovers: Erotic Encounters in the Field.' In D. Kulick and M. Wilson (eds) in *Taboo: Sex, Identity and Erotic Subjectivity in Anthropological Fieldwork*. London & New York: Routledge. pp. 140–67.

Boynton, P. (2002) 'Life on the Streets: the Experiences of Community Researchers in a Study of Prostitution.' *Journal of Community and Applied Social Psychology* 12: 1–12.

Brewer, D. (2000) 'Prostitution and the Sex Discrepancy in Reported Number of Sexual Partners.' *Proceedings of the National Academy Science* 97: 12385–88.

Brewis, J. and Linstead, S. (2000a) '"The Worst Thing is the Screwing" (1): Consumption and the Management of Identity in Sex Work.' *Gender, Work and Organization* 7: 84–97.

————. (2000b) '"The Worst Thing is the Screwing" (2): Context and Career in Sex Work. *Gender, Work and Organization* 7: 168–80.

Campbell, C. (1991) 'Prostitution, AIDS, and Preventive Health Behaviour.' *Social Science and Medicine* 32: 1367–78.

Chapkis, W. (1997) *Live Sex Acts: Women Performing Erotic Labour.* New York: Routledge.

Church, S., Henderson, M., Barnard, M. and Hart, G. (2001) 'Violence by Clients Towards Female Prostitutes in Different Work Settings: Questionnaire Survey.' *British Medical Journal*: 524–25.

Cockington, J. and Marlin, L. (1995) *Sex Inc.: True Tales from the Australian Sex Industry.* Sydney: Ironback Pan Macmillan.

Coffey, A. (1999) *The Ethnographic Self: Fieldwork and the Representation of Reality.* London: Sage.

Cooper, K., Kilvington, J., Day, S., Ziersch, A., and Ward, H. (2001) 'HIV Prevention and Sexual Health Services for Sex Workers in the UK.' *Health Education Journal* 60: 26–34.

Cressey, P. (1932) *The Taxi Dance Halls.* Chicago: University of Chicago Press.

Cusick, L. (1998) 'Non-use of Condoms by Prostitute Women.' *Occupational Health and Industrial Medicine* 35: (1)1.

Day, S. (1994) 'What Counts as Rape? Physical Assault and Broken Contracts: Contrasting Views of Rape amongst London Sex Workers.' In P. Harvey and P. Gow (eds) *Sex and Violence: Issues in Representation and Experience.* London: Routledge. pp. 172–89.

Day, S. and Ward, H. (1990) 'The Praed Street Project: a Cohort of Prostitute Women in London.' In M. Plant (ed.) *AIDS, Drugs and Prostitution.* London: Routledge. pp. 61–75.

Delacoste, F. and P. Alexander. (1988) *Sex Work: Writings by Women in the Sex Industry.* London: Virago.

Denzin, N. (1997) *Interpretive Ethnography: Ethnographic Practices for the 21st Century.* Thousand Oaks, CA: Sage.

Ditton, J. (1977) 'Alibis and Aliases.' *Sociology* 11: 233–56.

Dodds, S. (1997) 'Dance and Erotica: the Construction of the Female Stripper.' In H. Thomas (ed.) *Dance in the City.* London: Macmillan. pp. 218–33.

Douglas, J.D., Rasmussen, P.K. and Flanagan, C.A. (1977) *The Nude Beach.* Beverley Hills CA: Sage.

Downe, P. (1999) 'Laughing when it Hurts: Humour and Violence in the Lives of Costa Rican Prostitutes.' *Women's Studies International Forum* 22: 63–78.

Durkin, K. and C. Bryant. (1995) '"Log on to Sex": Some Notes on the Carnale Computer and Erotic Cyberspace as an Emerging Research Frontier.' *Deviant Behaviour* 16: 179–200.

Edwards, S. (1993) 'Selling the Body, Keeping the Soul: Sexuality, Power and the Theories and Realities of Prostitution.' In S. Scott and D. Morgan (eds) *Body Matters.* London: Falmer Press. pp. 89–104.

Efthimiou-Mordant, A. (2002) 'Sex Working Drug Users: Out of the Shadows at Last.' *Feminist Review* 72: 82–83.

Epele, M. (2001) 'Excess, Scarcity and Desire among Drug-using Sex Workers.' *Body & Society* 7: 161–79.

Evans, C. and Lambert, H. (1997) 'Health Seeking Strategies and Sexual Health among Female Sex Workers in Urban India: Implications for Research and Service Provision.' *Social Science and Medicine* 44: 1791–803.

Farley, M., Baral, I. Kiremire, M. and Sezgin, M. (1998) 'Prostitution in Five Countries: Violence and Post-Traumatic Stress Disorder.' *Feminism and Psychology* 8: 405–26.

Faugier, J. (1996) 'Descriptive Study of Drug-using Prostitutes and their Clients.' Unpublished PhD dissertation. Department of Social Sciences, University of Manchester.

Faugier, J. and M. Sargeant. (1997) 'Sampling Hard to Reach Populations.' *Journal of Advanced Nursing* 26: 790–97.

Fetterman, D. (1991) 'A Walk Through the Wilderness: Learning to Find Your Way.' In

W. Shaffir and R. Stebbins (eds) *Experiencing Fieldwork: An Inside View of Qualitative Research.* London: Sage. pp. 87–106.

Finnegan, F. (1979) *Poverty and Prostitution: A Study of Victorian Prostitutes in York.* Cambridge: Cambridge University Press.

Funari, V. (1997) 'Naked, Naughty and Nasty.' In J. Nagel (ed.) *Whores and Other Feminists.* London: Routledge. pp. 19–35.

Goffman, E. (1963) *Stigma: Notes on the Management of Spoiled Identity.* Engelwood Cliffs, NJ: Prentice-Hill.

———. (1968) *Asylum.* Harmondsworth: Penguin.

Gold, R.L. (1958) 'Roles in Sociological Fieldwork', *Social Forces* 36(2): 217–23.

Goode, E. (2003) 'Sexual Involvement and Social Research in a Fat Civil Rights Organization.' *Qualitative Sociology* 25: 501–34.

Gossop, M., Powis, B., Griffiths, P. and Strang, J. (1994) 'Sexual Behaviour and its Relationship to Drug Taking Among Prostitutes in South London.' *Addiction* 89: 961–70.

Green, A., Day, S. and Ward, H. (2000) 'Crack Cocaine and Prostitution in London in the 1990s.' *Sociology of Health and Illness* 22: 27–39.

Gysels, M., Pool, R. and Nsalusiba, B. (2002) 'Women Who Sell Sex in a Ugandan Trading Town: Life Histories, Survival Strategies and Risk.' *Social Science and Medicine* 54: 179–92.

Harding, S. (1986) *The Science Question in Feminism.* Ithaca, NY: Cornell University Press.

Hart, A. (1998) *Buying and Selling Power: Anthropological Reflections on Prostitution in Spain.* Boulder, CO & Oxford: Westview Press.

Hausbeck, K. and B. Brents. (2000) 'Inside Nevada's Brothel Industry.' In R. Weitzer (ed.) *Sex for Sale.* London: Routledge. pp. 217–43.

Heyl, B. (1979) *The Madam as Entrepreneur.* New Brunswick, NJ: Transaction Books.

Hine, C. (2000) *Virtual Ethnography.* London: Sage.

———. (2004) *Virtual Methods in Social Research on the Internet.* Oxford: Berg.

Hobbs, D. (2001) 'Ethnography and the Study of Deviance.' In P. Atkinson, A. Coffey, S. Delamont, J. Lofland, and L. Lofland (eds) *The Handbook of Ethnography.* London: Sage. pp. 204–19.

Hoigard, C. and L. Finstad. (1992) *Backstreets: Prostitution, Money and Love.* Cambridge: Polity Press.

Hubbard, P. (1999) 'Researching Female Sex Work: Reflections on Geographical Exclusion, Critical Methodologies and 'Useful' Knowledge.' *Area* 31: 229–37.

Humphreys, L. (1970) *The Tearoom Trade: a Study of Homosexual Encounters in Public Places.* London: Duckworth.

Jaget, C. (1980) *Prostitutes: Our Life.* London: Falling Wall Press.

James, J. (1974) 'Motivation for Entrance into Prostitution.' In L. Crithes (ed.) *The Female Offender.* London: Heath. pp. 177–205.

Jewell Rich, G. and Guidroz, K. (2000) 'Smart Girls Who Like Sex: Telephone Sex Workers.' In R. Weitzer (ed.) *Sex for Sale.* London: Routledge. pp. 35–48.

Kaplan, C., Korf, D. and Sterk, C. (1987) 'Temporal and Social Context of Heroin-using Populations: an Illustration of the Snowball Sampling Technique.' *Journal of Nervous Mental Disorders* 175: 566–74.

Kempadoo, K. and Doezema, J. (1999) *Global Sex Workers.* London: Routledge.

Killick, A.P. (1995) 'The Penetrating Intellect: on Being White, Straight and Male in Korea.' In D. Kulick and M. Wilson (eds) *Taboo: Sex, Identity and Erotic Subjectivity in Anthropological Fieldwork.* London: Routledge. pp. 76–106.

Kinnell, H. (1991) 'Prostitutes' Perceptions of Risk and Factors Related to Risk-taking.' In P. Aggelton, G. Hart, and P. Davies (eds) *AIDS Responses, Interventions and Care.* London: Falmer. pp. 79–94.

Kirkpatrick, K. (2000) 'Provider-Client Models of Individual Outreach and Collective Behavioural Change: the Delivery of Sexual Health Promotion among Sex Workers.' *Health Education Journal* 59: 39–49.

Kleinman, S. (1991) 'Field-workers' Feelings: What We Feel, Who We Are, How We Analyse.' In W. Shaffir and R. Stebbins (eds) *Experiencing Fieldwork: An Inside View of Qualitative Research.* London: Sage. pp. 184–95.

Kohler Riessman, C. (1991) 'When Gender is Not Enough: Women Interviewing Women.' In J. Lober and S. Farrel (eds) *The Social Construction of Gender.* London: Sage. pp. 217–36.

Lever, J. and Dolnick, D. (2000) 'Clients and Call Girls: Seeking Sex and Intimacy.' In R. Weitzer (eds) *Sex for Sale.* London: Routledge. pp. 85–100.

Levine, J. and L. Madden. (1988) *Lyn: a Story of Prostitution.* London: The Women's Press.

Lewis, J. and E. Maticka-Tyndale. (2000) 'Licensing Sex Work: Public Policy and Women's Lives.' *Canadian Public Policy* 26: 437–49.

Liebling, A. and Stanko, B. (2001) 'Allegiance and Ambivalence: Some Dilemmas in Researching Disorder and Violence.' *British Journal of Criminology* 41: 421–30.

Liepe-Levinson, K. (2002) *Stripshows: Performances of Gender and Desire.* London: Routledge.

Logan, M. and Huntley, H. (2001) 'Gender and Power in the Research Process.' *Women's Studies International Forum* 24: 623–35.

Lowman, J. (2000) 'Violence and the Outlaw Status of (Street) Prostitution in Canada.' *Violence Against Women* 6: 987–1011.

Luff, D. (1999) '"Dialogue across the divides": Moments of Rapport" and Power in Feminist Research with Anti-Feminist Women.' *Sociology* 33: 687–703.

Maher, L. (2000) *Sexed Work: Gender, Race and Resistance in a Brooklyn Drug Market.* Oxford: Oxford University Press.

Malinowski, B. (1929/1987) *The Sexual Life of Savages.* Boston: Beacon Press.

Mansson, S.A. and Hedin, U. (1999) 'Breaking the Matthew Effect: on Women Leaving Prostitution.' *International Journal of Social Welfare* 8: 67–77.

Matthews, R. (1997) 'Prostitution in London: an Audit.' Department of Social Sciences, Middlesex University, London.

Mattley, C. (1997) 'Field Research with Phone Fantasy Sex Workers: Managing the Researcher's Emotions.' In M. Schwartz (ed.) *Researching Violence Against Women.* Thousand Oaks, CA: Sage. pp. 101–14.

———. (1998) '(Dis) Courtesy Stigma: Fieldwork among Phone Fantasy Workers.' In J. Ferrell and M. Hamm (eds) *Ethnography at the Edge.* Boston: Northeastern University Press. pp. 146–58.

May, T., Edmunds, M. and Hough, M. (1999) 'Street Business: the Links between Sex and Drug Markets.' *Police Research Series.* Paper 118. London: Home office.

May, T., Harocopos, A. and Hough, M. (2000) 'For Love or Money: Pimps and the Management of Sex Work.' *Police Research Series* Paper 134. London: Home Office.

McKeganey, N. and M. Barnard. (1996) *Sex Work on the Streets.* Buckingham: Open University Press.

McKeganey, N., M. Barnard, A. Leyland, I. Coote, and E. Follet. (1992) 'Female Streetworking Prostitution and HIV Infection in Glasgow.' *British Medical Journal* 305: 801–05.

McLeod, E. (1982) *Working Women: Prostitution Now.* London: Croom Helm.

Mead, M. (1928/1949) *The Coming of Age in Samoa: a Psychological Study of Primitive Youth for Western Civilization.* New York: Mentor Books.

Miller, J. (1995) 'Gender and Power on the Streets.' *Journal of Contemporary Ethnography* 24: 427–51.

———. (1997) 'Researching Violence against Street Prostitutes.' In M. Schwartz (ed.) *Researching Sexual Violence Against Women.* Thousand Oaks, CA: Sage. pp. 144–56.

Miller, J. and R. Tewksbury. (2001) *Extreme Methods: Innovative Approaches to Social Science Research.* Boston: Allyn & Bacon.

Mitchell Jr, R. (1991) 'Secrecy and Disclosure in Fieldwork.' In W. Shaffir and R. Stebbins (eds) *Experiencing Fieldwork: An Inside View of Qualitative Research.* London: Sage. pp. 97–108.

Montemurro, B. (2001) 'Strippers and Screamers: the Emergence of Social Control in a Noninstitutionalized Setting.' *Journal of Contemporary Ethnography* 30: 275–304.

Monto, M. (2000) 'Why Men Seek Out Prostitutes.' In R. Weitzer (ed.) *Sex for Sale.* Routledge: London. pp. 67–83.

———. (2004) 'Female Prostitution, Customers and Violence.' *Violence Against Women* 10: 160–88.

Monto, M. and Hotaling, N. (2001) 'Predictors of Rape Myth Acceptance among Male Clients of Female Street Prostitution.' *Violence Against Women* 7: 275–93.

Morgan Thomas, R., Plant, M.A., Plant, M.L. and Sales, D. (1989) 'Risks of AIDS among Workers in the 'Sex Industry': Some Initial Results from a Scottish Study.' *British Medical Journal* 299: 148–49.

Murphy, A. (2003) 'The Dialectical Gaze: Exploring the Subject–Object Tension in the Performances of Women who Strip.' *Journal of Contemporary Ethnography* 32: 305–35.

Nagel, J. (1997) *Whores and Other Feminists.* London: Routledge.

Nencel, L. (2001) *Ethnography and Prostitution in Peru*. London: Pluto Press.

Norton-Hawk, M. (2004) 'A Comparison of Pimp- and Non-Pimp Controlled Women.' *Violence Against Women* 10: 189–94.

Oakley, A. (1981) 'Interviewing Women – a Contradiction in Terms.' In H. Roberts (ed.) *Doing Feminist Research*. London: Routledge. pp. 30–61.

O'Connell Davidson, J. (1998) *Prostitution, Power and Freedom*. London: Polity Pess.

O'Connell Davidson, J. and Layder, D. (1994) *Methods, Sex and Madness*. London: Routledge.

O'Neill, M. (1996) 'Researching Prostitution and Violence: Towards a Feminist Praxis.' In M. Hester, L. Kelly, and J. Radford (eds) *Women, Violence and Male Power*. London: Open University Press. pp. 130–47

_____. (2001) *Prostitution and Feminism*. London: Polity Press.

O'Neill, M. and Barbaret, R. (2000). 'Victimisation and the Social Organisation of Prostitution in England and Spain.' In R. Weitzer (ed.) *Sex for Sale*. London: Routledge. pp. 123–37.

O'Neill, M. and Campbell, R. (2001) 'Working Together to Create Change.' Staffordshire University and Liverpool Hope University, Walsall Consultation Research. Unpublished report.

Parry, O. (1982) 'Campaign for Respectability: a Study of Organised British Naturism.' MSc Econ dissertation, University College, Cardiff.

Pasko, L. (2002). 'Naked Power: the Pratice of Stripping as a Confidence Game.' *Sexualities* 5: 49–66.

Phoenix, J. (1999). *Making Sense of Prostitution*. London: Macmillan.

Plummer, K. (1995) *Telling Sexual Stories: Power, Change and Social Worlds*. London: Routledge.

Plumridge, E., Chetwynd, S.J. and Reed, A. (1997) 'Control and Condoms in Commercial Sex: Client Perspectives.' *Sociology of Health and Illness* 19: 228–43.

Porter, J. and Bonilla, L. (2000) 'Drug Use, HIV and the Ecology of Street Prostitution.' In R. Weitzer (ed.) *Sex for Sale*. London: Routledge. pp. 103–12.

Pyett, P. and Warr, D. (1997) 'Vulnerability on the Streets: Female Sex Workers and HIV Risk.' *AIDS Care* 9: 539–47.

Rao, V., Gupta, I., Lokshin, M. and Jana, S. (2003) 'Sex Workers and the Cost of Safe Sex: the Compensating Differential for Condom Use among Calcutta Prostitutes.' *Journal of Development Economics* 28: 1–19.

Raphael, J. and Shapiro, D. (2004) 'Violence in Indoor and Outdoor Prostitution Venues.' *Violence Against Women* 10: 126–39.

Reckless, W.C. (1933) *Vice in Chicago*. Chicago: Chicago University Press.

Rickard, W. (2001) '"Been there, seen it, done it, I've got the T-shirt": British Sex Workers Reflect on Jobs.' *Feminist Review* 67: 111–32.

Romans, S., Potter, K., Martin, J. and Herbison, P. (2001) 'The Mental and Physical Health of Female Sex Workers: a Comparative Study.' *Australian and New Zealand Journal of Psychiatry* 35: 75–80.

Ronai, C. (1992) 'The Reflective Self Through Narrative.' In C. Ellis and M. Flaherty (eds) *Investigating Subjectivity: Research on Lived Experience*. Newbury Park, CA: Sage. pp. 102–25.

Ronai, C. and Ellis, C. (1989) 'Turn-On's for Money: Interactional Strategies of the Table Dancers.' *Journal of Contemporary Ethnography* 18: 271–98.

Sanders, T. (2001) 'Female Street Sex Workers, Sexual Violence and Protection Strategies.' *Journal of Sexual Aggression* 7: 5–18.

_____. (2004a) 'Controllable Laughter: Managing Sex Work Through Humour.' *Sociology* 38: 273–91.

_____. (2004b) 'Researching the Online Sex Work Community.' In C. Hine (ed.) *Virtual Methods in Social Research on the Internet*. Oxford: Berg. pp. 66–79.

_____. (2005) *Sex Work: A Risky Business*. Cullompton, UK: Willan.

Shaffir, W. (1991) 'Managing a Convincing Self-Presentation: Some Personal Reflections on Entering the Field.' In W. Shaffir and R. Stebbins (eds) *Experiencing Fieldwork: An Inside View of Qualitative Research*. London: Sage. pp. 72–82.

Sharp, K. and Earle, S. (2003) 'Cyberpunters and Cyberwhores: Prostitution on the Internet.' In Y. Jewkes (ed.) *Dot Cons: Crime, Deviance and Identity on the Internet*. Cullompton, UK: Willan. pp. 36–52.

Sharpe, K. (2000) 'Sad, Bad and (Sometimes) Dangerous to Know: Street Corner Research with Prostitutes, Punters and the Police.' In R. King and E. Wincup (eds) *Doing Research on Crime and Justice*. Oxford: Oxford University Press. pp. 362–372.

Silbert, A. and Pines, M. (1982) 'Victimization of Street Prostitutes.' *Victimology: An International Journal* 1(4): 122–33.

Smart, C. (1984) *The Ties That Bind Us: Law, Marriage and the Reproduction of Patriarchal Relationships.* London: Routledge and Kegan Paul.

Smith, C. 2002. 'Shiny Chests and Heaving G-Strings: a Night Out with the Chippendales.' *Sexualities* 5: 67–89.

Smith, C. and Wincup, E. (2000) 'Breaking In: Researching Criminal Justice Institutions for Women.' In R. King and E. Wincup (eds) *Doing Research on Crime and Justice.* Oxford: Oxford University Press. pp. 331–49.

Stacey, J. (1988) 'Can There be a Feminist Ethnography?' *Women's Studies International Forum* 11: 21–27.

Stebbins, R. (1991) 'Do We Ever Leave the Field? Notes on Secondary Fieldwork Involvements.' In W. Shaffir and R. Stebbins (eds) *Experiencing Fieldwork: An Inside View of Qualitative Research.* London: Sage. pp. 248–55.

Sterk, C. (2000) *Tricking and Tripping: Prostitution in the Era of AIDS.* New York: Social Change Press.

Suttles, G. (1968) *The Social Order of the Slum.* Chicago: University of Chicago Press.

Thompson, W. and Harred, J. (1992) 'Topless Dancers: Managing Stigma in a Deviant Occupation.' *Deviant Behaviour* 13: 291–311.

van Mannen, J. (1988) *Tales from the Field: On Writing Ethnography.* Chicago: University of Chicago Press.

van Meter, K. (1990) 'Methodological and Design Issues: Techniques for Assessing the Representatives of Snowball Samples.' *National Institute on Drug Abuse: Research Monographs* 98: 31–43.

Walkowitz, J. (1980) *Prostitution and Victorian Society: Women, Class, and the State.* Cambridge: Cambridge University Press.

Ward, H., Day, S. and Weber, J. (1999) 'Risky Business: Health and Safety in the Sex Industry over a 9-year Period.' *Sexually Transmitted Infections* 75: 340–43.

Whittaker, D. and Hart, G. (1996) 'Research Note. Managing Risks: the Social Organisation of Indoor Sex Work.' *Sociology of Health and Illness* 18: 399–413.

Williamson, C. and Cluse-Tolar, T. (2002) 'Pimp-controlled Prostitution: Still an Integral Part of Street Life.' *Violence Against Women* 8: 1074–92.

Wojcicki, J. and Malala, J. (2001) 'Condom Use, Power and HIV/AIDS Risk: Sex-workers Bargain for Survival in Hillbrow/Joubert Park/Berea, Johannsburg.' *Social Science and Medicine* 53: 99–121.

Wood, E. (2000) 'Working in the Fantasy Factory: the Attention Hypothesis and the Enacting of Masculine Power in Strip Clubs.' *Journal of Contemporary Ethnography* 29: 5–31.

Young, E. and Lee, R. (1997) 'Fieldworker Feelings as Data: "Emotion Work" and "Feeling Rules" in First-Person Accounts of Sociological Fieldwork.' In V. James and J. Gabe (eds) *Health and the Sociology of the Emotions.* Oxford: Blackwell. pp. 42–63.

Zussman, R. (2003) 'Editor's Introduction: Sex in Research.' *Qualitative Sociology* 25: 473–77.

Part 7

Embodiment and Identity

14

Fieldwork and the Body: Reflections on an Embodied Ethnography

LEE F. MONAGHAN

The human body is in many respects intensely personal and private, yet it is also intertwined with the very fabric, structure and organization of society. C. Wright Mills's (1970) famous sociological dictum concerning the interrelationship between the private and public spheres is clearly exemplified by the body–society nexus. Whether discussing the body as a lifestyle accessory in consumer culture, the politicization of the gendered body in patriarchy, the impact of innovative health technologies in 'risk society' (Beck, 1992) or (at the time of writing) the horrific consequences of 'precision' US military bombing on children in Iraq, bodies are clearly a central element of the social.

Sociological calls over the past decade to 'bring the body in' have largely been heeded (Williams, 2003). A burgeoning theoretical literature (Shilling, 2003; Turner, 1996), the launch of the journal *Body & Society* by Sage in 1995, and a conference on the body by the British Sociological Association in 1998, all indicate, and contribute towards, a 'somatic turn' within mainstream social science. Yet,

while important empirical work is emerging on the body in everyday life (e.g. Nettleton and Watson, 1998), contributors have bemoaned the often abstract, sterile and overly theoretical character of this enterprise (Watson, 2000). Even so, this lacuna is not absolute. Whether exploring the embodied worlds of professional boxers (Wacquant, 1995), ecologists (Roth and Bowen, 2001), schoolgirls (Delamont, 1998), police officers (Westmarland, 2001) or dying patients (Lawton, 1998), bodies are explicit topics of analysis in recent qualitative research. Similar to social anthropology, which has long brought the social dimensions of the body to ethnographic attention (Brain, 1979), this recent literature foregrounds the obdurate reality of flesh and blood bodies.

Referring to my recent ethnography on doorwork, violence and risk, this chapter similarly makes the body a focus of enquiry and supports arguments for an embodied fieldwork perspective. In short, it discusses the significance of the 'lived body' (Williams and Bendelow, 1998) as a topic of, and resource in, fieldwork. The latter method-ological concern is especially important; not 'all ethnographical accounts have silenced the body [but] little has been made of the embodied nature of the fieldwork task' (Coffey, 1999: 75). Grounded in the inescapable corporeality, emotional vicissi-tudes and sometimes violent 'aesthetics' (Stranger, 1999) of nightclub security work, this chapter considers some of the ways in which bodies are central in writing about and doing fieldwork. Far from having an 'absent presence' (Shilling, 2003), issues con-cerning bodies and embodiment are made explicit throughout.

Doorwork, besides representing a site for exploring key social scientific concerns such as masculinities and risk, lends itself especially well to the study of the body and method-ological reflections on embodied fieldwork. Taking as its point of departure the paucity of body discourses in methodological writings (Coffey, 1999), this chapter explores various embodied themes and issues in four main sections. First, I briefly describe the fieldwork, or 'embodied ethnography', which I under-took in Britain's night-time leisure economy. Second, the body of 'the other' (i.e. doorstaff or 'bouncers') is made explicit. Here reference is made to physical risk, the social construc-tion of occupational competence, plural workplace masculinities and embodied limits to their violence. Third, I focus upon how my own body was as a resource for undertaking and writing an ethnography 'at the edge' (Ferrell and Hamm, 1998). Here I recount a particular violent incident, representing a 'fateful moment', which dramatically threat-ened my own bodily integrity and related 'ontological security' (Giddens, 1991). This leads me to reflect upon my emotional experi-ences of doing field/body/edgework and how using my body to research 'other bodies' in a risk environment was sociologically

valuable but also personally troublesome. The conclusion then provides a closing statement on the centrality of the body in ethnographic fieldwork.

DOORWORK, VIOLENCE AND RISK: AN EMBODIED ETHNOGRAPHY

Recent qualitative research provides impor-tant insights into a male-dominated practice that has hitherto eluded sociological and criminological attention; namely, the private policing of Britain's night-time economy by 'bouncers' (Hobbs et al. 2003) or 'door supervisors' as they call themselves. Between 1997 and 2001 I undertook a similar ethnog-raphy in seven city-centre licensed premises in southwest Britain. (No data were recorded in 1998 due to personal circumstances and contingencies. However, re-entry was facili-tated given my links with a head doorman who informally recruited and organized doorstaff.) Ethnography consisted of partic-ipant observation where I assumed an 'active membership role' (Adler and Adler, 1987); in short, and similar to Winlow (2001), this meant I actually became a working doorman. This role consisted of me posi-tioning my uniformed body inside, and at the entrances to, urban drinking venues – a physical presence that permitted first-hand acquaintance with private security work. Doorstaff with whom I regularly worked knew of my university affiliation and research interests, though, for all practical purposes, I was a doorman and was treated as such by others. Looking like, and being viewed by others as, a doorman is notewor-thy because 'the social role of the participant observer and the images which respondents have of him [sic] have a decisive influence on the character of the data collected' (Vidich, 1955: 354).

Before outlining the research (including characteristics of the study population, research sites and data analysis), it is necessary to offer a reflexive statement on the genesis, framing and accomplishment of this ethnography. Reference to my embodied 'biographical situation' (Schutz, 1962) is instructive in this respect. Space constraints prohibit detailed commentary, but it is worth locating this study in the context of my previous 'body-oriented' research, unfolding academic career and general bodily-being-in-the-world.

After obtaining a bachelor's degree in sociology in 1993, I worked as a researcher between 1994 and 1996 on an Economic and Social Research Council funded project on bodybuilding, steroids and violence. (Data from this ethnography, comprising participant observation and indepth interviews, were also used to complete a PhD in 1998. A revised version of the thesis was published as a monograph (Monaghan, 2001).) Towards the end of 1997, university funding for my PhD ceased and I required additional money to complete my studies. At this time I also considered my future employment situation and the fact that academic careers are dependent upon further research and publications. In short, as a 'rookie academic', I was acutely aware of, and anxious about, the intense competition that exists among people wishing to get onto 'the slippery pole' of academia (Hobbs, 1993: 46). I therefore needed another research avenue, in addition to the research I was completing on bodybuilding, drugs and risk. One option, open to relatively few academics (for exceptions, see Calvey 2000 and Winlow, 2001), was to enter the sphere of licensed premises security work. This would allow me to secure a part-time income in order to complete my PhD and hopefully generate some interesting ethnography which I could mine when (or, more

accurately, if) I became a 'licensed' academic. Doorwork was an obvious fieldwork option because I had established contacts with doormen through bodybuilding gyms, possessed necessary 'bodily capital' (Wacquant, 1995) following several years of physical exercise (boxing and lifting weights), was male, relatively young (under 30) and from a working-class background.

My readiness to engage in what, for many middle-class academics, would be considered a very risky (foolhardy) practice could *partially* be explained in terms of Bourdieu's (1977) notion of the habitus. This concept, which refers to socialized subjectivity, pertains to an 'acquired system of generative dispositions' (Bourdieu, 1977: 95) which manifest themselves in class-dependent ways of treating and relating to the body. Certainly, I did not feel my body was expendable, disposable or invincible – an instrument simply to be used for economic survival regardless of possible health consequences. I knew doorwork could be dangerous, even fatal (Hobbs et al. 2003; Monaghan, 2003). Yet, and however illusory, I felt able, given my own embodied history and bodily capital, to work in potentially violent situations and manage (not eliminate) other-imposed risk. Moreover, as research progressed, and I learnt that assaults against doorstaff were exceptional in venues where I worked, risk became habitualized as normal and acceptable to me over time (see Bloor, 1995, on the social phenomenology of risk).

Given my ability and willingness to get in and get on with doorwork (initially as an 'on the job' apprentice and probationer), I satisfied my own dual mandate as outlined above. I informed other doorstaff at my first research site of my university affiliation, my studies on steroids and violence, and that doorwork was not only an immediate source of income for me but also a possible topic for future research publications. However, my expressed academic interest (verbalized by me on occasions when it was situationally appropriate for such disclosure) never undermined my ability to maintain productive field relations and generate rich data. Admittedly, I was marginalized in particular door teams at particular times and places (compounded towards the latter stages of the study when I typically worked just one night per week) and I never naively assumed that my academic identity was personally, if not publicly, problematic for certain contacts. Nonetheless, fieldwork encounters were largely framed by embodied 'rules of irrelevance' (Goffman, 1961) which filtered my external university-related attributes. Even when I became a sociology lecturer in 1999, and informed workers at other sites, doors remained open. Social access – an ongoing practical accomplishment which is never guaranteed – was facilitated for various (embodied) reasons. In particular, a shared interest in physical exercise (manifest in my body build), shared experiences and emotions of doing doorwork in risky situations and, most crucially, my ability and willingness to effectively lend my body 'when it counted' facilitated ethnography in a highly insecure occupation where the larger body of doorstaff work at the head doorman's discretion and invitation (Monaghan, 2002a).

The above hopefully provides sufficient background knowledge concerning the genesis, framing and accomplishment of this study, and the centrality of the body in such processes. In qualifying the above I should stress that I am not endorsing 'the "cult of fieldwork" – as if "getting one's hands dirty" in the field were a heroic venture, or some kind of fashion-statement to complement the careworn office life of university teachers' (Pearson, 1993: xviii). Neither am I offering the general argument that the ethnographer must become competent as a group member,

achieving full membership by becoming 'one of them' (ibid.). However, in the context of my own study, Pearson's (1993: xviii) statement that ethnographers, like boxing commentators, do not need to risk a fight, and must remain content to 'talk a good fight', is literally implausible. Certainly, much of the craft of ethnography (as written product) entails relaying the experiences of others to an academic audience using social scientific concepts, theories and frameworks. Being an observer 'There', and the ability to re-present and interpret the field for others 'Here' is therefore requisite (Hobbs and May, 1993). Yet, in an ethnography of doorwork that aims (repeatedly) to go firsthand where the action is, a necessary condition for data generation is the researcher's willingness to risk (a level of) violence and personal bodily injury. An ethnographer of football hooliganism may be able to run away from a fight and still maintain productive field relations (Armstrong, 1993), but a male ethnographer obtaining privileged access to doorwork culture by actually working as 'one of them' has little option but to stand his ground and intervene if violence erupts inside licensed premises.[1] If not, access would quickly be terminated in that venue, doors would close at other sites in the locality and violence may even be meted out by co-workers for reneging on one's duty and increasing their risk of injury (similarly, see Winlow et al., 2001: 546). In such a context, being able to 'talk a good fight' may go someway in maintaining field relations, but, being able physically to control (potentially) violent situations is the bottom line (Hobbs et al. 2003). Correspondingly, in order to maintain both social access and a sense of 'ontological security' in risk contexts (Giddens, 1991), the ethnographer's own 'bodily capital' (body build, techniques of the body) and hexis (comportment, style) (Bourdieu, 1977) represent valuable resources for undertaking fieldwork on doorwork.

Other aspects of the research must also be noted. Importantly, and given the potentially sensitive nature of the study, I use pseudonyms when referring to licensed premises and contacts, and I have changed certain background details to preserve anonymity. Regarding fieldwork sites, establishments varied in their size, customer capacity, appearance, mood, opening times and number of doorstaff employed. Uncle Sam's, where I spent my longest stint of fieldwork (14 months), was a super-pub/sports bar that usually closed before midnight, often screened popular sports events (e.g. soccer and rugby matches), held up to 2,000 people and employed up to ten doorstaff. Oceanic was a dance club with a much later license (closed at 3am on Saturday night), holding up to 1,500 customers and employed around 12 doorstaff. While sites varied in their characteristics, all catered for a predominantly young (under 30), white, heterosexual clientele. All but one venue was located in the same city, employing a network of doormen and a few doorwomen who often knew or knew of each other. (The ratio of doormen to doorwomen was in the region of 10:1.) While sampling of sites was largely opportunistic, capitalizing upon informal links and employment opportunities, fieldwork was undertaken on a time-sampling basis, thus enhancing theoretical representativeness. Reference to ethnography conducted elsewhere in Britain (e.g. Hobbs et al., 2003; Winlow, 2001), occasional serendipitous discussions with doormen not included in my original sample (including doormen working in Manchester, Newcastle, Durham and Wakefield), and published insider accounts (e.g. Thompson, 2000) also lend greater external validity to knowledge claims made in this study.

Regarding the characteristics of doorstaff – a misnomer in that working 'on the doors' often entails working away from building access points – most contacts were young men from working-class backgrounds (similarly, see Winlow, 2001: 98). Ages ranged from 19 to 45. Most were in their late 20s/early 30s and white, though some were of ethnic minority status (e.g. Middle Eastern, African and Afro-Caribbean). Fieldwork stints, consisting of between one and five working visits per week, ranging between 3 and 14 hours per shift, brought me into contact with over 60 doormen. And while many contacts were fleeting (in an occupation with a high staff turnover), others were more prolonged and sustained. All contacts presented, in accord with hegemonic masculinity (Connell, 1995), an image of heterosexuality, including the few doorwomen with whom I regularly talked (N = 5). While a significant minority of contacts were 'officially' unemployed (especially younger doormen at Oceanic), most combined part-time doorwork with full-time employment in the formal economy. Occupations included: tax inspector, salesman, carpenter, scaffolder, gym owner, trainee accountant, office clerk, karate instructor, chef, mechanic and aircraft engineer. A few college and university students also worked the doors. Wages, usually paid 'cash in hand', were in the region of £7.50 per hour though head doormen with additional responsibilities, and others working in a context of heightened risk, earned higher rates.

A grounded theory approach (Glaser and Strauss, 1967) was adopted during concurrent data generation and analysis. Given the methodological concerns of this edited collection, it is worth clarifying that grounded theory need not bar the importation of concepts and analyses derived from other theoretical work. Grounded theory need not force researchers to wear 'theoretical blinkers' where the ethnographer 'remain[s] unaffected by earlier ideas and information (since) grounded theorists can (among other things) use extant theories to sensitize them to certain issues and processes in their data' (Charmaz and Mitchell, 2001: 169). Using this approach to grounded theory, I read and re-read field notes, leading to the identification of emergent themes and the development of a flexible coding scheme which, in turn, strategically informed subsequent fieldwork visits. This approach was particularly useful because it enabled me to modify and refine emerging substantive theory which I was constructing and submitting to academic journals towards the latter part of the fieldwork. Furthermore, the coding scheme served as a basis for segmenting, grouping, and indexing data which were then stored in computer-generated text files (Weaver and Atkinson, 1994). These data, indexed using general thematic codes (e.g. the body, violence, sexualities) and more specific, subordinate codes (e.g. bodily capital, doorstaff–customer violence, sexual risk), could then be readily accessed for systematic analysis. This qualitative approach, which endeavours to make sociological sense of the complexity and messiness of social life, is variously termed 'analytic induction' or 'deviant case analysis' (Bloor, 1978).

Finally, the partiality of the above should be stressed. Following Coffey's (1999: 59–75) discussion on the embodiment of fieldwork (and other ethnographies she cites), many relevant issues warrant attention. For example, much could be said about how the fieldworker's 'body looks' figure in the research, including skin colour (I am white and I was researching predominantly white bodies), hairstyle and colouring, clothing, body adornments and decoration (e.g. piercings, jewellery, tattoos), height, weight and the amount of body fat and muscle carried. With labour-intensive fieldwork there are also issues concerning bodily exhaustion (e.g. working on one's feet for up to 14 hours

in hot, noisy, potentially violent conditions and the need to keep an up-to-date field diary), feeling irritated and the social implications of embodied and enacted mood states. 'Participatory issues' (Coffey, 1999: 70–1) are also salient, including the ways in which the body is a prop or aid in negotiating field roles, the exposure and disclosure of the ethnographic body and how co-present bodies mediate (un)productive field relations. That said, while my methodological focus upon the body is partial, the bodily dimensions and sociological implications of facing physical danger (namely, a beer bottle being thrown at my head) are explored later in this chapter.

THE BODY AS TOPIC OF ENQUIRY: SOME EMERGENT THEMES

Academic literature describes how British city administrators have recently mobilized festivity, fun and the carnivalesque for purposes of urban revitalization. Hughes (1999), for example, describes the marketing of the night-time city as a consumption site where the inclusion of *bodily* pleasure is a formal objective of public sector intervention. Even the most casual observer visiting Britain's urban 'nightscapes' (Chatterton and Hollands, 2003) will see this objective manifest in the 'architectural structure' (Bourdieu, 1973) of many licensed premises: a relative absence of seating, the centrality of the dance floor(s), the stimulation to drink alcohol, dimmed overhead lighting, flashing disco lights and strobes, smoke machines and loud music. These are body-oriented contexts, especially during weekends and other festive periods, for sometimes fiery forms of 'effervescent sociality' (Mellor and Shilling, 1997).

Turner (1992), a key body theorist, has characterized contemporary society as a 'somatic society' which is crucially, perhaps critically, structured around regulating bodies. During this ethnography it was clear that the regulation of consuming/hedonistic/carnivalesque bodies was crucial to the commercial viability of the night-time economy; however, this task lay beyond the capabilities of the public police (similarly, see Hobbs et al., 2003). Correspondingly, a large market exists in private security, with typically large, male door supervisors hiring out their muscle for the purposes of regulating 'unruly' bodies in and around commercial space (Monaghan, 2002b). In undertaking qualitative research on doorwork, violence and risk, I aimed to understand this demonized occupation and contribute towards existing social theory on the body. And, in foregrounding bodily matters, I also heeded theoretical calls for an embodied sociology (Shilling, 2003; Williams and Bendelow, 1998) that incorporates other social scientific concerns such as risk, masculinities, health and illness.

In treating the body of 'the other' as an analytic topic, this section briefly outlines two overlapping empirical areas; namely, bodily risk attendant to doorwork and typifying occupational competence. Here I will highlight various socio-cultural and economic factors implicated in bodily harm for doorstaff and (potential) customers (Monaghan, 2003). I will also address the embodiment of plural workplace masculinities and normative limits to their violence (Monaghan, 2002c). Before proceeding, however, there are three points to make.

First, body boundaries between the ethnographer and the researched may become blurred during participant observation, prompting other academics to assume that 'you are what you study' (Kleinman and Copp, 1993: 6). While a courtesy honour or halo effect is likely to be experienced and embraced by those researching high-status

groups, fieldworkers studying dangerous groups may actually risk their career (Jipson and Litton, 2000). Certainly, there are many good reasons for avoiding complete immersion in (stigmatized) groups, but a good way to learn first-hand about any community – regardless of their standing on a hierarchy of virtue – is to subject one's own body, personality and social situation to the same petty contingencies to which group members are subject (Goffman, 1989). Because I hired my body to security agencies and, in the process, *actively embodied the field I was researching* (more so than Goffman, who never allowed himself to be committed to an asylum when studying the social situation of mental patients), this study inevitably entailed a blurring of self and other. That said, I should stress that heterogeneity among door supervisors (e.g. regarding orientations to violence, the degree to which their masculine identity is tied to their night-work), and a sustained focus on many 'other' working bodies, means that this study is not an auto-ethnography. Second, in focusing upon labouring bodies, I do not seek to reinforce negative stereotypes of 'bouncers' as 'all muscle and no brain' (similarly, see Monaghan, 2001). Such a negative reading would be to miss the non-dualist argument – evident in recent social theorizing (Williams and Bendelow, 1998) – that social actors are 'mindful bodies' even when co-constituting quasi-liminal, body-oriented contexts. Third, an embodied fieldwork perspective does not render other social scientific concerns irrelevant. Crucially, an embodied perspective must remain sociologically mindful, embedded and indebted. Hence, this study considers other issues such as members' 'situated accounts' or 'vocabularies of motive' (Mills, 1940), the political economy of violence (Hobbs et al., 2003), the social study of plural masculinities (Connell, 1995), and theoretical debates on risk (e.g. Bloor, 1995). However, as an embodied ethnography, various sociological concerns and analyses are (critically) incorporated into an approach that makes the bodily dimensions of social life explicit.

Danger on the doors: bodily risk in a demonized occupation

Because doorwork is structured around body regulation in quasi-liminal space (Monaghan, 2002b), various (embodied) risks are attendant to this trade. Whether referring to legal risk (police arrest and prosecution for assault), instant dismissal (as casual workers, doorstaff rarely have contracts), or personal bodily injury, risk and doorwork are intertwined. However, personal bodily damage through violence is perhaps the most thematic risk for doorstaff routinely exercising coercive authority. Although frequently stereotyped as dangerous, licensed thugs, doorstaff endeavouring to enforce commercial 'rules of the house' may themselves be in physical danger (Lister et al., 2001). In exploring bodily risk from the door supervisors' perspectives, various interrelated factors *may* amplify, attenuate or negate danger to these workers *and* (potential) customers. Here doorstaff may simultaneously be in danger and dangerous, although, from their viewpoint, their bodies are more likely to be targeted given the specifics of their work – a salient point when accounting for their 'work-related' violence to a largely condemnatory audience.

Individual agency and social structural considerations, which can only be separated arbitrarily for analytic purposes, are salient here (Monaghan, 2003: 14). For instance, doorstaff orientations to fighting (orientations which derive their gendered meanings in relation to other sex-specific bodies) may

amplify or minimize possible bodily injury to self and others. It may be increasingly incumbent in our surveillance society to enact the consciously restrained, 'civilized body' (Elias, 2000) – at least in 'frontstage regions' (Goffman, 1959) – but such modalities of bodily presentation may be situationally inappropriate, if not hazardous, among workers endeavouring to maintain control, credibility and 'face' in urban nightspots. Here, in making a virtue out of a necessity, doorstaff may attach kudos to their enactments of pugnacious masculinity and, more sensually, derive 'carnivalesque pleasure' (Presdee, 2000) in the process. In short, in an often monotonous and alienating work environment, doorstaff encountering (embracing, exacerbating) male-coded violence may derive 'edgework' (Lyng, 1990) thrills in chaotic situations (see discussion below). Collectively defined and institutionally supported, these 'violent masculinities' (Connell, 2000: 217) are implicated in 'shared risks' that are 'spread over more than one body/self' (Lupton and Tulloch, 2002a: 324).

Of course, violent injury may also be externally imposed and outside worker control, given management dictated doorstaff–customer ratios in a market geared towards profit maximization. (Too many customers, relative to doorstaff, may amplify the latter's real or imagined physical insecurity. This, in turn, may serve to justify their violence as a means of quickly negating risk to their own bodies, masculine integrity and occupational worth.) The political economy of violence, where 'bouncers' are hired to do the 'dirty work' of a densely populated yet under-policed night-time economy, is an important macro-structural theme explored by Hobbs et al. (2003). Other factors, which, from members' perspectives, are implicated in physical risk and are identified in my ethnography, include type of venue, for instance, 'thug bars' (Chatterton and Hollands, 2001) or 'dives' which attract a particular clientele (e.g. young, male, working-class customers keen to establish a reputation for violence). For many of my contacts, space and place figured in their topography of occupational risk, with 'other' venues in economically deprived areas representing 'hotspots' for unwelcome customer-initiated violence. Other emergent themes include the ways in which female doorstaff, in particular contexts, skilfully employ their gendered bodily capital and interpersonal skills in order to minimize or negate physical harm to themselves, their predominantly male colleagues and customers (Monaghan, 2003: 22–5). From these observations it is clear that 'danger on the doors' – a social relational concern embroiled in dynamics of gender and power – cannot be abstracted from sex-specific bodies (Collier, 1998) which, as stated by Shilling (2003), are the source, location and medium of society.

Hard men, shop boys and others: embodying occupational competence

The previous point is clearly exemplified when exploring the embodiment of competence in this masculinist occupation (Monaghan, 2002c). Similar to other manual workers labouring under conditions of deskilling and casualization (Connell, 1995: 55), doorstaff are largely defined in relation to their potentially forceful bodies: the physical body is their economic asset. For these predominantly male workers, 'bodily capital' (Wacquant ,1995), such as body build (size, weight, height and general appearance of the physique) and acquired 'techniques of the [violent] body' (Mauss, 1973), may be transformed into other forms of capital such as income and masculine validating recognition.

Status hierarchy among doorstaff finds expression in their body-oriented typifications. Labels such as 'hard men', 'shop boys' and others (e.g. 'bullies and 'nutters') refer to members' variable bodily capital and are related to in-group assessments of possible violence against themselves, the delineation of (flexible) boundaries for their own (in)appropriate violence against 'problematic' customers and the social construction of occupational worth. Certainly, not all doorstaff possess exemplary male bodies but bodily capital is extremely salient in relation to in-group typifications, relations and the forging of masculine identities in their enacted risk environment.

During fieldwork, body build, with its suggestion of commercially useful violence, was a common topic during in-group talk. Reference was made, among other things, to how door teams comprising large doormen were unlikely to experience trouble from violent customers and their ability effectively to deal with such trouble if it did arise. Reference was also made to how doorstaff recruitment and personal willingness to work at particular venues was influenced by body size (the size of one's own body and the size of other workers), how smaller doormen in certain situations may be exposed to greater danger and provide less effective team backup, and female door supervisors' evaluations of themselves and other (fe)male working bodies. In doorwork culture it was clear that group norms 'encourage people to develop their bodies in a manner which symbolises the *social* value placed on individual identities' and that bodily norms also enable workers not only to 'recognise and label others [but] to grade them hierarchically, and stigmatise them in a manner which facilitates discrimination' (Shilling, 2001: 333–7). Similarly, doorstaff with a reputation for being skilled in 'techniques of the forceful body' were valued and were engaged in the construction, presentation and performance of a situationally 'appropriate' (authoritative, dominant) self.

However, as suggested by the different values implied by members' typifications, doorstaff violence and talk about their violence occurs within and constitutes normative limits. Certainly, the precise boundaries of such violence (e.g. when to use it, against whom, what level is appropriate) are irresolvable (Winlow et al., 2001: 538). Even so, reference was made to general, though highly permeable and individualized bodily limits beyond which violence should not be used by competent workers. Here bodies subjected to coercive authority were divided and classified according to their perceived ability to inflict and absorb punishment. Vulnerable parts of the victim's sex-specific body (e.g. the head, nose, ears or eyes) were out of bounds for some using (un)acceptable parts of their own dominating bodies (e.g. the feet, teeth or right hand) at one time, only later to be reviewed given changing circumstances, experiences and definitions of the situation.

Exploring normative limits to doorstaff violence rendered other bodily matters thematic. For example, the appropriateness of non-violence against customers was determinable through 'shared vocabularies of body idiom' (Goffman, 1963). Drunken customers exhibiting a loss of self-control, sometimes becoming grotesque, leaky, carnivalesque bodies (Bakhtin, 1984), were often problematic for others (embarrassing, irritating, corporeally polluting) but this did not in and of itself render them legitimate targets for responsible doorstaff in my study. Some of my contacts, in enacting the 'civilized body' (Elias, 2000) or conformist models or masculinity, privately disparaged others for indiscriminately using force against intoxicated bodies. Others (admittedly a minority) were

condemned for routinely using unnecessary violence against physically smaller, non-threatening customers. Similar to football hooligans who forge definitions of correct conduct in an honour-based culture (King, 2001), doorstaff denigrated 'unmanly' colleagues for attacking unequals. They were, in their terms, 'bullies' who 'take liberties' and who thus should not be working the doors.

During fieldwork it therefore became clear that violence was normalized and routinized bodily labour among doorstaff, but it was also circumscribed. Occupational boundaries for violence – dependent upon socially located emotional/mindful bodies, body parts and shared vocabularies of body idiom (Goffman, 1963) – were permeable and flexible but they delineated limits of acceptability and figured in the social construction of competency. Even so, because doorstaff often present themselves as being sinned against rather than sinning, in-group tolerance exists for physically tough workers transgressing normative limits for (work-related) violence. Indeed, as will emerge below, it may have been relatively unusual for doorstaff deliberately to engage in violence with ejected customers outside commercial space but it was situationally acceptable for some, representing a heightened form of emotional 'edgework' (Lyng, 1990) on the doors. Discussing this further will hopefully underscore the relevance of an embodied fieldwork perspective where the goal is to learn first-hand about social life by putting one's body 'where the action is' (Goffman, 1961).

RISKY FIELDWORK AS EMBODIED/EMOTIONAL EDGEWORK

Urban ethnographies from the Chicago School onwards and recent writings on fieldwork risk (Lee-Treweek and Linkogle, 2000) usefully draw attention to the relationship between social research and danger. I would add, along with ethnographers such as Westmarland (2000), that it is also important to make the fieldworker's 'lived body' explicit in methodological writings on risky fieldwork. All fieldwork is dependent upon the researcher's bodily insertion and participation in a sometimes emotionally charged social world, but this is exemplified in ethnographies of risk where the researcher's body, as a piece of 'consequential equipment' (Goffman, 1967), is literally put on the line.

This section underscores the methodological and epistemological significance of the ethnographer's body by examining the ways in which physically risky fieldwork is, even if only by association, a form of embodied/ emotional edgework. To be clear, this discussion should not be read as an endorsement of adrenalizing, illicit thrill-seeking: ethnographers should observe caution, taking steps to ensure their own safety and well-being (Winlow et al., 2001: 537). Indeed, as Lee (1995) elaborates in his methodological writings, timidity may not serve ethnographers well but there is a strong need to exercise prudence given the many (gendered) dangers of fieldwork (e.g. sexual assault, violent conflict, biological and environmental hazards). Rather, my argument here is that ethnographic knowledge is constructed in and through an embodied, emotional – one might say aesthetically reflexive (Stranger, 1999) – engagement with a sometimes ineffable and disorderly social world. In making this claim more concrete I will recount a particular violent episode which occurred during fieldwork and which threatened my own sense of 'ontological security' (Giddens, 1991). First, however, it is necessary to explain the embodied significance of emotions when undertaking reflexive 'ethnography at the edge' (Ferrell and Hamm, 1998).

Criminologists such as Ferrell and Hamm (1998) draw upon Lyng's (1990) concept of 'edgework' when studying the affective dimensions of crime and deviance. Central to Lyng's study of voluntary risk-taking among skydivers, edgework involves 'a clearly observable threat to one's physical or mental well-being or one's sense of an ordered existence' (1990: 857). Importantly, edgework entails stepping outside one's 'comfort zone' and requires the 'ability to maintain control over a situation that verges on complete chaos' (Lyng, 1990: 859). Edgeworkers, in negotiating the boundary between order and disorder, derive a sense of exhilaration, excitement and experiential knowledge from their activities – a sense of being which is not easily grasped through everyday language. By deliberately entering a potentially dangerous and ineffable zone, voluntary risk-takers hope to return unharmed to their quotidian realities with feelings of aliveness, agency and insight. Far from being the preserve of 'cultural dopes' (Garfinkel, 1967), edgework is a skilled performance that consists of a socially situated rationality and sensuality and is thus related to the experiences of the emotional/mindful body.

For Lyng (1990), this micro-social (Median) analysis is combined with a Marxist critique of the political economy: it is a critical approach to risk that makes connections between individual sensations and feelings and the macro-social structure of late capitalist society. In short, edgework is conceptualized as a means of asserting agency in the context of dehumanized and alienated labour. Such research does not explicitly draw on the sociology of the body but it is compatible with an embodied sociological perspective where 'the lived experience and management of emotions as embodied modes of being in the world [is related] to macro-structural issues of power, domination and control' (Williams and

Bendelow, 1998: 132). Here it becomes apparent that emotions, similar to the body to which they are tied, actually matter despite traditional Western (rationalist) epistemology that has long banished these to the margins of scholarly thought (Williams and Bendelow, 1998: 131). By extension, I would maintain that ethnographic fieldwork, and methodological reflection upon this craft, is dependent upon an embodied engagement with the social world in a manner that effectively blurs key dichotomies such as mind and body, reason and emotion. As I hope to demonstrate, ethnography on risk in the night-time economy makes this especially clear.

The following field diary excerpt, wherein risk is thematic in both talk and practice, literally captures the embodied meanings of 'ethnography at the edge' (Ferrell and Hamm, 1998). In accord with the 'civilized body' (Elias, 2000), my own aversion to 'excessive risk' was discursively shared by the first doorman (Mr. T): a stance similar to that posited by Beck (1992) where risk is construed as negative. I may have 'chosen' (albeit under conditions not of my own choosing) to undertake ethnography in a risk domain, but there were (spatial, legal, moral, bodily) boundaries circumscribing the risks I was willing to take. More specifically, I hoped to avoid door-related conflict outside commercial space, using (unreasonable) force inside such space, risking police arrest and prosecution or being the victim of grievous bodily harm. Yet, and similar to Lyng's (1990) edge-workers, a small minority of doorstaff I encountered were enchanted by the 'sensual seductions' (Katz, 1988) of risk-taking, and deliberately courted physical and legal danger outside the relative safety of the night-club. (Similarly, see Presdee (2000), on the carnival of crime where pleasure is derived on the streets by joy-riders, rioters and others precisely because their illegal enactments are

in opposition to the authority of municipal ownership.) My own observations of the following incident were obviously constrained by my changing bodily location and immediate pragmatic concerns; research interests were not at the forefront of my mind (similarly, see Winlow et al., 2001: 546). However, as this 'cacophony of sensory stimulation' climaxed, I obtained a clearer 'ringside' view of 'the aesthetics of risk' (Stranger, 1999). Here I literally stood on the border between order and disorder, witnessing an unusual episode where three doormen transgressed occupational boundaries delimiting appropriate violence. By engaging in field/body/edgework on the doors, I literally faced danger, yet I was also in a 'privileged' position to make some sense of the (embodied) meanings that lay behind the brief, inarticulate and seemingly absurd words of a leading player (Charlie) in the incident after it ceased:

I talked to Mr. T, a postgraduate cum doorman. Mr. T has recently completed his Masters degree and is awaiting his results. I asked him what he'd do after obtaining his degree – would he continue working as a doorman? He said he would probably do 'something with computers' and would also continue with his doorwork: 'Yeah, probably do one or two nights a week. The money is good and there's no real trouble. I worked in this pub [outside the city centre], just two of us worked it, and there was trouble all the time. Not like this place'. I understood Mr. T's 'complacency' about the 'dangers' of doorwork at Oceanic. Violence was relatively unusual and I never felt I was risking life and limb. (That doesn't mean to say another researcher wouldn't have felt at risk.) However, violence, serious physical injury (and social risks, such as police arrest) are always possible for door supervisors plying their trade.

Later that night the manager requested a group, consisting of six young men, to leave the club for allegedly causing trouble. They were escorted out of the club via the fire escape by an equal number of doormen. I arrived on the scene just as the men were entering the fire escape. There was some pushing and shoving on each side, which resulted in one of the customers breaking an unwritten rule: he threw a punch at a working doorman in full view of other doormen. As expected this resulted in swift retaliation from several doormen. This was immediately followed by a (limited) violent response from the soon to be ejected customers. Events happened extremely quickly and I have difficulty recalling exactly what happened; my main concern was to shield my own body from any potential blows! That said, the violence – which resulted in a trail of customers' blood leading up the stairs to the fire exit – was not protracted despite the volatility of the situation. As we moved up the stairs there were heated claims, counter-claims and threats from both groups. As part of the procession (I was towards the front end) reached the top of the stairs, and the fire escape doors were flung open, violence again erupted as one of the customers challenged the doormen: 'Come on then, if you want to go, let's go outside!' Three doormen brushed past me, spilling onto the main street. Standing on the threshold of the fire escape, I immediately saw the fluorescent coats of two police officers who were facing the opposite direction. There was absolutely no way I was going into the street to fight and risk police arrest and/or injury! As one of the ejected pugnacious customers fell into the police, the officers turned around, grabbed hold of him and struggled with him to the ground. Another ejected customer, who was on the opposite side of the road, had tipped a bin over and decided to launch a missile. A beer bottle, thrown with extreme force, hurtled inches past my face and smashed against the fire escape doors. Shocked, I stayed where I was, feeling the effects of adrenaline while hurriedly casting my eyes around in case there was another bottle heading my way. Within seconds a police car pulled up as another doorman (Charlie) was about to punch an ejected customer who had just attempted unsuccessfully to hit him. Charlie, upon seeing the police car, ceased his attack: the officer quickly got out of the car and restrained this other ejected customer who had been too preoccupied with his advancing opponent. Charlie returned to the door beside me, waited for a few seconds to see the police arrest several members of the ejected group, before returning inside the club. Not wanting to risk another bottle or police arrest, I followed hot on his heels.

Later I learnt that all of the doormen escaped police arrest. I talked to Charlie and he had little idea about what had caused the incident (I only learned after talking to the manager who was directly involved) and he didn't seem to care either. With a huge grin, this experienced martial artist just said: 'Funny as fuck, that was'. Afterwards, as I stood inside the club alone, I reflected upon what had happened and the seriousness of the injuries I'd have sustained if the hurtling bottle had hit me full force in the face. The bloody consequences did not fit with my idea of 'fun' and I had serious doubts about continuing with the ethnography. Nonetheless, the episode was instructive, contributing to my first-hand knowledge of the field. Without trivializing the risks I literally faced, it was clear that I, along with the other doormen, had entered a danger zone, retained self-control, and returned unharmed. I was alive and well. Charlie's apparently nonsensical comment, his

seemingly absurd presentation of self after the incident, made sense to me as a result of being there. I definitely did not share his conception of fun, but I felt I understood it. (Saturday 23 June 2001: Oceanic.)

Analytically, much could be said about this risk (carnivalesque) episode. Similar to professional boxers, for example, doormen such as Charlie could be viewed as stepping on 'a stage on which to affirm (their) moral valor and construct a heroic, transcendent self which allows (them) to escape the status of "non-person" (Goffman, 1959: 151–2) to which (sub)proletarians like (them) are typically consigned' (Wacquant, 2001: 188). However, regarding methodology, I would stress how my own bodily co-presence and emotional involvement during fieldwork was intimately linked to the sociological task of making sense of (illicit) social action. For many doormen, among whom types and levels of violence are normalized, Charlie and his two colleagues would be considered foolhardy for practising their violent (exciting) craft in public space amidst CCTV surveillance and the police. Nonetheless, the embodied meanings of this voluntary risk-taking would be lost if the researcher simply dismissed such action as pathological, the product of an inadequate personality. By risking my own body in combative situations, by experiencing the physical and emotional vicissitudes of this dangerous yet largely monotonous trade, I was able to appreciate why violent crime is seductive for certain people in certain contexts. From my own personal standpoint, and in contrast to Charlie, for whom violence had significant meaning, the sublime character of this risk episode was eclipsed by a feeling of disconcertment and ontological insecurity. Nonetheless, and by proxy, I *felt* able to allocate 'meaning' to this ineffable risk-taking not necessarily through an intellectual process but through an affectual one that literally incorporated an aesthetic of sensation, the prioritization of images over words (Stranger, 1999).

Finally, in enacting the 'mindful body', I have asked myself: 'What price am I willing to pay for these ethnographic observations on risk?' The body of the fieldworker is, after all, potentially vulnerable and the management of physical risk is to an extent illusory (Lyng, 1990) – a point which nearly hit me full force in the face. While a continuing ethnographic presence could be accounted for in terms of 'a certain status' attached to the masculinist cult of fieldwork (Hobbs 1993, cited by Westmarland, 2000: 33), I eventually exited the door in a context of diminishing marginal returns, exigencies in the field, changes in my personal and professional life, and memories of my 'body under attack'. The 'lived body' may be a vital resource in fieldwork, but when such work may dramatically and painfully consume one's body it is probably wise to leave as soon as is practicable (or never go there in the first place) and return to the care-worn life of the university office. This is my current position where the aestheticization of risk is subjugated by my concerns for an easier, less hazardous life. This may seem 'pretty dull' (Lupton and Tulloch, 2002b) or boring for those who enjoy risk, but it is nonetheless a choice (relative luxury) which is closed to many 'dirty workers' in the night-time economy (Hobbs et al., 2003). I certainly enjoyed aspects of my fieldwork experience (bodies are vehicles of pleasure as well as pain), but I am glad I now have the option of earning my living punching a keyboard rather than risking a punch (or bottle) in the face.

CONCLUSION

Following the 'somatic turn' in the social sciences, this chapter discussed the relationship between fieldwork (risk) and the body. Reference to a recently completed 'embodied ethnography' of doorwork, violence and risk grounded methodological discussion in the inescapable corporeality, emotional vicissitudes and aesthetic reflexivity of social life. Admittedly, when researching a masculinist occupation such as security work, an analytic concern with the (emotional) body may initially seem peculiar: within Western culture, the norm of masculinity 'implicitly requires that the body and all its material and emotional vulnerabilities be denied, hidden or transcended' (Davis 2002: 59). Similarly, bodily denial – the tendency to bracket out the embodied nature of the fieldwork task in methodological writings (Coffey, 1999: 75) – is likely to be compounded given the 'masculinist cult of fieldwork' (Westmarland, 2000) mentioned above. However, it is difficult to imagine how the intellectual and affectual task of doing 'risky' fieldwork on doorwork could proceed without 'bringing the body in' (Frank, 1990). Here the multidimensional body becomes a topic of, and resource in, ethnographic fieldwork.

By undertaking participation observation among doorstaff in situations of bodily co-presence, I obtained a grounded understanding of their embodied social world alongside the significance of my own corporeality for generating ethnographic understandings. Relevant issues and themes to emerge during this research included the ways in which the body is the central yet exhaustible instrument in fieldwork; how 'body looks' and gendered physical pursuits (e.g. lifting weights) mediate field relations; the embodiment of a habitus comprising class-related dispositions and modalities of bodily action; how the phenomenology of the body is implicated in shifting perceptions and understandings of risk; how constructions of plural workplace masculinities and competency centre upon bodily capital, techniques and embodied limits to violence; and, as explored in the penultimate section, how 'the emotional body at the edge' is integral to methodological and epistemological reflection. Other embodied themes which are worth mentioning, and are detailed elsewhere, include the regulation of 'unruly bodies' in and around commercial space (Monaghan, 2002b); the embodiment of worker solidarity, contested hierarchy and cool loyalties (Monaghan, 2002a); and the significance of the body in the performance of urban male heterosexualities, opportunities, pleasures and risks (Monaghan, 2002d). Far from having an 'absent presence' (Shilling, 2003), the bodies in this research have a sustained and visible presence as lived, flesh-and-blood entities embroiled in larger social dynamics, processes and concerns.

Moving from substantive to more general, formal concerns, discussing the body and emotionality may also seem incongruous with (traditionally male-dominated) academic thought that has traditionally privileged the disembodied, rational mind (Turner, 1992). Yet, as made clear within the recent sociology of embodiment (and longer established feminist scholarship), Western (rationalist) epistemology is hamstrung by unhelpful dichotomies that posit an oppositional and hierarchical (rather than mutually constitutive) relationship between mind and body, reason and emotion (Williams and Bendelow, 1998). Moving from the specifics of the present ethnography, it is clear that all fieldwork is dependent upon our bodily insertion and participation in a lived, sometimes emotionally fraught, social world. Correspondingly, the body is a necessary, yet often taken-for-granted and neglected, condition for generating knowledge of social realities and actions. Bodies, and associated emotions, matter (Kleinman and Copp, 1993). For that reason, and in conclusion, I concur with Williams and Bendelow (1998: 212) when they state that 'sociologists – as embodied practitioners and living, thinking, feeling agents – [must] put minds back into

bodies, bodies back into society, and society back into the body'. To neglect the bodily dimensions of social life or, more inclusively, the embodiment of the social in our fieldwork would be to ride roughshod over a 'somatic' (Turner, 1992) or 'risk society' (Beck, 1992) that lives, breathes, fights and bleeds.

NOTE

1 Violence outside licensed premises often has a different meaning. The street is public and therefore state police territory. Doorstaff stepping outside their work role and fighting in the streets amplify their risk of police arrest.

REFERENCES

Adler, P.A. and Adler, P. (1987), *Membership Roles in Field Research*, London: Sage.

Armstrong, G. (1993), 'Like that Desmond Morris?', in D. Hobbs and T. May (eds), *Interpreting the Field: Accounts of Ethnography*, Oxford: Oxford University Press.

Bakhtin, M. (1984), *Rabelais and His World*, Cambridge, MA: MIT Press.

Beck, U. (1992), *Risk Society: Towards a New Modernity*, London: Sage.

Bloor, M. (1978) 'On the Analysis of Observational Data: A Discussion of the Worth and Uses of Inductive Techniques and Respondent Validation', *Sociology*, 12: 542–52.

_____. (1995), *The Sociology of HIV Transmission*, London: Sage.

Bourdieu, P. (1973), 'The Berber House', in M. Douglas (ed.), *Rules and Meanings*, Harmondsworth: Penguin.

_____. (1977), *Outline of a Theory of Practice*, Cambridge: Cambridge University Press.

Brain, R. (1979), *The Decorated Body*, New York: Harper & Row.

Calvey, D. (2000), 'Getting on the Door and Staying There: A Covert Participant Observational Study of Bouncers', in G. Lee-Treweek and S. Linkogle (eds), *Danger in the Field: Risk and Ethics in Social Research*, London: Routledge.

Charmaz, K. and Mitchell, R. (2001), 'Grounded Theory in Ethnography', in P. Atkinson, A. Coffey, S. Delamont, J. Lofland, and L. Lofland (eds), *Handbook of Ethnography*, London: Sage.

Chatterton, P. and Hollands, R. (2001) *Changing Our 'Toon': Youth, Nightlife and Urban Change in Newcastle*, University of Newcastle: Newcastle upon Tyne.

_____. (2003), *Urban Nightscapes: Youth Cultures, Pleasure Spaces and Corporate Power*, London: Routledge.

Coffey, A. (1999), *The Ethnographic Self: Fieldwork and the Representation of Identity*, London: Sage.

Collier, R. (1998), *Masculinities, Crime and Criminology*, London: Sage.

Connell, R. (1995), *Masculinities*, Cambridge: Polity Press.

_____. (2000), *The Men and the Boys*, Cambridge: Polity Press.

Davis, K. (2002), '"A Dubious Equality": Men, Women and Cosmetic Surgery', *Body & Society*, 8(1): 49–65.

Delamont, S. (1998), '"You Need the Leotard": Revisiting the First PE Lesson', in J. Richardson and A. Shaw (eds), *The Body in Qualitative Research*, Ashgate: Aldershot.

Elias, N. (2000), *The Civilizing Process: Sociogenetic and Psychogenetic Investigations*, (revised edn), Oxford: Blackwell (Orig. 1939.)

Ferrell, J. and Hamm, M. (eds) (1998), *Ethnography at the Edge*, Boston: Northeastern University Press.

Frank, A. (1990), 'Bringing Bodies Back In: A Decade Review', *Theory, Culture and Society*, 7(1): 131–62.

Garfinkel, H. (1967), *Studies in Ethnomethodology*, New York: Prentice-Hall.

Giddens, A. (1991), *Modernity and Self-Identity: Self and Society in the Late Modern Age*, Cambridge: Polity Press.

Glaser, B. and Strauss, A. (1967), *The Discovery of Grounded Theory*, Chicago: Aldine.

Goffman, E. (1959), *The Presentation of Self in Everyday Life*, New York. Doubleday.

Goffman, E. (1961), *Encounters: Two Studies in the Sociology of Interaction*, Indianapolis: Bobbs-Merrill.

Goffman, E. (1963) *Behavior in Public Places: Notes on the Social Organization of Gatherings*. New York: The Free Press.

Goffman, E. (1967), *Interaction Ritual: Essays on Face-to-Face Behaviour*, New York: Doubleday.

_____. (1989), 'On Fieldwork', *Journal of Contemporary Ethnography*, 18(2): 123–32.

Hobbs, D. (1993), 'Peers, Careers, and Academic Fears: Writing as Field-Work', in D. Hobbs and T. May (eds), *Interpreting the Field: Accounts of Ethnography*, Oxford: Oxford University Press.

Hobbs, D., Hadfield, P., Lister, S. and Winlow, S. (2003), *Bouncers: Violence and Governance in the Night-time Economy*, Oxford: Oxford University Press.

Hobbs, D. and May, T. (eds) (1993), *Interpreting the Field: Accounts of Ethnography*, Oxford: Oxford University Press.

Hughes, G. (1999), 'Urban Revitalization: The Use of Festive Time Strategies', *Leisure Studies*, 18: 119–35.

Jipson, A. and Litton, C. (2000), 'Body, Career and Community: The Implications of Researching Dangerous Groups', in G. Lee-Treweek and S. Linkogle (eds), *Danger in the Field: Risk and Ethics in Social Research*, London: Routledge.

Katz, J. (1988), *Seductions of Crime: Moral and Sensuous Attractions of Doing Evil*, New York: Basic Books.

King, A. (2001), 'Violent Pasts: Collective Memory and Football Hooliganism', *The Sociological Review*, 49(4): 568–85.

Kleinman, S. and Copp, M. (1993), *Emotions and Fieldwork*. London: Sage.

Lawton, J. (1998), 'Contemporary Hospice Care: The Sequestration of the Unbounded Body and "Dirty Dying"', *Sociology of Health and Illness*, 20(2): 121–43.

Lee, R. (1995), *Dangerous Fieldwork*, London: Sage.

Lee-Treweek, G. and Linkogle, S. (eds) (2000), *Danger in the Field: Risk and Ethics in Social Research*, London: Routledge.

Lister, S., Hadfield, P., Hobbs, D. and Winlow, S. (2001), 'Accounting for Bouncers: Occupational Licensing as a Mechanism for Regulation', *Criminal Justice*, 1(4): 363–84.

Lupton, D. and Tulloch, J. (2002a), '"Risk is Part of Your Life": Risk Epistemologies among a Group of Australians', *Sociology*, 36(2): 317–34.

Lupton, D. and Tulloch, J. (2002b), '"Life Would Be Pretty Dull Without Risk": Voluntary Risk-taking and its Pleasures', *Health, Risk and Society*, 4(2): 113–24.

Lyng, S. (1990), 'Edgework: A Social Psychological Analysis of Voluntary Risk-taking', *American Journal of Sociology*, 95: 887–921.

Mauss, M. (1973), 'Techniques of the Body', *Economy and Society*, 2(1): 70–88. (Orig. 1934.)

Mellor, P. and Shilling, C. (1997) *Re-forming the Body: Religion, Community and Modernity*, London: Sage.

Mills, C.W. (1940), 'Situated Actions and Vocabularies of Motive', *American Sociological Review*, 5(6): 904–13.

———. (1970), *The Sociological Imagination*, New York: Penguin. (Orig. 1959.)

Monaghan, L. (2001), *Bodybuilding, Drugs and Risk*, London: Routledge.

———. (2002a), 'Embodying Gender, Work and Organization: Solidarity, Cool Loyalties and Contested Hierarchy in a Masculinist Occupation', *Gender, Work & Organization*, 9(5): 504–36.

———. (2002b), 'Regulating "Unruly" Bodies: Work Tasks, Conflict and Violence in Britain's Night-time Economy', *The British Journal of Sociology*, 53(3): 403–29.

———. (2002c) 'Hard Men, Shop Boys and Others: Embodying Competence in a Masculinist Occupation', *The Sociological Review*, 50(3): 334–55.

———. (2002d), 'Opportunity, Pleasure and Risk: An Ethnography of Urban Male Hetero-sexualities', *Journal of Contemporary Ethnography*, 31(4): 440–77.

———. (2003) 'Danger on the Doors: Bodily Risk in a Demonised Occupation', *Health, Risk & Society*, 5(1): 11–31.

Nettleton, S. and Watson, J. (eds) (1998), *The Body in Everyday Life*, London: Routledge.

Pearson, G. (1993), 'Talking a Good Fight: Authenticity and Distance in the Ethnographer's Craft', in D. Hobbs and T. May (eds), *Interpreting the Field: Accounts of Ethnography*, Oxford: Oxford University Press.

Presdee, M. (2000), *Cultural Criminology and the Carnival of Crime*, London: Routledge.

Roth, W. and Bowen, G. (2001), 'Of Disciplined Minds and Disciplined Bodies: On Becoming an Ecologist', *Qualitative Sociology*, 24(4): 459–81.

Schutz, A. (1962), *Collected Papers I: The Problem of Social Reality*, The Hague: Martinus Nijhoff.

Shilling, C. (2001), 'Embodiment, Experience and Theory: In Defence of the Sociological Tradition', *The Sociological Review*, 49(3): 327–44.

———. (2003), *The Body and Social Theory* (2nd edn), London: Sage.

Stranger, M. (1999), 'The Aesthetics of Risk: A Study of Surfing', *International Review for the Sociology of Sport*, 34(3): 265–76.

Thompson, G. (2000), *Watch My Back*, Sussex: Summersdale.

Turner, B. (1992), *Regulating Bodies: Essays in Medical Sociology*, London: Routledge.

———. (1996), *The Body and Society* (2nd edn), London: Sage.

Vidich, A. (1955), 'Participant Observation and the Collection and Interpretation of Data', *American Journal of Sociology*, 60: 354–60.

Wacquant, L. (1995), 'Pugs at Work: Bodily Capital and Bodily Labour among Professional Boxers', *Body & Society*, 1(1): 65–93.

———. (2001), 'Whores, Slaves and Stallions: Languages of Exploitation and Accommodation among Boxers', *Body & Society*, 7(2–3): 181–94.

Watson, J. (2000), *Male Bodies: Health, Culture and Identity*, Buckingham: Open University Press.

Weaver, A. and Atkinson, P. (1994), *Micro-Computing and Data Analysis*, Aldershot: Avebury.

Westmarland, L. (2000), 'Taking the Flak: Operational Policing, Fear and Violence', in G. Lee-Treweek and S. Linkogle (eds), *Danger in the Field: Risk and Ethics in Social Research*, London: Routledge.

———. (2001) *Gender and Policing: Sex, Power and Police Culture*, Cullompton, UK: Willan.

Williams, S. (2003), *Medicine and the Body*, London: Sage.

Williams, S. and Bendelow, G. (1998), *The Lived Body: Sociological Themes, Embodied Issues*, London: Routledge.

Winlow, S. (2001), *Badfellas: Crime, Tradition and New Masculinities*, Oxford: Berg.

Winlow, S., Hobbs, D., Lister, S. and Hadfield, P. (2001), 'Get Ready to Duck: Bouncers and the Realities of Ethnographic Research on Violent Groups', *British Journal of Criminology*, 41: 536–48.

15

Sport Ethnography: A Personal Account

SUSAN BROWNELL

More than any other discipline, cultural anthropology is defined by the research method of intensive ethnographic fieldwork, or participant observation. Since Bronislaw Malinowski spent his famous three years in the Trobriand Islands while interned there during the First World War, research through one to two years of immersion in a non-Western culture has become the standard rite of passage for attaining a PhD in the discipline in the United States and Great Britain. New PhDs lacking this conventional fieldwork experience are commonly disadvantaged in the job market. With the postmodern turn in the 1980s, anthropology as a discipline began to intensively re-examine its colonialist and imperialist past along with the traditional notions of 'ethnographic fieldwork' and 'fieldsite.' In this chapter, I situate my own sport ethnography in the People's Republic of China from 1985 to 1988 within these developments in the discipline. I do this in order to make two points: the first is that my choice of sport as an ethnographic

method was so particular and contingent that it can hardly be considered a generalizable method; the second is that, nevertheless, there were some unique characteristics of sport ethnography that allowed me to negotiate the difficult contingencies of my situation better than other kinds of ethnography might have allowed.

I use sport ethnography to refer to ethnographic fieldwork that is primarily carried out through active participation in some kind of 'sport,' broadly defined. Although it is not always the case, sport ethnography usually starts with a person who has some degree of expertise in a sport. Occasionally some brave soul attempts to play a sport in which he has no prior experience, such as Loïc Wacquant's boxing at a gym in a black Chicago neighbourhood, described in *Body and Soul: Notebooks of an Appentice Boxer* (2003). When I first went to China in 1985, I was in the 12th of my 16 years competing in track and field, and was still competing at a national level in the United States.

THE POSTMODERN CRITIQUE OF ETHNOGRAPHY

Ethnography as a research method was derived from the natural history model out of which anthropology had emerged as a discipline at the end of the nineteenth century, under colonialist conditions that provided a supply of observable subjects. This model had imagined ethnography as an 'objective' scientific endeavor involving a detached observer and to-be-observed subjects. The two key texts that initiated the critique of this model of ethnography in the 1980s were James Clifford and George E. Marcus (eds), *Writing Culture: The Poetics and Politics of Ethnography* (1986) and Clifford Geertz, *Works and Lives: The Anthropologist as Author* (1988). Both books focused on the process by which lived experience is transformed into written text, but used that as a starting point to 'reach beyond texts to contexts of power, resistance, institutional constraint, and innovation' (Clifford, 1986: 2). As a result of the debates stimulated by these and other works, anthropologists became more aware that we bring all of our personal history with us into the field, and that it necessarily plays a role in our interactions with our informants, who are, after all, also living human beings with their own personal histories. Critics of the old, natural-history style of writing called for a more honest account of the 'position' of the anthropologist within his/her own research, and by the 1990s it had become much more common for anthropologists to begin their dissertations or books with a description of their own personal investment in the project, as well as to include themselves in the first person in parts of the narrative where appropriate.

In this chapter, I situate my discussion of my own sport ethnography within this postmodern turn. I hesitate to make general statements about 'sport ethnography' as an abstract category when my own choice of sport as an ethnographic method for research in the People's Republic of China in the 1980s was so intensely personal, and so closely bound to a particular historical moment in time, that it could not possibly be put forward as a general method for others to use.

THE POSTCOLONIALIST CRITIQUE OF ETHNOGRAPHY

The postcolonialist turn constitutes a second trend that is relevant to this chapter. The critique of ethnography also made us more conscious that anthropology was strongly implicated in the history of colonialism. British, US, and French colonies had been a major source of the colonial subjects who were researched, and access to the subjects had been made possible because anthropologists were backed by powerful states. The same was true of research among Native Americans in the United States, another source of influential studies in the discipline. Geertz notes, in his essay on E.E. Evans-Pritchard, who studied the Nuer of the Sudan just after they had been pacified by the British, that 'This loss of confidence, and the crisis in ethnographic writing that goes with it, is a contemporary phenomenon and is due to contemporary developments. It is how things stand with us these days. It is not how they stood for Sir Edward Evan Evans-Pritchard' (Geertz, 1988: 72).

In stark contrast with Evans-Pritchard, I did my fieldwork in 1980s China, closely monitored by a government that had successfully thrown out foreign nations with colonial aspirations in the Communist takeover of 1949, and which since that time had stringently guarded its political and cultural sovereignty against all agents of imperialism, including Christian missionaries, foreign-owned businesses, Hollywood films – and foreign ethnographers. Those of us who did field-work in 1980s China found ourselves in the midst of a political power dynamic that was very different from that experienced by the preceding generation of China scholars, who had no access to the Mainland, and so did their fieldwork in Hong Kong, the New Territories, Taiwan, and Singapore, backed by the colonialist presences of the US and British governments.

THE CRITIQUE OF 'THE FIELDSITE'

The third trend that is relevant to this chapter is the critique of the notion of the 'field' that followed the previous two critiques. The key text was *Anthropological Locations: Boundaries and Grounds of a Field Science* (1997a), edited by Akhil Gupta and James Ferguson. In their introduction, the editors observed that the imperative to examine the idea of 'the field' 'follows from a now widely expressed doubt about the adequacy of traditional ethnographic concepts and methods to the intellectual and political challenges of the contemporary postcolonial world' (Gupta and Ferguson, 1997a: 3). This inadequacy stemmed from the fact that the traditional practice of 'going to the field' to study a bounded, territorially-grounded 'culture' was no longer workable in a world in which people and ideas flow across local, national, and regional boundaries with unprecedented speed, and in which global capitalism and transnational culture have extended their reach into even the most isolated areas. In fact, it is not clear that the notion of studying a bounded culture was ever entirely accurate, but the increasing interconnectedness of the world from the 1980s on made the problem more pressing. Marcus called for 'multi-locale ethnography'

(1986: 171–2), and Gupta and Ferguson argued that the notion of the 'bounded field' must be discarded for something more fluid (1997b: 38–9). 'Multi-sited ethnography' has now become common in anthropology, but when I began my research in 1985 it was not. Since the elite athletes that were my primary research group constituted a national net-work with nodes all over China, situated within a global network of international sports, my research was necessarily multi-sited. I spent most of my time at the center of that network, the capital city of Beijing, site of the National Team training center and of the State Sports Commission. However, I also traveled to provincial and municipal team headquarters and attended national competitions outside Beijing. Elite sports are also intimately intertwined with the mass media, and my research on sports journalism and sports telecasting involved interviews in Hong Kong, the United States, and Beijing, while the Olympic telecasts themselves reached all of Asia, or about one-third of the world's population.

ETHNOGRAPHY IN 1980s CHINA

I had been a nationally-ranked track and field athlete in the United States since 1978. My event was the pentathlon and, after 1980, when two more events were added, the heptathlon. I had been a high school state champion and a Division I collegiate All-American, had been nationally-ranked as high as eighth, competed internationally, and took part in the 1980 and 1984 Olympic Trials. I had limited my graduate school applications to those programs that were located near top coaches, and that is how I ended up at the University of California, Santa Barbara, where I trained under the head coach there, Sam Adams, with the then-national record-holder, Jane Frederick, as a training partner. I arrived in Santa Barbara in 1982 with definite plans to train for the 1984 Los Angeles Olympics but only a fuzzy idea of what I wanted to study in graduate school.

In 1981, the People's Republic of China had just opened up to US anthropologists who wished to do research there. The Communist takeover had been in 1949, and the anti-rightist campaigns of the 1950s and the Cultural Revolution of 1966–76 had been periods of political attacks on intellectuals within China and isolation from the international academic community outside China. From the 1950s to the 1980s, anthropologists who wished to study 'China' had been forced to do their fieldwork in Taiwan, Hong Kong, Singapore, and among overseas Chinese. Sino-US diplomatic relations were restored in 1979. The US and Chinese governments established an exchange program which was administered on the US side by an organization called the Committee on Scholarly Communication with the PRC (CSCPRC, or CSC for short). This organization, which was under the auspices of the National Academy of Sciences, and which also administered the Fulbright Program in China, was the single channel by which US citizens could obtain official permission to carry out doctoral research in China until the late 1980s. CSC offered an annual competition for grants, which was open to all disciplines, including anthropology. The first class of grantees went to China in 1981. As it happened, one of my classmates in the UCSB anthropology program, William Jankowiak, was in that first class of grantees and was thus one of the first anthropologists to do ethnographic fieldwork in the People's Republic of China. Because of his pioneering status, he was something of a legend among the graduate students at UCSB. He spent two years in Huhhot, Inner Mongolia, and

eventually wrote the first urban ethnography from the PRC, *Sex, Death and Hierarchy in a Chinese City* (1993). When I arrived at UCSB and heard about him, I was motivated to become a China scholar myself. I had long been interested in China, had taken Chinese history and art history courses as an undergraduate, and had a family history of connection with China by virtue of the fact that my great-grandfather, a one-time governor of Mississippi, had been the lawyer for the Mississippi Chinese Association in the 1910s. During a time when my professors were pessimistic about the prospects on the academic job market but there was great excitement about 'the China market,' I thought that by specializing in China I would not only have the chance to be one of the first anthropologists to do fieldwork in China, but also I would have other job options besides an academic job. I spent my first year in graduate school taking basic anthropology courses and mulling over my choice of a fieldsite.

The pivotal moment occurred in the summer of 1983 at the Olympic Training Center (OTC) in Colorado Springs. I had an abysmal track season due to a foot injury, but had been invited to an elite heptathlon training camp at the OTC. In our final lecture, the head coach, Lyle Knudson, gave us a speech in which he called upon us to demand of ourselves excellence in all areas of our lives and not to settle for simply being good athletes. This speech hit me at the end of a year in which I had slowly adjusted myself to the idea that I probably did not have enough talent to realize my long-term dream of making an Olympic team. Afterwards, as I sat under the ring of international flags at the entrance to the OTC, waiting for the bus to take me to the airport, I resolved to take my graduate studies seriously and to specialize in China.

In the fall of 1983 I began to study Mandarin Chinese and to take classes on

China. In the summer of 1984 I was placed eleventh in the Olympic Trials heptathlon. In the winter of 1984 Bill Jankowiak had returned from his fieldwork and I learned about the complications of doing participant observation in China. Even when the Chinese government granted the visa and the permission to do fieldwork, it was still difficult to carry out traditional anthropological fieldwork as proposed. Since ethnographic fieldwork was an unfamiliar research method, the Chinese authorities regarded it with suspicion: it looked an awful lot like espionage. Many groups and places were off limits to foreigners. Despite having obtained official Chinese government approval for his project through CSCPRC, Jankowiak never got the proper permits from local officials to do fieldwork among herders on the Mongolian grasslands as originally proposed. Stuck in the capital city of Huhhot, he made the best of it and carried out urban ethnography, improvising methods as he went along.

Traditionally, rural village studies have been the mainstay of anthropology, since ethnographic fieldwork is best suited to studying face-to-face communities. In 1981, the vast majority of Chinese anthropologists had written village ethnographies, and so there was not much precedent for research done in urban settings. However, villages were precisely where the Chinese authorities did not want anthropologists to go, since they were concerned about the loss of 'face' entailed by revealing poverty and 'backwardness' to foreigners. Those anthropologists who later got permission to do fieldwork in villages were accompanied by the ubiquitous *peitong*, in theory an interpreter and guide, in practice an employee of the local government who reported the anthropologist's every move to his or her superiors, and whose translations of controversial informant statements were often less than accurate, if they were conveyed at all.

The shift back toward fieldwork in Mainland China led to an immediate change: China scholars needed to master Mandarin Chinese. In Taiwan, Hong Kong, and Singapore, one could get around using only English, converse with academic colleagues in English, and conduct one's fieldwork with the help of a reliable and competent interpreter. In China, Russian had been the required foreign language for 40 years and the only people who spoke competent English were old men educated in missionary schools and Western universities before 1949, and young students at the elite universities, which were just beginning to establish English classes. For ethnographic fieldwork in particular, Chinese was indispensable.

SPORT ETHNOGRAPHY IN CHINA

I arrived at Beijing University in the fall of 1985 to study Chinese in a program administered by the Committee on International Educational Exchange (CIEE). Immediately after my arrival, I approached the head coach of the track team, Gong Lei, to inquire about joining the track team. He began by asking me for my personal best performances and, when he heard them, observed that they must be from years ago, since surely I had retired to concentrate on my studies. With some difficulty, due to my then-rudimentary Chinese and his thick Shandong accent, I told him that in fact I had just been placed fifth in US nationals and competed in an international meet two months previously. This was hard for him to grasp, since at that time Chinese athletes at my level were almost all state-supported, full-time athletes, and the notion of the student-athlete was novel. However, after he realized what fate had dropped on his doorstep, he jumped at the opportunity. I stepped into the middle of a situation that

I only later came to understand. As it happened, the second National College Games were scheduled for the spring of 1986. These games were a symbolic marker of a major social change that had begun with the era of reform in 1978. National games echoed the class ideology of the Party-state. The first National Soldiers' Games took place in 1952, the first National Minorities Games in 1953, and the first National Workers' Games in 1955. The first Chinese National Games had taken place in 1959. These games marked the groups favored by the national government: soldiers, workers, ethnic minorities, and 'the Chinese people.' Intellectuals were not one of the favored groups until the first National College Games in 1982. In preparation for the 1986 Games, colleges nationwide had begun recruiting top athletes by lowering their admission standards on the National College Entrance Examination, and in some cases waiving the admission requirements. Beijing University, as the top liberal arts university in the nation, refused to give anything but minor concessions to athletes, and as a result the Physical Education Division was panicked that Beijing University teams would do poorly in the Beijing City and national games, causing the university to 'lose face.' And then I appeared on the scene – a legitimate student who was capable of winning multiple medals and setting multiple records at the National Games (records as well as medals were rewarded with points toward the team championship). The only complication was that I was enrolled in an 'advanced studies' (*jinxiu*) program, not a Bachelor's degree program. This was 'fixed' by my coaches through their contacts at the State Education Commission, who warned me not to show anyone my student ID and, if I was asked, to say that I was studying in the Chinese Department, and not the Center for Teaching Chinese to Foreigners.

For my part, I had hoped that I could use sports as a way of doing the kind of intensive ethnography that was expected in anthropology, but which was very difficult under the conditions in China. A senior anthropologist who had attempted to carry out a research project in China in the late 1970s had warned me not to plan to do my dissertation research in the Mainland, because, he said, 'For your dissertation, you need to be sure that you can do the research.' I ran the risk of delaying my graduate studies for several years if something went wrong. He advised me to carry out dissertation research in Taiwan and then move to the Mainland. However, I had a keen interest in the Mainland and little interest in Taiwan. I reasoned that sports would be perceived as a less politically-sensitive topic than others; that I had an expertise that might be viewed as useful; that since the Ping Pong Diplomacy of the 1970s, sports had been the key realm in which interaction with foreigners had been allowed. I also knew that participation on a sports team would provide the kinds of intense everyday social interactions that were expected in fieldwork. I had therefore committed myself to studying sports in China by writing two masters degree theses on the topic before arriving at Beijing University. Joining the track team was the first step in my plan to write a dissertation on Chinese sports. As it happened, everything went according to plan.

The foreign students and visiting professors at Beijing University were housed in the 'foreign ghetto,' the Shaoyuan dormitory complex on the western edge of the university, backed up against the wall that encircled the entire university campus, walls and supervised gates being a standard architectural feature at all 'work units.' Any Chinese student who wanted to visit a foreign student in her dormitory had to register at the front door. After a few visits, it was likely that his or her class supervisor would pay a visit to ask about why she/he had visited a foreigner, and to discourage further visits. Chinese female students who visited foreign male students were monitored more strictly than the other way around, which gave me a bit more freedom as a foreign female. Foreign students took classes along with other foreign students. It could thus be difficult to meet Chinese people. Relationships between Chinese and foreigners were regarded with suspicion and I knew both Chinese and Western friends who were detained for 'self-criticism' at the local police station to respond to accusations of extra-marital sex (which was illegal), espionage, or other such activities.

In short, far from the colonialist context that had eased the research of previous generations of anthropologists around the world, China scholars in the 1980s carried out their fieldwork in an intensely anti-colonial, anti-imperialist atmosphere. Personally, I was comfortable with this atmosphere, because I felt it limited the potential for abuse that existed in colonial contexts.

However, since I trained every day with my teammates, I had a way of meeting Chinese students and a reason to engage in daily interaction with them. My Chinese language skills quickly surpassed those of my classmates, who were spending most of their time with other foreigners. I joined my teammates in their own dormitories for conversations in the evenings after practice, and I often ate with them in their own horrendous cafeterias, where the food was quite poor compared to that offered to foreigners – but was considerably cheaper. I hung out with my teammates and coaches during the intramural and the Beijing City track meets, where I was the only foreigner among several hundred Chinese. I spent time at the Beijing City Team Center and the National Team Center in Beijing. These team centers were regarded as part of the national defense system and foreigners were not allowed to enter them at will; in addition, the employees and athletes were prohibited from communicating certain kinds of information to foreigners because information about the sports system was regarded as a low-level state secret. However, I was able to enter either as an athlete or with the introduction of my coaches.

Based on my performance in the Beijing City collegiate track and field meet, I was selected to represent Beijing City at the 1986 National College Games. In preparation for those games, I joined my teammates for a two-and-a-half month training camp, which was held at the Beijing Institute of Aeronautics and Aviation. Because of the secret research carried out there, this institute did not allow foreigners to pass through its gates. I had to use a small gate in the back wall to come and go, since the gatekeepers there had been notified about me. I, eight coaches, and my 28 teammates, one of whom was another American, James Thomas, lived in a small dormitory building and observed the military-style discipline that was common on Chinese sports teams through the 1990s. Our daily schedule consisted of:

6:20am	roll call
6:30–7:00am	morning exercises
7:00–7:30am	eat breakfast
8:30–10:00am	train
12:00–12:30pm	eat lunch
12:30–2:30	siesta (*xiuxi*)
3:30–5:30pm	train
6:30–7:00pm	eat supper
11:00pm	lights out

Showers: Tuesday through Saturday 3–8 pm. We were allotted 20 tickets per month for the communal shower hall, which was a generous allotment because it allowed us to shower five days per week.

We were given mimeographed copies of a pamphlet entitled 'Things to Know Before the Meet' printed by the Beijing College Team Secretariat, and instructed to study it. The team leaders reviewed it during our first team meeting. The goal of the meet was a 'proper competition atmosphere, strict and impartial discipline, good performances, a whole new look.' The guiding slogan of the Games was: 'Civilization, Unity, Learning, Vigorous Progress.' Our assignment was to 'increase knowledge, improve friendship, receive education.' The rules listed in the pamphlet included a dress code, one of the restrictions being against long, loose hair; curfews; rules against eating food from street vendors; rules about obeying coaches; and rules against smoking, drinking, and fighting. We were expected to memorize the official meet song and we practiced it in team meetings so that we could demonstrate the enthusiasm expected of the capital city while singing it at the opening ceremonies and other occasions:

> As majestic as the dragon,
> As brave as the tiger,
> Our mother is China.
> Facing the world, facing the future,
> We give our best in the struggle for national unity.
> We give our best in the struggle for national dignity.
> Civilization, learning, unity, progress,
> Our banner glistens beneath the sun's rays,
> College students of the '80s,
> Carry out your great task.

Every other morning after roll call, we walked to the sportsfield to practice our technique for the Parade of Athletes in the opening ceremonies. We were to shout slogans in time with our goose steps as we passed the reviewing stand where the high officials sat.

> Train the body! [This was shouted out by our march leader, followed by a response by the rest of us. Our responses were:]
> Study diligently!

> Bravely scale the peaks!
> Carry out the Four Modernizations!
> Defend the Nation!

Our performance was considered technically difficult because it entailed cradling flowers in one arm, shouting slogans, and unfurling banners, all while goose stepping. Our successful execution of this level of difficulty was an important part of our bid for a 'spiritual civilization award.'

We also filled out self-evaluation forms, which were to be the basis for selecting the recipients of the individual 'spiritual civilization' awards. Self-evaluations were a frequent requirement in everyday Chinese life; most work units required their regular submission. The style was highly formalized and full of key jargon words. Since I was unfamiliar with the proper language, I asked two teammates to help me. One of them began by reeling off the phrase, 'Under the correct guidance of the Party and the leaders...' The other interrupted him, pointing out that I was a foreigner and not a Party member, so I didn't have to say that. He agreed, so they deleted it and proceeded as I wrote down:

> Since joining the Beijing City collegiate group training, I have been able to obey the directions of the leaders and coaches, actively join in on all the activities organized by the team, train strenuously, and assiduously improve my sports technique. I have respected the coaches and made many friends, despite the fact that I wasn't accustomed to the food and drink and other aspects; but I was able to overcome the difficulties. As a foreign student, I very much want to work hard to improve the friendship between college students of the two nations of America and China, and I am determined to spread the fighting spirit during this college student meet, and to win glory for Beijing's college students.

These self-evaluations were later examined during a meeting of the team leaders, captains, and officers, and six semi-finalists were announced at the next meeting of the entire Beijing team. During the College Games themselves, all of the Beijing semi-finalists' self-evaluations were submitted to the national committee and finalists were selected. Perhaps not surprisingly, I was one of the finalists. The names of the finalists were read out at the closing ceremonies, and six teams with the largest numbers of finalists were designated 'spiritual civilization teams.' Individuals were awarded certificates and teams were awarded trophies.

It should be clear by now that the greater part of my experience in sport ethnography was shaped by factors so particular to my own situation that it could hardly be touted as a generalizable method. At the same time, there were some aspects of my experience that would be common to other sport ethnographers, and it is those that I will now discuss.

THE SPORT ETHNOGRAPHER AS A 'PLAYER'

First, one of the unique features of sport ethnography is that, within the microcosmic structure of the game, the anthropologist is as much a 'player' as everyone else. She has a stake in the outcome, and the other players have a stake in her performance. This situation is rare in ethnographic fieldwork, where it is more likely that the anthropologist is an alienated observer who pops in to extract enough 'data' to build a professional career, and then returns home to exploit it. Similar situations of personal investment can be found in 'insider' ethnography by scholars who study their own cultures; in 'advocacy' anthropology by scholars who are politically involved in their fieldwork; and among the sizeable number of anthropologists who marry natives. In my case, my coaches received substantial financial bonuses for each medal that I won and record that I broke. They also had a stake in the overall

placement of the team. Therefore, they wanted to make sure that I performed as well as possible, and so they pressured me to follow regimens that they believed would help me do this. They believed that the militarized discipline of the training camp, including the political study sessions, would help me, while I found them to be more of a distraction than a help. Although I did receive some concessions as a foreigner, on the whole, I was held to the same disciplinary standards as a Chinese athlete.

This was not without its challenges for my own dual identity as athlete and researcher. As I stood lined up with my teammates behind the Beijing City flag in the middle of the field during the opening ceremonies of the College Games, with 50,000 pairs of eyes converging on us, it occurred to me that I had actually become Bao Sushan, 'the American girl who wants to win glory for Beijing' (as one of many newspaper headlines had described me). In the course of the training camp, my world had progressively shrunk until, lying in bed that night, I realized with some self-disgust that I had come halfway around the world only to find myself engaging in the same mental routine that I always used to prepare for competitions in the United States. I thought to myself, 'Here I am on the other side of the world, and all I can think about is running faster, jumping higher, throwing farther, beating people.' At that point in time these goals seemed terribly trivial, but I could not escape them because my coaches, my teammates, and the high officials of sports in Beijing expected me to win and I didn't want to let them down. Not only did I fail to take detailed field notes during the week-long period of the games themselves, I could not even bring myself to write down anything until several months after returning to the United States. This illustrates the flip side of being a 'player': sport ethnography is notorious for lacking 'distance' or 'objectivity.' Sports participation, especially at a high level, demands that the participant live very much within the moment. To convert this into social scientific analysis involves an almost painful process of detachment.

In the end, I fulfilled my duty. I won the heptathlon, setting a national college record. In the last event, the 800 meters, I ran alone out front, hearing only the sound of my own footsteps and one singular yell from the stands: 'Add gas, foreigner!' I ran on two silver-medal relay teams. Beijing's women placed second overall. I was given a spirit award. A magazine article captured my double identity well when it quoted me as responding, 'To use the American formula, I want to say, "Thank you." To use the Chinese formula, I want to say I still haven't done enough!' (Chu, 1987: 27).

SPORT ETHNOGRAPHY AS A REGISTER OF CULTURAL DIFFERENCE

A second unique aspect of sport ethnography is that because it is so intensely physical, in some ways it acts as a more sensitive register of cultural difference than other kinds of ethnographic interaction. Roy Wagner has argued that:

> When we speak of people belonging to different cultures, ... we are referring to a very basic kind of difference between them, suggesting that there are specific varieties of the phenomenon of [humankind]. ... [T]he anthropologist is forced to include himself and his own way of life in his subject matter, and study himself. More accurately, since we speak of a person's total capability as "culture," the anthropologist uses his own culture to study others, and to study culture in general.' (Wagner, 1981: 2)

This means that there can be no absolute 'objectivity' in the study of culture, but only a relative objectivity based on the characteristics of one's own culture. Understanding another culture involves creating a relationship between it and one's own culture, resulting in an understanding that embraces both cultures. An anthropologist experiences the subject of her study through the world of his own meanings. The anthropologist 'invents' the culture she believes herself to be studying, and the relationship between it and her own culture is more 'real' than the thing it 'relates' (Wagner, 1981: 3–4). Wagner has labeled this process 'the invention of culture,' and he calls for an anthropology that is more self-aware of this process, rather than one that simply consigns cultural difference to the category of exoticism, where it can be rationalized, repressed, ignored, and 'not seen' (Wagner, 1981: x).

To illustrate his points, I will describe one example of how sport ethnography forced me to see something uncomfortable that I would not have otherwise seen. It forced me to see it because the realization hit me at a visceral level, bypassing the already carefully-constructed categories that were present in my conscious thoughts. This epiphany occurred with respect to the disciplinary regime described above. Like most Americans raised during the Cold War, I had pre-existing notions about authoritarian, militarized, 'Communist' discipline. I saw the discipline on sports teams, including that which I experienced, as a quintessential example of this kind of 'Communist' discipline, which I assumed to be antithetical to the 'democratic' regimes of a 'free' society. During the Beijing City College Team training camp, however, I had to re-evaluate my assumption of cultural difference because I noticed that I was perhaps the most disciplined athlete on the team. I obeyed the rules more strictly than most of my teammates. They consistently violated the rules when they felt they had more important things to do. They were more cynical than the team leaders. The main problem with the regime of discipline was boredom and they were not content to remain bored. As my roommate complained to me, it seemed like all we did was sleep, eat, train, and sleep again. The main sanctions were criticism and the threat of a negative entry in their dossiers, but they felt confident that a good performance in the meet would override them and did not seem to take the threat seriously. Not being Chinese, I did not fear a negative entry in my dossier – and so I asked myself, why am I obeying these rules? I reluctantly concluded that I was obeying them because they were familiar to me. Obeying the rules seemed to be easier for me than for my teammates. I had lived this life before, in the United States.

The experience was most similar to a girls' sailing camp I attended one summer at the age of 16. This camp also had morning roll calls, curfews, sanitation checks, a talent show, and inspirational singing after lunch and dinner. As the oldest cabin, we were told it was our duty to lead by example, just as the Beijing team was told that it was our duty as the capital city to lead by example. The camp explicitly promoted not Communist ideology, but rather the ideology of 'Jane Achiever' along with Christian ideology. This camp was founded and run by the YMCA. The YMCA had more responsibility than any other single source for introducing Western sports into China at the turn of the twentieth century; what I thought of as 'Communist' sports discipline had its roots in the Christian missionizing of the early twentieth century.

The national heptathlon training camps that I attended at the US Olympic Training Center in Colorado Springs utilized somewhat different disciplinary regimes, which in certain respects were more draconian than the YMCA regime. We did not sing songs and

shout slogans, which were practices that were relatively easy to contest and question. The youngest coach on the Beijing team once commented:

> Why do you always have to shout slogans? Of course we all want to 'win glory for Beijing.' But do you think Beijing really cares whether you win points for it or not? Most of Beijing doesn't even know who you are. If you do badly, is Beijing going to console you? No, but you have to live with it. So we're all really performing for ourselves.

By contrast, in the US Olympic Training Center, we ate every meal surrounded by the flags of the world strung around the cafeteria, and every time we left the front gate we passed under the American and Olympic flags – reinforcing an ideology of nationalism within world peace that would have required much more sophisticated reasoning for us to contest, even if we were so inclined. Instead of political study meetings where we were subject to 'thought education' such as memorizing the meet rules and anthem, we endured even more interminable sessions in which our bodies were weighed underwater, tested on machines, and measured. We analyzed videotapes of our training sessions, publicly dissecting our own bodies according to the principles of momentum, levers, center of gravity, and so on. I found this process far more invasive and humiliating than the self-evaluation I wrote in Beijing: 'science' is such an ultimate voice of authority that one feels absolutely defenseless under its gaze.

In sum, my bodily experience of 'Communist' sport discipline forced me to acknowledge that the dichotomy between 'Communist' and 'democratic' discipline that I had constructed as a way of making sense of cultural difference simply did not hold up to scrutiny. Ever since that moment of insight, I have asked myself, 'Who is really more "free," after all?' I do not think that I would have arrived at this question if I had not personally experienced a lifestyle that I had assumed would make me feel imprisoned, but which did not.

SUMMARY: WHAT SPORT ETHNOGRAPHY CAN AND CAN'T DO

In the spirit of the postmodern and postcolonialist critiques of ethnographic fieldwork, I have tried to show how my own sport ethnography cannot be taken as a generalizable formula for research because it was so closely tied to an individual with a particular personal history who happened to do research in China at a particular point in time. I was lucky to have this opportunity, out of which I produced one of the first detailed ethnographies to emerge out of China in the post-Mao era. Sport ethnography made it possible, but that was because of my own history as an athlete, because sports diplomacy happened to receive a great deal of government attention in China, and because I happened to arrive at Beijing University in the year of the second National College Games. If I were to begin dissertation research in China now, in the absence of the constraints on fieldwork in the 1980s, I might well choose to do a village study more in keeping with the anthropological tradition. On the other hand, a traditional village study would probably not have challenged my worldview in the way that sport anthropology did. I might have been able to maintain a comfortable set of neatly ordered systems of cultural differences. Instead, I now have a much more fluid notion of cultural difference – we may be different, but we are never different for the reasons that we think we are different.

REFERENCES

Chu Zi (1987) 'Rexin Zhongguo tiyude Meiguo guniang' ['The American girl who warmly loves Chinese sports']. *Tiyu bolan* [*Sports Vision*], March, pp. 26–7.

Clifford, James (1986) 'Introduction: Partial Truths.' In James, Clifford and George E., Marcus, (eds), *Writing Culture: The Poetics and Politics of Ethnography.* Berkeley: University of California Press. pp. 1–26.

Clifford, James, and Marcus, George E. (eds) (1986) *Writing Culture: The Poetics and Politics of Ethnography.* Berkeley: University of California Press.

Geertz, Clifford (1988) *Works and Lives: The Anthropologist as Author.* Stanford, CA: Stanford: University Press.

Gupta, Akhil, and Ferguson, James (eds) (1997a) *Anthropological Locations: Boundaries and Grounds of a Field Science.* Berkeley: University of California Press.

Gupta, Akhil, and Ferguson, James (1997b) 'Discipline and Practice: "The Field" as Site, Method, and Location in Anthropology.' In Akhil Gupta and James Ferguson (eds), *Anthropological Locations: Boundaries and Grounds of a Field Science.* Berkeley: University of California Press. pp. 1–46.

Jankowiak, William (1993) *Sex, Death, and Hierarchy in a Chinese City: An Anthropological Account.* New York: Columbia University Press.

Marcus, George E. (1986) 'Contemporary Problems of Ethnography in the Modern World System.' In James, Clifford, and George E. Marcus (eds), *Writing Culture: The Poetics and Politics of Ethnography.* Berkeley: University of California Press. pp. 165–93.

Wacquant, Loïc (2003) *Body and Soul: Notebooks of an Apprentice Boxer.* Oxford: Oxford University Press.

Wagner, Roy (1981) *The Invention of Culture.* Chicago: University of Chicago Press.

16

Hidden Identities and Personal Stories: International Research about Women in Sport

JENNIFER HARGREAVES

PERSONAL AND FEMINIST RESEARCH

Doing research is always personal, often solitary, and sometimes highly emotional. It can be hugely rewarding, but difficult and frustrating as well; full of possibilities, but also riddled with problems; it can both illuminate and obfuscate. This chapter is about all these feelings and characteristics. It is about research carried out over six years, between 1994 and 2000, resulting in a 120,000-word monograph entitled *Heroines of Sport: The Politics of Difference and Identity* (Hargreaves, 2000). Research for the book was tied to my personal history (Alasuutari, 1995: 159) and to my theoretical and political interests about women in sport. The story starts with the inception and then the manipulation of a research idea, and includes a discussion about the rationale, the selection of participants, and the mixed methods that were used, focusing in particular on interviews carried out with women in different international contexts. The epistemological and methodological orientation of the research, making sense of the data, and the ethical implications of my role as researcher are also intrinsic to the project as a whole.

I have used the personal pronoun 'I', acknowledging my agency throughout the research process. But while aiming to be 'scientific' and scholarly, I do not claim some spurious position of neutrality, but rather, have worked with 'passionate objectivity' (Hargreaves, 1992; Maykut and Morehouse, 1994). *Heroines of Sport* is positioned firmly within the feminist tradition of scholarship which places women at the centre of the research process and allows them, as far as is possible, to have an authentic voice in the final product (Stanley and Wise, 1990, 1993).

THE TOPIC

This project was in part a response to pressure put on academics to produce high-level research in order for universities to get government money[1], but, working within that imperative, I had considerable autonomy to decide *what* research to do and *how* to do it. The choice was a natural progression from my work in the general field of sport, culture and ideology (Hargreaves, 1982), and in the specific areas of equity issues and gender discrimination (notably Hargreaves, 1994). Situated within the feminist cultural studies tradition which recognizes that 'culture is itself constituted in relation to gender and other social and political categories' (Lury, 1995: 33), I had examined issues of difference and discrimination in the history of women's sport in the UK linked to such social variables as age, class, disability, ethnicity, and sexuality.

The focus on difference in the UK context led me to extend the scope of my work to include investigations of women in sport from a wider range of groups, including those from outside the west. A very basic examination of sport history and sociology literature reveals that most texts are either *exclusively about* men's sport, or *focus predominantly on* men's sport (Hargreaves, 1994: 1–2, 2000: 5–6), but a worrying tendency in the proportionately limited number of books about female sport is to treat 'women in sport' as if they are a homogeneous group with a shared culture. Furthermore, it is commonplace in academic texts about women's sport for generalizations to be made from the experiences of western women who are white, middle-class, able-bodied, and heterosexual. The end result is that women who come from minority groups and from countries outside the west have been marginalized – treated as 'different', as 'Others'. It is a process of exclusion which, according to Cassidy and her colleagues:

> includes thinking, imagining, and speaking as if whiteness describes the world. Racism, for example, engenders white solipsism by allowing White women the power to make it seem as if their own experience is wholly representative of all women's experience. Black women, Native women, disabled women, in fact, most other women, are left out without anyone noticing they are absent. (Cassidy et al., 1995: 32–3)

A few feminist scholars of sport have been critical of exclusionary 'white' research. For example, Birrell (1989, 1990) and Smith (1992) from the United States were two of the first. They represent a slowly emerging field of feminist scholarship about women from non-hegemonic groups. But the body of work remains *very small.*

My growing interest in the politics of difference and identity coincided with an invitation to write a book about heroines of sport in order to provide the female equivalent of a book about heroes in sport! I agreed to write the book on the condition that I could redefine the conventional concept of heroine (Hargreaves, 2000: 1–5). The creation of sporting heroines is normally a very public affair, synonymous with stardom and commodification, linked to winning medals and images of nationhood that typically mask differences between different groups of women both within nations and between nations. I wanted instead to find out about the 'unsung' heroines of sport, those women from minority groups who have been marginalized in mainstream accounts, and who have had to struggle to overcome difficult barriers. My intention was to focus on women from across the world and through doing so to revisit 'the politics of difference and identity' as well as the complexities and multiplicities of late capitalist/postmodern/postcolonial societies.

So who were to be *my* heroines? Initially, I had many categories of women in mind and carried out exploratory research on one or two groups only to find out that for logistical reasons it would be unlikely that I could get enough data in a reasonable time span. For example, I started to investigate the participation of women in the British Workers' Sports Federation (BWSF) during the 1920s and 1930s using the archives at the London School of Economics. I wanted to provide a gender balance to the research that had been done on men in the BWSF (Jones, 1988), but apart from one or two working-class women portrayed as 'stars', details about female participation were minimal in relation to the full reports about men's sports and the ideologies underpinning them.

I finally made a decision about which participant groups to include and how to conduct the research based on accessibility, personal contacts with key people connected to the groups, and opportunities that opened up for travel to Australia, Canada, Egypt, Holland, and South Africa.

There were five main groups, each of which became the focus for one of the five central chapters of the published book: Black women in South Africa (Chapter 2); Muslim women in the Middle East (Chapter 3); Aboriginal women in Australia and Canada (Chapter 4); lesbian women (Chapter 5) and disabled women (Chapter 6) across the world. The first chapter places the participant groups into the context of research that is breaking with the conventional ethno-/Euro-/American-centrism of most previous research and discusses the significance of difference and identity and other theoretical and methodological issues. The final chapter (Chapter 7) concerns a number of organizations that together comprise what I have characterized as the Women's International Sport Movement and asks key questions about whether such organizations adequately represent groups of women that are marginalized in mainstream sport and, further, relates their development to colonialism and neo-colonialism.

DISCOURSES OF EPISTEMOLOGY AND METHODOLOGY

The fieldwork for this project evolved in relation to discourses of episotomology and methodology. The project fitted with the mid-1990s emphasis in feminist methodology on the individual and the cultural which, Celia Lury (1995: 42) argued at the time, had not led to 'an abandonment of previous methods of interpretation and analysis in feminist research', but that discourse analysis had simply been added to 'textual interpretation, life histories, interviews, questionnaires and ethnography, which together comprise[d] the most prevalent techniques in feminist cultural studies'. Lury went on to discuss different theoretical implications drawn from the use of such techniques and argued for 'the development of historically-specific understandings of the cultural, which neither assume that it is gendered through a universal process of sexual difference, nor assume that it is a gender-neutral field', and for 'a feminist methodology that is sensitive to both social *and* cultural specificity' (Lury, 1995: 43). Further, the connections between culture, systems of meaning, and questions of power and politics (Alasuutari, 1995: 2) provided a basis for the way in which the project was conceived and carried out.

Feminist methodology is conventionally coupled with interpretative interactionism (Denzin, 1989) which, Bruce (2001: 40) suggests, is 'particularly suited to interpreting the experiences of groups whose perspectives [are] marginalized'. Such a position recognizes the transformative interventionist potential of academic sport feminism – that if individuals and groups of women can tell their stories, bring to light problems and constraints, get their voices heard, then there is a chance, however small, for change. With this in mind, the project involved the meticulous collection of detailed personal narratives about the experiences – and meanings placed on those experiences – of individual women and groups of women. An outcome of the research was to write about the hidden histories of these women and to speak out wherever possible about their struggles and aspirations in forums where decisions about women's sport development were being made. Characterized as 'a focus *on* women, in research carried out *by* women who [are] feminist, *for* other women', feminist research is linked ideologically to social justice and emancipatory politics (Stanley and Wise, 1990: 21) and its working imperative is to cement together theory, research and praxis. Such an approach addresses the often overlooked feature of academic politics: struggles come from knowledge and ideas.

It was essential, however, to address the problem arising from speaking 'for and on behalf of others' (Aitchison, 2000: 136). This is a major concern of postcolonial feminists and Black feminists because of the risk of appropriation of the voices of the 'Other' by white feminists (Hill Collins, 1990; hooks 1990; Mohanty, 1991, 1995; Spivak, 1987). Referring to difference, bell hooks argues that: 'It is not just important what we speak about, but how and why we speak' (hooks, 1990: 15). My approach was to avoid the use of 'generalized/homogenized', and to recognize the diversity of lived experiences and subjectivities.

LITERATURE REVIEW

A literature review is an essential preparatory technique that provides invaluable information about the general field of investigation, in turn providing a knowledge base from which to plan the logistics of the fieldwork.

For example, through the immersion into books about the politics of: apartheid (Chapter 2); Islam (Chapter 3); Aboriginality (Chapter 4); sexuality (Chapter 5); and disability (Chapter 6), it was possible for informed questions to be formulated for interviews with Black South African, Muslim, Aboriginal, lesbian, and disabled women, respectively. Most importantly for international research was searching for and referring to publications that were written by authors from the participants' countries or with similar backgrounds, for example, books written by Muslim and South African feminists, Islamic scholars, Aboriginal activists, and lesbian sportswomen. Doing so created the potential for a more authentic analysis.

Reading background secondary texts – about theory as well as context – should always be an ongoing process throughout the research period so that development takes place at the level of ideas, and in response to the analyses and interpretations of others. Secondary sources helped with the processes of investigation and the development of theoretical and conceptual frameworks, as well as facilitating insightful analysis.

INVESTIGATING THE UNKNOWN

In common with other feminist researchers, I have used varied investigative techniques or methods (Harding, 1987: 2), namely, examining historical traces and records; observing girls and women in different contexts; and collecting the stories, opinions and feelings of participants. Exploring previously unexplored territory requires dedicated 'detective' work: constantly searching for clues, sometimes in unlikely situations; spending hours and hours on the telephone; sending and receiving letters and e-mails; scrutinizing newspapers, magazines, pamphlets and websites; seeking help from friends and colleagues; and using networks to reach significant informers and potential participants. During the life-span of the project hardly a day went by when no ideas about the research were triggered off, no information received, no new contacts made. In other words, the research was constantly in process and central in my life. Gathering original information from numerous and varied sources ensured that the final written account was as full and as rich as possible and incorporated different and complex ideas and examples.

Qualitative methods were supported by quantitative data. For example, in order to be able to comment on the scale of the 'problem' of Olympic competition for Muslim women (Chapter 3), it was useful to calculate the number of countries that have sent no female competitors to the Olympic Games, to ascertain which of those countries are Islamic, which Islamic countries *did* send female competitors, and in which events and according to which dress codes those women took part. The British Olympic Association has archival material to make such calculations possible. This is one example of important background information against which the personal experiences and opinions of Muslim women about Olympic participation could be made. There is no intrinsic objection in a feminist approach to quantitative methods; they have been opposed previously only because of the discriminatory and biased ways in which they have been used (Jayaratne and Stewart, 1991: 88–9; Oakley, 1998).

RESEARCH LOGISTICS:
TIME AND SPACE

Original data was collected from numerous different sources and people (mostly women) located in different countries across the world. In order for the data collection to be successful, complex and time-consuming planning took place. Many of the arrangements depended on the help of friends, colleagues, or sports contacts. South Africa (Chapter 2) provides a good exemplar. Introductory letters and e-mails were sent months in advance of a six-week visit, followed in some cases by telephone calls and e-mails. A skeleton itinerary was fixed before arriving. I divided most of my time between Johannesburg, Cape Town, and Durban, and other locations relatively close by. I was dependent on South African friends and contacts, both for hospitality and for making detailed arrangements, including booking venues, finding knowledgeable participants, and setting up interviews. Sometimes I had group meetings in universities, did observation and interviews in people's homes, in hotel lobbies, at conferences, on the netball court in Soweto, in a karate club in Cape Town, in a sports hall in Guguletu (a township outside Cape Town), and so on. Most of the time I was chauffeured to and from venues, and for safety reasons this was essential, especially when visiting townships, such as Soweto and Guguletu. But when I was invited to go to the University of Zululand, against advice I hired a car and drove on my own for over 200 miles through Kwazulu Natal. It was the only viable method of travelling from Durban to the university.

Sometimes I made *ad hoc* arrangements. For example, in 1994 I attended the first-ever international conference on women and sport entitled 'Women and Sport: the Challenge of Change', in Brighton, UK. There were 280 delegates from 82 countries, including women from the developing world. Leaders of the Women's International Sport Movement were there, and most of the delegates were sport policy- and decision-makers in their respective countries (Chapter 7). I only had the four-day conference period to identify participants from across the world, get their permission, confirm a time and place, and conduct interviews. On-the-spot decisions were made under huge pressure in order to fit in as many interviews as possible and to make the most of a unique opportunity. I focused on foreign delegates, as many from the developing world as possible, interviewing leaders of the Women's International Sport Movement on a later occasion.

These two examples are indicators of the varied and complex arrangements needed to complete the fieldwork for this study. It was necessary throughout the six years to be creative in making contacts, flexible in terms of time and space, and responsive to opportunities, grasping them whenever they arose.

DOCUMENTARY EVIDENCE

Original documentary evidence provided invaluable information about economic, political, and religious features and ideologies; particular situations and events; personal and public opinions; and other aspects of the social and cultural worlds in which the five groups of women lived and played their sports. Much of the primary source material was historical, including archival evidence and information from personal letters and other memorabilia, newspaper articles, official reports, pamphlets, competition programmes, and contemporary books. I also saw photographs and video and film footage.

Although during the six years I had access to, or was given, a wealth of documentary material, getting hold of it was frequently fraught with frustration, but at other times presented amazing surprises and pleasure. The following examples occurred in South Africa (Chapter 2). First, through a mutual friend, an appointment was made with the Deputy Director of the National Library of South Africa in Cape Town in order to look for material about Black women (used here to denote all non-white women in South Africa) in sport during the apartheid years (1948–91). Together, we spent around six hours searching in every conceivable book, magazine, sports report, and we found an unending amount of information about white men's sport, a fair amount about white women's sport, a smattering about Black men's sport, but *nothing* about Black women's sport. *Absolutely nothing.* Through this experience, the concept about women being 'hidden from history' (Rowbotham, 1973) was concretized in the specific context of apartheid South Africa, and the theoretical implications of the particular relationship between gender and 'race' also came alive. This example illustrates the importance of looking for theoretical and analytical clues throughout the whole of the research process, letting the data (in this case the lack of data) 'speak for itself'.

The second example followed the depressing library visit. Although I knew from anti-apartheid friends in London about some Black African, coloured, and Indian women who had taken part in non-racial sport during the period of apartheid, I was facing the likelihood that I would find no documentary evidence of their participation. But then, co-incidentally, I learned about the Women's Bureau of South Africa Resource Centre. I visited the Centre and found, among other publications, past copies of *The Sowetan*, which contained regular articles about Black African female athletes. I photocopied as many articles as possible and then accepted the offer of help from one of the Centre's staff, who photocopied all the remaining articles about Black women's sport and sent them to me in England. The Women's Bureau had never before had requests for material about sport.

The third example of documentary evidence was also unexpected. During an interview with two 'coloured' women who had been active members of the South African Council on Sport (SACOS – the non-racial anti-apartheid sports organization located inside South Africa), they presented me with *SACOSSPORT Festival '88* (SACOS, 1988), a unique commemorative volume of a celebratory event, popularly called the 'Black Olympics', which symbolized the past struggles of Black people against the pernicious apartheid regime. For the two women who told me their story, it was an invaluable record of their personal histories. But when I demurred about accepting such a gift, they were insistent because, they said, '*You* are the only person who will write our history and we want to help you'. The volume included written details and photographs of non-racial women's netball, softball and track and field competitions. The photographs showed that the 'sportswear' of many competitors comprised pieced-together items of clothing and that most of the African women ran in bare feet, and one of the feature articles recorded the anti-sexist, anti-racist, and feminist philosophies of the SACOS women, who claimed that even in non-racial sport they were treated as 'sex objects', their events were trivialized, and there was a lack of women's participation in decision-making.

In relation to Chapter 6, the only method available to trace women's participation in the Stoke Mandeville Games (precursor of the Paralympic Games) was to trawl meticulously through copies of *The Cord* and some other disability-specific 1940s and 1950s publications. Content analysis revealed that there was relatively little information about women's sports in relation men's sports, but enough to construct an outline account of the frequency and character of the participation of women with spinal cord injuries.

Lesbian friends who competed in the 1998 Gay Games in Amsterdam came back with a huge number of publicity pamphlets and specially-produced newspapers, booklets and other written and visual materials, relevant to Chapter 5. It was possible to extract comprehensive background information about the philosophy and aims of the Games, their historical, political, financial, cultural, and social significance, the surrounding discourses of sexuality and homophobia, transcripts of speeches, numbers of participants, details of events and associated cultural and political activities, and so on. By scrutinizing written material, it was possible to comment on different features of the Gay Games – for example, the acute homophobia faced by lesbians in the developing world and the sponsored outreach programmes enabling their (secret) attendance at the Games.

The discourses of the Gay Games allowed for textual analysis, and photographs and videos showed colourful parades and details of dance and theatre performances incorporating visual signifiers of lesbian and gay sexualities. In other words, documentary and visual imagery enabled events to 'come alive', and afterwards it was possible by means of interviews to gather the personal reactions and interpretations of lesbian athletes to these events.

The internet was another source of original documentary material. In relation to Chapter 3, it was possible to collect a wealth of data from internet documents about the founding of the Islamic Countries' Women's Sports Solidarity Games, first held in Tehran in 1993. I was dependent on the help of a third-year undergraduate student from Iran, who translated from Arabic and Persian into English details about the conception, rationale, ideology and organization of the Solidarity Games, particulars of the opening ceremony, numbers and nationalities of competitors, and speeches given by the

President of Iran and the Head of the Physical Education Organization of Iran.

The examples above give some idea of how varied the documentary material was in terms of type of evidence, age of the evidence, and use of language and illustration. Although documentary data was used for every chapter of the book and greatly enhanced the data from observation and interactive methods of investigation described below, nevertheless, it was critically investigated, carefully used and not automatically accepted as literal recordings of events (Yin, 1984: 80).

OBSERVATIONS

Observations for this project were generally unplanned, occurring spontaneously during visits around interviews and to different places and events. For example, I watched Black African girls playing netball on the only properly surfaced netball court in Soweto and I listened to their emotional claims and descriptions of racism both on and off the court; I saw the vast and expensive sport facilities at Stellenbosch University, which had been previously exclusively for white students and then I saw the impoverished facilities for girls' and women's sport in the Black townships; I observed a gymnastics demonstration involving girls and boys and men and women from different communities and from all ethnic backgrounds; and I visited a karate club which was also multi-ethnic. These observations helped me to understand the continuing legacy of apartheid alongside the tremendous efforts that were being made to establish non-racial sport.

Observations of the other participant groups provided examples of sport participation, organization, media coverage, images of the female body, rituals and symbols,

relations of power, discourses of difference, and so on. The data generated from observations complemented the interview data that was collected in parallel, providing a better feeling for the actual contexts in which the participants practised sport and lived their lives. Observations were ongoing throughout the six years, often throwing up unexpected examples of the construction of individual and group identities articulated fully in the interviews.

INTERVIEWS AS FEMINIST RESEARCH

It is claimed that one of the 'prime tasks of academic feminism in the social sciences' is to make links between 'beliefs, life and research' through investigating 'material differences', that is 'real events and experiences' in women's lives (Stanley and Wise, 1983: 192–3). This perspective reflects the historical break by feminists with the scientized conventions of positivist research that led to the development of biography/life history/oral history as their preferred methodological approach (Anderson et al., 1990; Bertaux, 1981; Birrell, 1989) and the break with conventional divisions between participant and researcher (Oakley, 1981) as their preferred interview technique. Anderson et al. argue that:

> Oral history is a basic tool in our (feminist) efforts to incorporate the previously overlooked lives, activities, and feelings of women into our understanding of the past and of the present. When women speak for themselves they reveal hidden realities: new experiences and new perspectives emerge that challenge the 'truths' of official accounts and cast doubt upon established theories. (Anderson et al., 1990: 95)

There were two convincing reasons for using a biography/life history/oral history approach for this particular project: first, because the participants came from varied personal, cultural and political contexts it would have been impossible to standardize their responses and, second, a sensitive interactive exchange was the most likely way to uncover such experiences as personal and institutional discrimination linked to ableism, homophobia, racism, and sexism. Referring to the significance of the individual woman's story and her sense of self and identity, Victor Seidler makes the important point that:

> The personal voice is irreducible because it reflects a particular level of experience, a qualitative connection to self. For what is being explored is the ongoing dialectic between what has been experienced and the relationships within which she is living. Here there is a space and time for acknowledging differences between women, even celebrating difference. (Seidler, 1994: viii)

Interactive interviewing was the key technique of investigation throughout this project (Cook and Fonow, 1990; Oakley, 1981). Participants were positioned at the centre of enquiry by encouraging them to talk freely about their experiences of, and feelings about, female sport. I was able to speak in person to women from all ethnic backgrounds when in South Africa; to Muslim women when at a conference in Egypt; to Aboriginal women in different locations in Australia and Canada; to lesbian women in Holland and the UK; to disabled women mostly in the UK; and to women involved in the Women's International Sport Movement at two international conferences and at locations in the UK. I carried out face-to-face interviews with individuals and groups, telephone interviews and 'e-mail interviews'. In all, I conducted around 150 interviews.

SELECTING PARTICIPANTS

It was a challenge to find authentic representatives of all the participant groups and so, from the start, a purposive sampling procedure was adopted. Through my background in sport sociology over many years and my work on gender and discrimination, I already had contacts with people who could help me to access potential participants. Many were personal friends who had specialist knowledge about one or other group. For example, in relation to South Africa (SA), I knew Sam Ramsamy (Chairman of SANROC until 1991 and then President of the (new) National Olympic Committee of SA) and Jasmat Soma (member of SACOS, non-racial tennis champion of SA, subsequently a member of SANROC in London, still in contact with friends from SACOS, and in his present role as GB Over-55 Tennis Champion, he has new contacts in South Africa. In relation to Muslim women, at a conference in Alexandria, Egypt, there were delegates from many different Islamic countries, including Bahrain, Iran, Iraq, Jordan, Kuwait, Syria, and Nigeria, as well as Egypt. In relation to Aboriginal sport, I knew the leading Canadian sports sociologist doing research about First Nation women in sport, and at conferences in Australia colleagues put me in touch directly with Aboriginal women. In relation to disability sport, an ex-student of mine was a Paralympic gold-medal swimmer, working now with the GB Paralympic team, and I knew staff in several disability-sport organizations. In relation to lesbian sportswomen, my initial contact was a friend who had taken part in each Gay Games since their inception in 1982. Finally, contacting the leaders of the International Women's Sports Movement was straightforward since several of them are friends of mine.

In addition to personal contacts, I wrote 'out of the blue' to numerous relevant people requesting help, such as university academics, authors of key texts, leaders of (female) sport-specific organizations, directors of state-run sport agencies, and individual sportswomen. Following a snowball effect, I secured enough contacts to carry out a viable investigation for each chapter. All interview participants received a written statement incorporating a message of introduction, an explanation about the research, and an assurance of confidentiality. In this way, a process of informed consent was followed.

Without exception, people were exceptionally generous of their time and help and unequivocally supportive of the research idea and purpose. Many of them went out of their way to put me in touch with other people, providing transport to and from venues, giving me hospitality in their own homes, and driving me to venues where I carried out interviews.

INTERVIEW PROCEDURES

The purpose of the interviews was to collect original data which, together with information from other sources, would enable me to piece together new and different stories about women in sport who had been hidden from, or marginalized, in earlier accounts. To this end, creating a relaxed and friendly atmosphere in order to deconstruct the common-sense feeling of being a researcher who was *the* authority figure was essential. Whenever possible, questions were open-ended, encouraging participants to talk freely, tell their own stories, and elaborate in their own ways. Only the introductions were somewhat formalized, in order to elicit brief personal and sport details. Characterized as non-standardized, in-depth interviews, they were, in essence, like conversations, including exchanges of ideas and political discussions.

However, the interactive interviews did not exclude having a guide for questions covering key issues and thematic areas in order to ensure that nothing significant was left out. Some probing occurred which in practice was more like mutual communication that guar-

anteed a fuller narrative. All the interviews were concerned with past achievements and future possibilities, struggles and discrimination. However, they also had numerous different orientations because of the varied social backgrounds of the participants and their specific histories. All the interviews were audio-taped and transcribed.

There were very few problems getting information by this method. All participants were *willing* to talk, almost all of them *wanted* to talk, and in some cases they had to be *stopped* from talking and kept on track! Most of the participants had experienced specific forms of discrimination, such as ableism, homophobia, racism and sexism, and, as a result, were highly politicized. For example, urban Australian Aboriginal women were aware of ongoing human rights discourses about Aboriginality in their country and linked their experiences of racism in sport to their political beliefs about constructions of national identity (Glowczewski, 1998: 347; Tonkinson, 1998: 298). In fact, the discourse of identity politics was relevant to every interview, even through the very process of the interview itself, by bringing women from the minority groups to the centre of the story of sport, that is, through making women who had been invisible, visible.

FOCUS-GROUP INTERVIEWS

Group interviews enabled the collection of much more data from many more people in far less time than would have been possible solely through individual interviews. For example, in Guguletu, there were 13 Black women in the group and although the session lasted for over two hours, the women were surprisingly self-disciplined, highly focused, spontaneously ensured that everyone had a chance to speak, and they did not spend unnecessary time repeating the comments and experiences of others. They sparked each other off, built on each other's stories, embellished, gave more examples, interrupted to say, 'Yes, yes, you're right'; 'No, it's not like that'; 'Do you remember?'; 'Oh yes, it happened to me as well'; 'No – I don't see it like that'; 'Things were much worse for us'; 'In my school the system was rather different'. These were women who were political in their thinking and were prepared to speak out openly and without hesitation. They were making connections between sport and their political and gendered experiences – of abuse in the home, problems of travel and safety, lack of access and funding, child-care problems and poor facilities, etc. They had stories to tell that no one else had ever listened to.

Sometimes the venues for group interviews were noisy and cramped. On one occasion, there were insufficient chairs for everyone and so I sat on the floor with several of the participants and others sat on windowsills and radiators. In Guguletu, the group interview took place in a room overlooking a ramshackle sports hall that echoed with the sounds of basketballs bouncing and men running. The focus-group women told me straight away that this was a typical situation – the men always used the indoor space and the women could never get access to it. So the actual venue became a starting point for a lengthy discussion about gender relations of power in life and in sport.

The groups varied in composition – sometimes members all came from the same location, sometimes from different parts of the same country, two groups incorporated women from different countries. The groups were relatively cohesive in the sense that they were made up entirely of women, usually of similar ages, and with a common *focus* on sport. Some of them knew each other very well and were part of the same training squad, or members of the same sports committee, but in other groups there were women who had never met each other before. In relation to Chapter 6, I interviewed a group of disabled athletes at the Stoke Mandeville Games. Although they came from different parts of the country and had different social backgrounds, they were all elite competitors, focused on winning medals, with forceful opinions about the problems of being disabled athletes, and who made informed comments about the politics of disability in general. They all defined themselves as *sports*women and constructed their identities first and foremost through sport and physical *ability*, and not through disability.

In each group there was some unevenness of participation. Self-made group 'leaders' were generally more articulate and outspoken than the others, and there were participants who said very little, but nodded approval and smiled to indicate that they agreed with what was being said. I did everything I could to be sensitive to the group dynamics, to pull in everyone on at least one or two occasions, and to check that some of the quieter members had nothing more to say. I agree with Mann and Stewart, who say that:

> In any group situation, it is almost inevitable that some members will contribute more than others to a discussion. But does this matter in the specific context of focus groups? In FTF [face-to-face] focus groups, the uneven contribution of group members may have little impact upon the quality of the data obtained. Those who are vocal may bring valuable insights to the discussion of the focus group topic. (Mann and Stewart, 2000: 114)

As in individual interviews, focus-group participants talked about real-life experiences, attitudes, values, opinions, and feelings. They revealed a diversity of views with agreements and disagreements. Sensitive issues evoked emotional responses and sometimes participants revealed very personal experiences that they had clearly never talked about in front of other people before.

I found the least satisfactory way of conducting interviews was over the telephone with recording equipment attached to it. On some occasions the sound was distorted or there were transmission breaks, and because there was no possibility of eye contact or visible facial expression, it was impossible to 'set the scene' in any way other than with the use of the voice. I chose e-mail communications as my preferred way of distance interviewing, confirming what Denzin and Lincoln (2000: 10) point out, that it is possible to use written, (as well as) narrative and oral methods in order to capture the ways in which women 'live and give meanings to their lives'.

E-MAIL EXCHANGES

Computer-mediated communication (CMC) has transformed the ways in which we are able to interact with research participants and is an invaluable resource for international research. E-mail interviews supplemented the face-to-face interviews and enabled me to get additional data from women in different countries and continents, some of whom lived in remote areas that I was unable to visit, minimizing the usual constraints of time and space (Mann and Stewart, 2000: 5).

The 'electronic word' has been characterized as a stand-alone category distinct from, but sharing qualities with, the spoken *and* the written word (Mann and Stewart, 2000: 183). I certainly found that e-mail exchanges were very much like having a conversation. I gathered data by asking a few questions only at a time, or asking for comment on just one issue at a time. I started by asking for personal details about family background and sporting

status, then, over time, moved towards more sensitive questions. Participants normally typed out responses as if they were talking, and I responded in conversational style also. Problems of understanding rarely occurred, but when necessary, I clarified questions or probed participants, thus deepening understanding and detail. Because participants have more time 'to study, analyse and reflect on incoming messages', they are able 'to compose responses carefully', usually resulting in 'thoughtful, organized, detailed information' (Mann and Stewart, 2000: 182). Trust can also be built up and closeness developed between researcher and participant over the extended time between e-mail exchanges and, moreover, 'the written account can also serve to evoke emotion, tension, and irony in its interactive qualities' (Temple, 1994: 38).

In one case, I had exchanged e-mails with an Aboriginal basketball player in Australia over some months. She was busy with a young child, pregnant with her second baby, and working full-time, but she still wanted to tell me her story and although her responses were delayed, they were always articulate and comprehensive. A point was reached when I asked about her experiences of racism in mainstream sport. This is an extract from her reply: 'Oh, Jenny! How I wish I could talk to you in person. I have so much to tell you. Would you mind if I recorded my experiences of racism and sent you the tape?' Three weeks later I received a tape, together with two photographs – one in her basketball kit and the other with her daughter. The recording was graphic and emotional, providing rich and detailed data of racism experienced at the level of the personal and the institutional. Whereas for some women the anonymity in the use of technology provided a screen for the communication of sensitive issues, for my Aboriginal friend it was the extended time span that had helped her, as she put it, 'confront my demons' and speak out for the first time about her anger, hurt, and sense of powerlessness in the face of both explicit and subtle forms of racism. She would not have responded in this way in a one-off, face-to-face interview.

When a project extends over years, follow-up e-mails are useful to bring the research up-to-date, to make additional queries, further clarify issues, and for participants to make fresh comments. Women who had face-to-face interviews in the first place can also use e-mails in this way. They are a facility that can be established, lapsed, and re-established, building up a 'history' of communication, making the gathering of data a process over time. Furthermore, it is easy to keep a textual record and then to be able to cut and paste when using the data for the analysis and write-up.

Some researchers value the spontaneous qualities of speech which, they argue, are lost in written exchanges and they further claim that CMC hinders the exploration of meaning that can occur easily in face-to-face interviews (Denzin, 1999). I did not find this to be the case and, arguably, the positive aspects of talking need not be lost. The following e-mail, sent by a participant, sums up the benefits to my research of e-mail exchanges:

> Hi Jenny
> The more information I send you, the more easy it becomes to express myself. In fact I'm really enjoying it. I didn't know how good it would feel to get my feelings off my chest and I never thought I'd have so much to say! Thanks for asking me to take part in your project. I think it's really important. So here goes again!

In relation to all the types of interviewing used in this research, I suggest that woman-to-woman interaction may be the most likely to elicit personal, intimate and sensitive exchanges, and to lead to lasting friendships. All-female interaction was especially significant because most of the women spoke about patriarchal relations of power in the family and in sport contexts as the greatest problem for female sport development. There was also a

sense in which the participants in this project knew I was 'on their side', that I identified with their difficulties, and that although I was not an organic member of their groups, I understood their specific struggles.

However, there is never absolute reliability of interview data; it has to be compared with alternative findings and assessed in relation to all the evidence available. For example, it was known to me that some Muslim participants from Islamic countries took part in mixed sport when they travelled abroad to study or holiday in the west, but in interviews they were in denial about the pull between local and global cultures and about exercising in western sports gear in mixed venues. Investigating the politics of the female body and the ways in which gendered identities in sport are linked to other aspects of identity, such as disability, ethnicity, 'race' and sexuality, is intrinsically sensitive and polemical and there can be no certainty that data are always accurate.

MAKING SENSE OF THE DATA: THEORY AND ANALYSIS

Content analysis and coding of all the evidence collected from documentary material, observations and interviews showed what data there was and what themes were emerging. Another process that was ongoing throughout the project was the exploration of relationships between women's sporting experiences and particular theories and concepts (Lury, 1995: 34). Although it is clear that I embarked on the research with theoretical preferences, I tried to keep an open mind about allowing the analysis to evolve from the women's narratives about their material realities, as in standpoint epistemologies (Hill Collins, 1990; Stanley and Wise, 1993; Stanley and Wise, 1990). Second, I worked with the concern to 'historicize the cultural' (Lury, 1995: 41). I believe with Andersen et al. (1990: 106) that '[i]f we are to reconstruct theoretical accounts of society by seriously including women, we must begin to situate each individual woman's life history in its specific social and historical setting and show how women's actions and consciousness contribute to the structuring of social institutions' (Anderson et al. 1990: 106). Further, I took account of the observation that '[t]he social contexts within which different kinds of women live, work, struggle and make sense of their lives differ widely across the world and between different groupings of women' (Stanley and Wise, 1990: 22). The aim was to make sense of the ways in which women's experiences in sport are linked to specific cultural, economic, ideological, political and religious contexts. In other words, to relate private lives and personal problems to wider social structures and public issues.

Another focus for analysis was the particular constructions of difference and identity of women in sport in relation to class, culture, disability, ethnicity, nation, 'race', religion and sexual orientation, taking account of the particular, as opposed to the general, relations of power, and the dialectical relation between agency and constraint. I was influenced by Avtar Brah's answer to her own question, 'How may "difference" be conceptualized?', when she says:

> At the most general level 'difference' may be construed as a social relation constructed within systems of power underlying structures of class, racism, gender and sexuality. At this level of abstraction we are concerned with the ways in which our social position is circumscribed by the broad parameters set by the social structures of a given society. ... Difference may also be conceptualized as experiential diversity. Here the focus is on the many and different manifestations of ideological and institutional practices in our everyday life. (Brah, 1991: 171)

Brah is pointing here to the way in which difference is constructed at different levels, at the level of the subject (personal) and at the level of ideology, institutions and politics. I wanted to explore this definition of difference in all its complexities in relation to the experiences of the participants (Hill Collins, 1990; hooks, 1990; Olesen, 2000). To focus on differences in terms of experience alone 'encourages benign description which concentrates largely on distinctions in lifestyle, cultural practices etc.' In contrast, the analysis for this project incorporated 'detailed structural explorations of how specific forms of oppression are legitimated and maintained' and interrelationhips between different categories of difference (Maynard, 1994: 24).

In summary, my analytical approach followed a feminist cultural studies perspective, linking empirical material to theoretical ideas, history to sociology, and private to public, treating women as distinctly heterogeneous and focusing on the importance of the politics of difference and identity.

POSITIONING THE RESEARCHER: ETHICAL COMMENTS

I share common beliefs with other feminists that 'the researcher's "personal" is absolutely central to the research process' (Stanley and Wise, 1983: 200), and that 'the personality and biases of the researcher clearly enter into the process to affect the outcome' (Anderson et al., 1990: 102). Knowledge about and understanding of the pervasive influence of gender divisions in social life is a defining characteristic of feminist research in general (Maynard, 1994: 15) and, in relation to this project, knowledge about gender relations of power in sport in the west, together with my growing interest in the politics of gender in different countries across the world, were crucial in the conceptualization of the project in the first place. It is also clear that connections with different people involved in the politics of difference and identity in sport were fundamental to the way in which the research was carried out and the findings theorized. Further, working within the interactionist tradition, centralizing women's experiences, being sensitive to the confusions, contradictions and ambivalences thrown up by the data that points to them being intrinsic to experience and identity was a personal, preferred approach to making sense of the world of women's sports. Du Bois makes the point that:

> Social scientists are certainly no more able than others to pursue inquiry free of the assumptions and values of their own societies. In fact, the closer our subject matter to our own life and experience, the more we can probably expect our own beliefs about the world to enter into and shape our work – to influence the very questions we pose, our conception of how to approach these questions, and the interpretations we generate from our findings. (Du Bois, 1983: 105)

But a more fundamental question is whether a white, western, heterosexual, able-bodied woman who is not an organic member of any of the groups being studied should have done the research in the first place. There are different possible responses to feminist criticisms regarding the homogenization of women. One response is to revert to cultural relativism, remaining silent about 'Others' who are 'separate', 'different', or 'marginalized', thus leaving traditional hegemonies intact (Ahmed, 2000: 166–7). The other response, articulated by hooks (1984: 6), and which I share, is for privileged people to make alliances with the disadvantaged and to accept responsibility for fighting oppressions that may not directly affect them as individuals. Referring specifically to South Africa, Flax (1992: 460) urges feminists 'to learn to make claims on our own and others' behalf and to listen to those which differ from ours', and Spivak (1987, 1993) challenges those white feminists who

she claims support universalism by refusing on ethical grounds to speak out on behalf of those who are less privileged.

The participants frequently believed that I had power to help their cause. 'We don't get invited to important conferences to tell our stories', they said, 'so you will have to do it for us'. But although I have recorded their histories and spoken out on their behalf whenever possible, I do not wield decision-making power and they still lack power. Nevertheless, I have avoided the 'widespread engagement with postmodernism and (the) concomitant disengagement with social and material analyses of power' (Aitchison, 2000: 127) with the express intention of aligning with emancipatory politics (Klein, 1983: 90).

Another ethical comment relates to what Stacey identifies as 'the dissonance between fieldwork practice and ethnographic product' in that:

> ethnographic method appears to (and often does) place the researcher and her informants in a collaborative, reciprocal quest for understanding, but the research product is ultimately that of the researcher, however modified or influenced by informants. With very rare exceptions it is the researcher who narrates, who 'authors' the ethnography. In the last instance an ethnography is a written document structured primarily by a researcher's purposes, offering a researcher's interpretations, registered in a researcher's voice. (Stacey, 1988: 23)

This is true of *Heroines of Sport* (Hargreaves, 2000). Although I tried to give the participants an authentic voice, to make the book as far as possible 'their story', the orientation and analysis are mine. Incompleteness is also a characteristic of all biographies because the researcher can never know all there is to know. In relation to this project, a selection of data was made from the huge amount collected, resulting in an inherently partial account. For example, although I remember reading somewhere that the Australian track and field star, Cathy Freeman (the first-ever Aboriginal Olympic gold medallist) was raised in a Bahá'í family, I omitted this part of her biography from my account. The invisibility of Freeman's Bahá'í identity in Chapter 4 is defined by van den Hoonaard (2004) as biographical zoning which refers to the process whereby an author privileges particular biographical information at the expense of other biographical data.

CONCLUSION

At the level of methodological assumptions, Kelly-Gadol (1987: 15–16) sees 'traditional history most deeply challenged by the task of explaining and understanding a world that must now be perceived to include women as fully historical persons' and that 'women's history has revitalized theory' by recognizing 'the relation between the sexes as a social and not a natural one.' It is hoped that *Heroines of Sport* represents something of a challenge to the hegemony of male sport history. This project has also striven to address the critiques of Black and Third World feminists about the universalizing of women from the perspective of white, privileged academics.

The process of carrying out the research for *Heroines of Sport*, communicating with women who face struggles and discrimination in their lives on a daily basis, was a very humbling experience. It illustrates convincingly that the existing, very limited history of women's sport is partial and biased and that young researchers should be urged to investigate further the sporting lives of women that we still know so little about. The task of re-writing women's sports history is an urgent one because already much of the rich oral source for women's sport has disappeared.

NOTE

1 The Research Assessment Exercise (RAE) is a government-inspired investigation carried out every few years. It is intended to assess the quality of research in universities and colleges in the UK in order for the higher education funding bodies to distribute public funds for research selectively on the basis of quality. Those institutions judged to have conducted the highest quality research receive a larger proportion of the available grant so that the infrastructure for the top level of research in the UK is protected and developed. Along with three other publications, *Heroines of Sport* was submitted by the university I was working at for the 2001 RAE.

BIBLIOGRAPHY

Ahmed, S. (2000), 'Strange Encounters: Embodied Others in Post-Coloniality', in M. McNeil, L. Pearce and B. Skeggs (eds), *Transformations: Thinking Through Feminism*, London: Routledge: pp. 161–81.

Aitchison, C. (2000), 'Poststructural Feminist Theories of Representing Others: a Response to the "Crisis" in Leisure Studies' Discourse', in *Leisure Studies*, 19: 127–44.

Alasuutari, P. (1995), *Researching Culture: Qualitative Method and Cultural Studies*, London: Sage Publications.

Anderson, K., Armitage, S., Jack, D. and Wittner, J. (1990), 'Beginning Where We Are: Feminist Methodology in Oral History', in J.M. Nielsen, (ed), *Feminist Research Method: Exemplar Readings in the Social Sciences*, Boulder, San Francisco: Westview Press: pp. 94–113.

Bertaux, D. (ed) (1981), *Biography and Society*, Beverley Hills, CA: Sage.

Birrell, S. (1989), 'Racial Relations Theories and Sport: Suggestions for a More Critical Analysis', *Sociology of Sport*, 6: 212–17.

Birrell, S. (1990), 'Women of Color, Critical Autobiography and Sport', in M. Messner and D. Sabo (eds), *Sport, Men, and the Gender Order*, Champaign, Il: Human Kinetics: pp.185–200.

Bruce, T. (2001), 'Second Sight: Experiencing Life Through the Eyes of Women Sports Writers', in C. Hallinan and J. Hughson (eds), *Sporting Tales: Ethnographic Fieldwork Experiences*, Australian

Society for Sports History No 12: Sydney NSW: Kwik Copy Printing Centre: pp. 31–44.

Bryman, A. and Burgess, R.G. (eds) (1999) *Qualitative Research,* London: Sage.

Cassidy, B., Lord, R. and Mandell, N. (1995), 'Silenced and Forgotten Women: Race, Poverty, and Disability', in N. Mandell (ed.), *Feminist Issues,* Ontario: Prentice Hall: pp. 32–66.

Clifford, J. (1986), 'Introduction: Partial Truths', in J. Clifford and G.E. Marcus (eds), *Writing Culture,* Berkeley, CA: University of California Press: pp. 1–26.

Cook, S.A. and Fonow, M.M. (1990), 'Knowledge and Women's Interests: Issues of Epistemology and Methodology in Feminist Sociological Research', in J.M. Nielsen (ed.), *Feminist Research Methods: Exemplar Readings in the Social Sciences,* Boulder, San Francisco: Westview Press: pp. 69–93.

Denzin, N. (1989), *Interpretive Interactionism,* Newbury Park, CA: Sage Publications.

Denzin, N. (1999), 'Cybertalk and the method of instances', in S. Jones (ed.), *Doing Internet Research,* Thousand Oaks, CA and London: Sage.

Denzin, N. and Lincoln, Y. (eds) (2nd edition) (2000) *Handbook of Qualitative Research,* London: Sage.

Du Bois, B. (1983), 'Passionate Scholarship: Notes on Values, Knowing and Method in Feminist Social Science', in G. Bowles and R.D. Klein (eds), *Theories of Women's Studies,* London: Routledge and Kegan Paul: pp. 105–16.

Flax, J. (1992), 'Feminists Theorize the Political', in J. Butler and J. Scott (eds), *Feminists Theorize the Political,* London: Routledge: pp. 450–68.

Glowczewski, B. (1998), '"All One but Different": Aboriginality: National Identity versus Local Diversification in Australia', in J. Wassmann (ed.), *Pacific Answers to Western Hegemony,* Oxford/New York: Berg: pp. 335–54.

Gratton, C. and Jones, I. (2004), *Research Methods for Sport Studies,* London and New York: Routledge.

Hall, M.A. (1996), *Feminism and Sporting Bodies: Essays on Theory and Practice,* Champaign, Il: Human Kinetics.

Hammersley, M. and Atkinson, P. (1995), *Ethnography: Principles in Practice,* New York: Routledge.

Harding, S. (1987), *Feminism and Methodology,* Bloomington: Indiana University Press.

Harding, S. (1987), 'Is there a Feminist Method?', in S. Harding (ed.), *Feminism and Methodology,* Bloomington: Indiana University Press: pp. 1–14.

Hargreaves, J.A. (ed.) (1982), *Sport, Culture and Ideology,* London: Routledge and Kegan Paul.

Hargreaves, J.A. (1992), *Sporting Females: Issues in the History and Sociology of Women's Sports,* London: Routledge.

Hargreaves, J.A. (1992), 'Sex, Gender and the Body in Sport and Leisure: Has There Been a Civilizing Process?', in E. Dunning and C. Rojek (eds), *Sport and Leisure in the Civilizing Process: Critique and Counter Critique',* London: Macmillan: pp. 161–82.

Hargreaves, J.A. (1993), 'Bodies Matter! Images of Sport and Female Sexualization', in C. Brackenridge (ed.), *Body Matters,* Leisure Studies Association Publication No. 47: 60–66.

Hargreaves, J.A. (2000), *Heroines of Sport: The Politics of Difference and Identity,* London: Routledge.

Hargreaves, J.A. (2004), 'Querying Sport Feminisms: Personal or Political?', in R. Giulianotti (ed.), *Sport and Modern Social Theorists,* London: Palgrave: pp. 187–206.

Hill Collins, P. (1990), *Black Feminist Thought: Knowledge, Consciousness and the Politics of Empowerment,* Boston: Unwin Hyman.

hooks, b. (1984), *Feminist Theory: From Margin to Center,* Boston: South End.

hooks, b. (1990), 'The Politics of Radical Black Subjectivity', in b. hooks *Yearning: Race, Gender and Cultural Politics,* Boston: South End: pp. 15–22.

Jayaratne, T.E. and A.J. Stewart (1991), 'Quantitative and Qualitative Methods in the Social Sciences: Current Feminist Issues and Practical Strategies', in M.M. Fonow and J.A. Cook (eds), *Beyond Methodology: Feminist Scholarship as Lived Research,* Bloomington, Indiana: Indiana University Press: pp. 85–105.

Jones, S. (1988), *Sport, Politics and the Working Class,* Manchester: Manchester University Press.

Kelly-Gadol, J. (1987), 'The Social Relation of the Sexes: Methodological Implications of Women's History', in S. Harding (ed.), *Feminism and Methodology,* Bloomington, Indiana: Indiana University Press: pp. 15–28.

Klein, R.D. (1983), 'How To Do What We Want To Do: Thoughts about Feminist Methodology', in G. Bowles and R.D. Klein, *Theories of Women's*

Studies, London: Routledge and Kegan Paul: pp. 88–104.

Lury, C. (1995), 'The Rights and Wrongs of Culture: Issues of Theory and Methodology', in B. Skeggs (ed.), *Feminist Cultural Theory*, Manchester: Manchester University Press: pp. 33–45.

Mann, C. and Stewart, F. (2000), *Internet Communication and Qualitative Research*, London: Sage Publications.

May, T. (2001), *Social Research: Issues, Methods and Process*, (3rd edn), Buckingham: Open University Press.

May, T. (ed.) (2002), *Qualitative Research in Action*, London: Sage.

Maykut, P. and Morehouse, R. (1994), *Beginning Qualitative Research: A Philosophical and Practical Guide*, London: Falmer Press.

Maynard, M. (1994), 'Methods, Practice, and Epistemology: The Debate About Feminism and Research', in M. Maynard and J. Purvis (eds), *Researching Women's Lives from a Feminist Perspective*, London: Taylor and Francis: pp. 10–26.

Meis, M. (1991), 'Women's Research or Feminist Research? The Debate Surrounding Feminist Science and Methodology', in M.M. Fenow and J.A. Cook (eds), *Beyond Methodology: Feminist Scholarship as Lived Research*, Bloomington, Indiana: Indiana University Press: pp. 60–84.

Mohanty, C. (1991), 'Cartographies of Struggle: Third World Women and the Politics of Feminism', in C. Mohanty, A. Russo and L. Torres (eds), *Third World Women and the Politics of Feminism*, Bloomington: Indiana University Press: pp. 1–47.

Mohanty, C. (1995), 'Under Western Eyes: Feminist Scholarship and Colonial Discourses', in B. Ashcroft G. Griffiths and H. Tiffin (eds), *The Post-Colonial Studies Reader*, London: Routledge: pp. 259–63.

Oakley, A. (1981), 'Interviewing Women: A Contradiction in Terms', in H. Roberts *Doing Feminist Research*, New York and London: pp. 30–61.

Oakley, A. (1998), 'Gender, Methodology and People's Ways of Knowing: Some Problems with Feminism and the Paradigm Debate in Social Science', in *Sociology*, 32(4) 707–31.

Olesen, V. (2000), 'Feminisms and Qualitative Research At and Into the Millenium', in N.K. Denzin and Y.S. Lincoln (eds), (2nd ed), *Handbook of Qualitative Research*, London: Sage Publications: pp. 215–53.

Ritchie, J. and Lewis, J. (eds) (2003), *Qualitative Research Practice: A Guide for Social Science Students and Researchers*, London; Thousand Oaks, CA: Sage Publications.

Rowbotham, S. (1973), *Hidden From History: 300 Years of Women's Oppression and the Fight Against It*, London: Pluto Press.

SACOS (1988), *SACOSSPORT Festival '88*, Cape Town: Bachu Books.

Said, E. (1993), *Culture and Imperialism*, London: Chato and Windus.

Seidler, V. (1994), *Recovering the Self*, London: Routledge.

Scraton, S and Flintoff, A. (1992), 'Feminist Research and Physical Education', in A. Sparkes (ed.), *Research in Physical Education and Sport: Exploring Alternative Visions*, London: The Falmer Press: pp. 167–87.

Smith, D. (1987), *The Everyday World as Problematic: a Feminist Sociology*, Boston, Mass: Milton Keynes: Open University Press.

Smith, Y. (1992) 'Women of Color in Society and Sport', *Quest*, 44: 228–50.

Sparkes, A. (ed.) (1992), *Research in Physical Education and Sport: Exploring Alternative Visions*, London: Falmer.

Sparkes, A. (1994), 'Writing people: Reflections on the Dual Crisis of Representation and Legitimation in Qualitative Inquiry', in *Quest*, 47: 158–95.

Sparkes, A. and S. Squires (1996), 'Circles of Silence: Sexual Identity in Physical Education and Sport', in *Sport, Education and Society*, I, 77–101.

Spivak, G.C. (1987), *In Other Worlds: Essays in Cultural Politics*, London: Routledge.

Spivak, G.C. (1993), *Outside in the Teaching Machine*, London: Routledge.

Stacey, J. (1988), 'Can there be a Feminist Ethnography?', *Women's Studies International Forum*, 11(1): 21–27.

Stanley, L. and Wise, S. (1983), ' "Back into the Personal": or Our Attempt to Construct "Feminist Research" ', in G. Bowles and R.D. Klein (eds), *Theories of Women's Studies*, London: Routledge and Kegan Paul: pp. 192–209.

Stanley, L. and Wise, S. (1990), 'Method, Methodology and Epistemology in Feminist research Processes', in L. Stanley and S. Wise (eds), *Feminist Praxis, Research, Theory and*

Epistemology in Feminist Sociology', London: Routledge: pp. 20–60.

Stanley, L. and Wise, S. (1993), *Breaking Out Again: Feminist Ontology and Epistemology,* New York: Routledge.

Stevenson, D. (2002), 'Women, Sport, and Globalisation: Competing Discourses of Sexuality and Nation', *Journal of Sport and Social Issues,* 26(2): 209–25.

Temple, B. (1994), 'The message and the medium: Oraland Written Accounts of Lives', in *Auto/ Biography,* 3:1: British Sociological Association Study Groups Publication.

Thomas, J.R. and Nelson, J.K. (1996) *Research Methods in Physical Activity,* (3rd edn) Champaign, Illinois: Human Kinetics.

Tonkinson, R. (1998), 'National Identity: Australia After Mabo', in J. Wassmann (ed.), *Pacific Answers to Western Hegemony,* Oxford/New York: Berg: pp. 287–310.

van den Hoonaard, W. (2004) 'Biographical Zoning and Baha'i Biographical Writing: The Case of Rose Henderson' in *Baha'i Studies Review.*

Yin, R. (1984), *Case Study Research: Design and Methods,* London: Sage.

Young, I. (1990), 'Throwing Like a Girl: A Pheno-menology of Feminine Body Comportment, Motility and Spatiality', in I.M. Young, *Throwing Like a Girl and Other Essays in Feminist Philosophy and Social Theory,* Indianapolis: Indiana University Press: pp. 141–59.

Part 8

Fieldwork in Organizations

17

Fieldwork and Policework

NIGEL FIELDING

Over half of complaints against the police concern aggressive behaviour: some 18% assault, and 11% oppressive conduct (Maguire and Corbett, 1991).

> I hate violence, I'm a pacificist. There's no place for violence but if it's offered you, well, you'd better be good at it. But explanation is the biggest part. In there [charge room] or outside. I find that if you take them through what you have to do and why, then 90% of them are as good as gold. (interview, woman police sergeant)

14.00–14.15. Canteen.
All settling with tea when a 'shout' (officer-in-distress call) comes through; the ripple of officers responding works its way down the canteen in 20 seconds.

14.15–14.35. Officer in distress.
Dave is having trouble with his gear and is last away. Everyone hurtles down the two flights of stairs two at a time. ... The call was from _____ Park, east entrance. On arrival the area car is up on the grass 100 yards inside the entrance; officers are running to it. As Dave and I get out, the van cruises past us. ... The area car driver has hold of one arm of a violently struggling male black youth in black leather jacket and jeans, his other arm held by a young blond female. She is wearing a bomber jacket and slacks, and inside the jacket hangs a police radio, squawking. They wheel the youth around and the van operator joins them, steering the now physically subdued but shouting youth into the back of the van. The doors bang shut behind him and three of the officers – the area car driver, van operator and another officer. 'I think they're helping him to his seat', an officer remarks as howls and banging emanate from the van. The van is rocking on its springs. But around its front,

all is tranquil, as officers discuss the turnout. Dave chats with the blond. 'All it was was a stop, but now it's an assault'. The youth gave lip when she stopped him to search for car-breaking tools, then she sensed him getting seriously aggressive and issued the shout. ... Our talk is interrupted by another priority call ...

14.35–14.45 Sensitive address alarm.
... the area car driver approached, sucking the blood off a bad cut on his thumb. 'I'm injured', he joked, 'but justice has been done', confirming the retribution received by the youth in the van.

Qualitative research seeks to balance documentation of action in natural settings with insight into its meaning to those involved. The idea of 'appreciation' central to the 'naturalistic' approach, which emphasizes seeing things from the perspective of those studied before stepping back to make a more detached assessment, holds that an adequate knowledge of social behaviour requires understanding of the 'symbolic world' in which people live, the meanings developed through patterns of behaviour which are in some way distinctive. The authority of fieldwork-based inquiry stems from depth of exposure to the subject of study, the ability to directly capture the 'reality' of action in the setting, and the multidimensionality of analysis that fieldwork's mix of methods can support. But fieldwork's *authority* stands in tension with its *range*. Since analysis requires comparison between settings in which similar activities occur, field research is usually not confined to a single setting, but samples remain small. Fieldwork can expose knowledge that is both unexpected and telling, but we are often left asking (or being asked) if what we have seen is 'typical'. We may feel that a dramatic incident of the sort above 'says it all' about some aspect of policing in a way other methods do not, but our audiences will usually want to know if it is 'generalizable'.

QUIS CUSTODIES CUSTODIET:
FIELDWORK IN POLICE RESEARCH

Police research is big business for researchers of every methodological stripe. However, even in large-sample research designs, field observation and interviewing have been prominent among the methods used (e.g., Black and Reiss, 1967; Sampson and Raudenbush, 1999). Fieldwork enjoys its position because of the way it addresses the questions that animate inquiry into policing. Crime and criminal justice consistently register towards the top of the public's concerns. In matters of high importance and, particularly, where society suspects things are going wrong, field methods bring us right up close to the action.

On both sides of the Atlantic, the opening of the police organization to research was prompted by public concern over policing scandals. In Britain, the 1962 Royal Commission followed such public concern and, shortly afterward, the first empirical study of British policing was published (Banton, 1964). It employed detailed observation. Banton (1964), along with Westley

(1970) in the United States, effectively established the field of police research, and both based their analyses on fieldwork. Concern with biased police discretion culminated in Reiss and Black's large-scale observational study for the 1967 Presidential Commission on Law Enforcement (Black and Reiss, 1967; Reiss, 1971). While Banton applied observational method to the police, Black and Reiss introduced observation of the context of police/public interaction.

Field observation played an important part in one of the most sustained programmes of research into policing, evaluating Chicago's Alternative Policing Strategy (CAPS). Observation was compared to survey response, supporting assessment of how well CAPS was working in each beat (Chicago Community Policing Evaluation Consortium 1997). In Britain, fieldwork has been used by organizations like the Policy Studies Institute (Smith, 1983), the Police Foundation (Irving, 1989), and the Home Office (e.g., research into stop-and-search practices following the Macpherson Report on police/ethnic minority relations). Individual forces have employed fieldwork to evaluate innovations such as the joint investigation of child sexual abuse cases (Fielding et al., 1990). Thus, fieldwork, and particularly observation, has a long and legitimate lineage in research on policing, and methodological innovations in fieldwork techniques, such as Systematic Social Observation (Sampson and Raudenbush, 1999), were developed specifically for police research.

One task of research is to think the unthinkable, or at least the uncomfortable. Fieldwork is a research tradition that has often debunked, demystified and destabilized the conventional wisdom. For example, it has counteracted police claims that their working lives are a continuous frenzy of crime-busting, and has revealed the reality behind forces' assurances of equal treatment for all. For Reiner (1989: 4), police research 'opens up rather than forecloses the analytic problems of what in particular social contexts the function, impact and legitimacy of the police might be'. Fieldwork underpins police research because its methods are sensitive to the situated practice of policing ('particular social contexts'), can detect the latent or counter-intuitive effects of policing ('function', 'impact'), and makes it apparent that consent to policing is actively negotiated ('legitimacy'). Much police research is responsive to police or government concerns. This does not mean such policy-relevant research has not been 'critical', exposing problems and pursuing concerns expressed by the wider public. Weatheritt (1989: 42) observes that 'the purpose of research may often be to uncover impediments to action and to demonstrate how shaky are the assumptions on which action is based'. In the academic domain, fieldwork has provided the major empirical input for the conceptualization of formal social control.

When we place police research against its several audiences, we see three principal roles for research on policing: informing and *evaluating policy*; monitoring and *civil accountability*; and *conceptual knowledge*. In their way, each is a 'critical' function. It is not that policing is an institution that has somehow 'gone wrong'. The need for critical oversight is inherent in the nature of the police institution. As Manning observes (1999: 117), its requirement to take immediate remedial action 'enables the police to do their work, but the expectation's generality and urgency lay the foundation for ambiguous interpretations of the law that can lead the police to overstep the boundaries of their legitimate authority'.

WHY FIELDWORK?

Fieldwork has different resonances when applied to the three roles of police research. In *policy-oriented* research, fieldwork is directed to policy development and evaluation, for example, the balance between crime control and other police services. Policymakers of the 1990s imposed a mechanistic 'stopwatch' approach, setting priorities centrally without reference to local conditions or public perception, and evaluating this work by numerical targets. The fact that measuring how long it takes for the front desk to answer the phone has limited influence on public satisfaction became apparent in fieldwork-based findings from FitzGerald and Hough (2002: 1), who report that:

> the failure of the [Metropolitan Police] to be more responsive to local need, and the fall in staff morale, can both be traced ... to performance management regimes that emphasise quantified performance targets and as a result ignore the complexities of police work. ... The current emphasis on quantitative measures is distorting performance and reducing the quality of service.

A theme of police fieldwork is that 'the ranks' can so translate policies into practice that they lose their original character, sometimes producing the opposite of what was intended. In a street robbery initiative, managers intended that officers should undertake surveillance from vehicles until suspects were caught in the act (Holdaway, 1994). Officers' customary practice, much resented by ethnic minorities, was to randomly stop and search on 'fishing expeditions' for evidence. Holdaway found that the new vehicles were simply used as convenient locations to interrogate minority people. Chatterton and Rogers' fieldwork on computer-based crime pattern analysis showed how 'the lower ranks began to distinguish between uses of the computer which protected or furthered their interests and those they were suspicious of' (Chatterton and Rogers, 1989: 77).

While all occupations develop ways of 'normalizing' deviance, and afford members means to rationalize mistakes, the police are uniquely related to the sacred legal institutions of the state, consequently facing demands for high standards, and their frontline work is uniquely non-accountable, largely free of effective supervision and only knowable via records created by frontline workers themselves, enabling a police deviance which is 'largely invisible, concealed and difficult to study' (Manning, 1999: 119). Fieldwork has shown that occupational deviance is a feature of criminal investigation (Hobbs, 1988, 1995) and has exposed the negotiated nature of detective work in serious fraud (Levi, 1981, 1998). Field research played a major role in reforming interrogation practice to counter duress, false confessions and oppressive tactics: Irving's field study (1980) influenced the Royal Commission on Criminal Procedure, whose outcomes included the Police and Criminal Evidence Act 1984 and the Crown Prosecution Service. Observational research on interrogating the mentally ill and vulnerable (Gudjonssen and MacKeith, 1982; Tully and Cahill, 1984) and investigating child abuse cases (Fielding and Conroy, 1992) influenced the Royal Commission on Criminal Justice.

Fieldwork has a 'safeguard' function for *civil accountability*, being used by the media and by police to gauge acceptance of policies. In Waddington's (1994) assessment, police acceptance of research on public order reflects their confidence in how they maintain the 'boundaries of freedom of protest'. His observations of sensitive public order policing revealed how police 'incorporate' organizers of demonstrations and protests. Punch's field studies reveal the moral rhetoric police use to justify adopting illegal means to 'beat the criminal' and reconcile contradictory demands (e.g., Punch, 1997).

Field research can be a deterrent to abuses of power but can also reveal the more subtle, tangled relations that grow up in divided communities such as South Africa (Dyzenhaus, 1998) and Northern Ireland (Weitzer, 1993). Brewer's (1991) field research reported the skills Belfast folk developed in appearing to abuse officers (for the benefit of paramilitary onlookers) while actually seeking their assistance, and the obstinate attempts to do 'routine beatwork' when 'community bobbies' had to be accompanied by rifle-carrying soldiers and even helicopters. Weitzer's fieldwork (1995) reported police/public attitudes which contradict a divided society model that would 'paint communal divisions in black and white', including substantial Catholic support for the then-RUC (Royal Ulster Constabulary).

Fieldwork is the major source of our *conceptual understanding* of policing. An instance is the tradition of research into police occupational culture, nearly all of it fieldwork-based. Work on occupational culture shows much variety, from research on machismo in police culture (Fielding, 1994) to work on homosexual police (Burke, 1993). While early conceptualization was interactionist (Holdaway, 1989), the concept was adopted by Marxists (Jefferson, 1990), dramaturgical analysts (Manning, 1977, 2001), and feminists (Brown, 1997). These are not purely analytic interests. Occupational culture has been referred to in legal cases brought against forces by minority officers, and managers have blamed problems on 'canteen culture'. That work on culture is no mere academic parlour-game is apparent in Chan's study (1997) of the New South Wales police, who drew on analysis of local police culture to combat longstanding brutalized relations with ethnic minorities. Occupational culture is plainly a useful and multiplex heuristic.

Some depictions of police culture are overdrawn for effect, implying a monolithic culture whereas there are many cultures. Much work on police culture was prompted by a transatlantic interest in police decision-making, a context in which consistencies of occupational culture have been used to 'read off' likely police action. Discordant themes in culture are as important as unifying themes. Culture is a resource upon which officers actively draw to negotiate their way through the occupation (Fielding, 1989). Individuals' mediation of culture, experience, and the particularities of the station and working group, are too little acknowledged. A useful heuristic should not become a stereotype.

While I hope to have demonstrated the manifold importance of police fieldwork, there are limits on any method. A principal limit of fieldwork is generalizability. I will return to this, but now we need to turn from the question of 'Why fieldwork?' to how we do police fieldwork.

'JUST BE CAREFUL OUT THERE': THE NATURE OF ACCESS IN POLICE FIELDWORK

> [T]he research role (and the ethnographic one in particular) carries with it a social stigma that can potentially discredit the person who embodies the role. From this perspective much of an ethnographer's behaviour in the field can be understood as an attempt to manage this stigma. (van Maanen, 1981: 472)

Van Maanen's remark arose from musing on trust in police fieldwork. While the police often claim to be 'over-researched', it is generally as a result of internal surveys and most are unlikely to have directly encountered a fieldworker before, so our presence will usually be conditional rather than simply taken on trust. The police is a large organization whose complexity has been augmented by

moves towards 'modern management'. Its quasi-military hierarchy is now cross-cut by bolted-on special sections and large numbers of civilian employees. This organizational complexity amplifies a characteristic of fieldwork, that access is not negotiated once-and-for-all but continually.

Van Maanen captures this unpredictability, remarking that:

> in the abstract, relations in the field are such that the researcher is provided with trusted information of the sort necessary to both understand and empathize with the observed, but the researcher's presence itself creates little change or disturbance … [C]oncretely, however, such relations wax and wane over the course of a study, approach or exceed the upper and lower limits with different individuals … and vary according to the practical situation. (van Maanen, 1982: 138)

Thus, initial access negotiations, likely to be with a relatively senior officer, may lay down ground rules for the fieldwork but these have a symbolic as much as a practical function. Their function is to satisfy both sides that trust is possible, but we cannot expect that fieldwork will proceed precisely as suggested by the terms of access nor that the granting of access at senior level will secure access at all others. There is a difference between access and cooperation. Further, those who indicate a general willingness to cooperate are not offering a blanket receptiveness.

Every organization and working group has offstage practices it wishes to conceal. But as Dalton (1954) recognized, resistance to research carries messages about organizations and their members. Evasion, obstruction, truncated accounts and other troubles can reveal analytically significant facets of the culture being researched. This is a far cry from faith in 'trust' as guarantor of access to the gospel truths of policing, but the post-Watergate era has questioned such icons of American naturalism (Douglas, 1976). Trust has to be earned – by both parties. The point is that real access is more than a preliminary negotiation. One can enhance the likelihood of cooperation by respecting refusals (albeit filing them for analysis), and by displaying a measured independence from the superior officers who have granted access (van Maanen, 1981: 475).

One reality of police fieldwork is that access-givers (and those subject to field-work) worry that fieldwork may uncover the dirt. Despite being charged with upholding the law, the police have their own white lies and dark secrets. The key thing is being able to distinguish the professional foul from the unforgivable sin. It is common when negoti-ating access to enact what we might call 'threshold agreements' on witnessed mal-practice, in which both parties specify the level of malpractice above which fieldwork-ers should report what they have seen not as research data but with a view to disciplinary action.

The incident at the beginning of this chapter occurred during fieldwork bound by such an agreement. It has plainly been used as data. I should explain why. While I wit-nessed what was clearly the beating of a citizen by police, with the van's doors shut during the beating, I could not say who had administered the blows or whether the area car driver's injury was from self-defence or assault. Legally, then, there would have been little prospect that my testimony would have enabled disciplinary action. On the basis solely of the law 'in the books', I witnessed a possible crime and should have reported it, just as should any other bystander. But the relevant 'law' was the evidential standard required for disciplinary charges and on that basis there was no point in proceeding. Practically, of course, if I had acted on the agreement, cooperation by the patrol offi-cers who were the subject of the research would have been withdrawn and the field-work would have ceased. Intellectually, I

could understand the circumstances of the beating. The officer who was assaulted was undercover attempting to identify car-breakers operating in the area. When she identified herself as a police officer and asked to search the suspect, he had assaulted her. A 'shout' from an unarmed female con-stable inevitably elicits an all-out response. If the administration of 'street justice' was not justifiable, it was at least understandable.

While threshold agreements are impor-tant, like any formal rule they must be inter-preted with discretion. Analogous to the application of professional codes of research ethics, their interpretation must reflect the contingencies and particularities of the situ-ation to which they are applied (Duster et al., 1979). A reasoned judgement about what it is right to do when presented with a test of the threshold agreement requires that we balance the several consequences of a decision to invoke the agreement, although the essential starting point is the *effective* legal position.

DATA: YOUR FLEXIBLE FRIEND

In fieldwork we expect much from members of the setting but have little to contribute. In a world governed by exchange relationships, fieldworkers have few gifts to bring; van Maanen (1981: 475) observes that we can sel-dom offer cures to police problems, useful knowledge, or help with careers. The 'let's make this as painless as possible' tack helps, agreeing arrangements that suit participants regardless of convenience to oneself, keeping interviews short or, better, working questions into periods of observation so interviews are unnecessary, and adopting a maximally agreeable demeanour. Always laugh at their jokes. Police culture is replete with 'frat house'-type pranks (standardly a trip to the morgue, on which there are numerous variations). Though you may sense it is a wind-up, have had it done to you before and even designed superior versions of your own, if you sense you are about to be the butt of one of these, take it for the compliment it is and play along. Remember that pranks are normally tests for novice members of the culture: if you are the butt, it is the best possible signal about how members are seeking to place you. Likewise, if the chief pulls a bottle of scotch out of the filing cabinet first thing in the morning, share the offered drink.

Listen keenly to every story, no matter how redundant or irrelevant, and express your appreciation with gusto. Accept social invites. At the social event, be aware that what is said may not be said in innocence. Never censure, and do not gossip unless certain of your ground. Like many organizations except universities, organizational underlife is lubricated by racist, sexist, and nationalist 'humour'. If you are troubled by this and know you will be unable to resist 'taking a stand', re-consider fieldwork. Nowadays most such humour is preceded by 'I'm not a racist but ...' statements. I take these as sincere. A friend's brother is a police officer in a large US city. He is of upper middle-class origin, politically liberal and highly educated. He was working a permanent 'midnight' shift when I accompanied him on patrol in a gay red-light district. The description he gave of a man who lurched towards our car was among the most creatively abusive I have ever heard. When he rolled the window down I have seldom heard a citizen so graciously treated. It is important to remember that 'abuse' is often used to blow off steam (on the occasion mentioned, my friend's brother had just been chewed out by his lesbian Sergeant). Sometimes other members of the setting will challenge prejudiced 'humour'. When this happens it permits one to take sides. There is a difference between '-ist humour' and real bigotry. Know it. The latter may call for action under the threshold agreement.

Relationship-building is aided by shared personal and practical concerns. Sport is the lingua franca of male police culture (and many females follow suit). Even fieldworkers largely indifferent to sport may vaguely follow one, in which case this should be played up. No matter how obscure it is, you are likely to find someone who is also interested, and you may gain credibility as an expert on it instead of the ubiquitous football. At higher echelons scan offices for pendants or trophy-like objects. These usually relate to football (but sometimes golf, tennis or even cricket) and a strategically placed reference to one's admiration for the game can crack the ice. Other bonding topics include celebrity gossip, cars, TV, holidays and politics. While politics is for the truly desperate, there is usually a little mileage in denouncing the Home Secretary.

Van Maanen is not entirely right that there is little we can do of practical use for participants. Most academics have better knowledge of IT than most police. In our research on community policing, familiarity with word processors was a useful quid pro quo. We facilitated the preparation of crime reports and other documents, and where these related to incidents we had observed it had the additional benefit that we could see what the officers were reporting. This strategy should not be tried until members are comfortable with the fieldworker's presence, and should not be discussed outside the working group. Other favours depend on one's skills; in the same study one of us with profound counselling skills offered emotional support to constables with personal troubles. We all functioned as another pair of hands on patrol, fetching and carrying at incidents, map-reading and the like, and sometimes intervening more directly (usually by offering an opinion during the incident or reporting something we had picked up that officers had missed, but occasionally physically, as where I – purely instinctively – helped restrain an individual who was attempting to lasso the officer and I with a still-plugged-in electric fire).

In short, the police fieldworker wishes 'to be seen as comparable to others, not unique; as supportive of (the) police contact's worldly concerns, not threatening; as a regular participant in the mundane matters of everyday life, not aloof or distant' (van Maanen, 1981: 476). This does not mean one should come over as a cipher or mindless fan. Police often express strong views. They respect that in others. In police fieldwork long periods are spent doing little: being good company is valued. Police often find satisfaction in helping others get a job done. Referring periodically to one's own work helps them feel part of the effort, and comparing work demands, rewards, bosses and so on can give rise to illuminating data. Some participants may also want to take the opportunity to sound off 'through' the fieldworker.

While the organization is changing, its culture remains machismo-oriented: tough-minded, action-oriented and physical. Women now comprise a significant share of police personnel but it remains moot whether the presence of women changes the organization or the organization changes the women (Fielding and Fielding, 1992). In frontline fieldwork it still helps to be male, fit and physically imposing (van Maanen, 1981: 480), but what matters most is displayed personal fortitude. This should not mean taking undue risks: foolhardiness is as despised as cowardice. A tenet of frontline policing is being able to rely on one's colleagues: level-headedness and a dispassionate demeanour are valued. Further pointers on

personal style are discussed by Hunt (1984), Punch (1989) and van Maanen (1981) in respect of policing and by Goodale (1996), Lee (1994), Polsky (1971) and Whyte (1985) more generally.

COVERING YOUR BACK

This heading is the demure form of the universal police practice known as 'covering your ass'. The idea is to be alert to the fact that any situation can rebound and cause 'within-the-job' trouble. One might stop a speeding driver only to discover he is chauffeuring one's own chief constable (*Surrey Advertiser*, 5 January 2001). Like police officers who learn always to be on guard, fieldworkers need to cultivate a Zen-like awareness of the effect of their own presence and to document everything. This can help in assessing one's own effect on the data. 'Ethnography as a research style involves a heightened and continual concern for the consequences of one's social and personal identity upon the observed situations' (van Maanen, 1981: 474). Ultimately we need to document the research sufficiently well to rebut challenges to its legitimacy.

The literature offers guidelines on self-monitoring fieldwork and organizing accounts of procedure. For example, in Lofland and Lofland's account (1994), the first consideration is the directness of the report; direct observation is more reliable than second-hand observation. Second is the observer's spatial location. Third, problems arise from the skewing of reported views by the informants' social location: informants may not have said the same to others. Means to validate anecdotal testimony include identifying a third party who can confirm the account. Developed in a study of policing, Reuss-Ianni's (1983) system for determining whether a given informant's testimony is reliable employs a grid that cross-cuts directness of source with a reliability assessment based on their previous testimony. Fourth, one needs to guard against self-serving error in describing events by considering whether the observations fit too neatly into one's analytic schema. Fifth are plain errors in description: one may not be an accurate observer. It is better to leave something out than to include doubtful information. Sixth and seventh are problems of internal and external consistency. One's findings need to be internally coherent, while external consistency is evaluated by checking agreement against independent studies.

TREADING ON TOES

Part of the lore of policing is that one progresses by designing (or taking the credit for) an innovation, implementing it, and reaping career advantage quickly before its demerits become apparent. Whatever the truth of this cultural tenet, the police organization is at any time subject to numerous experimental programmes. These require evaluation, and in-house research is unreliable. As Weatheritt found, 'virtually all of [it] … is used to legitimate the activity to which it is addressed rather than to critically evaluate it' (Weatheritt, 1989: 37). As this suggests, innovations attract vested interests. Earlier we considered the ability of 'the troops' to distort innovations to suit their own ends. Again, this bespeaks interests which are vested in particular ways of working. The external researcher challenges both kinds of vested interest. Research can expose knowledge that undermines pet projects and practices. Such disturbance is not confined to field relationships but can be entangled in the intellectual disagreements of the research world, as illustrated by the policing of intimacy.

Matters like domestic violence and child abuse are highly sensitive and fieldwork enables inquiry to be shaped closely by respondents' reactions. Field research has evaluated the use of video in taking victim statements, barriers to prosecutions for domestic violence, and the operation of rape crisis suites and domestic violence refuges. It has also documented the replication of stereotypes by police, where child abuse cases are still regarded as female detectives' work and beliefs endure that 'attending "domestics" and dealing with rape between intimates are family problems and not the proper function of police' (Edwards 1994: 132). Multi-agency work is now conventional wisdom in the policing of intimacy, but research reports much friction between agencies and inflated claims about the success of new procedures.

Child abuse investigators regularly videotape interviews with suspected victims. We found micro-analysis techniques to be powerful tools for analyzing such data (Fielding and Conroy, 1992). We showed that, despite the claims of psychologists to train investigators to conduct 'neutral' interviews with child victims, so that inferences about their testimony could be made on the basis that leading questions and other interrogatory behaviours did not intrude, in practice investigators could not sustain a neutral practice of interviewing. Invalid assumptions were made about what children could reliably recall, answers were suggested by the interviewers, and gross behaviours (such as placing the child on one's lap and manipulating their limbs to simulate particular actions) were indulged which would not have been apparent in transcribed testimony (Fielding, 1999a).

While fieldwork can involve 'treading on toes' and give rise to a range of problems, it is also a problem if we don't have this problem.

If our research passes off unproblematically, we encounter no surprises in the field, and our findings are warmly received by all, we have probably been deceived, or have deceived ourselves.

INCORPORATION, SYMPATHIES AND OTHER TIES THAT BIND

Fieldwork strives for an authoritative, verifiable account. The perspective of 'naturalism' associated with the original constructions of fieldwork saw the achievement of trust as securing such an account. Emphasis was on gaining rapport, employing empathy to gain insight into members' perspectives, and faithfully reporting 'the truth'. Wittgensteinian/ Winchian perspectives have problematized naturalism. Nevertheless, the unpublished discourse of fieldwork continues to register a preoccupation with trust and truth. While all research can be read as a moral process, fieldwork wears its morality on its sleeve. Trustworthiness is an inescapable nuance of every field interaction.

In the social world we regard trust as a quality of individuals: some are trustworthy, others not. But trust is a dynamic quality that grows incrementally, can evaporate suddenly, and has always to be carefully worked at.

> [T]rust ultimately hinges on a fieldworker's (or informant's) compliance with the taken-for-granted expectancies of daily life within the social world under study. ... In the field, trust ... emerges slowly, as an ethnographer displays a ... more or less visible conformance to the expectations of 'proper form(s)' held by those he would like to call his informants. (van Maanen, 1981: 473)

These qualities make trust a dangerous tool which can subvert the tenets of inquiry it was called into being to satisfy. For much of the fieldwork the researcher's main anxiety will be about 'fitting in' and not disturbing the setting. Certainly one will evaluate data

as they are collected (qualitative method involves 'sequential analysis'; Becker, 1971), and the pursuit of a role with which members are comfortable does not mean one has to be credulous, but when our first objective is to remain on the scene the incentive is to adopt the 'appreciative stance'. Most friendly relationships can withstand a measure of quarrelling but the next time you quarrel with a friend notice how much effort goes into signalling that this temporary disagreement does not impugn the relationship itself. In police fieldwork, the effect is that we invest in presenting ourselves as someone who will not disrupt the setting, and the intended product of our fieldwork is something we prefer to keep in the shadows.

As a moral practice, then, fieldwork pulls one towards appreciative, even sympathetic relations with members. Some have gone further, taking a stance closer to incorporation than mere sympathy. There are cases of fieldworkers whose enthusiasm for their police associates has led them to interventions against citizens that were considerably more gung-ho than the officers they were accompanying. We should also remember that some police researchers are former police, for whom the appreciative stance poses special dilemmas.

In this context, the final stage of fieldwork is awkward and troubling. Added to one's own self-questioning, those with whom one has achieved friendly relations can suddenly become preoccupied with 'what you found', and their interest is not intellectual but motivated by the need to know if your work may be consequential for them or the organization. I mentioned that our efforts to pass make for a playing down of reference to our ultimate purpose – to craft an account which takes the product of empathetic field relations and uses it as 'data'. This is a guilt-producing process. For one thing, much of the 'data' will not even be used. Further, one finds oneself weighing 'the data' and becoming aware of contradictions, evasion and orientation to other agendas in the accounts offered by the buddies whose respect one felt one had earned in frontline incidents, canteen conversations, and after-hours boozing.

It helps to remember that hearing a variety of versions is why you went to the field in the first place. You may still need to reconcile these into an integrated interpretation, but competing versions are not in themselves a sign of bad faith or lack of trust. The police has factions and individual rivalries like any complex organization. Discreditable information about other organizational segments is often freely given. Collecting 'information shaded by its source' is the consequence of sampling different organizational segments and sources, and, as van Maanen observed, '[w]ithout such inconsistent information the researcher would not be able to go beyond trivialities, clichés and literal performances as a description of the scene' (1981: 484–5). However, that 'playing the field' involves moral dilemmas and is likely to impact on our emotions is also to be acknowledged, for 'the suspicion of duplicity, deception and evasiveness tends to become the private attitude of the fieldworker toward many of his informants' (van Maanen, 1981: 485). At each stage – access, fieldwork, and exit – this style of research exploits ties that bind.

THE FRACTIONATED AUDIENCE

Fieldwork is often begun with no clear idea of when it will end. The unpredictability of the field makes for uncertainty, as does the contingent nature of qualitative inquiry: fieldwork can conclude when there is enough data to support 'the analysis' but quite how quickly the data will flow, and exactly what analysis will emerge, is unpredictable. Often fieldwork is concluded by brute facts: the grant runs out, or other work intrudes. Departure is often unplanned or discrepant with the original plan, and sometimes abrupt. But the graceful exit is also obstructed by a quite different sort of trouble.

Fieldwork can involve close, even intimate, field relations. Indeed, many regard such relations as criterial to the adequacy of field data. The work that we and our participants do in these relations is unlike any other relationship, while, in drawing on the negotiation of trust, it invokes some of humankind's most volatile qualities. Against the context of the intellectual and emotional ties discussed above, far from being graceful, exit may elicit feelings of betrayal. Unless one is both thick-skinned and not planning to remain in the field of study, it is not sensible to indulge in kiss-and-tell sociology.

When informants become intimates, it is important to give account: to say what one has taken from the field, what one will do with it, and what may happen as a result. In the slow emergence of trust in the field, as the fieldworker displays practical competence in documenting but not disturbing the setting, and participants demonstrate the faithfulness of their testimony, the focus has been on negotiating the immediate. When it shifts to negotiating the consequences, diminished accountability to participants usually coincides with an end to regular (or any) contact. It may be helpful to plan one or two meetings to 'brief' participants on the 'findings' if there is special concern about the consequences. If research has been bound by best practice standards, now is the time to remind participants of the terms of research consent and honour any conditions that were agreed (e.g., providing a transcript of any formal interview, demonstrating that data have been anonymized, etc.). Where the bind of collective ties is felt, the fieldworker will also want to attest the debt they owe members and perhaps offer a small token (standing a round of drinks is usually appreciated but all-female groups may prefer confectionery). The parenthetical comment perhaps sounds twee but points to the central fact: the fieldwork relationship is a *relationship* and should be marked as such. Such ritual not only goes towards marking the close of what may have been quite intense contacts, but can help meet upset that may be caused when members see what we have written about them (particularly where it has been agreed to provide preliminary drafts to participants; Lawless, 1991).

Participants are, of course, only one audience for our output. Since the categories of research for policy, civil accountability and academic knowledge overlap, the work may be applied for purposes other than the original primary orientation. The fieldworker's dissemination strategy should be attuned to several audiences with different interests. This is especially important where one is seeking or maintaining a long-term presence in the field. For example, my study of police recruit socialization (Fielding, 1988) was driven by an analytic interest in the relative influence of formal and informal socialization but it also happened to be the only longitudinal study of change in British police officers undergoing training. In light of the recurrent view that the demerits of policing could best be addressed by better selection and training, the study gained considerable notice among those officially responsible for police training.

CONCLUSION: AUTHORITY AND SCOPE

In terms of the classic methodological distinction between validity and reliability, fieldwork produces data that are generally regarded as having high validity: the data are pertinent to the phenomenon of interest and accurately represent its qualities. Methodologists distinguish between internal reliability – the consistency of data over the course of the research in the sample site(s) – and external reliability – the agreement between independent reports of the phenomenon gathered at different sites by different researchers. Internal reliability is somewhat problematic in field research, as we become aware in the field that exceptions to routine or 'normal' events do occur but it can be difficult to assess how significant they may be. However, this can be addressed by investing sufficient time in the field, and using key informants who can help us interpret unusual occurrences and testify to what is normal or typical.

External reliability is a different matter. It is unusual for follow-up studies to take place in the same setting with the intention of comparing findings to previous studies of that setting. In fact, it is not common for follow-up studies to take place even in other settings similar to the original setting and pursuing similar analytic interests. Even where there is a concerted research effort, as with research on occupational culture, different nuances tend to be addressed. Interest in discovering new insights exceeds that in replication. Logically, even if one wished to conduct a replication, pursued identical analytical interests, and went back to the same setting as the original study, it would not be possible to satisfy the requirements of replication, because time does not stand still and settings change, and one would have to allow for the fact that conducting the original study will have had effects on the setting and its members. Research subjects are increasingly consumers of research about themselves (a particularly strong trend in life history research, a genre in which interviewees speak to their native world through their accounts; Blackman, 1992) and there are instances of police research where subjects of an original study have proved still to be oriented to it when researchers return for further work (van Maanen, 1982), so that behaviour in the setting is informed by the researcher's previous actions.

Another aspect of external reliability is problematic in fieldwork. Qualitative research tends to produce conceptual interpretations of empirical phenomena that are claimed to apply to a range of settings which at first blush may seem to have little empirical relation. For example, Kidder's (1981) analysis of hypnotism workshops employed a conceptual apparatus derived from Becker's analysis of how marijuana users learn to regard the effects of the drug as pleasurable. Kidder suggests that the applicability of Becker's conceptualization to the hypnotism workshops validates the concept. There is more interest in qualitative research in the derivation and application of concepts than there is in testing whether the concept was securely derived from the empirical data from which it originated. In other words, validation reads differently in fieldwork than it does in the canons of positivist inquiry that are largely oriented to statistical inference from survey data.

Because the validity/reliability heuristic reflects positivist canons of method, its relevance to qualitative work is contested. However, the alternative criteria so far put forward for evaluating field data, such as those offered by postmodernists, do not yet represent an effective alternative (Engel, 2002; Fielding, 1999b). The audiences of police fieldwork are likely to be impatient with research that equivocates on the basis of polyvocality, subjectivity, and the other disturbances to producing a stable and comprehensible account. It is not easy to get access and conduct fieldwork in police settings, and

audiences will want to know what one found, having taken the trouble to conduct such work. Responses on the lines of 'it all depends on what you mean by a finding' get short shrift. Yet there are good epistemological reasons for reservations about the applicability of a heuristic developed to validate quantitative research. External reliability remains a problem and the way the field has responded has changed remarkably little in 50 years: fieldwork-based analyses are regarded as conceptually productive but their generalizability is doubted.

This is, however, well-understood by policy audiences and the research community. Our research into community policing was based on observation of community and regular police over a two-year period. When we went into print (Fielding, 1995) other researchers suggested the work was unrepresentative, although we had made no claim to generalizability. Our critics felt that as we had only studied three sites and had not employed a control design, we could not show for certain that community policing was any better than regular policing or that the factors we identified as making for success did not obtain elsewhere without improvements in police performance. However, we were interested in how community policing is accomplished, not whether it 'succeeded'. Our work has since been used by policy-makers, police trainers and police forces. Their interest was not in whether our analysis was generalizable, but whether it identified factors that affected practice in the fieldwork sites. Police audiences may be particularly sympathetic to fieldwork-based knowledge because of its parallels to their own working practices. A single study is seldom the full answer to a given issue, and it is important both for researchers to be clear on what analytic claims their research design can support and for audiences to evaluate research on its own terms.

Sometimes field researchers have responded to critics by asserting that, because they were in the setting, their interpretation cannot be gainsaid. But ultimately there remain existential differences between being 'of' a social world and participating in it for research purposes. One gains insight into the police world from fieldwork, but this differs from that held by members. It is held in awareness of its construction and contingency, whereas the member's knowledge is taken for granted and may not even be recognized as knowledge but merely as 'what is'. Capturing what outsiders don't know and members can't articulate is why you are there, but a convincing analysis is one whose construction is transparent.

REFERENCES

Banton, M. (1964) *The Policeman in the Community*, London: Tavistock.

Becker, H. (1971) *Sociological Work*, London: Allen Lane.

Black, D. and Reiss, A. (1967) 'Patterns of behaviour in police and citizen transactions', in US President's Commission on Law Enforcement and the Administration of Justice, *Studies in Crime and Law Enforcement in Major Metropolitan Areas*, Washington, DC: US Government Printing Office.

Blackman, M. (1992) 'The Afterlife of Life History', *Journal of Narrative and Life History*, 2(1): 1–9.

Brewer, J. with Magee, K. (1991) *Inside the RUC: Routine Policing in a Divided Society*, Oxford: Clarendon Press.

Brown, J. (1997) 'Equal opportunities in policing', in P. Francis et al. (eds), *Futures of Police and Policing*, Basingstoke: Macmillan.

Burke, M. (1993) *Coming Out of the Blue*, London: Cassell.

Chan, J. (1997) *Changing Police Culture*, Cambridge: Cambridge University Press.

Chatterton, M. and Rogers, M. (1989) 'Focussed policing', in R. Morgan and D. Smith (eds), *Coming to Terms with Policing*, London: Routledge.

Chicago Community Policing Evaluation Consortium (1997) *Community Policing in Chicago, Year 4*, Chicago: Illinois Criminal Justice Information Authority.

Dalton, M. (1959) *Men who Manage*, New York: Riley.

Douglas, J. (1976) *Investigative Social Research*, London: Sage.

Duster, T., Matza, D. and Wellman, D. (1979) 'Fieldwork and the protection of human subjects', *American Sociologist*, 14(3): 136–42.

Dyzenhaus, D. (1998) *Judging the Judges, Judging Ourselves: Truth, Reconciliation and the Apartheid Legal Order*, Oxford: Hart.

Edwards, S. (1994) 'Domestic violence and sexual assault', in M. Stephens and S. Becker (eds), *Police Force, Police Service*, Basingstoke: Macmillan.

Engel, P. (2002) *Truth*, Chesham: Acumen.

Fielding, N. (1988) *Joining Forces*, London: Routledge.

Fielding, N. (1989) 'Police culture and police practice', in M. Weatheritt (ed.), *Police Research: Some Future Prospects*, Aldershot: Avebury.

Fielding, N. (1994) 'Cop canteen culture', in E. Stanko and T. Newburn (eds), *Just Boys Doing Business*, London: Routledge.

Fielding, N. (1995) *Community Policing*, Oxford: Clarendon Press.

Fielding, N. (1999a) 'Social science perspectives on the analysis of investigative interviews', in D. Canter and L. Alison (eds), *Profiling in Policy and Practice*, Aldershot: Ashgate.

Fielding, N. (1999b) 'The norm and the text', *British Journal of Sociology*, 50(3): 523–32.

Fielding, N. and Conroy, S. (1992) 'Interviewing child victims', *Sociology*, 26(1): 103–24.

Fielding, N., Conroy, S. and Tunstill, J. (1990) *Investigating Child Sexual Abuse*, London: Policy Studies Institute.

Fielding, N. and Fielding, J. (1992) 'A comparative minority', *Policing and Society*, 2(4): 205–18.

FitzGerald, M. and Hough, M. (2002) *Policing for London*, Cullompton, UK: Willan.

Goodale, J. (1996) *Experiencing Fieldwork*, New York: Rowman & Littlefield.

Gudjonssen, G. and MacKeith, J. (1982) 'False confessions', in A. Trankell (ed.), *Reconstructing the Past: The Role of Psychologists in Criminal Trials*, Stockholm: Norstedt.

Hobbs, R. (1988) *Doing the Business*, Oxford: Oxford University Press.

Hobbs, R. (1995) *Bad Business*, Oxford: Oxford University Press.

Holdaway, S. (1989) 'Discovering structure: studies of the British police occupational culture', in M. Weatheritt (ed.), *Police Research: Some Future prospects*, Aldershot: Avebury.

Holdaway, S. (1994) 'Recruitment, race and the police subculture', in M. Stephens and S. Becker (eds), *Police Force, Police Service*, Basingstoke: Macmillan.

Hunt, J. (1984) 'The development of rapport through the negotiation of gender in fieldwork among police', *Human organisation*, 43(4): 283–96.

Irving, B. (1980) 'Police interrogation: a case study', *Royal Commission on Criminal Procedure, Research Study 2*, London: HMSO.

Irving, B. (1989). *Neighbourhood policing*, London: Police Foundation.

Jefferson, T. (1990) *The Case against Paramilitary Policing*, Buckingham: Open University Press.

Kidder, L.H. (1981) 'Qualitative research and quasi-experimental frameworks', in M. Brewer and B. Collins (eds), *Scientific Inquiry and the Social Sciences*, San Francisco: Jossey-Bass.

Lawless, E.J. (1991) 'Women's life stories and reciprocal ethnography as feminist and emergent', *Journal of Folklore Research*, 28: 35–60.

Lee, R.M. (1994) *Dangerous Fieldwork*, London: Sage.

Levi, M. (1981) *The Phantom Capitalists*, London: Heinemann.

Levi, M. (1998) 'Organising plastic fraud', *Howard Journal of Criminal Justice*, 37(4): 423–38.

Lofland, J. and Lofland, L. (1994) *Analyzing Social Settings* (3rd edn), Belmont, CA: Wadsworth.

Maguire, M. and Corbett, C. (1991) *A Study of the Police Complaints System*, London: HMSO.

Manning, P. (1977) *Police Work*, Boston: MIT Press.

Manning, P. (1999) 'Structure and control: "deviance" in police organizations', *Research in the Sociology of Work*, 8: 117–38.

Manning, P. (2001) 'Theorizing policing: the drama and myth of crime control in the NYPD', *Theoretical Criminology*, 5(3): 315–44.

Polsky, N. (1971) *Hustlers, Beats and Others*, London: Penguin.

Punch, M. (1989) 'Researching police deviance', *British Journal of Sociology*, 40(2): 177–204.

Punch, M. (1997) *Dirty Business: Exploring Corporate Misconduct*, London: Sage.

Reiner, R. (1989) 'The politics of police research in Britain', in M. Weatheritt (ed.), *Police Research: Some Future Prospects*, Aldershot: Avebury.

Reiss, A.J. (1971) *The Police and the Public*, New Haven, CT: Yale University Press.

Reuss-Ianni, E.R. (1983) *Two Cultures of Policing*, London: Transaction.

Sampson, R. and Raudenbush, S. (1999) 'Systematic social observation of public spaces', *American Journal of Sociology*, 105(3): 603–51.

Smith, D. (1983) *Police and People in London*, London: Policy Studies Institute.

Tully, B. and Cahill, D. (1984) *Policing Interviewing of the Mentally Handicapped*, London: Police Foundation.

van Maanen, J. (1981) 'The informant game', *Urban Life*, 9(4): 469–94.

van Maanen, J. (1982) 'Fieldwork on the beat', in J. van Maanen (ed.), *Varieties of Qualitative Research*, London: Sage.

Waddington, P. (1994) *Liberty and Order*, London: UCL Press.

Weatheritt, M. (1989) 'Why should the police use police research?', in M. Weatheritt (ed.), *Police Research: Some Future Prospects*, Aldershot: Avebury.

Weitzer, R. (1993) 'Transforming the South African police', *Police Studies*, 16(1): 1–10.

Weitzer, R. (1995) *Policing under Fire*, Albany, NY: State University of New York Press.

Westley, W. (1970) *Violence and the Police*, Cambridge, MA: MIT Press.

Whyte, W.F. (1985) *Learning from the Field*, Beverly Hills, CA: Sage.

18

An Ethnographer's Tale: A Personal View of Educational Ethnography

ROBERT G. BURGESS

Thirty years ago it would not have been possible to have written or found an account of this kind. The field of educational ethnography was only in a very preliminary stage within the UK and there were only a relatively small number of studies that had been conducted in the United States, and even in that instance they were not brought together under the term 'educational ethnography'. Second, it was rare to find essays that contained reflections on the process of research – this was a development that came late in the 1970s (Bell and Newby, 1977) and for educational ethnography in the 1980s (Burgess, 1984a). It has subsequently grown into a particular genre in the literature of social research methodology. Third, for those who engaged in studies of schools, classrooms and curricula, it was usual that they turned to accounts from ethnographers working in the tradition of social anthropology, where studies had been conducted of various tribal societies (Malinowski, 1922, 1935; Evans-Pritchard, 1940) or, in a more contemporary form, anthropology had 'come home' through studies of the urban world (Pons, 1969). In

addition, some of the literature of urban sociology and 'community studies' also provided lessons for the developing field of ethnography applied to educational settings (Stacey, 1960). This raises a number of questions. First, what counts as ethnography? Second, what constitutes educational ethnography? Third, what are the processes associated with it and how does the researcher link process and method together?

WHAT COUNTS AS ETHNOGRAPHY?

Ethnography is based on the study of cultures and has involved a transition from the study of whole societies through to small-scale interactions, either in particular urban settings or in particular institutions in urban areas, such as factories, hospitals and schools. However, we might ask what are the key characteristics associated with the conduct of ethnographic enquiry? First and foremost is the researcher who engages with the participants in the setting under study. In the history of ethnographic work there are classic studies, where ethnographers have joined a particular group with a view to understanding the culture of that group from the perspective of the participants (Whyte, 1955; Liebow, 1967). At one level this may seem straightforward. However, there are several issues that need to be considered. First, the age, gender, ethnicity and social class of the researcher will influence the kind of data that the ethnographer is able to collect. Indeed, even the same ethnographer may be involved at different periods of his or her life in collecting different data, given the vantage point that he or she may have. For example, I engaged in two studies of an urban comprehensive school that I called Bishop McGregor School (Burgess, 1983). In the first study I was a young postgraduate who had trained to be a schoolteacher. This gave me access not only to the school but also to particular classrooms. However, the vantage point that I had of the school and the classroom was that of a young teacher, so gaining access to senior staff was more difficult to achieve. Ten years later I conducted a second study of Bishop McGregor School. This time not only was I ten years' older but I was also a senior lecturer in the university in which I was located and was about to become the Head of the Department of Sociology. On this occasion, I found it more difficult to gain access to the world of school students and this, in part, determined that I would focus on teachers and their work. I found that it was much easier to gain access to teachers in middle and senior management positions rather than those who were just starting out as they were at a similar stage of their careers to my own. I found that some teachers, whom I had studied and worked alongside ten years earlier, were now in middle management and senior positions in the school so they constituted a natural peer group. However, ethnographers also need to consider how other attributes may assist or impede particular subjects of study and be reflexive about their work.

It is essential that a critical stance is taken to the field in which the individual is working and the roles, actions and activities in which it is possible to engage while being in the field.

A second feature that I associate with the conduct of ethnographic enquiry is the use of key informants; that is, particular individuals with whom the researcher associates and who will assist him or her in the collection and analysis of data about events in the field (Casagrande, 1960; Burgess, 1985). However, once again it is important for the researcher to consider very carefully who his or her key informants are – does the researcher choose the key informants or the key informants choose the researcher? In any field study both situations may occur. However, it is very important that the researcher is in control of the situation, so that the research is not limited by the range of people with whom the researcher is working. If a researcher aligns with one group in a school staff room, it may mean that it prevents him or her from sitting with, or getting to know, another group of teachers. The choice of key informants will therefore have a direct impact upon the study. However, key informants can also take the researcher into social situations where otherwise he or she would not gain access. Indeed, in some instances key informants might act as unpaid research assistants, as indicated by the comment that a teacher once made to me during the course of a period of fieldwork at Bishop McGregor School. Several events were occurring and one teacher decided to seek me out in the staff room to talk me through her interpretation of the events that were unfolding. At the end of our conversation, she told me that she thought she needed to tell me all this as she knew it was my job 'to collect all the gossip'. This remark alone would rate as one of my favourite statements about how ethnographers may be perceived by their informants. But, it also contains a very important message, namely that those who engage in ethnographic enquiry are collecting accounts of the way in which the social world is defined, developed, constructed and analysed by participants.

A third feature that I associate with ethnographic work is methodological. Given that the focus of ethnographic work for me is upon the researcher and his or her informants, it automatically means that the key research instrument in any investigation is the researcher himself or herself. Automatically, the key approaches that are used in any enquiry are based on observation and on talk, either through informal conversations or more systematic approaches through the interview. However, it seems to me that it is important that researchers use a wide range of 'methods' in their field studies. Among the methods used is the collection of documentary materials, given that educational institutions are often crammed with paper that is used to communicate policies and which can also be of great assistance to the researcher. However, there are other ways in which the researcher can work with documentary material. For example, documents such as diaries may be commissioned that relate to the participant's view of the situation under study. Participants' personal diaries can be used as a basis for interview and discussion in order to retrieve the perceptions that individuals have of a social situation (Burgess, 1984b). Alongside written documentary materials there is also considerable benefit from gaining access to photographs and films as photographs can be used to obtain a narrative account of a situation in which an individual has participated (Walker and Wiedel, 1985). There are many different characteristics associated with ethnographic work when used in a variety of social settings. However, we now turn to the study of educational settings in particular.

WHAT IS EDUCATIONAL ETHNOGRAPHY?

The work of educational ethnographers is often associated with the study of schools, classrooms and curricula. Within this framework very particular features can be examined. If I take my own research, I can illustrate it in a number of ways:

- *Studying schools.* First and foremost in my research career has been the study of Bishop McGregor School (Burgess, 1983). I was indeed fortunate to have the possibility of studying this institution on two occasions in a decade. The first occasion allowed me access to management and school structure, together with access to classrooms where I acted as a class teacher with a particular group of students. In the second study the focus shifted to examine the world of teachers' work as pupil perspectives were not considered to form the focus of the study.

- *Studies of the curriculum: food and eating.* In the early 1990s I became interested in a particular aspect of schooling, namely the position of food and eating as a means of understanding aspects of the school curriculum and school culture (Burgess and Morrison, 1995). One study in particular allowed comparative work to be conducted between four schools, two primary and two secondary, and in each case one school in a rural location and the other in an urban setting. This allowed comparisons to be made. For example, in examining a multicultural urban primary school it allowed the ethnographer to understand the way in which different cultures were represented in the school and the way in which children switched between cultures through their food choices (Burgess and Morrison, 1998).

- *Studying patterns of teaching and learning.* In Bishop McGregor School I looked at those students who did not enjoy their schooling and who found formal aspects of education problematic (Burgess, 1983). In this study, it was essential to focus on the way in which teachers attempted to provide a curriculum that was of relevance while in turn also examining ways in which the students challenged that curriculum.

In other case studies, work was conducted that involved comparisons between schools in the state and independent sectors by looking at ways in which students were prepared for examinations and the kind of culture that surrounded school work within these different settings (Scott, 1991).

Libraries and library use was also studied, not only in relation to teaching and learning but also in an attempt to understand the position of the library in the context of the school and other institutions (Morrison et al., 1998). Again comparative studies were conducted, looking at primary and secondary schooling.

Even this range of work demonstrates gaps. I was aware through my work in the higher education community, that colleges and universities were completely hidden from view as very few sociological studies had been conducted on the patterns and processes associated with the higher education sector. It was therefore my intention to fill this gap in our knowledge by extending the approach I had developed in schools to the study of higher education. Among the studies that I have conducted are:

- *A study of postgraduate education and training* in 18 higher education institutions across the UK, looking at the way in which postgraduate students have been socialised into their disciplines and into postgraduate studies through a research training in the social sciences and the physical sciences respectively as well as through supervision (Burgess, 1994).
- *A comparative study of postgraduate education and training* in a range of European countries. In this study different educational traditions and different cultures could be observed whereby what may seem unproblematic in one culture is problematic in another. For example, in this particular study defining what constituted a postgraduate and what constituted doctoral research became part of the object of study.

Another gap involving comparative work was filled through:

- *Comparative work in schools in another society: Japanese schooling.* Comparative studies also yield opportunities to think about ethnography and the study of culture so, for example, an opportunity that arose to study Japanese schooling also presented me with a huge problem, given that no members of our team spoke Japanese. So, how might this be handled? In this particular instance the team needed to focus on areas that would be accessible in terms of verbal and non-verbal behaviour. Accordingly, the studies that were conducted in Japanese schools focused upon the teaching of English as a Foreign Language and more practical classes, including physical education, art and science lessons where demonstrations occurred (Burgess, 2000).

This gives a flavour of the educational ethnographies in which I have been involved in different capacities and on which I will draw throughout this chapter. These have been influenced by my own personal biography and by my sociological interests as a researcher. Overall, I would argue it is important for ethnographers to think about the study of educational settings rather than educational institutions as this will give access to a whole range of processes, both formal and informal, that will allow us to understand education and educational activity much more clearly.

The material on which I draw is taken from a career as a researcher working from different vantage points: first, as a lone researcher; second, working in teams; third, acting as a manager of projects; and fourth, commissioning projects. Some of the familiar themes that arise in the study of ethnography will be looked at from the perspective of the researcher adopting a series of different roles in order to illustrate the ways in which ethnographic work confronts a series of major problems and how these can be dealt with on a day-to-day basis. Some of the topics that will be covered tend to be hidden from view or, at best, assumed in the methodological literature. Some aspects of this chapter will therefore address some of the work that occurs in the 'back region' of the research process. We begin by looking at how research is sponsored and commissioned.

SPONSORING AND COMMISSIONING RESEARCH

Research sponsorship takes many forms and includes commissioning and funding research. Sponsorship also takes place through the process of gatekeeping, that is through a key individual who can grant or withhold access to a research site. Over the course of a research career I have been involved in all these aspects of ethnographic work. My most recent experience of ethnographic enquiry has involved commissioning projects for the Higher Education Funding Council's Equal Opportunities Research Programme. The programme has been designed in such a way that a range of methodological tools are used in order to explore the practice and implementation of equal opportunities policies in higher education institutions. The programme involves the collection of secondary data, that is those data that are routinely collected by higher education institutions in connection with gender, race and disability. A survey across the sector provides quantitative data about the patterns of equal opportunities work, but it is the ethnographic studies that are being conducted that will give insight into the perceptions of individuals located in different workplaces within higher education. The case studies attempt to focus on the perceptions of academic, academic-related, clerical, technical and manual workers regardless of whether they are employed on a full-time or part-time basis. As the chair of the panel who commissioned the research, I see it as important to encourage the research teams to think about how their different forms of data collection complement each other and shed greater light on the practice of equal opportunities work within higher education than could be obtained by one method alone. Funding is provided by the Higher Education Funding Council. This adds a further dimension to the studies, which could not be described as basic or fundamental work (although it is anticipated that the researchers will publish findings of this kind). The main purpose of the funding is to influence policy and practice within higher education so as to bring about changes in equal opportunities work within the higher education sector (HEFCE, 2005).

This raises the whole question of sponsorship in the form of research funding. Obviously, ethnographic work is sponsored by a range of different organisations. Over the years, I have conducted work that has been funded by the Economic and Social Research Council, where the projects concerned have contributed to the development of sociological and educational studies as well as having implications for policy and practice within the school system. It could be argued that this has also been the case with some of the work that I have completed on postgraduate education and training and also on food use in schools. Funding has also been obtained from a range of other bodies. For example, sponsorship from Warwickshire Local Education Authority on records of achievement resulted in work that could contribute to the implementation of policy and practice within Warwickshire schools. Case studies were also published that contributed to the sociological study of education (Pole, 1993) and in turn methodological papers were produced, including a paper that looked at data analysis in the context of multi-site case study (Burgess et al., 1994). Sponsorship may, therefore, have implications not only for the conduct of research, but for its dissemination. This demonstrates that ethnographic research cannot be conducted in discreet steps and stages, but is a continuous process with questions about publication and dissemination arising at the point of funding as the kind of sponsorship that is provided may well lead to particular forms of dissemination that are appropriate for communication with policy-makers and practitioners.

But sponsorship, as I have indicated, takes many forms. In some instances the sponsor acts as the gatekeeper who provides access to the research site. For example, in the early 1970s, I was invited by the head of the co-educational comprehensive school, which I called Bishop McGregor, to study that particular institution. While the head gave me permission to go into the school and to go anywhere I wanted and to examine anything I liked, this did not give automatic entry to all pupils and all teachers. Indeed, individuals were still free to decide for themselves whether they wished to participate in the research. However, I would argue that the head of Bishop McGregor School was an important gatekeeper who enabled me to conduct two studies in the institution, first in the 1970s, when I focused on school structures and the teaching of less able pupils and subsequently in the 1980s, when I focused on teachers' work as opposed to work that occurred with pupils in school classrooms. In each instance, it was the head of the school who sponsored and supported my work by granting access to the institution. However, this did not automatically imply that I could have ease of access to all areas within the school.

Now that I head an institution I find that I am in receipt of requests to conduct studies in different parts of the university. Obviously, as someone who has spent a research career relying on the successful negotiation of research access, I am persuaded that if we are to learn more about higher education, one needs to give access to institutions, but I am also conscious of the fact that individual staff and students must be free to decide whether they wish to grant or withhold access to a particular setting in which they are located – just because the head of the institution may agree that research can be conducted does not automatically mean that this will provide the researcher with complete freedom to go wherever he or she wishes within an institution.

GAINING ACCESS TO RESEARCH SITES AND PRINCIPLES OF SELECTION

The literature of social research tends to suggest that gaining access occurs at the beginning of any study, yet I would argue that access is gained throughout an investigation as the researcher follows up particular leads and works with different individuals and groups. This prompts a series of questions: Access to what?; Access to whom?; Access for what purpose? Each time the researcher attempts to negotiate access, these questions need to be addressed as they influence the design of the study and the data that are available for analysis. Gaining access to particular institutions or aspects of institutions influences the shape that the study will take. In Bishop McGregor School, gaining access to a particular department influenced my studies of the school curriculum, that is work that occurred with less able pupils in the school, rather than those who were following subjects for examination purposes. However, it is not just access to particular locations that become important, but also access to particular people within the educational setting under study. In Bishop McGregor School, having access to a group of young teachers who were being socialised into the profession of teaching was an important element of the first study, in part determined by my role as a researcher, my age and the age of those with whom I associated.

In studying postgraduate education and training within higher education, it became important to focus on particular groups of people, and most particularly staff groups including supervisors, the graduate dean or the sub-dean for postgraduate study and senior administrators associated with the development of postgraduate work. The study was focused through the choice of individuals with whom we negotiated in order to conduct similar studies across institutions. The important point was to make sure that similar groups of people were studied across all higher education institutions so as to collect rich data on specific themes. It was also important to ensure that the study was not so broadly defined that it became

impossible to say anything that was meaningful about the postgraduate work that was being done. This leads to a further question for the researcher. It is often easy to gain access to large numbers of people within the institution that is under study but it is very important to consider the question 'access for what purpose?'. This highlights another aspect of research design. The design of a project is not a blueprint that is established at the beginning of the investigation. Instead, it develops throughout different phases of the study. It is in these different phases that access is also linked with questions concerning selection and sampling.

The ethnographic researcher is involved in selection throughout the course of fieldwork. Choices have to be made in some instances before entering the field but the fieldwork will also involve choices being made *in situ* so that the researcher determines the field of study that is to become the focus of the investigation. This means access to sites, to people and to documentary evidence. The choice of research site is often determined by the research purpose and the research question that the investigator wishes to pose. The studies of Bishop McGregor School required access to one location and allowed me to discuss in depth the process of schooling in a co-educational comprehensive school. Subsequently, in further studies in the school system, I was interested in making comparisons along a range of dimensions so, for example, in conducting studies of food use among school students it seemed natural to choose two primary and two secondary schools, two urban and two rural locations so that comparisons could be made between primary and secondary schools and between urban and rural schooling both in the primary and secondary age phases.

In any research project the selection of the people with whom the researcher works is critical. In some instances the researcher engaged in ethnographic fieldwork finds that it is not just those people whom he or she chooses to work with that become informants, but in turn individuals seek out the researcher with whom they wish to form a bond and to work alongside. However, this is not always done for altruistic reasons and the researcher may be used in the politics of the setting under study. In these instances, it becomes important for the researcher to discover why a particular person wishes to participate in a study in order to guard against the researcher and the research being used for particular local political purposes. However, there are other issues that need to be considered, for example, teachers within schools may carry similar labels, such as 'senior teacher', but one needs to interrogate the label that is used as the job that two teachers are doing may not be identical. No assumptions can be made about similarities. It is the task of the ethnographic researcher to question the familiar in the settings that are studied. Similarly, I have found in conducting studies in higher education institutions in the UK that terms such as 'faculties', 'deans', 'sub-deans' and so on may exist in many institutions but the researcher cannot make the assumption that they carry out the same role. For example, some institutions may refer to an individual being dean of a faculty while other institutions may refer to the role as being chair of a faculty. For the ethnographic researcher, it is essential to get behind the titles that are used to describe the parts of a higher education institution and the duties of those who perform particular roles. It is this questioning stance that becomes essential for the ethnographer to adopt in exploring a field of study.

Finally, there is the question of selection of documentary material. Institutions, whether

they are schools or universities, are crammed full of paper. It is fortunate for the researcher that the paperless office does not yet exist as documents give insights into the ways in which educational institutions are structured, policies developed and plans implemented. Indeed, it allows comparisons to be made between what is seen, what is discussed and what has been planned. In my Bishop McGregor School studies I found that I was given access to whatever materials I wished to have. As a consequence, I found it difficult to decide what was appropriate. The selection of documents needed to be organised around some of the themes that were developing in my fieldwork. Once again, data analysis influenced the collection of data rather than data analysis following data collection. It also became important to decide what to include and what to exclude. A similar problem also existed when conducting a piece of research on the development of the University of Warwick (Burgess, 1991). I was given complete access to the university's archives, but for anyone who has done archival research it quickly becomes apparent that the researcher is involved in questions of selection. Often, wider reading of documentary evidence may be required in order to situate events under study in a broader context. It becomes important to select thematically the documents that are appropriate for the fieldwork. In this particular instance I was interviewing a selection of founding professors in the university in order to ascertain ways in which they defined and developed their particular disciplines by establishing new academic departments. Looking at the documentary evidence that they produced became vital in supporting the interview data that were obtained through face-to-face interviews. The principles of selection do not only apply to written material but also to photographic evidence. Many research projects have now used photographs in order to talk to students and teachers about a particular social situation in the classroom or to examine particular events and to get the individual to describe what is happening in the pictures that have been taken (Walker and Wiedel, 1985). Yet it is important to remember that photographs freeze images at a particular point in time. It is therefore important to consider who is taking the picture, the perspective from which it is taken and the way in which the choice of photograph is a selection from all the activity that surrounds the researcher and the research. In this respect, issues of selection using photographs are very similar to the issues associated with selection while conducting fieldwork when the ethnographer is conducting participant observation.

DOING PARTICIPANT OBSERVATION

Of all the approaches associated with fieldwork, participant observation is the most frequently used. As a consequence, there are numerous discussions in the literature on fieldwork about the use of participant observation and, in particular, the roles that individuals play (Burgess, 1982, 1984b; Hammersley and Atkinson, 1995). A common topology is that which talks about the complete participant through to the complete observer with roles as participant as observer and observer as participant standing between the roles at extreme poles (Gold, 1958). Yet we need to ask, does this particular approach, with the researcher adopting a set role, exist in reality? I would argue that the researcher takes different roles in the course of conducting fieldwork and needs to think about the different styles of work which are appropriate to the setting under study. In the Bishop McGregor studies,

I have been involved in working with key informants, observing school-wide events and talking to teachers and pupils about these events. I have also asked teachers to keep diaries of the situations that I have also observed or, in some instances, situations where I could not be present. Such diaries helped me to understand teachers' perspectives of classroom life. In addition, my own experience of taking the role of a classroom teacher has provided insights into the dynamics of what happens in school classrooms that can be subjected to sociological analysis. When the researcher is working as a classroom teacher, it may mean that the role adopted is closer to that of the complete participant while in other instances the role may move towards that of the complete observer (or very close to it) when recording the actions and activities of other participants. But participant observation is much more and it is important that the researcher uses a wide range of approaches in order to gain access to data. One particular technique that I have always liked to use has been the research diary.

Diaries take many forms. They can be a simple aide-memoire, a log of events, or they can be reflective, giving the individual an opportunity to discuss situations in which he or she has been located. In the Bishop McGregor School study I invited teachers to keep diaries of their work with less able students so that I obtained an insight into work within the classroom and in turn established a database from which I could invite teachers to discuss their work in some detail using the diary as a key element of a diary interview (Burgess, 1984b). In other studies, the diary has been used in a different way. For example, in establishing patterns of children's eating in the primary school, an attempt was made to provide novel stationery for primary-age children in order to encourage them to keep a food diary which would provide data upon different patterns of eating (Burgess and Morrison, 1995). In this instance, the food diary provided a basis upon which to investigate contrasting settings and also to make comparisons between different cultures. It was evident that different cultural traditions became intertwined through patterns of eating within and beyond the urban primary school (Burgess and Morrison, 1998).

Comparative studies are very important in ethnographic work as comparison is a way in which patterns are derived from data. In studying Japanese schools, our team was given the opportunity by a visiting scholar from Japan to engage in studies in Japanese schools with a Japanese team who were also studying English schooling. While the Japanese team had linguistic proficiency in English, the same could not be said for our team, who did not possess a word of Japanese between us. This posed an issue as to how the research was going to be done in Japanese schools. Participant observation may have been 'the answer'. However, the question was how do you make accessible another culture expressed through another language, as much can be lost in translation. First, we decided that we should focus on particular classes in Japanese schools through the teaching of English as a Foreign Language, as this would give us a familiar linguistic base. Second, we looked at practical lessons and physical education was an obvious example. Third, as one of our team was specifically interested in the teaching of science, we decided that those science classes involving practical work would again give access to interactions that could be studied by an observer. These studies focused more on the complete observer role than on the researcher being a participant, but even in this instance some participation was involved given the researcher's presence in the classroom. However, it also meant that

pre-eminence was being given to non-verbal behaviour rather than verbal behaviour, and careful planning was required to think about the kinds of observation that could be made, the kinds of field notes that could be taken and the kinds of evidence that could be collected. In this study, it was not only important to be able to describe the classrooms and the activities that occurred, but also to portray the lessons, with many photographs being taken to assist in reconstructing the events that had been observed first-hand by the researcher.

Observation is but one element of ethnographic work and talk constitutes another important dimension of the research experience. Among the most popular approaches to social investigation is the use of interviews or, as I prefer to call them (after Sidney and Beatrice Webb, 1932), conversations with a purpose (Burgess, 1988). In many instances, schools, higher education institutions and other educational settings give rise to opportunities for the researcher to engage in informal discussion with those who work in schools and classrooms and those who are students. In other instances, the conversations are developed around an interview, which is organised in terms of themes. The themes have been derived from the participation and observation which the researcher has conducted and give rise to an interview agenda that can be used with teachers and students within a range of educational settings. One area of consideration is whether to use individual or group interviews. It has always been my view that if working with pupils in school, it is important to consider the role of the adult, whether cast in the role of researcher or that of researcher taking the role of teacher. Adult status confers a particular attribute on the individual which in turn may influence data collection and data analysis. I have always favoured the conduct of group interviews with students as the data have proved richer as the participants engage in conversations with each other (Burgess, 1984b).

ANALYSING DATA

There are now numerous accounts of the ways in which computers and software programs can be used to analyse data (Burgess, 1995). It is appropriate to examine the potential of software packages in handling data and to examine the experience of researchers using the computer to analyse their data. However, it is essential to evaluate the advantages and disadvantages of this approach and to look at the massive advances that have taken place on an annual basis. Even with the use of a computer, there is no substitute for the creativity of the researcher exercising the sociological imagination to develop research themes. While software packages can be used to develop codes, indexes and very efficient ways of retrieving data, it is only the researcher who can engage in the rich conceptualisation of the work that he or she has been doing. In this respect, accounts on the use of the computer in social research rapidly become dated. So, how might themes be developed?

Among the essays that I have found most useful in thinking about the role of the researcher in the analysis of ethnographic data is the work of Blanche Geer, who studied students in the Kansas Medical School. On the basis of her fieldwork and the production of very detailed field notes, Geer produced an article entitled 'First Days in the Field' (Geer, 1964). In this article, she reports ways in which she developed topics and themes within her field notes, which were then used as a means of exploring her data to develop further fieldwork and further

categories in her writing. It is this approach that can be used by the researcher to think about data analysis right from the beginning of a field study, rather than to leave it as a discreet body of work that needs to be done towards the end of a project. Writing an account of the first days in the field allows the researcher the opportunity to engage in preliminary analysis which points to further fieldwork that needs to be done, categories that can be developed and theorising that can be explored. Yet there are other ways in which one can begin to explore the data. For me, this has often meant the study of critical incidents which I have used and developed since my initial study of Bishop McGregor School.

During the course of the fieldwork for the Bishop McGregor School study the first marriage of Princess Anne took place. It was decided by the local authority in which Bishop McGregor was located, that a day's holiday would not be granted to pupils. As a consequence, the pupils of Bishop McGregor School decided to take collective action and to walk out of school on the day of Princess Anne's wedding. For me, the events surrounding the walkout constituted part of a chapter of my study entitled 'The Princess Anne Affair'. I was able, through an analysis of the plans that the pupils had to walk out of school, together with the walkout and the actions taken by the head teacher, his senior management team and other teachers, to begin to explore the patterns of social relations and the power structures within Bishop McGregor School (Burgess, 1983). In this respect, the Princess Anne Affair was not a mere description of a walkout by 600–700 school pupils, rather it was an event that exposed the raw nerve endings of the social structure of the school and facilitated a study of the relationships that existed in the senior echelons of school management, the way in which teachers perceived senior managers operating and student perspectives on the day and the actions that followed. This provided an account of the school from yet another vantage point. This approach can be used in many studies to explore the routine patterns of everyday life, as exposed through critical incidents. However, it is one thing to analyse data, to identify key themes and to think about ways to conceptualise and theorise, but it is essential to also consider how the data are to be interpreted and written up.

WRITING ON AND WRITING UP

In recent years it has become much more common for sections of books devoted to qualitative research and ethnographic studies to discuss writing (Pole and Morrison, 2003). Indeed, there are also a number of specialist books to go alongside the technical manuals that discuss the writing process (Wolcott, 2001). Often, in courses devoted to ethnography, writing is either omitted from view or at best assumed rather than being taken as an important topic which is crucial to the whole of the research process. Writing is not something that should be confined to the end of a research project, but should take place throughout a study. Researchers are often engaged in different pieces of writing, from the initial period when the research design is established through field notes and field diaries that are written. So, in what ways do these different pieces of writing influence the style in which ethnographers engage in their craft?

The research design is the formal statement that may be written by the researcher prior to the beginning of the project. It is often the statement that is produced in order that funding can be achieved and also establishes the key objectives of the project, but it is important to remember that it will undergo change and

may be a piece of writing that can be drawn upon in the final study to demonstrate the way in which shifts have occurred in the research programme. A second important source of writing constitutes field notes. These are the observations recorded by the researcher having spent a period in the field. They are often first-person accounts, which are drawn on in a verbatim way in the published study. Field notes contain material that can be coded, analysed and developed by the researcher to focus on particular themes. In contrast, the field diary is a set of personal reflections that the researcher can call upon in order to develop insights into the conduct of inquiry and the way in which that inquiry may be moved forward. It is also an exercise in which the researcher may be involved in 'talking to' themselves. The diary becomes an opportunity to reflect on practice and to outline the problems and pitfalls associated with the conduct of social research. But what kinds of writing might be engaged in within the final study? The advantage of engaging in an ethnographic approach is the richness of the description that can be provided of the situations in which the researcher has participated. In this respect, researchers can begin to investigate ways in which they can move between description, analysis and interpretation during the course of their investigations. But much depends on audience as to the kinds of ways in which the ethnographer thinks about writing up the study. In this respect, it brings us back to a question that needs to be raised under research design, namely, what constitutes the focus of the study and for whom is it produced? Once this has been decided it will influence the kind of writing that is produced and the way it is developed during the course of a study. But there is more to producing ethnographic studies than written text.

In any cross-site comparative study it would not be unusual for a researcher to produce

20,000–30,000 words for each study. Four studies would therefore constitute a huge volume of material that would need to be assimilated. Indeed, in a policy arena it may mean that those to whom the researcher is reporting are too busy to read the detailed studies and need to rely on executive summaries which provide an account of the work that has been done. But what other forms can dissemination take? Workshops, conferences, briefings and so on can be developed and different formats also need to be explored for different audiences. For example, in a study of libraries, the mode of dissemination did not take the form of a case study in each instance. If this had been done it would have been far too long, and would not have engaged the appropriate audience. Instead, a brochure was produced which contained a number of inserts, each containing a set of panels where key elements of data could be disseminated (Morrison et al., 1998). The sponsor decided that this was an ideal approach to reach a group of professional librarians and, as a consequence, printed 30,000 copies of the dissemination document – a much larger print run than any ethnographer could expect a publisher to provide, even in the case of a best-selling ethnographic study! Yet, for the research team this form of dissemination was not without its problems. For example, one needs to ask in what ways will the material that has been produced for professionals also meet the requirements of an academic audience. In this way, books, articles and policy documents derived from ethnographic enquiry need to engage with different audiences.

CONCLUSION

This chapter has provided an opportunity to reflect on the process of 'doing fieldwork' in the course of studying a range of educational settings. The illustrations highlight the different ways in which field studies are conducted and the range of ways in which fieldwork can be developed. It is the hallmark of ethnographic work in educational settings that the researcher is central to the enquiry and develops the study not through mere technique, but through the use of creativity, imagination and sociological flair. As familiar problems are solved, so new issues arise. For example, ethnographers will need to examine the impact of contemporary legislation concerning children and young people on ethnographic enquiries. Similarly, the creation of university ethics committees will lead to developments in the practice of ethnographic work. There is still much for the researcher to explore while developing fieldwork in educational settings.

ACKNOWLEDGEMENTS

An earlier version of this chapter was presented to the staff and students on the Doctorate in Education Programme at the Open University in October 2004. I am very grateful to those who commented on the paper, especially Hilary Burgess, who has improved the presentation. Finally, I am indebted to Jo Wood who efficiently and effectively turned various drafts into a manuscript for publication.

REFERENCES

Bell, C. and Newby H. (eds) (1977) *Doing Sociological Research*. London: Allen & Unwin.
Burgess, R.G. (ed.) (1982) *Field Research: A Sourcebook and Field Manual*. London: Allen & Unwin.
Burgess, R.G. (1983) *Experiencing Comprehensive Education: A Study of Bishop McGregor School*. London: Methuen.

Burgess, R.G. (ed.) (1984a) *The Research Process in Educational Settings: Ten Case Studies.* Lewes: Falmer Press.

Burgess, R.G. (1984b) *In the Field: An Introduction to Field Research.* London: Allen & Unwin.

Burgess, R.G. (1985) 'In the company of teachers', in R.G. Burgess (ed.), *Strategies of Educational Research.* Lewes: Falmer Press. pp. 79–100.

Burgess, R.G. (1988) 'Conversations with a purpose? The ethnographic interview in educational research', in R.G. Burgess (ed.), *Conducting Qualitative Research.* London: JAI Press. pp. 137–155.

Burgess, R.G. (1991) 'Working and researching at the limits of knowledge', in M.L. Shattock (ed.), *Making a University: A Celebration of Warwick's First 25 Years.* Coventry: University of Warwick, pp. 94–112 and pp. 115–16.

Burgess, R.G. (ed.) (1994) *Postgraduate Education and Training in the Social Sciences: Processes and Products.* London: Jessica Kingsley.

Burgess, R.G. (ed.) (1995) *Computing and Qualitative Research.* London: JAI Press.

Burgess, R.G. (2000) 'Some issues and problems in cross-cultural case study research', in C.J. Pole and R.G. Burgess (eds), *Cross-Cultural Case Study.* Oxford: Elsevier for JAI Press. pp. 43–52.

Burgess, R.G. and Morrison, M. (1995) *Teaching and Learning about Food and Nutrition in Schools.* Report to the ESRC on Grant No. L209252006, Swindon: Economic and Social Research Council.

Burgess, R.G. and Morrison, M. (1998) 'Ethnographies of eating in an urban primary school', in A. Murcott (ed.), *The Nation's Diet: The Social Science of Food Choice.* London: Longman.

Burgess, R.G., Pole, C.J., Evans, K. and Priestley, C.J. (1994) 'Four studies from one or one study from four? Multi-site case study research', in A. Bryman and R.G. Burgess (eds), *Analysing Qualitative Data.* London: Routledge.

Casagrande, J. (ed.) (1960) *In the Company of Man.* New York: Harper & Row.

Evans-Pritchard, E.E. (1940) *The Nuer.* Oxford: Oxford University Press.

Geer, B. (1964) 'First days in the field', in P. Hammond (ed.), *Sociologists at Work.* New York: Basic Books.

Gold, R. (1958) 'Roles in sociological field observation', *Social Forces,* 36(3): 217–23.

Hammersley, M. and Atkinson, P. (1995) *Ethnography: Principles in Practice* (2nd edn). London: Tavistock.

Higher Education Funding Council for England (2005) *Equal Opportunities and Diversity for Staff in Higher Education.* Bristol: Higher Education Funding Council (HEFCE).

Liebow, E. (1967) *Tally's Corner: A Study of Negro Street Corner Men.* Boston: LittleBrown.

Malinowski, B. (1922) *Argonauts of the Western Pacific.* London: Routledge.

Malinowski, B. (1935) *Coral Gardens and their Magic* (Vols 1 and 2). London: Routledge and Kegan Paul.

Morrison, M., Burgess, R.G., Band, S., Costley, D. and Wardle, K. (1998) *The Role of Libraries in a Learning Society.* London: Library and Information Commission.

Pole, C.J. (1993) *Assessing and Recording Achievement: Implementing a New Approach in a School.* Buckingham: Open University Press.

Pole, C.J. and Morrison, M. (2003) *Ethnography for Education.* Buckingham: Open University Press.

Pons, V. (1969) *Stanleyville: An African Urban Community under Belgian Administration.* London: Oxford University Press for the International African Institute.

Scott, D. (1991) 'Issues and themes: coursework and coursework assessment in the GCSE', *Research Papers in Education,* 6(1): 3–20.

Stacey, M. (1960) *Tradition and Change: A Study of Banbury.* Oxford: Oxford University Press.

Walker, R. and Wiedel, J. (1985) 'Using pictures in a discipline of words', in R.G. Burgess (ed.), *Field Methods in the Study of Education.* Lewes: Falmer Press, pp. 191–216.

Webb, S. and Webb, B. (1932) *Methods of Social Study.* London: Longman.

Whyte, W.F. (1955) *Street Corner Society* (2nd edn). Chicago: University of Chicago Press.

Wolcott, H. (2001) *Writing Up Qualitative Research.* Thousand Oaks, CA: Sage.

Part 9

Fieldwork, Science and Technology

19

Software and Fieldwork

SUSANNE FRIESE

The aim of the chapter is to give you an introduction to Computer-Aided Qualitative Data Analysis Software (CAQDAS) and how it can be utilised in fieldwork. To set the stage, I review the almost 20 year long history of qualitative computing and provide some anecdotes based on my personal experience with the field. Then I provide some examples on how qualitative computing software can be put into use while in the field or when returning from the field. With this as background information, we look at the linkage between software and method. I present a general model of qualitative data analysis and explain how the various steps can be translated into computer functions and a computer-aided analysis. This gives a first impression which computer function might be important and necessary for which purpose. In the section 'What to look for when deciding on a package' the central functions of CAQDAS and their variations are explained. The aim is to sharpen the view and to enable the reader to make a better informed decision when it comes to matching personal and project requirements with a particular package. The last part of the chapter is devoted to a description

of four popular programs (in alphabetical order): ATLAS.ti 5, The Ethnograph v 5.08, MAXqda, and QSR Nud*ist 6. The software descriptions are structured around the central functions so that a comparison becomes possible.

LOOKING BACK AT ALMOST 20 YEARS OF QUALITATIVE COMPUTING

The first programme developed for the purpose of supporting qualitative data analysis was The Ethnograph (http://www.qualis research.com). The programme was first launched in 1985. Thus, we can look back at a history of nearly 20 years of computer-supported qualitative data analysis. At the beginning of the 1990s, a number of additional software packages were launched like Nud.ist 3, MAX, HyperResearch and ATLAS.ti. At this time, all programmes were DOS-based and offered basic code and retrieve functions. Nevertheless, they were not all the same. The developers or designers were often researchers who needed computer support for a particular project. As a consequence, the requirements posed by the data at hand, the research questions and the chosen methodological approach guided the development and the design of the software. The study motivating the development of N4, for example, included large amounts of open-ended questions from a survey. This necessitated a tool that allowed for automatic data processing on the basis of command files. The first version of MAX was originally also developed to support the analysis of open-ended questions in survey questionnaires. However, the features of Nud.ist 3 and MAX were not the same as the methodological approach differed. MAX was designed to support the methodological approach of case-oriented quantification based on the works of Max Weber and Alfred Schütz (Kuckartz, 1995). The development of ATLAS.ti was guided by project needs as well as by a combination of various methods, that is, phenomenology, hermeneutics and Grounded Theory (Böhm et al., 1992). This heritage is still obvious today in certain features like the 'code family' or in menu labels like 'open coding'. Thus, there is a story to tell about all programmes and their development. Let me finish with an anecdote that led to the development of the pioneer of all programmes, The Ethnograph.

John Seidel, a sociologist by training, developed The Ethnograph while he was working on this PhD thesis. At the time, personal computers were not as widespread as today. Software for statistical analyses ran on large mainframe computers and, in order to obtain results, it was necessary to type in an appropriate syntax to tell the computer what to do. This was not the same as programming software but very similar to it. John worked as an assistant in the research lab supporting statistical applications, but for his PhD he collected qualitative data. His raw data consisted of many pages of transcripts. All

readers who have conducted a qualitative data analysis by hand know what this entails. Piles of paper need to be ordered and sorted, cut into smaller units, pasted on to different papers according to themes, sorted and ordered again, and so on. John, while in the midst of making sense of his data, however, lived not alone. There were also two cats in the house. They loved to stroll around the stacks of paper, though not always respecting that there was a particular order to them that should not be messed up. Before a catastrophe could occur (at least from the viewpoint of a PhD student), John utilized his skills gained from working with mainframe computers to literally move his piles of paper from the floor into the computer. This resulted in the development of The Ethnograph 1.0. Fellow students and colleagues were amazed to see that computers could also be used to support qualitative data analysis. When demonstrating his software and creating an output of segments sorted by selected code words, they gathered around the dot-matrix printer to celebrate the wonders of computer technology. Based on popular demand, John continued to develop the programme that was originally intended to only serve his PhD research. Version 2 was made available to colleagues and friends, and version 3 was the first commercial version released in 1985.

Since 1985 development has not stopped. In 1995, Prein, Kelle and Bird provided an overview of twelve CAQDAS programmes; Weitzman and Miles (1995) described ten programmes. Today most of them still exist, joined by a number of new packages. All programmes have been developed further and today most of them are no longer DOS but Windows-based programmes, supplemented by a few native Macintosh programmes.[1] The distribution of these programmes varies. Some are not spread much beyond country boundaries like Kwalitan, which is mainly used in

The Netherlands, or AQUAD, which is mainly used in Germany. Others, such as QSR NVivo and N6, MAXqda or ATLAS.ti, have a worldwide user group. These programmes offer sophisticated features and up-to-date technology. On the downside, the learning curve is steeper and users need to invest more time to become skilled at handling these packages.

With increasing development of CAQDAS, some diversification has taken place. The main features of CAQDAS in the early days of qualitative computing were the code and retrieve functions. Today a number of the programs have become quite sophisticated and offer a variety of other features (see 'Software Description', page 318 below). There are still software packages that offer just basic code and retrieve functions, some of them are distributed as freeware. For certain groups of users such packages are entirely adequate, offering all the functionality they need.

The diversification of CAQDAS has some positive but also some negative side-effects. The focus on different features above and beyond basic code and retrieve functions have made it easier to advise potential users which package to choose. For example, there are only a few programmes that support the analysis of photographs, audio and video data (e.g., HyperResearch and ATLAS.ti). Some programmes offer features or add-on modules to combine qualitative and quantitative content analysis, such as MAXqda or C-I-SAID. Others, like NVivo, are strong in supporting analyses based on a combination of codes, data attributes and cross-tabulation. On the negative side, it becomes more and more difficult for one person, even though an expert in CAQDAS, to stay on top of the development and to know all available programs in detail. Comparative reviews will therefore become

scarcer in the future or limited to fewer programs.

USER ADAPTATION OF CAQDAS IN THE TWENTY-FIRST CENTURY

Gathering around a dot-matrix printer and celebrating a computer printout may sound ridiculous to (at least some) computer users today. But even in 2004, there are qualitative researchers who refuse to use computer programs to support their research. Such a refusal is adequate in some cases because not all qualitative methods call for a code and retrieve approach (e.g., sequential analytic approaches or objective hermeneutic). In other cases, the negative response to software is related to the belief that the researcher would lose the closeness to the data, or that software would automatically code and analyse the data and thus take away the analysis from the human interpreter, or that software would lead to shallow analyses. These are prejudices based on an incomplete understanding of what qualitative computing is all about.[2] CAQDAS does not analyse data. Moreover, the software is a tool that (only) supports the process of qualitative data analysis. Computers are generally very good at finding things like strings of characters or coded data segments in a large variety of combinations. But it is still the researcher who needs to tell the computer which data segment has which meaning by way of coding. Let's look once more at the acronym that was introduced at the beginning of this chapter: CAQDAS. It stands for Computer-Aided Qualitative Data Analysis Software. It is a somewhat lengthy acronym as compared to 'QDA Software', a short form that can also be found in the literature. The latter stands for Qualitative Data Analysis software and may be responsible for some of the misunderstandings and misperceptions related to CAQDAS.[3]

This explanation is at times also used as an argument against using software according to the following logic: if the computer doesn't do the coding, then what is it good for? And without 'test driving' a CAQDAS package, they judge software as not something to be used in a qualitative research context and return to their manual methods of using colour pencils and filing cabinets. To my mind, they forego an opportunity to improve the validity of their research. Software, used appropriately, offers the possibility to verify or falsify ideas, hypotheses, theoretical constructs or models at any stage of the research process because the data can easily be accessed, they can effortlessly be grouped and regrouped, compared and contrasted. It is no problem to rename, modify or merge codes if one gains more and more insights into the data. One's thoughts about the data are likely to be different three or six months into the analysis as compared to the very early stages and modification of codes and concepts is an inert part of qualitative data analysis. But this is not the only advantage. With the aid of computers, this process can also be easily documented. The steps of analysis can be traced and the entire process does not remain inside a black box, as often is the case.

Thus, even if you don't have cats or kids or other intervening forces that can mess up your carefully sorted piles of transcripts or field notes, software offers clear advantages over manual techniques. It frees the user from those tasks that a machine can do much more effectively, such as modifying code words and coded segments, retrieving data based on various criteria, searching for words, integrating all material at one place, attaching notes and finding them again, counting the numbers of coded incidences, offering overviews at various stages of a project, and so on. When using software, it becomes much easier to analyse data systematically and to ask questions that otherwise would not be asked because the manual tasks involved would be too time-consuming. Even large volumes of data, and data of various media types can be structured and integrated very quickly with the aid of software. In addition, a carefully conducted computer-aided qualitative data analysis also increases the validity of research results. Especially when one has reached the conceptual stage of an analysis, it is easy to 'forget' the raw data behind the concepts. In case of a manual analysis, it is quite laborious to get back into the data. In a software-supported analysis, the raw data are only a few mouse clicks away and it is much easier to remind oneself and to verify or falsify one's developing theoretical thoughts about the data.

THE USE OF SOFTWARE IN FIELDWORK

As the title of this chapter implies, CAQDAS can not only be used after data have already been collected, but also during the data collection process. This does not apply to all studies, but there are a number of research situations where it can make sense to utilise a CAQDAS package from the very beginning. An example would be a research project where a variety of data types are collected over an extended period of time, as the case in ethnographic studies, for instance. Field notes can be directly typed into a CAQDAS package, arising interpretative thoughts into memos. Pictures can be assigned, organised into groups according to specific criteria, such as, dates and themes. Comments and descriptions can immediately be added to develop a picture archive. The same can be done with short sequences of video footage. Interviews may be recorded on a laptop and immediately archived into the growing database inside the CAQDAS package. At this stage, no detailed analysis is yet taking place, but valuable thoughts that might otherwise be forgotten can immediately be written down in the form of comments and memos and attached to the data.

This requires some technical know-how and adequate technical equipment, especially if one works with multimedia data. In recent years, though, multimedia technology has become much more accessible and affordable also for the 'lay' user. Most laptops already include the possibility to record and to save the outcome in the form of a digital file; the use of digital cameras and the skill to download pictures on to a computer has entered the mainstream, and with the right software you also no longer have to be an expert to download and work on video footage.

CAQDAS offers the possibility to integrate all relevant data materials into one place to create a growing database already during the process of data collection. This can, of course, also be done without collecting multimedia data. Instead of writing field notes and comments into a word-processing package or a note book, they can be typed directly into an editor provided by almost all CAQDAS packages. A further advantage is that in addition to the raw data, comments and memos can be included.

Another under-explored usage of CAQDAS is its support in terms of data representation, as has already been suggested by Coffey, Holbrook and Atkinson (1996). At present, only ATLAS.ti offers an HTML and XML output option.[4] But others may follow suit. This allows for projects to be published independently of the software either as Web hypermedia presentations or distributed on CD-ROMs or DVDs (see Pink, 2001). Examples of hypermedia presentations can be found at the following sites: http://www.lboro.ac.uk/departments/ss/visualising_ethnography/index.html and http://lucy.ukc.ac.uk/Stirling/index.html.

As far as the usage of image, audio and video in such presentation is concerned, a number of new ethical issues need to be considered. This might be a reason why one today rarely finds hypermedia presentations. But it may also be a matter of timing related to advances in computer technology (price) and user friendliness. It only has recently become feasible to even think of 'home made' multi- and hypermedia productions without having to involve experts.

SOFTWARE AND METHODS

A common question of novices is whether particular software packages are suitable for a specific methodological approach such as grounded theory. The answer to this question is simple: one can use any of the software packages for any approach that involves coding. It is a myth that some packages can or cannot be used in conjunction with a particular methodological approach. Related to this myth is the implicit assumption that a methodological approach somehow magically emerges just because one enters and codes data in a CAQDAS package. The disenchanting truth is that learning a methodological approach and a software that supports the analysis process are two distinct, even if related, processes. You should have at least some basic knowledge about qualitative data analysis techniques before you embark on a computer-aided analysis. The purpose of CAQDAS is not to manipulate or direct your analysis; its purpose is simply to support it. The user should be the one manipulating the software to make it perform those tasks that best suit the selected methodological approach. This sounds logical, but everyday reality often looks different. Therefore, below, a very basic model of qualitative data analysis is presented, followed by an explanation of

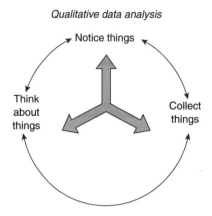

Qualitative data analysis

Figure 19.1   *The three basic steps of qualitative data analysis (Seidel, 1998: 2)*

how it can be translated into a computer-supported analysis.

According to Seidel (1998), the general idea behind an analysis method that is based on a code-and-retrieve approach is that data are broken up, separated or disassembled into pieces, parts, elements or units. The purpose of it is to end up with manageable pieces of data sorted by themes or concepts. This greatly facilitates comparing and contrasting and thinking about the data. The researcher can then sort and sift the pieces, searching for example for patterns, classes, sequences, types or processes with the aim to assemble or reconstruct the data in a meaningful and comprehensible fashion. This process involves three basic steps: noticing things, collecting things and thinking about things (see Figure 19.1 above).

These three basic steps can be found in almost any qualitative data analysis approach. When reading your data, you start noticing things. You are likely to mark those things in the margins and add a few notes. Over time, you find other instances of the same noteworthy things in your data and you start collecting those things under the same name. You begin to create code words. Over time

you build up a coding system. The next logical step is to think about those things you have noticed and collected. For this to be possible you need to find and retrieve these instances in your data. In this process the underlying structure of your data will become more and more obvious. You will be able to see sequences, patterns, hierarchies, and wholes that had been hidden before in the mass of your data. While you are thinking about your data, you may want to go back to the original not-fragmented text, you may want to re-code some passages, add new code words or get rid of some old ones. The following section shows how this process can be translated into a computer-aided analysis.

THE COMPUTER-AIDED QUALITATIVE DATA ANALYSIS PROCESS

Noticing things – creating a project and reading your data files

If you use a software package for analysing your qualitative data, then the preparation of one or more data files will be your first task during or after collecting the data. Text data can be prepared within any of the commonly used word processors, such as MS Word, WordPerfect, etc. Depending on the software package, you need to observe certain formatting rules. Some packages still only allow you to work with text-only data, other packages also accept Word or Rich Text files.

After you have prepared your data files, the next step is to create a project and to import your data files into the program. Now you can embark on the task of reading your data files.

Collecting things – coding data files

When reading through your data, soon you will start noticing multiple instances of certain occurrences and you will want to mark them with a code word. In order to do so, you highlight the data segment in question with a mouse and assign one or more code words to it. Some software packages restrict the number of codes you can assign to one data segment, others have no limitation. But even if a restriction applies, the restrictions are generous enough so that you probably won't notice that there is one. All packages allow overlapping or nested segments as it is common when working with qualitative data that meaning is ambiguous and not always confined to whole sentences or paragraphs. Therefore being able to apply overlapping codes is essential and one of the many advantages of using a software package. Nonetheless, coding the data material and developing a suitable coding system is a laborious task also when analysing the data with the aid of software. As mentioned above, computers cannot think and therefore this task has to be undertaken with much care. This said, software packages are also superior to manual techniques during this part of the analysis. With the aid of software, it is much easier to modify coded data segments, to rename codes globally or locally, or to reverse coding. Notes, including first interpretations or clarification, can be attached to data segments and one does not end up with post-it notes or scribbled handwriting all over the place. With the help of the retrieval functions that the software packages provide, it is also very easy to find these notes again.

Thinking about things – searching data files

Once a coding system has been developed and the data have been coded, data segments can be searched, retrieved and displayed in a number of ways. A search operation can be very simple, that is only being based on a single code word. It is, however, also possible to build more complicated search requests, which consist of multiple code words linked by Boolean, proximity, or contextual operators. Such requests can also be combined with variables like gender, age, education or other data attributes.

The retrieval of data segments makes it easier to see things in your data and to think about them. It helps the researcher to recognise relationships that previously went unnoticed because they were disguised by too much noise in the data. Some packages allow the visualisation of the established relationships in form of networks or graphic models.

WHAT TO LOOK FOR WHEN DECIDING ON A PACKAGE

Prerequisites

As mentioned above, when wanting to use CAQDAS, it is essential to work with a method that is based on a code-and-retrieve approach. A clear distinction needs to be made between quantitative content analysis programs, such as Sonar Professional, Folio VIEWS, etc., and the here described CAQDAS packages. The focus of CAQDAS is on thick descriptions, *verstehen* and context-rich analysis, and not on the quantification of qualitative data. Therefore the first question that needs to be answered before deciding on a software package is what kind of method should be applied to *collect* and *analyse* data. A well-known method is the grounded theory approach originally developed by Glaser und Strauss (1967). Other approaches are biographical life history research, case studies, phenomenology or ethnography. Within each of these methods various ways of data collection and data analysis are described (see Creswell, 1998, for an overview). After you have decided that CAQDAS is suitable for the kind of analysis that you intend to conduct, looking at the following program features can help you to select a package that fits your needs.[5]

Data entry

With regard to data entry, it is worthwhile investigating the following questions: What kind of data do you want to analyse and is this a format supported by the software? Some programmes can only handle text documents; others also support the analysis of graphic images, photographs, audio and video data. If you only want to analyse text documents, it may be worth investigating the fit of programs that require documents in text-only format versus those that allow to import Rich Text or Word documents. The learning curve for the latter is often steeper as these programs generally offer more features and are more complex. For some purposes, a simple program might also be sufficient. Another issue to look at is the possibility to edit the data material once it is imported into the package and coded.

Coding

The issues to look for here are: What is the smallest chunk of text that can be coded? How are coded data segments and code words displayed? Can I use codes that are not linked to any data segment (e.g., for the purpose of structuring code lists or when developing models and theory)? Is automatic coding possible?

Memos and comments

Analysing qualitative data means writing a lot. A great deal of analysis happens while you write notes in the form of comments and memos. Therefore, it is vital to look at the features that the various software packages provide in order to support this process. What kind of notes can you write? Is there a distinction between writing code definitions (= a short comment) and memos, or is the same technical solution offered independent of content? Look for what kinds of object comments and memos can be written for and where? How can you track that you have attached or inserted a memo or comment somewhere? Is it made visible and how? Further analytic support is provided when you can link memos and comments to other objects. Is this possible?

Data retrieval

The search functions and features are essential as it is here where the computer power can be fully utilised. Investigate what can be searched and how search results are displayed? Can you search for words, strings of text or text patterns? Can the finds be coded automatically? The purpose of the text search and auto coding is to allow you to 'dive' into your data and to give you a quick feel for what is there and what to look for. Another application is to code structured information like the responses to entire questions, or speaker turns in focus-group transcripts.

Searching for coded data segments is a significant part of your analysis after having coded the data. Therefore you need to look out for the ways this is facilitated by the software package. How conveniently can coded data passages be accessed? Can they be displayed in context? What kinds of search operator are available? They allow you to ask questions such as: Show me all data passages where Code_A and Code_B overlap/where B follows A/all passages coded with child codes (lower order) of A, etc. Another important search function is the ability to restrict searches to particular document codes, or data attributes. This allows you to ask questions such as: Show me all data passages where Code_A and Code_B overlap, but only in interviews with female respondents, age 21–30.

Output and display options

You may not necessarily always want to work in front of the computer. You may miss going through stacks of real paper, and at some point in time you want to be able to transfer your analytic work to a word-processing program to write the final report. For all of this, you need output functions that facilitate the transfer from the CAQDAS package to a printer or another software application. Therefore, you should pay attention to the output destinations offered by the software. Can output be displayed in an editor, saved to a disk, and printed on paper? Is it saved in text-only or Rich Text format. Some packages also provide a quantitative overview of your data that can be outputted in an Excel-compatible format. Other issues to look for are: Can you select only parts of a result for reviewing, editing or saving? Is there an easy way to access the context of search results? Is it easy to identify where retrieved data passages come from, how specific is the source tag? In addition, a number of packages provide export functions to interface with other programs, such as SPSS or mapping software. Depending of your chosen method and analysis aims, these might also be features to look out for.

Other features

Some users prefer to organise their coding system in a hierarchical manner. Most programs allow for this, but all in different ways.

Thus, if you are interested in a hierarchical representation, pay attention to how this is realised and what best suits your needs and working style.

Team work is also supported in different ways by different packages. When working in teams, it is important that a program offers a merge function to combine work done by various team members. Another issue to pay attention to is whether it is possible to distinguish work done by different team members.

Further decision criteria

There are simpler, and thus easier-to-learn packages, and more complex programs with a steeper learning curve that may best be learned when attending a professional training session. Therefore, you should ask yourself what kind of computer user you are. If you think of yourself as a novice or not very experienced user, insecure in issues related to data management, a simpler program may be a better choice for you. This may also be the case if you only need some basic functions and do not need the advanced options provided by the more sophisticated packages.

A further decision criterion should be whether the software is only to be used for a single project, or also in the future for other projects and possibly by other users. If it is to be only chosen for a specific project, then a program that fits the specific requirements of that project is needed. If one is buying for the long term, it may be better to choose a package that offers additional features, even if they may not be required at present.

Last but not least ...

Rely on your intuition when deciding on a program. All companies offer a demo version and tutorial that can be downloaded from their respective websites. Look at the demo versions and go step-by-step through the provided tutorials and sample project(s). The time invested will be worthwhile. A program may provide all the features that you need, but you may feel uncomfortable with the user interface and the ways the data are handled. This is something you can only find out by gaining some hands-on experience yourself. Reading this chapter or the program descriptions on the company websites can never substitute your personal experience.

SOFTWARE DESCRIPTION

The functions considered in the program description below are: data entry, coding, text search and auto coding, memos and comments, data retrieval, mapping and team support. If applicable, special features that only apply to a specific program, and thus distinguish it from others, are described at the end of each section.[6]

ATLAS.ti 5

Data entry

Four document media types are supported: text, graphic, audio and video data. Text documents can be imported as text-only documents, as Rich Text files (RTF), or as Word documents. If documents are not yet converted to Rich Text, ATLAS.ti 5 provides automatic conversion of word documents to RTF. OLE support is offered as well. This means other objects, like tables, images etc., can be embedded into a (rich) text document and coded as one unit. This is in addition to supporting the detailed coding of original audio, video and image source files. As documents are assigned to a project and

not imported, they do not become part of the project file and thus file size does not play a role. ATLAS.ti can handle large data sets, and large video files also do not create a problem. The overview (which can be found at www.qualisresearch. com/QDA.htm) lists the multimedia file formats that are accepted by ATLAS.ti.

Documents can be grouped into so-called families. This is a way to assign variables by creating, for example, a female family, a male family, families containing interviews from respondents between the ages of 21 and 30, between the ages 31 and 40, and so on. These can later be used to restrict or filter search results.

Documents that have been assigned to ATLAS.ti can be edited at all stages of the project.

Coding

Coding is an interactive process and the results are immediately visible on the screen. Code words are displayed in the margins and the length of the coded data passage (=quote) is marked by a bracket. The smallest text unit that can be coded is one character; the smallest unit in audio files is a millisecond, in video files a frame. Graphical quotes are rectangular sections of the original image.

There are no restrictions with regard to the number of levels that can be coded or the length of a code word. All code words in ATLAS.ti are interactive. If you click on a code word once, the text passage coded with this code word is highlighted. If you double-click on a code word, the code word's comment is displayed. The modification of already coded data segments is quick and easy.

Many drag and drop operations are available to facilitate coding, the modification of coded data passages, and the unlinking and exchanging of code words. For novices, an option is provided to deactivate the many

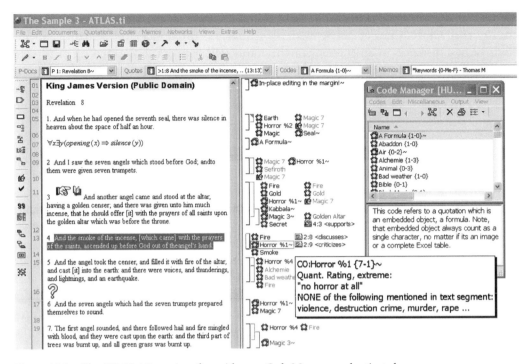

Figure 19.2 *The ATLAS.ti 5 user interface with open Code Manager and activated code and code definition*

drag and drop operations to make it easier to concentrate on the basics first.

A code word list is automatically created and updated while you code your data. Behind each code word, two numbers are displayed: the first number tells you how often a code word is used, indicating the frequency or groundedness of a code word; the second number informs you about the links that exist to the code word, thus indicating the density of a code word. A code manager offers additional functions to manage your code word list conveniently. Codes can be grouped in so-called code families and data segments can be retrieved based on their family membership. Furthermore, codes can be ordered hierarchically with the aid of the network tools (see 'Mapping', below).

Figure 19.2 above shows the ATLAS.ti 5 user interface. A coded document is loaded. In addition to codes, hyperlinks and memos are also shown in the margin. This can be recognised by the different symbols used. The code 'Horror %1' is highlighted in context and the code definition has been activated via a double click. The Code Manager is open, as is commonly the case when coding a document.

Text search and auto coding

You can search all primary documents using a procedure that is similar to what you might know from word-processing programs. To find instances that are anchored at the beginning or end of a line or sentence, certain number patterns, etc. GREP expressions can be used. Search patterns that are potentially used more than once, can be saved. The text search function only searches through primary data, not through other texts, such as comments or memos. In order to search through all texts, the so-called Object Crawler can be used. It finds all first instances of an entered search term in all specified object types.

Text search can be combined with auto coding. This means that you can search for a string of characters in the text and code the hits, the surrounding word, sentence or paragraph automatically with a selected code word. This process can run fully automatically, or you can control it by deciding each time a match is found whether or not you want to code the instance.

Memos and comments

For virtually every object in ATLAS.ti you can write a memo or a comment. Comments are directly attached to the object they relate to and cannot be handled independently. A comment can be written for the entire project, each primary document, quote, and code word. Commented objects are indicated by a tilde sign (~) in the respective object lists. Memos are independent objects and can be attached to quotes, codes and other memos. When attached to quotes, this is indicated in the margin next to the coded segment (see Figure 19.2). When linked to codes or other memos, this can be made visible in the network editor (see below). As a way to facilitate memo management, memo types can be defined and used for sorting and filtering purposes.

Both memos and comments can be formatted as Rich Text, just like primary documents, including embedded objects.

Data retrieval

ATLAS.ti offers you a wide variety of options to search for coded data segments – all

in all there are 14 operators, including Boolean, proximity and semantic operators. Hit lists can be cleaned up or filtered according to specified criteria, such as only those quotes from interviews with female respondents. All finds can be displayed in context or reviewed in an editor, saved to disk or printed. The output contains clear source tags, but unfortunately these cannot easily be removed to display a generic view, if desired. Each query can be saved in the form of a super code. A super code contains the query and each time you click on a super code, the query is executed again. This is a useful feature when using more complex queries that you want to re-run or re-use at a later time in your analysis. Super codes can also be turned into regular codes, presenting a snapshot of the present stage of the analysis.

Mapping

A distinct feature of ATLAS.ti is the way the various objects of an ATLAS.ti project can be visualised and linked to each other in so-called network views. Unlike in other programs that offer a mapping or modelling feature, connections between codes and connections between quotes can be named. The program offers seven relation types, but these can be edited or new ones can be defined. Objects can be linked visually in an network editor, but also via menu functions.

The place of objects in a network editor is not static. In other words, all objects can be moved around freely without having to obey a default structure. From a network view you can access your primary data directly and display them in context. Figure 19.3 shows an example network view. Frequency and density are displayed in numbers. Also shown are a linked memo, the context menu for a code

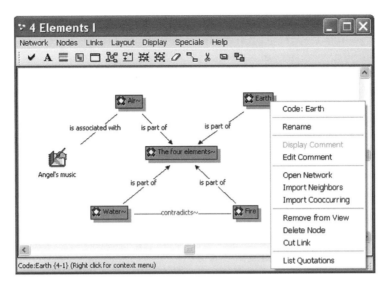

Figure 19.3   *An ATLAS.ti network view*

node, and the type of relation between two connected codes (i.e., is part of, contradicts). A comment has been written for the contradicts relation, as indicated by the tilde sign (~).

Network views can be saved as graphic files and edited in a graphic program. They can also be copied to the clipboard and directly inserted into Word files or PowerPoint presentations.

You can create a hierarchical view of your coding system by linking codes either in network views, by using the link menu option or per drag and drop in the Code Manager. The hierarchy of codes can then be displayed in the form of a sideways tree, similar to the display of folders and files in Windows Explorer (Figure 19.4). However, codes cannot be manipulated in the tree view, only via the above mentioned functions.

Team support

ATLAS.ti supports team work. All users can be given a user name and if logged in, all new entries are 'stamped' with the name of the logged-in user. Thus, all work done on a project, such as creating code words, memos, etc., carries the name of the current user (=author). In this way it is possible to trace the analytic steps of the various team members. Documents can be analysed simultaneously when working on a shared network drive, given that each user works on his/her own project file. When documents are edited, the modifications are propagated to all users of the same document and the affected document will be synchronised. All affected coded data segments will be adjusted. When splitting a project into sub-

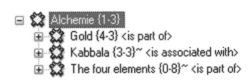

Figure 19.4   *Hierarchical display of codes in ATLAS.ti*

parts, these can be put together using the ATLAS.ti merge function. The ATLAS.ti merge function offers a variety of strategies to either add or merge the various object types, such as documents, quotes, codes, memos, networks or families.

Other features

Hypertext

ATLAS.ti offers the possibility to link quotes within and across documents, thus creating a hypertext structure this way. The original sequential document is de-linearised, broken down into pieces, which are then reconnected, making it possible to traverse from one piece of data to another piece of data regardless of their original positions.

Additional output and export options

Projects can be saved as a HTML document and published on a website. In addition, a XML export option is available. This offers the possibility to represent data in a form that does not restrict their usability to the context and output options provided by ATLAS.ti. With the aid of style sheets, users can then create their own reports, beyond the options ATLAS.ti offers.

A further output option is to export the entire coding system in the form of a SPSS syntax file. When run by SPSS, a data matrix is created containing all codes as variables and all coded segments (quotes) as cases.

Word frequencies

The ATLAS.ti Word Cruncher creates a list of words for the selected or all primary document. This feature is useful for a simple quantitative content analysis. A stop list can be used to exclude certain words, characters

or patterns from the frequency count. Results can directly be opened in Excel.

Summary

ATLAS.ti 5 is one of the more complex CAQDAS packages, offering a large number of tools and options for analysing qualitative data. In order to learn the software, you need to set aside some time or, if possible, go on a training session. However, if you invest the time, you have made a decision for a product that incorporates up-to-date Windows technology, offering you powerful tools to analyse your data. Some of the highlights are that you can assign Word or Rich Text documents, image, sound and video files. The interactive display and handling of codes and coded text passages as well as the hypertext and network functions are unique in ATLAS.ti. You may not utilise all functions in a first project when still learning the program, and not all tools may always be exploited in all projects, but with this package you certainly have software that can be extended for future use.

MAXqda2

Data entry

In MAXqda you can analyse text documents in Rich Text format including OLE support. This means you can embed objects like tables, PowerPoint presentations, audio, video or graphic files, but you can only code them as one unit. Documents can be assigned to certain text groups, such as articles, documents, interviews, etc., and organised into sets, such as interviews with female or males, documents from 1950 to 1960, etc. Text groups and sets serve in later stages of the analysis as filter devices to retrieve coded segments that match certain specified criteria, such as only responses from female interviewees working as teachers in primary schools.

Documents that have been imported into MAXqda can be edited at all stages of a project. Certain precautions have to be taken into account when working in teams.

Codesystem		118
simultaneous world.		2
media	🖉	16
characteristics		1
cold - hot		5
nature		4
learn		1
communication	📄	12
ritual		2
information		3

Figure 19.5   *Code system in MAXqda*

Coding

The smallest unit of text you can code is one character. Text is selected by highlighting the appropriate passage with the mouse. All code words are represented in form of a sideways tree hierarchy, similar to the kind of tree structure in the Windows Explorer (Figure 19.5).

The structure of the tree can be manipulated by dragging and dropping codes to other places in the tree. Symbols next to the code words indicate whether a memo has been written for a code. Code frequencies are listed at the right of the code system window.

There is no limit with regard to the number of code words you can use or the number of nests and overlaps that result from the coding process. The code word tree can be up to ten levels deep. Modifications of the coding system is possible by copying or moving all coded text at a code word to another code word. The code words of individual coded text passages cannot be modified. If this should become necessary, you first need to delete them and assign them again.

A coded text in MAXqda can be seen in Figure 19.6.

In the left margin of the displayed text, MAXqda offers three types of information. In the first column of the left margin, you see the codes displayed against the text. The

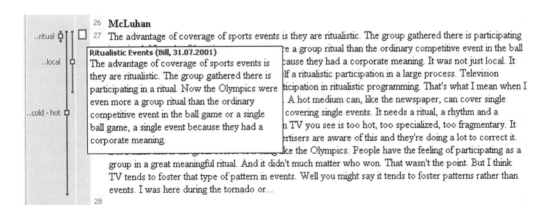

Figure 19.6   *Coded text and activated memo in MAXqda*

coded segments are referenced by a straight line with a little square box in the middle. When moving the cursor to this box, the code word for this segment is displayed. After attaching a memo to a text passage, a yellow post-it symbol is shown in the second column. When moving with the cursor over this symbol, the memo text is displayed. The third column lists paragraph numbers.

Memos

Memos can be attached to documents, codes and coded text passages. Each memo is date and time stamped. Optionally, an author and code words can be associated. This information can be used to filter, search and sort the memos. A further option is to define memo types by selecting different memo icons. Memos are in Rich Text format.

Text search and auto coding

MAXqda offers you a number of options to search the text. You can search in all or only selected documents or document passages, in retrieved text passages or in memos. Entered search strings can be combined using the logic operators AND and OR. The results are displayed in a table, which can be sorted by headers. When clicking on a result in the table, the match is highlighted in context. Search results can also be saved and exported as Rich Text files. Rather than just exporting the found search string, additional context can be exported as well.

The result table also offers a function to code the search results with a selected code word. One can either code just the hits or select x number of paragraphs surrounding the found search string.

Data retrieval

The retrieval of coded text segments follows a simple logic, which is particular to MAXqda. The retrieval logic is based on activating codes and documents. If one wants to retrieve all coded segments of Code_A from interviews 1 and 5, one needs to activate Code_A and interviews 1 and 5. The coded segments are immediately displayed in a separate window. A retrieved segment is clearly indicated by a source tag and when selected is displayed in context. The results of a search can be saved under a new code word.

It is also possible to conduct some more complex retrievals using Boolean and proximity operators. A total of ten logic operators, such as OR, intersection, if inside, if outside, followed by, etc., are available. In addition, you can use variables as filters in a search. For instance, you could ask for all occurrences of Code_A where it overlaps with Code_B in all the responses of men, age category 5, living in Munich. Variables can be managed in tables and exported or imported as text (tab-delimited) files.

Team support

MAXqda offers team support in two ways. Team members can either work with the same master version of a project (option A), or the different members of the team divide their work (option B). When choosing option A, team members can never work simultaneously on a project; only one person at a time can code a text and then the entire project has to be given to the other team members. When choosing option B, team members can work simultaneously on a project, but only on different parts. When a team member has coded a particular text or part of a text, this text can be transferred to other team members. The same applies to memos.

Another option is to merge two projects. New texts and all memos will be inserted, codes and variables will be merged.

Other features

Scoring relevance

Each coded segment can be given a weight between 0 and 100. This can be used as an indicator of how relevant or how typical a code is for a certain category. Depending on the kind of analysis, the weights can be treated as fuzzy variables. When creating a table for all codings or for the codings at a particular code, the relevance scorces (weights) are included.

Quantitative content analysis functions

If you are interested in quantitative content analysis, MAXqda offers the add-on module MAXdictio. This module allows you to analyse vocabulary and to create dictionaries. You can examine the vocabulary used in the text to find out which words can be found in which text passages or the full text. For example, among the offered functions are the creation of word frequency lists of the whole text, of marked passages, in-text groups or in-text sets, the creation of an index of selected words of one or more texts, the building-up of word-based dictionaries, the export and import of dictionaries from MS Office programs like Excel, or the further processing of the results in SPSS and Excel. All content analytic functions can be integrated into the functionality of MAXqda. Thus, if you are interested in a combination of quantitative and qualitative content analysis, the combination of MAXqda with the add-on module might be the right choice for you.

Summary

MAXqda convinces due to its simple logic and structure. It is likely to appeal to users who prefer to think of their coding system as a hierarchical construct consisting of higher and lower order codes. Conceptual-level relationships cannot be mapped within the software. Nonetheless, the software provides all necessary features to perform a qualitative data analysis and, by keeping it simple, the learning curve is not as steep as for other software packages.

The add-on module MAXdictio gives the software a unique profile, allowing for the combination of qualitative and quantitative content analysis methods.

THE ETHNOGRAPH v5.08

Data entry

The Ethnograph supports the analysis of text data. Before importing the data, it is necessary to format them in a particular way. An Ethnograph data file has a 40-character line and hanging paragraph indents. All of your data must be saved as ASCII text. The program provides an editor that facilitates the creation and re-formatting of data files into format required by The Ethnograph. The special formatting rules allow the program to identify speaker or section turns. Thus, there is no need to code speaker or other sections and variables can be directly attached to them.

Coding

It is possible to code your data interactively. This means that you can view and read the text of your data files on screen while you are coding. For each coded segment the

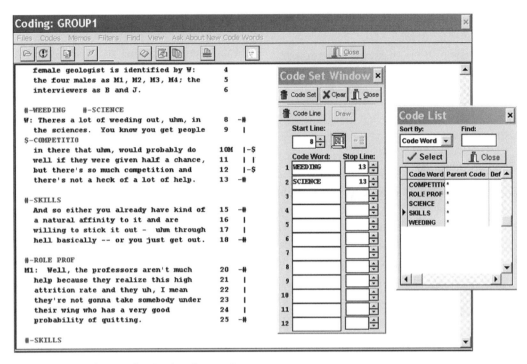

Figure 19.7   *Coding window in The Ethnograph*

boundaries are marked in the margin and the code word appears one line above the coded text segment. Code words can be conveniently selected from either the Code Book or the Tree View. Both are automatically created and updated when coding.

The smallest size of a text segment you can code is one line; the maximum length of code words is ten characters. This is a necessary restriction, otherwise it would be impossible to display all of your code words within the text (see Figure 19.7). Longer definitions of up to 500 characters (roughly half a page) can be written into the Code Book. Each coded segment can be defined by up to 12 code words and these code words can be nested or overlapped up to seven levels deep.

Within the Coding Window simple text search and code search functions are available. The coding system can be structured hierarchically by assigning parent and child codes in the Code Book, or by dragging and dropping codes in the Tree View. Parent codes are higher-level and child codes lower-level. A code can be both a parent code of a subgroup of codes and a child code of a super-ordinate code.

A hierarchical presentation of the coding system is possible in the Tree View, which displays the codes in the form of a side-ways tree. You can either view just the Tree or both the Code Book and the Tree side by side (see Figure 19.8 opposite). By collapsing or opening the various branches of the Tree View, it is possible to focus one's view on just a particular area of the coding system.

Memos

Three types of memos are available: text memos, project memos and file memos. You can attach up to 26 memos to each line in a

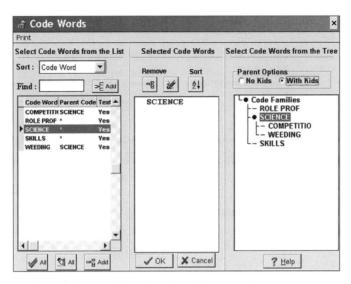

Figure 19.8   *Single code search showing the Code Book and the Tree View*

data file, up to 1,000 memos to a project and up to 1,000 memos to each data file. Each memo can be up to 32 pages in length and is date and time stamped. In addition, the initials of the author can be entered, memo categories can be defined and up to three code words can be associated with a code word. The memo categories, code words, line numbers, date and time of creation/modification, author's name and memo title can be used as sorting devices.

All memos can be accessed from a variety of places in the project. Text memos for example are identified by the letter M, which is displayed next to the first line number of the segment the memo is attached to (see Figure 19.7). A double click on the M opens the memo window.

Data retrieval

The Ethnograph search tool nicely integrates the various search options and filters that can be used in a search. You can search for segments coded by a single code word, or for segments coded by multiple code words. In the latter case, Boolean and proximity operators can be used to combine a string of up to five code words. Multiple code word searches can be saved and called up again, reused or edited for later searches.

Figure 19.8 shows the selection window for codes in a single code search. Codes can either be selected from the Code Book or the Tree View. The parent/child structure of the coding system allows you to use the equivalent of a semantic DOWN operator (i.e., SCIENCE with kids).

In addition to codes, speaker or section identifiers can be used in a search; variables and file codes can be used to restrict searches to certain documents or attributes. An identifier search retrieves all instances of a certain speaker or of text passages marked with a specific tag. Identifiers are defined in the process of transcribing the data (see 'Data entry' on page 325). A common use of identifiers is to mark speaker turns, for example the name of the interviewee or the names of participants in a focus group. Those identifiers are referred to as Speaker Identifiers. If your data consists of documents like letters or newspaper articles, you can identify them by date and source. These types of identifiers are called Section Identifiers. When employed as part of a search, both Speaker and Section Identifiers can be used as if they were code words.

For each identifier, variables such as gender, age, occupation, and so on, can be entered. In a search, this information can be utilised by retrieving text passages coded by single or multiple code words in combination with selected variables. Thus, you can, for instance, ask for all comments about a particular topic that can be attributed to only male interviewees between the ages of 25 and 30 with an income of at least $50,000 per year. Variables in The Ethnograph allow fine-grained searches in that you cannot only choose categories but enter continuous numeric values.

File codes also serve as variables in that they permit you to attach specific attributes to an entire document. File codes, like variables, can be combined by AND, OR and NOT operators. The difference between file codes and variables attached to identifiers is that you can assign up to 16,000 file codes to a data file but only 40 variables to an identifier. Thus, the program offers more than enough options to restrict and filter searchers. Search results can be reviewed on screen, printed or saved to disk, and displayed in three different ways:

- In the form of coded text segments (with or without the surrounding context, line numbers, boundaries, code words or memos).
- In the form of summary reports. Summary reports give you a count of all hits. An additional option is to display all of the start and stop lines of the coded segments that have been found.
- As frequency counts. Frequency outputs list the percentages of all hits within and across data files.

Before saving or printing search results, segments of interest can be marked and the output can be restricted to only the marked segments. Text output is saved in ASCII text format, all quantitative output is saved in the form of tables and can be imported to a statistical package for further analysis.

The entire search results or only selected segments can be saved as a new data file, which is automatically imported into the project and available for further analysis and coding.

Other features

Splitting and combining files

It is possible to split data files and to combine data files. When you combine data files, you have the option of combining only selected parts of the data files, for example lines 1 to 500 from data file X and lines 350 to 1,300 from data file Y. Inserted sub-headers inform you of the original source. Splitting and combining data files can be done on the basis of numbered or coded versions of your data files. This process does not affect the coding. You can save and print numbered, coded or generic versions of your data files.

Summary

The Ethnograph is one of the simpler programs to analyse qualitative data and it is probably the easiest of all programs to learn. The procedures are straightforward and by design they are strictly separated, so that one does not get lost or confused by multiple overlapping windows. However, experienced Windows users might expect more in terms of user friendliness. The DOS roots of the program are still noticeable. File and folder names that are longer than eight characters are not accepted or are abbreviated. Data, code, search and memo procedures cannot be run side by side. For instance, one cannot add additional files to a project while the coding or search window is open. One cannot search while the coding or memo window is still open, etc. This may not be experienced as a problem and some may even appreciate the clear separation of functions. The Ethnograph certainly offers very good search functions in combination with easy-to-handle variables. The option to work with Section and Speaker Identifiers is a unique feature of The Ethnograph. Other programs offer similar but less elegant solutions. All in all, The Ethnograph is a programme that offers good value for money; it is the least expensive of all programs discussed here.

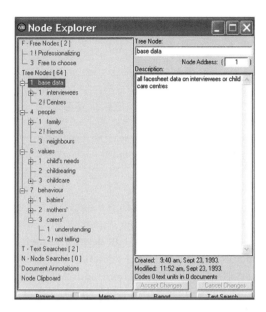

Figure 19.9   *QSR N6 Node Explorer displaying free nodes and index tree*

QSR N6

Data entry

QSR N6 can be used to analyse text data. The required format for importing data into N6 is plain text. The smallest segment that can be coded is a text unit, which can be set to lines, sentences or paragraphs. A paragraph is defined as two successive hard returns. This needs to be taken into account when transcribing or formatting the data. New data can be appended to existing documents and already imported documents can be edited. This includes inserting or removing text units, sub-headers and annotations.

Coding

Coding can be done interactively while you read the text on screen or, if you prefer, on a hard copy of your data. Coding done on paper can be transferred to the computer by using text unit numbers as reference points. All coded segments are stored in a so-called node. Coded segments are not indicated inside the text or in the margin area. They can only be made visible by specifically requesting a report that includes coding stripes for selected code words (= nodes).

Nodes can be understood as containers that have a node address and node title. There are different types of node, those holding coded data segments, results of text or node searchers, document annotations or the content of the clipboard when cutting or copying node contents. Nodes containing coded text passages can either be handled as 'free' node or can be integrated into the index tree. The index tree offers the possibility to structure and organise your codes hierarchically. All nodes are displayed in the Node Explorer (see Figure 19.9). A description for each node can be entered into the right window pane of the Node Explorer.

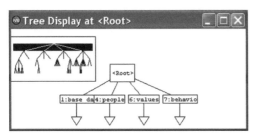

Figure 19.10   *Tree display in N6*

The Node Explorer offers a sideways representation of the coding system. Within the Node Explorer you can cut, delete and merge nodes, you can browse the text that is coded at a node, you can change node addresses, write and review memos or modify the coding at a node. In addition, the Node Explorer is a very handy device when it comes to searching. From there you have direct access to the results of the search operations (see Search Functions). To efficiently build up a hierarchical index system, certain rules should be followed. For a introduction to creating a hierarchical category scheme, see Richards and Richards (1995).

The index tree can also be displayed graphically in the form of an upside-down tree. The top of the index tree is the root and from there all the branches ramify. An overview of the entire tree is provided. However, the user can only access two levels at a time (see Figure 19.10). Nodes can be manipulated in either the side-ways or the graphical display.

It is possible to create the tree before you start coding your data. In fact, it is very common to set up certain parts of the index tree at the start of a project. This part of the tree is generally referred to as the base data tree. It can be used for coding factual information such as gender, age, race, occupation, or time series. Since this is a fairly routine task, this process can be automated by using command files. If the factual information is available in the form of a spread sheet, you can use the Import Table function for generating the base data tree and to code your data. This feature of the program allows you to link quantitative information that you have about your data with the qualitative-rich content. Document base or case data and coding at a particular node can be exported as plain text or tab-separated tables.

Memos and annotations

In addition to writing a description for each document and note, you can attach one memo to each document and node. Memos are indicated with an exclamation mark (!) before the object they belong to and their content in plain text format can be cut and pasted somewhere else. Memos can be retrieved via the context menu or when creating a report.

Annotations are short notes that can be attached as a text-unit to any text-unit in a document. All annotations are coded automatically at the Document Annotation node in the node system. In order to distinguish annotations from the rest of the text in your documents, they are put into <<brackets>>.

Text search and auto coding

In N6 you can search for words or phrases in either the documents or the coded text segments. The search can be restricted by a number of criteria. In addition, GREP expressions can be used for pattern searches. You can keep all finds or review the finds first and decide which ones you want to keep. The resulting hits are automatically coded at a new node in the Text Search area of the node system.

Data retrieval

The search engine in N6 is a very powerful tool. It offers 17 different ways of asking questions about your data, including Boolean, context, sequence, proximity, matrix and vector searches. The results of a search are saved to the node clipboard. In addition, a node containing the search results is automatically created and saved in the Node Search area of the node systems. Results of matrix or vector searches can be exported as plain text or tab-separated tables.

Node searches can be restricted to selected documents and nodes. As in N6, the text coded at the base data nodes is a form of defining data attributes or variables. This is a way to combine codes with variables, thus being able to ask questions such as: Give me all text related to attitude x, but only from female respondents of age group 1.

Having the results of a search saved at a node, you can ask further questions about specific parts of your data. This way it becomes possible to build up more and more layers of analysis and to go deeper and deeper into your data.

For utilizing the search functions in N6 in the most efficient manner, you are advised to build up the index system following the rules of hierarchical category schemes.

Team support

QSR offers a free companion tool as an add-on to N6 to merge projects. This tool allows you to compare and contrast two different projects or to build a central project from multiple sites. It is also possible to use the merge tool across different platforms (i.e., Macintosh and PC platforms).

Other features

Command files

Many processes in N6 can be automated by using command files. Command files contain written instructions that can be executed by

N6 to carry out different processes, such as importing documents, setting up the base data tree, adding and deleting coding, copying and pasting parts of the tree, deleting nodes, displaying the tree, searching text and nodes, setting restrictions, or making and printing reports. N6 makes the use of command files fairly simple by providing a number of templates. Thus, command files can be written without knowledge of the underlying syntax.

Model-building – exporting the index tree

N6 does not offer a model-building function itself, but the index tree can be exported to either Decision Explorer or Inspiration. This allows you to break away from the hierarchical structure enforced by N6 and to freely play around with the nodes, thus to enter the phase of model-building. While you lose direct access to your raw data, you can still view and edit memos.

Summary

QSR N6 is a good choice for those who prefer to organise their coding system in a hierarchically manner, or who have data that lend themselves to such a structure. Even though N6 (as compared to previous versions) offers the inclusion of free nodes into the index system, the program would lose much of its power if you do not choose to utilise the tree. Comparable to the The Ethnograph, N6 has recognisable DOS roots. File and folder names can be no longer than eight characters or have to be abbreviated. All imported documents need to be saved as plain text; output formats are also plain or tab-separated texts. Unique to the QSR products (i.e., N6 and NVivo) are the matrix and vector searches and the possibility to display and export the search results as tables. Another distinctive feature is that all text and node searches are automatically saved at a node and can easily be subjected to further analysis.

You may teach yourself the program with the help of the provided tutorial, but a professional training session is especially useful to start on the right foot in terms of setting up the index system.

NOTES

1 On the following website you find a list of free and commercial CAQDAS packages: http://caqdas.soc.surrey.ac.uk/links1.htm

2 Interesting to read in the context of arguing for or against computer technology in the qualitative data analysis process is the book chapter by John Seidel: 'Methods and Madness in the Application of Computer Technology to Qualitative Data Analysis' (Seidel, 1991).

3 The acronym CAQDAS was developed by the directors of the CAQDAS networking project at the University of Surrey, Guildford, UK. http://caqdas.soc.surrey.ac.uk/.

4 See 'ATLAS.ti goes XML' at http://www.atlasti.de/xml/.

5 Further advice in deciding between software packages can also be found on the website of the CAQDAS networking project: http://caqdas.soc.surrey.ac.uk/.

6 Other descriptions and software overviews can be found in: Friese, S. (2004) Qualitative research and consulting, at http://www.quarc.de/software_overview_table.pdf. Alexa and Zuell (1999) Commonalities, differences and limitations of text analysis software: the results of a review, at http://www.gesis.org/Publikationen/Berichte/ZUMA_Arbeitsberichte/99/99_06abs.htm.

REFERENCES

Alexa, M. and Zuell, C. (1999). 'Commonalities, differences and limitations of text analysis software: The results of a review', *ZUMA-Arbeitsbericht* No. 99/06. http://www.gesis.org/Publikationen/Berichte/ZUMA_Arbeitsberichte/99/99_06abs.htm (last accessed 4 July 2004).

Böhm, A., Legewie, H. and Muhr, T. (1992). 'Kursus Textinterpretation. Globalauswertung und Grounded Theory'. Unpublished manuscript, Technical University Berlin, Germany.

Coffey, A., Holbrook, B. and Atkinson, P. (1996) 'Qualitative data analysis: technologies and representations', *Sociological Research Online*, vol. 1, 1(1), http://www.socresonline.org.uk/socresonline/1/1/4.html (last accessed 4 July 2004).

Creswell, J.W. (1998). *Qualitative Inquiry and Research Design: Choosing among Five Traditions*. London: Sage.

Friese, S. (2004). 'Qualitative research and consulting', http://www.quarc.de/software_overview_table.pdf.

Glaser, B.G. and Strauss, A.L. (1967). *The Discovery of Grounded Theory: Strategies for Qualitative Research*. Chicago: Aldine.

Kuckartz, U. (1995). 'Case-oriented quantification'. in U. Kelle (ed.), *Computer-Aided Qualitative Data Analysis*. London: Sage, pp. 158–66.

Pink, S. (2001). *Doing Visual Ethnography*. London: Sage.

Prein, G., Kelle, U. and Bird, K. (1995). 'An overview of software', in: U. Kelle (ed.), *Computer-Aided Qualitative Data Analysis*. London: Sage, pp. 190–210.

Richards, T. and Richards, L. (1995). 'Using hierarchical categories in qualitative data analysis'. in U. Kelle (ed.), *Computer-Aided Qualitative Data Analysis*. London: Sage, pp. 80–95.

Seidel, J. (1991). 'Methods and madness in the application of computer technology to qualitative data analysis'. in N. Fielding and R. Lee (eds), *Using Computers in Qualitative Research*. London: Sage, part two.

Seidel, J. (1998). 'Qualitative Data Analysis'. Available at: http://www.qualisresearch.com (last accessed 4 July 2004).

Weitzman, E.A. and Miles, M.B. (1995). *A Software Sourcebook: Computer Programs for Qualitative Data Analysis*. London: Sage.

SOFTWARE

ATLAS.ti	http::/www.atlasti.com
MAXqda	http://www.maxqda.com
The Ethnograph	http://www.qualisresearch.com
QSR N6	http://www.qsr.com.au

20

Seeking Science in the Field: Life Beyond the Laboratory

STEVE FULLER

PHILOSOPHY BY SOCIOLOGICAL MEANS: STS AS FIELDWORK

There is a ready-made formula for translating philosophical concerns about science into topics of field research in Science and Technology Studies (STS): what philosophers regard as *problems*, STS researchers treat simply as *facts*. Philosophers are often misled by the import of STS's fixation on the 'social construction of scientific facts', to quote the notorious subtitle of the first edition of Latour and Woolgar (1986). Much more telling than showing that facts are socially constructed is that what is socially constructed are facts. In other words, STS takes the existence of facts as unproblematic, once they have been constructed. If the relevant scientists deem that a certain social construction constitutes a fact, then *ipso facto* it is a fact, with no philosophical questions left to be asked about it. Here STS's debt to a late Wittgensteinian style of empiricism is most keenly felt, whereby the main task of fieldwork is to enable us to observe without epistemological prejudice

(Lynch, 1993). Of course, the scientists under study may query a fact according to approved discipline-based methods, but such queries are not available to a free-ranging philosophical critic, let alone sceptic, who might wish to ground the fact in principles of knowledge that could ground any conceivable fact. Even in matters as basic and universal as logic, STS fieldworkers are inclined to reserve judgement, interpreting those who *prima facie* commit contradictions as 'contextually sensitive reasoners'. In the old scholastic saying, every contradiction is a distinction waiting to be drawn; every erroneous conception is in reality an action yet to be completed.

STS fieldwork typically draws on the sociological method of 'grounded theory', according to which the inquirer introduces a theoretical concept or perspective only if the agents under study also do so (Glaser and Strauss, 1967). Grounded theory was originally developed as an inductivist response to the hypothetico-deductive method favoured by the main school of US sociology, structural-functionalism, associated with Talcott

Parsons and Robert Merton. In particular, structural-functionalists postulated that *deviance* was a well-defined role with specific functions in the social system. In contrast, grounded theorists argued that the deviant role, say, in the context of asylums and hospitals, must be constructed from moment to moment, as there is no clear observable difference between the behaviour of so-called normals and deviants. The groundbreaking, albeit perverse, insight of STS fieldwork is that this approach to deviance may be applied to people on the *positive* as well as the negative extreme of a normal distribution curve. Thus, in their daily laboratory tasks, scientists do not sound or look especially different from people working in an industrial environment subject to an intensive division of labour. Nevertheless, scientists are socially constructed as exceptionally rational, producing knowledge that commands authority throughout society. How, then, do their thoughts, actions and outputs acquire such a superior status? According to STS, the general answer lies in the 'made for export' language scientists use to describe their activities and the specific distribution channels in which that language, as expressed in journal articles, preprints, and press releases, circulates. (Still the best methodological introduction to this 'discourse analytic' side of STS is Gilbert and Mulkay (1984)). This produces a forward momentum, involving many other people, laboratories, interests, and so forth, that eventually turns a unique set of events into a universally recognizable fact (Latour and Woolgar, 1986: Chapter 6).

At one level, STS's research orientation reveals a remarkable sympathy for the inquired: The burden of proof is always on the inquirer to demonstrate that she has not cut short the inquired by passing judgement on the latter's actions before their consequences are fully known. Such sympathy

makes for a peculiar but disciplined form of inquiry, one in principle willing to suspend judgement indefinitely as the inquirer records the vicissitudes undergone by the inquired. This is the spirit in which to understand Bruno Latour's (1987) injunction to 'follow the actors'. It is worth observing just how diametrically opposed this mode of inquiry is from the inquirer-centred approach championed by the hypothetico-deductive method (see Table 20.1).

The broadly positivist philosophy associated with the hypothetico-deductive method would concentrate all the power (or 'agency', to use the politically correct term) in the inquirer and none in the inquired. The positivists were willing to treat the inquired as mere things, passive entities awaiting their natures to be revealed by active inquirers. Of course, the positivists themselves understood the matter in a more ethically flattering light: inquirers take full responsibility for their inquiries, in that if their theories turn out to be in error, then they have only themselves to blame. In contrast, in STS's moral universe, the locus of responsibility remains unclear because it is distributed among a plethora of agents in the sphere of inquiry. Indeed, the only clear responsibility the STS inquirer takes for his/her account is at the brute proprietary level that the account belongs to him/her and not to the inquired, a stance familiar from the annals of ethnomethodology (e.g. Sharrock, 1974).

If philosophers with their explicit normative appeals to truth, rationality and objectivity behave like legislators and judges, STS researchers act more like ventriloquists and impersonators. Thus, philosophers treat inquiry as a matter of upholding and meeting standards that may exceed ordinary scientific behaviour, whereas STS researchers emulate the view of inquiry they ascribe to the scientists they study, namely, the manufacture of endless

Table 20.1   *How should research be grounded?*

Standpoint	Inquirer-based	Inquired-based
Frame of inquiry	Theory-laden observation	Object-centred sociality
Social epistemology	Sovereignty of inquirer's standpoint	Distribution of knowledge among the inquired
Inquirer's default attitude	Resistant to the environment	Adaptive to the environment
Inquirer's philosophical position	Relationism (i.e. shift to whatever is critical of the presumptive standpoint)	Relativism (i.e. mirror whatever is the presumptive standpoint)
Goal of inquiry	Reveal the limits of the inquired's sphere of action	Reveal the extent of the inquired's sphere of action
Overall normative goal	Expand the inquired's sphere of action	Normalize the inquired's sphere of action
Inquirer's response to inquired's self-images	Iconoclast (i.e. they are likely self-deceptive)	Iconophile (i.e. they are likely self-empowering)
Where the inquirer is rigid	Her own theoretical framework	Her adherence to the inquired's perspective
Where the inquirer is flexible	Her own attitude to the inquired's situation	Those who pay her to study the inquired's perspective

products whose success or failure is determined by their intended consumers.

Not surprisingly, when pushed back into philosophy, STS researchers instinctively convert epistemological issues to ontological ones. Epistemology presupposes that reality sets a standard that is met to varying degrees by different modes of cognitive access, whereas ontology presupposes that reality constitutes a domain with different kinds of objects that are encountered equally. In quantitative terms, knowledge is measured, while entities are counted. Thus, it is standard practice among STS fieldworkers, having completed the study of one research site, they do not test their findings for their generalizability to other research sites; rather they use the findings as a template to explore new sites, the deviations from which then provide the basis for generating new findings (Knorr-Cetina, 1999: 252).

STS's broadly empiricist – 'seeing is believing' – rhetoric tends to privilege methods involving face-to-face encounters with subjects in or around the subjects' native knowl-edge production sites. Encounters with subjects by more spatially and temporally mediated means – such as their writings in the archives, their behaviour under experimental conditions, or statistics collected about them – are regarded with greater suspicion. It might have been expected that this radical empiricism would end in tears, or at least scepticism, as STS researchers would have little reason to trust the word of their own colleagues without themselves having first inspected the research site to check their observations. For example, the logical positivists quickly realized that such hyper-verificationism would render science impossible, or at least impossibly slow. Consequently, they generally gravitated towards a 'conventionalist' epistemology, in which theories are initially imposed on reality (as 'hypotheses') and then judged according to the consequences ('predictions') they yield. In such a regime, as Karl Popper especially stressed, even error may turn out to be instructive and, in that sense, worth having been committed. In contrast, the general STS solution to the problem of verification is what Steven Shapin (1994) has called 'virtual witnessing', a meta-method that he himself learned 'retro-reflexively', so to speak, by imitating those he studied archivally, namely, such seventeenth-century English experimentalists as Robert Boyle, Robert Hooke and Isaac Newton, who practised virtual witnessing as a distinct rhetoric for persuading those absent from the laboratory that the experimenter's eyes provide a reliable lens through which to view the reported events.

STS FIELDWORK AS A REFLECTION OF THE SHIFTING MATERIAL CONDITIONS OF SCIENTIFIC WORK

It would be hard to imagine another group of subjects who have reacted so violently to the sociologists studying them as scientists. Yet, the reaction has been by no means uniform across the scientific community. The purer the science and the older the scientist, the greater the suspicion of sociologists, especially those social constructivist practitioners of STS who study scientists in their work sites. In contrast, for younger, typically client-centred, contract-based researchers who work in interdisciplinary and applied fields, sociological fieldwork is often a bracing antidote to gerontocratic pretensions of a nostalgic golden age of inquiry that continue to dominate the bastions of scientific professionalism. After all, a central conclusion of recent STS, backed by both historical and ethnographic inquiries, is that science has always been implicated in wider social, political and economic processes. However, the legitimation of science has traditionally involved minimizing the attention drawn to these entanglements, usually with the help of philosophically inspired 'methodological' discourse that refers only to 'logic' and 'evidence' in the presence of complicated machinery and datasheets. This conclusion has now even seeped into European science policy thinking, which proclaims a 'new production of knowledge' that is epitomized by the younger generation of researchers, so-called 'Mode 2' knowledge producers, for whom 'science' is tantamount to the entire technical infrastructure of contemporary social life, or simply 'technoscience'. Accordingly, those older scientists who cling on to the traditional mode of legitimating science are relegated to 'Mode 1' (Gibbons et al., 1994; Nowotny et al., 2001).

At the outset we should take the measure of this sea change in the social legitimation of science. In Mode 1 it is unseemly to justify research in terms of the income streams it generates – let alone the costs generated by its very pursuit. If anything, the material bases of research had been regarded as inversely related to its epistemic merit. The idea goes back to Aristotle and Newton: science aims to explain the most by the least. In science's heroic age, one clever experiment or one neat proof could lay to rest a host of uncertainties and controversies. In the case of more naturalistic research, whose painstaking character required concentrated effort over long periods, the expectation was that it would be undertaken only by people like Charles Darwin, whose inherited wealth afforded them adequate leisure. Darwin rushed *Origin of the Species* into print in 1859 after a 'mere' 20 years of effort, not because a desperate funder had pestered him for 'outputs', but because he feared being scooped by Alfred Russel Wallace in their highbrow gentlemen's game to explain organic evolution. In Darwin's day, laboured efforts that required the indulgence of funders – be they private or public – raised suspicions of researcher incompetence or, perhaps worse, researchers interested more in lucrative applications than edifying insights. Traditionally, the persuasiveness of state support for so-called curiosity-driven science has been that the level of material support – specifically, the time and equipment – required for its conduct would be minimal *vis-à-vis* its long-term returns. However, as the entry costs for sustaining such curiosity have risen, so too has the desire for the returns to be larger and appear sooner.

Science has been traditionally justified as a somewhat other-worldly enterprise very clearly distinguished from technology. The philosophically sanctified discourses of objectivity and rationality that continue to prevail in scientific journal articles may be understood – and certainly was by the early STS fieldworkers – as a symbolic recoding of the fairly pedestrian set of routines that constitute 'laboratory life' (Knorr-Cetina, 1981; Latour and Woolgar, 1986). As the fieldworkers saw it, scientists write about enchanted realms of 'quarks' and 'alleles', hidden causes – the source of the blurry traces found in photographic plates and Petri dishes – whose subtle effects can be found throughout the material world. Readers of such fieldwork would be forgiven for being reminded of a shaman's divination of a bird's entrails. Indeed, one of the original ethnographers (Lynch, 1988) provocatively, but no less usefully, compared the divergence between science's traditional – and still official – descriptions of its laboratory practices and how things appear to the observant fieldworker with an agnostic's perception of the Catholic doctrine of transubstantiation, whereby the priest (scientist) claims to convert ordinary bread and wine (technically mediated samples) to the body and blood of Jesus (scientifically real entities) in the Holy Mass (an experiment).

However, as scientists have been increasingly forced to justify themselves in terms of the sheer material character of their activities, they have come to look more favourably upon the fieldworker's perspective. In this Mode 2 state, a greater proportion of a senior scientist's effort is spent on activities that would have been previously regarded as peripheral or auxiliary to 'science as such'. These include incessant grant-writing, the day-to-day management and coordination of a non-trivial number of specialized researchers, not to mention conference presentations to potential funders – as well as colleagues. These are no longer seen as regrettable but necessary means to a nobler end, such as a Nobel Prize-winning discovery. Rather, the perpetuation of the research programme – more precisely, the livelihoods of the major stakeholders in the research team – has become an end in itself. As suits the fieldworker whose eyes are firmly 'on the ground', the working aim of science is self-maintenance not self-transcendence. Accordingly, the magical philosophical discourse that traditionally legitimated science metamorphoses into an expertise in rhetoric, one typically possessed by senior scientists herself, given her responsibility for launching the research programme, promoting its virtues and, hopefully, boosting its fortunes. Knows how to assemble speech and writing to organize the lab's disparate activities into a credible quantum of new knowledge. This involves both the selection of an appropriate set of theoretical and empirical precedents in which to embed the team's findings and the construction of an appropriate, typically mathematical, representation of the team's data that reveals a good – but not suspiciously too good – fit with the hypotheses under consideration.

Knorr-Cetina (1981) and Latour and Woolgar (1986) accessed this rhetorical dimension by alternative means. The former examined successive drafts of a single research article intended for publication, while the latter followed the streamlining of a published finding as it came to frame the basis on which subsequent researchers constructed their findings. Whereas Knorr-Cetina chased the paper trail back to the researchers' rubbish bin, Latour and Woolgar turned to the serials section of the university library. Together they provide two crucial dimensions for fathoming the social construction of a scientific fact. In terms of developmental biology, Knorr-Cetina studied the 'ontogenesis', and Latour and Woolgar the 'phylogenesis', of that peculiar species of scientific life, *the fact*. The overall image one gets of this process is that regardless of what actually transpires at the laboratory site, the scientist's prime rhetorical objective is to convey the impression that she has made the most of her situation. Knorr-Cetina dubbed this the 'logic of opportunism', but it is most naturally interpreted as an *ethic of productivity*. The best advertisement for the continuation of one's research programme is the demonstration that the time and money spent in the lab was optimal for its results. Thus, as much as possible, one tries to minimize the appearance of waste or idleness. Again, the contrast with more traditional scientific modes of justification is striking. Perhaps the last great defence of a Mode 1 political economy for science, Polanyi (1957), explicitly tied free inquiry to the ability to waste resources with impunity, since if natural reality is truly independent of human designs, then there is no reason to think that it will conform to scientists' work patterns, let alone deadlines. At most, through their disciplinary training, scientists can mentally prepare themselves just in case a glimpse of reality should come their way as a 'discovery'. On this traditional view, knowledge is more a matter of being *receptive* than *productive* (for a critique, see Fuller, 2002: 16–20; Fuller and Collier, 2004: 229–30).

Here is a good way to epitomize the difference in mentalities between science in Mode 1 and Mode 2 in terms of the conduct of laboratory life: Mode 1 scientists seek *prizes*, that is, recognition for specific achievements that imply nothing about the material conditions under which they were made. In contrast, Mode 2 scientists seek *grants*, that is, extended licences to the material conditions of knowledge production before any achievements have been made (Fuller, 2002: Chapter 1). The contrast in mentalities also parallels the two main empirical methodologies of STS, *archival history* and *ethnographic fieldwork*. A prize-centred study of science typically works backwards to explain an achievement, whereas a grant-centred study typically follows the flow of action and documents its consequences. The former studies science already made, the latter science in the making. An old scholastic distinction comes in handy at this point. In Mode 1 the order of knowing reverses the order of being, whereas in Mode 2 the order of knowing corresponds to the order of being (see Fuller, 1993: 95–6). The implied epistemological distinction is realist versus constructivist. From a social epistemological standpoint, the most interesting feature of this set of transitions is that constructivism's vaunted 'anti-establishment' view of science tracks the emergence of the neo-liberal political economy in which science is increasingly embedded. In other words, constructivism breaks with more rationalist and realist philosophies of science not because they are insufficiently critical of science but, on the contrary, because they fail to reflect the current state of science. Thus, constructivism provides ideological support for the emerging scientific orthodoxy as it criticizes the old philosophical orthodoxy (Fuller and Collier, 2004: xiii–xiv).

NEW HORIZONS FOR LABORATORY LIFE: SCIENCE AS A SITE OF GENERATIONAL CONFLICT AND JURISDICTIONAL AMBIGUITY

The STS researcher entering a scientific work site steps into a scene of smouldering conflict, what Marxists used to call a 'structural contradiction'. Whether the origins of this conflict are traced to the end of the Cold War or the fiscal crisis of the welfare state, both in the 1980s, the effects are manifest. The conflict is epitomized as a generational gap in how scientists relate to each other and their work. (As science has lost its lifelong 'vocational' character, the differences in generations no longer correspond so neatly with age cohorts. Generational membership begins with receipt of the terminal academic degree.) Roughly speaking, the more institutionally secure scientists explain their work in terms of the logic of a research programme that is justified on intellectual grounds, as evidenced in peer-reviewed journal publications. For them, the primary 'users and beneficiaries' of their work are people very much like themselves, though they expect that eventually the work will contribute to public enlightenment and practical applications. However, these are distinctly non-scientific activities, usually better performed by others. In contrast, less institutionally secure scientists explain their work in terms of a more diffuse set of market attractors that, to be sure, still include scientific colleagues but also more openly address the needs of 'users and beneficiaries' outside the professional community. These others, though euphemistically called 'the public', are often more accurately described as 'stakeholders', 'consumers' or, more brutally, 'clients'. In short, from a political economy standpoint, the younger scientists see their 'manufacture of knowledge' in the laboratory as closer to service delivery

than capital development. It would seem, then, that the transition from Mode 1 to Mode 2 tracks this generational shift.

Of special interest here is the tendency of the younger generation to identify their 'freedom' and even 'autonomy' with the relative ease with which they can shift research orientation, rather than an ability to follow through a line of research to its logical conclusion. This point of difference raises profound questions of interpretation for the STS fieldworker. Older scientists may resent that their work is increasingly evaluated at the point of delivery, forcing them to produce results 'just in time' instead of 'just in case'. Yet, their younger colleagues appreciate the more tangible rewards – both in terms of recognition and remuneration – that such direct exposure to the market brings. For them, the professional autonomy strenuously defended by their elders looks like an 'old boys club' shrouded in mystique, reminiscent of the worst features of trade guilds. To the elders, of course, the juniors appear to be 'selling out', or at least lowering their professional aspirations. Given this vast difference in perspectives, it would seem that the distinctive sense of 'free inquiry' invoked across generations of scientists may be identified in two rather contradictory ways: either a certain sort of steadfastness (the older view) or a certain sort of flexibility (the younger view). Do these two interpretations offer alternative contextualizations of the same norm (say 'research autonomy') or signal a subtle but fundamental shift in the normative structure of science itself?

The alternative contextualizations view is supported by Thomas Kuhn's (1970) understanding of the sources of incommensurability in the scientific enterprise. According to Kuhn, the normative features of science most clearly linked to its knowledge-producing functions – simplicity, fecundity, intelligibility, novelty, etc. – are not expressed the same way across different paradigms. For example, what one paradigm counts as the simpler hypothesis may appear the more complex from the standpoint of another paradigm with different background theories and interests. This divergence in interpretations renders the paradigms incommensurable. Kuhn's deepest, and least appreciated, insight is that the history of the natural sciences (as opposed to, say, the history of politics or even of the humanities or social sciences) can be easily told as one of continuous progress only because those disciplines have maintained a fairly fixed normative repertoire, typically expressed in terms of what philosophers call a 'logic of justification', in the face of the ever-changing research conditions in which the repertoire must be deployed. This insight helps to explain Kuhn's continuing popularity with ethnomethodologists, despite the historical limitations of his model (Sharrock and Read, 2002). Nevertheless, it remains somewhat mysterious the sense in which science's normative repertoire exerts constraint over what scientists do if its effects can turn out to be so diffuse (Fuller, 1993: 191–207; Fuller and Collier, 2004: 274–78).

In contrast, the view that generational shift corresponds to a fundamental normative shift is rooted in the classical sociology of knowledge, though the thesis was originally developed with political parties, not scientific paradigms, in mind (Mannheim, 1936). According to this view, scientists are always trying to shore up the legitimacy of their position in a world over which they have limited control. Moreover, each new generation of scientists enters a world already populated by senior scientists who expect that their successors pay homage to their achievements, which may have themselves come to be part of why the larger society continues to

support science. However, once the elders lose their grip over the juniors (through death, retirement, or institutional displacement), the juniors are free to adapt more directly to their world, which invariably requires a selective appropriation of the language that the elders had used to justify their position in an earlier time. But this is done more in the spirit of what evolutionary biologists call 'protective colouration' than 'showing one's true colours'. From the fieldworker's standpoint, the philosophically sanctified discourse of science's normative repertoire would thus appear as potentially diverting from the real causes of action, which may be linked to a reward structure that is maintained outside the scientific field. Put crudely but not inaccurately, according to this view, philosophy simply *is* ideology, when it comes from the mouths of scientists.

It is difficult to decide between these two accounts of the normative implications of generational change in science because the *jurisdiction* of the 'scientific community' supposedly constituted by the 'normative structure of science' remains radically unclear. Indeed, this may be the most glaring conceptual problem facing STS fieldworkers today. To be sure, talk of 'scientific community' and the 'normative structure of science' is now common parlance across several disciplines. Nevertheless, these two phrases came into use only in the 1950s, as coinages associated with Michael Polanyi (1957) and Robert Merton (1957). From somewhat different ideological positions, they were concerned with protecting the autonomy of science from government interference in the Cold War era (Hollinger, 1990; Fuller, 2000b: 70–1, 235–38).

Were it not for this external threat to scientific autonomy, 'community' would not be the most obvious term in the sociological lexicon for capturing science's social dimension. The historic exemplar of scientific inquiry has tended to be a maverick and myth-destroyer, like Galileo, who by the end of the nineteenth century had become a stock character in literature as, to quote the title of Ibsen's famous play, 'an enemy of the people'. Yet, the idea of community suggests a bounded region where mutually recognized members organize their activities into meaningful practices that serve to maintain the community's integrity across several generations. Communities tend to be held together by strong kin or kin-like bonds, as in the case of master–apprentice, which simulates features of the parent–child relationship. The strong sense of self-protection and self-perpetuation implied in community appears alien to the often self-sacrificing spirit of the exemplary scientist. Not surprisingly, Karl Popper (1981) insisted to his deathbed that the scientist was the ultimate 'permanent revolutionary'.

Of course, with a little metaphorical extension, the 'laboratory life' model of science favoured by STS fieldworkers may be regarded as a community in the strict sociological sense, especially given the increasing use of the postdoctoral fellowship to stagger the entry of scientists into regular academic employment. The 'postdoc' is a category of scientist who acquires additional professional training by engaging in front-line research. However, the role expectations of such a scientist are ill-defined: Are they autonomous inquirers or glorified lab technicians? Do they bring skills otherwise absent from the lab or do they lack skills that only the lab can provide? In any case, the number of scientists in this category has increased markedly in the aftermath of the Cold War, as the number of permanent academic posts has generally shrunk. When the US Congress's old research arm, the Office of Technology Assessment, first recognized the proliferation of postdocs, they were dubbed the 'unfaculty', which invites comparison

with the 'undead' (Fuller, 2000a: 127). In this potentially unsavoury context of a changing labour market, communitarian rhetoric has functioned as protective colouration. Seen in the round, laboratory life prosthetically extends home life by creating new dependency relations between the lab director and the postdocs that reinforce relations of authority and deference long after the completion of formal academic requirements, indeed sometimes marking scientists as the spawn of the prestigious research environments that typically sponsor postdoctoral fellowships (Fuller, 2003: 65–7). In this respect, postdocs are 'born again' scientists.

Nevertheless, the laboratory does not exhaust – or perhaps even epitomize – the social character of science. The point cuts in two opposing ways, which together define the terms of the ongoing 'Science Wars' (Ross, 1996). On the one hand, it encourages fieldworkers to cast doubt on science's purported normative structure for its failure to capture the communal character of laboratory practice. On the other hand, scientists themselves appear to locate their normative structure outside the immediate environment. Their talk of what Merton identified as 'communism', 'organized scepticism', 'universalism' and 'disinterestedness' refers to what in the Enlightenment was called the 'republic of letters', a virtual community held together by regular correspondence, punctuated by a few life-defining face-to-face encounters. In its original eighteenth-century incarnation, the sentiment constituting this republic often amounted to little more than 'my enemy's enemy is my friend', specifically common persecution by religious and civil authorities. Thus, when Voltaire famously claimed he would risk his life to defend his opponent's right to speak against him, he was implicitly acknowledging the threat of state censorship they both shared. As science became more technologically enhanced and politically relevant, the republic of letters underwent mutation. Movements towards the internationalization of scientific communication, the unification of scientific knowledge, as well as the unionization of scientists themselves, all of which enjoyed their heyday from about 1870 to 1970, were safeguards against the pressures scientists faced to perform in a patriotic and otherwise sectarian fashion in an increasingly militarized global environment (Schroeder-Gudehus, 1990).

An unintended consequence of the end of the Cold War has been a weakening of both the nation-states and global organizations that had grounded the dialectic of scientific jurisdiction. It would be easy, therefore, to conclude that the corresponding normative pulls traditionally exerted on the scientist would similarly diminish. However, this has not been the case. To be sure, today's partial replacement of military with commercial concerns has somewhat lowered the stakes of the struggle. Nevertheless, the struggle retains its original intensity, albeit expressed in less absolute terms. On the one hand, the call of worldwide movements typically infused with the grandiose philosophical ambitions of positivism or Marxism (or both) has been sublimated into the imperative to publish in internationally oriented, peer-reviewed journals. In effect, the republic of letters has lost its older imperial ambitions to become the template for societal transformation. Now it mainly worries about securing its own borders from those who would corrupt the peer review process. On the other hand, the nationalist mentality prone to interpret scientists' cross-border associations as potential acts of espionage or treason has yielded to a less consistently stoked paranoia about unprotected intellectual property and unexploited economic opportunities. Although there is little clear relationship between the sheer acquisition of intellectual property rights and financial gain, the mere failure or reluctance to patent research can render a scientist a source of suspicion in the eyes of today's academic administrators and research managers.

How might the fieldworker translate these tectonic shifts in the macro-social context of scientific work into something that might be obtained from observing and interviewing scientists? An interesting angle into this question is to consider how principled disputes about the nature of jurisdiction are resolved by judges in particular cases. When a crime is committed, there are two ways of determining jurisdiction: either by the location of the crime or the nationality of the criminal. Common law countries favour the former criterion, civil law countries the latter. Moreover, differences in jurisdiction may exist cooperatively, as in mutual extradition treaties, or competitively, as in duties to family, religion or profession that are in conflict with those of the state. By analogy, the fieldworker might try to get the scientist to talk about situations in which local lab allegiances cut against wider normative commitments, and how these are resolved. The point would be to acquire a sense of science's exact jurisdiction over some *prima facie* scientific activity, since scientists, as full-bodied human beings, are not always responding to what they regard as specifically 'scientific' imperatives.

The fieldworker might start by inquiring into the parameters of the scientist's sense of 'scientific community'. Two distinct lines of inquiry are implied here: To what extent is this term indexed to the scientist's work site? To what extent is this term indexed to a set of non-work activities?

The first question addresses whether the scientist sees him/herself as primarily relating to the people he/she encounters everyday in the lab or the people to whom he/she would like his/her work to make a difference. To be sure, the two groups may overlap but they are probably not identical. Differences between the two groups may explain, for example, why the scientist fears but does not respect the lab director, tolerates colleagues, but feels he/she comes into their own only in cyberspace or at conferences. However, the two groups may increase in overlap as disciplinary norms weaken and lab members see themselves as sealed in a common fate, for example, an inter-disciplinary research team (typically in environmental or biomedical science) in need of renewed funding to complete a project that has taken them outside the mainstream of their respective disciplines for several years (Lazenby, 2002). The second question concerns the depth of the scientist's conception of community: Does a sense of community among scientists extend to, say, matters of politics and culture? The burgeoning social capital literature suggests that the most productive communities are ones whose members have common interests outside the work environment, which then help to sustain work-based relations, especially through difficult times.

When researching both questions, the fieldworker might find of use the model of a 'community of faith' whose members struggle to uphold their beliefs against ambient local resistance. It might thus be worth asking a pointed question: *To whom are you ultimately accountable for the quality of your research?* For example, it would be interesting to see whether the lab director, or whoever happens to be the scientist's paymaster, figures in the answer. The idea that the scientific community might be constituted more like a religion than, say, a neighbourhood or a tribe is supported by the free-floating character of the Mertonian norms, which operate more as professions or justifications than as constraints on actual conduct. Something similar may also be said of

recent philosophical attempts to incorporate science within an overall distribution of knowledge in society (e.g. Putnam, 1975). Here science tends to function as an all-purpose arbiter of disagreements – be they semantic or political – that manage to elude the local means of dispute resolution. The jurisprudential precedent for this sense of 'normative structure' is, of course, *natural law theory*, which was historically invoked in just this fashion, especially before the Peace of Westphalia in 1648 established the precedent of identifying jurisdiction with territorial sovereignty (Fuller, 2004). Not surprisingly, increasing calls for 'science courts' and 'research ethics panels' to decide cases of alleged violations of normatively acceptable research practice often seem to be inspired by international courts of justice, perhaps the last refuge of natural law theory in the contemporary world.

More than a quarter-century has passed since the first ethnographies of the laboratory were published. The intervening period has been marked by considerable institutional, and some intellectual, growth for the STS field. However, the field remains largely anchored in its original anti-philosophical stance. This, in turn, has discouraged field-workers from asking foundational questions about how exactly the inquirer is to infer the 'governance of science' from the laboratory environment, especially in a time when laboratory life is embedded in environments that are at odds not merely with, say, positivist or functionalist understandings of science, but more importantly with the training and expectations of the scientists to whom the fieldworker is likely to encounter. That Merton's proposed 'normative structure of science' does not capture what transpires on the ground is by now obvious, and it may mean, of course, that his theory is false. But equally it could mean that science today leads a fugitive existence, as its adherents live and work in a state of quasi-captivity. Future forays into the laboratory would do well to try to tell the difference.

REFERENCES

Fuller, S. (1993). *Philosophy of Science and Its Discontents* (2nd edn; orig. 1989). New York: Guilford Press.

Fuller, S. (2000a). *The Governance of Science*. Milton Keynes: Open University Press.

Fuller, S. (2000b). *Thomas Kuhn: A Philosophical History for Our Times*. Chicago: University of Chicago Press.

Fuller, S. (2002). *Knowledge Management Foundations*. Woburn, MA: Butterworth-Heinemann.

Fuller, S. (2003). 'In Search of Vehicles for Knowledge Governance: On the Need for Institutions that Creatively Destroy Social Capital'. In N. Stehr (ed.), *The Governance of Knowledge* New Brunswick, NJ: Transaction Books. pp. 41–76.

Fuller, S. (2004). 'Descriptive vs Revisionary Social Epistemology: The Former as Seen by the Latter', *Episteme* 1(1): 23–34.

Fuller, S. and J. Collier (2004). *Philosophy, Rhetoric and the End of Knowledge: A New Beginning for Science & Technology Studies* (2nd edn; orig. 1993). Hillsdale, NJ: Lawrence Erlbaum Associates.

Gibbons, M. et al. (1994). *The New Production of Knowledge*. London: Sage.

Gilbert, N. and M. Mulkay (1984). *Opening Pandora's Box*. Cambridge: Cambridge University Press.

Glaser, B. and A. Strauss (1967). *The Discovery of Grounded Theory: Strategies for Qualitative Research Practice*. Chicago: Aldine.

Hollinger, D. (1990). 'Free Enterprise and Free Inquiry: The Emergence of Laissez-faire Communitarianism in the Ideology of Science in the United States', *New Literary History* 21: 897–919.

Knorr-Cetina, K. (1981). *The Manufacture of Knowledge*. Oxford: Pergamon.

Knorr-Cetina, K. (1999). *Epistemic Cultures*. Cambridge, MA: Harvard University Press.

Kuhn, T.S. (1970). *The Structure of Scientific Revolutions* (2nd edn; orig. 1962). Chicago: University of Chicago Press.

Latour, B. (1987). *Science in Action*. Milton Keynes: Open University Press.

Latour, B. and S. Woolgar (1986). *Laboratory Life: The Construction of Scientific Facts* (2nd edn; orig. 1979). Princeton, NJ: Princeton University Press.

Lazenby, J.A. (2002). 'Climates of Collaboration', PhD dissertation in History & Philosophy of Science, University of Toronto, Toronto.

Lynch, M.E. (1988). 'Sacrifice and the Transformation of the Animal Body into a Scientific Object: Laboratory Culture and Ritual Practice in the Neurosciences'. *Social Studies of Science* 18: 265–89.

Lynch, M.E. (1993). *Scientific Practice and Ordinary Action*. Cambridge: Cambridge University Press.

Mannheim, K. (1936). *Ideology and Utopia* (orig. 1929). New York: Harcourt, Brace & World.

Merton, R.K. (1957). *Social Theory and Social Structure*, New York: Free Press.

Nowotny, H. et al. (2001). *Re-Thinking Science: Knowledge and the Public in an Age of Uncertainty*. Cambridge: Polity Press.

Polanyi, M. (1957). *Personal Knowledge*. Chicago: University of Chicago Press.

Popper, K. (1981) 'The Rationality of Scientific Revolutions'. I. Hacking (ed.) Scientific Revolutions. Oxford: Oxford University Press. pp. 80–116

Putnam, H. (1975). *Mind, Language and Reality: Collected Papers* (Vol. 2). Cambridge: Cambridge University Press.

Ross, A. (ed.) (1996). *Science Wars*. Durham, NC: Duke University Press.

Schroeder-Gudehus, B. (1990). 'Nationalism and Internationalism'. In R.C. Olby et al. (eds), *Companion to the History of Modern Science* London: Routledge. pp. 909–19.

Shapin, S. (1994). *The Social History of Truth*. Chicago: University of Chicago Press.

Sharrock, W. (1974). 'On Owning Knowledge'. In R. Turner (ed.), *Ethnomethodology*. Harmondsworth: Penguin. pp. 45–53.

Sharrock, W. and R. Read (2002). *Kuhn: Philosopher of Scientific Revolution*. Cambridge: Polity Press.

Part 10

Locating Fresh Fields

21

Postmodern Field Relations in Health Research

NICK J. FOX

There is, of course, no such thing – in any essential sense – as 'the field'. The 'field' is constructed out of the practices of certain human beings who designate themselves as social researchers, define others as subjects and (with luck) persuade a further group to fund the former to inspect, categorise, analyse and interpret the latter. Fieldwork is both the sum of these processes and a performance characterised by a particular, self-conscious set of behaviours, including stoicism in the face of one's own discomfort or others' procrastination and a willingness to accept the bizarre or outrageous as commonplace and morally neutral (Barley, 1986).

Fieldwork (as a particular kind of systematic research practice based on naturalistic observation) is a typically modern enterprise, one that in its short life has reflected, refracted and maybe even helped constitute the dominant politics, ethics and social relations of the broader society that spawned it. It is certainly constitutive of an 'archive' (Foucault, 1974) that documents the social behaviour of people in our communities and cultures (I will have more to say about this 'archive' later). This *Handbook* is documentary proof of its significance and the growing impact of fieldwork as a methodology of knowledge creation.

So the critiques of modernism, science and in particular the epistemology of research knowledge that have been shepherded together under the banners of postmodernism and post-structuralism[1] will have much to say about research activity and, as I shall show in these pages, will offer a different agenda for the set of practices that we call 'fieldwork', including both the relations that we have with the people we interact with in 'the field' and the forms of interpretation that we place on our field data. In this chapter, I want to reflect on how the 'postmodern turn' in social theory affects the philosophy, politics and social relations of field research, and what it may mean for those of us who work from within the postmodern critique for the ways we engage with 'the field'.

I shall look first at three bodies of work in which postmodern and post-structuralist thought has touched field relations in the social sciences: the 'writing culture' critique of ethnographic objectivity (Clifford and Marcus, 1986), the acknowledgement of the autobiographic character of fieldwork (Okely and Callaway, 1992), and the research approach known as 'action research'. Then, with the assistance of some notes on the role of the informant from an ethnography of surgical work, I draw out the divergences of postmodern field relations in terms of how it fulfils the individual and collective needs of research audiences and fieldwork participants. I conclude with some thoughts on the politics of fieldwork in this postmodern 'mood'.

THE CRITIQUE OF ETHNOGRAPHIC OBJECTIVITY

The postmodern turn in the theory and practice of ethnographic fieldwork impacted most significantly within anthropology, which, as a subject, has had most to grapple with in terms of its colonial roots and questions of epistemology in its constitution of its subject. As a discipline, it has emerged as more self-conscious, less confident in its authority and more open to self-critique as complicit in western ethnocentrism (see, for example, James et al., 1997).

Books rarely have the impact that the collection called *Writing Culture* (Clifford and Marcus, 1986) has had on a discipline. This book – still on bookshop shelves – was a deconstruction of the textual activities that fieldworkers use to represent their subject matter. It was a pivotal text, acting as judge, jury and executioner for anthropology as an 'objective' discipline documenting the truths about the exotic. Metonymic for this book's content was its cover picture of anthropologist

Stephen Tyler writing notes, while seated on the stoup of his tent during fieldwork in India in 1963. Behind him, a figure – most likely a local man – sits impassively (Clifford, 1986: 1). As a student of mine also noted (although this is not mentioned in Clifford's discussion of the photograph), in the shadows a female figure also sits, almost invisible to the lens. As Clifford comments, this is an unusual anthropological picture in that it focuses on the writing activity that eventually constituted the ethnographic text of Tyler's fieldwork. It is usually the locals who are pictured, perhaps with the anthropologist participating in some cultural activity.

Writing Culture made visible the processes whereby ethnographic fieldwork is translated into social science knowledge, and, in so doing, proclaimed a crisis in anthropology's ability to validly represent 'the other' (Clifford, 1986: 3). The book brought together a series of critiques of anthropological epistemology that were overwhelming in their import. Within the collection, it exposed the rhetorical methods used in fieldwork accounts to make them 'believable' and establish the authority of the fieldworker (Crapanzano, 1986; Marcus, 1986), the power relations between wealthy western ethnographer and impoverished native and how this affected the emergent ethnography (Rosaldo, 1986). It raises problems of cross-cultural and between-language translation (Asad, 1986). Tyler (1986) argues against the epistemology of representationism that underpins ethnographic writing, in favour of a poetics that 'evokes' rather than tries to achieve correspondence in a realist sense.

Clifford suggests that the writers in the collection shared the view that the ideology of representation had 'crumbled', and instead considered that culture is

composed of seriously contested codes and representations; … that the poetic and the political are inseparable; that science is in, not above, historical and linguistic processes. They assume that academic and literary genres interpenetrate and that the writing of cultural descriptions is properly experimental and ethical. Their focus on text making and rhetoric serves to highlight the constructed, artificial nature of cultural accounts ... [and] reach beyond texts to contexts of power, resistance, institutional constraints and innovation. (Clifford, 1986: 2)

Clifford and Marcus's book is not the only one to have raised issues concerning the constructionism of scientific accounts. Atkinson (1990) unpacks sociological ethnography to expose the rhetorical devices that establish textual authority, while in a rather different context, Latour and Woolgar (1979) show how scientific laboratories are 'inscription devices' which turn 'reality' into scientific 'knowledge'. All are 'postmodern' in their doubts over realist claims of correspondence between the world and the text that purports to describe it. For fieldwork, the challenge to 'objectivity' that emerges is not insignificant. Anthropology emerged chastened, more self-conscious about its roots in colonialism and racism, more aware that fieldworkers must address the needs of the peoples they work with, and that the dynamic aspirational struggles of these people for self-determination and economic development were more important to them than the academic explorations of cultural values and social structures (Marcus and Fischer, 1999).

THE INVISIBLE FIELDWORKER

The second contribution to this analysis that I will consider is another edited collection: Okely and Callaway's (1992) *Anthropology and Autobiography*. This volume also looks at the accounts of fieldwork that emerge from ethnographic activities, but focuses on recent efforts to redress the absence of the anthropologist themselves from fieldwork narratives. It raises questions about the fieldworker's personal biography in relation to

their accounts of the field, and reminds us that fieldworkers are not simply mechanisms for recording field data.

For Callaway (1992), the embodied, emotional selfhood of the ethnographer must be acknowledged, and in her analysis she emphasises the need to re-introduce the gendered identity of the fieldworker as relevant to the social relations of the ethnographer to those she studies. She suggests that many accounts by women of 'the field' (for instance, those written by wives of anthropologists) were excluded from the ethnographic canon because they breached rules by introducing reflexive elements or adopting fictional genres.[2]

Hastrup (1992) argues that the ethnographer and his/her subjects are engaged in mutual constitution of, and challenges to, subjectivity during fieldwork encounters. Fieldwork stands between autobiography and anthropological (or for that matter sociological) knowledge, and the experience of fieldwork is not the unmediated world of the respondent but a world between the self and the other, and '[o]ur results are deeply marked by this betweenness [*sic*] and there is no way, epistemologically, to overcome its implications' (Hastrup, 1992: 117). The main lesson of fieldwork is that the distinction between observer and observed is 'a modernist artifact ... subject and object are categories of thought, not discrete entities' (ibid.).

Hendry, Crick and Rapport (all 1992) write separately about the strange nature of fieldwork interactions with informants, whose 'friendship' is always already situated in unequal relations of power, but may have a dynamic that extends across long periods of time as informants' lives unfold and develop in a changing culture. For Caplan (1992) it was, for example, a surprise to her to learn that her long-term informant Mohammed was himself an ethnographer: a diarist and documenter of his own culture.

His needs were, needless to say, not identical to her own as a fieldworker. Caplan's study is of particular relevance to the field data I will discuss later in this chapter.

The papers in *Anthropology and Autobiography* establish the situated nature of fieldwork by revealing the embodied character of field-working itself, and the impact of personal biographies, including and perhaps especially those of the fieldworkers themselves, on the knowledge that is created. They remind us of the identities that fieldworkers carry with them, identities which are constructed from and may indeed transmit cultural norms, including colonialism, racism, social class and so on. Informants and respondents in field settings similarly carry with them and trans-mit their own cultural tags.

These two takes on the enterprise of field-work establish many of the epistemological challenges for the fieldworker. They may use-fully be complemented by a short reflection on a methodology of research that addresses some of the same issues.

ACTION AND PRACTITIONER RESEARCH

Action and practitioner research implicitly link research to 'real life' within a field, but despite a long history within the social sciences, have been marginalised and often ignored in methodology texts. Action research grew up in the 1940s and 1950s, with the underpinning principles that theory would be developed and tested by practical interven-tions or actions; that there would be consis-tency between project means and desired ends; and that ends and means were grounded in guidelines established by the host commu-nity (Stull and Schensul, 1987).

While acknowledging the importance of the perspectives of the researched subjects,

such an advocacy model for fieldwork retains a distinction between researcher and researched. This distinction is elided in practitioner research (Nixon, 1981), which focuses on changing practice and involves practitioners in the field in innovating practice. Practice becomes a form of research, and vice versa (Elliott, 1995). Action research in 'emancipatory mood' (Carr and Kemmis, 1986) moves beyond collabora-tion between fieldworker and subjects, to a model in which the researcher takes on the role of a 'process moderator', assisting participants to undertake the research themselves.

Zuber-Skerritt (1991) suggests that within this paradigm, action research is participative and collaborative, emancipatory, interpreta-tive and critical. Stronach and MacLure's (1997) postmodern action research adopts the notion of 'transgressive validity' as out-lined by Lather (1993: 676; see also Richardson, 1993). In this perspective, the 'validity' of research is a function of its capa-city to transgress, challenge or subvert exist-ing conceptions. In the context of field relations, it is an appropriate postmodern counterpoint to the ways in which fieldwork has been used to archive the social world (Foucault, 1974: 130).

Such a model of transgressive action research offers a template for fieldwork com-mitted to engagement with practical con-cerns in the field, to collaboration with participants and to difference: that it should engage with a wider project of *resistance* to power and control. Together, these commit-ments indicate a fieldwork that is implicitly and explicitly engaged and as such must be seen as political, both at the micro-level of interpersonal power and sometimes also at the level of struggles and resistance.[3]

Having considered fieldwork through these three lenses, I want to turn to the implications for doing fieldwork, in particular in health and social care. My focus is on the relations which inhere in the field, between the fieldworker and his/her interlocutors. I am interested to examine the power relations, the differing needs of the various parties and how these may influence the fieldwork enterprise.

Although some of the studies that have been considered thus far relate to 'other-culture' studies in anthropology, there is relevance for our own culture studies too. Be it a study of 'street corner society', of work in a car factory, of criminals and police, or of medicine, science and technology, there is a strong sense for many social scientists that their fieldwork has carried them into a different culture, with its own mores, tenets and rules. Our informants are part of that culture and they have their own agendas and particular needs and commitments. Working with people in the field must acknowledge this skein of needs and work with them, not against the grain. The data I report below was from my own 'home culture', but one that was still alien: the world of the surgical operating theatre (room).

DR J AND I: OBSERVING THE FIELD OF SURGERY

In the late 1980s, I met Dr J,[4] an anaesthetist at 'Western Hospital', a large teaching hospital somewhere in the United Kingdom. It was a chance encounter, in the hospital's newly open museum of medical history. I was a PhD student and a part-time anthropology lecturer, and having heard of the museum I was spending an enjoyable hour looking at all the medical paraphernalia from bygone eras that had been gathered together. The museum was housed in a modern rotunda, and it was clear that much effort and enthusiasm had graced its inception.

Having pretty much completed my tour, I noticed the only other person present in the museum, and somehow we fell into conversation. Dr J, it turned out, was the brains behind the project and had raised the cash and devoted himself to getting the exhibits together and the displays mounted. I was effusive about the results, and he soon asked me more about myself. I was doing a doctorate on the sociology of surgery at the University of Warwick, I explained. 'Really?' Dr J responded. 'I'm actually a consultant anaesthetist when I'm not doing this.' He asked me how my research was going and I told him how I had started by observing ward rounds and was due to begin fieldwork in the operating theatre at nearby University Hospital. We talked for some minutes about our shared interests in surgery: me as a researcher, he as a participant. Eventually I said I should be going, and Dr J gave me a card and told me to get in touch if he could be of any help to me.

Six weeks later, I dug out Dr J's card. Things at University Hospital were not going well. I was not getting the access I needed, and I felt that my contact there, a general surgeon, was having second thoughts about allowing a social scientist access to his patients and operating theatres. I called Dr J and asked if he remembered me. Yes, he replied. Could I come to talk to him, I asked. He agreed and we met a week later. During my interview with Dr J, which generated a mass of valuable information, we discussed the possibility that I might observe in the surgical operating theatres at Western Hospital. His response initiated a period of fieldwork and a research relationship that lasted for over a year, during which time Dr J and I talked very many times, I was introduced to – and interviewed – many other staff (surgeons, anaesthetists, nurses) and I observed more than 70 operations in most sub-specialties of surgery, from the trivial to the life-threatening. Dr J eased me into settings I would never have been able to access without his seniority and sponsorship behind me. He helped me learn the rules of the setting, and he was a known figure in an alien world: no one questioned my presence because I was perceived as Dr J's protégé.

From the start, Dr J was fascinated by my project. Unlike many other medics with whom I had had contact during the fieldwork, he seemed to grasp why a social scientist might want to study a setting like an operating theatre, and in what I might be interested (the social interactions rather than the technical proficiency of the surgeon). He was keen to pass on information he thought I would find useful (it almost always was), and used me to bounce around some ideas of his own.

Once inside the operating theatre, I understood more about Dr J's interest. As an anaesthetist, he spent most of his time watching things: looking on while the surgeons cut, watching dials on the monitors and the clock, sitting back and watching the intensive and sometimes frenetic activity around the surgical wound while he carefully guarded the airways and circulatory access of his impassive, somnolent patients. Anaesthetists' work is characterised by long periods of virtual inactivity, punctuated only by occasional note-taking. During long procedures, they may have little or nothing to do. Only a deviation from the norms, as measured on their various instruments, will result in any action. The work of the anaesthetist seemed much like the 'fieldwork mode' described by Barley (1986), which enables long frustrating periods of delay to be survived by, adopting a stoic detachment from reality. Any distraction was welcome, and an inquisitive fieldworker was an entertaining diversion.

A favourite topic of Dr J's was the perceived shortcomings of surgeons and the superior intellectual capacities of anaesthetists. Surgeons, in Dr J's view, were technicians, skilled in the narrow expertise of cutting, but unable to see the whole patient, and to work within a bigger picture of what was needed from the surgical service. Surgeons as managers were laughable, Dr J considered, blinkered by their desire to do interesting and varied work, and incapable of seeing other points of view. Dr J, on the other hand, saw himself as management material, and would often gossip with the nurse managers who administered the theatres.

Dr J was the perfect key informant in that he saw me as an ally in his struggle against surgical authority. He would tell me stories that inevitably showed surgeons in a bad light. He regarded his work as constrained by the irrationality and selfishness of surgeons, and often used my presence as a sounding-board, to test out ideas to improve the rationality of what happened in his world. These conversations happened under the noses of those he was criticising. On one occasion, as I was walking along a corridor near the operating theatre, an arm reached out from the linen cupboard and pulled me inside. It was Dr J, who was ensconced with the surgical charge nurse. They proceeded to tell me the latest absurdity that had happened that day as a result of apparent surgical managerial incompetence, and documented a litany of similar events.

When I finally left the field, it was with a sense that I had made a friend, although he felt also like patron and mentor, and maybe, given our relative ages, something like a kindly uncle too! I think he was sorry to see me go, as I had perhaps alleviated the tedium of daily surgical lists. When the book of the work was finally published (Fox, 1992), I sent him a copy. I don't know whether he read it, but he wrote me a letter saying he thought it a 'very fair' account.

I do not wish to claim anything special for this account of a field relationship – there are many others in the literature that would do as well – but it does raise some important issues and illustrates the theoretical analysis discussed earlier. First, the power relations within the field are complex. As a young PhD student I was dependent upon Dr J and his colleagues to provide me with the access that I needed to get my research completed successfully. In an alien environment, I had little or no authority, and was excluded on one occasion (when I did not have Dr J's patronage) from an operating theatre simply for being 'an outsider'. On the other hand, as a fieldworker I had freedom to go where I wanted, when I wanted, while my interlocutors were constrained by their job descriptions and the requirements of the daily routine. I could document what I wished, and exclude or ignore other aspects of the field. Ultimately, the account that emerged and would form part of the sociological archive would be mine and mine alone.

My second point is related to this. It concerns Dr J's role as a naive ethnographer of surgery. As I have indicated, he was a great observer, a role that grew out of the watchfulness of the anesthetist (elsewhere (Fox 1994) I have described the anaesthetist as the watchful advocate of the unconscious patient in the face of the surgical assault). But Dr J had become interested in the social relations of surgery as well as the technicalities. He was an observer of the surgical character, a repository of ironies he collected as he saw, day by day, the managerial absurdities of the uncertain and unpredictable activity of surgery. While other anaesthetists read books or the paper, Dr J watched the comings and goings with a cynical eye. My presence gave him an audience, someone with whom to test out his ideas and share his observations. I would try out my ideas too,

and the dialogue was productive for us both. The relish with which he accounted the latest incident he had witnessed indicated that we had a bargain: we were both refining our understandings, for our own purposes. Like Caplan's (1992) Mohammed, Dr J was using another's fieldwork activity to help him make sense of his world. The outside view (mine) grew from an insider's understanding (Dr J's), but also fuelled the latter, giving it a framework and enabling it to grow in sophistication.

Third, the activity of fieldwork is embodied, tied in to the biographies and corporeality not just of the participants, but also to that of the ethnographic fieldworker. In 'the field', I occupied space, and in a limited space like an operating theatre, finding a place to stand was a problem. My embodied observations are a function of 'being there', of physically occupying space and all that goes with having a body: wearing the uniform of surgery, adhering to the customs of sterility and so on, keeping out of the way as much as possible, and occasionally being dragged into the action to hold an instrument or move a piece of non-sterile equipment (see Fox, 1992 for examples). I was physically present from nine in the morning to the end of the list, I would share the routines of coffee and sandwich lunches in the theatre complex, I would make small talk and try to present myself as a worthy observer of the mysteries. I was also aware on occasions of my emotional and physical reactions to the phenomena I witnessed, and these emotional responses coloured my 'objectivity' in how I reported the ethnographic data (Fox, 1995).

Finally, my ethnography of surgery pales into insignificance in comparison with the daily activities of the people in the field, whose actions led to the amelioration of suffering, enhancement of well-being and extension of life for most of those who were the objects of surgery. The fieldwork I undertook was parasitic on this generally benevolent and beneficial activity, and it is only by acknowledging the personal relations such as those with Dr J that the fieldwork seems ethically legitimate. As fieldworkers we do touch the lives of those we work with and we need to ensure those contacts are grounded in a framework that is collaborative and participatory, that can assist our interlocutors to address their situation and where feasible change it for the better.

DISCUSSION: DISSOLVING THE FIELD?

From this consideration of field relations – intentionally grounded in one small (though crucial) aspect of an ethnographic study – I want to address the broader implications of the 'postmodern turn' in social research for fieldwork. Postmodernism is suspicious of and rejects 'grand narratives' that offer a unified or monolithic perspective on the world, human-ness, or knowledge in general (Lyotard, 1984). Derrida (1976) describes these grand narratives as *logocentrisms*, whose objective is to achieve the *logos* – unmediated truth about the world. During its short history (a history itself constitutive of the modernist project), social science has moved from empiricist roots which aped natural science in teasing out 'social facts', to epistemologies that problematise the relation between observation and reality in approaches such as interpretative sociology, ethnomethodology and post-structuralism (Denzin and Lincoln, 1998). Despite this, the desire for the *logos* – truth about the object of study – underpins discussions of research methodology (Feinstein, 1992).

The postmodern turn sees both 'internal validity' (the extent to which a study measures what it claims to be measuring) and 'external validity' (the generalisablility of study findings) as articulating a scientific *logocentrism* based in the premises of a discipline. Methodology makes reality accessible, minimising distortions that methods of observation or analysis may introduce. Similarly, it offers the prospect of inference from specific to generality, and offers a privilege to methodologically rigorous research over anecdote or practitioners' own experiences (Fox, 2003).

Research methodology is therefore not just a matter of technique, but stems from pronouncements on epistemology: of how we may legitimately 'get to truth' (Denzin and Lincoln, 1998; Lakatos, 1978; Popper, 1982). Different scientific disciplines have developed their own methodologies that they accept as legitimate: these disciplines variously confer validity on the findings of studies conducted in accordance with their own methodological norms. Methods texts are science's equivalent of a religion's holy book, setting out the right way to do things and the 'threats to validity' that derive from transgressing prescriptions and precedents. Novices learn through research experience and by demonstrably applying this holy writ of methodology to their own research.

Inevitably, 'fieldwork' has been part of this modernist logocentrism for social researchers in areas such as health and social care. Fieldwork is one among several means of data collection, and while viewed cautiously by some (Greenhalgh, 1997; see also Denzin and Lincoln, 1998: 7), is often given great privilege as a methodological approach by its proponents. Because of its apparently direct access to 'what is going on' in a setting, fieldwork accounts are offered as justification of a study's conclusions, because the work is demonstrably 'relevant' and 'authentic' and therefore 'valid' (truthful).

However, in postmodern mood, the privilege of 'fieldwork' will be downplayed as a means to gain 'truth' about the world. That is not to say that we may not gain knowledge of the world, but rather that there are many 'truths' which are highly historically and setting-contingent. It also follows that research reports of fieldwork are not representations (accurate or flawed) of the world, but contested claims to speak 'the truth' about something that happened in 'the field' (that is, the world). Necessarily, this challenges fieldworkers' privilege to speak authoritatively (Game, 1991:18). But at the same time, this analysis opens up possibilities for a fieldwork practice no longer obsessed by efforts to attain transparent truth, to be perhaps 'evocative' rather than representative (Flax, 1990; Hutcheon, 1989; Sanger, 1995; Tyler, 1986).

On another tack, post-structuralism and postmodernist social theory have re-theorised power, making its connections with knowledge and knowing explicit. Authority is associated with authorship, with the rendering of 'archives' (Foucault, 1974) to support disciplinary regimes through the establishing of authoritative 'bodies of knowledge' (Armstrong, 1994). This post-structuralist understanding has provided not only a means to explore the power of systems of thought such as medicine, the law and social welfare (Armstrong, 1983; Harris, 1999; Lewis et al., 2000; Morrall, 1999; Rose, 1989), but also to look reflexively at the power plays involved in the archival work that is social research itself.

The social sciences are strongly implicated in the archiving of human activity (Donnelly, 1986; Fox, 1993). Indeed, Foucault argued (1970) that it was the rise of the social sciences that made human beings the object of study for the first time. In today's world, our 'ethics of daily life', as defined by disciplines of political philosophy, social welfare, the public health, criminology, education and so forth, are based in a social research enterprise which is slowly but surely creating an 'evidence-based existence'. Power in society is coming to inhere in the progressive archiving of what it is to be a healthy, wealthy and wise individual (Fox, 1999; Nettleton, 1997).

There are crucial implications of this archiving of human life for those involved in fieldwork. Fieldwork supplies the raw material for this archive of existence, and Foucault's gaze of power is precisely the gaze of the ethnographer over his/her 'people' – traditionally, from the door of his [*sic*] tent (Rosaldo, 1986), but always with the safety of the academic office to which to retreat. There the transcription of raw lived experiences (those of the ethnographer as well as of the subjects) begins the production of the archive that will inform society's understanding of itself, be it in relation to social theory, welfare policy, public health or more sinister social movements.

Together, these two commentaries offer a critique of some premises of modernist fieldwork practices and suggest reasons to reassess field relations from a postmodern perspective. In an introduction to the revised second edition of their classic *Anthropology as Cultural Critique* (first published in 1986), Marcus and Fischer (1999) document the radical changes which have taken place in their discipline as a consequence of the postmodern turn of the 1980s, and suggest that this has provided the basis for a renewal of the anthropological project, within a new political and epistemological context (1999: xxii). That which in the 1980s was a challenging critique of a subject in crisis (1999: xi) has become 'mainstream', establishing new emphases upon issues of identity and reflexivity on one hand, and upon globalisation and the historical and political contexts of fieldwork on the other (1999: xxiii).

Marcus and Fischer (1999) offer a further reflection on postmodern fieldwork in this revision of their work. Noting their emphasis on a collaborative approach to fieldwork, they add that field settings are 'not just rich ethnographic arenas to be described within the traditional practices of fieldwork, but (also) arenas that are puzzling to all collaborators – informants and experts as well as ethnographers and cultural translators' (1999: xvii). Collaborators in fieldwork cease to be simply informants, they go on, and social science fieldwork is no longer simply 'the discovery of new worlds and the translation of the exotic into the familiar'. Instead, it entails the 'discovery of worlds which are familiar or fully understood by no one, and that all are in search of puzzling out' (1999: xvii). This acknowledgment of what has also been called the 'double hermeneutic' (the dual meaning–attribution which occurs both as actors make sense of their world and as researchers try to make sense of that sense-making) establishes a new politics of the field setting and of field relations. This may be fleshed out to reflect more fully on the consequences of this new collaborative relationship between actor/informant, ethnographer and reader.

What may be drawn into the research enterprise are the endless readings of the social world which inhere in the practical activities of those who live and breathe a 'research field', the people who in modernist research were called 'subjects'. Suddenly, research cannot be seen as separate from this world of practice, nor can the researcher's perspective be privileged in any way (Lather, 1993), because the researcher is now part of the world that s/he explores and translates

into research reports (Richardson, 1993). If no privilege is attached to particular research epistemologies, 'researchers' may explore a new richness of 'data' generated in novel and unending combinations.

Part of the re-privileging of the 'subject' of fieldwork is a de-privileging of the fieldworker *qua* fieldworker him/herself. One aspect of this is to acknowledge the human being who goes 'into the field', lives 'in the field' and writes 'about the field' yet who was traditionally absent from fieldwork accounts. The emotional context of fieldwork and the embodied character of the fieldwork enterprise (Callaway, 1992: 30) become legitimate, nay essential, content for field reports that bring back the fieldworker as co-participant in the production of field reality.

If researchers no longer stand apart from their research setting, it follows that their relationship with 'subjects' should be wider than simply that of researcher/researched. Consequently, the researcher must adopt an ethical and political position that structures the engagement that s/he has with the subjects of research. Part of this ethical engagement concerns the 'silent voices' in a field setting, those of the people whose position for some reason prevents them from being heard. Lyotard (1988) speaks of the 'differend' that denies others the possibility to speak authoritatively or authentically. Medical dominance, patriarchy and religious fundamentalism are all *differends* that deny other voices. The postmodern fieldworker can help these voices be heard through the research text: to turn 'subjects' into participants, empowered through the fieldwork connection. My work may have empowered Dr J: I regret now that its impact was so limited on the silent, sleeping surgical patients.

Similarly, reporting fieldwork changes from efforts to represent the field to a reflexive action which is itself part of the field. Indeed, the form of the research output may be radicalised, offering polyvocality (for example, Curt, 1994; Mulkay, 1985), or direct engagement (for example, teaching, therapy or protest). Whatever form is chosen, the research becomes part of the setting it is exploring, and fieldwork a facet of the field, inextricably tied up with the wider issues of political engagement, power and justice. It is no longer possible to 'enter' or 'leave' a 'field' because the field no longer exists as a reality separate from that in which participants' lives unfold from day to day.

Fieldwork can 'write against the archive', to challenge systems of thought rather than contribute to the progressive codification of 'evidence-based existence'. It can establish nodes of resistance, alliances and collaborations, and can also work to empower people to write their own lives, or to write accounts that contradict or challenge powerful systems of thought. Fieldworkers must reflect on the consequences of writing culture down (and 'up'), and perhaps on the priorities that may drive publication in the academic media that comprise the archive.

CONCLUDING REMARKS

The postmodern critique of fieldwork pushes towards and exceeds the limits of what has been called the 'crisis of representation' in modern research. While some have taken the postmodern turn to imply the end of representation, I have preferred to focus on the transformation of power relations that the position implies. It adds a radicalised vision of the fieldworker as collaborator, which should not be distasteful to those who have seen fieldwork research as a democratic, emancipatory process. Building on the analysis of fieldwork above leads to a number of propositions concerning relations in 'the field' (the world).

First, pursuit of knowledge should be considered as a *local and contingent* matter. While understanding of the 'field' may be achieved through observation and inductive reasoning, it cannot be assumed that these observations or this reasoning can be translated to other settings, or even from the research setting to 'real life'. Gaining understanding of a locale does not mean that such understanding will inform other settings. Indeed, a commitment to difference requires that no such assumptions be made.

Second, field relations should be *constitutive of difference* rather than demonstrative of similarity (for example, generalisability). Traditionally, a fieldworker seeks mastery (White, 1991) of her/his setting, pigeonholing phenomena into categories based on their qualities or hierarchical positioning in relation to each other. In contrast, fieldwork that is constitutive of difference acknowledges different qualities, yet accepts them as of equal value rather than hierarchically or oppositionally privileged in relation to each other. This political engagement with the world means that research avoids legitimating or repressing particular aspects of the world it observes (Brown and Duguid, 1991).

Third, *theory building*, while necessarily part of any activity of 'understanding', should be seen not as an end in itself. The value of theory will be in its applicability in immediate practical activities in settings in which it has been developed. Understanding makes sense only if data are placed in context (Mauthner et al., 1998). The modernist privileging of abstracted theory is replaced with a collaborative *bricolage* as 'researcher' and 'researched' work together to make sense of the 'field'.

NOTES

1 I use the term 'postmodern' to refer not to a period following modernity but to a critique of the modern commitments to science, rationality and western thought as privileged as a means to know the world. The critique draws heavily on the insights of post-structuralism on the relation between knowledge and power, but adds a political dimension, arguing for difference over identity, transgression and resistance over conformity and consensus in both epistemology and social relations. Within the social sciences, postmodern approaches include constructivist alternatives to realism and articulate with the kinds of post-positivist research approaches that have grown from the bodies of ethnographic work described in this chapter as well as engaged research in science studies, gender, race and disability studies and certain threads in the sociology of health and illness.

2 Callaway also notes that many of the 'innovations' argued for by contributors to *Writing Culture* were already established in feminist ethnographic texts.

3 This model of fieldwork articulates with other bodies of work which have argued for an engaged research practice, including feminist research, queer theory and disability studies. For example, Ramazanoglu has argued (1992: 209) that feminist methodologies are the outcome of power struggles over what it means to 'know', and what counts as valid research. Feminist commitments to resisting patriarchy has led to a suspicion of grand narratives (Holmwood, 1995: 416), and a preference for research which is local, engages with the concerns of women, and values experience (Gelsthorpe, 1992: 214, Oakley, 1998). Currently, postmodern research methods are being applied in a range of disciplines, including sociology, psychology, social work, geography, criminology, business studies and organisation studies (Allen, 2000; Brannigan, 1997; Cheek, 2000; Daly, 1997; Hamel, 1999; Healy, 2001; Payne, 2000; Pratt, 1999; Sanders, 1999; Scheurich, 1997; Tierney, 2001; Weiss, 2000).

4 Not his real name. The hospitals have also been disguised.

REFERENCES

Allen, K.R. (2000). 'A conscious and inclusive family studies', *Journal of Marriage and the Family*, 62: 4–17.

Armstrong, D. (1983). *The Political Anatomy of the Body*. Cambridge: Cambridge University Press.

Armstrong, D. (1994). 'Bodies of knowledge/knowledge of bodies'. In C. Jones and R. Potter (eds), *Reassessing Foucault*. London: Routledge.

Asad, T. (1986). 'The concept of cultural translation in British social anthropology'. In J. Clifford and G.E. Marcus (eds), *Writing Culture: the Poetics and Politics of Ethnography*. Berkeley: University of California Press.

Atkinson, P. (1990). *The Ethnographic Imagination*. London: Routledge.

Barley, N. (1986). *The Innocent Anthropologist*. London: Penguin.

Bauman, Z. (1993). *Intimations of Postmodernity*. London: Routledge.

Brannigan, A. (1997). 'The postmodern experiment: science and ontology in experimentatl social psychology', *British Journal of Sociology*, 48: 594–610.

Brown, J.S. and Duguid, P. (1991). 'Organizational learning and communities of practice: towards a unified view of working, learning and innovation', *Organization Science*, 2: 40–57.

Callaway, H. (1992). 'Ethnography and experience: gender implications in fieldwork and texts'. In J. Okely and H. Callaway (eds), *Anthropology and Autobiography*. London: Routledge.

Carr, W. and Kemmis, S. (1986). *Becoming Critical: Knowing through Action Research*. London: Falmer Press.

Cheek, J. (2000). *Postmodern and Poststructural Approaches to Nursing Research*. London: Sage.

Clifford, J. (1986). 'Introduction: partial truths'. In J. Clifford and G.E. Marcus (eds), *Writing Culture: The Poetics and Politics of Ethnography*. Berkeley: University of California Press.

Clifford, J. and Marcus, G.E. (eds) (1986). *Writing Culture: the Poetics and Politics of Ethnography*. Berkeley: University of California Press.

Crapanzano, V. (1986). 'Hermes' dilemma: the masking of subversion in ethnographic description'. In J. Clifford and G.E. Marcus (eds), *Writing Culture: the Poetics and Politics of Ethnography*. Berkeley: University of California Press.

Crick, M. (1992). 'Ali and me: an essay in street corner anthropology'. In J. Okely and H. Callaway (eds), *Anthropology and Autobiography*. London: Routledge.

Curt, B. (1994). *Textuality and Tectonics: Troubling Social and Psychological Science* Buckingham: Open University Press.

Daly, K. (1997). 'Re-placing theory in ethnography: a postmodern view', *Qualitative Inquiry*, 3: 343–65.

Denzin, N. and Lincoln, Y.S. (1998). 'Introduction'. In N. Denzin and Y.S. Lincoln (eds), *Collecting and Interpreting Qualitative Materials*. Newbury Park, CA: Sage.

Derrida, J. (1976). *Of Grammatology*. Baltimore, MD: Johns Hopkins University Press.

Donnelly, M. (1986). 'Foucault's genealogy of the human sciences'. In M. Gane (ed.), *Towards a Critique of Foucault*. London: Routledge and Kegan Paul.

Elliott, J. (1995). 'What is good action research?', *Action Researcher*, 2: 10–11.

Feinstein, A.R. (1992). 'Invidious comparisons and unmet clinical challenges', *American Journal of Medicine*, 92: 117–20.

Flax, J. (1990). *Thinking Fragments*. Berkeley: University of California Press.

Foucault, M. (1970). *The Order of Things*. London: Tavistock.

Foucault, M. (1974). *The Archaeology of Knowledge*. London: Tavistock.

Fox, N.J. (1992). *The Social Meaning of Surgery*. Buckingham: Open University Press.

Fox, N.J. (1993). *Postmodernism, Sociology and Health*. Buckingham: Open University Press.

Fox, N.J. (1994). 'Anaesthetists, the discourse on patient fitness and the organisation of surgery', *Sociology of Health & Illness*, 16: 1–18.

Fox, N.J. (1995). 'Intertextuality and the writing of social research', *Electronic Journal of Sociology*, 1(3): no page numbers.

Fox, N.J. (1999). *Beyond Health: Postmodernism and Embodiment*. London: Free Association Books.

Fox, N.J. (2003). 'Practice-based evidence: towards collaborative and transgressive research', *Sociology* 37: 81–102.

Game, A. (1989). *Undoing the Social*. Buckingham: Open University Press.

Gelsthorpe, L. (1992). 'Response to Martyn Hammersley's paper "On feminist methodology"', *Sociology*, 26: 213–18.

Greenhalgh, T. (1997). 'How to read a paper: papers that report diagnostic or screening tests', *British Medical Journal*, 315: 540–43.

Hamel, J. (1999). 'The dilemma of science in anthropology and sociology: pros and cons of postmodern thought', *Social Science Information*, 38: 5–27.

Harris, P. (1999). 'Public welfare and liberal governance'. In A. Petersen, I. Barns, J. Dudley and P. Harris (eds), *Poststructuralism, Citizenship and Social Policy*. London: Routledge.

Hastrup, K. (1992). 'Writing ethnography: state of the art'. In J. Okely and H. Callaway (eds), *Anthropology and Autobiography*. London: Routledge.

Healy, K. (2001). 'Participatory action research and social work: a critical appraisal', *International Social Work*, 44: 93–105.

Hendry, J. (1992). 'The paradox of friendship in the field: analysis of an Anglo-Japanese relationship'. In J. Okely and H. Callaway (eds), *Anthropology and Autobiography*. London: Routledge.

Holmwood, J. (1995). 'Feminism and epistemology: what kind of successor science?', *Sociology*, 29: 411–28.

Hutcheon, L. (1989). *The Politics of Postmodernism*. London: Routledge.

James, A., Hockey, J. and Dawson, D. (eds) (1997). *After Writing Culture*. London: Routledge.

Lakatos, I. (1978). 'Introduction'. In J. Worrall and G. Currie (eds) *Philosophical Papers of Imre Lakatos, vol. 1. The Methodology of Scientific Research Programmes*. Cambridge: Cambridge University Press.

Lather, P. (1993). 'Fertile obsession: validity after poststructuralism', *Sociological Quarterly*, 34: 673–93.

Latour, B. and Woolgar, S. (1979). *Laboratory Life: The Construction of Scientific Facts*. Beverley Hills: Sage.

Lewis, G., Hughes, G. and Savage, E. (2000). 'The body of social policy: social policy and the body'. In L. McKie and N. Watson (eds), *Organizing Bodies: Policy, Institutions and Work*. Basingstoke: Macmillan.

Lyotard, J. (1984). *The Postmodern Condition: A Report on Knowledge*. Minneapolis: University of Minnesota Press.

Lyotard, J. (1988). *The Differend: Phrases in Dispute*. Minneapolis: University of Minnesota Press.

Marcus, G.E. (1986). 'Contemporary problems in ethnography in the modern world'. In J. Clifford and G.E. Marcus (eds), *Writing Culture: the Poetics and Politics of Ethnography*. Berkeley: University of California Press.

Marcus, G.E. and Fischer, M. (1999). *Anthropology as Cultural Critique* (2nd edn). Chicago: University of Chicago Press.

Mauthner, N.S., Parry, O. and Backett-Milburn, K. (1998). 'The data are out there, or are they? Implications for archiving and revisiting qualitative data', *Sociology*, 32: 733–45.

Morrall, P.A. (1999). 'Social exclusion and madness: the complicity of psychiatric medicine and nursing'. In M. Purdy and D. Banks (eds), *Health and Exclusion*. London: Routledge.

Mulkay, M.J. (1985). *The Word and the World*. London: George Allen and Unwin.

Nettleton, S. (1997). 'Governing the risky self: how to become healthy, wealthy and wise'. In A. Petersen and R. Bunton (eds), *Foucault, Health and Medicine*. London: Routledge.

Nixon, J. (1981). *A Teacher's Guide to Action Research*. London: Grant McIntyre.

Oakley, A. (1998). 'Gender, methodology and people's ways of knowing: some problems with feminism and the paradigm debate in social science', *Sociology*, 32: 707–31.

Okely, J. and Callaway, H. (eds) (1992). *Anthropology and Autobiography*. London: Routledge.

Payne, S.L. (2000). 'Challenges to research ethics and moral knowledge construction in applied social sciences', *Journal of Business Ethics*, 26: 307–18.

Popper, K. (1982). 'Science: conjectures and refutations'. In P. Grim (ed.), *The Philosophy of Science and the Occult*. Albany, NY: University of New York Press.

Pratt, J. (1999). 'The return of the wheelbarrow man, or the arrival of postmodern penality?' *British Journal of Criminology*, 40: 127–45.

Ramazanoglu, C. (1992). 'On feminist methodology: male reason versus female empowerment', *Sociology*, 26: 207–12.

Rapport, N. (1992). 'From affect to analysis: the biography of an interaction in an English village'. In J. Okely and H. Callaway (eds), *Anthropology and Autobiography*. London: Routledge.

Richardson, L. (1993). 'Poetics, dramatics and transgression. The case of the skipped line', *Sociological Quarterly*, 34: 695–710.

Rosaldo, R. (1986). 'From the door of his tent: the fieldworker and the inquisitor'. In J. Clifford and G.E. Marcus (eds), *Writing Culture: the Poetics and Politics of Ethnography*. Berkeley: University of California Press.

Rose, N. (1989). *Governing the Soul*. London: Routledge.

Sanders, C.R. (1999). 'Prospects for a post-modern ethnography', *Journals of Contemporary Ethnography*, 26: 669–75.

Sanger, J. (1995). 'Five easy pieces: the deconstruction of illuminatory data in research writing', *British Educational Research Journal*, 21: 89–97.

Scheurich, J. (1997). *Research Methods in the Postmodern*. London: Falmer.

Stronach, I. and MacLure, M. (1997). *Educational Research Undone: the Postmodern Embrace*. Buckingham: Open University Press.

Stull, D.D. and Schensul, J.J. (eds) (1987). *Collaborative Research and Social Change*. Boulder, CO: Westview Press.

Tierney, W.G. (2001). 'The autonomy of knowledge and the decline of the subject: postmodernism and the reformation of the university', *Higher Education*, 41: 353–72.

Tyler, S.A. (1986). 'Postmodern ethnography'. In J. Clifford and G.E. Marcus (eds), *Writing Culture: the Poetics and Politics of Ethnography*. Berkeley: University of California Press.

Weiss, R.M. (2000). 'Taking science out of organisation science: how would postmodernism reconstruct the analysis of organisations?', *Organisation Science*, 11: 709–31.

White, S. (1991). *Political Theory and Postmodernism*. Cambridge: Cambridge University Press.

Zuber-Skerritt, O. (1991). *Action Research in Higher Education*. Brisbane: Centre for Advancement of Learning and Teaching.

22

Fieldwork in Transition[1]

PETER KIRBY MANNING

Chronicling movements in thought with respect to fieldwork obscures some basic dilemmas of the technical sort emphasized since Malinowski's first fieldwork published in *Argonauts of the Western Pacific* (1922). These technical dilemmas include how to establish, maintain and polish: field notes; a chronology of decisions and choices; a register of informants and interviews. Also relevant is how to extract and then elaborate and specify categories within the field notes that emerge over the course of time in the field, how to write a natural history of the research, including problem identification, site, entry, access, egress, role relations in the field, and post-fieldwork social relations. The situation of reflection – writing and its constraints – often surfaces ethical and personal dilemmas for the fieldworker. Validity and reliability can be addressed with respect to any of these points, as can questions of sampling and codification. In addition, tensions punctuate the phase called 'writing up', such as constructing the narrative, undertaking and completing the analysis. These tensions include delineating the functional aspects of the problem (e.g., how people do the things of interest,

such as rituals), the instrumental dimensions of it, the expressive or symbolic aspects, locating agency – in the group, the person (typically leaders of some kind), or other rather nebulous matters (e.g., equilibrium, pattern maintenance). How does one integrate a series of concrete observations with the analytic framework that is either inferred or imposed on the data? How does one capture the form as well as the content of key exchanges, and the generality of the findings? For example, how widely do they apply and what are the scope conditions of the theorizing.

It is clear from this set of questions and issues that modern fieldwork is in the shadow of positivism and statistical enumeration. The technical trumps the insightful and the imaginative. A concern for rhetoric and narrative is not inconsistent with 'dust bowl empiricism' as C. Wright Mills labeled modern sociology. Very rarely, at least in the last 50 years, has this hegemony been challenged, and never once successfully. The technique-focus remains in the major texts and collections on fieldwork, and virtually none discuss the more fundamental question of problem finding, naming and refining. A recent concern with writing up has surfaced (van Maanen, 1998; Wollcott, 2001). The technique-focus replicates positivism and erodes the putative strength of qualitative fieldwork. I should like to emphasize here that the questions shaping fieldwork in the coming years should be driven by inferences we draw from the world. Unfortunately, we can no longer rely on the urgings of Park to 'go out and look at the world' (paraphrase) and the parallel advice given to all fledging writers, 'write about what you know.' This advice is no longer effective because the social sciences in the United States and the UK are now populated almost entirely by middle-class people of small town, city and suburban origins. While there is more diversity in color and gender, and perhaps orientation to lifestyles, there is less variation in class origins, education and generational location (e.g., the educational level of parents and grandparents). The primary arenas in which the major studies of the last century were done – large cities and their niches, areas, and occupations – is primarily unknown to those under the age of 60 with a few exceptions. The great generation before mine, many of whom were refugee Europeans, are retired, sick, dying or dead. This demographic shift has significant consequences for the unfolding of our craft. Epistemological questions that arise from the changes in the composition of the social sciences, and the effects of gender on research practices exist, and these are vexing, but they do not bear on the questions that might be asked, once these matters are better understood and communicated. In many ways, the narrowed vision and experience of young social scientists make a focus on problem defining more challenging.

I want to suggest that understanding ordering and order still remains our quest. The complexity of modern society and rapid surface change blurs many traditional concepts, such as class, status and gender. Implicit in this change, however, is the abiding role of differentiation and the inevitability of stratification and inequality. It is important that any serious exploration of ordering begins with identifiable practices that characterize social interactions of interest. This means looking through the conventional façades of good and evil, distinctions such as 'legal' and 'extra-legal,' and other a priori concepts that reify processes and practices.

I propose to use studies of organized crime to illustrate the utility of the concepts of configuration, meaningful social space, networks, social worlds and games. I consider a game as a sub-part of a social world and social worlds residing within configurations. These are slightly nested notions and very difficult to disentangle, especially over time. It is also necessary to include the notions of situated or episodic action, exchange and exchange networks, and social differentiation (vertical and horizontal). In these activities, the shadow of the law remains as the needs and desires of people are never satisfied, and certainly never within the boundaries of the dominant legal order. The activities of control agents, their targets, collaborators, and informants, shape and give life to the provision of nominally prohibited goods and services – gambling, sex, and drugs. I think the configuration described here, which links enforcers and targets, the larger economic and political system of differential investigation of crimes, and the symbiotic nature of organized crime, reveals basic issues of inequality.

TRANSITION

Perhaps several general conclusions about the situation of fieldwork in the first few years of the present century are warranted.

One glance at *Sociology, American Sociological Review,* the *British Journal of Sociology,* or *American Journal of Sociology* will convince any reader that research-based, published sociology since the mid-1980s is a pseudo-economic, macro-statistical, model-based discipline. There is more diversity in other journals and some journals in the UK and Canada are not so myopic. Positivism and logical positivism, when linked with statistical enumeration, rules the elite segment of the discipline. The rich news of qualitative work is found in interdisciplinary units and in cross-disciplinary projects. A few marginalized social science groups (outside anthropology, which is defined by its field method) continue to publish qualitative work in journals such the *Journal of Contemporary Ethnography, Qualitative Sociology, Human Organization,* and *Symbolic Interaction.* Many innovative qualitative studies are now sent to specific journals specializing in victimization, violence, theory, corrections, social psychology, or gender. The qualitative work that remains alive, keeps the tradition developing, and is challenging, is compromised and marginalized in the social sciences for its putative descriptive bias, and its resistance to hypothesis testing, validity and reliability conundrums and emulative statistical modeling. Abstracted theorizing and modeling is preferred to close analysis of what people do, say, think and create. This is a misleading preoccupation. Even when close analysis is urged, the research is cast in new and challenging epistemologies, such as standpoint theory, semiotics, or queer theory, which are unfamiliar to some students and many researchers.

The last few years have seen a profusion of studies that reflect the lifestyles of the well-educated yet slightly bohemian middle classes in North America. In the 1950s, David Riesman and colleagues wrote an important book of lasting significance, *The Lonely Crowd* (1956), in which they pointed out that the American character, as a result of affluence, differentiation and urbanization, was becoming 'other directed' rather than 'inner directed.' This suggested to them a movement in sensitivity to others based in the here and now, the immediate, and an abiding feeling of being alone and slightly uprooted. Identity rested with others and with their responses. Efforts to find integration and well-being, whether in religion, politics, cults, or in the retreatist, family-focused, lifestyle of the suburbs, failed once it encountered the profound, ingrained American style individualism. These themes are documented further in the case studies in Robert Bellah's *Habits of the Heart* (1996). Published fieldwork work of the last ten years seems passively outer directed and moved more by sentimentality than theorizing or mannered testing of ideas. The studies reflect lifestyles based on comfort and affluence and mannered distance from the poverty, violence, and dread that exists in rural pockets and in inner cities of the United States. I would gloss these studies in a rather unkind way, as seen below. Some works, not all:

- capture moments at the edges of US middle-class life – the rural life as a stage for tourists, summer dwellers and visitors (Hannigan, 1998; Denzin, 2001; Jonas et al., 2003), brief amusements of the middle classes – cooking and fine dining (Fine, 1996 on kitchens), video games (Fine, 1983) and play (Turkle, 1991; Danet, 2003), leisure (Fine, 1998), dust (Fine and Hallett, 2003) and 'health and beauty rhetoric in health and fitness classes' (MacNevin, 2003). These studies are iconic indications of middle-class avoidance of the brutal, harsh politics of inner cities, of prison, jails, and violence (outside the context of middle-class females as victims).

- flatter and elevate the perceptions, feelings and perceptions of the observer over the attitudes, practices, and behaviors of the observed group (Ellis, 1994). Such work as rendered stands in bafflement before birth, death and tragic circumstances.
- are avowedly poetic (Richardson, 1998) and resonate with emotions. Unfortunately, they lack analysis, and neither display a poetic craft-like approach to rhyme or meter, nor explicate the sociological context or point (see Schwalbe, 1995). Social science aims to open conventionalized, encoded and narrowly reflective meanings so that they are more broadly understood. Poetic works rely on codes and rules of rhyme, meter, and inference (usually to classical or well-known sources of meanings – other poets, or poems, classical myths), and most readers have but limited access. The use of unique words and combinations to evoke well-known feelings closes off some conventional meanings and opens up others, some of which may 'feel' unique to a reader. No such agreement stands in ethnography, and ethnography is what ethnographers do. Interpreting ethnographic work of this style becomes more like W.H. Auden's characterization of analyzing poetry as a matter of disentangling metonymic metaphor, or 'a puzzle of knowledge.'
- are often romantic in favor of the underdog. They equate one standpoint, the perspective of the marginal on the more powerful, as an intellectual antidote to the conventional wisdom (Waquant, 2002).
- are conceptually difficult. They claim that the observer should be both inside the experience of the observed and outside

at the same time. They suggest further that this operation is best done by those inside the standpoint (DeVault, 1999).

In these stylistic and content-based moves, qualitative work is torn from empirically verifiable materials and becomes a mixture of observers' sensate and cognitive data, with some *ad hoc* reference to the others' performing. It may not be social science in the usual sense, but its practitioners are all PhD social scientists (mostly sociologists). It may be a new form of consciousness-raising and epistemology that rejects the canons of positivism (the notion that social science studies objective, external, shared social forms in a detached and stylistic fashion that insures 'good work'). Such studies reflect the loss of concern for problem finding and display temerity in seeking topics. One reason that positivism has vanquished challengers in social science is that it holds up standards (derived from statistics, physics, and logic) by which consensus can be reached on what is 'good work.'

FRONTIERS

In the coming years, a number of areas of fieldwork require either revisiting or 'replication.' Some need deeper drilling into the nuances of previous findings, and some new areas need opening. Elaboration of key concepts – configurations and situated actions and practices – may be needed. New areas cannot be mapped with conventional positivist methods. Mailed or phone surveys, official data, and observations or interviews alone are inadequate to study what I shall call, following Norbert Elias (1998), configurations, situated action and practices. This is patently true when the activity is semi-legal, often violent, and therefore concealed from the observation of social controllers whenever possible. It is also embedded in secrecy, bribery and deception, and out of sight and outside the sensibilities of most contemporary observers.

CONFIGURATIONS

My sketch of a challenge in fieldwork is meant as a *icon*, or miniature representation of problem domains, not merely an identification of questions of technique. Although the key studies of US organized crime are now more than 30 years old, and do require revisiting, I am not arguing for further study of 'organized crime' *per se*, although I call on its rich literature (Whyte, 1943/1981; Cressey, 1969: x–xi; Schelling, 1969; Smith, 1970; Ianni and Reuss-Ianni, 1972; Levi, 2002; Naylor, 2002; Hobbs, 1988). I am not debating the morality of the processes at the heart of the work – the use of violence to organize a market in illegal or legal goods or services. My aim is to use enterprise or transactional crime as an arena for urging more conceptually refined fieldwork. While ethnography and biography combined with the concept of criminal careers brought much rich descriptive work to criminology and sociology,[2] in truth, criminal careers should be seen as meshed with careers of police officers, federal and local, as well as conventional markets for illegal and legal goods and services, business and other criminals. Organized crime is a primitive configuration – it is twinned with social control forces competing for prestige. Controllers and controlled are bound together in a network of relationships and transactions, including gifts, money, goods and services. They focus and use the same skills and adopt a game-like attitude.

Norbert Elias' work (1998) is an attempt to dismiss the dominant functionalism of his day, and to substitute an elegant, contextual, historical analysis based in large part on studies of the European courts, Roman society and sport in the ancient world.[3] Configurations are action patterns that have meaning, are repeated, and cannot be reduced to 'structures,' 'processes' or 'functions.' These are labels for the outcomes of configured action. Situated action, arising from many motives and sources, becomes sedimented and reproduced. Elias argues that a configuration is an adjustment of people in interaction within a social space over time, with competition for status, both horizontal and vertical, in which participants are valued in some fashion. A configuration (Elias used both 'configuration' and 'figuration') is determined by the flow and source of prestige at the time, competition between persons in the figuration, and produces power that exceeds the function of the initial actions (Elias, 1998: 87). It is not, in short, about instrumental practices, but about doing something, action which includes its communicative, ritual aspects, as well as its outcomes. A configuration, in his words, 'points to the way that persons drawn into it form an especially intense and specialized competition for the power associated with status and prestige' (Elias, 1998: 93). Elias argues that any system of face-to-face relations contains modes of dramatizing status or marking it, non-verbal and verbal gestures, and actions that reflect the dynamics of the configuration. These modes are woven through the visible tasks performed – dancing, singing, courting, dressing and socializing broadly. This kind of emulation and solidarity, Elias argues, diffuses in such a way that democratic practices become generally admired, and differentiation unfolds. These modes of doing that animate the configuration must be plucked out, and rest on observation and observation of the observations of others. Above all, it begins in actions and practices that in due time become marked or symbolized. They arise, it would appear, from the shared sentiments of courtly society, but the practices are not sustained in due course by these same sentiments, but by others.

If we are to apply the concept of configuration to organized crime, it must be elaborated and refined. The configuration of interest is that which binds together in competition for status and prestige among law enforcement (a set of groups) and organized crime figures as a second set. They are in many ways closer to each other in sentimental terms than to members of the conventional society that surrounds them (Young, 1991: 189). Analysis of a configuration must take into account its opposites, or the relevant differences within that count in shaping it, as well as the way it reflects or opposes a larger context or society. In some ways, this oppositional juxtaposition is a source of dramatizations that set the configuration apart from 'society.' I suggest in the case of crime and deviance, that analysis of a configuration must also include the role of formal and differentiated modes of control, for example, the police, state, local and federal, in shaping the networks and actions. The internal dynamics of a configuration become 'networked.' That is, they include *networks of relations* between people through which exchanges take place.[4] Networks of interconnected actors, with dominant and subordinate nodes (clusters of connections between actors), are not permanent, but are occasioned or activated by situations. Networks 'come into action as the situation demands' (Mack, 1964: 41). In other words, jobs, tasks, threats and new opportunities stimulate connectedness among otherwise loosely linked actors (Stebbins, 1969).

This concept implies, of course, that a network is connected, or linked, and the points are actors, or participants. The idea is based on the notion that unlike a group in which all members share connections, a network connects but is not exclusive. Not all members of a network share connections with all others. There may be clusters, stars, or isolates. In the materials discussed below, the center of the network is usually a named figure and includes as a possible range of connections all those known to him and his associates. These can also be called 'action sets' or propensities to act, and can generate other kinds of relations that Boissevain (1968) calls 'non-groups' because they come into being as a result of situated contingencies. The nature of the *linkages* can vary from positive to negative, in *strength* and *density*, and in the content or *transactions* they carry.[5] A concept of less general scope is a *game*, or a series of interconnected transactions with acknowledged rules, roles and conventions. One can examine specific concrete games, businesses or operations of networked people, within a configuration. Examples of games characteristic of organized crime, for example, are loans at high interest and related violence, extortion, drug selling, policy or numbers, gambling establishments, and legitimate businesses such as travel agencies, used car lots, restaurants, and real estate (Ianni and Reuss-Ianni, 1972: 103). Running legitimate businesses, making and taking bribes and corrupting politicians, are crude skills or specializations that are a basis for stratification within the criminal networks (Ianni and Reuss-Ianni, 1972: 176). Further, although I would argue that while modern configurations stretch across time and space, the prominent shaping influences remain forces of formal social control as manifested within the limited ecological spaces in which people are regulated. This implies the importance of neighborhood in urban settings, ties of ethnicity, class and religion that bind as well as differentiate, social worlds (beliefs) that arise with given themes, for example, risk-taking, action, anti-authoritarianism, family centrality, and the routines and exchanges characteristic of the participants. These, I should emphasize, are displayed in action patterns understood by the relevant audiences.

Consider some additional factors that shape a configuration I will call 'organized crime–law enforcement.' Perhaps obviously, there are key ecological factors, neighborhoods of birth, places for socializing, and for 'doing business.' These may include business as fronts, bars and restaurants, liquor stores, and parks. They are ecologically patterned and linked into larger city processes, as Park and Burgess (1924) first noted. There are usually ethnic, religious and kin ties, in part based on neighborhood of origin. This place-based interaction is a basis for modeling behavior, observation and emulation. This configuration, composed of networks that are regional or neighborhood-based, include the police, both local and federal. There are networks of criminals as well as networks of law enforcers (to use a general term covering state, local and federal officers), and they are linked by known, regular, repeated transactions and exchanges of information, money, goods, people and services. These are, as Mauss argued so eloquently, totalistic in nature. That is, they display aesthetic, economic, political, moral and other aspects of institutions, and 'catch the fleeting moment when the society and its members take emotional stock of themselves and their situation as regards others' (Mauss, 1967: 77–8). Perhaps the most important matter that is exchanged, the content that flows along the links between groups and networks, is information (facts that are placed in a context).

Key in these information exchanges are paid or unpaid protected informants, double agents who inform both sides of the others' activities. While organized crime is not possible without police cooperation, investigation of organized crime is not possible without informants. As Goffman (1969) reminds us, the roles players take in strategic games vary, but the basis of the interactions is moral and tacit rather than explicit. A hierarchy of prestige obtains within and across the networks. High-status criminals and high-status federal agents are given deference for similar reasons – their propensity for violence, their authority and power, resources, and access to other important people such as politicians. They share values and clusters of values or themes such as status-seeking and envy, which are the phenomenological product of repeated, situated, joint action and opposition to and by the conventional world. Their practices define and display 'success.'[6] The roles played by actors within the networks varies. Contests for leadership and prestige, scarce matters, as Elias argues, provide the dynamics of striving. These networks are typically organized around a noted leader, much as the King and Queen functioned in 'court societies' (Elias, 1998: 83–94). Cliques of leaders form action sets that reside within a total network, as does a fluid division of labor based on skills. Clearly, such configurations are characterized by leadership that is multimodal and not based on a single dimension or network.[7] In summary, rather than investigating police and criminals, or police deviance, one should study configurations based on mutual interdependence, informants, exchanges and the politics of order and ordering (Brodeur, 1983). Crime is an intimate part of politics, and politics an intimate part of crime.

ORGANIZED CRIME AND POLICING AS A SINGLE CONFIGURATION

My primary (secondary) source here is material gathered by a journalist team from the *Boston Globe*, Dick Lehr and Gerard O'Neil

(1989, 2001), who created a rich descriptive tapestry of the relationships between the FBI, local law enforcement, and several organized crime groups in Boston over a 25-year period beginning in the mid-1970s. I build on the work of W.F. Whyte (1943), Herbert Gans (1973), and Frances Ianni and Elizabeth Reuss-Ianni (1972) because they studied similar social forms, and in the case of Gans and Whyte, studied contiguous social areas in Boston. I accept these renditions of social life in the North End, the Italian section of Boston, South Boston ('Southie'), the Irish section of Boston, and the former West End of Boston (a victim of urban renewal), a mixture of Italian and other ethnic groups, because it is stylish, imaginative and credible fieldwork.[8] The work of Frances Ianni and Elizabeth Reuss-Ianni (1972) on an Italian crime family in New York complements the Boston work, and adds insights to the notion of organized crime as a metaphoric creation and a police– criminal configuration. These fieldworkers, Gans, Whyte, Ianni and Reuss-Ianni, accomplished their fieldwork because although they were outsiders to the groups studied, they were able to take the role or perspective of the groups and people studied. They developed and maintained access and spent years in the field. They sustained their relationships long after they left the field. They were trusted to tell only the second or third worst thing that happened, and concealed names, precise locations and activity (e.g., actual crimes). They remained focused on the dynamics of the groups they studied. Their view was situational and situated in that key events, turning points in the action, were seen as the result of unanticipated actions to which leaders had to respond creatively, alter routines, and cope. They brought forward the ironies and contradictions that they uncovered.

Consider the organized crime–law enforcement configuration in Boston (Lehr and O'Neil, 1989, 2001). We can extract and chart interaction among seven networks within the configuration in Boston, especially in the North End and South Boston. The initial stimulus for the eventual configuration, according to Lehr and O'Neil, was that the FBI, after Robert Kennedy became US Attorney General, was pressured to have information and informants in the organized crime world. They had but little experience in investigating organized crime, having focused on bank robberies, communists, civil rights activities, and visible interstate crimes like kidnapping. The pressure to succeed was strong, and the target was defined in time as the 'mafia,' 'Cosa Nostra,' or 'Italian gangsters' and seen as operating through families and gangs in the North End. The FBI's strategy, then, was to cultivate as informants former neighbors, Irish-Americans from Southie, and through them and their contacts in the North End groups, to monitor and investigate organized crime in Boston from 1975 on. The key FBI agent in this drama was John Connolly, who cultivated and 'ran' Whitely Bulger and Stephen Flemmi for almost 25 years.[9]

The authors draw on interviews with informants and archives to describe the fate of Irishmen from the traditional Irish area of South Boston, and Italian organized crime figures in the North End, several gangs who are interconnected, rise and fall, and the machinations of the FBI, DEA (Drug Enforcement Agency), and local police. The thesis, well-demonstrated in the book, is that the FBI protected known Irish criminal gangs in order to penetrate and erode the power of the Italian organized crime figures in Boston's North End. The key figures were habitués of either the North End or Southie (including the key players, Flemmi, Bulger, Connolly and the leaders of the Italian group – see opposite). Socializing and meeting took place in restaurants, hotels, motels and

Network *Bulger*
Flemmi
Bulger
Femja
Weeks
O'Neil
Nee
Yerardi
Kaufman (front)

Network *North End 80's*
G. Angiulo
Zannino
D. Angiulo
M. Angiulo
J.R. Russo
Ferrar
Carozza

Network *Winter Hill Gang*
Bulger and Flemmi
Winter
Mortorano
Bamoski
Sims
McDonald
Ciulla
Halloran

Network *Mafia in the 90s*
Salemme

Network *FBI*
Sarhall, early 80s
Greenleaf, mid 80s
Ahearn, late 80s
Rico, organized crime squad
Morris, supervisor organized crime squad
Connolly
Condon, organized crime squad

Network *MA State Police*

Network *US Justice Department Prosecutors*

Figure 22.1 *List of the members of 7 networks, Boston 1980–2000*

homes in each locale, and Bulger owned a liquor store (obtained by extortion) where several of his associates spent time. New members were recruited from Southie, acted deferentially, and were treated in a feudal, patrimonial fashion. Loyalty was to the senior person – a matter that changed over time – Bulger and Flemmi, and, in the Italian group, the Anguilo family members and Jack Salemme.

The configuration includes the networks linking the crime figures to each other as well as to the federal, state and local police. The networks are shown in Figure 22.1, and include some seven groups – Mafia 1 and Mafia 2 based in the North End; the Irish Winter Hill mob (headed in time by Bulger); DEA; FBI; local police, Massachusetts state police, and federal prosecutors. I have grouped them (in Figure 22.1) into two arbitrary action sets – OCG (the organized crime set) and the LEG (the law enforcement set).

In general terms, the enforcers (networks 5–7) have a denser interaction within than between. The interactions shown in Figure 22.2 link them to the other networks (1–4). The flow within the links include information, misinformation, disinformation, tips, covering up crime, doing superficial investigation of alleged possible corruption, bribes, gifts, money and favors. False information was given to other FBI agents about what tips Bulger and Flemmi had given to the FBI (to enhance their status in the FBI's hierarchy) and additional misleading information was placed in records and given orally to conceal their crimes, their locations and movements. For example, Flemmi fled twice after being given an FBI tip that he might be arrested (he was arrested and convicted in 2002); Bulger fled in 1995 as a result of a tip-off and has not been seen since.

A hierarchy of prestige orders the networks, with federal and state agencies having higher status than local police, and the networks compete for status, with the Bulger group emerging as superordinate (in part because of FBI protection for their crimes). Transactions link sections of the networks: high-status FBI agents dealt with high-status informants

		1	2	3	4	5	6	7		+	0	−	
Bulger	1	0	+	−	+	+	0	+		4	1	1	6
Mafia 1	2	+	0	−	+	−	−	−		2	0	4	6
Winter Hill	3	+	−	0	0	−	−	−		1	1	3	5
Mafia 2	4	+	+	−	0	−	−	−		2	0	4	6
FBI	5	+	0	−	−	0	−	−		2	0	4	6
MA State Police	6	−	0	−	−	−	0	−		0	2	4	6
US Dept. Pros.	7	+	0	−	−	+	−	0		1	2	3	6

Figure 22.2   *Matrix of Network Relations in Boston, 1986–2000*

in the criminal networks. There was also a hierarchy of power in the cluster of networks (enforcers cluster), and relationships were based on the resources and ability to carry out an investigation. Investigations by the DEA, the FBI, New York City office, Quincy, Massachusetts police, and at least three state police investigations were foiled by tips or false information given by the FBI to the criminal networks (primarily by agent John Connolly, but also by agent Morris). Pressure was put on judges for leniency in trials; records were falsified concerning the activities of the Irish informants; other records did not include meetings and agreements, gifts and parties given by each group for the other. Gifts served to bind networks as well as individuals – they produced obligation, reciprocity, and readings of intentions and character.

If we consider the attraction and mutual respect valences between the networks, we see that some ironies emerge in that the Bulger group had the greatest number of positive signs, followed by the Mafia 1 network, while the FBI, Mafia 2 and the Massachusetts state police had the highest number of negative valences within the entire configuration. The weakest networks are the Massachusetts state police and the Winter Hill Mob (in part because they disbanded). The power of the Bulger network is shown by the high number of positives, mainly because they had a positive relationship with the FBI and an ambivalent relationship with the US Attorney's office (which supported the FBI).

Sponsorship and recruitment also pattern the networks and the configuration, as the younger members of the gangs came from the traditional ethnic neighborhoods, as did several of the FBI agents.

Here are two examples of how the loose networks within the configuration worked, how action sets were activated, how exchanges took place, what was exchanged and with what known consequence.

1. Feb. 1980. Whitey Bulger and Stephen Flemmi set up a loan sharking game based in the Lancaster Auto Body shop in Cambridge. A Massachusetts state trooper sees activity, notes it in his surveillance notes, and later obtains a search warrant to tap the phone lines of the body shop. Surveillance also reveals a link to a North End head of a crime family, G. Anguilo, but no other relevant information. Soon, the workers in the shop drove off and begin making their phone calls from public pay phones. The Massachusetts state police suspects that the FBI is tipping off Bulger. In August of that same year a 'law enforcement summit' is called to discuss the possible intrusion of the FBI on a planned state police sting at the Lancaster Body Shop. During this time (1980–81), the FBI outside Boston were calling for a 'suitability

review' of Flemmi and Bulger as informants, but two FBI agents, John Connolly and Morris, rebuffed a full review and protected Flemmi and Bulger. There is a review, and Flemmi is suspended (but not informed of this change in status by the FBI).

The enforcer cluster of networks is divided while the FBI–crime network (Connelly–Bulger–Flemmi) is activated. The FBI informs the criminals and foils the Massachusetts state police investigation. This action protects their informants as well as the loan sharking game being run by Bulger.

2. Feb 1981–June 1982. Gifts of wine, dinners, and cigars flow between the FBI agents and Bulger and Flemmi. Connolly hears from an informant that a man named B. Halloran is dealing drugs and talking publicly about Bulger being a drug dealer and an FBI informant. FBI Agent Morris is sent to Georgia for training, and asks Connolly to give Morris's girlfriend $1000 for an air ticket to come to visit him. This money is given by Bulger to Connolly who in turn gives it to Morris's girlfriend. Connolly then warns Bulger that Halloran is talking. Halloran is found dead and Bulger is suspected of the murder.

In this example, exchanges take place within the FBI network and as a result of an exchange with the Irish criminal network. Gifts and information (warnings, tips) were exchanged and their sources concealed. Bulger's drug game was protected and Halloran sacrificed. In a sense, the games, extortion, loan sharking (lending at high interest rates on the street and using violence to sustain compliance), and later drugs, are manifestations of the existence of the networks and show what is played and why. Violence plays a constant role in that it shapes outcomes, is tolerated by the powerful as used against the less powerful, lurks in every relationship as a conflict resolution mode, and is thought of as a tool or resource within the games. Secrecy protects the members of the entire configuration, because some secrets are shared, some are differentially shared, but no one knows all the secrets.[10]

These ideas are consistent with the Iannis's detailed ethnographic study of organized crime in New York City in a similar period. The configuration of crime and law in this case also includes both the dominant society (as a kind of opposition) and the Italian-American culture with its adaptation of family patterns to politics as a resource for trust and mobilizing resources. Lehr and O' Neil suggest that the relationships between organized crime groups and police in Boston show that transition and succession comes in part as a result of age (generational transition) and in part through intervention and control forces (arrest, imprisonment, close surveillance) by the police. These generalizations also held true in the Italian organized crime family studied by the Iannis. If we consider this configuration a *social world*, based in part on beliefs that are built up through exchanges and practices, the meaningful values and themes that obtain, we see that the FBI agents, the police and crime figures share themes and values, in part because they share similar lower middle-class origins, and experiences in neighborhoods, ethnicity and the Catholic religion.

There are a number of further generalizations one can draw from the studies of organized crime of the Italian and Irish sort. These suggest why a concept with general applicability like a configuration is more useful than more restrictive and morally loaded ideas like notions such as 'deviance,' 'police deviance,' or even Mafia.

- The experience of immigrant families and their peasant origins makes family loyalty central to survival, secrecy and distrust of government and distant politicians common, ambivalent attitude toward the middle class and conventional kinds of social mobility (based on education) shared, and a common shaping influence on the exchanges between politicians, law enforcers, and organized crime figures (see especially Gans, 1973: 229–80).

- 'Family' is the dominant metaphor that denotes vertical and horizontal relationships. Age and generation pattern respect; within generations, closeness to the central figure (the patrilineal line is dominant) obtains.
- Exchanges bind together the legal and illegal actors – politicians, law enforcement and the criminal groups. These include gifts of money, drink, dinners and entertainment at parties, information (warnings of ongoing investigations, raids and potential indictments).
- The social worlds of the two are compatible in values and prestige; a kind of mirror-image in that both action sets value toughness, secrecy, loyalty, betrayal (very negatively defined, but essential the work both sets of people do) and reject conventional values concerning success even while they are envious of celebrities and conventionally successful businessman and politicians.
- The games within the social world are well-identified and the players envy the respectable classes. These are handled by 'specialists', for example, corruption, violence, fixing horse races, and quasi-legal businesses (funded by illegal ones serving as money laundering sites).
- The exchanges are multi-leveled and connote ties between ethnic groups, Catholics, neighborhoods, friends, and are indicative of trust and implicit contractual relationships. These displays, visible and based on face-to-face relations, pin down trust in the problematic work that sustains this configuration.
- Leadership is somewhat stable, but subject to violent transitions and succession struggles since the basis of loyalty is personal and clique-based.
- Exchanges within and across the networks are touched off episodically, and are not structured tightly by formal ranks, names or duties. Choices arise within these situations.

TRUST AND CONFIGURATIONS

The unifying sources of such apparently diverse exchanges within the configuration are, as noted above, in addition to interaction itself, ethnicity, religion, social location (an ecological region) and family ties. The necessity of such trust-based ties is elevated in importance because the work is illegal and the secrets kept are potentially highly damaging to the business. Violence pervades the work. Organized crime, as in Boston, is part of a configuration protected by and sustained by the police. The metaphor of family is used within and across the enforcers, for example, the police family, and the criminals. It is in part a linguistic tool that sets the boundaries of the configuration and indicates an elastic sense of loyalty.[11] The Iannis, Whyte, Gans and the *Boston Globe* writers all note that the idea of 'family' is powerful and works at several levels. It works as a metaphor for closeness and loyalty to each other. It works as a denotative term pointing to the male head of the family as an authority and power figure. It works as a denotative term to honor the family line that is dominant within the set of businesses run by family members and associates. It works to create a generationally based hierarchy and thus patterns sucession to power.

The Iannis's fieldwork extracted some rules for organizing their materials and to which actors were oriented. These are inferences from action sets they observed, rather than rigid and exclusive ideas. Because relations within the configuration are personalized, or based on loyalty to specific people, changes in authority change the meaning and direction of the rules. Enforcement depends on the combination of rule, 'violator,' the person who applies the sanction and the source of authority. The Iannis argue that in the family they studied there were three basic rules:

- 'loyalty to family';
- 'act like a man' (submissive to authority, able to be authoritative);
- 'keeping secrets'.

These rules insulate and isolate family members from those outside the configuration. The centrality of the family, and of rules that govern the protection and orientation of family members as well as the family businesses, gives the network an acceptable metaphoric cover. The actual 'core' of family may be of variable strength. In Boston, the Winter Hill gang was part Italian and part Irish. John 'Whitey' Bulger, the key member of this gang, was the brother of the Head of the Massachusetts state Senate (later President of the University of Massachusetts). The Anguilo family was handed down to a weak family member and disintegrated around 1989 (See Lehr and O'Neil, 1989). The Salemme family tried to hand down power to the next generation, but eventually fell under the control of the Bulger-led Irish group. This resulted in part because Bulger and his mates were protected by the FBI while the Salemme family were not.

In many respects, the role of the configuration of interest here can be generalized. Its key theme is the mobilizing of a collective, anti-state action called crime or self-help (Black, 1983), a compromise formation with the police and federal agencies, and an activity mirroring the family as a metaphoric icon. It resembles banditry and other forms arising in chaotic periods or places where the state's authority is weak or where the state is in complicity with the criminal figures for other reasons. It has a resemblance to guerilla warfare in that the lines between forces are blurred and unclear, defections are frequent, and terrorism is used as a tactic. Essential questions of power and authority arise since the configurations are indirect consequences of the authority of the state withdrawing from some areas and leaving them to informal modes of control (Venkatesh, 1998, 2000), or acting in complicity with vigilante gang groups. The culture of control (Garland, 2001), with its incarceration-driven model of 'governmentality,' deregulation of capital markets, and privatizing of security in many housing estates (Rigakos, 2002), leads to a parallel in modern cities to the situation of bandits described by Hobsbawn (1969). Clearly, the gangs and habitual criminals in Boston, who worked in the configuration with the police, were protected for their information and tips as informants, and were rooted in a political environment and neighborhoods where their activities were well known, if not sanctioned (MacDonald, 2001). Crime networks are service providers in impoverished, service-deprived areas, that are also crime-dependent, and when the young in particular lack legitimate employment. The networks of criminals provide a version of order and self-help. Like many gangsters and gang members, the leaders have prestige and, like bandits, serve many ordering purposes, even while terrorizing other groups.

COMMENT

If we are to move fieldwork to advanced theorizing, we should apply our energies to studying the major problems of our times – justice, security, inequality, and violence – in their concrete manifestations. We must use the techniques we have mastered and which conventional survey research, interviewing and official data cannot and will not grasp. Using official data perpetuates the blindness of those in authority and their perspectives, as reflected in the data gathered, available and used. One of the rather ignored aspects of modernity and postmodernity has been theorizing situated actions and practices (Rawls, 2003). This is essential, for our larger theories – functionalism, Marxism, and structuralisms – cannot penetrate the subtleties of the interpretations that sustain and mark the practices of interest. To elaborate this point, I mean that when society is constituted of, on the surface, a rapidly changing set of configurations, not structures or functionally integrated entities, the underlying order and ordering is subtle and attempts to 'pin it down' are unsuccessful. The quest for the functional integration of societies should be terminated, the quest for those things that indicate order, practices, doings, performances and games should be chosen for analysis.

In the examples used here as a kind of icon, I have argued that configurations, action-based forms, are a way of framing choices. These choices, indicated in potential by the networks, can be traced out by their effects among participants. Networks are subjectively touched off by situations in which something must be done. They are virtual until that time. The social worlds that surround action choices and practices are stimulated and sustained, marked by these action choices. I have suggested that the concept of a game can be used to identify the little but very valued exchanges that exist. We search for the 'there' that is out of sight, and it is easy to glance aside, or cast a look away, only to be lost in the middle distance.

NOTES

1 I am grateful to Rosanna Hertz and Anne Rawls for pointed suggestions and helpful comments, and to Maria Marcucilli, Stephanie Saia, and Claire Rambo for research assistance.

2 This aspect of the problematic of crime has only been touched upon. Four important studies have been done, studies that use a personal career to explicate sociological concepts: Sutherland (1937) on the professional thief; Cressey (1953) on the embezzler; Klockars (1974) on the fence; and Chambliss and King (1972/1984) on the safe cracker. Each of these is notably dated, and were dated at the time of publication since they were interviews with aging criminals. While they touched on the network of relations within which the criminals worked, they were centered on the careers of the central character, rather than the configuration of police and criminal enterprise.

3 Elias argued that court society produced a proto-democratic demeanor. This model of comportment and demeanor, somewhat forgiving and equalitarian as the roles shifted frequently, became a pattern emulated by the middle classes or rising bourgeoisie.

4 Elizabeth Bott (1971: 319–21) is generally viewed as the author of the concept of a network, or a set of connections between people that is not closed, but overlapping. Leach's brilliant work on the political systems of highland Burma makes a similar point in great and delicate detail (Leach, 1954).

5 I mention these as avenues to explore. The fieldwork required to chart them would be extensive and demanding. To some degree, it is possible to plot the relationships within networks in a sociometric matrix.

6 The point here is that while the idea of success is shared and the conventional world is envied for its modes and appearances of success and related symbols, this configuration converts the term 'success' through their practices that distinguish them from the 'straight world.'

7 A full ethnography might include rules of conduct which cross-cut the legal and illegal, and are part of the configuration generally.

8 The two projects of Whyte and Gans are among the most significant in sociology. William Whyte's *Street Corner Society* (1943/1981) is a classic of fieldwork. He shows the interconnectedness of a neighborhood (the North End of Boston), ethnicity (Italians of southern Sicilian and northern origin), religion (the Catholic church), and age-graded cohorts (my term) or corner boys and college boys, in dynamic relationship to racketeering and politics. The book begins with an overture of some 75 pages, which describes several key scenarios in which Whyte played a role and showed how the factors of interest to him were displayed in collective action (meetings, bowling, elections). The latter part of the book includes analysis of the social structure of racketeering, political campaigns and why the configuration located in the North End had sustainability.

Key to the work is the way that the corner boys were deeply implicated in the rackets (policy, numbers, to a lesser degree horse-race betting), politics, and social clubs. They stood ready for this because the street corner society is based on a male–female divide socially and an age grading that makes unemployed people (in school or out of work) active participants in the street culture. This is also the finding of Herbert Gans (1973), who worked in the West End of Boston (which adjoins the North End) in the late 1950s, some 25 years later. While the family remains the key social unit, complemented by the institutional structure, the public culture remained powerful and that, in turn, was linked to betting, gambling, politics and corruption.

9 The former FBI agent, John Connolly, was arrested, indicted, tried and convicted of obstruction of justice and went to Federal prison in September 2002.

10 Bruce Jacobs (2000), in his fine ethnographic study of crack cocaine dealers in East St Louis, argues that violence, based on revenge, self-protection, sustaining reputation and protecting customers, is more significant in shaping drug market dynamics (entry, exit, success, failure) than the actions of formal law enforcement.

11 I am grateful to Rosanna Hertz for suggesting this point.

REFERENCES

Bellah, Robert et al. (1996). *Habits of the Heart*. Berkley: University of California Press.

Black, Donald (1983). 'Crime as Social Control.' *American Sociological Review* 48: 34–45.

Boissevian, J. (1968). 'The Place of Non Groups in the Social Sciences.' *Man* 3: 542–56.

Bott, Elizabeth (1971). *Family and Social Network* (2nd edn). New York: Free Press.

Brodeur, J.P. (1983). 'High Policing and Low Policing.' *Social Problems* 30: 507–20.

Chambliss, William, J. and King. (1972/1984). *Box Man*. New York: Harper & Row.

Cressey, Donald (1953). *Other Peoples' Money*. Glencoe, IL: Free Press.

Cressey, Donald (1969). *The Theft of the Nation*. New York: Harper & Row.

Danet, B. 2003. *Cyberplay*. Oxford: Berg.

Denzin, N. (2001). 'Cowboys and Indians.' *Symbolic Interaction* 25: 251–61.

DeVault, M. (1999). 'Talking Back to Sociology.' *Annual Review of Sociology* 22: 29–50.

Elias, Norbert (1998). *Norbert Elias on Civilization, Power and Knowledge*. Edited by Stephen Mennell and Johan Goudsblom. Chicago: University of Chicago Press.

Ellis, Carolyn (1994). *Fatal Illness*. New Brunswick, NJ: Rutgers University Press.

Fine, Gary (1983). *Shared Fantasy: Role Playing Games as Social Worlds*. Chicago: University of Chicago Press.

Fine, Gary (1996) *Kitchens: The Culture of Restaurant Work*. Berkeley: University of California.

Fine, Gary (1998). *Morel Tales: The Culture of Mushrooming*. Cambridge, MA: Harvard University Press.

Fine, Gary and Hallett, Tim 2003. 'Dust.' *The Sociological Quarterly* 44: 1–15.

Gans, Herbert (1973). *Urban Villagers*. New York: Free Press.

Garland, David (2001). *The Culture of Control*. Chicago: University of Chicago Press.

Goffman, E. 1969. *Strategic Interaction*. Philadelphia: University of Pennsylvania Press.

Hannigan, John (1998). *Fantasy City*. London: Routledge, Kegan Paul.

Hobbs, R. (1988). *Doing the Business*. Oxford: Clarenden Press.

Hobsbawn, Eric (1969). *Bandits*. New York: DeLacorte Press.

Ianni, F. and Reuss-Ianni, E. (1972). *A Family Business*. New York: Mentor.

Jacobs, Bruce (2000). *Robbing Drug Dealers*. New York: Aldine.

Jonas, Lillian, Stewart, W.P and Larkin, K. (2003). 'Entertaining Heidi: Audience for a Wilderness Adventure Identity.' *Journal of Contemporary Ethnography* 32: 403–31.

Leach, E. (1954). *Political Systems of Highland Burma*. London: Athlone Press.

Lehr, Dick and O'Neil, Gerard (1989). *Underboss*. New York: St Martins Press.

Lehr, Dick and O'Neil, Gerard (2001). *Black Mass*. New York: Perennial.

Levi, Mike (2002). 'Elite Crime.' In *Oxford Handbook of Criminology* (2nd edn). Oxford: Oxford University Press.

MacDonald, Michael (2001). *All Souls*. New York: Ballantine.

MacNevin, Audrey (2003). 'Exercising Options: Holistic Health and Technical Beauty in Gendered Accounts of Bodywork.' *The Sociological Quarterly* 44: 271–81.

Malinowski, B. (1922). *Argonauts of the Western Pacific*. London: Routledge.

Mauss, M. (1967). *The Gift.* Translated by Ian Cunnison. New York: Norton.

Naylor, R. (2002). *Organized Crime.* Ithaca, NY: Cornell University Press.

Park, Robert and Burgess, Ernest (1924) *Introduction to the Science of Sociology.* Chicago: University of Chicago Press.

Rawls, Anne Warfield (ed.) (2003). 'Editor's Introduction.' In A.W. Rawls (ed.), *Ethnomethodology's Program.* Lanham, MD: Roman & Littlefield.

Richardson, Laurel (1998). *Fields of Play.* New Brunswick, NJ: Rutgers University Press.

Riesman, David, Glazer N. and Denney, M. (1956) *The Lonely Crowd.* New York: Doubleday Anchor.

Rigakos, George (2002). *Parapolice.* Toronto: University of Toronto Press.

Schelling, J. 1969. 'What is the Business of Organized Crime?' Working paper, Presidents Crime Commission. Washington DC: US Government Printing Office.

Schwalbe, M. (1995). 'The Responsibilities of Sociological Poets.' *Qualitative Sociology* 18: 393–413.

Smith, Dwight (1970). *The Mafia Mystique.* New York: Basic Books.

Stebbins, Robert (1969). 'On Networks as a subjective construct.' *Canadian Review of Sociology and Anthropology* 6: 1–14.

Sutherland, Edward (1937). *The Professional Thief.* Chicago: University of Chicago Press.

Turkle, S. (1991). *The Second Self.* New York: Simon & Schuster.

van Maanen, John (1998). *Tales of the Field.* Chicago: University of Chicago Press.

Venkatesh, S. (1997). 'The Social Organization of Street Gang Activity in an Urban Ghetto.' *American Journal of Sociology.* 103: 82–111.

Venkatesh, S. (2000). *American Project.* Cambridge: Harvard University Press.

Wacquant, Luc (2002). 'Scrutinizing the Street: Poverty, Morality, and the Pitfalls of Urban Ethnography.' *American Journal of Sociology.* 107: 1468–532.

Whyte, W.F. (1943/1981). *Street Corner Society.* Chicago: University of Chicago Press.

Wollcott, H. (2001). *Writing Up Qualitative Research.* Thousand Oaks, CA: Sage.

Young, Malcolm (1991). *An Inside Job.* Oxford: Clarendon Press.

Author Biographies

Elijah Anderson is the Charles and William L. Day Distinguished Professor of the Social Sciences and Professor of Sociology at the University of Pennsylvania. An expert on the sociology of black America, he is the author of the classic sociological work, *A Place on the Corner: A Study of Black Street Corner Men* (1978; 2003) and numerous articles on the black experience. Dr. Anderson is director of the Philadelphia Ethnography Project, associate editor of *Qualitative Sociology*, and other professional journals, a member of the Board of Directors of the American Academy of Political and Social Science, and the past Vice President of the American Sociological Association. He was a member of the National Research Council's Panel on the Understanding and Control of Violent Behavior, which published its report in 1993.

Susan Brownell is Associate Professor and Chair of the Department of Anthropology at the University of Missouri-St. Louis. She was a nationally-ranked track and field athlete in the U.S. before she went to China for a year of language study, joined the track team at Beijing University, and won the heptathlon in the 1986 Chinese National College Games. This experience was the basis for her book, *Training the Body for China: Sports in the Moral Order of the People's Republic* (1995). She is also the co-editor of *Chinese Femininities/ Chinese Masculinities: A Reader* (2002). Her recent research concerns the 2008 Beijing Olympic Games.

Carole Browner is Professor in both the Department of Anthropology and the Department of Psychiatry and Biobehavioral Sciences at UCLA. Her research interests include comparative medical systems and reproductive politics in Latin America and the US.

Robert Burgess is Vice-Chancellor of UCAS, the University of Leicester and Chair of the Research Information Network, the UUK/SCOP Teacher Education Advisory Group, ESRC/Funding Council's Teaching and Learning Research Programme and the UUK/SCOP enquiry on Measuring and Recording Student Achievement. He has been President of the British Sociological Association and the Association for the Teaching of the Social Sciences, Founding Chair of the UK Council for Graduate Education and a member of the Council and Chair of the Postgraduate Training Board of the Economic and Social Research Council. He has published widely on the sociology of education and social research methodology.

Joseph Carrier has been a pioneer in the ethnographic study of male homosexuality since the late 1960s. His groundbreaking fieldwork in Mexico, which began in the summer of 1968 and continues to date, paved the way for the ethnographic study of men who have sex with men in Latin America and internationally. Since the beginning of the AIDS epidemic, his ethnographically based fieldwork helped provide the basis for an extension of ethnographic methods to the study of sexual behaviors in relation to HIV prevention programs. He received his Ph.D. in Social Sciences from the University of California, Irvine.

Ben Crewe is a Senior Research Associate at the Institute of Criminology, Cambridge, and a Fellow of Robinson College. In recent years, he has been engaged in ethnographic research in a medium-security prison, where his aim has been to explore the everyday social world and culture of the institution. He has written on various methodological and substantive issues in this area, including the role of heroin in the prisoner society, and the 'inmate code'. In previous work, his focus was on cultures of masculinity within the sphere of media production.

Mary Dodge is an Associate Professor at the Graduate School of Public Affairs, University of Colorado at Denver and Health Sciences Center. Her articles have appeared in *Courts and Justice, Contemporary Issues in Criminology, International Journal of the Sociology of Law, The Prison Journal, Police Quarterly, Journal of Contemporary Criminal Justice,* and the *Encyclopedia of White-Collar and Corporate Crime.* She and Gilbert Geis co-edited the book *Lessons of Criminology* (2002) and share authorship on the book *Stealing Dreams: A Fertility Clinic Scandal* (2003). Her research and writing interests include women in the criminal justice system, white-collar crime, policing, prostitution, and courts.

Nigel G. Fielding is Professor of Sociology at the University of Surrey, co-Director of the Institute of Social Research, and co-Director of the ESRC-supported CAQDAS Networking Project, which provides training and support in the use of computers in qualitative data analysis. He was editor of the *Howard Journal of Criminal Justice* from 1985 to 1998 and is co-editor of the *New Technologies for Social Research* series (Sage).

His main research interests are in qualitative research methods, new technologies for social research, and criminal justice. He has authored or edited 17 books, 47 journal articles, 47 chapters in edited books and 145 other publications. In research methodology his books include a study of methodological integration/triangulation (*Linking Data,* 1986, Sage; with Jane Fielding), an influential book on qualitative software (*Using Computers in Qualitative Research,* 1991, Sage; editor, with Ray Lee), a study of the role of computer technology in qualitative research (*Computer Analysis and Qualitative Research,* 1998, Sage, with Ray Lee) and a four volume set, *Interviewing* (2002, Sage; editor). He is presently researching the application of Grid/ high performance computing applications to qualitative methods, and the impact of community policing on public reassurance.

Nick J. Fox is Reader in Sociology of Health and the Body in the School of Health and Related Research at the University of Sheffield. His research interests are in postmodern social theory; health technologies, embodiment and subjectivity; and the social impact of information and communication technologies on health and health care. *Beyond Health: Postmodernism and Embodiment* was published by Free Association Books in 1999 and other recent journal publications continue to develop constructivist approaches to issues around health, embodiment, governance and research.

Susanne Friese is director of the IT and media centre at the University of Hannover, Faculty of Philosophy, Germany. She also works as a consultant for Qualitative Research & Consulting. Her special interest is in qualitative data analysis with an emphasis on software supported analysis. More recently she has been exploring the possibilities of collecting and analysing digital multimedia data. Her background is in social sciences and most of her academic research is related to the field of consumer behaviour. Previously she worked in various positions for Qualis Reseach Associates, Oregon, USA; University of Sussex, Brighton, UK; University of Hohenheim, Stuttgart, Germany; and Copenhagen Business School, Copenhagen, Denmark.

Steve Fuller is Professor of Sociology at the University of Warwick. He is best known for his work on 'social epistemology', which is also the title of a journal he founded in 1987 and the first of his nine published books. He recently published *The Intellectual* (Icon, 2005), which is modelled on Machiavelli's *The Prince*. His next books are *The New Sociological Imagination* (Sage, 2006) and *The Philosophy of Science and Technology Studies* (Routledge 2005). Fuller is currently working on the future of the university as a site for knowledge production and a comprehensive history of epistemology.

Gilbert Geis is a Professor Emeritus, Department of Criminology, Law and Society, University of California, Irvine. He is a former president of the American Society of Criminology, and recipient of the Society's Edwin H. Sutherland Award for Outstanding Research Achievement. Geis has written extensively on white-collar crime, going back to the 1950s. His current books are: *Criminal Justice and Moral Issues: Prostitution, Abortion, Drugs, Homosexuality, Pornography and Gambling*, with Robert F. Meier (Roxbury, 2005), and *White-Collar and Corporate Crime* (Prentice-Hall, 2006).

Jennifer Hargreaves is Visiting Professor of Sport and Gender Politics at the University of Brighton. She has played a pioneering role in the development of sport sociology and is considered a world authority in the field. Her particular interests are sport and gender politics; the social construction of the sporting body; and issues of exclusion and discrimination in sport. Among her publications is the watershed edited text, *Sport, Culture and Ideology* (1982); and *Sporting Females: Critical Issues in the History and Sociology of Women's Sports* (1994) which was awarded the best sports sociology book of the year by the North American Society of Sports Sociology (NASSS). Her second monograph, *Heroines of Sport: the Politics of Difference and Identity* (2000) resulted from several years of original research focusing on women from historically marginalised groups. Jennifer is joint editor of the book series, *Routledge Critical Studies in Sport*, and is co-editing a book for the series entitled, *Physical Culture, Power, and the Body*. Jennifer has worked as a guest professor in Germany, Hong Kong and Japan, she lectures in venues around the world, is on the editorial boards of international refereed journals, and does consultancy work for sport organisations and for the media.

Chris Haywood is a lecturer in Communication and Cultural Studies in the School of Education, Communication and Language Sciences, University of Newcastle-upon-Tyne. He has written in the areas of sexuality, masculinity and schooling and is currently completing his Ph.D. entitled, 'Sexuality and Schooling: A Cultural Politics of Desire.' This doctoral work explores the relationship between post-structuralism, epistemology and the possibilities of knowing. Alongside this, he has recently been a joint director with Mairtin Mac an Ghaill, on a Joseph Rowntree Foundation funded project examining young people's transitions to adulthood.

Dick Hobbs is Professor of Sociology at the London School of Economics, having previously taught at Durham University. He has published on deviance, ethnographic methods, policing, organised crime, professional crime, drugs, violence, private security, working class entrepreneurship, and the night-time economy. He is currently working on a project looking at female doorstaff in the night-time economy, and a project on organised crime in Europe. His main publications are *Doing the Business* (1988) which won the Philip Abrams Prize, *Bad Business* (1995), and, with Philip Hadfield, Stuart Lister and Simon Winlow, *Bouncers* (2003).

Bruce A. Jacobs is Associate Professor of Crime and Justice Studies at the University of Texas-Dallas. Jacobs has authored two books and numerous peer-reviewed articles on the decision-making processes of active street offenders.

Mairtin Mac an Ghaill is Professor of Sociology in the Department of Sociology, University of Birmingham. He teaches in the areas of ethnicity, masculinity and sexuality. He is author of *The Making of Men* (1994) (OUP); *Understanding Masculinities* (1996) (OUP); *Contemporary Racisms and Ethnicities* (1999) (OUP) and *Men and Masculinities* (2003) (OUP) with Chris Haywood.

Peter K. Manning holds the Elmer V. H. and Eileen M. Brooks trustees Chair in the College of Criminal Justice at Northeastern University, Boston, MA. He has taught at Michigan State, MIT, Oxford, the University of Michigan and elsewhere, and was a Fellow of the National Institute of Justice, Balliol and Wolfson Colleges, Oxford, the American Bar Foundation, the Rockefeller Villa (Bellagio), and the Centre for Socio-Legal Studies, Wolfson College, Oxford.

Listed in *Who's Who in America*, and *Who's Who in the World*, he has been awarded many contracts and grants, the Bruce W. Smith and the O.W. Wilson Awards from the Academy of Criminal Justice Sciences, and the Charles Horton Cooley Award from the Michigan Sociological Association. The author and editor of some 13 books, including *Privatization of Policing: Two Views* (with Brian Forst) (Georgetown University Press, 2000). The second edition of *Narcs' Game* [1979], appeared in 2004 (Waveland Press). His monograph, *Policing Contingencies*, was published in 2003 by the University of Chicago Press, and *Technology's Ways* in 2006.

Shadd Maruna is a Reader in Law and Criminology at Queen's University Belfast. Previously he has taught at the University of Cambridge and the State University of New York. His book, *Making Good: How Ex-Convicts Reform and Rebuild Their Lives* (APA Books, 2001) was named the Outstanding Contribution to Criminology by the American Society of Criminology in 2001. He is the co-editor of two new books, *After Crime and Punishment* (2004) and *The Effects of Imprisonment* (2005), both with Willan Publishing.

Christine Mattley is Associate Professor of Sociology & Anthropology at Ohio University. She has published numerous articles and book chapters on a variety of topics including battered women, gender performance, the temporality of emotion, stigma and sex work. She continues to explore facets of sex work and is beginning to investigate embodiment, stigma and privilege.

George J. McCall is Professor Emeritus of Sociology and Public Policy Administration University of Missouri-St. Louis. His professional interests include Social Psychology,

Methodology, and Conflict Resolution. Recent publications include 'The Me and the Not-Me: Positive and Negative Poles of Identity,' (2003) in Peter J. Burke, Timothy J. Owens, Richard Serpe, and Peggy A. Thoits (eds) *Advances in Identity Theory and Research.* New York: Kluwer Academic-Plenum Press, 2003. pp. 11–26; George J. McCall and Patricia Resick (2003) 'A Pilot Study of PTSD Among Kalahari Bushmen,' *Journal of Traumatic Stress,* 5:445–50; 'Interaction,' (2003) in Larry T. Reynolds and Nancy J. Herman (eds) *Handbook of Symbolic Interactionism.* Walnut Creek, CA: AltaMira Press. pp. 327–48.

Lee F. Monaghan is Senior Lecturer in Sociology at the University of Limerick, Ireland. His ethnographic research draws from, and contributes to, the sociology of the body and embodied sociology. He is the author of *Bodybuilding, Drugs and Risk* (2001, Routledge) and numerous articles on doorwork and risk in Britain's night-time economy. His current research critically engages with the obesity debate, exploring the ways in which fat is or is not a male relevant issue. His research has been published in *The British Journal of Sociology, Journal of Contemporary Ethnography, Body and Society, Sociology of Health & Illness, The Sociological Review, Health, Risk & Society, Social Science & Medicine, Social & Legal Studies* and *Gender, Work & Organization.*

H. Mabel Preloran has over 25 years experience working in the field of cultural anthropology in the United States and Latin America. She has published extensively in scientific sources such as the *American Journal of Public Health;* and books like '*Aguantando la Caída: familias argentinas venciendo la desocupación*' ('*Enduring the Fall: Argentine Families Conquering Unemployment*'). She is currently working as a Research

Anthropologist at UCLA Department of Social Psychiatry, Center for Culture and Health. Her current research focuses on decision-making about genetic testing for neurological disorders.

Teela Sanders is a lecturer in the School of Sociology and Social Policy at the University of Leeds and specialises in regulation, illegal economies, crime and deviance. Her main research interests are in the adult female sex industry examining the social organisation of sex work, regulation regimes and men who buy sex. She is also interested in qualitative research methods, in particular ethnography. She has recently published in journals such as *Sociology, Urban Studies,* the *Sociology of Health and Illness* and *Gender, Work and Organization.* She has recently published her first book '*Sex Work: A Risky Business*' (Willan, 2005).

Gary Shank is Associate Professor of Educational Psychology at Duquesne University in Pittsburgh. Professor Shank has lectured and published extensively in the fields of semiotics and qualitative research methodology, and is the author of *Qualitative Research: A Personal Skills Approach,* second edition (Prentice Hall, 2005).

Bob Simpson is a senior lecturer in anthropology at the University of Durham. His research interests are mostly linked by a focus on kinship and family relations. He has carried out research into the transmission of ritual knowledge in Sri Lanka and worked extensively on changing family forms in the UK. In 1998 he published *Changing Families: An Ethnographic Approach to Divorce and Separation* (Berg). More recently he has carried out research into the ethical social and legal implications of the new reproductive and genetic technologies both in Sri Lanka and the UK.

Michael Stein is a Professor of Sociology at Lindenwood University, St. Charles, Missouri, USA. His research interests have generally focused on Qualitative Methods, Dramaturgy and Popular Culture. He has a special interest in notions of place, especially as regards the domains of public and private. Published works include an appreciation of Erving Goffman, and have involved such ethnographic settings as adult bookstores, college classrooms, and soup kitchens.

Richard Wright is Curators' Professor of Criminology and Criminal Justice at the University of Missouri-St. Louis. He has conducted numerous field-based studies of offenders actively involved in the commission of serious street crimes such as armed robbery, residential burglary, and carjacking. His current research focuses on the role of criminal retaliation in the spread and containment of urban violence.

Name Index

Abbott, Andrew 11
Abbott, S. 205, 208
Abrahamson, Mark 66
ACOG (American College of Obstetricians
    and Gynecologists) 94
Adams, Richard N. 12
Adler, Emily Stier 59
Adler, P. 158, 207, 209, 210–11, 226
Adler, P.A. 207, 209, 210–11, 226
Agar, Michael 16, 60
Agnew, Neil 59
Ahmed, S. 269
Aitchison, C. 258, 269
Alasuutari, P. 255, 257
Albesson, - 203
Alexa, M. 332
Alexander, Priscilla 142, 204
Allen, K.R. 358
Allison, A. 207
Altork, K. 201
Anderson, Elijah 13, 39–58, 61, 67, 70, 72, 377
Anderson, K. 262, 268
Anderson, Nels 7
Appadurai, Arjun 65
Applebome, Peter 79
Archard, P. 163, 166
Arcury, T.A. 93
Arean, P.A. 97
Arendell, Terry 164
Arensberg, Conrad 10
Armstrong, D. 355
Armstrong, Gary 158, 163, 228
Arrom, J. 93, 97
Asad, T. 348
Asamoah-Amu, C. 205
Ashworth, G. 203
Atkinson, Paul 16, 23, 60, 70, 190, 230, 301, 313, 349
Atkinson, R. 206
Ayala, A. 182

Babbie, Earl 59
Bailey, Carol A. 16
Bakhtin, M. 234
Banfield, Edward C. 66
Banton, M. 278
Barbaret, R. 204
Barley, N. 347, 351
Barnard, M. 205–6, 210, 213

Barthes, R. 26
Barton, B. 208, 214
Baumeister, Roy F. 113
Bechhofer, Frank, 84
Beck, U. 225, 236, 239
Becker, Howard S. 10, 11–12, 13, 15, 16, 51, 90, 286
Bell, C. 293
Bell, D. 127
Bellah, Robert 363
Bendelow, G. 225, 231, 236, 239
Benedict, Ruth 10
Bennett, John W. 9
Bensimon, E.M. 193
Bensman, Joseph 10–11, 12
Benson, C. 203
Benson, Michael L. 86
Ben-Yehuda, N. 196
Berg, Bruce L. 60
Berger, Peter 62
Bernard, H.R. 93
Bernard, Jesse 9
Bertaux, Daniel 110, 112, 262
Bettelheim, Bruno 10
Bird, K. 310
Birrell, S. 256, 262
Black, D. 278, 373
Blackman, M. 289
Blackwood, E. 201
Bland, L. 186
Blau, Peter M. 11–12
Blee, Kathleen M. 158
Bloor, M. 206, 209, 227, 230, 232
Blumenthal, D.S. 93
Blumer, Herbert 14
Boas, F. 15, 23
Bochner, A.P. 24
Bogdan, R. 93
Böhm, A. 310
Boissevian, J. 366
Bolton, R. 191, 201
Bonilla, L. 204, 205
Bonvicini, K.A. 93, 97
Booth, Charles 5
Bott, Elizabeth 374
Bourdieu, P. 126–7, 227–8, 230
Bourgois, Philippe 158, 160
Bowen, G. 225
Bowman, G. 190

Boynton, P. 203
Brah, Avtah 268
Brain, R. 225
Braithwaite, John 84
Brannigan, A. 358
Brent, B. 204
Brewer, D. 204
Brewer, J. 280
Brewis, J. 212
Bright, Margaret 83
Bristow, J. 187
Broadhead, Robert S. 166
Brodeur, J.P. 367
Brown, J. 280
Brown, J.S. 357
Brownell, Susan 243–54, 377
Browner, Carole H. 93–106, 377
Bruce, T. 257
Bruner, Jerome S. 109
Bryant, C. 206
Buchanan, I. 190
Bucher, Rue 11
Bulmer, Martin 9, 12
Burawoy, Michael 13, 15
Burgess, Ernest W. 5, 7, 9, 367
Burgess, Robert G. 13, 377
Burke, M. 280
Butler, J. 197

Cahill, D. 289
Callaway, H. 348, 349, 356
Callero, P.L. 189, 198
Calvey, D. 227
Campbell, C. 205, 215
Cantú, L. 182
Caplan, - 349–50, 353
Cardwell, J.D. 68
Carr, W. 350
Carrier, Joseph 171–83, 377–8
Carrillo, H. 182
Carroll, Leo 110
Casagrande, J. 294
Casey, K.M. 97
Caspi, Avshalom 112
Cassidy, B. 256
Caughey, John L. 148–9, 151
Cavan, Sherri 12, 68
Chambliss, William 374
Chan, J. 280
Chapkis, Wendy 208
Chapoulie, Jean-Michel 7
Charmaz, K. 230
Chatterton, M. 279–80
Chatterton, P. 230, 233
Cheek, J. 358
Chu Zi 252
Church, S. 204

Clark, Roger 59
Clemmer, Donald 110
Clifford, James 24, 244, 348–9
Clinard, Marshall B. 85–6
Cluse-Tolar, T. 208
Cockington, J. 204
Coffey, A. 127, 202–3, 212, 226, 230, 238, 313
Coleman, S. 127
Collier, J. 338, 340
Collier, R. 233
Connell, R. 229, 231, 232
Conroy, S. 280, 285
Cook, Thomas D. 14
Cooper, K. 204
Copp, M. 158, 231, 239
Coppleston, F. 23
Corbett, C. 277
Crandall, B.F. 94
Crapanzano, V. 348
Cressey, Donald 86–7, 365, 374
Cressey, Paul G. 7–8, 201
Creswell, J.W. 316
Crewe, Ben 109–23, 378
Crick, M. 349
Croall, Hazel 82
Cunningham, D.J. 26–7
Curt, B. 357
Cushing, Frank 5
Cushing, Harvey 87
Cusick, L. 210

Dalton, Melville 12, 281
Daly, K. 358
Danet, B. 363
Darwin, Charles 336
Davis, Allison 10
Davis, Fred 10, 11
Davis, K. 238
Day, S. 203, 205
Dean, John P. 10–11
Dean, T. 189, 196
Decker, Scott 61, 70, 73, 158, 161, 165
Delacoste, F. 204
Delamont, S. 225
Denzin, Norman K. 14, 15, 203, 257, 266, 267, 354, 363
Derrida, J. 354
DeVault, M. 364
DeWalt, Billie R. 4, 16
DeWalt, Kathleen M. 4, 16
Dexter, Lewis Anthony 84
Dirksen, S.R. 93
Dissanayake, V.H.W. 133, 136
Ditton, J. 207
Doan, L. 186
Doby, John T. 11
Dodds, S. 208

Dodge, Mary 79–92, 378
Doezema, J. 204
Dollard, John 84
Dolnick, D. 204, 206, 210, 213
Donnelly, M. 355
Doocey, Jeffrey H. 82
Douglas, J. 281
Douglas, Jack D. 12, 201
Downe, Peter 205, 208
Du Bois, B. 269
Ducharme, Lori J. 10, 11
Duguid, P. 357
Durkheim, Emile 6
Durkin, K. 206
Duster, T. 282
Dyzenhaus, D. 280

Earle, S. 206
Eco, U. 25, 26
Edmunds, M. 213
Edwards, J. 136
Edwards, S. 202, 211, 285
Efthimiou-Mordant, A. 204
Egger, Steven A. 88
Eisner, E. 188
Elias, Norbert 232, 234, 236, 364, 365–7
Elliott, J. 350
Ellis, C. 24, 207
Ellis, Carolyn 364
Ellis, Havelock 186
Emerson, Robert M. 9, 15, 16
Engel, P. 289
Epele, M. 205, 208
Epstein, Seymour 112
Epston, David 112
Erikson, Kai T. 12
Erlich, Danuta 11
Erskine, Nancy 112
Esterberg, Kristin G. 164
Evans, C. 204
Evans-Pritchard, Edward Evan 293

Fann, K.T. 25
Farley, M. 204
Faugier, J. 203, 206
Fawcett, B. 192
Feinstein, A.R. 354
Ferguson, James 245
Ferrell, Jeff 158, 166–7, 226, 235–6
Festinger, Leon 11
Fetterman, D. 207
Fielding, Nigel G. 277–91, 378
Filstead, William J. 13, 60
Fine, Gary Alan 10, 11, 143, 148, 363
Fine, Michelle 148
Finkler, K. 136
Finnegan, F. 204

Finstad, L. 205
Fischer, M. 349, 355–6
Fisher, T. 196
FitzGerald, M. 279
Flax, J. 269, 355
Fleisher, Mark S. 165
Flint, J. 206
Flowers, Amy 143, 152
Fog-Olwick, K. 127
Fonow, M.M. 263
Ford, Larry R. 65
Foucault, Michel 185, 186, 347, 350, 355
Fox, Kathryn J. 166
Fox, Nick J. 347–60, 378
Francis, B. 187–9
Francis, Mark 66
Frank, A. 238
Franklin, S. 136
Freilich, Morris 13
Freud, Sigmund 186
Friese, Susanne 309–32, 378–9
Fromm, Erich 109
Fuller, Steve 333–44, 379
Funari, V. 207

Gagne, Patricia 167
Gagnon, J.H. 188
Gallagher-Thompson, D. 97
Game, A. 355
Gans, Herbert 12, 368, 372, 374–5
Gardner, Burleigh 9–10
Gardner, Mary R. 10
Garfinkel, Harold 13, 235
Garland, David 373
Gaziano, Emanuel 11
Geer, Blanche 10, 11–12, 303
Geertz, Clifford 14, 23, 125, 244
Geis, Gilbert 79–92, 166, 379
Geis, Robley 88
Gelsthorpe, L. 358
Gergen, Kenneth 112
Gibbons, M. 336
Giddens, Anthony 109, 112, 226, 228, 235
Gilbert, N. 334
Gill, Brendan 81
Gillen, - 5
Glascock, Jack 152
Glaser, Barney G. 11–12, 23, 229, 315, 333
Glesne, C. 163
Glowczewski, B. 264
Goffman, Erving 10, 12, 23, 68, 70, 111, 163, 202, 207, 228, 231, 232, 234, 235, 237, 367
Gold, Raymond L. 10, 208, 301
Golde, Peggy 13
Golden, Frederic 91
Goldenberg, Sheldon 59–60, 69
Goodale, J. 284

Goode, Erich 12, 196, 201, 209
Goode, William J. 11
Gossop, M. 205–6
Gould, Stephen Jay 90
Gouldner, Alvin 11
Green, A. 203, 205
Greenhalgh, T. 354
Guba, Egon 14, 194
Gubrium, Jaber F. 80
Gudjonssen, G. 280
Guidroz, K. 204, 205
Gupta, Akhil 245
Gusfield, Joseph 10
Guyer, J.I. 95
Gysels, M. 205

Habenstein, Robert W. 10, 13
Hacker, E.A. 23
Hallett, Tim 363
Hamel, J. 358
Hamm, Mark S. 166–7, 226, 235–6
Hammersley, Martyn 15, 23, 60, 70, 301
Hammond, Philip 12
Hannigan, John 363
Hanson, R.N. 25
Harding, S. 258
Hargreaves, Jennifer A. 255–73, 379
Harman, G.H. 25
Harocopos, A. 205
Harred, J. 208
Harrington, Brooke 160, 163–5
Harris, Marvin 15
Harris, P. 355
Harrison, Shelby 5
Hart, A. 206
Hart, G. 204, 210
Hastrup, K. 127, 349
Hatt, Paul K. 11
Hausbeck, K. 204
Haywood, Chris 185–200, 379–80
Healy, K. 358
Hearn, J. 192
Hedin, U. 205
Heiser, J.F. 93
Hendry, J. 349
Henry, Frances 12
Henslin, James M. 12, 167
Herskovitz, Melville J. 11
Hesse-Biber, Sharlene 60
Heyl, B. 205
Hill Collins, P. 258, 267–8
Hine, C. 206
Hinkle, Gisela J. 5, 6
Hinkle, Roscoe C., Jr. 5, 6
Hirchsfield, Magnus 186
Hiss, Tony 64
Hobbs, Dick 158, 163, 203, 226–9, 231, 232, 238, 380

Hobbs, R. 280
Hobsbawn, Eric 373
Hochschild, Arlie R. 141
Hodson, Randy 15
Hoigard, C. 205
Holbrook, B. 313
Holdaway, S. 279–80
Hollands, R. 230, 233
Hollinger, D. 340
Hollway, Wendy 115
Holmwood, J. 358
Holstein, James A. 80
Homans, George C. 10
Hooker, E. 174
Hooks, B. 258, 268
Hotaling, N. 205
Hough, M. 205, 213, 279
Howard, J.A. 189, 198
Hubbard, P. 204, 214
Huberman, A. Michael 15
Hughes, Everett C. 7, 9, 11
Hughes, G. 230
Humphreys, Laud 12, 71, 201
Hunt, J. 284
Huntley, H. 214
Huston, Ted L. 80
Hutcheon, L. 355
Hymes, Dell 13

Ianni, Frances 365–6, 368, 372–3
Inciardi, James A. 158
Irving, B. 278, 280
Irwin, John 12, 163

Jackson, Bruce 60
Jacobs, Bruce A. 157–68, 374, 380
Jacobs, Jane 67
Jaget, C. 204
Jahoda, Marie 11
Jakle, John 61, 65
James, A. 348
James, J. 204
Janes, Robert W. 12
Jankowiak, William 246–7
Janowitz, Morris 12
Jayaratne, T.E. 259
Jeffcutt, P. 189
Jefferson, Tony 115, 280
Jeffries, Stuart 62
Jesilow, Paul 87, 88
Jewell Rich, G. 204, 205
Jipson, A. 231
Johnson, John M. 13
Jonas, Lillian 363
Jones, S. 257
Jorgenson, D. 163, 165
Josephson, J.R. 25

Josephson, S.G. 25
Josselson, Ruthellen 113
Junker, Buford H. 12

Kanfer, Stefan 83
Kapferer, B. 128
Kaplan, Abraham 24
Kaplan, C. 206
Kats, B.B. 93
Katz, Daniel 11
Katz, Jack 15, 236
Kehily, M. 190
Keiser, Robert 12
Kelle, U. 310
Kellogg, Paul U. 5
Kelly-Gadol, J. 270
Kemmis, S. 350
Kempadoo, K. 204
Kidder, L.H. 289
Killick, A.P. 201
King, J. 374
King, A. 234
Kinkaid, Harry V. 83
Kinnell, H. 203, 206
Kinsey, A.C. 174, 187
Kirkpatrick, K. 204
Klein, R.D. 269
Kleinman, S. 158, 215, 231, 239
Klockars, - 374
Kluckhohn, Florence 9–10
Kneale, M. 23
Kneale, W. 23
Knorr-Cetina, K. 335, 337–8
Kohler Riessman, C. 214
Kondo, D.K. 127
Konrad, M. 136
Kornblum,William 13
Kuckartz, U. 310
Kuhn, Thomas S. 339–40
Kuznar, Lawrence A. 15
Kvale, S. 194

Lakatos, I. 354
Lambert, H. 204
Langer, S.K. 23
Laqueur, T.W. 186
Lareau, A. 126
LaRose, Robert 152
Lather, P. 350, 356
Latour, Bruno 333–5, 337–8, 349
Lawless, E.J. 288
Lawton, J. 225
Layder, D. 202, 204, 205–6, 207–9, 214
Lazarsfeld, Paul F. 83
Lazenby, J.A. 340
Leach, E. 374
Leach, James 16

Leakey, Mary 91
Leavy, Patricia 60
Leck, G. 196
LeCompte, M.D. 23
Lee, R.M. 215, 235, 284
Lee-Treweek, G. 234
Lehr, Dick 367–8, 371, 373
Lever, J. 204, 206, 210, 213
Levi, Mike 280, 365
LeVine, E. 97
Levine, J. 204
Lévi-Strauss, C. 26
Lewis, G. 355
Lewis, J. 205, 208
Lewis, Oscar 11, 12
Leyland, A. 205
Lidz, Charles 163
Lieblich, Amia 80–1, 113, 215
Liebow, Elliott 12, 294
Liepe-Levinson, K. 208
Lincoln, Yvonne S. 14, 15, 194, 266, 354
Lindeman, Eduard C. 6
Linkogle, S. 234
Linstead, S. 212
Lister, S. 232
Litton, C. 231
Lofland, John 12, 13, 16, 60, 68, 70, 166, 284
Lofland, Lyn 60, 66, 68–9, 70, 73, 284
Logan, M. 214
Lohman, Joseph D. 8
Looby, C. 187
Lowman, J. 204
Luckmann, Thomas 62
Luff, D. 214
Lupton, D. 232, 238
Lury, Celia 256, 267–8
Lyman, Stanford M. 68, 111
Lynch, M.E. 333, 337
Lynd, Helen Merrell 7, 11
Lynd, Robert S. 7, 11
Lyng, Stephen 158, 232, 234, 235–6, 238
Lyotard, J. 354, 356

Mac an Ghaill, Mairtin 185–200, 380
MacDonald, Michael 373
Mack, - 366
MacKeith, J. 280
MacLure, M. 350
MacNevin, Audrey 363
Madden, L. 204
Maguire, M. 277
Maher, L. 202, 203, 205–6, 207, 210, 213–15
Malala, J. 204
Malinowski, Bronislaw 5–6, 7, 23, 201, 243, 293, 361
Mann, C. 265, 266
Mann, Kenneth 82

Mannheim, K. 340
Manning, Peter Kirby 12, 87, 279–80, 361–82, 380
Mansson, S.A. 205
Marcus, George E. 14, 126–7, 131, 244, 245,
    348–9, 355–6
Marlin, L. 204
Martin, C.E. 187
Martineau, Harriet 7
Maruna, Shadd 109–23, 380
Mathiesen, Thomas 110
Maticka-Tyndale, E. 205, 208
Matthews, R. 203, 204
Mattley, Christine 141–56, 166–7, 202–3, 207, 380
Mauss, M. 233, 367
Mauthner, N.S. 357
Maxwell, J.A. 191
May, T. 205, 213, 228
Maykut, P. 255
Maynard, M. 268
McAdams, Dan P. 109, 111–12, 113
McCall, George J. 12, 13, 60, 380–1
McCarry, Charles 79
McClintock, Anne 142–3
McCurdy, David W. 13
McIntosh, Mary 142, 192
McKay, Henry 67
McKeganey, N. 205, 210
McLeod, E. 205
Mead, Margaret 5, 7–8, 10, 201
Meinig, D.W. 64, 65
Melbin, Murray 61
Mellor, P. 230
Merton, Robert K. 10–11, 334, 340
Miles, Matthew B. 15, 310
Miller, J. Mitchell 155, 202, 203, 205–6,
    207, 214
Miller, S. 95
Miller, S.M. 10
Mills, C. Wright 225, 231, 361
Mitchell, R. 230
Mitchell, R., Jr., 211, 212
Mitchell, Richard G. 143–4
Moffitt, Terrie E. 112
Monaghan, Lee F. 225–41, 381
Money, J. 189
Montemurro, B. 205, 208, 212
Monto, M. 203, 205–6
Morehouse, R. 255
Morgan Thomas, R. 205
Morrall, P.A. 355
Morrison, M. 295–6, 302, 304–5
Moss, C.M. 27
Mulkay, M.J. 334, 357
Mullins, Nicholas 68
Murphy, A. 202, 205, 208, 211
Murray, Stephen O. 14
Myrdal, Gunnar 11

Nader, L. 132
Nader, Ralph 79
Nagel, Jill 142, 204
Naranjo, L.E. 93
Naroll, Raoul 12, 13
Naylor, R. 365
Nencel, L. 208
Netting, R.M. 95
Nettler, Gwynne 87
Nettleton, S. 225, 355
Newby H. 293
Nixon, J. 350
Noriega, G. 182
Norton-Hawk, M. 203, 206
Nowotny, H. 336
Nugent, S. 131

O'Connell Davidson, J. 202, 204, 205–6, 207–9, 214
O'Neil, Gerard 367–8, 371, 373
O'Neill, M. 202, 204, 205–6, 207, 210, 214–15
Oakley, A. 214, 259, 262–3, 358
Okely, J. 348, 349
Oldenburg, Ray 69
Olesen, V. 268
Orenstein, A. 171
Osler, William 87

Padilla, A. 97
Palen, John J. 66–7
Palmer, Vivien M. 7
Park, Robert E. 5, 7–8, 67, 367
Parkin, D. 127
Parry, O. 201
Parry, W.T. 23
Parsons, Talcott 10, 333–4
Pasko, L. 205
Patrick, J.H. 97
Patrick, James 158
Patton, M.Q. 93
Paul, Benjamin 11
Payne, Connie 88–9
Payne, S.L. 358
Pearson, G. 228
Peirce, Charles S. 25–9
Pelto, Gretel H. 13
Pelto, Pertti J. 13
Peshkin, A. 163
Peters, P.E. 95
Phillips, W. 171
Phoenix, J. 205
Pines, M. 205–6
Platt, Jennifer 9
Plummer, K. 203
Plumridge, E. 206
Polanyi, Michael 338, 340
Pole, C.J. 298, 304
Polsky, Ned 158, 159, 284

Pomeroy, W.B. 187
Pons, V. 293
Poole, H. 198
Popper, K. 335, 341, 354
Porter, J. 204, 205
Posner, Richard 85
Powdermaker, Hortense 12
Pratt, J. 358
Prein, G. 310
Preiss, Jack J. 12
Preissle, J. 23
Preloran, H.M. 93–106, 381
Presdee, M. 232, 236
Prieur, A. 182
Propp, V. 26
Pryce, Ken 158
Punch, Maurice 141, 142, 144, 280, 284
Pyett, P. 206, 210
Pyke, Sandra 59

Quandt, S.A. 93
Quinlivan, K. 192

Rabinow, P. 134, 186
Radcliffe-Brown, A.R. 7
Ragoné, H. 136
Ramazanoglu, C. 358
Ramsden, Derek 111
Rao, V. 206
Raphael, J. 206
Rapp, R. 94, 136
Rapport, N. 349
Raudenbush, S. 278
Rawls, Anne Warfield 374
Read, R. 340
Reckless, W.C. 201
Redfield, Robert 7, 9, 11
Reed-Danahay, D. 127
Reichardt, Charles S. 14
Reimer, Hans 8
Reimer, Jeffery 72
Reiner, R. 279
Reinharz, Shulamit 14, 143
Reisk, Theodor 84
Reisman, David 83
Reiss, A. 278
Relph, Edward 60, 64
Remmick, David 81
Resta, R.G. 94
Reuss-Ianni, Elizabeth R. 365–6, 368, 372–3
Richards, Audrey I. 9
Richards, L. 330
Richards, T. 330
Richardson, L. 185
Richardson, Laurel 350, 356, 364
Rickard,W. 205
Riecken, Henry W. 11

Riesman, David, N. 363
Rigakos, George 373
Rofes, E. 193
Rogers, M. 192, 279–80
Romans, S. 205
Ronai, C. 207
Rorty, R. 186
Rosaldo, R. 348, 355
Rose, N. 355
Rosoff, Stephen M. 88
Ross, A. 341
Roth, Julius A. 10, 11–12
Roth, W. 225
Rothman, B.K. 94
Rowbotham, S. 260
Roy, Donald 10
Russell, B.H. 98
Ryan, B. 128

Saberwal, Satish 12
Sampson, R. 278
Sanders, C.R. 358
Sanders, Clinton 70
Sanders, Teela 201–22, 381
Sanger, J. 355
Sanjek, Roger 15
Sapir, Edward 7
Sarbin, Theodore R. 81, 109
Sargeant, M. 206
Sartre, Jean-Paul 109–10
Saussure, F. 26
Scarce, R. 158
Schacter, Stanley 11
Schatzman, Leonard 11, 13, 23
Schelling, J. 365
Schensul, J.J. 350
Scheurich, J. 358
Schoepfle, G.M. 15
Schofield, M. 174
Schroeder-Gudehus, B. 342
Schumann, Howard 83
Schütz, A. 227
Schütz, Alfred 310
Schütz, Astrid 113
Schwalbe, M. 364
Schwandt, T. 194
Schwartz, Barry 68
Schwartz, Charlotte Green 10
Schwartz, Morris S. 10
Scott, D. 296
Scott, Marvin B. 12, 68, 111
Scultz, J. 126
Seamon, David 60, 65
Sebeok, T.A. 25
Segal, Lynne 142
Seidel, John 310, 314
Seidler, V. 263

Shaffir, Wiliam B. 60, 163, 209
Shank, Gary 23–36, 381
Shapin, S. 336
Shapiro, D. 206
Shapiro, Gilbert 10
Sharp, K. 206
Sharpe, K. 202, 203, 208, 211, 213–15
Sharrock, W. 335, 340
Shaw, Clifford R. 7, 67
Shedlin, M. 181
Shilling, C. 225–6, 230–1, 233, 239
Shore, C. 131
Shortridge, James R. 61, 65
Silbert, A. 205–6
Simmel, Georg 164
Simmons, J.L. 12, 13, 60
Simon, W. 188
Simpson, B. 125–37, 381
Singer, M. 98
Skelton, C. 187–9
Skoldberg, - 203
Sluka, Jeffrey A. 167
Small, Albion W. 5
Smalley,W.A. 12
Smart, C. 204
Smith, C. 211
Smith, Charles P. 113
Smith, D. 278
Smith, Dwight 365
Smith, Y. 256
Solway, I. 160
Sopher, David E. 64
Sparkes, A.C. 193
Spencer, - 5
Spindler, George D. 13
Spivak, G.C. 269
Spradley, James P. 12, 13, 23, 60, 70, 98
Stacey, J. 214, 269
Stacey, M. 293
Stake, R.E. 24
Stanko, B. 215
Stanley, L. 193, 255, 262, 267–8
Stark, Rodney 67
Stebbins, Robert 366
Stebbins, Roberta 60, 216
Stein, E. 189
Stein, Maurice R. 11, 12
Stein, Michael 59–75, 381
Sterk, C. 205, 211
Stewart, Abigail J. 112, 259
Stewart, F. 265, 266
Stimson, Gerry V. 60
Stocking, George W., Jr. 5
Stoddart, K. 163
Stranack, J. 198
Stranger, M. 226, 235–7
Strathern, Marilyn 126, 130, 136

Strauss, Anselm L. 10, 11, 13, 23, 229, 315, 333
Street, David 12–13
Stronach, I. 350
Stull, D.D. 350
Sudnow, David 12
Sutherland, Edward 374
Sutherland, Edwin H. 80
Suttles, Gerald D. 12–13, 207
Sykes, Gresham 110, 120
Szockyj, Elizabeth 80
Szwajkowski, Eugene 85

Taylor, C. 182
Taylor, S.J. 93
Temple, B. 266
Tewksbury, Richard 167, 207
Thagard, P.R.
Thielens, Wagner Jr., 83
Thomas, - 112
Thomas, - 112
Thompson, G. 229
Thompson, W. 208
Thrasher, Frederick M. 7–8
Tierney, W.G. 358
Tonkinson, R. 264
Town, S. 192
Traub, James 61
Trotter, J. 193
Tuan,Yi-Fu 60–1, 63–4, 65
Tucker, G. 94
Tulloch, J. 232, 238
Tully, B. 289
Turkle, S. 363
Turner, Alice K. 63
Turner, B. 225, 230, 239
Turner, Ralph H. 10
Tyler, Stephen A. 13, 348, 355

Ulrichs, Karl 186
Usher, R. 188

Van Den Hoonaard, W. 270
Van Maanen, John 24, 126, 158, 202, 211, 281–4,
    286–7, 289, 362
Van Meter, K. 206
Vaughan, Diane 84–5
Ventakesh, S. 373
Vidich, Arthur J. 10–12, 226
Von Kraft-Ebing, Richard 186

Wacquant, Loïc 243, 225, 227, 233, 237, 364
Waddington, P. 280
Wagner, Roy 252
Walker, A. 163
Walker, R. 295
Walkerdine, V. 191
Walkowitz, J. 204

Wallace, Sam 12
Waller, Willard 6
Walter, E.V. 60–1, 63, 65
Ward, H. 203, 205
Warner, Lloyd 7, 9
Warr, D. 206, 210
Warren, Carol A.B., 164
Waters, J. 160
Watson, J. 225
Wax, Murray 10
Wax, Rosalie H. 5, 9, 10, 13
Weatherford, Jack 70
Weatheritt, M. 279, 285
Weaver, A. 230
Webb, Beatrice 5, 7–8, 302
Webb, Sidney 5, 7, 302
Weber, M. 191, 310
Weeks, J. 186, 188, 194
Weiss, R.M. 358
Weitzer, R. 280
Weitzman, Eben A. 15, 310
Werner, Oswald 15
Wesnes, K.A. 93
Westley, W. 278
Westmarland, L. 225, 235, 238
White, Michael 112
White, S. 357
Whiteside, Thomas 79
Whittaker, D. 204, 210
Whyte, William Foote 10–12, 23, 50, 67, 110,
     165, 284, 294, 365, 368, 372, 374
Wiedel, J. 295

Wierzbicki, Zbigniew T. 11
Wilcox, C.S. 93
Wilk, R. 95
Williams, S. 225, 231, 235–6, 239
Williams, Thomas R. 12
Williamson, C. 208
Wilson, C. 182
Wincup, E. 211
Winlow, S. 226–9, 234, 235–6
Wise, S. 193, 255, 262, 267–8
Wiseman, Jackie 12
Wojcicki, J. 204
Wolcott, Harry F. 16, 304
Wolf, D. 163
Wolff, Kurt 11, 12
Wollcott, H. 362
Wood, E. 208
Woolgar, S. 333–4, 337–8, 349
Wright, Richard 61, 70, 73, 158–9, 161, 165, 382
Wysocki, Diane Kholos 59

Yin, R. 262
Young, E. 215
Young, Malcolm 366

Zelditch, M. 176
Zelditch, Morris, Jr. 12
Zietz, Dorothy 86–7
Zorbaugh, Harvey 7, 67
Zuber-Skerritt, O. 350
Zuell, C. 332
Zussman, R. 216

Subject Index

abductive reasoning 24–7, 30–2
Aborigines 264
acceptance rituals 211
access 8, 71
   health research 353
   police research 281
   schools 294, 298–301
   white-collar criminals 81, 89
accountability 280, 342–3
action research 350–1
aesthetic reflexivity 235
agency 235, 335
AIDS 181–2
alienation 65
amniocentesis decisions 94–104
analytic induction 54, 86, 230
anthropological tradition 5–16, 65, 348–9
Anthropology and Autobiography (Okely
   and Callaway) 349
Anthropology as Cultural Critique (Marcus
   and Fischer) 355–6
anti-science 16
apartheid 260
archiving 355
arrogance 87–8
Asch, Ricardo 89
ATLAS.ti computer programme 310, 311, 318–22
attachment 64–5
authority
   fieldwork 277–8
   scientific method 334
authorship 269

'babe in the woods' approach 80–1
Balmaceda, Jose 89–90
barrio studies 179–81
befriending participants 97–9
   see also insider research
beneficiaries of research 339
Berava community, Sri Lanka 128–30, 132–4
biases 11, 56, 93–4, 95–6, 100
binary categorisation 196
bioethics 131, 134
biographical zoning 270
black culture 39–58, 261
bodily capital 228, 233
bouncers 226–39
boundaries 61, 66, 68–9

'breaking the third wall' 154
British Workers' Sports Federation (BWSF) 257
brochure dissemination 305
'brokering' recruitment strategy 95, 97, 100, 102
bullying 119–20
BWSF *see* British Workers' Sports Federation

C-I-SAID computer programme 311
CAQDAS *see* Computer-Aided Qualitative Data
   Analysis Software
'carnival of crime' 232, 236
case study method 6
caste system 133–4
categorisation 196
causation 6
Centre for Contemporary Cultural Studies 189–90
Challenger disaster 85
Chicago School 7, 9–13, 67
child abuse 285
child participants 196–7
'chimeras' 185
the city 65–7
civil accountability 280
clues 32
CMC *see* computer-mediated communication
co-recruitment 95, 97, 100, 102
code-and-retrieve 311, 314
coding systems 230, 309–32
cognitive anthropology 13
coherence 33
cohort effects 8–9
'cold access' 159, 204, 263–4
collaborative approach 356
collective subjectivities 190–1
comadrismo 98–9, 103–4
combining data files 328
command files 331
commissioning research 297–8
commitment to data 32–3
common-sense understandings 189, 198
'community of faith' model 343
'community restudy problem' 10–11
comparative studies 302
complexity of research 125–6
Computer-Aided Qualitative Data Analysis Software
   (CAQDAS) 309–32
computer-mediated communication
   (CMC) 266–7

conceptual memos 56
conceptual problems 364
configurations 365–74
conjectural abduction 30–1
consent 98, 264
consistency *see* reliability
constructivism 15, 16, 338
contemporary society 230–1
content analysis 113
contextual issues 15–16, 190–1, 268
controversies 10–11, 13–14, 16
conventionalist epistemology 335
conversational data 53–4, 264
couples research 94–5
courtesy stigma 148, 202
courtroom observations 82
'covering your back' 284–5
covert research 70–1, 143–4, 154–5, 208–9
    see also 'insider' research;
        participant observation
criminality
    dangerous fieldwork 157–68
    organized crime 365–74
    self-narratives 111–22
    white-collar criminals 79–92
    see also deviance
'crisis of representation' 14, 357
critical incident technique 303
critical theory 13
cross-cultural comparisons 174
cultural anthropology 189–90
cultural geography 65
cultural relativism 269
cultural scripts 97–101, 103–4
cultural turn 194
culturalist epistemology 189–91
culture 4
    feminist tradition 256
    occupational culture 280–1, 284
    other-culture studies 351
    place 68, 70
    schools research 295, 302

dangerous fieldwork 157–68, 214–15, 227,
    228, 232–3
data
    analysis 15, 303–4
    files 314–15, 316, 318, 322–3, 325, 329
    quality control 12
    researcher commitment 32–3
    searching 315, 316, 319, 324, 327–8, 330–1
deception 144
deductive reasoning 23, 29–30
demographic characteristics
    researchers 14, 294
    study populations 362
'detective' work 258–9

deviance
    covert research 71
    grounded theory 334
    history of fieldwork 12
    policework 280
    self-narratives 111
    sex work 143
    structural functionalism 334
    see also criminality
deviant case analysis 230
diaries 295, 301–2, 304
'difference' 256, 268, 357
differends 356
disability 265
discourse analysis 257
dissemination of findings 288, 298, 305
distance metaphors 191
divinatory abduction 31
doctors 87–90, 127–8, 130–4
documentary sources 260–2, 295, 300
doorwork 225–39
double consciousness 8
double hermeneutic 356
dramaturgy 68
dress style 79–80
drug dealers 157–60
drummer caste, Sri Lanka 127–30

e-mail interviews 266–7
Economic and Social Research
    Council 297–8
edgework 232, 234–8
educational research 185–98, 293–306
egomania 88
'electronic word' 266
elitism 131, 133–4
embezzlers 86–7
embodied ethnography 189, 225–41, 350,
    353, 356
emic perspective 8, 13, 14
emotions 141, 214, 234–8
empiricist epistemology 187–9
endings 287–8
epistemic issues 11, 13, 14
epistemological approaches 185–200, 206, 257–8,
    335, 354
eroticism 185
'essential space' 186, 188
ethic of productivity 338
ethical issues
    covert research 70, 143–4, 208–9
    'going native' 72, 209
    health research 354
    history of fieldwork 12
    homosexuality studies 172–4, 176–7
    online research 206
    physician interviews 89

ethical issues *cont.*
    recruiting participants 98
    researcher's position 268–70
    see also moral issues
ethnocentrism 8
The Ethnograph computer programme
    309–10, 325–9
ethnographic present 15
ethnographic self 127
ethnography, definition 4
ethnomethodology 13
etic perspective 8
evidential induction 30
exchanges 372
exclusionary research 256
exotic settings 70–1
expenses 8
experiential approach 23, 40
experimental methods 3
'expert' role 69, 126, 193
explanations 32
explanatory abduction 32
external reliability 285, 288–9
external validity 354
eye contact 161

facts 333, 338
factual induction 30
families 114–15, 372–3
fantasy 141–56
favours 283–4
FBI 368–71
fear 65
feedback 90
feminist approaches 142–3, 188,
    193, 255–70
fertility clinic scandal 89–90
field experiments 3
field relations 11, 14, 282–3, 287–8, 347–60
fieldnotes 5, 15, 55–7, 71–2, 303, 304
financial incentives 99, 210
'fish out of water' 73
focus groups 264–6
follow-up studies 288–9
football hooligans 234
formal induction 30
formal social control 279, 366
freedom of inquiry 339
Freeman, Cathy 269–70
frequency data 187, 322
functionalism 6, 10, 15
funding for research 70, 142, 154, 166,
    297–8, 336–7

games 362, 366, 372
gatekeepers 163, 203–4, 297, 298
Gay Games 261

gender
    culture 257
    doorwork 233
    sex work 214
    sexuality 192
General Motors lawsuit 79
generalizability 278, 357, 371–2
Generation X 14
generational conflict 339–40
geographical issues 59–75
Gestalt psychology 6, 15
'getting in' 40–5, 144–5
'going native' 8, 72, 73, 201
    see also 'insider' research
grand narratives 354
grand theory 8
grounded theory 11, 14, 15, 229–30, 333–4
group interviews 264–6, 302–3
group membership 48–50
guided conversations 205

Habits of the Heart (Bellah) 363–4
habitus 227
halo effect 231
Hawthorne effect 63
health research 347–60
health risks 215
hegemonic masculinity 229
Heroines of Sport (Hargreaves) 255–70
heterosexuality 187, 190, 192, 193, 229
hexis 228
'historicizing the cultural' 268
history of fieldwork 5–16
HIV/AIDS 181–2
holism 6, 15–16
'home' 64, 66
homosexuality 171–83, 191–3
hoodlums 52
house buying 62
human body 225–41
human nature 186
humour 282–3
hunches 30–1, 163
hypermedia presentations 313
HyperResearch computer programme 311
hypertext 322
hypothetico-deductive method 333–5

ice-breaking 98, 283
identity
    group membership 49–50
    place 60–1
    researchers 213–14
    self-narratives 109–22
    standpoint epistemologies 192–3
    symbolic interactionism 68
    women in sport 264, 265

'impact factor' 166
incarcerated criminals 82, 110–22
incentives 99, 210
incompleteness of data 269
individuality 188–9
inductive reasoning 8, 23, 30, 54, 86, 230
inference 23–36
informal social control 162
informants
    field relations 349–50
    homosexuality research 173–4, 175
    Jelly's Place study 40
    organized crime 367, 373
    other-culture studies 351
    recruiting 176
    schools research 294–5, 300
    validating testimony 284–5
informed consent 98, 264
initiation rituals 211
'inquirer' versus 'inquired' 334–5
insider research 69–73
    bouncers 226–39
    considerations 293–5
    fantasy 141–56
    history of fieldwork 7–8
    homosexuality 171–83, 191
    Jelly's Place study 39–58
    sex work 207–8
    sport ethnography 255–73
    see also covert research; participant observation
intellectual property 342
intellectual trends 15–16
interactive interviewing 263, 264
interdisciplinary studies 10
internal reliability 285, 288
internal validity 354
International Review Board (IRB) 98
internet research 206, 261
interpretative interactionism 257
interviews
    child abuse victims 285
    educational ethnography 302–3
    empowerment 164–5
    feminist research 262–3, 264–7
    group interviews 302–3
    logistics 71
    mediated ethnography 160–1
    reliability 267
    self-narratives 113, 115–19
    sex work 205–6
    sexual behaviour 187
    white-collar criminals 79–92
investigative abduction 32
IRB see International Review Board

Japanese schooling 296, 302
Jelly's Place study 39–58

journal publications 10–11, 12, 13, 363
jurisdiction of science 340–2

kinship 133
knowledge 16, 56–7, 125–35, 355
kudos 129, 132

labeling theories 12
laboratory research 60, 69, 341
language
    metynomic language 197
    question wording 83
    semiotic theory 26
    symbols 4
Latino participants 93–106
'layered access' 204
legal issues 158, 162, 213, 215, 232, 282
legitimation of science 165, 336–8
lesbianism 192–3, 195, 261
levels of order 34
liberal philosophies 198
life history method 110, 112–13, 204, 205, 262–3
Listening with the Third Ear (Reisk) 84
literature reviews 258
Local Education Authority sponsorship 298
logic-in-use 24
logical reasoning 23–36
logistics of research 71, 259–60
logos 354
longitudinal studies 81
love 64
Lucas, Henry Lee 88

mapping software 320–1
maps of meaning 189
'marginal man' 8
marginalization 192–3, 196, 256
    see also stigmatization
Marxist approaches 235
masculinity 231–2, 238
MAX computer programme 310
MAXqda computer programme 311, 322–5
meaning
    place 60–8
    reasoning toward 25–6, 32–3
    self-narratives 111
media reports 84–5
mediated ethnography 160–1
Medicaid fraud case 88–9
member validation 14
memos 316, 320, 324, 326–7, 330
men
    amniocentesis decisions 94, 100
    cultural scripts 100–1
    homosexuality 171–83
    recruitment strategies 99–100
meta-analysis 15

metaphoric abduction 31
metaphors 31, 61, 191
methodogenesis 163
methodology
    approaches 295
    appropriateness 194, 198
    epistemology 354
    feminist research 257–8
metynomic language 197
Mexico 171–83
middle-class fieldwork 362, 363–4
'middle range' theories 8
Middletown study 7
military research 9–10
Mississippi River 61, 64
mixed-method research 4, 14
Mode 1/Mode 2 science 336–9
model-building 331
modernity 109
moral issues 14, 141–56, 286–7, 335
    see also ethical issues
motivating participants 97–101
multi-method research 4, 205, 295, 311
multimedia data 313
multiple causation 6

N4 computer programme 310
nakedness 202, 212–13
narrative psychology 109–10
natural history 6
natural law theory 343
naturalistic studies 3
neighborhoods 62
neo-Marxism 13, 16
networks 366–74
new ethnography 14
new reproductive technologies 130–1
night-time economy 230–1
non-experimental methods 3
normative structure of science 339–40, 343–4
North American fieldwork 190, 363
Northern Ireland policework 280
nursery schools 191
NVivo computer programme 311

objectivation 126–7, 130, 135
objectivity
    anthropology critique 348–9
    history of fieldwork 5
    ontological objectivity 188
    sexuality research 187
    statistical method 6
    white-collar criminal research 83, 90
objects of desire 194
observational studies 3, 208, 262
    see also participant observation
occupational culture 280–1, 284

omens 31
on-the-spot recruitment 95, 97, 99, 102
online research 206, 261
ontological approaches 188, 335
ontological security 228
operating theatres 352
oppression 192–3, 269
order 34, 362, 374
organized crime 362, 365–73
other-culture studies 351
output, computer-aided analysis 317, 322
outsider research 7–8, 69, 70, 72–3
ownership of knowledge 130

Pacific Island studies 5
paradigms 340
Paralympic Games 261
parochial realm 69, 70
participant observation
    conceptual limitations 127
    current trends 16
    educational ethnography 301–2
    history of fieldwork 7–8, 11, 13
    sex work studies 207–10
    see also covert research; insider research
participants
    children 196–7
    compliance determinants 204
    empowerment 356
    recruiting 93–106, 159–60, 263–4
    research process involvement 193
    selecting 299–300
    testing the researcher 211–12, 283
pathologization
    fantasy 149
    sexuality 192
pattern abduction 32
peripheral research 208
personal risks 157–8, 162, 215, 228, 232–3
personality
    researchers 141
    studies 15
phenomenology 68
philosophical issues 333–44
photographs 295, 300–1
place 59–75
poderismo 101, 103–4
poetics 364
policework 277–90, 367–72
policy-making 279
political issues 13, 16, 141–56, 206
postdoctoral scientists 341
postgraduate education 296, 299
postmodernism 15, 16, 347–60
post-structuralism 355
power–knowledge relations 125–34, 355
practitioner research 350–1

praxical reasoning 23–36
praxis 193
preliminary research 172
primary sources 260–2
'The Princess Anne Affair' 303–4
prison life 110–22
private realm 68–9
probabilistic laws 25–6
problem focus 361–2, 364
productivity 335, 338
program evaluation 14
prostitution 205
psychoanalysis 15
public realm 68–9, 70
Public Research Interest Group 79
publications 8, 10–12, 13, 59–60, 363

QSR N6 computer programme 329–32
Qualitative Data Analysis Software see Computer-Aided
    Qualitative Data Analysis Software
qualitative research
    aims 277
    external reliability 289
    history of fieldwork 14
    journal publications 363
    participant observation 4
    questionnaires 205
    software 309–32
    subjectivity 364
    surveys 310
    see also interviews
quantitative research
    criminology 165
    feminist approaches 259
    history of fieldwork 6, 14
    sex work 204–5
    software 325
    see also scientific method; statistical method
question wording 83
questioning stance 300
questionnaires 205

RAE see Research Assessment Exercise
rapport 98–9, 103
realism 338
reasoning 23–36
reasons for participation 96, 102
reconstructed logic 24
recruiting participants 93–106, 159–60, 263–4
reflexivity 3–4
    aesthetic reflexivity 235
    moral issues 14
    publications 8, 12, 13
    sex work studies 202–3, 294
refusal to participate 95–6
relational identity 114
relativism 14, 16

reliability 191, 267, 285, 288–9
replication of studies 288–9, 364
'republic of letters' 341–2
Research Assessment Exercise (RAE) 270
research bargain 210
research design brief 304
researchers
    commitment to data 32–3
    demographic characteristics 14
    participant empowerment 356
    personal danger 157–8
    personality 141
    reflexivity 202–3
    roles 7–8, 10, 12, 14, 297, 302
    service provision 210
    stigmatization 148, 166–7
    subjectivity 268–9
    trials and tests 211–12, 283
resistance to research 281–2
rhetoric 337–8
rights of membership 49, 53–4
rituals 49, 63, 128–30, 211
'rocking-chair' approach 85
roles 7–8, 12, 14, 69, 297, 302
'rules of irrelevance' 228
rural settings 66

sacred places 63–4
safety 162
sampling
    bias 93–4, 95–6, 100
    purposive sampling 263
    sex work studies 206
    snowball sampling 159–60, 206
schools research 185–98, 293–306
Science and Technology Studies (STS) 333–44
scientific community 340–3
scientific method
    authority 334
    dangerous fieldwork 165
    history of fieldwork 5
    legitimation 336–8
    sexuality research 186
    see also quantitative research; statistical method
scripts
    cultural 97–101, 103–4
    sexual 188
secondary sources 258, 297
secrecy 143–4, 155
selecting participants 299–300
self-monitoring 284–5
self-narratives 109–23, 257–8
self-serving error 285
semiotic theory 26–7
sensuality 230, 236
service provision 210
sex work 141–56, 201–21

sexual scripts 188
sexuality
　fantasy 141–56
　heterosexuality 187, 190, 192, 193
　homosexuality 171–83, 191–3
　lesbianism 192–3, 195, 261
　research frameworks 185–200
shopping 62
signs 26–32
'silent voices' 356
situated action 374
Small Town in Mass Society study 11
snowball sampling 159–60, 206
social construction
　facts 333, 338
　fantasy 141–56
　reality 16, 62
social control 162, 279, 366
social position
　dress style 79–80
　Jelly's Place study 46–7
　place 61, 62, 63
　power–knowledge relations 130, 133
Social Problems journal 12
social surveys 5
sociological tradition 5–16
sociology of knowledge 16, 340
software 15, 303, 309–32
solo fieldwork 8
somatic turn 225
South Africa 260–1
spirituality 63
splitting data files 328
sponsorship 297–8
sport ethnography 255–73
Sri Lankan community studies 125–37
stage theories 5
standpoint epistemologies 192–3, 267
statistical method 6, 85, 91
　see also quantitative research;
　　scientific method
Stewart, Martha 80
stigmatization 148, 166–7, 202, 281
　see also marginalization
Stoke Mandeville Games 261
Stone, Sergio 89
'stranger phenomenon' 164
Street Corner Society study 50
structural functionalism 333–4
STS *see* Science and Technology Studies
student participants 159–60
'studying up' versus 'studying down' 132, 133
subcultures 12, 119–22, 190
subjectivation 126–7, 130, 135
subjectivity
　collective subjectivities 190–1
　criminology 165

subjectivity *cont.*
　fantasy 149
　qualitative research 364
　researchers 268–9
　sexuality research 203
the suburb 66–7
survey research 310
suspension of disbelief 148, 151
sustained immersion method 110, 113
swearing 50
syllogisms 25–6
symbolic interactionism 68, 112
'symbolic worlds' 4, 277
synchronic accounts 15

tainting 166
tandem interviews 83–4
tape recordings 53–4
teachers 187–8, 193
team work 8, 317, 321–2, 324–5, 331
technical issues 361–2
telephone interviews 266
textbook publications 11–12, 13, 59–60
'texts' 14
The Lonely Crowd (Riesman) 363
theory
　building 357
　reasoning toward 30, 33
'third ear' 84
'third places' 68–9
threshold agreements 282
time and space 61, 127
Times Square, New York 61
totalitarianism 10
tradition 130
traditional fieldwork 3–21
transgressive approaches 185, 194–6, 350
'treading on toes' 285–6
trends, intellectual life 15–16
trust 286
truth effects 188–9
'truths' 355

Unsafe at Any Speed (Nader) 79
Urban Life and Culture journal 13
urban planning 67
urban sociology 66

validation hermeneutics 191
validity 191
　computer-aided analysis 312
　dangerous fieldwork 162–5
　external/internal 354
　qualitative research 289
　transgressive validity 350
vantage points 297
Vehstehn 191

verification 335–6
verisimilitude 187
vested interests 285
violence 234, 277
virtual witnessing 336

white-collar criminals 79–92
'white flight' 62, 67
'white' research 256
women
  bouncers 233
  cultural scripts 97–9
  embezzlers 87
  physicians 88

women *cont.*
  policework 284
  prisoner attitudes 120–2
  sexuality 192
  sport ethnography 255–73
  see also lesbianism
word frequency data 322
wording questions 83
work 62–3, 80
'working the hyphen' 148
World War I 5
World War II 9–10
Writing Culture (Clifford) 348–9
writing up 14, 15, 55–8, 304–5, 361–2